Smoke

Smoke

A Global History of Smoking

edited by Sander L. Gilman and Zhou Xun

REAKTION BOOKS

Published by REAKTION BOOKS LTD
79 Farringdon Road
London EC1M 3JU, UK

www.reaktionbooks.co.uk

First published 2004

Copyright © Reaktion Books 2004

Printed in Hong Kong

British Library Cataloguing in Publication Data

Smoke: a global history of smoking
   1. Smoking 2. Drugs of abuse - Social aspects
   3. Tobacco - Physiological effect 4. Drugs of abuse -
   Physiological effect 5. Smoking paraphernalia
   6. Smoking in art 7. Smoking in literature 8. Smoking
   in motion pictures 9. Smoking in popular music
   I. Gilman, Sander L. II. Zhou, Xun
   394.14

ISBN 1 86189 200 4

above: An early tobacconist's, with prototype 'cigar store Indian'.

opposite page: One of Christie's specialist staff smokes a meerschaum pipe with a gentleman's head design at the Alfred Dunhill private collection of pipes, 2004.

Contents

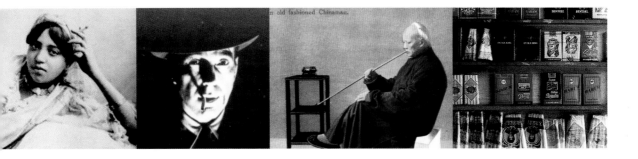

The Colossal Cigar representing the quantity of tobacco consumed by a smoker over 50 years.

Introduction

SANDER L. GILMAN AND ZHOU XUN

On 6 November 1492 two members of Columbus's crew returned from their adventures in the interior of Cuba. They reported an encounter with the natives in which they had smoked dried leaves like those that Columbus had been offered as a present a month earlier, on 15 October 1492. Luis de Torres and Rodrigo de Jerez, in inhaling the smoke from these burning leaves, became the first Europeans to smoke tobacco. This marked the beginning of a series of encounters between the two cultures of smoking.

According to the account of Bartolomé de Las Casas, the priest who in 1514 edited the lost manuscript of Columbus's travels, the people they found 'took certain herbs to take their smokes'. They 'lit [them] at one end and at the other chew or suck or take it in with their breath that smoke which dulls their flesh and as it were intoxicates and so they say that they do not feel weariness.'[1] The dried leaves were from the plant *Nicotiana tabacum* (Columbus's gift, grown in the upper half of South America, Central America and the Caribbean), but the Spaniards misheard its indigenous name as *tabaco*, which was actually the tube or pipe in which the Indians smoked the plant.[2] The plant was already widely cultivated throughout the Americas, from northern Mexico to southern Canada in the form of *Nicotiana rustica*.

The plant had been smoked as part of ritual practices in North and South America well before it began to be cultivated, during the period from 5,000 to 3,000 BCE. The Mayans, the Aztecs and the Caribs, and numerous other peoples in the Western Hemisphere, smoked one form of tobacco or another. Although tobacco could also be chewed, drunk as a tea, inhaled as a powder (snuff), inserted as a liquid enema and consumed as a jelly, it was smoking, the burning of the herb to produce smoke, that quickly became part of a priestly healing ritual both to diagnose and cure illness, as well as to drive out the evil spirits that had supposedly caused it. Smoking provided the intoxication that was inherent to the ritual, as Girola Benonzi notes in his *History of the New World* of 1565. The smoke also served as the food for the spirits that inhabited the shamans. Smoke, ineffable yet perceivable; real yet illusionary; present yet transient; breathable yet intoxicating. It was smoke that captured the European's imagination. It was an experience for which they had initially no vocabulary and to which they sought (and continue to seek) to give meaning.

Smoking was a cure, but it soon became a passion. As with most instances of the religious or medical use of stimulants, this meant that the elites soon began to smoke for pleasure. This also seems to have been true among the peoples of the South and North Americas. What begins with ritual and medicine (often the same thing) comes to be part of elite culture, and is eventually adopted throughout society. For Europeans, smoking, inhaling the residue of burning materials using an implement, was something that was perceived as new. One story about Sir Walter Raleigh (that exemplary smoker) first coined in the eighteenth century

A Mayan priest smoking, in a carving from the Temple at Palenque, Mexico.

much preparation apart from drying. Inhaling it into the miles of tissue in the lungs meant that a dose of nicotine and other chemicals was immediately deposited in the bloodstream. Neither taking snuff nor enemas nor teas nor tobacco jellies supplied as quick a delivery as did inhalation. (Nicotine and *Nicotiana* were named after Jean Nicot, the French ambassador to the Portuguese court who brought tobacco and smoking to the French court in the mid-sixteenth century as a medicine.)

While many stories have been told about the European discovery of the 'New World', very little is known about their first experience of smoking and their reaction to the magic smoke. Las Casas's account remained unpublished until the nineteenth century. In 1557 André Thevet described for the 'Old World' the still-fascinating smoking practices of the peoples of the 'New World', as it had come to be labelled:

> When [the tobacco plant] is dry they enclose a quantity of it in a palm leaf, which is rather large, and roll it up about the length of a candle. They light it at one end and take in the smoke by the nose and mouth. They say it is very good to drive forth and consume the superfluous moisture in the head. Besides, when taken in this way, it makes it possible to endure hunger and thirst for some time. Therefore they use it often, even when they are taking counsel they inhale this smoke and then speak; this they do ordinarily one after the other in war, where it is very useful. Women do not use it at all. It is true that if they take too much of this smoke or perfume it will go to their head and make then drunk like the smell of strong wine.[3]

relates how, on his return to England, he was quietly smoking his pipe when his servant threw a pint of ale at him, thinking that his master's face was on fire. Smoking was understood to be a new idea, a new experience – and one chiefly reserved for those who could afford it, the elite.

Such a luxury, however, was soon made available to the rest of the populace. For the rolls of tobacco that the indigenous peoples of Central and South America smoked provided even those who were not part of a priestly cult with quick, uncomplicated access to the pleasures of those chemicals that tobacco provided. Tobacco could be smoked without

In 1571 Nicolas Monardes, a renowned physician of Seville, pronounced to the Old World the 'virtues' and 'greatness' of the 'holy herb' tobacco: it could cure ailments and drive out evil; in fact, 'this herb is so general a human need, not only for the sick but for the healthy'. He also noted that

'The Earliest Representation in the West of a Tobacco Plant and the Operation of Smoking', c. 1570.

smoking tobacco could reduce weariness and help one to relax.[4] Indeed, it was seen as a remedy for at least the symptoms of that other great import from the New World, syphilis! In 1535 Gonzalo Fernandez de Oviedo, the military governor of Hispaniola after Columbus's discovery, condemned the natives' use of the weed, thinking that it made them lazy and useless. He acknowledges, however, that 'some Christians have already adopted the habit, especially those who have contracted syphilis, for they state that in the ecstasy caused by the smoke they no longer feel their pain.'[5] Smoking is an efficient delivery of the potent chemical nicotine. But smoking itself also seemed to have a magical aura. Girolamo Fracastoro, who coined the term 'syphilis' in 1530, thought that if germs could spread disease through the air, maybe smoke could cure it.

In 1586 Thomas Hariot, the English scientist who accompanied Ralph Lane's expedition to North America, took a copy of Monardes's work on the voyage and marvelled at the healing power of the 'holy smoke':

> they use to take the fume or smoker there of, by sucking it through pipes made of claie, into their stomacke and head; from whence it purgeth superfluous fleame & other grosse humors, openeth all the pores & passages of the body: by which meanes the use thereof, not only preserveth the body from obstructions; but also if any be, so that they have not beene of too long continuance, in short time breaketh them: wherby their bodies are notably preserved in health, & know not many greevous diseases wherewithal wee in England are oftentimes afflicted.[6]

Nicotine intoxication shown in Girolama Benzoni, *Dell'histoire del mondo nuovo* [History of the New World] (Venice, 1565/1572).

Hariot was so bewitched by the magic smoke that he turned into a habitual smoker and died from a cancer of the nose.[7] Smoking had become a pleasure, if a life-threatening one, for the European elites: for Hariot and his contemporaries in Spain, Portugal and France, who could obtain the still rare and expensive plant. Anthony Chute, who wrote the first English work entirely on tobacco in 1595 (not surprisingly entitled *Tobaco*), treated it as a medical herb, citing among others Monardes. But by the sixth edition of his book in 1626 he had condemned smoking for mere pleasure as a wasteful and vicious habit.[8]

Pipes of white ball-clay were first manufactured by the English towards the end of the sixteenth century. This marked the arrival in Europe from the New World of a new delivery system. It putatively came with Sir Walter Raleigh, who indeed carried a pipe to the scaffold when he was beheaded in 1618. The magic smoke of *tabaco* soon caught the fancy of Europeans, and by 1598 descriptions of smoking appeared in European literature and art. The fashion soon spread throughout the continent and the rest of the world. Robert Harcourt was quite right when he wrote in 1613 that 'this commodity Tobacco (so much sought after and desired) will bring as great a benefit and profit . . . as ever the Spaniards gained by the best and richest Silver mine in all their Indies considering the charge of both'.[9] But it was smoking that drove the interest in tobacco as a commodity. Without the wisp of smoke, tobacco would have remained a herb to treat a wide range of ailments.

Within the next fifty years, tobacco plants were grown in most parts of the world, from Siberia to Java and West Africa to Tibet – and the four corners of earth have been bewitched by its magical smoke ever since. What began as a ritual and medical practice in the Americas and the Caribbean came to be the preferred form of consuming tobacco and many other substances. Tobacco conquered the world via the magic of smoke.

Today a world without smoking seems almost unimaginable. We smoke tobacco, but also a wide range of other things, some legal, some illicit. The spirit of the magic smoke has haunted human souls and bodies since the beginning of time, long before the discovery of the New World. It has to do with nostalgia for a lost world through our nose and our sense of smell – one of the most fundamental senses of our being. Smoke satisfies our craving for pleasant odours, warms our skins, comforts our souls, heals our sorrows and brings back the sweet memories of childhood. Smoke had been always part of culture.

The Egyptians, the Babylonians and the Hindus offered incense to their deities, and the Native Americans smoked tobacco to communicate with the spirits. In the Temple in Jerusalem, incense was burned day and night outside the Holy of Holies, and it was in offering incense to their God that the Israelites escaped a life-threatening plague.[10] The Roman Catholic Church, which continued this practice throughout Europe and then the 'New World', burned incense at each High Mass. The great Gothic cathedrals were full of highly scented smoke. Incense accompanied Columbus on his voyages. The ancient Chinese, on the other hand, had burnt *moxa* to chase out demons and to preserve health. In ancient Greece, the inhalation of fumes was widely recommended as a healing practice. It was also used ritually: according to recent readings of Greek prophetic traditions, such as the Oracle at Delphi, the priestesses inhaled fumes from a natural bore in the earth and became so intoxicated that they spoke their prophecies in a sort of drug haze. But for the Greeks, this ritual form of healing was also a source of pleasure. The ancient Scythians, according to Herodotus, once took some hemp seed, crept into their tent and threw the seed on to the hot stones: 'At once it begins to smoke, giving off a vapour unsurpassed by any vapour-bath one could find in Greece. The Scythians enjoy it so much that they howl with pleasure.'[11] The Europeans may have 'discovered' the New World, but they did not 'discover' smoking. They simply remembered the world of smoke. What surprised them was the mode of delivery. No longer were rooms full of smoke, but individuals inhaled from rolls of tobacco or by means of pipes. When Jacques Cartier discovered the Iroquois (in present-day Canada) smoking in 1535 and tried it himself, he found that the smoke seemed as if 'they had filled it [the pipe] with pepper dust it is so hot'.[12] The Europeans soon got used to this form of smoking.

The proliferation of smoking also had much to do with its putative healing power. While much of the history of smoking has concentrated on the miracle plant of tobacco, little attention has been paid to the attraction of smoking – a novelty at the time – and its impact. There is no doubt that the Old World was excited by tobacco because of the belief in the wondrous curative power of the plants that were smoked. It is, however, equally true that it was smoking that produced the feeling of comfort and ease, a sense of well-being. Most of all – and this was noted from the very beginning – it seemed to assuage hunger and enable people to work harder and longer. But it was in its smoked form that tobacco conquered: from herbs to incense, from tobacco to opium, hashish, *qat* and so on, mankind had never lived without smoking.

Seventeenth-century European merchants recognized unlimited potential in exploiting the commodities found in the New World. They imported 'iron-wood' to cure syphilis, but it failed and this market soon dried up. Humankind, who had never lived without smoking, also continually craved cheap panaceas and sources of pleasure. Thus, the market for the magical healing herb that one could smoke continued to grow. Since tobacco was cultivated all over the world, smoking – a practice, a ritual, and a delivery system – was turned into a commodity. While tobacco made more fortunes than all the silver of the Indies — first for the Spanish and the Portuguese, perhaps even among the Jews exiled from Portugal and Spain by the Inquisition, and then for the Dutch and the English – smoking spread and became fashionable. In Europe, the smell of pipe smoke was identified as 'a gentleman-like smell', and Paul Hentzer, a German traveller in London around 1600, observed that by then almost everyone,

A 'savage of the nation of the Onneiothehage', from the *Codex Canadensis*, c. 1700. 'He smokes tobacco in honour of the sun, whom he adores as his particular god.'

including the rich and the poor, men and women, all puffed at long clay pipes.[13] Horatio Busion, another visitor to London around the year 1618, was impressed by the city's pipe ritual:

> It is in such frequent use that not only at every hour of the day but even at night they keep the pipe and steel at their pillow and gratify their longings. Amongst themselves, they are in the habit of circulating toasts, passing the pipe from one to the other with much grace, just as they here do with good wind, but more often with beer. Gentlewomen moreover and virtuous women accustom themselves to take it as medicine, but in secret. The others do it at pleasure.[14]

Different people with different status smoked different tobaccos, however, in different settings with different pipes. As the culture of smoking spread, smoking paraphernalia became more elaborate, and could be made of valuable materials. A culture of *objets d'art* for smoking developed. While ordinary folk smoked plain clay pipes, extravagantly carved and decorated pipes, some even made of silver, also appeared. Tobacco boxes, made of wood, metals or exotic materials such as ivory, also became indispensable items to carry around. They contained all the necessary accessories for smoking, flint, steel, ember tongs and, of course, tobacco. The boxes were soon given as friendship or diplomatic tokens, and travelled across the oceans far and wide with the 'holy smoke' and the 'holy herb'. By the beginning of the seventeenth century, the word for what the Jesuit preacher Jakob Balde had called 'Dry Drunkenness' in his anti-smoking treatise of 1658 had been coined. What everyone was doing was 'smoking'. The term took almost 200 years to become established.

Outside Europe, across the Ottoman dominions to Asia and Africa, smoking spread rapidly. It was the latest fashion. In central Asia and in India, under the Moguls, the locals adopted smoking as an art form with great inventiveness. They mixed tobacco with other more familiar leaves, spices and sandalwood, and smoked through a water pipe, known as a *hookah*. By passing through water, the smoke was cooled down and produced a cool whiff, which was most welcome in a hot climate. The *hookah* soon blossomed into an article of display. Pipe smoking also spread quickly throughout the African Continent, facilitated by Portuguese and French traders. By the end of the sixteenth century, it had already produced a rich local smoking culture, which extended into social rituals (e.g. weddings) and religious rites.[15]

According to Japanese records, pipe smoking entered Japan in April 1600 with the travelling Englishman William Adams.[16] Just a decade later, around 1615, it was observed that men, women and children had all taken up the habit of smoking.[17] Japanese art of the early Ukiyo-e, the dawn of the Floating World (1650–1765), presented the act of smoking as part of the world of the courtesan. In

Engraved title-page of Jakob Balde, *Die trunckene Trunkenheit* (Nürnberg, 1658).

Okumura Mansanobu's print from the mid-1740s of a courtesan holding a pipe, the sensuality of the woman is emphasized by the placement of a long pipe on the diagonal, literally cutting the image in half. Earlier, in the work of Omori Yoshikiyo of Kyoto, there are scenes in places of assignation, where pipes and tobacco trays designate the space as a brothel.[18]

The Spanish and Portuguese also brought tobacco smoking to China, via the South China Sea and Japan. The Chinese soon fell in love with this new practice and found that it was an intoxicating experience. Smoking rapidly became an integral part of the existing tea culture. Social elites further praised the medicinal qualities of smoking, from malaria prevention to treating rheumatism and common colds.[19] Within a single generation, China had acquired an all-engulfing smoking culture. The celebrated writer Quan Zuwang (1705–1755), in his famous essay on tobacco, claimed that 'the essence of tobacco smoke is not to provide warmth but pure pleasure and spiritual sublimity. When depressed, it can cheer the spirit, guide the *qi* and open up spiritual passages . . . It can sober up the drunk, as well as being intoxicating . . . It can dispel boredom and preoccupation, a necessity for daily life.'[20] The idea that smoke was part of the regime of modern life, a life in which it was possible to exercise control over the body, illness, sadness and drunkenness, was as much purported in the West as in China. In a French treatise of 1700 it was claimed that smoking tobacco 'makes the brain and the nerves drier and steadier. This conduces a sound faculty of judgement, a clearer, more circumspect faculty of reason and a greater constancy of soul.'[21] West and East agreed about the bountiful results of smoking.

A daily necessity, a fashionable leisure activity and a panacea, by the middle of the seventeenth century tobacco smoking had become endemic, rapidly crossing social divides. It also paved the way for smoking opium, which transformed China into one of the highest populations of smokers in the world. While it was the Europeans who were responsible for introducing the American tradition of smoking to the rest of the world, it soon became a global practice. Crossing continents, people began to experiment and make their skills, methods and techniques of smoking more sophisticated. They incorporated smoking into their culture and gave it a function in local traditions and rituals. In a world widely divided by geographic distance, religions, customs and social status, smoking became a common practice among many and stimulated social interaction.

While smoking dissolved cultural and social barriers, it also enforced them. As smoking became more and more a part of the life of ordinary people, a problem arose, which had to do with pleasure. Smoking gives pleasure, but this was to be enjoyed by royalty, by the privileged and by the elites, not by the self-respecting working masses, whose preoccupations were supposed to be work, productivity and discipline. In response to the claim that tobacco smoking increased the capacity for work came the answer that smoking was a leisure activity that caused workers to ignore their duties. Pleasure for the majority was too great a threat to social control, a 'terror' within that could potentially lead to social instability, especially when the ruling status quo was under challenge or on the way to collapse. When seen as a threat to social order, smoking became a crime that deserved punishment. Medical debates over the harmful effects of smoking and tobacco had been around since the early seventeenth century, both in Europe and in the East, although, as with drinking, the problem lay elsewhere. Often, as in the tract by Jacob Balde, the negative effects of drinking and smoking were seen as identical: both turned respectful, orderly workers into individuals interested in their own pleasures. The state often tried to regulate such pleasure-giving substances, to ensure social and economic stability.

The Ottoman sultan Murad IV (*reg.* 1623–40) was among the first rulers to ban smoking, for it was seen as a threat to morals and health. He even tried to close the coffee houses where smokers gathered. In China, the Chongzhen emperor (*reg.* 1627–44) lamented over the doom of the Ming dynasty. Two years before he hanged himself on the top of Corn Hill while watching the peasant rebels besiege the Imperial Palace, he issued an edict prohibiting tobacco smoking. Those 'common people' who broke the edict 'would be punished in a similar way as treason with barbarians'.[22] Similar prohibitions were repeated by the following dynasty, the Manchu, when smoking was considered to be 'a more heinous crime than even that of neglecting archery'.[23] In 1634 the Patriarch of Moscow forbade the sale of tobacco and sentenced both men and women who smoked to having their nostrils slit or whipped so badly that no skin remained on their backs. In 1642 Urban VII condemned smoking in a papal bull because 'persons of both sexes, yea even priests and clerics . . . during the actual celebration of Holy Mass . . . do not shrink from taking tobacco through the mouth or nostrils'. (Over time, however, the Church created a tobacco monopoly and then forbade the distribution of anti-smoking literature in its sphere of influence.)

In England, James I condemned tobacco smoking as early as 1604 based more or less on the same argument: smoking, a custom that came from the 'barbarous and beastly manners of the wild, godless, and slavish Indians', was blamed because England was seen as having fallen from its former glory. It caused the clergy to grow lax, the nobility to sink into idleness and *hoi polloi* were on a steep moral decline. According to Ben Jonson in 1621, it was the devil's fart: 'That the scent of the vapour before and behind, / Hath foully perfumed most part of the isle. / Tobacco, the learned suppose, / Which since in country, court, and town, / In the devil's glister-pipe smokes at the nose / Of polecat and madam, or gallant and clown.'[24] Given that there were more than 7,000 establishments selling tobacco in London at the time, there may have been a kernel of truth to this argument! A contemporary pamphlet, however, urged the replacement of the foreign weed with a true English product: 'Better be chokt with English hemp, then poisoned with Indian tobacco!'[25] Smoking would remain an option even for those crusading against tobacco consumption.

Yet even those prohibitions that threatened state action and bodily harm did not stop people from smoking. The masses were not as malleable as their rulers imaged them to be. They always made their choices. If they could not choose their leaders, they could at least fool them. Even though Moses brought them the Ten Commandments, they have always followed the Eleventh: 'Thou shall find a way out.' Once the masses have tasted pleasure, they

J. K. Föhl, *Still Life with Pipe and Tobacco-Packet*, 1789, watercolour.

will not easily give it up. As the prohibition against tobacco intensified, people's desire to smoke increased. Unable to suppress smoking, rulers turned to controlling it through state monopoly. Through such a monopoly, tobacco and smoking brought them wealth, eased social tension and strengthened their rule. Everybody was happy. Peter the Great even included smoking in his drive to propel the Russian feudal state into the arms of the West, the Enlightenment and tobacco. In England during the reign of William of Orange and Mary, which began in 1689, not only was the Dutch court fashion for smoking imported along with Dutch courtiers, but also the artistic tradition of Dutch genre painting, seen in works by Adriaen van Ostade and more formal portraits, in which pipes rarely fail to appear. The pipe or cigar had become a staple of how middle-class men and women were to be seen. This was true even in James Gillray's caricatures of high fashion in London; it was a mark of being fashionable. And there was little doubt that smoking and tobacco had accelerated international trade and contact, which in turn forged the world ahead into modernity.

In the eighteenth century, however, tobacco as an object to be smoked remained a commodity associated with a pre-modern delivery system. Introduced into Europe in the form of smoked tobacco, it ignored the wider range of means of consumption that had been used in the Americas.

An engraving of
a smoking club in
England, c. 1792.

(No craze for tobacco enemas was ever recorded in
Europe!) By then, smoking tobacco was no longer a
vogue, but a norm. It suddenly faced the rivalry of
snuff – inhaled tobacco – the fashion phenomenon
of the time. Snuff was modern. Pipe smokers held
on for dear life. William Cowper in 1782 noted that
the pipe smoker's 'breath is as sweet as the breath
of blown roses, / While you [the snuff taker] are a
nuisance where'er you appear; / There is noting [sic]
but sniveling and blowing of noses, / Such a noise
as turns any man's stomach to hear . . .'.[26] Better
the quiet contemplation of the pipe, an aid to
thought and writing, than the fashion of drooling
and sneezing.

The cigar is a prime example of how tobacco
continued to re-invent itself, enchanting the world
once more – and at its roots was one of the original
ways of consumption. The cigar became fashionable first in Spain, then in Britain and other parts
of Europe. It was first conceived of in Cuba and
was launched into full swing by the Spanish in the
Philippines. A not-too-distant cousin of the way
that the Cubans had smoked when they met
Columbus's sailors, it was pure smoke. Unlike
the ornamented, solid meerschaum or briar pipe,
it vanished as it transformed itself into smoke.
It became like smoke itself — an object of pure

essence. While the eighteenth century was described
as the century of snuff, by the early nineteenth
century the appeal of the cigar had become so
enormous that smoking rooms emerged throughout Europe. Lord Byron praised 'Sublime Tobacco!
Which from East to West / Cheer's the tar's labour
or the Turkman's rest . . . / Yet thy true lovers more
admire by far / Thy naked beauty – Give me a cigar!'
in 1823.[27] It was observed that 'In those where
civilization has made most advances, old habits and
modern delicacy are in some measure reconciled by
appropriating rooms exclusively to the smokers.'[28]
As cigars became more and more a mark of status
for aristocrats, the privileged, the wealthy and the
social elites, the 'dirty old pipe' also underwent a
revival among the masses. In addition to cigars and
pipes, Europeans were soon offered the choice of
cigarettes. By this point the gendered practice of
tobacco smoking had begun to vanish, since both
men and women took snuff (in different ways, in
different places and with different utensils). Ben
Jonson's Ursula in *Bartholomew Fair* (1614) could
demand: 'I can but hold life and soul together with
this . . . and a whiff of tobacco. Where's my pipe
now? Not filled? Thou arrant incubee!' Over time,
smoking cigars and cigarettes became associated
only with men, or became a marker of specific

types of women whose place was rarely in the home. Smoking and sex have had a long history together. William Makepeace Thackeray, writing in the *Fitzboodle Papers* (1842–3), states boldly: 'The fact is, that the cigar is a rival to the ladies, and their conqueror, too.' Charles Lamb compared his last cigar to the end of a marriage: 'Or, as men, constrain'd to part / With what's nearest to their heart, . . . / Whence they feel it death to sever, / Though it be, as they, perforce, / Guiltless of the sad divorce. / For thy sake, TOBACCO, I / Would do any thing but die . . .'. It is the smoke that defines for Lamb the experience he is abandoning: 'Thou in such a cloud dost bind us / That our worst foes cannot find us . . . / While each man, through they height'ning steam, / Does like a smoking Etna seem . . .'. Tobacco smoke is the lover abandoned but constantly desired. Women rarely consumed cigars; only their suitors did. Charles Dickens wrote from Geneva in 1846 about an evening with French and American women smoking cigars, but he concluded that 'I never saw a woman – not a basket woman or a gipsy – smoke before!' Perhaps not in polite British society, but women of all classes in the United States in the early nineteenth century smoked. Indeed the wives of two presidents, Andrew Jackson and Zachary Taylor, smoked in the White House! But as the cigar conquered smoking it did so in the hands of men.

Outside modern Europe, the Chinese had meanwhile perfected their skills in opium smoking. Having learned from the Javanese to smoke a mixture of tobacco and opium, the Chinese soon opted for the latter, partly because of the imperial ban on tobacco smoking. More importantly, smoking opium gave a much more intense pleasure and seemed more beneficial to the smoker's health. With their great technological genius, which focused on improving the art of living, the Chinese turned opium smoking into a real and unparalleled art. Smoking became a ritual for the consumers of the magic smoke of opium, and with ritual goes ritual implements. Apart from the high demand on the quality of opium and the strict procedure for its preparation, the opium pipe, also known as the 'Smoking Gun', is surprisingly unique. It is designed to distil rather than burn substances, and hence consists of two parts, the smoking tube and the distillation bowl or 'damper'. The wick must be properly trimmed to produce just the right flame; the bowl must be held at the right distance and angle from the heat; and the smoker must draw the pipe properly, so that the opium pellet will slowly vaporize rather than burn: it should produce a distinctive sizzling sound that echoes in the bowl. As the opium gradually vaporizes, it is transformed into a dense, bluish white smoke that rushes through the tiny pinhole attached to the pellet and into the bowl. The hot smoke expands suddenly then cools down in the bowl, causing the solids to precipitate from the smoke and form a crusty residue known as 'dross'. The remaining smoke now contains only the purest volatile and the most aromatic elements of opium, which enters the smoker's lip and descends down to the lungs as a velvet, fragrant and soothing fume.[29] The pleasure of pure smoke was the end result.

In Western Europe the rituals of smoking, as in the smokers' clubs in London and Berlin, were tied more closely to the socialization of individual smokers. Some of these clubs, such as those at the Berlin court of Frederick I (*reg.* 1701–13) and Frederick Wilhelm I (*reg.* 1713–40), were quite elaborate affairs, and their formal portraits resemble the Dutch formal portraits of medical and social organizations. Most, however, were middle-class affairs. These clubs served coffee or chocolate, the two drinks of pleasure in the eighteenth and nineteenth centuries. While the tamping, scraping, lighting and re-lighting of tobacco pipes did constitute a ritual, it was the context – the club with its conversation, libraries and meals – that provided greater rituals.[30] Among the working classes, public houses, inns and bars served much the same function. Smoking became part of a culture of drink in the working-class neighbourhoods of Europe and North America. In 1888, when Paul Gauguin painted his extraordinary *Night Café*

Frederick I of Prussia's 'Tobacco Club' (1701–13) in the castle in Berlin.

An opium den in Manila, Philippines, *c.* 1924.

depicting Marie Ginoux, the manager of an all-night drinking establishment in Arles, leaning in a philosophical pose against the bar, the room is full of smoke produced by her customers. Smoke defined the drinkers' world as much as drink.

In the Muslim and Indian worlds, smokers continued to enjoy the pleasure of the cool whiff produced by the *hookah*. With great knowledge of herbs and plants, they switched between various kinds of hashish, *qat* or tobacco, largely depending on choice and availability. In particular, hashish and *qat* played a pivotal role in poetry, music, architecture, social relations, wedding and funerary rites, fortune and misfortune, home furnishings, clothes, food and sex; smoking became a way of life more than ever before. The hashish smoking houses in Cairo were but one example of a space where all social events occurred.

Like eating, drinking and most other pleasurable activities, smoking is habit forming. For while we are unable to live without sustenance, the modern world demands more than bread and water. We have to breathe, but we do not have to inhale the residue of burning substances, as Bill Clinton claimed. Our dependency is, however, as much determined by our culture, or perhaps even more so, as a consequence of modernity, as it is a purely physiological one. While individual freedom found its expression in democracy, human beings have never been more trapped in a world of 'free choice'. Commodities are no longer just things to be enjoyed: they possess a power that can transform life. In the consumer world, it is believed that life can be enriched through purchasing, even though in reality one becomes poorer by spending. The key is to purchase those things that give pleasure in the most immediate and direct manner. Thus smoking with friends is more than a pleasure to be shared, but an occasion of glamour shaped by fashion and driven by envy. By sharing the experience with those who envy you, you may find a solitary form of reassurance, thus happiness. In addition, of course, most people find pleasure in the very act of inhaling substances such as

hemp or tobacco or opium. As money became the key to human capacity, the power to spend on smoking became the power to define smokers' lives. Smoking is therefore a sign of the fulfilment of a good life, the 'Cinderella dream' for the working class. (In 1888 W. D. & H. O. Wills launched Britain's first machine-made brand of cigarettes, called 'Cinderella'.) This promise was as ineffable as smoke itself.

The dependency on smoke was and still is created by the tobacco industry and the tobacco trade. The profit generated by the trade stimulated the growth of the industry. The bigger the industry, the wider the products and varieties, thus the more smokers / consumers and the greater the profits. By the end of the nineteenth century, smoking had become big business. In 1889 James Buchanan 'Buck' Duke spent $800,000 marketing his cigarette around the world. It was he more than anyone else who created the craze for cigarettes (through his American Tobacco Company). He was also the first to recognize that advertising, including the inclusion of collectable cigarette cards, was as important as the product itself (cards had appeared as early as 1885 to stiffen the soft packs, but it was Duke who made them into 'collectables'). Duke mechanized the manufacture of cigarettes with the new Bonsack automatic rolling machine, and could turn out 120,000 cigarettes in a ten-hour day, the equivalent of 40 hand rollers rolling five cigarettes a minute for ten hours. But there is no doubt that the explosion of interest in cigarette smoking was furthered by the birth of modern advertising.

During the 1880s improvements in transportation, manufacturing volume and packaging led to the ability to sell the same branded product first throughout the United States, then worldwide. As a result advertising was born. Advertising agencies sprouted like wildflowers. The most advertised products throughout most of the nineteenth century included elixirs and 'all cure' patent medicines. Tobacco products, however, became one of the prime objects for the new vehicle of global sales.

The Smoker's Textbook.

Smoking had to be made into a fashion for everyone and in every place.

The power of modern advertising was rooted in the cutting-edge psychological and sociological theories of its day. It used the explosion of cheap newspapers and magazines, of public images on billboards and sandwich boards, to convey its message. One of the most striking early tools of tobacco advertising was *Cope's Tobacco Plant*, a periodical published in London by Cope's Tobacco Company between 1870 and 1884. What is of the greatest interest is that it is more than a periodical devoted to tobacco smoking. Baudelaire's essay 'On Hasheesh' appeared there in English in October 1875 and Théophile Gautier's 'On Opium' a month later. The periodical was devoted to all forms of smoking pleasure in which gentlemen smokers indulged. Aimed at a new suburban or provincial middle class, it at least claimed this. How much more central to the self-image of the middle class was Lewis Carroll's *Alice in Wonderland* when it appeared in 1865 – it contained the extraordinary image by John Tenniel of the moment when 'the Caterpillar and Alice looked at each other for some time in silence: at last the Caterpillar took the hookah out of its mouth . . .'.

Advertising had become the life and the dream of modern culture in an age of roaring capitalism. Capitalism survives by tempting the majority to define their own interests as narrowly as possible. Samuel Gompers recognized this in 1873 when he organized the cigar workers in the United States. The beginning of the modern American labour movement was rooted in smoke. But even the cigar rollers depended on advertising to spread the word of their movement and to sell the product that they were manufacturing. Through advertising, all consumers are united in their pursuit of objects defined as desirable for everybody. Thus, by smoking the same brands, all the hopes of smokers / consumers are gathered together, made homogeneous, simplified. The brands provide a means by which images are used to define not the tobacco product but the very act of smoking itself. Advertising imagery became the place where twentieth-century fantasies about the power of smoking to provide status, desirability or pleasure were defined. With every purchase, consumers were offered an intense yet vague, magical yet repeatable promise: they too could be like the smokers illustrated in the advertisements. No other kind of hope or satisfaction or pleasure could any longer be envisaged. The nostalgia felt in seeing these images was no longer about the warmth or personal pleasure of smoking, but the power to control the present and buy or sell to the future. Thus cigars were sold under the name of powerful ancient monarchies, or cigarettes promised a 'Wedding Cake', whereas opiates in China were dispensed in the guise of traditional alchemical pills assuring immortality.

Modern advertising also turned women and children into new potential consumers of magic smoke,

The *hookah* and the Caterpillar, from Lewis Carroll's *Alice in Wonderland* (London, 1865).

ironically with the offer of liberation through smoking, now seen as the 'Torches of Freedom'. Although one may argue that women had smoked publicly as early as men, at least up to the beginning of the nineteenth century, and privately after that, throughout the world the thought of women smoking in public had been considered socially unacceptable and distasteful. Closely associated with promiscuity and prostitution in the late nineteenth century, the image of the smoking woman haunted the literary and artistic fantasy of both Western Europe (and the Americas) and the Middle East. With the advent of the First World War and the establishment of suffrage as a basic issue in Europe and the Americas, the attitude changed. The issue of women smoking became an arena where struggle over women's liberation took place. It had been the stuff of humour beginning in the 1840s with the first Women's Rights meeting in Seneca Falls, New York. Although many of the women present were also both abolitionists and advocates of temperance, they were caricatured as demanding the right to smoke. Smoking became as much a sign of the dangers of women's rights infringing upon traditional male activities as the clothing reform advocated by women such as Clara Bloomer. Indeed, by the close of the nineteenth century, there was a spate of images illustrating the levelling effect of smoking. Even international conflicts could be solved over a cigar! Equality was a good thing for many, and equality meant smoking. (Lucy Page Gaston, who founded the Anti-Cigarette League in 1899 in Chicago, disagreed vehemently.)

As the cigarette replaced the cigar, women across the social spectrum also began to smoke. In the United Kingdom in 1900 four-fifths of the tobacco smoked was in the form of cigars; by 1950 four-fifths was in the form of cigarettes. But the consumers of smoke had also radically shifted. Women of the upper and middle classes were smoking more and more of the cigarettes, if only in private. It was the sign of the 'New Woman' in 1915 when T. S. Eliot's 'Miss Nancy Elliot smoked / And danced all the modern dances; / And her aunts were not quite sure how they felt about it, / But they knew that it was modern'. In 1928 George Washington Hill, then the president of the American Tobacco Company, decided to launch an all-out campaign to get women to smoke the company's Lucky Strike cigarettes. With the help of Edward Bernays (Sigmund Freud's nephew) as the social engineer, Lucky Strike was hailed as the 'Torch of Freedom' for women, who must 'combat the silly prejudice' enforced upon them. In 1929 ten New York debutantes, recruited by Bernays, walked down Fifth Avenue in New York City smoking Lucky Strikes. It was also suggested that women 'Reach for a Lucky instead of a sweet', which reinforced the century-old belief that smoking was an aid in weight reduction or at least hunger control. The slim, androgynous body was the other sign of the 'New Woman'. The result was a great success, at least for the company. Lucky Strike's sales were boosted to 43.2 billion in comparison to 13.7 billion three years earlier. Since Lucky Strike promised women 'freedom', smoking became a 'must' among 'liberated' women.

John Leech, 'Bloomerism – an American custom', a cartoon from *Punch*, 1851. Some American women appeared in the streets of London in a tunic and trousers, confirming a certain brassy stereotype.

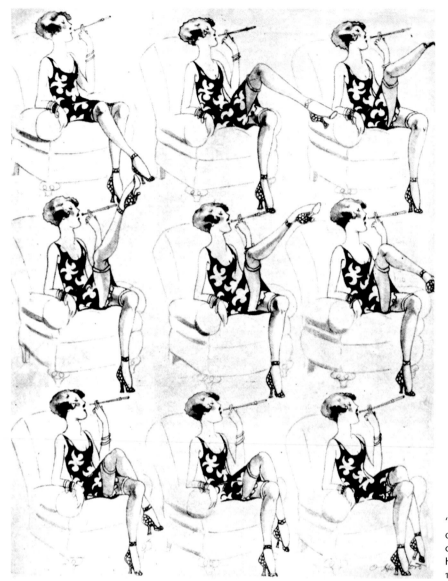

'Slow–motion picture of a John Held Girl crossing her legs', Oliver Herford's cartoon in *Life*, 1927.

At the same time, the increased pressure of modern life forced many smokers to crave a puff to release their daily strain even more desperately. If smoking had always been contested between those who saw it as a pleasure or a cure and those who saw it as a vice and a cause of illness, tobacco's danger to health was clearly recognized by the medical establishment in the nineteenth century. The analogy of this was that other major import for which tobacco was seen as amelioration, syphilis. While from the time of the first modern epidemic of syphilis in Italy in the late fifteenth century there had been an awareness of the association of the transmission of the disease with the sexual act, it was only in the early twentieth century that science proved the actual connection. Tobacco had been sensed as unhealthy more because of its moral than its physiological significance. In the seventeenth century James I had called forth a debate in Oxford about smoking, in which the opponents produced the blackened brains and viscera of smokers to prove the dangers. But it was clear that his objection was primarily a moral one. There had been suggestions about the dangers of smoke distinct from the moral attack on smoking. In 1761 John Hill had specifically associated smoking with cancer of the nasal passages. This soon became a popular 'fact'. In the 1830s Honoré de Balzac, in his extraordinary 'Pathology of the Social Life', a theoretical pendant to his life-long series of novels, *La Comédie humaine*, devoted his longest section to tobacco. There he notes its unlimited attraction for everyone across all levels of society, but also its deadly effect on the smoker's nose and throat.[31] It was only in the middle of the nineteenth century that scientists such as Etienne-Frédéric Bousisson in Montpellier started to do epidemiological studies that associated cancer of the mouth (popularly called *cancer des fumeurs*) with smoking pipes. Over the course of the nineteenth century science began to examine the effect of smoking tobacco (as well as other things) on health. In 1857 J. B. Neil asked in the *Lancet* whether insurance companies will be 'taking the precaution of inquiring . . . if he is an habitual and inveterate smoker?' By focusing on the changes on the cellular level, the changes in the organism that smoking caused became more and more seen as a public health problem. And smokers reacted by ignoring the growing suspicion about the dangers of smoking. The following appeared in one of the many anthologies of tobacco texts in the late nineteenth century:

In spite of my physician, who is, *entre nous*,
    a fogy
And for every little pleasure has some pathologic
    bogy,
Who will bear with no small vices, and grows
    dismally prophetic
If I wander from the weary way of virtue dietetic;

In spite of dire forewarnings that my brains will
    all be scattered,

My memory extinguished, and my nervous
    system shattered,
That my hand all take to trembling, and my heart
    begin to flutter,
My digestion turn a rebel to my very bread and
    butter;

As I puff this mild Havana, and its ashes slowly
    lengthen,
I feel my courage gather and my resolution
    strengthen . . .
I will smoke, and, I will praise you, my cigar, and
    I will light you
With tobacco-phobic pamphlets by the learnéd
    prigs who fight you![32]

Even with the increased awareness in the late nineteenth century that smoking was related to various forms of cellular change, it remained strongly associated with moral failing. J. H. Kellogg, the health reformer, stated in 1903 that smoking 'undermines both the health and morals in a most certain way . . . It is a savage practice, without a single redeeming feature [introduced by] the American savage.'[33] Needless to say, R.S.S. Baden-Powell, the creator of the Boy Scouts, condemned smoking, for 'a scout does not smoke. Any boy can smoke; it is not such a very wonderful thing to do. But a scout will not do it because he is not such a fool.' This was the message in his *Scouting for Boys* of 1909. With all of the moral and scientific discussion it was only after the Second World War, in 1948, that Sir Richard Doll began to work on the deleterious effects of smoking on health. It was his series of epidemiological studies of lung cancer that convinced both the British and the American public health authorities that smoking (of all substances) was bad for your health.

The public health campaign against smoking began at this time. It corresponded with other anti-drug movements that had arisen in the early twentieth century. Anti-drug laws were firmly in place in Europe and the United States by the early twentieth century. Smoking opium was seen as a curse, and smoking marijuana was already labelled as both immoral and life threatening by the 1930s. Marijuana was the devil's instrument, which seemed inevitably to lead to the injection of heroin. (Before this marijuana was generally seen as a medicine, being available as an extract in drugstores or in the form of cigarettes to be smoked by asthmatics.) According to Harry Anslinger, the implacable Commissioner of the United States Bureau of Narcotics in 1953: 'While opium can be a blessing or a curse, depending on its use, marijuana is only and always a scourge which undermines its victims and degrades them mentally and morally . . .'.[34] Smoking was bad, no matter what was being smoked. Tobacco, marijuana and opium were all now sources of danger to the health of the individual and the nation. When the systematic suppression of the sale of marijuana in the United States began in 1969, drug traffickers turned from one smoke to another in the 1970s and '80s. With the development of smokable cocaine, the rhetoric of anti-smoking and the anxiety about drugs was so powerful that 'crack cocaine' was immediately labelled a public health epidemic to no little degree because it was inhaled.[35]

By the year 2000, 1.1 billion people smoked. More than three times the number of men than women smoke. The greatest number of smokers today, 340 million, are in China, averaging 1,791 cigarettes each a year. Over the twentieth century, the Chinese smoked cigarettes in ever-greater numbers. They smoked 0.3 billion cigarettes in 1902, 4 billion in 1924 and 28 billion in 1928; many were sold through the joint British American Tobacco Company.[36] And, in a survey of 1996 by the Chinese Academy of Preventive Medicine, most of those who smoked in China (61 per cent) believed that smoking caused little harm. Still the Government banned smoking from most public places in May 1997, and virtually all advertising in the electronic and print media vanished three years earlier under governmental decree. The World Health Organization began work that year toward an international anti-smoking treaty, to be

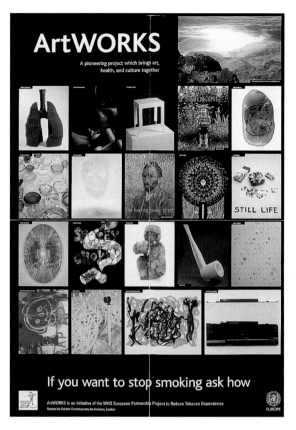

Poster from a Press packet for the Artworks project on smoking sponsored by the World Health Organization.

in place by the year 2003. Many nations had already begun to isolate smokers or ban smoking. The anti-smoking campaign was often one of moral objection to smoking and just as often used visual imagery. And this continues in the early twenty-first century.

'Can Art Make You Give Up Smoking? Artists Create Works for The World Health Organization' shouts the press release of the World Health Organization's regional office for Europe.[37] This is an odd claim. 'What do a hundred Murano glass ashtrays [by Stefano Arienti], a slice of embroidered ham [by Wim Delvoye] and a huge blue velvet sculpture of human lungs [by Milena Dopitova] all have in common?. The World Health Organization's exhibition, held in London and other European capitals in 2000–2001 'aim[ed] to raise awareness of the health risks of smoking, the benefits of quitting, the difficulty people have in successfully quitting, and how people can be supported by health providers to quit.' Can art be an instrument of health policy or can it cure? The materials for the exhibition make the goal clear. There are no claims for ethereal beauty and the sublime in this art. Rather, hard statistical reasoning: 'Research has shown that 70 per cent of the UK's 12 million smokers already want to give up.' And what is the role of art in helping them to accomplish this? It is 'to reduce tobacco-related death and disease among tobacco-dependent smokers and to prevent non-smokers from starting to smoke.' If, the rationale goes, the global tobacco industry has sold us smoking through images, then artistic images will scare and wean us from cigarettes. Does post-modern art serve here as an advertising surrogate? Twentieth-century artists such as Andy Warhol parodied the devices of advertising art, including those of smoking. The intent here is not to highlight how advertising creates images to influence us, but to empower us with images to take control over our actions. But just to make sure, the creators of this exhibition provide us with 'top tips for giving up smoking', which begin with 'don't go it alone'. And the person you should call on is 'your family doctor, a high street chemist or another expert', but not your local art gallery or print maker or performance artist. How strange. Art cures? But 'nicotine replacement therapy' is also effective, states one of the other handouts, which advocates some type of medical or psychological treatment for tobacco addiction.

Will seeing a painting cure the craving for an Uppman cigar after dinner? Will Gavin Turk's video and photographs of a smoking monkey doll persuade the viewer that (1) even monkeys can be addicted; (2) that he or she is no better than a monkey since they cannot reject my cigar; or (3) that they are much better than a monkey because through rational choice they can see the benefit of giving up smoking? Do these works of art really have the same power that the Philip Morris page had in the 1950s (when early television viewers

Knut Hansen, *Ash Wednesday*, an 1890s caricature.

imagined they could be really 'hip' sitting in an expensive hotel listening to him 'Calling Philip Morris')? Will they persuade today's Chinese, in the lead in world tobacco consumption as they eagerly ascend the smoky clouds of 'Red Pagoda Mountains'? (Hong Tashan is the most famous cigarette brand in China and the company ranks at the top of China's stock market.)

Art may not cure, for weaning oneself from smoking anything, including tobacco, is difficult.

Two protestors agreeing to differ at the 2003 Labour Party conference in Bournemouth.

Bartolomé de Las Casas noted in *History of the Indies* in 1535 that 'after I reprimanded [smokers] saying that it was a vice, they answered that they were unable to stop taking it . . .'. Smoking is a pleasure and a vice, a source of great relief and much danger. In 1923 the great Italian-Jewish novelist Italo Svevo wrote his *Confessions of Zeno*, the greatest novel to recount a protagonist's withdrawal from smoking. 'Now that I am old and no one expects anything of me, I continue to pass from cigarette to resolution and back again. What is the point of such resolution today? Perhaps I am like that aged dyspeptic in Goldoni, who wanted to die healthy after having been ill all his life.' But just after one more puff, perhaps while looking at some wonderful works of anti-smoking art!

Be it for or against the idea of smoking, in ritual or daily use, for pleasure or for cure, the competing perceptions of smoking have assaulted our sensibil-ities since its inception. According to Columbus's *Book of Prophecies*, which he wrote in Spain in 1501–2, the voyage that had resulted in the discovery of the Americas was motivated by his own mystical visions that he thought would lead to gold, thus funding for Spain a new crusade to retake the Holy Land.[38] Even he could not possibly have imagined the wealth, influence and mystique that another one of his imports, tobacco, has had. Although the inhalation of burning herbs has been part of the human experience for millennia, the smoking of tobacco has shaped invention and culture, capturing the imagination like nothing else in history. It has allowed us to imagine smoking a wide range of other plants and substances in various times and places. Be it a panacea or bane, icon or commodity, the magic of smoking and the images surrounding it continue to shape and be shaped by our changing perception of our world.

Smoking in History and Culture

Ritual Smoking in Central America

FRANCIS ROBICSEK

The first written report on tobacco in a European language is that of Christopher Columbus, who on 12 October 1492 noted in his journal that when he reached the beaches of San Salvador, 'the natives brought fruit, wooden spears, and certain dried leaves [tobacco] which gave off a distinct fragrance'. As the Spaniards cut their way with sword and cunning across the New World territory, they encountered the custom of tobacco smoking wherever they went.

The newly discovered plant, tobacco, was not only an item of luxury that played an important part in Mesoamerican social activity, but was also used extensively in everyday life. According to Francisco Javier Clavijero, the Jesuit historian, the custom of the after-dinner smoke was well known even in pre-Columbian times, and after meals the Aztec lords 'composed themselves to sleep with the smoke of tobacco'.[1]

TOBACCO AND THE MAYAS

Early records relating to the use of tobacco among the Mayas at the time of the Spanish Conquest are, to say the least, highly questionable and often confusing. The first Western recorded observer of Maya smoking habits was Juan Díaz, chaplain of Juan de Grijalva's expedition, which landed on the island of Cozumel, off the coast of Yucatán, in 1518. Diaz reported that the natives presented to Captain Grijalva reeds that 'gave off delicate odour on being burned'.[2]

During these first contacts with the Mayas, the Spaniards found them smoking primitive cigars made of long, thick leaves, similar to those smoked today by the Lacandón Indians. The preferred cigar in Central America – then as now – has three parts: filler, binder and wrapper. The filler is the inner core that forms the body and shape of the cigar. The binder is the leaf known as the 'cigar bunch'. The wrapper or outer covering consists of a ribbon leaf wrapped spirally around the bunch.

The smoking habits of the ancient Mayas probably derived from the incense ceremonies of the medicine men and priests. Contrary to the natives of North America, who smoked tobacco with a pipe, the Mayas were exclusively cigar and cigarette smokers. The absence of the pipe from the Maya area is also noteworthy in both artistic representations and archaeological finds.

A Lacandon Indian.

Several different types of cigars are mentioned in early manuscripts, some of them made entirely of tobacco, others rolled in leaves of other plants. As far as cigarettes are concerned, it would be a tempting evolutionary scheme to suggest that in ancient Central America, just as in Europe, the earlier method of tobacco use was in the form of the cigar and that from it evolved the cigarette. Pictorial evidence on ceramics, however, indicates that the Mayas may have smoked cigarettes even during the Classic times.

In this aboriginal cigarette, the tobacco filling was wrapped in a corn-leaf wrapper, a method that is still used throughout Mesoamerica. Another variety of aboriginal cigarette is the so-called cane cigarette that was popular not only in the Maya realm but also with their northern neighbours, the Aztec. This 'cigarette' is made by stuffing a short piece of reed or cane with powdered tobacco. A band of fabric or string is then tied to it, with a flap left free to grasp. Some regarded the cane cigarette as an intermediate form between the crude cigar and the pipe, but it is probably an individual development of one particular area.

Nowadays, the Mayas' smoking habits are changing rapidly. More and more of them, especially those living in and around cities, smoke commercial cigarettes. Some members of the highland Maya nations now also smoke pipes.

Polychrome vase. Maya culture, Late Classic Period (AD 800–900) from Guatemala's Peten Region. It is painted with a complex mythological scene which includes the figure of a seated Lord smoking a cigarette.

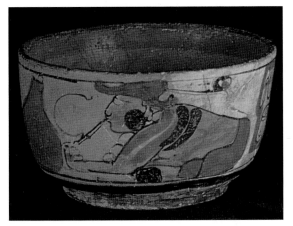

Shallow bowl from Yucatan Mexico. Maya Culture, Late Classic Period (AD 900–1000). It shows a seated figure smoking a cigarette.

Polychrome vase, Tikal area Guatemala. Maya Culture Middle Classic Period (AD 600–800). It depicts a seated Lord smoking a cigarette.

Plants that alter the mental state of the user have always been regarded by the natives of the New World as being endowed with supernatural powers. Such plants, including tobacco, played an important part in ceremonies and folklore. Tobacco was eminently fitted for religious rituals: 'It was aromatic and therefore suitable as an incense; it was beautiful in bloom; and it was consumed by fire – the cleanser; it mysteriously disappeared into the great void, the abode of gods and departed spirits, to whom the breath of its smoke was sweet.'[3]

It is probable that the use of tobacco was at first only esoteric and was confined to shamans, priests and medicine men. Only later did the plant pass from its ceremonious exclusiveness to general use, through migrations, the interchange of tribal customs due to the abundance of tobacco in some areas, the ease by which the practice of smoking was acquired, and European influence.

Tobacco was an important ceremonial object among the Aztecs, who regarded it as the incarnation of the goddess Cihuacoahuatl. They believed that the body of the goddess was composed of tobacco, and also used tobacco in the rites that honoured their war god, Huitzilopochtli. Tobacco, tobacco gourds and pouches have been described as symbols of divinity among several other Mesoamerican nations. Tobacco gourds were a part of the ceremonial garb of the Aztec priests who prepared the victim to be sacrificed to the Goddess Toci.

Other Mexican tribes, among them the Cuicatecs, used wild tobacco in their religious rituals. The ceremonies were usually performed in caves or on hilltops and were accompanied by prayers and supplications to the gods. Tobacco also played an important role in the ceremony of declaration of war in Michoacán. Among the Mazatecs, another Mesoamerican Indian nation, the *curandero* uses 'paste of powdered tobacco and lime to render pregnant women invulnerable to witchcraft'. Besides using tobacco as a protection against witchcraft, the

Polychrome vase from Tikal (Tikal Museum), Maya Culture Late Classic period (AD 800–950). It shows a scantily dressed Maya Lord smoking a cigarette.

Polychrome plate from Yucatan Mexico. Late Classic Period (AD 800–950). This plate is decorated with the scene of a Maya lady preparing dough while a smoking figure, seated nearby, watches her.

Aztecs also believed that it could be used to cast spells and to protect them from wild animals. It was thought to be especially effective against the poisonous ones, such as scorpions and snakes.

Even though our knowledge of ancient Maya rituals is incomplete, it is possible that tobacco was used in religious ceremonies very early in Maya history. It plays an important part today among the rituals of the Lacandones, a few hundred Maya Indians who still preserve the ancient ways. They grow their own tobacco, dry it on racks and store it in large funnel-shaped bundles. Similar bundles, presumably of tobacco, are shown the pre-Conquest *Codex Vindobonensis Mexicanus*, where they are being presented to Seven Flower, an important deity who was associated with sacred mushrooms, tobacco and other precious substances.

The Lacandón Mayas are heavy smokers, and they also use their wrapped cigars as trade articles in neighbouring towns. At the seasons of tobacco harvest the Lacandón performs his tobacco ritual. He takes the first leaves of his crop, rolls a cigar and lights it with a 'new fire' ignited by sun rays concentrated by a crystal lens. First the cigar is held in front of the sacred *olla*, and then it is offered to the god whose image decorates the incense burner ('god pot'). The god is usually pictured smoking and sitting on the sign for the earth (*caban*). In the past, the Lacandón Mayas of Cholti, a tribe with the same name but living in a different location, celebrates the Hicsión, the 'Feast of Cigars'. This ceremony was

View from the Temple of the Cross, Palenque Chiapas, Mexico.

The eastern door-jamb at the Temple of the Cross, Palenque Chiapas, Mexico. The carving shows an old Mayan deity smoking a large cigar. Late Classic Culture (AD 800–900).

described in a Spanish manuscript written in 1696 by three missionaries, which not only gives the factual description of the festivities but also provides insight into a truly democratic aboriginal society.[4]

Formal offerings of tobacco to the 'old gods' has now largely disappeared from both the Lacandón and Yucatec *milpa* ceremonies. In modern Maya folklore, however, ceremonies such as the New Year celebration in the Tzeltal town Oxchuc still include, among other things, the ritual offering of thirteen calabashes of tobacco. Native tobacco is considered a traditional defence against supernatural forces of evil among the Tzotzils of Chalho, Chamula, Husitán, Huitiupán, Pantelho, Venustiano, Carranza and Zinacantán. The Tzotzils of Larrainzar (formerly San Andrés Istacostoc) still attribute magic powers to

Red background polychrome vase showing the dancing God of Death smoking a cigarette. Maya Culture, Late Classic Period (AD 800–950). Northern Peten, Guatemala.

repeated until the patient gets well or dies. A similar custom exists among the Indians of the Amazon jungle. There the shaman healer drinks *natema*, a mixture of tobacco juice and another herbal extract called *piripiri*, which permits him to see into the body of the patient as 'though it were glass'. He then regurgitates over the body of his patient to rid him of the disease.[5]

Tobacco is also the magic tool of the Chorti diviner, the *ah q'in*. The *ah q'in* is a specialist in predicting future events, finding lost objects or animals, and determining the causes of sickness, either magical or natural in origin, and then recommending the best cure for it. He is also considered a good and respectable man who receives his power and information directly from the benevolent Sun God. He is called upon to counteract malignant spells caused by sorcerers, to predict whether it will rain and how much, to foretell whether the crops will be good, and so on. To facilitate his work, the *ah q'in*, like Aladdin in the fairytale, conveniently carries with him his personal genie, the *sahorin*, housed in the right calf of the *ah q'in*. A custom very similar to that of invoking the *sahorin* exists among the Chibcha and Puinavi Indians of Columbia. They, however, do not rub the tobacco on their bodies but eat it, and if certain joints of their body move, this is regarded as a sign that they will have good – or bad – luck.[6]

TOBACCO AS MEDICINE

In the life of the ancient – and to some degree also of the contemporary – human, religion, superstition and medicine cannot be completely dissociated. This principle certainly appears to be true with tobacco.

When the Spaniards arrived in Yucatán, they found a rich medical lore among the Mayas. The Mayans believed that supernatural forces set ailments as a punishment for their sins, and it was to the gods that they prayed for a cure. For the Mayas, religion and medicine, priest and physicians were inseparable. A considerable body of medical literat-

tobacco. They sprinkle powdered tobacco on the chest and face of the very ill to protect them from Pucah, the Demon of Death. The Chorti also hold their tobacco and tobacco utensils in great respect. When they die, they are placed in their graves.

An unusual and certainly unappetizing application of tobacco in folk healing is performed by the Chorti Maya *ah huht*, translated literally as 'spitter'. The *ah huht* is called to cure seizures, ward off the evil eye or treat 'strong blood', especially in children, which makes him something of a paediatric shaman. The *ah huht* chews different herbs, such as rue, sage and artemisia, but most often tobacco, and spits it on to the patient from head to toe. If the illness is especially severe, he sprays his saliva-mixed tobacco in the form of a cross from head to crotch and shoulder-to-shoulder. This treatment is ure was written on Maya medicine. Unfortunately, the earliest manuscripts date only from the eighteenth century. Tobacco as a remedy for physical and mental ills is mentioned in the *Princeton Codex*, or, as it is better known, *Ritual of the Bacabs*. It contains a mixture of incantations and straightforward medical prescriptions. It recommends tobacco for toothaches, chills, lung, kidney and eye diseases, and so on. For eruptions, fever and seizures, it is to be drunk with two peppers, a little honey and a little tobacco juice. Another famous Maya medical treatise is the *Yerbas y hechicerías del Yucatán* (Herbs and Magic Spells of Yucatán),[7] where tobacco, especially its green leaves, is the ingredient in various concoctions for such maladies as lack of strength, pain in the bones, snakebite, abdominal pains, pain in the heart, recurring chills, convulsions, loss of speech, sore eye, buboes, various kinds of pox, and retention of urine. Tobacco is also listed as a medicine to prevent miscarriage: it was mixed with lime and then smeared on the abdomen and massaged into it.

In the Maya community of Cham Kom, present-day use of tobacco in curing ceremonies has been reported. A widely practised 'curing' with tobacco can be seen by travellers in Petén. It is thought to be an excellent remedy for scorpion and tarantula bites.

UNEXPLAINED EFFECTS OF TOBACCO

Some records of early observers who described the drunken behaviour of those who smoked tobacco are puzzling. How could the *N. tabacum* plant, which is smoked today by millions without any of these effects, have made the Indians 'intoxicated', behave 'foolishly', 'lose their judgement', 'fall down as if they were dead' and 'invoke demons'?[8]

To explain this apparent contradiction, several possibilities must be considered.

1. The Mayans may have smoked a tobacco that was more potent than the presently commercially available species. While commercially grown *N. tabacum* seldom contains more than 2 to 3 per cent nicotine, *N. rustica*, a variety well known to the Mayans, contains as much as 10 per cent nicotine in the leaf. Nicotine is also by no means the only bioactive substance in the tobacco leaf.

2. The Mayans could have consumed the same species of tobacco that is smoked today but in much larger quantities. Records note Indians smoking cigars measuring from 34 to 75 centimetres in length.

3. The Mayas may have potentiated the effect of tobacco by non-pharmacological means. There is ample ethnographic evidence that the Maya shamans used (and in some areas still use) reverberation, chants, dancing and different forms of music either to induce or to potentiate trancelike states. Even more important is data indicating that in ancient times both fasting and penitential self-torture were widely practised among the Mayas.

4. The last and probably most likely hypothesis is that the Mayas may have consumed herbs other than tobacco with psychotropic properties, in conjunction with or instead of tobacco. It is probable that the early Spaniards, being only vaguely aware of these herbs but having learned the use of tobacco on the Caribbean Islands on which they first landed, thought everything that the Mayas smoked or chewed was tobacco and labelled it as such. It is also possible, however, that we unjustly criticize some of the early historians as poor observers when we should blame some of our contemporary scholars instead. Many of the modern translators of ancient Spanish manuscripts took considerable liberty in their interpretations. They freely translated such Spanish expressions as 'smoking reed', 'odoriferous herb' and 'smoke' as 'tobacco'. This naturally gives the impression that the natives smoked nothing but tobacco.

The ancient Mayas were passionate smokers, and so were their gods. In archaeological finds, many lordly figures smoking or holding cigars are shown in paintings in manuscripts and on ceramic vessels or in carvings on stone monuments. Whether some, most or all of these figures represent supernatural beings is a question long debated and still unresolved. While the smoking figures in manuscripts are certainly deities, a number of painted ceramics show smoking lords with human characteristics who probably represent rulers and their entourages.

Among the deities, God L appears to be a heavy smoker, while Gods A, B, D, F and N could be characterized as occasional indulgers. Among the mythical animals, monkeys have a strong lead in smoking, with jaguars second and frogs a distant third.

Peculiar groups of small gods on different Classic stone monuments have been documented, and the Flare God – also Schellhas's God K – first received attention because of its proboscis.[9]

A smoking Maya Lord wearing a deer headdress. Jaina Island, Yukatan, Mexico. Maya Culture, Late Classic Period (AD 800–950).

Shell carving of a Maya Lord wearing a dear headdress. Jaina Island, Yucatan Mexico. The carving is now in the Field Museum of Natural History, Chicago. Late Classic Period (AD 800–950).

Recently, however, interest has focused on his tube-and-coils forehead ornament that probably represents a cigar, and the flamelike appendage rising from the tube as smoke – an iconographic complex indicating power and divinity. A disturbing feature of this very attractive cigar theory is the great variety – some tubular like the modern-day cigar, others funnel-shaped or rhomboid – portrayed on ancient Maya monuments and ceramics. It is certainly possible that a deity such as God K may have had various implements at his disposal, and, depending on the occasion, placed in his forehead short cigars, long cigars, smoking cigars, torches or even flints or other objects. It is also conceivable that the shape, size and identity of the forehead ornament

Polychrome Maya vase. Maya Culture, Late Classic Period (AD 800–950), Usumacinta River Valley, Guatemala. It shows a standing monkey smoking a cigarette.

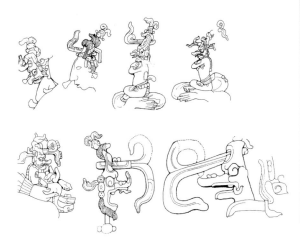

Flare Gods at Palenque, Mexico. The drawing shows designs on different structures at this Maya site.

reflect the particular role that the god is playing. Does God κ with a short, round cigar mean one thing and the same figure with a large non-smoking celt-shaped object mean something – or someone – else? My answer to all these questions is a cautious yes.[10]

CONCLUSION

According to ethnological and historical data, tobacco smoking played an important role in ancient Maya religion, folklore and healing. The examples in Maya art and other archaeological artefacts prove beyond doubt that the tobacco and the act of smoking not only had a deep religious meaning in the life of the ancient Mayas but also deeply penetrated art and had important significance in iconography. Performed by persons of apparently high rank, smoking was probably an activity of considerable importance rather than just a pleasurable act. The possibility that smoking for pleasure was also a widespread custom among the ancient Maya population can be neither proved nor disproved. The lives of ordinary people were simply not considered important enough to record and preserve for posterity.

Small container (*poisonero*) carved with a figure of an aged deity holding a tobacco leaf. Montaguo Valley, Honduras or Guatemala. Maya Culture, Late Classic Period (AD 800–950).

The Pleasures and Perils of Smoking in Early Modern England

TANYA POLLARD

The onset of smoking tobacco in late sixteenth-century England occupies a pivotal historical position as the beginning of a complex convergence of medicinal and recreational uses of drugs in English culture. Strange though it may seem from a modern perspective, smoking was ushered into England primarily through the rhetoric of medical benefits.[1] Its rapid and dramatic popularity, widely attributed to its addictive pleasures, can be seen as both symptom and cause of broader changes in the role of drugs in contemporary medicine and culture. Tobacco was the first of a series of new drugs from foreign countries to move from medical to recreational use, laying a foundation for the imminent rise of tea, coffee, cocoa, distilled liquors and opium.[2] The new substance mesmerized the public, but also met with fierce medical and moral controversies. Extravagant claims about its medical powers incurred scepticism, parody and fears of side effects. Despite its reputation for masculinity and potency, the association of tobacco with pleasurable intoxication led to attacks on what many saw as the feminine passivity and powerlessness induced by its addictive and narcotic qualities. Its novelty and exotic origins, meanwhile, intensified concerns about its eerie and unfamiliar nature.[3] Blurring the lines between medicine and pleasure, and producing unsettling new effects on body and mind, smoking offers a microcosm for the status of drugs in early modern England.

Smoking became an institution in England with the arrival of tobacco.[4] After catching the attention of sailors in the New World with Columbus in 1492, tobacco gradually made its way to Europe over the course of the sixteenth century, entering England in the 1560s and exploding into popularity in the 1590s.[5] English smokers emulated customs conveyed from the Americas: the most common form of consuming tobacco was to dry it, light it in pipes (generally of clay) and inhale or 'drink' it.[6] Prescribed by physicians and purchased from apothecaries, it was introduced as a medicine, its benefits heralded with an outpouring of euphoric praise.[7] In *Joyfull Newes out of the newe founde worlde* (1577, Spanish original 1571), Nicholas Monardes, a physician from Seville, wrote: 'In any maner of griefe that is in the bodie or any parte therof it healpeth . . . it taketh it awaie, not without great admiration.'[8] Treatise after treatise echoed Monardes's wisdom: in 1587 Giles Everard identified tobacco as the long-sought panacea, cure for everything.[9] The glory of tobacco took on near-religious associations: in 1610 the physician Edmund Gardiner wrote: 'By this wee may see the wonderfull workes of God, how that he can make things strange, great, and incomprehensible and wonderfull to mans iudgement.'[10]

Claims for the health benefits of smoking rested in large part on the logic of humouralism, the dominant medical philosophy inherited from Galen and ancient Greek medicine.[11] Galenic doctrine held that the body was composed of hot, cold, wet and dry humours, and that the secret to health lay in balancing these oppositions. Some balances, however, were better than others: cold and wet humours, associated with women, were characterized as slow, sluggish and particularly likely to bring about bad health.[12] Smoking, exploiting the extreme and literal dry heat of fire, was accordingly understood to heat and dry the body to a state of manly vigour, driving out all manner of ills.

To a certain extent, the popularity of smoking tobacco drew on pre-existing ideas about the medical use of fumes. The physician William Barclay argued in 1614 that 'Suffumigation or receauing of smoake, is not a newe inuented remedie, it is an old and well approoued forme of medicine in many diseases.'[13] He is echoed in his claim by Capnistus, the pro-smoking character in John Deacon's *Tobacco Tortured* of 1616, who similarly insists that 'there are many sorts of *fumes* inuented and taught by the Physitions themselues . . .'.[14] Barclay refers to medical use of the smoke of tussilago, musk, amber, insquiam and cinnabar,[15] and Capnistus adds red arsenic, quicksilver and orpiment to the list.[16] Other medical writers support these claims: Hippocrates, who was much cited in the Renaissance, suggests applying smoke near the female genitals as a cure for hysteria;[17] the Italian physician Leonardo Fioravanti refers to 'fumes against the Pore' as one way of preparing cinnabar;[18] and Monardes refers in passing to medical uses of the smoke of amber.[19] Smoke, then, was understood to be an effective vehicle for conveying remedies through the pores and orifices into the body's interior.

Despite this history of the medical uses of smoke, however, smoking as a public and recreational act was new, apparently at times startlingly so: in its early days, two men who saw Richard Tarlton smoking, 'neuer seeing the like, wondreth at it: and seeing the vapour come out of Tarltons nose cryed out, Fire, fire, and threw a cup of Wine in Tarltons face.'[20] Tobacco, moreover, as a drug labelled extremely hot and dry, was understood to intensify the medical power of smoke to balance the bodily humours.[21] In 1621 the physician Tobias Venner wrote that smoking tobacco

> helpeth the braine that is ouer cold and moist, . . . it taketh away rheumes and windinesse of the head, and is profitable for all colde effects of the braine and sinews, by resoluing and consuming the crude and windie superfluities of those partes . . . it preuenteth putrefaction of humours, by drying vp the crudities of the body, and is very profitable vpon taking of colde, and for all colde and moist effects of the stomake, breast, and lungs.[22]

Through his insistent repetition of active verbs (helpeth, taketh, preuenteth), Venner implicitly personifies tobacco smoke, identifying it with the forceful virility that it was meant to inspire. His claims echo standard arguments about the powers of tobacco's dry heat, portraying the consequences of cold and damp as corrupting matter ('putrefaction', 'crudities') interfering with the body's system, with refined heat as the cleansing solution. Smoke, in this model, invades and transforms the body, distilling and purifying its contents.

The euphoric tone of medical claims for tobacco lent themselves easily to parody. Witless blissful smokers quickly populated all genres of English literature; Ben Jonson, with his stockcasts of city gallants, especially revelled in mocking tobacco and its consumers.[23] Captain Bobadill, in *Every Man in his Humour* (1601), offers particularly expansive claims: 'It makes an Antidote, that (had you taken the most deadly poysonous simple in all Italy), it should expell it, and clarifie you, with as much ease as I speak . . . I could say what I know of the vertue of it'. He continues:

> for the exposing of rewmes, raw humours, crudities, obstructions, with a thousand of this kind, but I professe my selfe no quacke-saluer: only, thus much: by *Hercules* I doe holde it, and will affirme it . . . to be the most soueraigne, and pretious herbe, that euer the earth tendred to the vse of man.[24]

Willem Buytewech, *Merry Company*, 1617–20, oil on canvas.

Bobadill's fitful praise, for all its comic hyperbole, is in fact not far from actual paeans to tobacco's glories.[25] Like Venner, he emphasizes tobacco's effect on the products of cold and damp humours – rheumes, crudities and obstructions – as evidence for his accolades. Bobadill's glorious oaths and epithets, however, are undermined in the play by failings such as his inability to pay his rent; Jonson, with typical cynicism, identifies the glorious smoke of tobacco with the hot air of its proponents.

As Jonson's satire suggests, the extravagance of claims for tobacco incurred scepticism. Despite his own high praise for smoking, Gardiner worried that unrealistic claims for tobacco could lead to misunderstanding and misuse: 'they doe commend

it too much aboue measure, attributing to it so many great and excellent vertues, as I thinke is scarse possible to finde in any one hearbe.'[26] Joseph Hall, in 1601, agreed, arguing that 'no one kinde of remedie can aptly be applied to all maladies, no more then one shooe can wel serue all mens feete'.[27] King James I, an ardent opponent of tobacco, marvelled ironically at tobacco's manifold and contradictory powers:

such is the miraculous omnipotencie of our strong tasted *Tobacco*, as it cures al sorts of diseases (which neuer any drugge could do before) in all persons, and at all times . . . It cures the gowt in the feet, and (which is miraculous) in

A tobacco plant, with head of a native smoking, clearly adapted from that in Lobel's earlier *Plantarus seu stirpium Historia* (1570).

that very instant when the smoke thereof as light, flies vp into the head, the vertue therof, as heauy, runs down to the litle toe . . . It makes a man sober that was drunk. It refreshes a weary man, and yet makes a man hungry. Being taken when they goe to bed, it makes one sleepe soundly, and yet being taken when a man is sleepie and drowsie, it will, as they say, awake his braine, and quicken his vnderstanding.[28]

The king's witty catalogue of cures points to the incoherence of the contrasting characteristics attributed to tobacco. Its smoke, in his caricatured formulation, is personified into a quasi-magical entity flitting through the body, from foot to head and back, instantly resolving any and all problems, regardless of their unrelated and even opposing natures.

For all their playful humour, parodic critiques of tobacco's apparent omnipotence raised serious questions about the nature of medicine. How could a medicine serve both one function and its opposite: cure the head and the feet; satiate and make hungry; invigorate and lull to sleep? Medicinal drugs were understood to be powerful transformative agents, designed to attack a bodily dysfunction; the idea of ongoing use for general health and pleasure stirred worries. 'Medicine hath that vertue', James wrote,

that it neuer leaues a man in that state wherein it finds him: it makes a sicke man whole, but a whole man sicke: And as Medicine helps nature being taken at times of necessitie, so being euer and continually vsed, it doeth but weaken, weary, and weare nature.[29]

To use drugs when not sick, then, is to invite unforeseeable and dangerous consequences, as medical supporters of tobacco, such as Venner, insisted: 'the vse of it is only tollerable by way of physicke, not for pleasure, or an idle custome'.[30] James's concern about the intrinsic ambivalence of medicines is significant, not least because it is representative of the broad cultural anxieties about medicine at this time in history. In the context of recent pharmaceutical upheavals, triggered by new diseases and plants from the New World, new translations of classical medical texts, and especially the growth of chemical medicine led by Paracelsus and other Continental scientists, medicines were becoming more powerful and more uncertain than ever, leading to higher levels of both interest and risk.[31] The dramatic popularity of smoking meant that this remedy was being taken by perfectly healthy people. As Barnabe Rich scoffed: 'if all be diseased that doth vse to take Tobacco, God helpe *England*, it is wonderfully infected, and his Maiestie hath but a few subiects that be healthfull in his whole dominions'.[32] Accordingly, the drug was seen as threatening, mysterious and capable of catastrophic transformations.

There were, in fact, sweeping disagreements about the nature of these transformations. One of the more controversial medical claims about tobacco was that it could cure melancholy, an illness of great concern in the period.[33] As much identified with pleasure as with physical health, tobacco seemed an apt match for melancholy, an affliction hovering liminally between the bodily and the mental: Barclay argued, with many, that 'there is such hostilitie betweene it & melancholie, that it is the only medicament in the world ordained by nature to entertaine good companie ...'.[34] As with other claims about tobacco, however, this one incurred as many refutations as confirmations. Hall argued that smoking tobacco 'is a great encreaser of melancholy in vs, and thereby disposeth our bodies to all melancholy impressions and effects proceeding of that humour',[35] and Venner agreed, advising 'all such as are of a melancholericke constitution, vtterly to shunne the taking of Tobacco'.[36]

Arguments about smoking's effect on melancholy point to explicit contradictions in claims about tobacco. Melancholy, or black bile, a product of the cold and wet humours, should theoretically respond to the heating and drying effects of smoke, but other commentaries on tobacco pointed to its powerful effects, which led to oblivion and stupefaction. Gardiner noted that it brought about 'an infirmitie like vnto drunkennes, & many times sleep, as after the taking of *Opium*';[37] Henry Buttes wrote that it 'Mortifieth and benummeth: causeth drowsinesse: troubleth & dulleth the sences: makes (as it were) drunke';[38] and Venner found that 'it ouerthroweth the spirites, perverteth the vnderstanding, and confoundeth the senses with a sodayne astonishment and stupidity of the whole body.'[39] Despite its association with the manly vigour of dry heat, then, tobacco was simultaneously understood as intensifying, rather than countering, the problems of damp and drowsy dispositions, ultimately inducing the very passivity it promised to conquer. Barclay noted its contradictions with wonder and curiosity: 'So *Tabacco* is hote, because it hath acrimonie', he wrote;

> yet, it is cold because it is narcoticke and stupefactiue, it maketh drunken, and refresheth, it maketh hungrie and filleth, it maketh thirstie, and quencheth thirst. Finallie to bring man to health, it changeth as many formes as *Iuppiter* does change shapes to conuey himselfe to his Mistresse ...[40]

Barclay's identification of tobacco with the seductive metamorphoses of Jupiter mystifies, and compensates for, the drug's myriad contradictions; armed with power and divinity, it cannot be held to ordinary standards of conduct. The metaphor is problematic, though; if tobacco is Jupiter, and the consumer is one of his mistresses, the relationship between smoke and smoker is ultimately equated to rape, and with a wildly unequal power differential: the king of the gods versus a mortal, or a minor deity. While tobacco's virility was imagined by many as seeping into the consumer and reproducing itself, to others it held out precisely the opposite threat: smoke would effeminize, infantilize and paralyse its victims. The dispute over melancholy highlighted tobacco's paradoxical identification with both empowerment and enslavement.

Concerns about tobacco's narcotic effects, and the escalating debates about its medical powers, underlined the fact that smokers quickly began turning to tobacco for pleasure rather than medical need. The drug quickly spread from apothecaries' shops to social spaces. In 1599 a visitor from Basle, Thomas Platter, commented that 'In the taverns tobacco or a species of wound-wort are also obtainable for one's money, and the powder is lit in a small pipe, the smoke sucked into the mouth, and the saliva is allowed to run freely, after which a good draught of Spanish wine follows.'[41] As Platter suggests, tobacco quickly became associated with taverns and companionship; Barclay similarly claimed that tobacco 'worketh neuer so well, as when it is giuen from man to man, as a pledge of friendshippe and amitie.'[42] Just as tobacco's dry heat identified it physiologically with masculinity, so its social use reinforced male bonds; the capacity of smoke to infiltrate the body seems to have been reflected in an ability to erase borders between people. Yet this ubiquitous association was itself troubling to some: James I complained that 'a man cannot heartily welcome his friend now, but straight they must be in hand with *Tobacco*'.[43] As an increasingly indispensable prop for friendly meetings, tobacco could be seen as displacing and nullifying the value of unadorned social relations, to the point at which ordinary life could not function without it.

In fact, both critics and supporters of tobacco turned to proto-modern discourses of addiction to describe motives for smoking. '[M]any in this kingdome', James wrote, 'haue had such a continuall vse of taking this vnsauorie smoake, as now they are not able to forbeare the same, no more then an old drunkard can abide to be long sober . . .'.[44]

Explaining this tendency in further detail, Gardiner worried that 'Tabacco is a fantasticall attracter, and glutton-feeder of the appetite, rather taken of many for wantonesse, when they haue nothing else to doe, than of any absolute or necessarie vse . . .'.[45] Venner similarly worried that 'this custome of taking the fume, hath so far bewitched . . . many of our people as that they also often-times, take it for wantonnesse and delight, wherein they haue so great a pleasure, as that they desire nothing more then to make themselues drunken and drowsie with Tobacco.'[46]

Gardiner and Venner depict tobacco's hold over consumers in terms of magic ('fantasticall', 'bewitched') and sensual, even erotic pleasures ('appetite', 'wantonnesse', 'delight'), an idea echoed by James's claim that smoking enslaved users with its 'bewitching qualitie'.[47] Similarly, supporters and critics alike described smoking in tones of awe and enchantment. The poet Sir John Beaumont proclaimed it 'The sweete and sole delight of mortall men, / The *Cornu-copia* of all earthly pleasure'.[48] Barclay described its effects as 'a certaine mellilfouous delicacie, which deliteth the senses, & spirits of man with a mindful obliuion, insomuch that it maketh & induceth . . . the forgetting of all sorrowes & miseries'.[49] In 1612 the physician John Cotta wrote that smoking brought on 'some present bewitching feeling of ease, or momentarie imagined release from paine at some time', intriguingly attributing these effects more to consumers' perceptions ('feeling', 'imagined') than to the drug's actual powers.[50]

Reports of the narcotic effects of tobacco, and the awed (if potentially illusory) subjection of smokers, repeatedly blurred the lines between medicinal and religious effects. In his account of native American use of tobacco, Monardes explained that matters of urgent business were taken to a chief priest, who would inhale tobacco smoke for inspiration:

and in takyng of it, he fell doune vppon the grounde, as a dedde manne, and remainyng so, accordyng to the quantitie of the smoke that he had taken, and when the hearbe had doen his woorke, he did reuiue and awake, and gaue them their aunsweres, according to the visions, and

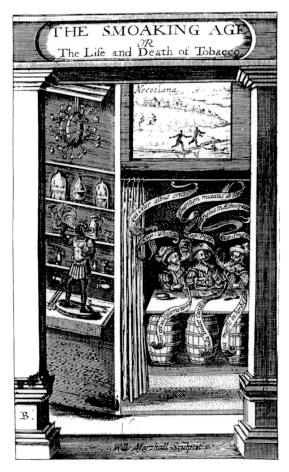

William Marshall, woodcut for Richard Braithwait's *The Smoking Age* (London, 1617).

dependence and passivity into a narrative of spiritual takeover. The image of the smoker lying 'doune vppon the grounde, as a dedde manne' both confirmed accusations against tobacco's dangerously soporific effects, and offered other-worldly explanations for them.

This analogy proved popular, and the association with Indians and prophetical rituals led to multiple accusations of paganism and strange gods, literalizing the period's many awed references to tobacco as a 'divine' drug.[53] Many critics of tobacco depicted it as an evil demi-god enslaving mortal souls; in Richard Brathwait's strange and colourful mythology of the drug's origin, tobacco is a bastard son born to Proserpine, enraging her husband Pluto, god of the underworld. Pluto comes to accept the situation, however, when he realizes the child's potential to enlarge the kingdom of death: 'thou playest Minister to Pluto, and estates me in an ample Government; thy smoake shall be the conveyance to hale those snuffing Prodigalls to my smoking Dominions . . .'.[54] More commonly, accusations of paganism merged with charges of Catholicism and idolatry:[55] Joshua Sylvester described tobacco as 'a Weed; / Which to their *Idols, Pagans* sacrifice, / And *Christians* (heer) doe wel-nigh *Idolize* . . .'.[56] George Chapman's Monsieur D'Olive reports on a Puritan who 'Said t'was a pagan plant, a prophane weede /And a most sinful smoke'.[57] Joseph Hall addresses it as 'thou Pagan Idol: tawnie weede', and claimed that 'the first author and finder hereof was the Diuell, and the first practisers of the same were the Diuells Priests, and therefore not to be vsed of vs Christians.'[58] As these examples suggest, attributions of quasi-religious power to tobacco were commonplace, bordering on obsessive: for better and for worse, tobacco's powers to enchant, bewitch and transform seemed to require constant reversion to the rhetoric of the supernatural.

As these recurring references to paganism and idolatry indicate, moreover, the lurid reports of tobacco's eerie religious status drew not only on its uncanny power, but also on its foreign origin, a source of intense controversy in early modern England. Tobacco's clear identification with the

illusions whiche he sawe, whiles he was rapte of the same maner, and he did interprete to them, as to hym semed beste, or as the Deuill had counsailed hym, giuyng theim continually doubtfull aunsweres, in such sorte, that how soeuer it fell out, thei might saie that it was the same, which was declared, and the aunswere that thei made.[51]

Monardes's anecdote clearly made a significant impact on English commentators on tobacco, many of whom reproduced this passage almost verbatim in their accounts.[52] His description of smoke-induced oblivion as demonic possession offers a vocabulary for translating fears about narcotic

'Occidental Indias' of the New World,[59] and its popularity with 'barbarous people',[60] were the cause of both celebration and consternation. Associated with magic, novelty and exoticism, the New World clearly exerted a powerful appeal, and equally powerful condemnation.[61] Rich lamented 'an inconsiderate and foolish affectation of nouelties, drawne from a people, that are infidels and Aliens to God, truely reputed to bee the very refuse of the world'.[62] His yoking of desire, novelty and dangerous foreignness was shared by many. 'Doe we not daily see', James similarly asked, 'that a man can no sooner bring ouer from beyond the seas any new forme of apparell, but that he cannot be thought a man of spirit, that would not presently imitate the same? And so from hand to hand it spreads till it be prac-tised by all, not for any commodity that is in it, but only because it is come to be the fashion . . .'.[63] James's complaint against the allure of novelty for its own sake wearily attributes the demand for newness to foolishness, but other critics went further to identify the allure of foreign novelties implicitly with self-destructive urges: Joseph Hall castigates 'our smoky gallants, who hauing long time glutted themselues with the fond fopperies and fashions of our neighbour Countries: yet still desirous of nouelties, haue not stucke to trauell as farre as India to fetch a *Dulce venenum* [sweet poison], a graecian Helen, an insatiate Messaline, and hugge a stinging serpent in their bosomes . . .'.[64] The appeal of tobacco, in his eyes, is equated with the dangerous temptations of poison, serpents and Helen; it invites tasters to another Trojan war, another fall from Eden.

The dismay voiced by Rich, James and Hall over tobacco's link to exotic climes points to broader anxieties about new drugs and the foreign cultures they represented. As a product of the New World, tobacco, like all new drugs, became a synecdochic stand-in for the promises and dangers of foreign shores. Smoke, the form through which it was primarily consumed, came to represent its quiet infiltration of boundaries and barriers. Just as the efficacy of smoking rested on its insinuation into the body, and its pleasures included the forging of social

bonds, so complaints about it emphasized its capacity for invasion and contamination. While James complained of men 'puffing of the smoke of *Tobacco* one to another, making the filthy smoke and stinke thereof, to exhale athwart the dishes, and infect the aire',[65] Deacon analogously ranted about Englishmen who 'borrow from the furthermost parts of *India* this stinking, infectious and venimous *smoke*, to expell that masse or sinke of humours from out of the body . . .'.[66] The idea of contagion led James to liken smoking to syphilis, another recent New World import: 'as from them was first brought into Christendome, that most detestable disease; so from them likewise was brought this vse of *Tobacco*'.[67] Moral, physical and cultural contaminations reinforced each other in this model; Deacon ascribed 'the pollutions of our minds and bodies (concerning religion and manners) to such carelesse entercourse of trafficking with the corruptions and customes of forreine countries . . .'.[68]

The intensity of the complaints against tobacco, combined with what seems to have been early evidence for its medical dangers – Platter wrote in 1599 that 'the inside of one man's veins after death was found to be covered in soot just like a chimney'[69] – might make its unfettered rise in popularity seem astonishing, particularly given the 4,000 per cent tax increase on tobacco imposed by James I in 1604.[70] For all the complaints, costs and disincent-ives, however, smoking's popularity rose steadily in early modern England. The magical qualities of the 'present bewitching feeling of ease' it bestowed on consumers, combined with its fashionable status and the fascination of the exotic New World it represented, held greater sway than its detractors. The controversies surrounding smoking four centuries ago were firmly rooted in the medical and cultural issues of the time, but their legacy is still powerfully visible today.

Smoking in Sub-Saharan Africa

ALLEN F. ROBERTS

Ceci n'est pas une pipe.
 Magritte

The history of smoking in Africa is receiving renewed attention. Ample ethnographic evidence suggests that herb smoking, smoke baths and fumigations were ancient therapeutic practices in many African societies, while smoking symbolically significant substances (that is, ones that are not necessarily or primarily chemically efficacious) has long been a feature of mystical procedures to promote and protect individuals, households and communities. Furthermore, for some Africans smoking appears to have been ideologically essential to the *performance* of pre-colonial technologies such as iron-smelting, salt-making and rain control.[1] That the act of smoking – whatever the substance – so often bears symbolic or historical allusions to other circumstances, practices, intentions and aspirations, suggests that Magritte's celebrated provocation, 'Ceci n'est pas une pipe', deserves elaboration when applied to African contexts.

An object that looks, feels, smells and tastes like a pipe may not be one, for, as Magritte asserted, 'everything leads one to believe that there is little relationship between an object and what it represents'.[2] In part this may be because objects can be 'promiscuous', possessing 'singular personal meanings at odds with their systemic significance', as Nicholas Thomas tells us; and these meanings can lead to a fan of 'entanglements' between otherwise opposed philosophies and practices.[3] But even though such associations can lead to far-reaching riffs of history and culture, and despite Magritte's further statement in his *La Trahison des images* drawing of 1952, that 'Ceci continue de ne pas être une pipe',[4] an object that serves other purposes and looks little if at all like a pipe, may be one just the same (see below). It is best, therefore, to seek relationships between smoking and other activities and ideas without forgetting that 'une pipe est quand même une pipe'. Indeed, such an object could not do the symbolic work it does were it *not* a pipe.

In the thirteenth century, or perhaps earlier still, Gujaratis and other visitors from the Indian Ocean rim introduced cannabis to what is now Ethiopia, and Arab sailors probably brought it to the east African coast at about the same time.[5] These were the fabled years when Sindbad plied the Indian Ocean, and one is left wondering if his storied

A Zulu (South Africa) wooden pipe for tobacco or cannabis. This fanciful pipe has three bowls and stands on a small box with a sliding door, meant to hold smoking and fire-making materials.

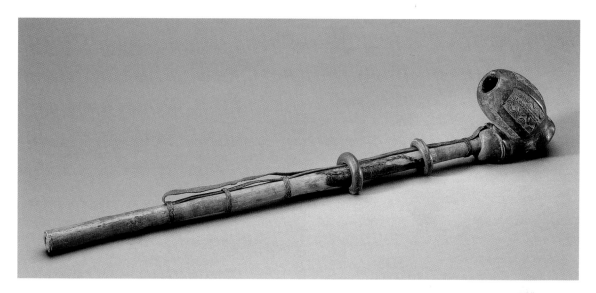

visions of jinns, giants and the mighty roc might
not have been clouded by too much time on the
hookah![6] Cannabis water pipes made from bottle
gourds and fitted with tubular terracotta bowls
appear to have been an early Ethiopian invention
that was spread to eastern, southern and central
Africa 'during medieval times on routes similar to
those used by coffee, another Ethiopian innovation'.[7]
Other sorts of smoking instruments were soon
invented and adapted elsewhere on the Continent.

Intriguing evidence suggests that tobacco was
first brought to coastal West Africa around 1600 by
French merchants, who introduced both *Nicotiana
rustica* and a distinctive form of terracotta pipe bowl
to what are now Senegal and the Gambia. The acute
angle and flattened foot of these 'elbow-bend' bowls
is similar to a Native American style from Louisiana,
where the French had been trading and would
establish a colony.[8] Footed bowls of the sort have
been discovered by archaeologists, and they are still
produced in many parts of west and north-central
Africa. In these same years, tobacco was carried
along caravan routes linking Timbuktu with
Morocco, and smoking tobacco quickly became
popular across the girth of Africa, as reflected in
linguistic study of the diffusion of *taba* as the root
term for 'tobacco' in many West African languages.[9]
Portuguese ships brought tobacco to southern

Frafra (Ghana) tobacco pipes with 'elbow-bend', footed
pipe bowls. One bowl (above) is in cast brass with a
bamboo stem and leather attachments, and dates from
c. 1900; the other (below) has a terracotta bowl sculpted
as a man's head and a wooden stem with leather fittings.

Africa long before the Dutch settled on the Cape, and by about 1650 it was in widespread use throughout the region.[10]

Although tobacco was grown locally where soil and climatic conditions permitted, the imported plant remained a common commodity of inter-regional trade throughout West Africa.[11] In particular, tobacco featured prominently in the transatlantic slave trade through the infamous triangle linking Europe, West Africa and the Americas. Business correspondence from the West African coast suggests that tobacco may have been 'absolutely necessary if any [slave] trading were to be done at all'.[12] Portuguese merchants established a monopoly in what is now Ghana by importing Brazilian tobacco that was 'slightly treated with syrup' to give it a distinctive taste, precluding easy duplication by competitors; and, when soaked in rum, Brazilian tobacco became a sumptuary luxury of Akan royalty.[13] Brazilian tobacco remained a commercial staple along the coast well into the twentieth century, until local affiliates of trans-national tobacco companies rose to their present prominence. Long-stemmed, white-clay, Dutch tobacco pipes were also important trade goods during the contact and early colonial periods, and they provide archaeologists with useful temporal indices.[14]

It did not take Africans long to incorporate cannabis into their own cultural practices. In southern Africa, cannabis smoking became a male prerogative in pre- and early colonial times. Water pipes were fashioned from gourds or animal horns, fitted with a hollow reed to hold a bowl made from stone, clay or leaves. Straight pipes or pipes with small bowls were also prevalent (below left), and early visitors to what is now South Africa recorded local people using 'pipes' created by making small tunnels into the earth, lying on the ground and drawing forth the intoxicating smoke.[15] In southern Africa, cannabis was associated with bellicosity and cattle-herding, but was also the basis for a widespread nineteenth-century pastime of blowing cannabis-produced saliva through a tube, from which it could be dripped into humorous images on the ground.[16] The Tabwa people of south-eastern Congo also feel that cannabis use leads to aggression among men but also among some animals. Bushbucks (*Tragelaphus scriptus*) are red-eyed, dangerously fierce and to be avoided as 'sorcerers' because they are said to eat cannabis, for example.[17]

Tobacco, too, was quickly incorporated into many local circumstances of commerce, politics and ritual. Smoking tobacco is an inherently collective enjoyment, and sharing a pipe implies trust that no harmful substances have been introduced or evil intentions are afoot. Elderly Tabwa men love nothing more than to pass around a water pipe among friends, and despite the idea that using one is supposed to cool the smoke and reduce bitter tars, tobacco is not considered 'good' unless it is strong enough to reduce the mightiest man to fits of deep coughing.

In the old days, tobacco often had established value in local and regional markets. Ten-metre-long rolls and horsetail braids of locally grown tobacco

A Tuareg (Mali) iron pipe and leather pouch, used for cannabis or tobacco.

A Bobo (Burkina Faso) tobacco pipe made from recycled aluminium cast as the head of an antelope, with a carved wooden stem.

A Tabwa (Congo) gourd water pipe with copper wire decoration, reed and terracotta bowl.

49

were traded along the great lakes and rivers of central Africa, and Tabwa and related peoples sometimes used them as currency tokens in bridewealth, ransom and a few other sorts of limited exchange.[18] Those living around the southern end of Lake Tanganika took to pounding locally grown tobacco and shaping it into loaves to make it easily portable. They still jokingly call these 'hippo excrement' – because of the visual analogy, one would hope!

The degree to which tobacco smoking has become Africanized is even more obvious in the brilliance of African pipes. It sometimes seems that no two African pipes are alike, both within a given society and between groups at some particular time or through history. Although specialist artists often produce pipes, it is likely that many individuals make or elaborate their own, as one finds with a few other personal possessions in Africa, such as walking sticks and headrests.[19] One may assume that the remarkable diversity of pipes reflects and fosters both idiosyncratic and collective references to beliefs, practices and contexts other than smoking itself.

A Chokwe (Angola and Zambia) wooden tobacco pipe depicting an antelope. When turned upside-down, the pipe serves as a headrest.

An Asante (Ghana) ceramic bowl in the shape of bird, for a pipe offered as a prestige gift at a wedding or funeral, c. 1900.

A Tikar (Cameroon) cast brass or bronze pipe bowl depicting a hunter with a gun standing over the head of an elephant.

In his two-volume compendium *Pipes d'Afrique noire*, Jean Lecluse provides hundreds of line drawings and photographs to emphasize this last point: African tobacco pipes have been constructed, carved or cast from leaves, basketry, bamboo, reeds, gourds, seeds, shells, sun-baked soil, fired clay, soft stone, bone, leather, horn, ivory, wood, forged iron, cast brass and aluminium and, more recently, recycled materials such as tin cans and plastic bottles.[20] Pipes have been decorated or magically enhanced with pigment, shells, beads and many other decorative or symbolically powerful materials. Some pipes are mnemonic or narrative, their iconography referring to relationships, anecdotes, animal metaphors, proverbs, myths and cosmology.[21] Others startle with their grandiose complexity, suggesting that anyone possessing such a pipe must be sufficiently wealthy and well-placed to afford to commission such a treasure. Some portray and offer sustenance to ancestors, cultural heroes or other spirits. Still others portray European colonizers or their technologies, perhaps to share in the aura of their political and economic powers, but as likely to caricature the attendant pretences.[22] As the examples illustrating this essay suggest, African pipes can be

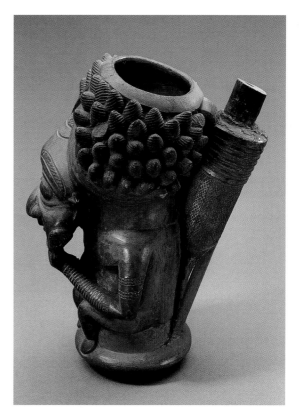

A Bamun (Cameroon) ceramic pipe bowl depicting a dignitary. This bowl is from the palace of King Njoya, 1931.

A ceramic pipe bowl depicting a man standing on an aeroplane with inset shell fragments, from an undetermined ethnic group in Adamawa Province, Nigeria.

A Frafra (Ghana) wooden pipe for cannabis or tobacco, lined with tin and shaped like an aeroplane with a removable nose.

astounding for their technical artistry, style, creativity, humour and wisdom.

Other than differences of personal genius, collective aesthetics, available materials and ethnic interactions, there may be sociological reasons for this remarkable diversity, especially as one considers the history of a specific region. Brian Vivian suggests that the archaeological progression of pipe types in southern Ghana proposed by Paul Ozanne, from those copying or clearly derivative of imported European models to later, singular, *tour de force* local creations, reflects historical and social realities: when the series began in the early seventeenth century, tobacco was a rare commodity; trade with Europeans was strictly controlled; and society was highly centralized, leading all goods and prerogatives to the king. But through the nineteenth century, as transatlantic slavery and later forms of long-distance and local trade brought wealth to ever-larger numbers of people, more could afford what had once been guarded goods and privileges – including the artistry of the most accomplished pipe makers.[23]

Smoking in Africa often implies a solidarity that may be limited to a particular group or community, but which may also extend across ethnic or other social boundaries. The intercultural entanglements and possible politics of smoking are made especially evident in the late nineteenth-century case of the Rasta-like Bena Diamba or 'People of Cannabis', living in Lubuko, the 'Land of Friendship' in what is now the Democratic Republic of the Congo. Johannes Fabian has recently retold this tale as he examined the ecstatic theatricality of early European imperialism in central Africa. What a mad lot the explorers could be, and how surreal were some Africans' reactions to them! In order to understand the circumstances of how Others – both colonizers and colonized – were created as objects of knowledge, Fabian brings facts to the fore that are nearly always glossed over in explorers' travelogues and early ethnographies: panic and the manic, to be sure, but also 'the effects of alcohol, drugs, illness, sex, brutality and terror, as well as the role of conviviality, friendship, play and performance'.[24]

Cannabis smoking appears to have been a feature of caravan travel, especially into the interior from the Swahili coast of East Africa. Such activity was more than matched by the drug abuse of many early European visitors to Central Africa, and indeed, as they found themselves isolated and fearful in strange lands, 'we are entitled to imagine our explorers "drugged", most of them some of the time, and perhaps some of them most of the time.'[25] Sincere friendship might result, but so could unmitigated brutality. Yet it is conceivable, Fabian holds, that the delirious effects of substance abuse allowed escape from the rigidities of European explorers' and Africans' own upbringings, and so *aided* whatever understanding of each other's cultures and customs – so frighteningly different from their own – that they may have achieved during the contact period.

Of these tales, that of the Bena Diamba from the 1880s stands as 'one of the strangest twists in the strange story of the exploration of central Africa'. Bena Diamba emerged as a politico-religious society among Lulua people (also called Shilange) living near what is now the city of Mbuji Mayi in southwestern Congo. In a context rife with violence due to jockeying for control of long-distance trade and raiding for slaves and ivory, a charismatic man named Kalamba Mukenge 'made cannabis a cultural and political symbol capable of creating a sense of identity among his followers and of obligating or pacifying other chiefs and officeholders in a fairly large area'.[26]

Mukenge and his sister and a close confidante, Sangula Meta, appear to have been very deliberate in inventing traditions. The distinctive greeting *Moyo!* ('Life!') was used among those inhabiting the Land of Friendship, for example. Earlier status and affiliations through kinship, clan and political organization were replaced by a new sense of crosscutting solidarity based upon cannabis as a source of spiritual power. Indeed, although it is not altogether clear from the fragmented sources that

Fabian had at his disposal, it appears that Cannabis may have been recognized as an animated presence – a deity, that is. Bena Diamba became pacifists in lands long torn by internecine strife, and they even refused to kill animals. They gave up palm wine and herbal medicines in favour of cannabis, and practised ritual nudity, shaving their heads and bodies to eschew all markers of former social identity. Architecture was altered to favour larger communal dwellings; villages were reorganized around a central plaza for cannabis smoking; and earlier material culture was destroyed. Huge water pipes made from gourds – some a metre in diameter – stood as the sole material vehicles for the Bena Diamba's nativistic movement. Hermann von Wissman and several other European visitors encouraged and sometimes joined the movement's ecstasies for reasons of personal pleasure informed by the goals of imperialist politics. Fabian ominously concludes that as a consequence of these odd encounters, the early European administrators of the Congo Free State lent an authority to the cannabis-inspired polity that set it against other groups in the emerging ethnic nationalism of the colonial period. The effects of this divisiveness continue to be dire more than forty years since Congolese independence.[27]

These unusual political purposes and outcomes are matched by many more benign examples of deep religiosity attached to the practices, substances and paraphernalia of smoking tobacco in Africa. In the Kingdom of Kom in the Grassfields region of south-western Cameroon, tobacco was considered a 'necessity' in the 1930s; in South Africa, it was 'comparable in importance to beer and meat'.[28] A Kom prayer implores the gods to protect one's progeny, prosperity and prestige, and as the missionary-ethnographer Paul Gebauer noted, 'prosperity' does not refer to material wealth as much as it does to goods necessary for basic dignity, with palm wine and tobacco chief among them. In the 1930s when Gebauer observed them, women took 'tobacco breaks' to 'help dispel the morning blues' and 'lighten farming chores', and 'unforgettable' were 'the single files of grassland women toiling uphill, followed by

a thin blue trail of smoke'. Men would stop work to smoke their pipes every other hour or so, 'to let their souls catch up with them'. Tobacco was planted close to homesteads, often on middens or abandoned housing sites where it was felt that 'the bones of the ancestors buried below' might 'add flavour to the leaves!'[29]

The association between smoking tobacco and the spirit world may be of far deeper significance than this may suggest. For a number of southern African peoples, tobacco is 'often shared, rarely taken alone', and is 'enjoyed equally by the living and the spirits of the dead'. Among the Sotho people of Lesotho, tobacco 'clears the head . . . allowing for the voices of the ancestors to be heard', and is an important 'food' for the spirits. Zulu offer tobacco to their ancestors; Xhosa consider a tobacco pipe 'a means of befriending the spiritual world'; and Fon of the Republic of Bénin place cigarettes in the mouths of spirit figures for their delectation.[30] The verb 'to smoke' (tobacco) in the Tabwa language is *kupepa*, which also means 'to offer sacrifices to the spirits'. Tabwa used to bury the dead with pipe and tobacco and sing plaintive songs equating the person's loss with an inability to smoke together any longer.[31] Nowadays they bring tobacco to funerals, where it is shared among those grieving, but presumably with ancestral spirits as well.

Smoking can also attract spirits for more particular reasons, and especially for divination. Many Tabwa speak Swahili and use the Swahili verb *kuvuta*, 'to pull or drag', to refer to smoking – presumably because one 'takes a drag' on one's pipe or, nowadays, on one's cigarette. The same verb can be used in the sense of drawing a spirit to oneself as a spirit medium (*ng'anga*) does to begin an inspired session of problem-solving. Chokwe diviners of Angola and Zambia smoke their water pipes in this way, as they welcome spirits to help them in their diagnoses of people's illnesses and other misfortunes. Similarly, Kabre earth-spirit priests of Togo smoke in their sacred shrines as they divine. Among the Xhosa of South Africa, pipes decorated with white beads are used by diviner-healers 'as a symbol of their

A Chokwe (Angola or Zambia) wooden pipe depicting a nobleman.

profession', and in the old days at least, Zulu diviners kept special tobacco patches called 'fields of the spirits', the crops from which were reserved for convening spirits. Tobacco was mixed with honey and burned in these same fields to honour the diviners' guardian ancestors.[32]

Other herbs or vegetable substances are sometimes smoked for similar purposes. Tabwa shamans (*Tulunga*) smoke *lubowe* (*Amaranthus dubius Mast*), a herb that does not appear to be hallucinogenic but which one Tulunga nonetheless reports to be so powerful that it allows him to 'see' sorcerers invisible to healers lacking the healers' special knowledge and abilities. Smoking psychoactive drugs appears to be very rare in Africa (discounting the possibility of a recent introduction of narcotics to urban centres), and so datura smoking by the Kotoko people of Chad seems a very localized practice. A scattering of groups take mind-altering drugs, as the Fang of Gabon do when they use *eboga* (*Tabernanthe iboga*) to 'see' their ancestors and receive from them 'all the imaginative elaborations of liturgy and belief' for their religion; but *eboga* is eaten rather than smoked.[33]

In more mundane circumstances, the sense of community that tobacco smoking fosters among people and spirits is convivial (for ancestors are not 'dead'), and, like many other African peoples, the Tabwa associate family cohesion with smoking:

those who smoke together stick together through ancestral sanction, and a descriptive term for divorce is 'to cut the tobacco'. Tobacco and smoking may also be associated with fertility, as the Sotho make very explicit. Their word for tobacco, *kwae*, is a euphemism for 'penis', and, as a Sotho saying has it, '*kwae* is a thing smoked at night by women'. *Kwae* also refers to the sheep slaughtered when a bride joins her husband's home, and so signifies the expectation of the new couple's sexual union.[34]

The anthropomorphism of some African pipes underscores analogies that may be drawn among smoking, sex and gender, but perhaps nowhere with as great drama as among the Luba, Tabwa and neighbouring Congolese peoples. Only a few such pipes are known in collections or from early colonial literature; but even water pipes made from bottle gourds are often decorated with inlaid copper wire in patterns suggesting human scarification, making these 'anthropomorphic' as well.

Two very rare, anthropomorphic pipes – a Luba one collected in the eastern borderlands between Luba and Tabwa in the 1890s and a nineteenth-century Tabwa water pipe – are such evocative sculptures that one wonders if Magritte were not correct after all: How *can* these be pipes?[35] Yet they are and must be just the same.

The posture, coiffure and scarification of the Luba water pipe recalls the stylistic features of several

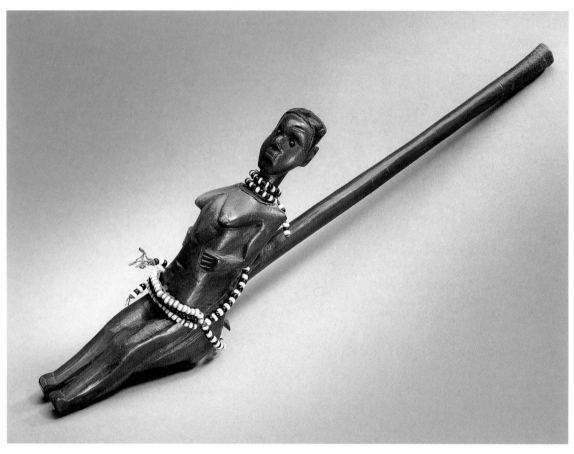

A Tsonga or Nguni (Mozambique or South Africa) wooden pipe portraying a woman wearing beads with her head used as a stopper for the bowl.

particular figures, and, more generally, the caryatid figures supporting Luba stools.[36] Here, the kneeling legs do not rest upon the base of a stool; rather, they are supported by the pipe's water chamber as an extension of the figure's genitals. The same is true of the Tabwa pipe. Luba and Tabwa female figures usually have pronounced pudenda, reflecting cultural practices to enhance a woman's sexual allure. But in this case the pipes make further reference to gender theatre and the politics of kinship.

Tabwa and eastern Luba observe matrilineal descent, and men find themselves subject to the dilemmas that anthropologists have called the 'matrilineal puzzle'. When kinship is traced through one's mother's line, a man's biological children are not his heirs. Instead, his sister's children fulfil such

roles. Men feel themselves torn between their love for the progeny residing in their own homes and their sisters' children, whom they must discipline, teach and otherwise bring to social maturity. Tensions, competing loyalties and occasional conflict result, for a political triangle results with a man at the apex and his wife and sister at the two basal points.

Tabwa consider the perplexities of their social organization through narratives and material culture, such as when they decorate objects with isosceles triangles in a motif called *balamwezi*, 'the rising of a new moon'.[37] The male moon moves through phases of light and darkness, but is also caught between the interests of the two most important women of his life, understood as the morning and evening apparitions of Venus in the east and west, respectively. Sometimes these same 'stars' are said to be the polygamous moon's first and second wives, but the narrative outcome is the same: a man is caught between opposing attributes of the women dearest to him.

The Tabwa and Luba anthropomorphic water pipes are 'object lessons', giving material representation to these very conundra. The water chambers of the female pipes are cool, dark, guarded and fertile. They soothe; they provide; they love. But such pipes possess two other essential parts – reed segments inserted into the depths of the water chambers, and the ceramic pipe bowls that the reeds bear on their opposite ends. The reeds are 'male' to Tabwa thinking, whereas the bowls are 'female'. Bowls contain tobacco (or cannabis) and the fire to light it. These 'women' are 'hot', and the fire they hold transforms tobacco into the smoke that the male reeds convey to the bowls' cool counterparts. Following triadic colour symbolism that is a 'mode of thought' for a great many African societies, these 'women' are 'red', denoting the enticing violence of change. Those 'women' are 'black' in secrecy, wisdom and fecundity. The 'men' forever culturally caught between the women are as 'white' as smoke, their powers ethereal but potent.[38]

This brief review skims the surface of African histories and cultures of smoking, yet it should be sufficiently clear that, in Africa, smoking has long been 'good to think' as well as to savour. What remains of these beliefs and practices in our times, though? Certainly in rural areas, people maintain some of the philosophy and activities described here; but elsewhere smoking has changed in pace with other aspects of globalization.

Industrially produced tobacco products have been available since well before the end of the colonial period, for although per capita income was and still is very low, potential markets have been obvious. Cigarettes were and still are imported, and with breweries, cigarette factories became among the earliest – and in some cases the only – industries created in the colonies. In recent years, locally produced cigarettes have met increased competition from trans-national companies eager to replace income lost in the health-conscious countries of Europe and the Americas. Yet despite the ravages of HIV/AIDS and endemic illnesses such as malaria and tuberculosis, a researcher at the US Center for Disease Control estimates that, by the year 2020, tobacco-related diseases will become Africa's biggest killers.[39] African governments and international agencies such as the World Health Organization are striving to assess and control tobacco-related mortality, sometimes against fierce opposition from trans-national companies and local people themselves. In Africa as elsewhere in the world, smoking is 'modern' and 'chic', but although these postures and presumptions are ends unto themselves, 'ceci est quand même une pipe.'

Tobacco in Iran

RUDI MATTHEE

It is known that tobacco first came to Iran during the rule of the Safavid dynasty (1501–1722 CE), following the European exploration of the American continent, although the source of transmission and diffusion remains unclear. Some have insisted that the Iranians learned about smoking from the Ottomans during the Safavid–Ottoman war of 1609, when Shah ᶜAbbas I, on hearing that his soldiers were spending much of their pay on tobacco, outlawed its use, cropping the noses and lips of violators of the ban. This was documented by the German traveller Adam Olearius, who visited Iran during the reign of ᶜAbbas's successor, Shah Safi.[1] Olearius, however, does not say that tobacco was *introduced* in this manner. Unfortunately, there are few eyewitness accounts of the actual use of tobacco during the reign of Shah ᶜAbbas, and the earliest one, from the hand of the Spanish envoy Don Garcia y Silva de Figueroa, is dated 1617.[2]

The eighteenth-century Persian pharmacological dictionary *Makhzan al-adviyah* may well be right in its claim that Portuguese merchants and sailors were responsible for the introduction of tobacco.[3] The allegedly earliest reference to the water pipe, *qalyan*, in Persian literature lends further credence to this argument. It is found in an early sixteenth-century *rubaᶜi* from the hand of an anonymous poet from Shiraz who died in 942 HQ/1535–6 CE:

From your lips the water pipe draws enjoyment
In your mouth the reed turns sweet as sugar cane
It is not tobacco smoke around your face

It is a cloud that circles around the moon[4]

The presumed date of this poem – before 1536 – the lack of other references to tobacco in Iran for the next half century, and indications that elsewhere in Asia tobacco was not introduced before 1600, cast doubt on the poem's authenticity, although not on the likelihood that the Portuguese were responsible for bringing smoking to Iran.[5]

A related issue is that of the provenance of the water pipe, the most popular smoking device in Iran, which is called *qalyan* in Persian, *huqqah* (lit. orb, jar, receptacle) in India and *nargilah* or *shishah* in the Arab lands. It is often assumed that the *qalyan* was an Iranian invention and that it spread from there across the Middle East.[6] Yet, apart from the fact that the water pipe over time became particularly popular in Iran, there is little proof that it originated there.[7] On etymological and physiological grounds, it is more likely that the water pipe was first developed in India. The term *qalyan* does not point to an Iranian origin, for it is a derivative of *ghalyan*, a word that, in turn, derives from the Arabic verb *ghala*, to 'boil' or to 'bubble'. The early water pipe was a simple device consisting of a hollowed-out coconut, into which a straight (bamboo) reed was inserted through which the tobacco smoke was filtered.[8] This type continued to be used by poor people in southern Iran and India alike for a long time.[9] The very word *nargilah*, meaning coconut in Sanskrit, refers to these origins.[10] Since the coconut is not indigenous to Iran but does grow in southern India it stands to reason

Seventeenth-century water
pipes, from Engelbert
Kaempfer's *Amoenitatum
Exoticarium politico-physico-
medicarum*, fac. v (Lemgo,
1712).

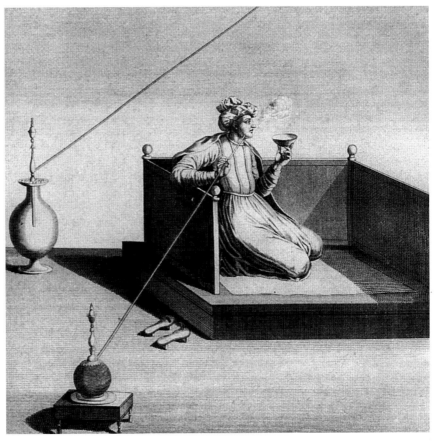

Water pipes with long
stems, used by clerics, from
Jean Chardin, *Voyages du
chevalier Chardin, en Perse et
autres lieux de l'Orient*,
10 vols (Paris, 1810–11).

Early image of a water pipe, from Johann Neander's
Tabacologia medico-cheururgico pharmaceutica (Leiden, 1622).

that the water pipe originated in the Subcontinent, where an Iranian physician is said to have been the first to use one.[11]

A final issue relates to the further development of the water pipe. A drawing of a Persian *qalyan* is included in the earliest European compendium on tobacco, the *Tabacologia*, written by Johann Neander and published in the Netherlands in 1622.[12] Contrary to what one might expect, the images are not of primitive and crude contraptions improvised from coconut shells, but of highly elaborate and intricate devices. The high-quality craftsmanship suggests a relatively long process of technical advancement and aesthetic refinement and might thus corroborate the timing of the early poetic reference. In sum, Safavid Iran may have been one of the first societies outside the New World and the Iberian peninsula where tobacco was diffused and became a commonplace article of consumption.

POPULARITY AND SOCIAL ASPECTS

Accepting the early diffusion of tobacco in Iran allows for the interpretation of the many references regarding the extraordinary popularity of tobacco in the country by the mid-seventeenth century. The German traveller Heinrich von Poser, visiting Qandahar in 1621, spoke of the 'excessive drinking of tobacco'.[13] Fifteen years later, Olearius noted that Iranians of all classes found so much pleasure in tobacco that they smoked it everywhere, even inside mosques. At that time tobacco was still imported. The term *inglis tanbaku* hints at imports by the English in the early seventeenth century. Iran also received supplies of mostly cheap grades from the Ottoman Empire and India.[14] By the mid-1600s foreign imports had largely come to an end and tobacco had turned into a cash crop that was cultivated all over Iran. *Tanbaku*, the fine tobacco used for water pipes, was mainly grown in the south-central parts of the country, with the best grades found around Isfahan and in Fars, while *tutun*, the coarser tobacco used for regular pipes, grew in the western regions.[15] Soon Iran was exporting its home-grown tobacco to India and the Ottoman Empire.[16]

So popular had the plant become by the mid-seventeenth century that Iranian soldiers brought their water pipes with them during campaigns and travellers carried the device with them on trips.[17] Most Iranians, noted the French traveller Jean-Baptiste Tavernier, would rather forego bread than tobacco, and the first thing they would do at the breaking of the fast during the month of Ramadan was to light their pipes.[18] The Englishman John Fryer concurred when he said that 'the Poor, have they but a Penny in the World, one half will go for Bread and dried Grapes, or Butter-milk, and the other for Snow and Tobacco'.[19] And the Dutchman Cornelis de Bruyn, visiting Iran in 1703–4, insisted that tobacco was the 'main delicacy and pastime of

Iranians smoking at a coffee house in the 17th century, from Tavernier's *Les six voyages de J.-B. Tavernier* (Paris, 1676).

the Iranians'.[20] The *qalyan* house, possibly synonymous with the coffee house, seems to have been a standard feature of Iranian towns in late Safavid times. Engelbert Kaempfer, passing through Rasht, the capital of the northern province of Gilan in 1683, noted that 'every third or definitely every fourth house here is a *qalyan* house, in which orators as well as beggars can be heard'. In many towns the *qalyan* houses were located in the heart of town, often flanking the main square.[21] In addition to the coffee and tobacco houses there were many shops, *dukkan-i tanbaku-furushi*, where tobacco was sold to passers-by.[22] Again, Iran seems to have been decades ahead of Europe in fully integrating tobacco and tobacco smoking into the texture of society and in turning tobacco into an article of mass consumption.

The subject of the rapid integration of tobacco smoking in Iran is furthered when it is considered in connection with other stimulants. It is tempting to try to find a causal link between the quick acceptance of tobacco and the near-simultaneous introduction of coffee in Iran. Smokers metabolize caffeine much faster than non-smokers and thus require a greater coffee intake to gain the same

effect.[23] However, to see one as the vector of the other in an effort to explain the speed of the process is merely to beg the question. Both became complementary accessories to life in Iran, in that tobacco calms while coffee stimulates.[24] A Persian saying has it that 'coffee without tobacco is like soup without salt.'[25] Yet there is no intrinsic reason why this should have been the case. The quick and total acceptance of tobacco by Iranians can possibly be explained as a form of convergence and fusion of a different order, involving other, pre-existing mind-altering drugs. Some of these had been widely used in Iran long before the introduction of tobacco. Among these is opium, which is a good example of fusion following rather than preceding the dissemination of tobacco smoking, since it was eaten rather than smoked before the nineteenth century. The same is not true for *bang*, or hashish, an intoxicant that had long been known to Iranians and whose widespread use may have facilitated the adoption of tobacco.[26] Tobacco and cannabis are highly complementary, and in Iran they have long been used together.[27] In suggesting a connection between tobacco and hashish, however, it has not

A water-pipe bearer on horseback, late Safavid period, from Cornelis de Bruyn's *Reizen over Moskovie, door Persie en indie* (Amsterdam, 1714).

been proven that the water pipe was used to smoke hashish before the introduction of tobacco. This then casts doubt on the possibility of a spontaneous invention of the water pipe in the world of Islam.[28] It is quite possible to entertain the idea that the water pipe, whether it originated in Iran or India, was an original invention, *and* to argue that the rapid acceptance of tobacco and the concomitant development and refinement of the water pipe followed a process of fusion between existing and newly introduced habits of hallucinogenic drug taking. For this to be the case, it is irrelevant as to whether hashish was ever smoked by way of a water pipe. That the two, tobacco and hashish, were consumed jointly in the seventeenth century merely strengthens this hypothesis.[29] Thus Fryer in the 1670s noted that the Iranians 'never smoked a pipe without the leaves of the intoxicating bang and flowers of the same mixed with their tobacco'.[30]

Unlike the situation in several Western European countries, where different social classes gravitated toward different forms of taking tobacco, class distinctions in Iran expressed themselves less in the choice between different forms of smoking than in the degree of refinement and decoration of the paraphernalia used, the elaborateness of the surrounding ritual and the social codes inscribed in a pastime that was sociable rather than individual in nature. The old, the rich and the poor, noblemen and commoners, all indulged in smoking with the same gusto.[31] The *qalyans* of the poor, however, were made with a base of coconut, or alternatively a gourd (*qabaq*).[32] The wealthy, by contrast, had their water pipes made of painted glass or chiselled silver or gold. Surviving examples suggest that, whether the *qalyan* originated in India or in Iran, it attained its acme of design and sophistication in the latter.[33] People of high rank also took to employing a *qalyandar*, or a water-pipe holder, who would follow them on horseback while carrying the various implements needed for smoking.[34] This phenomenon, incidentally, gave rise to further differentiation along religious and social lines, for in Safavid times Armenian Christians were prohibited from having

A Qajar official and his water-pipe bearer, early 19th century, from G. Drouville's *Voyage en Perse, fait en 1812 et 1813* (St Petersburg, 1819–20).

An Iranian woman and her wet nurse, late Qajar period, from J. Dieulafoy's *La Perse, la Chaldée et la Susania* (Paris, 1887).

10 Women with a water pipe in a private home, from H. Grothe's *Wanderugen in Persien* (Berlin, 1910).

A girl smoking, Muhammad Qasim, Isfahan, 17th century.

their tobacco gear thus carried behind them.[35] In the Qajar period (1796–1925) the wealthy similarly employed a servant whose sole task was to clean, move, light and recharge their *qalyans*.[36] The same sort of class distinction can be observed with regard to the regular tobacco pipe. 'Dry' smoking in Iran was done through long-stemmed pipes with a small bowl, which were quite similar to the ones used in England and the Netherlands. Originally made of clay, these pipes were known as *chupuq* or *chapuq* in Turkish and Persian, a cognate of the Persian word for wood, *chub*, and rendered in English as *chibouk*.[37] The wealthy over time took to using richly decorated pipes of engraved silver, while people of lesser means smoked simple wooden pipes. The poor usually assembled or fixed broken pipes.[38]

Unlike the situation in most early modern Western societies, no overt gender division seems to have existed in Safavid Iran with regard to tobacco smoking. Textual evidence and contemporary illustrations suggest that both men and women smoked.[39] As one observer noted: 'All people, men and women, smoke, indiscriminately and avidly, day and night.'[40] It was rather location that separated the sexes. While men enjoyed their pipes in the many coffee houses that sprang up in the Safavid urban centres, women rarely ventured outside and indulged in the confines of the private sphere.

A different kind of convergence and assimilation involves prevailing social customs of the time and traditions of ceremony and ritual. From the very beginning, smoking in Iran was not just a pastime and an addiction, but also a *habitus* that became closely interwoven with hospitality and conviviality. One seventeenth-century observer claimed that, while Iranians smoked tobacco as commonly as the Turks, they surrounded it with much more ceremony.[41] Part of this involves the strong tradition of hospitality and sociability in Iran, and the water pipe was a device that lent itself to social gathering. Thus tobacco became a symbol of social graciousness. Many foreign visitors noted that as soon as a guest entered the house of an Iranian he would be offered a water pipe and coffee or tea.[42] Tobacco, John Fryer noted, 'is a general companion, and to give them their due, they are conversable good-Fellows, sparing no one his Bowl in their turn.'[43] Observers of Qajar Iran further drew attention to the ritualized dimension of smoking in Iran, a pastime rich in the enactment of social status and hierarchy. S.G.W. Benjamin, America's first ambassador to Iran, in 1882–3, gives a good example of this:

[I]f one present outranks all the others, only one pipe is brought in, which is handed to him. Before smoking, he makes a feint of offering it in turn to all present, but woe to him who incautiously accepts before he of higher rank has smoked, for in that case he will be made to feel the withering scorn of which a Persian gentleman is capable. The Mestofi-Mamolek, the highest official in Persia after the King, has not

The mayor of Miyaneh, Iranian Azerbaijan, and his servants, late Qajar period, from J. Dieulafoy, *La Perse, la Chaldée et la Susania* (Paris, 1887).

smoked for forty years. He took a solemn resolution against tobacco, because, when a young man, the *kaliân* was on one occasion given in his presence to a man whom he considered of lower rank, before it was offered to him. When the pipe was presented to him he dashed it aside, and swore never to smoke again, in order to avoid the possibility of being a second time subjected to such an affront.[44]

The water pipe remained popular in Iran until the twentieth century, when it gradually fell out of favour, making room for cigarette smoking. Cigarettes were first smoked in the late nineteenth century and initially were an affectation of the sophisticated.[45] Cigarette smoking soon spread, however, and by 1890 the typical merchant in the

bazaar of Tehran could be seen with a cigarette in his mouth. At that time Russian firms had also opened cigarette manufactories in Gilan on the Caspian Sea.[46] In modern times almost all tobacco grown in Iran was manufactured into cigarettes, and by the 1960s two large domestic factories produced 10 billion cigarettes yearly.[47] Foreign cigarettes, above all Winston, were and remain to this day the most prized brands.

RESISTANCE: CRITICISM, PROSCRIPTION
AND RESIGNATION

As in many places around the world, tobacco in the early stage of its introduction in the Middle East aroused medical interest, provoked moral rebuke among clerics and caused economic anxiety on the part of bureaucrats. Like their counterparts in the West, Muslim physicians discussed the effect of smoking on physical health. Controversy surrounded the alleged effects of smoking on the body. As a supposedly hot and dry substance, it was held to be salutary for people with a humid disposition, although some believed that it weakened the brain.[48] Similar to European beliefs, tobacco smoke was thought to repel pestilence.[49] Overall, however, tobacco in Islamic lands never gained the medicinal reputation it enjoyed in early modern Europe.

Muslim scholars, on the other hand, showed themselves highly preoccupied with the potentially detrimental effects of the novelty on piety and propriety. Unable to find references to tobacco in the Koran, they resorted to analogical reasoning to determine whether smoking should be permitted or condemned. Since tobacco did not resemble any of the forbidden substances mentioned in the Koran and the sayings of the Prophet (*Hadith*), proscribing it was not a simple matter. Neither was it easy to 'prove' that tobacco in itself was bad, or harmful to one's health. One argument for proscription was to equate tobacco with the foul things that Sura VII: 157 (*al-Aᶜraf*) declares forbidden and to associate it with the 'avoidance of things evil' (*nahi ᶜan al-munkar*) contained in Sura III: 104 (al-ʿImran). Also, according to a *Hadith*, the Prophet appreciated sweet odours and would certainly have loathed tobacco's foul smell.[50]

In the Shia world tobacco inspired similar debates. A number of Iranian theologians wrote treatises that discussed the religious status of tobacco smoking, weighing the potential health benefits ascribed to it by some physicians against possible religious objections. Arguments for and against tobacco were often made in the context of the controversy between the representatives of orthodoxy, who rejected tobacco, and members of Sufi orders, who took to smoking. In Iran, most of those who spoke out against the habit seem to have adhered to Akhbarism, a theological school of thought that relied heavily on the sayings of the Prophet and the Shia Imams.[51] Following clerical disapproval, Safavid authorities issued decrees that outlawed smoking. Muslim rulers tended to present and articulate prohibitive measures as a 'return to the true faith'. It would be erroneous to take this lofty goal at face value, though, for the real motives typically went beyond mere considerations of piety. In their zeal to curb smoking, Safavid rulers were motivated by concerns about treasure rather than religious probity. Shah ʿAbbas banned smoking after reviewing his soldiers' wasteful spending habits, and his grandson and successor, Shah Safi (r. 1629–42), rescinded the ban on smoking shortly after taking power in 1629 as part of a series of measures designed to establish his legitimacy and to propitiate the population of his realm.[52] The same ruler is known to have banned tobacco several times during his reign, for reasons that remain unknown, but each time the effect was minimal and the measure temporary.[53]

But censure and proscription were unable to stop the advance of the herb. Even clerical authorities came to realize that fighting tobacco was an exercise in futility. As one of them observed at the end of the Safavid era: 'The *qalyan* is so well known in east and west that its removal is no longer possible. In former times a ruler proscribed it everywhere and ordered the execution of addicts, and people

were indeed killed on its account, but all to no avail.'[54] This is probably a reference to Shah ʿAbbas I, who apparently found so many violators of his ban that in the end he was forced to give in to the passion of his people and to permit tobacco to be planted in public.[55] The strongest incentive to connivance no doubt came from authority figures who had succumbed to the habit themselves. The best example is the influential and outspoken anti-Sufi and Akhbari theologian Muhammad Baqir Majlisi (d. 1699), who as Shaykh al-Islam of Isfahan was the most prominent cleric of his time and who considered smoking permissible. Like many of those who sanctioned tobacco, he was a fervent smoker himself, as was his father, Muhammad Taqi Majlisi. Of the latter it is said that he considered smoking permissible even during periods of voluntary fasting and that he refrained from smoking only at times of obligatory fasting so as to avoid controversy.[56]

The other impulse behind permitting or even encouraging smoking was the tax revenue it generated. Prohibitions, Tavernier noted, would never last long, for banning the sale and use of tobacco cost the shah a great deal of money. Isfahan alone, he explained, yielded 40,000 *tumans* in annual revenue from taxing tobacco, while Tabriz brought in 20,000 and Shiraz 10,000 *tumans*, formidable sums given total crown revenue of some 600,000 *tumans*.[57] Others corroborated the State involvement in trade and consumption by endorsing *pul-i tanbaku* (tobacco money) and 'a heavy tax laid upon tobacco'.[58]

In the mid- to late nineteenth century tobacco had become one of Iran's leading export products, going to India, the Ottoman Empire and Russia. By 1878 the total crop had increased to approximately one million kilograms.[59] It is therefore not surprising that the Qajar Government attempted to bring this lucrative product under greater central control. In 1886 Nasir al-Din Shah issued a royal decree (*farman*) that, under the guise of a State concerned to curb the negative effects of smoking on body and mind, sought to bring the cultivation and consumption of tobacco under governmental

A group of men smoking.

control.[60] Although the decree was quickly abandoned, it served as a precursor to the infamous tobacco concession that the shah in 1890 granted to the British Major Talbot, whose corporation received the rights to the sale, distribution and export of all Iranian tobacco.

This concession galvanized popular resentment of long-standing Government neglect, mismanagement and the exploiting of national resources, which sparked the famous Tobacco Revolt of 1891–2. Russia's representatives in Iran voiced their opposition to the concession and Iran's tobacco merchants were quick to put up resistance against it as well, but it was the leading *ulama* (religious leaders) who articulated this resistance in ideological terms by issuing a religious ban on the handling and smoking of tobacco. The boycott that followed was so successful – even the women in the shah's harem stopped smoking – that the shah was forced to repeal the concession.[61]

Immensely popular, tobacco by the nineteenth century had become firmly embedded in Iran's social texture. As a national consumer product, it cut through social classes and gender distinctions, while the ritual and accoutrements involved in smoking reinforced those same divisions. The economic importance of tobacco, and the fact that the best grades were cultivated in Iran, lent tobacco and its use a 'national' dimension. For Iranians, who had long jealously cherished the ideal of economic self-sufficiency and whose suspicion of import goods goes back to Safavid times, the tobacco concession touched an emotional nerve.

Smoking and Āyurvedic Medicine in India

P. RAM MANOHAR

Many ancient cultures share a belief in the beneficial effects of exposure to certain kinds of carefully prepared smoke. Indian tradition is no different. According to a legend narrated in Indian medical literature, the benefits of smoke were revealed to the sages by the fire god. By his grace, they discovered various methods to make smoke that successfully protected babies and children from malefic spirits.[1]

Purposeful exposure to smoke has various objectives, which include medicinal use, religious obligation, recreation, psychedelic experiences and de-addiction. Smoking is recommended by traditional systems of medicine such as Āyurveda for the prevention as well as cure of diseases, especially those affecting the respiratory tract. Smoking is sometimes an essential component of religious ceremonies. It may be merely a pleasurable activity for relief from stress, or it may become a means to induce altered states of consciousness. Herbal smoking is often resorted to for de-addiction, as an alternative to the habitual smoking of harmful substances such as tobacco and marijuana.

A close study of classical Sanskrit literature reveals that, in the Indian cultural context, exposure to special types of smoke not only benefited an individual's health but also impacted positively on the harmony of the environment. The smoking of marijuana and tobacco, as well as the use of the special smoking apparatus called *hookah*, were introduced into India at different periods. They do not, however, represent India's original contribution to smoking and are not extensively documented in its classical literature. The cultural pluralism and eclecticism of India make it difficult to distinguish between what is native and what is adopted, although a study of the classical literature can help to some extent.

Three methods of purposeful exposure to smoke are recognized in India. They are known as *homa* (fire offering), *dhūmapāna* (literally 'drinking smoke') or *dhūma* (the contracted form), and *dhūpa* (fumigation). *Homa*, the offering of clarified butter and grains in fire created by burning sacred plants, generates smoke that spreads over a large area. Its purpose is to make a profound impact on the environment and thereby the people living there.[2] It is also said to confer spiritual benefits. *Dhūma*, the active inhalation of smoke generated by burning smoking mixtures in a pipe, has a direct and profound impact on the individual.[3] *Dhūpa* or fumigation generates smoke that spreads over a small area, affecting an individual or individuals and their immediate vicinity. It is performed in winter to provide protection from cold, and during rains to fumigate clothes before use.[4] A major function is to drive away demons.[5]

Of these three methods, *homa* has a predominantly religious appeal and *dhūma* occupies a prominent place in the medical tradition. *Dhūpa* has religious and medicinal as well as social dimensions. *Homa* comes under the purview of magico-religious medicine, whereas *dhūma* is based on empirico-rational medical principles. *Dhūpa* has both magico-religious and empirico-

Apparatus for fumigation.

The gum of *Commiphora mukul* (guggulu) used for smoking since the Vedic period.

Apparatus for performing *homa*.

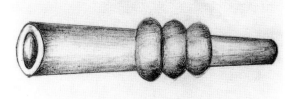

The Āyurvedic smoke pipe, a drawing by Hrishikesh Damle, 2001.

A *sadhu* (renouncer) smoking a *chillum*, 1992.

rational elements.[6] *Dhūmapāna* is akin to the modern practice of smoking and hence will be the focus of this essay.

Vedic literature abounds with detailed descriptions of *homas*.[7] *Hārīta Saṃhitā* is one of the few medical works that devotes a chapter for discussion on *homa*.[8] On the other hand, elaborate accounts of *dhūma* are found only in Āyurvedic literature. There are scattered mentions of *dhūpa* in various types of literature in India. An entire chapter in the *Kāśyapa Saṃhitā*, the classical treatise on pediatrics, deals with *dhupa*.[9] The use of the gum of *Commiphora mukul* for smoking perhaps began with the practice of fumigation to cure consumption mentioned in the *Atharva Veda*.[10]

Performance of *homa* and *dhūpa* has been in vogue for at least 3,000 years, and *Dhūmapāna* practised for more than 2,000. The practice of smoking was systematized at a very early stage in the evolutionary history of Āyurveda, which goes back to a few hundred years before the Common Era, and remained relatively unchanged, except for the addition of some new recipes and herbs. The present study is based on references from important Āyurvedic literature representing crucial landmarks in its historical development. *Caraka Saṃhitā*, *Suśruta Saṃhitā*, *Kāśyapa Saṃhitā* and *Bheḷa Saṃhitā* date back a few centuries before the Common Era, although these texts were edited and revised up to the fourth century CE. *Aṣṭāṅga Saṃgraha* and *Aṣṭāṅga Hṛdayaṃ* belong to the fifth and sixth centuries CE. *Dhanvantari Nighaṇṭu*, *Cikitsāsārasaṃgraha* and *Cakradatta* were composed in the tenth, eleventh and twelfth centuries, *Śārṅgadhara Saṃhitā* and *Kayyadeva Nighaṇṭu* in the thirteenth and fourteenth centuries and *Bhāvaprakāśa*, *Yogaratnākara* and *Rāja Nighaṇṭu* in the sixteenth and seventeenth centuries.

In Āyurvedic practices, smoking is an indispensable element in the daily routine for healthy living.[11] The six-pronged strategy is intended not only to ward off potential harm, but also to ensure maximum benefit from smoking. In addition to the thoughtful design of the smoke pipe and an intelligent way of smoking, it is important to recognize a legitimate purpose for smoking; check the fitness of the person who is to smoke; identify proper occasions for smoking; and select the ingredients for the smoking mixture carefully. Why, who, when, what and how are five questions that need to be answered before deciding to smoke.

Smoking as stipulated in Āyurveda aims primarily at reaping physical benefits and has only a mild effect on the mind. According to Āyurvedic practices, proper smoking can clear up the channels in the supra-clavicular region and the respiratory tract, thereby preventing as well as curing diseases in these regions. The effects of smoking can be fine-tuned by choosing appropriate ingredients, adjusting the length of the smoke pipe and making alterations in the method of smoking. Smoking has been classified in Āyurveda in two ways, since the smoking mixture is either lit up directly in the pipe or drawn through it after being lit in a closed crucible. Routine smoke, unctuous smoke and cleansing smoke are the three types of smoking that make direct use of the smoke pipe. Expectorant smoke, emetic smoke and wound fumigation make use of a closed crucible in addition to a pipe.[12] Some texts follow a different classification. For instance, *Suśruta* does not include wound fumigation as a type of smoking, and *Caraka* does not mention expectorant and emetic smoke, let alone wound fumigation.[13] Wound fumigation is included under *dhūma* because the smoke affects a specific part of the body. Others exclude it because the smoke is not inhaled here, inhalation being the true character of *dhūma* . In the literature, routine smoke has a wide range of effects on the mind and body. Unctuous smoke is regarded as nourishing, and cleansing smoke is believed to eject materials from clogged channels. Expectorant smoke is recommended for coughs and emetic smoke to induce therapeutic vomiting. Wound fumigation exposes wounds to smoke and is believed to promote healing.[14] The local and systemic effects of exposure to smoke are taken advantage of in these types of smoking.

According to Āyurveda, people afflicted by sorrow, exhaustion, fear, anger, heat, poison, disorders of the blood, delirium, giddiness, burning sensation, thirst, dryness of palate, vomiting, head injury, cataract, diabetes and ascites should not smoke. Neither should young children (less than 12 years of age), the elderly (more than 80 years of age), weak people, pregnant women and those who have taken purgatives, suffer from insomnia or consumed honey, clarified butter, curds, fish or alcohol.[15]

In the literature, there are strict guidelines about the use of smoke. Routine smoke may be performed on getting up, after urination, defecation, brushing teeth, sudation, nasal medication, eating, playing in water and surgery. Unctuous smoke is used when one is hungry, after sexual intercourse, when laughing, sitting for a long time, yawning, urinating, defecating, brushing teeth, irrigating eyes with medicated oil and surgery. Cleansing smoke may be performed after the application of nasal medication, collyrium, vomiting, bathing and after sleeping in the daytime.[16]

The benefits of smoking are then given. As maintained in Āyurveda, smoking immediately after waking up dries the accumulated mucus, activates the six sense organs (mind included) and facilitates the free movement of air through channels. It may alleviate diseases of the upper region, remove dislodged mucus and freshen and clean the mouth after brushing the teeth. It may also remove gum and dental diseases. Smoking after playing in water may be a quick cure for headache, earache and a running nose. After a meal, it is said to normalize the humours, clear the head and stabilize ingested food. Smoking after sneezing may clear blockages and ease air flow. It may normalize the flow in channels of the throat and head disturbed by the strain of defecation. A similar benefit is said to be obtained if performed after sexual intercourse. Smoking after vomiting may serve to dry up and clear the passages as well as neutralizing the pressure in the head.[17]

Āyurveda recommends the use of plant and animal as well as inorganic substances to make the smoke mixture. A number of plants are mentioned as ingredients in various smoking mixtures.[18]

Saussurea lappa and *Valeriana wallichii* are not recommended for smoking, although they are included in the aromatic group of drugs used for smoking, because their hot potency and sharpness can harm the brain.[19] Substances of animal origin are also mentioned as ingredients,[20] as are the inorganic substances orpiment and realgar[21] Some Āyurvedic recipes are also formulated for different types of smoking: there are recipes for routine smoke,[22] unctuous smoke,[23] cleansing smoke,[24] expectorant smoke,[25] emetic smoke[26] and wound fumigation.[27]

The pipe for such recipes is usually made out of metal, bamboo or dried petiole of castor leaf.[28] Metal is chosen if the pipe is used to burn the smoking mixture. The typical smoke pipe is a straight hollow tube with three prominent bulges in the middle. These correspond to three chambers in the pipe, the purpose of which is to slow down the smoke flow.[29] It should be possible to pass a grain of *Vigna cylindrica* through the aperture of the pipe. Each smoke pipe is personalized for the individual, a thumb thickness at one end and the thickness of a little finger at the other.[30] Pipes are 40, 32, 24, 10 and 8 fingers long for routine, unctuous, cleansing, expectorant, emetic and wound fumigation smoking respectively.[31] The length of the pipe regulates the impact of the smoke on the mucosal surface of the

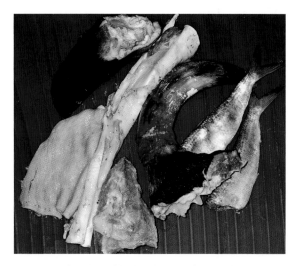

Ligament, skin, horn, hoof and meat of a cow along with fish used for emetic smoke.

Realgar (left) and orpiment (right) are ingredients of inorganic origin used in smoking mixtures.

Crucible for burning the smoking mixture and pipe made of dried petiole of castor.

mouth or nose. The shorter the smoke pipe, the greater the impact. Experts disagree slightly as to the desired length.[32]

When the smoking mixture is burnt in the smoke pipe directly, the ingredients must be ground into a fine paste. A stalk of *Saccharum munja* or *Desmostachya bipinnata* grass is kept immersed in water for 24 hours so that it swells up. Fifteen grams of the paste is applied in five layers to make the thickness of the thumb and the length of eight to twelve fingers. After drying in shade, the grass stalk is removed and the dried wick dipped in oil, burnt and put in the pipe.[33] When crucibles are used, the powder or tablet made out of the ingredients is placed on a crucible and burnt. Another crucible with a hole is placed over it, and smoke is drawn through the hole with the help of a pipe.

Āyurveda recommends brief episodes of nasal and oral smoking with measured puffs. One should smoke with a calm mind sitting in an erect posture. After a round of inhalation and exhalation, smoke should be drawn through one nostril while the other is kept closed. The inhaled smoke should be exhaled through the mouth. Alternatively, the smoke may be both drawn and exhaled through the mouth. Āyurvedic texts emphasize that exhaling smoke through the nostrils may harm the eyes.[34]

Stalks of *Desmostachya bipinnata* used to make suppositories for pipe smoking.

Smoking mixture ground to paste, applied on stalk and removed from it after drying.

In routine smoking, which is to be performed each day, smoke must be inhaled through one nostril two or three times and the process repeated through the other nostril. This may be done up to twice a day. It should be inhaled only through the nostrils.[35] In the case of unctuous smoke, which is performed only once a day, one inhales alternatively through each nostril three or four times, or until the eyes begin to water. A round of inhalation through the mouth may then follow. For diseases afflicting the regions above the throat, inhalation should first be done through the nostrils; for those affecting the throat, it must be done initially through the mouth.[36] Cleansing smoke may be carried out three to four times a day, and may be continued until one feels light-headed. It should be inhaled only through the nostrils.[37] Expectorant smoke must be inhaled only through the mouth – and must be drawn into the chest[38] – and emetic smoke should also be inhaled only through the mouth, after ingestion of emetic drugs and fluids.[39]

The Āyurvedic literature outlines the consequences of both proper and improper smoking. Proper smoking is characterized by the thinning and drying of mucus, and lightness of the chest,

throat and head.[40] Insufficient smoking is distinguished by muffled voice and persistent phlegm in the throat and head.[41] Excessive smoking causes dryness and burning in the palate, head and throat. It also leads to thirst, haemorrhage, giddiness, fainting, confusion and affects the sense organs.[42] Improper smoking may disturb the heat balance of the body and spoil the blood. It is also said to cause complications such as giddiness, fever and afflictions of the head, malfunctioning of the sense organs, dryness of the palate, vomiting, fainting, facial palsy and even death in some cases. If the smoke penetrates the channels, a persistent burning sensation, flatulence, eye diseases, asthma, cough, rhinitis, lethargy, loss of voice and hyperacidity will result.[43] Suggested remedies include the administration of medicated clarified butter, grapes, milk, sugar-cane juice, decoctions, nasal medication, ointments, collyriums and taking a shower. These cool the system and purify the blood to mitigate complications.[44]

Routine smoke, for the healthy, is preferably performed daily after the application of nasal drops, which mobilize clogged materials in the head channels for the smoke to act upon. It may

Shed snake skin used for fumigation in haemorrhoids.

also be done on other occasions, but no more than twice a day. The stated effects include calming and invigorating the mind, and strengthening the skull and sense organs. It is said to prevent diseases such as migraine, rhinitis, asthma, salivation, voice loss, throat afflictions, toothache, stiff neck, lock jaw, worm infestations, itching, hypersomnia, premature baldness, greying and hair loss.[45] Bhāvaprakāśa excludes smoking from the discussion of daily routine and treats it purely as a therapeutic measure along with body cleansing procedures.[46]

So far as smoking in disease is concerned in the classical literature of Āyurveda, homa is recommended as a therapeutic measure for relief from malarial fevers, intermittent fever, mental disorders and epilepsy.[47] Dhupa is recommended in the management of diseases such as malarial fever, haemorrhoids, demonic seizures, mental disorders, epilepsy and wounds.[48] dhūma is advised in the treatment of fevers, cough, asthma, mental diseases and epilepsy.[49] Leaves of turmeric, root of castor plant, raisins, orpiment, realgar, Cedrus deodara (wood) and Nardostachys jatamansi (roots) are ingredients of the smoking mixture used in the treatment of asthma.[50] The literature posits that smoking in asthma is effective only if

it is done after cleansing therapeutic measures, such as emesis and purgation. Choosing the right occasion is important for asthma, because smoking can trigger an asthmatic attack.[51] Shed snake skin is used as an ingredient in the smoking mixture for fumigation in haemorrhoids.[52]

As is evident from the above discussion, Āyurvedic smoking is characterized by the conspicuous absence of psychedelic ingredients in the smoking mixture. Smoking has never been recommended for relief from stress. In addition, people afflicted by sorrow, fear and exhaustion are deemed unfit for smoking. Acorus calamus and Nardostachys jatamansi are ingredients in the Āyurveda smoking mixtures that can produce mild psychotropic effects. Datura metal is a hallucinogen used in folk practices for smoking in the management of asthma. It does not, however, figure prominently in the classical Āyurvedic texts.

Indians knew Cannabis sativa, the source of marijuana, as early as the eleventh century CE because the plant is referred to in Vañgasena's Cikitsāsārasaṃgraha, which was written in this period. It is also mentioned in works such as Dhanvantari Nighaṇṭu, Śārṅgadhara Saṃhitā and Kayyadeva Nighaṇṭu. Cannabis is not an ingredient of the smoking recipes listed in the later literature of Āyurveda, in spite of the fact that it is used for various other medicinal purposes.[53]

Tobacco is first mentioned in the Yogaratnākara, which dates from the seventeenth century. Unlike

Acorus calamus (left) and Nardostachys jatamansi (right) used in smoking mixtures exhibit mild psychotropic action.

marijuana, tobacco, known as *tamākhu* in Sanskrit, is recognized as the smoke tree. It is known as smoke, smoke tree and the source of light in the smoke pipe. The tobacco plant is recognized as having big, greyish leaves with long reddish brown flowers and a cluster of fruits with many seeds. On internal use, its leaves are said to be hot and sharp, pacifying phlegm and wind. According to Āyurveda, there are many professed uses and effects for tobacco smoking. It is said to cure asthma and cough as well as flatulence. It is ascribed with diuretic action. It may ease the bowels, alleviate toothache, destroy worms, itching and increase heat, while also causing intoxication and giddiness. It can induce vomiting and purgation. It may damage the eyesight and increase menstrual flow. As an emetic, it is indicated in the management of scorpion bite and as a purgative in the management of diseases caused by wind and phlegm. Tobacco smoking is said to be bad for the heart and can cause impotency.[54] *Rāja Nighaṇṭu*, also composed in the seventeenth century, does not associate tobacco with smoking but describes its medicinal properties.[55]

Homa and *dhūpa* are still performed in modern India, although not strictly for medicinal purposes. Tobacco smoking, however, has overshadowed and completely replaced the classical *dhūmapāna*. In recent times, Āyurvedic smoking has begun to show signs of resurgence in the form of herbal cigarettes, which is a far cry from the original classical method.

A westernized Indian smoking a cigarette in a popular ad of *c.* 1990.

Tobacco Culture in Japan

BARNABAS TATSUYA SUZUKI

HOW TOBACCO SMOKING CAME TO JAPAN

The first Europeans to arrive in Japan were three Portuguese who reached Tanegashima Island in 1543 on a wrecked Chinese junk and the Jesuit priest St Francis Xavier, who arrived in 1549 and stayed two years. The Portuguese established regular trading with Japan in 1550, bringing Chinese raw silk to exchange for Japanese silver. They were the only Europeans to trade with Japan until the Dutch Trade Post was founded in Hirado in 1609. This was followed by the English Trade Post, which was established and operated in this city between 1613 and 1623.

The earliest references to tobacco smoking in Japan – in the form of cigars – were in *Razan Bunshu* (1661), an anthology by Razan Hayashi, and *Honcho Shokkan* (1692), an encyclopedia of Japanese food. From these sources it seems likely that tobacco smoking in the form of cigars was introduced by the Portuguese long before tobacco cultivation and pipe smoking began in Japan itself. Unfortunately, there is no extant source document that directly describes the 'Southern Barbarians', the name given by the Japanese to the meat-eating Portuguese and Spaniards visiting Japan, and their smoking rolled tobacco in Japan. There is, however, a letter dated 11 October 1620 (21 October in the Gregorian calendar) from Richard Cocks of the English Trading Post in Hirado, in which he describes that several letters 'rolled like tobacco' were found on two Portuguese prisoners.[1] The indirect implication is that some Portuguese were smoking tobacco cigars or cigarettes in Japan.

Japan, through trade and interaction with China, had already incorporated elements of Chinese culture. While the introduction of European culture was soon to take place, this process was interrupted by the banning of Christianity and the closing of the country.

To prevent Christian destruction of Japanese culture and to prevent Spanish or Portuguese invasion following Christian missionaries, attempts to prohibit Christianity were made for more than half a century after 1587, and it was banned completely in 1639. The prohibition against Portuguese and Spanish ships sailing to Japan and Japanese trade ships (*shuinsen*) going abroad was in full force by 1635. Japanese expatriates were also prevented from returning to their homeland.

Only Chinese and Dutch traders were allowed to do business with Japan, and then under strict governmental control. The single exception was an artificial island in Nagasaki for the licensed Dutch traders who operated there from 1641 to the mid-nineteenth century. This tiny island, called Dejima (or Deshima), was essentially the only nexus for Japanese and Western culture. Among those things introduced into Japan during the so-called Christian Century of Japan,[2] from 1549 to 1642, were the influences seen in the manners of the tea ceremony (*cha-no-yu*), adopted partly from the posture of Roman Catholic priests at mass, and in the social custom of smoking, which was developed after the introduction of pipe smoking, which came to accompany tea drinking in Japan. Also linked with the tea ceremony were the Japanese *kiseru* (smoking pipe), *tabako-bon* (tobacco tray), *tabako-ire* (tobacco case or pouch) and other uniquely designed and highly sophisticated accessories that evolved from quite simple European smoking instruments. No references from the period indicate how pipe smoking was introduced into Japan, however, except for a few legendary stories written in the late seventeenth or the beginning of the eighteenth century.[3]

New insights in the form of three long-ignored documents have recently shed some light on this subject.[4] First, the *Izumosaki-mura Omizucho*, a land-tax book of Izumosaki Village of 1576, indicates that a small-scale tobacco dealer was operating there. It is known that silver ingots were brought to this small village from mines located on an island off the coast, and that they were then transported to Hirado (before 1565) or Nagasaki (after 1570), where Portuguese traders accepted them in exchange for raw Chinese silk. Since Japanese merchants were dealing directly with the Portuguese without Government intervention before 1601, it is likely that they also transported a small quantity of expensive tobacco leaves to Izumosaki for sale to the rich miners of the island. Second, *Rokuon Nichiroku*, a diary kept by the priests of Rokuon-in Temple in Kyoto, lists tobacco as a gift on several occasions, the earliest being 1593.

There are some doubts as to the credibility of these two documents since they were written before smoking was prevalent in Portugal. Smoking in the form of a cigar or a cigarette, however, was a practice among sailors and merchants on Portuguese ships sailing between Brazil and their homeland. Discovery of the word *fumo* (smoke and tobacco for smoking) on a cargo manifest of 1548 of a ship sailing from Brazil to Portugal implies that sailors were already accustomed to smoking. It is also known that colonists in Brazil were cultivating tobacco as early as 1534.[5]

Third, *Ryukyu Ohrai*,[6] compiled by the Buddhist priest Taichu in 1603, was a textbook for the children of a courtier of the Ryukyu Kingdom (now Okinawa,

Japan). In the form of exchanged letters, Taichu described the things he saw in Kyoto. One chapter, entitled 'About Tobacco', states that tobacco came from the countries of the Southern Barbarians, that it was used to please guests and that the *kiseru* required frequent cleaning.

In addition to these previously unexplored texts, there are other references to smoking scattered through the literature. The *Saka Jochi-in Diary*, written in 1607 by a physician, mentions the prevalence of the smoking habit and the use of shredded tobacco. In 1612 Matheus de Couros SJ wrote a letter to Claudio Aquaviva, the Jesuit Father General in Rome, complaining that, in spite of a prohibition issued in 1607 or 1608 by Francisco Pasio, the Father Visitor, Japanese apprentices were smoking *tabaco* with an instrument.[7]

Another view holds that the Spaniards introduced smoking to the Japanese via the Philippines. This is based on a report about a Franciscan who had brought both tobacco seeds and a medicine made from tobacco to Japan in 1601.[8] This is less plausible, because Spaniards did not smoke pipes, in spite of the fact that pipes have been found in Mexico. According to J. Alden Mason, Assistant Curator of Mexican and South American Archaeology at the Field Museum of Natural History in Chicago, the pottery elbow pipes excavated in Mexico at the time of the Conquest are more characteristic of the Toltecs than of the Aztecs.[9] Spaniards observed more cigarette and tube-pipe smoking there. It is also known that the Spaniards preferred a cigar made of *Nicotiana tabacum* with a broad leaf, rather than a pipe filled with *Nicotiana rustica*, a stronger tobacco with a narrow-leaf configuration. Filipinos are still making cigars of the type that were introduced by the Spaniards in the sixteenth or seventeenth century.

There were considerably fewer Spanish visitors from the Philippines to Japan than there were Portuguese from Goa on the Indian subcontinent. Moreover, the first Spanish Franciscans from Manila arrived in 1584 in a Portuguese vessel. Hence, if the content of *Izumosaki-mura Omizucho* – the land-tax book – is true and accurate, then the Portuguese were the first to introduce tobacco to Japan, and before 1584.

PROPAGATION OF THE HABIT OF PIPE SMOKING

The custom of pipe smoking made a round-the-world trip from North America through Britain, the Netherlands, Japan, Korea, China, Siberia and Alaska, and back to the Native Americans living on the north-west coast of the United States. The Native Americans learned about pipe smoking from the Inuit. For this reason, the exportation of *kiseru* is discussed here in order to clarify how the concept of pipe smoking migrated from Japan to other parts of Asia.

The production of clay pipes in the Netherlands before 1630 is known to have met only local demand. Dutch traders stationed in Japan before 1642 could not therefore have received a sufficient supply of clay pipes before sailing, and they were not shipped to Japan. They were probably smoking *kiseru* before 1642. Smoking tobacco in a *kiseru* was already popular in Japan when the Dutch arrived in 1609. Dutch traders even supplied silver *kiseru* and finely shredded tobacco to their colleagues in other colonies or trading posts in Asia. The diaries of the Dutch Trade Post in Siam (now Thailand) recorded tobacco imported from Japan in 1634 and 1635.[10] In the journals of the Dutch Trade Post in Hirado there are several entries noting *kiseru* and tobacco for export to Taiwan in 1639 and 1641.[11] Dutch traders were thus extensively involved in the propagation and migration of pipe smoking into South-East Asia.

Licensed Japanese trade ships (*Shuinsen*) began to call on Asian ports in the late sixteenth century until the close of the country around 1635, and these merchants and sailors brought the custom of pipe smoking to South-East Asian countries. Japanese inhabitants there (at the time there were seven overseas Japanese towns) also smoked *kiseru* that were brought in by Japanese ships. Even after these Japanese expatriates were barred from their home-land in 1635, they sought their supply of both *kiseru* and finely cut tobacco from Chinese or Dutch ship merchants. The continuous supply of tobacco and *kiseru* to those countries even in the eighteenth century may indicate that the Japanese living abroad preferred the finely shredded Japanese tobacco to the local variety.

The Japanese influence on the habit of pipe smoking can be readily seen in many pipe shapes and styles indigenous to China, Korea, South-East Asia and the northern Philippines. Some of these pipes may have been influenced by Dutch or English clay pipes or in combination with the *kiseru*. It is said that smoking pipes were introduced to China before 1622 (or before 1613, depending on the sources) via at least four external sources: from Japan via Korea, from the Philippines, from Taiwan and from Vietnam.[12] Introduction from the Spanish Philippines, where people did not smoke pipes, is unlikely, and the two channels from Japan via Korea to the north-east and via Ryukyu to the south-east are the most probable sources for *kiseru* smoking in China.

Dutch traders stationed in Taiwan from 1624 to 1662 must have influenced the local people with their clay pipes when Dutch expatriates, who used to smoke Japanese *kiseru* supplied by their colleagues in Japan, started to receive a sufficient supply. This influence is apparent in some Taiwanese pipes. Although Spaniards who lived in Manila did not smoke pipes, the natives of the northern part of the Philippines learned pipe smoking from Japanese traders. The influence from Taiwan, some 400 kilometres north of the Philippines, however, cannot be overlooked, because some pipes from the northern region of the Philippines suggest the influence of Dutch as well as Japanese pipes.

THE TOBACCO CULTURE OF JAPAN

It is believed that pipe smoking was first introduced to Japanese high society, for example, to the samurai (warriors), the Buddhist priest classes and some rich merchants.[13] In these circles, the tea and incense

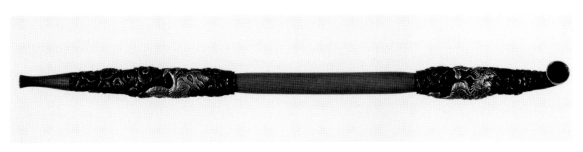

A 19th-century example of *kiseru*.

ceremonies, and writing or appreciating poetry, formed an essential part of the culture and education; for nobles especially, the use of incense and writing poetry were always considered important.

Tea leaves, used as medicine, were cited in a procurement memorandum of 739 CE kept at the Shoso-in Treasure House, but it is not clear whether this was the herb that is tea as we know it. In 805 CE the Buddhist priest Saicho brought tea seeds from China when he returned to Japan with a Japanese envoy. The serving of a cup of tea to Emperor Saga in 815 is recorded in *Nihon Koki* (Late Chronicle of Japan, 792–833). A Zen priest, Eisai, introduced powdered tea to Japan in 1191 when he returned from China with some that he had obtained there. Drinking powdered tea then became a common habit among the priests of the Zen sect of Buddhism; it prevailed among the samurai class in the early fourteenth century, and eventually among the noble class.[14] Masters of the tea or incense ceremony appeared for the first time during the period of Tenmon (1532–55).

Rikyu (Sen-no-Rikyu, 1522–91) established the tea ceremony in the most simple and humble way. He rejected luxury and ostentation, and paid more attention to locally available tea bowls and pots. It is believed that Rikyu adopted a part of the posture in the tea ceremony from the Roman Catholic mass, something that he might have observed at a Jesuit or Franciscan church in Kyoto or Sakai.[15] Although Rikyu was not considered a confirmed Christian, he had many Christian followers. After his death in 1591, the tea ceremony (*cha-no-yu*) became more popular among townspeople, particularly among nouveau riche merchants. Oribe Furuta (1544–1615) – one of Rikyu's ardent disciples – started to reform the ceremony by paying more attention to those things that Europeans had brought to Japan, especially tobacco smoking. He used a tea bowl that exhibited a mark in the shape of a cross, possibly derived from the Christian symbol; more notably, he commissioned tobacco pipes in porcelain to be made in his unique design and colour. Although there is no clear proof that he integrated the *tabako-bon* into the tea ceremony, the assumption that he introduced it coincides with the timing of other aspects related to the tea ceremony.

When tobacco smoking became popular in Japan, *kiseru* were produced in three parts: a bowl and a mouthpiece of metal, and a bamboo stem to connect them. Normally, the metal parts had chased decoration or fine inlaid carvings, which were a marked divergence from the simple and fragile clay pipes of the Netherlands and England. Further implements for the smoker, the *tabako-bon* (tobacco tray), *tabako-ire* (tobacco case or pouch) and *kiseru-zutsu* (*kiseru* case) were also elaborately decorated to express the unique smoking culture of Japan.

The *tabako-bon*, a tray used to serve tobacco at the beginning of the tea ceremony, was adapted from a *koh-bon* (incense tray) used in the incense ceremony. A *koh-bon* is a tray with an incense burner (*kohro*) accompanied by a pair of chopsticks to lift embers. Other components of the incense ceremony were converted for use with the *tabako-bon*: the incense burner became a tobacco embers pot (*hi-ire*); the incense cinder pot became an ash pot (*hai-otoshi* or *hai-fuki*); and the incense pot, or incense plate case, evolved into a tobacco case or pot. Two *kiseru* were placed on the *tabako-bon* in place of chopsticks (see below). Ash pots of bamboo were often called *togeppoh* after the name of a hill seen from the temple that, in the middle of the eighteenth century, was the first to use bamboo. The *tabako-bon* was seen in paintings as early as the Kan'ei Period (1624–44) after the death of Oribe Furuta (1615); this leads to the assumption that it was first used exclusively in the tea ceremony before it became popular in its own right. In later years, more practical *tabako-bons* were created in the form of box with a handle, a *kiseru* rack and drawers in which to keep tobacco and smoking implements.

In *Mesamashi-so* (Awaking herb), written in 1815 by Kiyonakatei, there is a passage that describes a precise ritual for serving tobacco to guests; he quotes from Shinmi's *Yaso-oh Chu Seki Wa* written during the Kyoho Period (1716–36):

In early days nobody was carrying tobacco. People smoked tobacco served on a tobacco-bon where he visited and the way they smoked is different from today. Nobody smoked until the host comes in the room and offers the tobacco. The guest first declines and tells the host that he should first start and repeats saying so twice or three times just like a manner of serving a cup of tea. Then, the host takes out a pocket paper and takes a kiseru and wipes it with the paper after removing a protecting rid [which prevented the mouthpiece from touching the floor] of the kiseru before offering it to the guest. The guest accepts it and after smoking one or two fills of tobacco, he wipes the kiseru and places it in front of him. Before he leaves the room, he again uses his pocket paper to wipe the kiseru and puts it back to the tabako-bon. The host will say to the guest, 'Please leave it.'[16]

Tabako-bon, an early style of design.

Kiyonakatei noted with regret that such good manners were no longer common. According to him, Shinmi's description pertained to the Manji and Kanbun eras (1658–73), a period just after the *tabako-bon* was first illustrated in paintings. The manner described above clearly shows the influences of the tea ceremony.

Initially, tobacco was sold as whole leaves, not shredded. It was cut at the tobacco shop at the customer's request, or the smoker shredded the tobacco leaves at home. Later, finely shredded tobacco became available in the market. Shredded tobacco was normally carried in a folded sheet of pocket paper; at home, it was kept in a box. The tobacco box is described as a gift in the diary of Richard Cocks, the general manager of the English Trade Post in Hirado on 20 January 1617 (30 January 1618 of the Gregorian calendar).[17]

Carrying folded sheets of pocket paper, called *tatoh*, *tatoh-gami* or *tatoh-shi*, was already a practice among nobles in the eighth century CE; they used this paper to write poems and to blow their nose. This paper is still used in the tea ceremony to receive

An illustration of
Mesamashi-so, 1815,
and a 'protective rid'.

Tabako-ire of the pouch type.

a sweet before the tea is served, or to wipe the lid of the bowl after drinking.

People of the samurai class carried an *inroh* on their sash by means of *netsuke* (an ornamental button for suspending a pouch) along with their swords; the *inroh* was originally used to carry a seal stamp and stamp ink. In the Edo Period (1600–1867), it was used more often to carry medicine. The idea of the *inroh* was applied when people began the custom of carrying a *kiseru* and tobacco. The common practice was to carry a pouch for the shredded tobacco and a *kiseru-zutsu*, a *kiseru* case made of leather or various other materials; both hung from the girdle or sash wrapped around the waist.

A purse made of oiled or crêpe paper or cloth was the typical container for tobacco until the *tabako-ire* of a pouch, purse or *inroh* type became popular. The noble class, however, did not consider that it was elegant to carry a tobacco pouch on the girdle, and instead used the traditional folded paper purse. The concept of the tobacco pouch

was probably borrowed from the flint pouch and then adopted for tobacco to replace the paper purse. Interestingly, in one famous Japanese painting depicting early smoking practices, a servant accompanying his master carries an exceptionally long *kiseru* on his shoulder, and tied on the pipe's stem is a folded paper containing tobacco. A purse made of leather or cloth (*kamasu*) and an *inroh* type made of wood (*tonkotsu*) came after the pouch.

When all the internal feuding was quelled, and the nation was united after 1600 under Ieyasu, the first Shogun of Tokugawa, economic stability created a new class of rich merchants. While the warrior class was still permitted to wear swords – as a status symbol – townspeople, including merchants, also sought symbols to denote their wealth. Many chose smoking utensils, such as *kiseru*, *tabako-bon*, *tabako-ire* and *kiseru-zutsu*. All types of fine arts and technologies were applied to create extremely luxurious smoking artefacts, often employing imported materials obtained from Dutch traders. In 1867, when the Imperial Restoration abolished the samurai class, the craftsmen who had decorated swords applied their skills to decorating *kiseru* or making

Tabako-ire of the purse type (*kamasu*).

buckles for *tabako-ire*. *Kiseru* and *tobacco-bons* are still manufactured in the Kyoto area on a very small scale, principally for use with the tea ceremony. Most of these modern *tobacco-bons* are in the form of a tray, with or without handles, and they are no longer made in a box shape. Today, the manufacture of *kiseru* for collectors is the domain of a few craftsmen on a very limited scale, and inexpensive models for souvenir hunters are mostly machine-made.

It is said that Y. Tsuchida was the first person to manufacture cigarettes in Tokyo in 1869, but he was unsuccessful. Cigarette smoking became popular only after M. Iwaya began to manufacture cigarettes in Tokyo in 1882, and 1890, when the Murai Brothers established a cigarette factory in Kyoto. A complete shift from *kiseru* to cigarette smoking, however, did not take place until after the Second World War. From the scattered early sources, it seems likely that the Portuguese introduced tobacco to Japan and that they probably smoked tobacco at this early stage in the form of cigars. Pipe smoking was probably introduced by the Dutch. It enjoyed a long history and was only overtaken after the Second World War.

Tabako-ire of the *inroh* type (*tonkotsu*) for ordinary people.

Smoking in Imperial China

TIMOTHY BROOK

How could I know that beyond the tastes of this world
There would be yet another worth tasting?
Cao Xibao (1719–1792)[1]

When a nine-year-old boy was installed as Emperor Wanli of the Ming dynasty in 1573, no one in China, with the possible exception of those trading with the Portuguese in the far south, had tasted the smoke of tobacco. Less than a century later, when a seven-year-old was installed as Emperor Kangxi of the Qing dynasty in 1662, the transformation of Chinese into smokers, and China into a smoking culture, was almost complete. What had arrived in China as a taste 'beyond the tastes of this world' was now a thing daily consumed and enjoyed.

Wanli never tried smoking, so far as we know, but Kangxi probably picked up a pipe before his seventh birthday. In an edict he issued in 1676 banning smoking in the palace – one of several prohibitions seventeenth-century emperors issued, to no effect – Kangxi mentions that he was 'well acquainted with smoking' at the home of his wet-nurse. The women who surrounded him in his infancy all smoked. So did the men. Great-uncle Dorgon, who had been his father's chief regent, was so keen a smoker that Korean ambassadors coming to Beijing made a point of bringing him some of their best.[2] Kangxi does not actually say when he started smoking, though people at the time saw no reason to withhold from children what adults were enjoying. He and his grandmother must eventually have come to some other under-standing about smoking in the palace, for in 1684 the emperor rephrased his prohibition to require only that people in the palace should not smoke carelessly.[3]

To learn about the beginning of smoking in China, we must read the puzzled reflections of seventeenth-century essayists who were up against the challenge of explaining something that was strangely popular while being foreign, without precedent, and not altogether pleasing in its effects. Consider, for instance, how the dissident scholar Fang Yizhi (1611–71) describes the arrival of what many called the 'southern herb' because of its presumed point of origin:

> Late in the reign of Emperor Wanli [*reg.* 1573–1620], people brought it to Zhangzhou and Quanzhou. The Ma family processed it, calling it *danrouguo* [fleshy fruit of the *danbagu*]. It gradually spread within all our borders, so that everyone now carries a long pipe and swallows the smoke after lighting it with fire; some have become drunken addicts.[4]

A late-19th-century postcard.

A Manchu nobleman, identified as the son of the Seventh Prince, on horseback in Beijing c. 1885, with a tobacco pouch and pipe on his belt.

and would eventually invade in 1644, were smokers before northern Chinese acquired the habit. They passed their taste for tobacco, and the tobacco itself, to the Chinese soldiers stationed there in the 1620s. There was some understanding that the Manchus learned to smoke from the Koreans, but we now know that the Manchus stood at the receiving end of a far wider global circuit. For the Koreans got tobacco from the Japanese, the Japanese from the Portuguese in Macao, and they in turn from their plantations in Brazil. Tobacco thus travelled to China along two routes that both began in South America, one passing through the colonial regime of the Portuguese and the other of the Spanish.

Wherever the herb entered China, domestication was immediate. Thus capital official Yang Shicong (1597– 1648) notes that 'within the last twenty years, many people in the Beijing area are growing it. What they make from planting one *mu* of tobacco is equal to what they can make from planting ten *mu* of grain fields. It has got to the point that there is no one who doesn't use it.'[6] Fujian retained a commercial edge as the source of the best 'smoke liquor', as Yang called it, although Manchurian tobacco was a close second. As another sojourner in the capital reported at the time, these two fetched the best prices in Beijing.[7] Besides confirming which brands were best, the comment implies not only that tobacco was being cultivated at both of its points of entry, but that cheaper varieties were being grown in other locations as well and shipped up to the smokers of Beijing. Indeed, when Yang Shicong first arrived in the capital in 1642, he was surprised to find 'tobaccanists on every street corner', especially as decapitation had been mandated in 1639 as the punishment for selling this morally dubious and money-wasting substance in the capital. A national market of production and consumption was forming even as a national pastime was taking shape, and no bans could stop the trend.

Fang was correct in identifying the two main ports in the south-east coastal province of Fujian as the places where tobacco entered China, for tobacco arrived there in the ships of Chinese merchants trading with the Spanish in Manila. Fang does not mention the Philippines, though other essayists do. An obscure mid-seventeenth-century essayist named Yao Lü, for instance, reported that farmers around Zhangzhou took up the cultivation of tobacco with enthusiasm, with the result that 'now there is more here than in Luzon, so they ship it to that country to sell it.'[5] One or two early commentators guessed that the plant was not native to the Philippines but had been brought from the Great Western Ocean on the far side of the world, and of course they were right.

The south-east coast was only one corridor of entry, however; the north-east border was another. The Manchus, who were massing on that border

Smoking leaves must have seemed a strangely exotic thing to do when Chinese first arrived in Quanzhou, Zhangzhou and Beijing puffing on pipes (which more closely resembled the pipes of

Native Americans than the styles Europeans would evolve). That aura was soon worn away by use, though not immediately in all cases. Ye Mengzhu was a native of Shanghai whose childhood in the 1640s spanned the Manchu conquest of China. The world changed greatly in his lifetime, as he noted again and again in his essay collection, *Yueshi bian* (A survey of the age). Smoking is one of his many examples. 'The tobacco plant first came from Fujian', he begins.

> When I was young, I heard my grandfathers say that there was tobacco in Fujian, and that you could get drunk smoking it. They called it 'dry liquor'. There was none in our region, however. During the Chongzhen era [1628–44], someone in the [Shanghai] county seat by the surname Peng got some seeds, from where I do not know, and planted them in this soil. He picked the leaves, dried them in the shade, then got workmen to cut them into fine shreds, which he consigned to traveling merchants to sell. Locals still did not dare to taste it.

So in Shanghai at least, tobacco became a commodity produced for markets elsewhere before smoking became an item consumed at home. The reticence of Shanghainese to take up smoking was reinforced for a time by a regional military official who banned it as something that only bandits consumed. When troops of the new dynasty arrived in 1645, writes Ye, 'there wasn't one soldier who didn't use it'. The effect on the Shanghai economy was immediate: 'Suddenly peddlars arrived from all corners, so the planters went back to planting and the profits they made doubled.'[8] The same effect was seen elsewhere in the Yangzi Delta. Wang Pu, a contemporary in the neighbouring county south-west of Shanghai, tells a similar tale: 'When I was a child I had no idea what tobacco was. At the end of the Chongzhen era people started planting it all over my home district. Customs suddenly changed, and all people, even boys not yet four feet tall, were smoking.'[9] Within the lifetimes of Wang Pu and Ye Mengzhu, the Shanghai region had become a smoking culture.

Wherever tobacco arrived, those who noted its arrival cast about for ways of making sense of it. Some treated tobacco as a herb which, like other 'medical' herbs, was ingested for its pharmacopoeic properties. This was Yao Lü's way of making sense of smoking: 'You use fire to burn a bowlful, then bring the pipe to your mouth', he explained. 'The smoke goes through the stem and down your throat', producing an effect similar to drunkenness, hence one of tobacco's popular epithets, 'golden-shred inebriant'. Tobacco had other effects, for Yao noted that 'it can also block malarial vapours'.[10] He also declared that its leaves could be pounded into a paste and rubbed into the scalp as a cure for head lice. But Yao Lü was not a pharmacologist. For him, tobacco was a curiosity that belonged in the company of all manner of things interesting, striking and amusing that caught his attention and found their way into his commonplace book. His entry on tobacco is followed by two entries about strange plants ('drake-cooked chrysanthemum' and 'earth betel-nut'), which might suggest a sustained curiosity about plants, but these in turn are followed by a series of stories about a copper Buddha that sweats, a bell that on cloudy days shows a man's outline on its surface, and an iron flute that sounds six different notes when you blow it. For Yao, tobacco may have had medicinal qualities, but it was first and foremost a curiosity.

Fang Yizhi did not lump his entry on tobacco in with sand chickens, sweating statues or magic flutes. Instead, he placed it in the section on plants and trees in his *Wuli xiaoshi* (Minor knowledge about things and their principles), his encyclopaedic compilation of information about the physical world. Fang thus framed tobacco as a thing in nature rather than a curiosity or omen. Like other plants, it had natural properties to nourish, poison and treat the human body.

> Its root is like potherb mustard, but its leaves are large like cabbage. When it is fermented and dried and then burned as 'fire liquor', it is called

'golden-shred smoke'. Northerners call it *danbagu*, or sometimes *danbugui*. It can be used to dispel dampness, but long usage heats up the lungs. Other medicines mostly have no effect. Those afflicted will suddenly vomit a yellowish liquid and die.[11]

Fang makes sense of tobacco by aligning it visually and pharmacologically with other plants. His assumption that death awaits the devoted smoker did not survive beyond the seventeenth century. The idea that smoking was a danger to health would only resurface in the 1980s in relation to the new, 'modern' medicalized body rather than the old pharmacopoeic body that Fang found familiar.

By the eighteenth century, smoking was being depicted in utterly different ways. There were no more bans, no more warnings about yellow vomit, no more puzzles to be solved, only a strong sense of the pleasures of tobacco and the habitual urge to smoke it. As the author of a handbook of edible plants observes, 'those who take it instead of tea or liquor cannot do without it however briefly, and to the end of their lives never tire of it.'[12] The century's great chronicler of the joys of smoking was a poet by the name of Chen Cong. The petted son of an old gentry family living west of Shanghai, he gained an early reputation as a brilliant poet and became a central figure in the elite cultural world of his county. Chen spent his adult life teaching in the county academy, writing poetry and building up a large personal library.[13] He also became a *yanke*, a 'guest of tobacco' ('devoted smoker' would be a more idiomatic translation), and turned his literary and bibliophilic talents to the subject. For two decades he culled material from 210 county gazetteers, essay collections, belles-lettres and poetry books, plus the writings of his friends, to produce *Yancao pu* (The tobacco manual) in 1805. Chen's goal was to create a book that had the cultural authority of the two great classics of refined consumption, *The Book of Tea* and *The History of Liquor*. He succeeded: his book is the largest compendium on tobacco to come out of the late-imperial period, and the fullest testimony to its pleasures.

A woodblock-printed frontispiece to Chen Cong's *Yancao pu* (1805) by Cheng Zhong of tobacco plants and an elderly smoker, probably Chen Cong himself.

Over half of the material in *The Tobacco Manual* is poetry, the production of which shows that Chinese elites in the eighteenth century had culturally appropriated smoking to their world. This poem by Shen Deqian (1673– 1769), which plays with the image of smoke's insubstantiality and extols the thrill of intoxication, is typical:

> Planted all over the eight prefectures of Fujian,
> Its clouds swirl throughout the nine layers of
>   heaven.
> Through my pipe I draw the fiery vapour,
> From out of my chest I spew white clouds.
> The attendants take away the ash,
> Bring some wine to add to the intoxication.
> I put the flame [to the bowl] to know its taste,
> Letting it burn in the elephant's tusk.[14]

He Qiwei wove similar images into a more moody invocation of melancholic pleasure:

> Laughing, I ask: among all under heaven
> Who can leave it even for a single moment?
> I also know it has not much flavour,
> Yet always I yearn for the taste.
> After the guest who came to chat has departed,
> Or as I sit in quite melancholy,
> Neither the tea caddy nor the wine sack
> Is as dear to me as this.

Wang Lu's set of six eight-line stanzas written in praise of his pipe is the longest Qing poem on smoking. In the fourth stanza he announces the pipe's arrival:

> Out of this emptiness comes the thing of substance:
> My servant boy reverently brings it out.
> Feeling its contours I know instinctively its familiar shape,
> So why not scrape out the remnant ash,
> Hold it in the moonlit evening while flowers are still in bloom,
> Keep it company within the screened walls of my tea pavilion,
> And without the slightest hesitation, let it hang from my teeth as always,
> Without any pause, my stick of jade and ivory?

Only in the fifth stanza does he actually get around to lighting the pipe:

> Thin mists and light clouds waft imperceptibly;
> The friends who have gathered here pass the pipe around.
> I know that there is no constancy in what is possible and what is not,
> Yet I do not believe that fire and ash are only fragments of time.
> As dawn sits astride the aboriginal hills, it disperses the miasmic vapours,
> As night frames the window where banana leaves rustle, it aids my thoughts.
> *Danbagu*: long I have known your name;
> Burning and dying out: you alone are my master.

These poems point to something that the seventeenth-century commentators on tobacco missed because they stood outside the practice of smoking: its sociability. Smoking was something people did together, something they shared, something through which social interaction was performed and social status marked. The gentlemen who wrote their poems about the 'herb of longing' inhabited an imag- inative world in which tobacco, properly enjoyed, was a token of elegance (like all the other tokens of elegance pictured in the frontispiece of Chen Cong's *Tobacco Manual*) that set them apart from their social inferiors, but that also placed them together in each other's company. As for stylish melancholy, that was all right in small private doses, but it was much more fun when shared with your friends.

If Chen Cong was the eighteenth century's chronicler of smoking, Lu Yao (1723–1785) was its arbiter of taste. In his *Yanpu* (Smoking manual), which he wrote about 1774, Lu declares that 'in recent times there has not been one gentleman who does not smoke'. Gentlemen should not smoke inappropriately, though, and so Lu goes on to list all sorts of rules that the refined smoker had to follow.[15] A gentleman does not smoke when listening to the zither (the preferred instrument of the elite), when feeding cranes (symbols of longevity), when dealing with subtle and refined matters, or when looking at plum blossoms. Nor should he be caught with a pipe in his mouth when performing a rite, appearing at an imperial audience, or sharing a bed with a beautiful woman. Knowing *when* to smoke thus became one more one component of the art of elegant living, though Lu Yao has some rather less refined advice for smokers, such as not smoking when coughing up phlegm, when having trouble breathing, or when your host cannot afford to offer you tobacco. Lu also works in some practical advice that Kangxi's grandmother would have approved, such as not lighting your pipe when walking on fallen leaves, riding in a reed boat, or standing next to a pile of old paper.

The smoking practices of the elite may have set them apart from mere farmers, but smoking cut across other status boundaries that one finds in other cultures, notably gender. As Lu Yao tells us, 'even women and children all have a pipe in their hands'. Europeans were struck by the freedom with which women smoked. An Englishman writing in 1878 noted: 'it is the fashion for girls of even eight or nine years of age to have as an appendage to their dress a silken purse or pocket to hold the pipe and tobacco to which they aspire, even if they do not already use them.'[16] To say everyone smoked is not to say that men and women smoked in the same ways, although differences are hard to detect. Chen Cong provides a glimpse when he quotes from an author writing about the customs in Suzhou, the cultural and commercial capital of central China, who observes that Suzhou women liked to smoke lying down. Those who slept till noon had to smoke several pipefuls as soon as they awoke, and since the business of doing their hair and make-up could interfere with this necessary pleasure, some had their maids arrange their coiffures while they were still asleep.[17] The scene is a little hard to imagine.

Where gender did intrude in the Chinese culture of smoking was in its pharmacological understanding. Being of the *yin* gender, women had to protect themselves against the excessive *yang* of tobacco more than men did, and therefore they were warned against hot smoke. This meant smoking pipes with longer stems. (Elderly men whose *yang* was decreasing also availed themselves of a longer pipe, which might double as a walking-stick or even as a cane to whack miscreants on the head.[18]) The stem of the females' pipe grew to such a length that it was as long as the smoker was tall. A woman poet refers to the inconvenience of her pipe when trying to smoke in her dressing room:

> This long stick of a tobacco pipe
> Is too big to put on my dressing-table;
> When I raise it, it tears the window paper,
> So I hook the moonlight and drag it in.[19]

Toward the end of the eighteenth century, the smoking fashion for women shifted from the long bamboo pipe to the water pipe. Designed simply to produce cooler smoke, these pipes turned into objects of showy consumption in their own right, and signs of their owners' wealth and status. When the Manchu princess Der Ling selected photographs to illustrate one of her books on the Empress Dowager Cixi (1835–1908), she chose one featuring what she labelled as the dowager's 'favourite pipe'.[20]

The water pipe belonging to the Empress Dowager Cixi.

The dowager liked to have her picture taken, but never, to my knowledge, did she allow herself to be photographed smoking. The image of the smoker, male or female, was not common before the advent of the camera. Occasionally one spots a figure in a genre painting holding a pipe, but smoking was not a subject that Chinese artists took up. It became common only in the mid-nineteenth century when Europeans commissioned Chinese professional artists to paint scenes of daily life to send or take home as souvenirs. Even then the depiction of smoking was often second-hand. When Tingqua, best-known of the mid-nineteenth-century export artists, painted dandies of mixed Chinese-Filipino ancestry strolling along with cigars between their fingers, he was simply producing copies of paintings by the Filipino artist Tristinian Asumpción, not painting anything he had seen in real life.[21] Cigars were interesting because they were smoked elsewhere. Nor was Tingqua persuaded to import smoking as a signifier into his own work.

A Mestizo Dandy, an 1850s copy (gouache on paper) by the Chinese export painter Tingqua after the Filipino artist Tristinian Asumpción.

The stalled representation of smoking picked up pace as cameras came into use. With the camera, the Western eye could more easily control and reproduce views of smoking. It peered into the corners of everyday life, although early shutter speeds were so slow that what was intended to look like daily life had to be posed to create that impression. The male smoker lounging against the courtyard wall in the accompanying illustration is an example of this posing. But what the Western eye most desired to see once it could rove with a camera was what Europeans regarded as the shameful sight of Chinese smoking opium. Photographs of prone addicts sucking opium pipes became popular with foreigner consumers. Most of the popular postcards of opium smokers were staged, often with the photographer himself posing as one of the smokers, but they sold well. These were as much documents of what Western viewers desired to see as they were archives of what Chinese did.

Opium came under increasing political and moral pressure toward the close of the nineteenth century, its depiction signifying all that was wrong with China and its eradication heralded as the goal

A smoker lounging in a courtyard, a late-19th-century photo.

A couple smoking, the husband opium, the wife tobacco, a photo published in S. Kojima's *View and Custom of North China* (Tianjin, 1910).

of the new modern state. Tobacco was free of such constraints. It remained an innocent pleasure. It might migrate to such new Western forms as industrially produced cigarettes or European-style pipes, but it would not retreat from Chinese social life until health warnings began slowly to curb consumption in the 1980s. Yuan Shikai, the first full-term president of the new republic, was not easy with the shift in smoking styles at the turn of the twentieth century, or at least those who arranged his funeral in 1916 were not. Among the weapons, clothes and objects of personal use were set out on tables to be burned as offerings could be seen a long pipe in the old style as well as several foreign smoking sets.[22] Yuan's descendants did not want him to get caught using the wrong sort of smoking utensil in the afterlife, or worse, of being deprived of the chance to smoke at all. The Kangxi emperor would have understood their concern.

長城牌香煙

長城香烟

旅行之良伴

客途有良伴
其名曰長城
青史久標名
變幻類煙雲
不虞盜賊侵
共倚此長城

昔年禦胡虜
今茲侍旅客
不為風雨阻
寄語旅行者
中國南洋兄弟烟草公司啓

An ad for *The 'Great Wall' Cigarettes* in the 1920 edition of the *Guide to Shanghai*.

Tobacco in Edo Period Japan

TIMON SCREECH

Tobacco entered the Japanese archipelago at about the same time as it entered Europe. At the end of the sixteenth century, traders originating from Spain, Portugal, the United Provinces and England visited Japanese ports via the Philippines or the Spanish Americas. A host of products were imported, carrying with them the label of *nanban*, a term referring to a mythical primitive people said to lie to the south of the Chinese cultural epicentre. The Europeans did appear from the southerly direction, so the designation, probably originally a joke, stuck. Smoking was one of the chief constituents of the hybrid '*nanban* culture' that emerged within the Japanese polity – at this time fractured into several hundred micro-states endemically at war. Other items on the regular import lists were cloth (velvet, woollens or trans-shipped Chinese silk), ivory, aromatic woods and sugar. The Europeans exported silver, copper and some lacquer.

The Europeans brought something else with them: Christianity. The rise and fall of the creed of the 'absurd person' (*jaso*, Jesus) has been amply documented, and does not need to be repeated here. Converts were many and obstreperous. In 1625 and 1636 the Iberians were expelled for over-zealous proselytization (Japanese rulers were aware of the fate of Mexico); the English had left in 1623, intending their absence to be temporary, but they never returned. After the 1630s, only the Protestant Dutch remained. The archipelago consolidated under the new shogunal house of Tokugawa, ruling in Edo (modern Tokyo) from 1615 to 1868. Much of *nanban* culture was subsequently eradicated or marginalized, and the radical diminution of tonnage arriving made for a great scarcity of goods.

Tobacco, though, did not go the way of velvet or wool because it could be grown perfectly well in many parts of the archipelago. So well in fact that it soon ousted more established crops, and in 1612 tobacco was already banned as a drain on food production.[1] Penalties, though stiff (sometimes including death), were laxly enforced, and tobacco continued to be grown. The Tokugawa shogunate tolerated moderate consumption, so long as the plant was raised in such a way as not to detract from food farming too obviously. Tobacco, though, had about it a slightly *louche* air, as we shall see.

TOBACCO AS A FOREIGN WEED

The island of Dejima (or Deshima), in Nagasaki Bay, was from 1641 to 1800 home to the Dutch East India Company factory, and then to a more informal trade that continued until 1868. Archaeologists have excavated the site and found that a considerable percentage of the soil is the detritus of discarded clay pipes.[2] A conjecture could be made that, for two and a half centuries, European traders paced the small island, filling their ledgers, writing letters home, receiving visitors – and relieving their general boredom by smoking, after which they trod their broken pipes into the earth. At about fifteen men stationed there all year round, swelling to two hundred when the two annual ships were in dock, for 227 years, the

An unsigned leaf from the album *Bankan-zu* ('Pictures of the Barbarian [European] Compound'), (?)1797.

amount of clay-pipe fragments is substantial. As the Swedish physician Carl Peter Thunberg wrote of his Dutch colleagues, 'the tobacco-pipe has too great charms for them'.[3] Thunberg, a pupil of Linnaeus, was perhaps the most energetic intellectual to visit Japan in the Edo Period, and he thought that dozy smoking had ruined the whole exciting prospect of East–West encounter. The Japanese also noted the extent to which the Dutch were reliant on the pipe, but the sharing of fire was (and still is) in Japan a gambit for initiating contact. Lights would be swapped, and perhaps tobacco, to lubricate social interaction and overcome language problems. There is plenty of pictorial evidence of this, and the often-made illustrations of life on Dejima (produced for interested Japanese viewers) invariably show the connections that smoking helped to make. This was especially important within the tight space of trading, where neither side fully trusted the other and the shogunate was convinced that all parties were conspiring to defraud the State. In addition, smoking paraphernalia made good gifts or bribes. This resulted in the establishment of Japanese collections of smoking-related objects from Europe and the rest of the world. One of the finest collections belonged to the shogunal advisor on Western matters, Ōtsuki Gentaku. In 1796 he published a book on this theme, *Enroku* (Treatise of smoking), which included a section of his and his friends' best pieces, and covered an impressive range.[4] Gentaku was a fluent writer on many themes, and it has been estimated that he wrote more on tobacco than any other person of the age.[5] His treatise followed the movement of the tobacco plant all over the world and discussed the different manners in which it could be consumed.

Gentaku, and others, noted that their own method of smoking differed from that of the

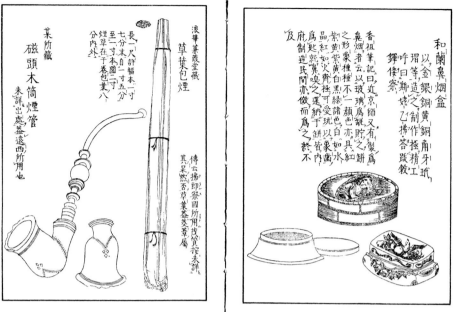

Ishikawa Tairō's illustration to Ōtsuki Gentaku's *Enroku* ('On Smoking'), a printed book of 1796.

Europeans. It is not clear when or how the two manners diverged; both may have been similar in the late sixteenth century. But by the mid-seventeenth century a specifically regional pipe had come into being – the *kiseru*. The origins of the *kiseru* are obscure, but Gentaku, among others, wrote much about it. It shared a closer resemblance with the Malay-style pipe than the Dutch fashion, being composed of metal with a long stem and a tiny bowl.[6] The length of the stem enabled the metal to remain cool at the place where the fingers gripped the pipe, and also ensured that the smoke had dropped in temperature before reaching the mouth. There was also a difference in handling, in that *kiseru* were not used horizontally or with the stem descending – as was the norm in Europe – but with the bowl raised; the stem sloped downwards towards the mouth, which meant coagulating nicotine dripped on to the tip of the tongue. In addition to smoking tobacco, there was also a kind of liquid consumption.

Kiseru evolved over time, gradually becoming smaller. The inordinate flamboyance of the *nanban* era gave way to the more manageable length of mid-Edo. Few sixteenth-century *kiseru* survive,

but pictorial evidence suggests that they might have reached up to some two metres in length. Such a pipe was truly cumbersome to fill and puff on, but was just right for showing off or for use as a weapon, which seems to have been two important functions they were put to. This was the era of the *kabuki-mono*, or 'bent people'. These were dandified thugs, who took advantage of the relative peace brought about by the newly installed shogunate in Edo. Their arch-rivals were the Toyotomi, who controlled the Osaka region until 1615, when they were effectively eliminated. *Kabuki-mono* wore fancy clothes (probably imported from China, Indonesia or England), they were rude to their elders, roughed people up for money, and often slung crucifixes around their necks as a final insult. They were dangerous products of the globalized age, and exaggerated smoking was prominent among their deplorable excesses. *Kabuki-mono* consorted with women of questionable repute, whose dancing, singing and post-performance extras grew into the *kabuki* theatre. A fine screen of about 1610 shows a more restrained group of men watching *kabuki* at the Temple of Kiyomizu in Kyoto, one individual with a massive golden pipe. As the English trader

Richard Cocks wrote in 1615: 'it is strange to see how these Japons, men women and children, are besotted in drinking that herb; and not ten years since it was in use first.'[7]

SMOKING AND PLEASURE

The removal of most foreigners from regular civic space, the banning of Christianity and other shogunal regulations dampened the individualistic behaviour of the *kabuki-mono*. Laws governing 'manners and customs' (*fûzoku*) were passed, and *kabuki* theatre in its original form was banned in 1629.[8] Tobacco remained in use as a serviceable tool during hard negotiations or breaks in work, and to the end was a pleasure of a grabbed moment – a rest on a journey, a breather from broom-pushing – but the business of filling and lighting a pipe resulted in the institutionalization of it. Extant smoking kits were quite heavy, with large ashtrays and tinderboxes

some 60 centimetres across that sat in place and did not move about with the person. Pipes became much shorter, with small tobacco pouches to sling from the waist. In addition, the hazard of fire in Japanese all-wooden towns and villages meant that care was required. One did not play with fire, but composed oneself and concentrated while smoking (Cocks reported the loss of a whole town, blamed on careless smoking).[9] Smaller pipes helped to achieve greater safety.

Tobacco migrated to the formalized world of official leisure – the Government-licensed pleasure districts. Most major cities had a single zone where all manner of entertainment was available for a man with money. The most celebrated of these was the Yoshiwara in Edo, established in 1618 but later moved further out of town (due to fire risks) in 1657. Edo was the largest city in the world by 1750 and its rich and fashionable went to the Yoshiwara to be seen. In a way the spiritual descendants of the

An unsigned detail (of a left-hand screen) from *Pleasures at the Kiyomizu Temple*, c. 1610, a pair of six-fold screens.

kabuki-mono, these men were now integrated into a bourgeois world, comfortable with the notion that money was earned rather than stolen. The Yoshiwara had its parallels in Osaka, Kyoto, Nagasaki and elsewhere, and it was in these districts that smoking became fashionable and where smoking implements continued to be developed. The euphemism 'courtesan-grass' (*keisei-sô*) was applied to tobacco, for it was in the company of such women that it was often used. Tobacco was a relaxant, but less in the private, ruminative way than as a social asset on an actual or aspirational trip to the pleasure district.

Edo should not be considered typical, for not only was it much larger, but it had one of the most forced demographics ever attempted. Roughly 260 *daimyō*, or hereditary regional lords, spent alternate years in Edo, leaving their wives there permanently. They paraded their way into the city with hundreds, sometimes thousands of retainers, who were all male, and whose womenfolk were left in the provinces. As a result, Edo did not have enough women to go around, which facilitated the development of the courtesan class.

Since smoking was an unnecessary excess, and because excessive behaviour was frowned upon other than in designated spaces of amusement, the careerist or the policed would refrain from smoking unless in the company of friends, most typically in the licensed districts. The final stretch of the path from Edo to the Yoshiwara was called *Emon-zaka*, 'clothing hill', for here men would pull fine tunics from their bags and change out of severe workplace garb. They would also pull out their most expensive pipe and pouch, one perhaps the work of a celebrated craftsman and the other sewn from Dutch embossed leather, both of which could not have been revealed within the city.

Inside the walls of the pleasure district, male–female liaisons began with an exchange of smoke. This might have been the case in male–male encounters at work, but now the desiderata were elegant display and refinement. There was nothing harried or hurried about such contexts, and the pipes and pouches used in the pleasure districts spoke of their owners' choices and self-definitions. This mode of self-expression could not be visible within the rest of the city where sumptuary laws were stringent. Fine pipes appear in many pictures of the pleasure districts, such as the title page of Santō Kyōden's 'Elegant Talks of Clothing Designs' (*Komon gawa*) of 1790, showing a refined smoker, trendily coiffed. For women, fine pipes and pouches were aspects of the feminine charms that, as courtesans, they could not succeed without.

ECONOMICS OF SMOKING

Prices varied according to the grade of the tobacco and quality of the smoking necessities, but it is certain that astronomical sums were spent. Different cities had different systems and, more interestingly, different norms of purchase and exchange. The smoker and senior samurai, Hōseidō Kisanji, visited Kyoto at the turn of the eighteenth century, and recorded with some shock what occurred when he sought to solicit tobacco from someone sitting beside him. 'When you use someone's ashtray in the street, or borrow a light from them for your pipe, it is normal enough to help yourself to a little of their tobacco too'; true, he conceded, it could be deemed vulgar,

> but looked at in the large picture, depriving them of their goods is hardly the primary intention. You could calculate it probably at one, two or three *zeni* and hand the money over and settle up there and then for what you had taken . . . but no Edoite would accept cash even if it amounted to a whole *hiki* [1 *hiki*=25 *zeni*].[10]

Chûryō was using the representative example of the 'borrowed' smoke to suggest a different outlook on finances, and by extension on life in general. In his view, the people of Edo (his city) were generous and those of Kyoto more tight-fisted with their tobacco. As a result, if someone expects a certain conviviality in regard to tobacco, the denial of this could be deemed a great insult. It is possible that the

An unsigned (Santō Kyōden) cover to Santō Kyōden's *Komon gawa*, a printed book of 1790.

reverse of gender balances between Edo and Kyoto played its part in this. Edo was some 80 per cent male, but Kyoto was reckoned at 60 per cent female.[11] It follows that with more women on the streets of Kyoto, the person of the courtesan became less of a fetish, which altered the importance attached to 'courtesan grass'. Visiting Edo-ites noted that Kyoto's pleasure district, the Shimabara, was not as lively as Edo's Yoshiwara. In Kyoto, smoking was not necessarily associated with leisure time spent with women, and so it was not part of the mythology of generous manhood.

Fortunes were to be made in the tobacco trade. One of the great tobacco dealers in Edo was Seichū-tei Tokushin, a fifth-generation seller, who also translated Gentaku's *Treatise on Smoking* into Japanese. The book had been written in classical Chinese – the formal literary mode – as befitted the text of a Government scholar. But Seichū-tei knew money resided in large markets, and so took the opportunity to make the treatise readily readable for use as a marketing tool. Before this, the difficult prose had seemed to others to be at odds with the relaxed associations of smoking. As one critic wrote: 'A gentleman by the name of Ōtsuki Gentaku, surgeon to the *daimyō* of Sendai and well-known in the field of European studies, recently wrote a book on the origins of tobacco, but put it all in Chinese [*kanbun*]. It is commoners and the uneducated who enjoy smoking so as a result everyone ridiculed his book.'[12]

Seichū-tei inserted additional commentary into Gentaku's work (with or without permission) and he offered, for example, the opinion that the singular advantage of smoking was that it did not dim the mind, as its kindred spirits tea or alcohol did. The drinker was soon incoherent or over-simulated, whereas the smoker could continue indefinitely, and 'never have the stuff away from hand and mouth'.[13]

There is a factual basis to this, but the claim has its economic thrust too. The incessant smoker puts more cash into the hands of the tobacco dealer than the swift-collapsing drinker does into the hands of the *sake* merchant, or the trembling over-consumer of green tea to the teaman. Seichū-tei was benifitting from addiction.

Lower down the scale of wealth, and operating out of a smaller establishment, was Kyōya Denjirō, better known by his pen name, Santō Kyōden, mentioned above. He was trained as an artist in the Floating World manner (the style associated with the pleasure districts), and was a writer of *gesaku* (Floating World fiction). In 1793, aged in his mid-thirties, he opened a tobacconist's shop in Edo's Kyōbashi district. His days were spent in the shop; his nights were given over to the pleasure districts; and in 1797 he bought out the contract of his favourite courtesan, Tama-no-i, whom he married as his second wife.[14] The only image of the couple together has Kyōden labouring at his desk and Tama sewing in the next room, in domestic bliss.[15] But in all probability, they would also have shared a smoke. It was the bringing of the pleasure district's 'floating' (*ukitaru*) norms into the home space that led to the downfall of many of the Floating World aficionados, notably Kyōden's publisher Tsuta-ya Jūzaburō and the artist Utamaro, who were severely punished for breaking implicit guidelines separating the two spheres of life. Kyōden escaped by deft retrenchment when a Government clampdown on luxurious expenditure began cutting swathes through pleasure district (and tobacco) culture. The image of him and Tama is from 1804, and so post-dates this period, and indeed may have been intended to reconstruct the famous sybarite as a modest family man.

The appearance of Kyōden's shop is known from several paintings, all executed by Floating World artists with whom he was on amicable terms, or even had trained with as a youth. These images were part of the established genre, but they also served very well as advertising. We see the awning and sign to the right; the shop is large and several men are on duty, while a manager fills in the ledger. All the customers are people in the height of fashion, and men and women are there together. The print's maker is Kyōden himself, signing with his artist's name, Kitao Masanobu.

Kitao Shigenobu (Santō Kyōden), *Santō Kyōden's Shop*, c. 1800, a multi-coloured woodblock print.

Kyōden was not averse to advertising his goods in his works of fiction, and often ended the story with an advertisement for his shop. He sometimes had his author's name appear on a title page as 'Kyōden who's waiting for you at his tobacco-pouch shop', and characters within the story would comment on what excellent value goods purchased from him always turn out to be.[16] Kyōden would also praise his publisher, Tsuta-ya Jûzaburō, and his astounding acumen. It became an assumption of the period that popular fiction would plug products in this way (just as *kabuki* actors inserted advice on where and what to buy into their stage dialogues) and endorse stock in exchange for a commission. But it was Kyōden who invented the advertisement that was put in exclusively for the direct financial gain of the author himself.[17]

The fineness of available equipment for tobacco, the knowledge that the leaf was grown at the expense of crops that might have fed the masses, and the direct link of pipes and pouches to the thrilling world of the pleasure district, all in a civic space in which luxury was repeatedly denounced, was enough to ensure that men with any spare resources at all spent it on smoking.

How Do We Smoke?: Accessories and Utensils

BEN RAPAPORT

For more than four centuries, smoking has had a tremendous impact on lifestyles and on society in general around the globe. Today, there is a worldwide effort to eradicate smoking; but whether it is the cigar, the pipe or the cigarette, smoking remains one of life's continuing personal pleasures. At one time, smoking was *de rigueur* – it was chic, even sophisticated – for adult men and women of all social classes and economic strata. Regardless of the eventual outcome of the current emotional, economic, health and often political battle, history will still have to record that this social custom prompted the creation of a panoply of *objets d'art* for smokers of every persuasion; on cursory inspection of these utensils, even the casual viewer must conclude that nothing was too rare or too beautiful for the cultists of smoke. Today, most of these smokers' accessories and accoutrements have fallen into disuse, for various reasons, among them changes in smoking preference, a better understanding of the health-related hazards and, surely, the fast pace of modern life.

Just as the subject of tobacco is endlessly fascinating to explore, so is the study of the innumerable utensils devised to prepare, carry, store, smoke or ingest, and dispose of tobacco in all its forms. As Philip Collins maintains: 'It is doubtful that any other industry has spawned as many allied consumer products . . . These objects echo a vast industry – and way of life – forever changed by scientific inquiry into the effects of smoking upon our health.'[1] Given tobacco's

enduring and ubiquitous use, it is not surprising that utensils and accessories were developed in response to each smoker's needs.

This chapter is devoted to illuminating these commonplace smokers' accessories, these utilitarian objects sold and seen wherever smokers communed, the many and varied accoutrements and utensils that were yesterday's tobacco *nécessaires*. Once an item becomes passé, it often metamorphoses into some other use, and many obsolete objects eventually enter the realm of collectibles; tobacco accessories are no exception. Smokers and non-smokers alike have been enticed by all the utensils, devices and ephemera once associated with tobacco. Writing about Near East water pipes in 1930, Robert Cudell noted: 'We can therefore expect that from now on this beautiful part of Asiatic culture will be associated only with antique dealers and collectors.'[2] Were Cudell alive today, he would see that not only is this type of pipe still in use in the Near East and in other parts of the world, but that many have begun to collect such ethnographic pipes, as well as assorted smoking-related artefacts.

A brief chronology of the introduction of the various forms of tobacco must come before any discussion of the implements used in conjunction with smoking. It is generally accepted that tobacco in ground (or grinded) form, as nasal snuff, spread throughout Europe sometime in the sixteenth century and became popular in the seventeenth century. The clay tobacco pipe was introduced in the sixteenth century, and subsequent pipes made of various less-than-pleasant-tasting woods, porcelain, meerschaum, corncob and the now ever-popular briar followed in the eighteenth and nineteenth centuries. By the end of the first quarter of the eighteenth century, the cigar was being produced in substantial numbers. The cigarette, the most popular tobacco product today, was born in 1832, when Egyptians were laying siege to Acre, which was then under Turkish control. Many believe that it was during the Crimean War (1854–6) that British military personnel first observed Turkish, Russian and perhaps Italian and French soldiers smoking fine-cut tobacco wrapped in paper, the *papalete*; from then on, the cigarette spread rapidly across Europe and the Atlantic to America.[3]

The rite of smoking, depending on the manner of tobacco used, has always required some equipment, and only dipping (moist) snuff, introduced in the second half of the nineteenth century, and chewing tobacco can be consumed without accessories. Accessories are optional pieces of equipment for convenience, comfort or appearance, and the smoking of yesteryear prompted a kaleidoscopic array of them, with an attendant lexicon, taxonomy or patois.[4]

Some idea of the breadth and range of smoker's utensils can be given by looking at those that the tobacco trade offered to the smoking public about a century or so ago. In the late 1800s to early 1900s Salmon & Gluckstein Ltd was the largest retail tobacconist in England, with head offices in London and more than 120 retail branches in the provinces.[5] In its 51-page catalogue of January 1899, the *Illustrated Guide for Smokers*, the company offered cigar and cigarette tubes, vesta cases and boxes, cigarette machines and papers, snuff boxes, wax matches, match stands, tobacco cutters and spinners and snuff grinders, as well as the expected assortment of packaged cigarettes and all manner of pipes, pipe tobacco and cigars. By comparison, around 1892 the George Zorn Co. of Philadelphia, which was one of the largest importers and manufacturers of tobacco products in America,[6] issued a 160-page catalogue, *Pipes & Smokers' Articles*, which contained

an even broader range of products: esoteric sundries and accoutrements such as smokers' trays and tables, ash receivers (known today as spittoons or cuspidors), steam-pipe cleaners, automatic match machines, parlour matches, counter-top cigar lamps, and even a tobacco clock!

Why all this smoking paraphernalia? Today's common cigarette merely requires a match or a cigarette lighter to get started, and a receptacle to dispose of the remains. But it is not quite so simple to partake in the several other forms of tobacco. Those who ingested nasal snuff or smoked a pipe or cigar required ancillary 'stuff' – smoker's requisites, as they were called – in order, first, to ensure that the smoking rite (or ritual) was conducted correctly and in a dignified manner and, second, to derive maximum enjoyment from the encounter. This resulted in the creation of utensils associated with smoke. Some still survive in their original or modified format, while others are no longer in use.

THE PIPE

The tobacco pipe, introduced in the late sixteenth century, has been in continuous use ever since, although its form and materials have changed significantly. The once-popular clay tobacco pipe produced in European countries has all but disappeared, as has the very ornate and majestic hand-carved meerschaum pipe. Only the relatively plain meerschaum pipes that are more in line with today's conservative tastes are still available, as well as reproductions of the ornately carved nineteenth-century originals, both of which are made in Turkey, from where they are exported.

Porcelain pipes have been produced in various formats and qualities for more than 250 years, from the leading manufactories such as Chantilly, Sèvres and Vincennes in France, and Bruckberg, Kopenhagen, Meissen and Nymphenburg in Germany, which produced hand-painted pipe-bowl gems, to the kitschy German regimental (*reservistenpfeife*) pipes made in the period between the Franco-Prussian War (1870–71) and the First

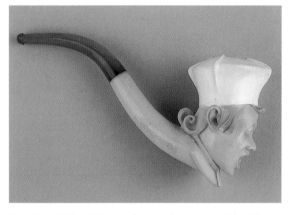

Bi-colour, high-relief carved meerschaum pipe, figurative head of singing *abbé* with amber mouthpiece, from the atelier of J. Sommer Frères, Paris, *c.* 1895.

World War. The mass-produced porcelains produced today in Germany and the Czech Republic bear decals of stags that appeal primarily to tourists. But because of the material's non-porosity, porcelain pipes never became popular outside France and Germany.

In other parts of the world, tobacco pipes have been fabricated from indigenous materials, such as metal, stone, bone, shell, horn and earthenware, but their popularity has never extended beyond those countries or regions in which they were used. Today, the briar, having supplanted pipes made of various other woods around the middle of the nineteenth century, remains the dominant medium for pipe smokers. Nearly every country in Western Europe,

Japan, Israel and the United States produces a broad assortment of briar pipes in various shapes, styles, finishes and price ranges. Attempts to market pipes in the twentieth century made from alternative woods – rosewood, olivewood, ebony, Bubinga, hickory and Manzanita and the corncob – were not successful among discerning pipe smokers.

Pipe smoking still requires the same minimal impedimenta that were employed 300 years ago: a means to light the tobacco; a stopper (or tamper) to tamp down the tobacco in the bowl; a poker-like device to remove the dottle (tobacco residue) and clean the bowl; a pocket tobacco pouch; and a tobacco jar in which to store tobacco. The earliest stoppers were made of ivory, brass, pewter, ceramic, glass and other materials; today, they are made of exotic woods, metal and acrylics. Tobacco jars composed of lead were first introduced in the second half of the seventeenth century; later, jars and pots became available in many other materials, including lead, brass, steel, wood, glass and pottery, and with a vast assortment of figural motifs. The heyday of their popularity was during the second half of the nineteenth century and the first quarter of the twentieth. Those with extensive pipe collections typically owned at least one piece of pipe furniture that served to display and protect the pipes, from custom-made stands, racks and cases to cabinets.

The earliest packaging format for pipe tobacco was paper or cardboard, but from the start of the

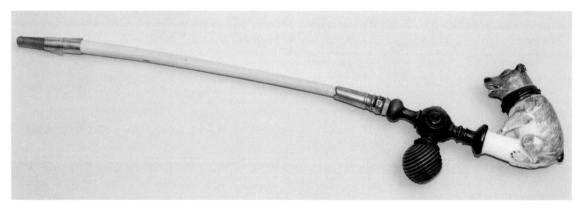

Figurative Meissen pipe bowl of a dog sejant, turned horn reservoir and ivory stem with silver and amber mouthpiece, *c.* 1800.

Assorted early figurative pipe tampers in brass, wood, ivory and mother of pearl. The wood tamper, centre top, a scholar leaning on a pedestal exhibiting the heads of various kings and queens of England at its base, is inscribed 'Cut By Salsbee Aged 74, 1777'.

twentieth century, when lithography and rolled tin were merged, myriad brands of pipe tobacco were packaged in vertical tin containers designed to fit in the pocket of a suit jacket, as well as an assortment of larger tin pails, bins and lunchbox-shaped canisters for home use, each with a distinctive, colourful and often humorous trade name.

CIGAR ACCESSORIES AND EPHEMERA

The cigar is a quite special form of pleasure. Like a cigarette, it is consumed almost entirely, but the conduct of its smoking requires some special devices: a pocket piercer, clipper or cutter, or a decorative desktop clipper (one popular desktop cutter was in a miniature, but functional, guillotine), to snip the tapered smoking end and create the draw hole; and a holder (see right). Other useful items include a cigar chest, or humidor, for home or office in which to store cigars and keep them fresh; a cigar dispenser, or a companion set used to display cigars and wood matches; a vest-pocket case containing

several cigars 'at the ready'; and, finally, the most engaged cigar smoker might own one or more figural desktop cigar lighters. All the better cigar stores had counter-top mechanical cigar cutters cum kerosene, gas, electric or jump-spark cigar lighters for the convenience of their clients.

One unique outgrowth of the cigar industry was the packaging and advertising of cigar brand names. With the introduction of limestone lithography by the Bavarian Aloys Senfelder in 1798, and the later improvements in colour printing – chromolithography – by the Frenchman Godefroi Engelman in 1836, the myriad brands and shapes of cigars were merchandized and distinguished through the creation of individual cigar-box labels and cigar bands.[7] Then thought of as mere

Ornate, footed, silver-plated brass cigar companion set, composed of dispenser, cutter and match holder, probably English, c. 1900.

advertising, today these labels and bands are relished and revered around the world for their individual art content, and have become the paper collectible *du jour*; they now command high prices at auction.[8] Clubs, trade shows, magazines and books devoted to cigar advertising abound, and the current enthusiasm for this once-ephemeral artwork of engravers and lithographers was probably never envisioned during the period in which they were produced. Not unexpectedly, the relics of brands that are no longer manufactured are particularly collectible: cedar and pressed-cardboard cigar boxes and the tin canisters in which the cigars were sold.

CIGARETTE CASES, HOLDERS AND MORE

Today, cigarette smoking is a rudimentary affair – one draws a cigarette from a soft pack or a flip-top box and lights it. But not so long ago cigarette smoking exuded flair, elegance and a *je ne sais quoi* character. The cigarette case and holder probably evolved for women, but both gained eventual impetus as the preferred accessories for male smokers as well. And, like so many other tobacco-related accessories, cigarette cases were made in an extensive array of materials, finishes, shapes and sizes to match the assorted lengths and diameters of different cigarettes produced in Europe, the Near East and the United States. Cigarette holders of the period in metal, Bakelite and other materials varied in length from as few as five centimetres to as many as fifteen, the shorter variety for men and, perhaps as a female affectation, the longer ones for women. Neither accessory is any longer in vogue, and they have both become the domain of the tobacciana collector. Like cigars, at home or in the office cigarettes were sometimes removed from their original factory packaging and placed into decorative dispensers, canisters, companion sets (cigarette cup and match holder) or server-retrievers made specifically for display and for guests. All these items are now relics of the past.

Just as pipe tobacco, cigar tins, cigar-box labels and cigar bands are now in demand as collectibles,

Cigarette case, painted enamel on silver, image of *Leda and the Swan*, Germany, *c.* 1910.

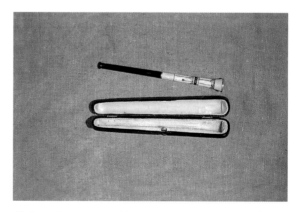

Cloisonné cigarette holder and etui, 'Austria Double', *c.* 1925.

Very unusual cigar holder, chrome-plated metal with ivory mouthpiece (Patent Number 188,992 of F.H.W. von Tiedemann, San Francisco, 27 March 1877). The leather etui has the embossed trademark of F.F.A. Fabricant, Paris.

Porcelain cigarette companion, or parlour set, hand-painted floral décor, comprising matching tray, dispenser, matchbox holder and ashtrays, Dresden, The Ouington Brothers Co., New York, c. 1900–20.

Two bellhop cigarette carriers, stylized enamel-coated metal figurative dispensers for cigarettes and matchbooks, c. 1930.

the cigarette packs of yesteryear in paper and cardboard, flat and round cigarette tins, and other cigarette packaging formats have also attracted collectors. Given the more than 120 years of cigarette production in the United States and elsewhere, one can only make an educated guess as to the total number of brands that are no longer produced, of unfiltered, filtered, mentholated, charcoal and flavoured cigarettes containing blended, burley, Egyptian, oriental, perique, Turkish, Virginia, or Yalta tobaccos; cigarettes marketed as regular, low-tar and light, in standard-, long-, king- and super king-size; and cigarettes contained in soft and hard packs, flats, round tins and other configurations. Cigarette pack art, as it is now called, has earned a rightful place in the worldwide image history and culture of tobacco.

ASHTRAYS

The ashtray, or ash pan, probably became popular at the same time as cigarette smoking became generally acceptable. Eventually, cigarette-specific ashtrays were designed for different locales, for example the parlour and the boudoir, and public places where cigarette smokers congregated, such as reception areas, lounges, elevator entrances and hotel lobbies. Further, specially configured ashtrays were designed and produced for the cigar and the pipe smoker, each requiring a slightly different style and shape. Over time, the ashtray evolved from a simple functional utensil of pressed tin to an art object in pottery, porcelain, glass, crystal, cast bronze, silver, copper, marble, onyx and innumerable other materials; it also evolved into novelty, figural and advertising ashtrays. Wherever smoking is still allowed, an ashtray is always within reach.

LIGHTING UP

Lastly, that which gives life to tobacco – fire. Since the beginning of time when fire making was discovered, the science of creating it has undergone revolutionary changes, with alterations in design ranging from fire pots and drills, to tinderboxes, tinder pistols and chuck-mucks, to friction lights (the sulphur and phosphorous match, lucifer, congreve, fuzee, vesta, vesuvian and safety match) and, finally, to flint, gasoline, methanol and methane, alcohol, battery, electric, gas, solar cell and piezo-ignition pocket and table lighters of every conceivable configuration and appearance.

Wood friction matches were in vogue from about the middle of the nineteenth century to about 1930, when wood safety matches, matchbooks and gas lighters became popular. To improve the presentation of these wood matches, a small storage container was devised – the vesta box or vesta case in England or, as it was called in the United States, the matchsafe. This box was originally intended to keep matches dry and to store them safely in a pocket, but it soon evolved into a remarkable personalized biblelot that assumed many different shapes, materials and designs. From about the 1870s to about the 1910s, the predominant matchsafe-producing countries were Britain and a few other European countries, the United States, Japan, China and India. In the United States alone, between 1856 and 1930 more than 1,000 matchsafe designs were registered at the US Patent Office, but many more thousands of designs were produced without being registered.[9] Jewellers, silversmiths, novelty companies, match manufacturers and a host of unheralded and unknown individuals produced an endless assortment of matchsafes, to the extent that, according to Sampson Shinn, 'The appeal . . . as small precious objects is irresistible, and their many amusing novelties are an enduring delight . . . A study of matchsafes is a study of design itself.'[10]

The historic evolution of both pocket and table lighters is a fascinating story of the marriage of science and art, and form and function. These ranged from the prototypical devices and imaginative and rare creations of Cartier, Dunhill and Tiffany in gold, to mass-market base-metal lighters such as Zippo, Ronson and Evans, to gimmick and disposable plastic lighters from Marksman and

Bruma (Press Easy) semi-automatic cigarette lighter with plunger-type mechanism, hand-chased and embossed .935 silver, patented in Germany and the United States in 1927.

Scripto, as well as a host of other models and brand names too numerous to mention. Most lighters produced in the twentieth century were fashioned as an accessory, and their design and decoration were influenced by the art of the period. Almost all the earliest fire-making contrivances are now relegated to museums and private collections. Paper matchbooks that continue in use today serve primarily the cigarette smoker, while those who smoke a pipe or cigar prefer either a wood match or a new-age lighter specifically designed to control the direction and intensity of the flame. Whether paper or wood match or lighter, fire remains an inseparable element in the rite of smoking.

CONCLUSION

The uninterrupted consumption of tobacco in a variety of forms in almost every corner of the civilized world for more than 400 years has spawned a plethora of necessary devices, utensils, accoutrements and accessories that have served their original purpose well. They have also enriched our lives, because this remarkable range of artful objects now testifies to the importance that smoking has had for many millions. In the aggregate, symbolically, all the aforementioned accessories represent a microcosmic insight into a once elegant and glamorous past.

The *Belle Epoque* of Opium

JOS TEN BERGE

For most of us, the word opium brings to mind images of opium smokers, even though by far the largest part of the history of opium does not belong to the history of smoking at all. Opium (*Papaver somniferum*) has been known to humanity since at least Neolithic times, but until some three centuries ago it was either eaten or drunk in dissolved form, but never smoked. The ancient Greeks ate or drank opium, but did not spread its use except to the Romans, who also mostly kept it to themselves. It was the Arabs who, from the seventh century CE onwards, recognized opium as an ideal item of merchandise. They carried it from the Middle East all the way through Persia, India and as far as China, where it found favour among the upper classes, who used it both as a medicine and a stimulant.

Then, from another corner of the world, smoking was introduced and spread quickly around the world. In the sixteenth and seventeenth centuries, sailors learned the habit from Native North Americans and brought it to Europe, India, China and South-East Asia. Tobacco smoking was very much frowned upon almost everywhere, but even the severest penalties were of no avail in China, where smoking tobacco was prohibited in 1644 and inveterate smokers quickly turned to opium as a substance that, when prepared in the right way, could be smoked as well. J. M. Scott, in 1969, called this marriage of opium, born in the Middle East, and the pipe, born in North America, an event of great historical importance.[1] More recently, another historian of opium, Martin Booth, called it one of

the most evil cultural exchanges in history.[2] Even so, it would take some two centuries before the new custom arrived on European shores.

Europe was reintroduced to opium during the eleventh and twelfth centuries when Venetian merchants traded it with the Arabs and the crusaders brought it back home from the Middle East. From the sixteenth to well into the nineteenth century, opium counted as the major panacea in Western medicine. It usually came in the form of laudanum – raw opium dissolved in alcohol. It was this drink to which Thomas De Quincey sang his praises in 1821: he was the first to confess that it created both pleasurable dreams and horrible nightmares. His reference to opium eating in the title of his famous book, *Confessions of an English Opium Eater*, is somewhat mysterious. Possibly he wanted to imply some kind of kinship with an exotic Turkish fraternity that, according to many Eastern and travellers' tales, ate their opium raw.[3] In any regard, De Quincey gave the use of opium a hitherto unknown – or rather unrecognized – dimension that proved very tempting to romantically inclined Europeans, coming close to identifying it with inspiration.

A NEW ERA, A NEW WAY

The late nineteenth century had been dominated by morphine usage. Primarily used for medicinal purposes after the Franco-Prussian War of 1871–2, many soldiers became dependent on it, and this was supplemented by another phenomenon: usage for

'A New Vice: Opium Dens in France', cover of *Le Petit Journal* (5 July 1903).

reasons of pleasure, hedonism and decadence. According to many Parisian physicians, journalists and writers of the 1880s and '90s, females especially seemed unable to resist the temptations of morphine, a theme that fitted in very well with the growing concern with feminism and the many misogynous clichés about the 'weaker sex' that pervaded the *fin de siècle*. The newspaper *Le Figaro* stated in 1886 that there were so few male morphine addicts because 'men were better able to resist, work and smoke [tobacco]'.[4] To many, morphine was symptomatic for the general decline of European civilization.

The turn of the century brought new vigour, and many felt that it was time to clear out all symptoms of decadence. This reaction took several forms. Some thought all drug use had to be eradicated once and for all, often adopting Max Nordau's medically inspired thesis of 1892, *Degeneration*, in which he indiscriminately attacked all that he deemed decadent and effeminate. Others, equally tired of effeminacy, but unwilling to give up the pleasures of drugs, chose a new method of opiate

Henry Vollet, *Le Vice d'Asie: fumerie d'opium*, as published in the *Catalogue illustré du Salon de 1909*.

use: smoking. Smoking opium was not entirely new to Europe at the time. Following the colonialization of South-East Asia, quite a few European sailors and officials adopted this exotic habit in the East. By the 1850s the first opium dens were established in the small enclaves of Asian immigrants in French, British and American harbour cities. As long as these catered only to an Asian clientele, nobody perceived much harm in them. But when it became apparent that European marine and government personnel returning from the East wanted to continue to enjoy the charms of opium dens, and that some white women fell for it as well, many perceived a new and great danger to Western civilization.[5]

The French were not as disquieted about the practice of *tirer sur le bambou* (sucking on the bamboo [pipe]) as the British or Americans – at least not until 1905, when it was disclosed that possibly more than half of all colonial personnel in Indo-China were smoking opium. The country was again shocked in 1907, first by the Ulmo Affair, when an addicted officer tried to sell military secrets to the Germans, and then when a naval ship commanded

by an opium-addicted captain rammed the quay wall of Toulon harbour. Opium seemed to incapacitate the country's ability to defend itself. The satirical magazine *L'Assiette au Beurre* summed up the situation with a caricature of two opium-smoking officers: 'We're sinking? . . . Well, so what ?'[6] Those interested had no trouble in finding one of the numerous opium dens in the French harbour cities. Brothels also adapted swiftly to the new wishes of their clientele. But like the British and the Americans before them, some Frenchmen perceived the establishment of opium dens as a subtle and pernicious plot, by means of which Indo-China was trying to take revenge for its physical occupation by enslaving the minds of its conquerors.[7]

Apart from the many representations of Asian opium smokers that were presented to Western audiences with the aura of a registration of an exotic custom, many illustrators and artists dedicated themselves to the disquieting theme of Westerners in opium dens. The paintings of Henry Vollet, for example, with significant titles such as *Le Vice d'Asie* and *Le Poison de Bouddah*, speak for themselves.

The first, presented to the Salon exhibition of 1909, shows an opium den with one sailor lighting his pipe, another despairingly raising his hands to his head, a third attempting to touch the visions that materialize over his head, while a European woman in the foreground stares vacantly into space. The whole scene of degradation is orchestrated by an Asian hostess, who seems to take satanic pleasure in wielding the opium sceptre over the minds of those who brutalized her country.

LITERARY INSPIRATIONS

Even though other drugs such as absinthe, ether and hashish remained ever popular in French literary and artistic circles, it was opium that overtook morphine use around 1900. In his *La Belle Epoque de l'opium* (1984) Arnould de Liedekerke concluded:

> Under the sign of opium and the opium den, the ties between the literary world and the drug were, for some fifteen years, until the declaration of war, numerous and of an unequalled richness. Less intense than morphine, less capricious than hashish, more aesthetic than ether, opium, that 'blissful poison of educated intelligence', had its Golden Age.[8]

Smoking opium became the focus of a new literary genre, just as injecting morphine had been in the 1880s. According to de Liedekerke, however, the main difference was that this time not only was the number of opium-dedicated writers larger, but their talent was also greater.[9]

French opium literature started in Indo-China itself, where writers tried to combat their home-sickness and colonial ennui with the drug. The first opium novel, *L'Opium*, by war correspondent Paul Bonnetain, was published in 1886. It still stressed the dangers, with a young decadent poet enjoying its 'vague and mysterious, profound and volatile inspirations' until he realizes that he needs the drug to fight off his nightmares and slowly but surely goes to ruin.[10] Bonnetain's widely praised realism,

however, contrasts sharply with most of the opium literature, in which, as a rule, the mystique and aesthetics of the opium den are praised.

THE CHARMS OF OPIUM: ITS REVERIE...

Representations and writings that emerged at this time soon tempted others to submit to the charms of this new 'oriental vice'. And its charms were many. A visit to an opium den was an expression of exotic and hedonistic desires for which, for the first time, absolutely no medical alibi could be offered. For this reason alone it had an aura of something forbidden and 'underground', even when there was as yet no law forbidding the drug or its use. Smoking instead of eating or drinking opium was a sign of wanton withdrawal from society's norms. It was also new and exotic, as well as somewhat dangerous and threatening, and like many drugs it seemed to create an 'in-group' of users who tended both to proselytism and contempt for non-users.[11] Many thought of opium as 'a true fatherland, a religion, a strong and jealous bond that brought people together', as Claude Farrère noted in his widely read and frequently reprinted and translated *Fumée d'opium* of 1904.[12]

The experience that they shared was first of all the opium reverie itself, the nature of which – according to those in the know – was only partly determined by the drug's morphine content. Roger Dupouy, in his 'clinical and medical-literary' study *Les Opiomanes: Mangeurs, buveurs et fumeurs d'opium* of 1912, claimed that the best *chandou* or smoking opium often contained 'the least morphine' and that injected morphine never gave as pure an intellectual stimulation as natural opium.[13] A good *chandou* consisted of purified and dissolved opium to which aromatic substances were added to give the smoke a unique flavour. Much of its morphine contents remained behind in the dross, the residue left in the pipe after it was smoked, and this was sold to those who were unable to afford the real thing.

According to Dupouy, during the three to four hours of opium intoxication, sensorial perception becomes so intense that loud noises and intense light cannot be tolerated. Only in the silence and dim lights of the opium den will the force, speed and subtlety of the intellect be raised to unknown heights. Clearly outlined ideas and memories will enter the consciousness without the smoker losing a sense of logic. After some eight to ten pipes one enters the state of *rêverie*, a lucid dream state in which the smoker loses all sense of his body. Thought processes speed up to become autonomous, uncontrolled by the smoker, unrelated to his earthly worries, though still mirroring his character or profession:

> The adventurer makes wondrous travels, the mathematician accomplishes complex calculations, the literary man works out eloquent speeches, the scientist courts wise dissertations, the libertine pursues licentious scenes, the actor personifies fictional characters in a magnificent way, the gambler construes playing systems that always win.[14]

But as Dupouy admitted, this charm of opium consists mainly of subjective and megalomaniac illusions. The smoker merely thinks that he is capable of great things and understands everything profoundly. Euphorically overestimating himself, he becomes deluded by the idea that he is more successful than he really is. To substantiate this conclusion, Dupouy pointed out that smokers become apathetic after a sleepless night of opium, having lost not only all energy and appetite for work, but also all memory of whatever it was that they had thought they had found in their reveries. Experimental subjects appeared unable to report on their experiences and could not remember a thing of the stories that were read to them during intoxication. And when notes were kept during reverie, either by the smoker himself or by witnesses, they invariably were unable to believe afterwards that the incoherent nonsense taken down was their own doing, as one of Dupouy's colleagues demonstrated by studying such writings.[15]

Nevertheless, the ever-ambivalent Dupouy had reservations. His colleague, he argued, had sketched an exaggerated picture because he had worked only with heavily addicted smokers. With occasional users, things weren't so bad. Moreover, Dupouy continued, one should distinguish between passive reveries, in which smokers merely surrender to their absurd thought processes and remain sterile, and active reveries, wherein the goal is predetermined and the development can be steered at will. It was these 'optimistic' and 'aesthetic' reveries that poets and artists aimed for and could profit by, Dupouy claimed, for there they could find things that 'exclusive and despotic' reason was unable to accommodate.[16] Unfortunately, however, occasional smokers tend to become regular smokers.

. . . AND ITS AESTHETICS

In addition to the nature of the opium reverie itself – with its pleasant illusions of power – opium smoking had other, equal or even more important charms. It was also, in the words of de Liedekerke:

> the strange decorum that surrounded the opium ceremony that attracted writers, the whole of inherited Asian aesthetics, with its wise gestures, its instruments, its lamps, pipes, needles, in short, the picturesque and wondrous milieu of the opium den, that is, another dimension of the artificial paradise, a dimension that was ignored completely by Baudelaire, Gautier and De Quincey.[17]

With the arrival of the opium den, drug use transcended the prosaic consumption of a draught of laudanum, a spoonful of hashish paste or an injection of morphine. Instead, it became an aesthetic ceremony performed in a *fumerie* that was especially designed for the purpose. 'With its refined rituals and its mysterious alchemy, its lacquer, its silk and its jade, with its dimmed light and the drug's odours, it offered the writer and poet an incomparably more dense matter.'[18]

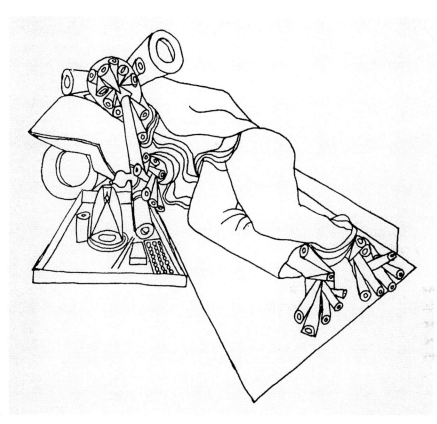

Jean Cocteau, an untitled drawing in indian ink on paper, from *Opium: Journal d'une désintoxication* (1930).

In many ways, opium smoking was not just the next rage in drug use, following morphomania. It was also a reaction against its predecessor. Users never failed to emphasize the differences. As Jean Cocteau put it in his *Opium: Journal d'une désintoxication* of 1930: 'Opium is the opposite of the hypodermic needle. It reassures. It reassures by its luxury, by its rituals, by the anti-medical elegance of the lamps, pipe-bowls, pipes, by the age-old institution of this exquisite poisoning'.[19] The opium den was a world apart, a hermetic, mysterious and smoky world, a shrine for the initiated, designed for the purpose of dreaming, an invitation *au voyage* that already on entering displaced a person, allowing no room for spleen or ennui. Chinese wallpaper, statues of the Buddha, dragons and lanterns, kimonos for customers, low cribs, small smoking tables and Asian servant boys – all this was part of the usual setting of a luxurious Parisian *fumerie*, and as such contrasted sharply with the miserable dens in which

most of the Chinese users huddled together. The opium literature contains many lyrical pages on the interiors of opium dens and the magical beauty of artistically crafted smoking paraphernalia made of bamboo, silver, ivory, jade and other exotic materials, even though some purists maintained that true smokers had no need for all this unnecessary decor.

And then there was the art of smoking. The proper preparation of an opium pipe had the status of a magical ceremony. 'Opium does not tolerate impatient adepts and people making a mess. It will turn its back on them and leave them nothing but morphine, heroin, suicide and death', according to Cocteau, who, as many like him, thought of opium smoking as an art form; when executed with care, it resulted in a 'perfect masterpiece, because it is fleeting, without form and without critics'.[20] First, the opium needle was run through the sticky *chandou* and then heated above an oil lamp until a pliable little ball was formed at its tip. This ball was then rolled into a cone on a heated plate. The cone was put into the pipe-bowl and the smoker, lying on his hip, held the pipe at a tilted angle above the lamp and inhaled the smoke. It was an art that demanded dedication, patience and experience before it could be practised correctly, but then the effects would show immediately. In the unequalled words of Cocteau: 'The smoker slowly ascends like a balloon, turns around slowly, and slowly descends again on a dead moon, the weak gravity of which prevents him from leaving.'[21]

Opium smoking not only contrasted with morphine for its superior effects and aesthetics, but also because it was deemed a thing for men. At the *fin de siècle*, morphine was a vice for women and effeminate aesthetes. Real men smoked their opium raw. This notion of the masculinity of opium smoking, though professed by many authors, was not mirrored in the visual arts. For marketing purposes, Salon artists favoured females, preferably nude ones, when representing opium smokers. Pierre Gourdault's *Rêverie d'opium*, exhibited at the Salon of 1903, depicted one of those typical Salon nudes, lying on pillows with the wanton smile of the femme fatale, while Cécile Paul-Baudry – a woman – presented the Salon of 1912 with a nude *Fumeuse d'opium*, enjoying her reveries without any apparent sense of shame. Albert Matignon, on the other hand, after having painted a very enticing scene of three lascivious lesbian 'morphinomaniacs'

in 1905, must have altered his view, for at the Salon of 1911 he showed a horrifying scene of addiction in the form of a clearly degenerate young woman with deep, junky-like eyes, attempting to raise herself from a dark alcove.

MONTMARTRE: OPIUM CAPITAL

According to Dupouy, it was in particular 'a certain category of brain workers that produced opium smokers, the category of men of imagination and feeling, that of poets and artists, in short, that of dreamers'.[22] Opium was seen a poetic substance compared to morphine. In his *La Noire idole* of 1930, Jean Dorsenne, for example, wrote: 'Morphine is the vice of hurried people, businessmen, while opium is that of sensual man, of artists.'[23]

Besides Salon artists looking for sensational subjects, many avant-garde artists felt attracted to the real charms of opium smoking. Following the French ports, Paris soon counted numerous opium dens, especially in artists' neighbourhoods such as the Latin Quarter, Montparnasse and Montmartre, each with its own more or less luxurious decor and more or less private clientele. In 1919 Francis Carco, that shrewd observer of the bohemian life, wrote disapprovingly about the new rage in Montmartre:

> Poor naïves, dedicated to extracting severe headaches from the bamboo, why should we

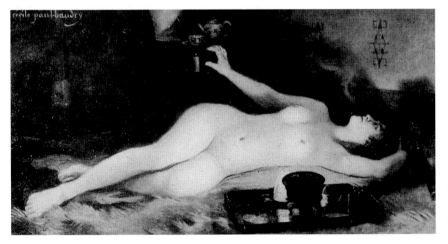

Cécile Paule-Baudry, 'Fumeuse d'opium', as published in the *Catalogue illustré du Salon de 1912*.

Albert Matignon, 'Réveil d'opium', as published in the *Catalogue illustré du Salon de 1911*.

take you seriously? One reads verses – and what kind of verses! – in the artists' dens, and the evil demon that Baudelaire praised without approaching it produces a whole mountain of silly and childish literature. Montmarte, capital of opium? No way ... That's not Montmartre. Montmartre has better things to offer than these unhealthy dreams.[24]

Despite Carco's admonitions, opium was one of the things for which Montmartre became famous. In his biography of Amadeo Modigliani, André Salmon asserted that it was the followers of the fifteenth-century poet François Villon who left their base in the Latin Quarter to come and sell drugs to the *baudelairians* of Montmartre, making Modigliani one of their prey.[25] It was more probably Modigliani's patron, the physician Paul Alexandre, who tempted him to try drugs, since he was convinced that hashish and opium stimulated the artistic imagination. For this purpose, Alexandre organized special parties for the group of artists that he had assembled around him.[26]

In any case, Modigliani did develop a taste for drugs and soon turned to a certain 'Baron' Pigeard, a well-to-do boat builder who dealt in hashish and ran an opium den in Montmartre. In this respect he went along with a fashion that may have started with one Paulette Philippi, who was introduced to opium smoking by a naval officer around 1905. Since this amorous girl did not like being alone, she invited writers and artist friends to come and smoke with her in her private *fumerie*, among them Salmon, Paul Fort, René Dalize, Guillaume Apollinaire and possibly the Cubist painters Georges Braque and Pablo Picasso.[27] From 1906 to 1909 the artists of Montmartre mostly called at Pigeard's, but the new fashion spread quickly among networks of friends. Soon the choice of opium dens enabled

'Une Fumerie d'opium à Montmartre', a photo published in 1910, in Richard Millant, *'La Drogue': Fumeurs et mangeurs d'opium*.

everyone to choose his or her own favourite *fumerie*, if they had not already set up a little smoking corner in their own apartments and studios. Alfred Jarry went with Léon-Paul Fargue; Dalize smoked at Salmon's; the writers Octave Mirbeau and Henry Bataille knew opium; Colette went to a certain Charlotte while her husband Willy had Paul-Jean Toulet ghost-write the drug-related passages in his *Lélie, fumeuse d'opium* of 1911. Max Jacob, famous for his taste for ether, was not averse to opium either, and went down the Parisian dens with Apollinaire, Dalize and Francis Picabia. The Fauve painter André Derain visited the local *fumeries* with his neighbour, Apollinaire, keeping each other informed about the latest developments in modern poetry and painting.[28]

The list seems endless, revealing time and again the same names in different combinations. Apollinaire, friend of Jarry, Salmon and Picasso, frequented a certain Madame Bargy, where he would 'smoke on Saturdays', usually accompanied by his secretary Jean Mollet. Mollet had made his entrance into literary circles through a *fumerie*, possibly that of Philippi, where – or so he related in his memoirs – one stayed eight to ten days at a stretch on the sole condition of bringing a basketful of oysters and two litres of berry dregs. One day he introduced Apollinaire as his excuse for extended absences.[29] Picabia stated that, during the last two years before the war, he and Apollinaire went to smoke opium at friends' 'almost every night'.[30] At the start of the war, Apollinaire took refuge in Nice, where opium, so he stated, transformed the war into an 'artificial paradise'. There he also created a calligram for his beloved Lou in the shape of an opium pipe. The text read: 'And behold the instrument with which I angle for the immense monster of your desire as a strange art that plunges itself into the lap of deep nights.'[31]

Picasso smoked opium two or three times a week between the summers of 1904 and 1908, as his mistress Fernande Olivier wrote in her memoirs.[32] They too may have been initially guests of Alexandre, Pigeard or Phillipi, but Picasso soon purchased the necessary smoking materials himself and sub-sequently invited friends to come over to his studio in the Bâteau Lavoir and have a smoke. According to his biographer John Richardson, it was not a belief in a 'derangement of the senses' *a là* Rimbaud but an innate curiosity that made Picasso try drugs. 'Opium flavours the themes and the mood of many late Blue and early Rose period works', Richardson observed, pointing out the sleepy, almost trancelike expressions of the faces in several paintings of 1905. One of these, the *Saltimbanques*, may have been inspired by a poem of this title that Apollinaire dedicated to the painter. It has the same subject and mood as the painting and speaks, in its first version, of 'Lethe's milk of oblivion', a clear reference to opium. Picasso abruptly renounced opium in June 1908, not just because nothing could impede his intense urge for renewal, as is often suggested, but also because he was profoundly shocked by the drug-related suicide of a confused housemate, for which he was unfairly blamed.[33]

THE GREAT WAR

With the outbreak of the Great War in 1914, the *belle époque* of opium came to an end. Hedonistic drug use, up until now tolerated as a 'social flaw', did not fit in well with times of war, and the disruption of international lines of distribution made life difficult for inveterate smokers. The French Government outlawed opium in 1916 and came down heavily on the dens after 1918, although not without some strong protests from the expected quarters. Claude Farrère especially fulminated in 1920 with a pamphlet entitled *L'Opium ou l'alcool?*, arguing that opium was clearly beneficial, both to the individual and to society, when compared to alcohol or tobacco. Opium smokers abstain from alcohol and never beat up their wives and children. He also deemed it plainly hypocritical to outlaw a drug at home while still making huge amounts of money from it elsewhere. The only reason why opium was forbidden, according to Farrère, was economic, in that it protected the interests of the 'assassins of France': wine and liquor merchants, who saw their

Georges Gros, 'Fumeries d'opium. Leur dernière arme: Sa Majesté la Drogue!', on the cover of *La Grimace* (22 July 1917).

Geo Dorival's cover illustration for the 1925 edition of Jules Boissière's *Fumeurs d'opium*, first published in 1909.

profitable dealings in sterility, violence, disease and death economically endangered by opium.[34]

Public opinion, however, chose to side with the law. Remembering the Ulmo Affair, opium meant a threat to the country, weakening resistance against the enemy. A picture on the cover of *La Grimace* in 1917 said it all. While a long-haired opium smoker in oriental dress prepares a new pipe, fiendish madness radiating from his eyes, in the background the shadowy figure of a German soldier looms up. Smoking opium, as the caption explains, is the enemy's 'latest weapon'. Still, the anti-opium campaign, reinforced by several international treaties, proved successful only very slowly. After the war a new generation let itself be charmed by opium, tempted by new books on the subject such as Louis Laloy's *Livre de la fumée* of 1913, by Surrealism's goal of uniting dreams with reality, and certainly by influential artists such as Jean Cocteau, who, from 1925 onwards, never tired of proselytising young admirers. But the *belle époque* of opium did not repeat itself. The 'roaring twenties' favoured other drugs and no longer had the patience for time-consuming smoking rituals. Opium smoking slowly returned to the Chinatowns until, at some point in the 1970s, it was not heard of again. The marriage between smoking and opium proved not to be durable, and faded out, along with its literature, its crafts and its lamps.

The Opium Den in Victorian London

BARRY MILLIGAN

For many modern readers, the words 'opium den' surely conjure images of a dingy hideout filled with clouds of narcotic smoke, where nefarious Asian masterminds lure unsuspecting victims to their doom. The textbook example of this type can be found in the Fu Manchu novels popular around the time of the First World War, the first of which describes a 'dope-shop in one of the burrows off the old Ratcliff Highway'. Amidst 'an atmosphere which was literally poisonous . . . being loaded with opium fumes', were a dozen bunks whose occupants 'were lying motionless, but one or two were squatting in their bunks noisily sucking at the little metal pipes'.[1] The hellishness of the scene is only enhanced by the narrator's fall through a trapdoor into a flaming pit shortly after observing it. Despite such penny-dreadful sensationalism, accounts such as this either matched or shaped contemporary perceptions to the degree that they were echoed in the supposedly factual press for a few decades afterwards, with headlines screaming of oriental syndicates seducing Londoners into drug-induced slavery.[2] Although it is not impossible that there was an Asian underground attempting to invade the West via a network of drug dens, an overview of the accounts beginning with their roots in the popular journalism of the mid-nineteenth century strongly suggests a different story. There clearly was opium smoking on a small scale in London, mainly as a casual pastime of visiting Asian seamen. But this relatively benign phenomenon was inflated into an insidious conspiracy by anxieties attending Britain's imperial activities in the East and the Victorian vogue for 'sensation' fiction.

Opium in itself was not exotic in nineteenth-century England. In its most familiar forms – as the active ingredient of laudanum and patent medicines such as Godfrey's Cordial and Mrs Winslow's Soothing Syrup, for instance – it was an unexceptional part of daily life, much as aspirin or Tylenol are today. All of these common forms of opium were taken orally; in the mid-nineteenth century, even the hypodermic injection of morphine (opium's most significant alkaloid) was a cutting-edge medical technology. Opium smoking would have been known to the average Briton only as an *outré* habit of characters in oriental tales, or, with greater resonance, as the vice of Chinese peasants, which was often invoked in debates over the so-called Opium Wars of 1839–42 and 1856–60, which were fought over the sale of Indian opium to China. The British East India Company exercised a monopoly over the poppy crops of Bengal, and, suffering a deficit of trade in tea and silk with China, British commercial firms would have been glad to pay down the balance with the abundant Indian opium had not the Chinese Government banned imports. When merchants smuggled the drug into Canton anyway, the Chinese responded by destroying their stock and Britain sent gunboats to 'open' the port. Some factions in England, such as the Society for the Suppression of the Opium Trade, warned that Britain could expect retribution for thus fuelling an epidemic of opium smoking, which they claimed was enslaving China's economic lower classes. When the first reports of opium smoking in the very heart of the British Empire appeared in the 1860s, then, they were culturally positioned to excite both titillation and anxiety.

The first accounts of opium dens in London, which appeared in popular periodicals, appealed to a broad readership on a number of levels. They served in part as a sort of cultural anthropology: given the exotic nature of opium smoking, reporters focused a good deal on the process itself. An elaborate series of steps was essential, for if smoked in its common form, opium would often merely induce nausea. The raw opium imported into Britain was the dried milk of the poppy's seed capsule, with whatever fragments of plant matter, dirt and other impurities that had been mixed in when it was harvested. Most opium that went to market had been boiled and filtered in at least a crude fashion, but many adjuncts remained. Chinese practitioners would shred the waxy opium into fine fragments, then boil it inside a piece of cloth, discarding the tea-leaf-like residue collected there. The dark, treacly substance remaining in the pot (sometimes called *chandu*) was rolled on to the point of a long metal wire or pin and roasted over a flame until it sizzled and congealed into a pea-sized, dark-brown ball. This pellet was then inserted into the end of an unusual pipe, which acquired quite a mystique of its own. The stem was usually a piece of bamboo about 45 centimetres long. A few centimetres from one end of this stem was an egg-shaped earthenware or metal bowl with a very small opening at the end opposite its junction with the bamboo stem. One famous variation was the pipe on which Charles Dickens supposedly based his account in *The Mystery of Edwin Drood* (1870): it substituted a penny ink bottle (or a brass doorknob, according to one account)[3] for the bowl. The pellet of sizzling opium was placed into the little hole in the bowl and the pipe was then turned so that the opening faced downward over the flame of a small oil lamp, which kept the opium burning. The smoker drew vigorously at the other end of the stem, exhaling as little of the smoke as

possible, until the pellet was consumed after about a minute and a half. Experimenters claim that a novice smoker would require a whole pipeful to feel light-headed and relaxed, several more to see dreamy visions, if ever. Seasoned smokers would go through as many as twelve bowls in an evening, each costing about a penny and a half, a price comparable to that of a drink in a pub. Conventionally, the smoker followed each opium pipe with a cigarette on the house.

The early journalistic accounts also fit within the tradition of 'slumming', or visiting the most sordid parts of the East End in shabby disguise with a police escort. Many reporters dwell on the details of donning seedy costume and joining a guide at the police station before journeying to the den, whose location is precisely the same in almost every account that specifies it: in a cramped court off a street known as Bluegate Fields, just north of the former Ratcliff Highway in Shadwell.[4] The area in general was infamous in the mid-nineteenth century as a 'spot where vice loses all its charms by appearing in all its grossness'.[5] Bluegate Fields in particular, chiefly a row of dance halls and gin palaces, was also known as 'Tiger Bay' after its ruthless denizens, who preyed upon sailors from the nearby London Docks. Shadwell's population consisted predominantly of immigrants, and the court in question, off Bluegate Fields through an archway near the Royal Sovereign pub, was favoured by Asian seamen who either were temporarily without ships or had settled in the area. This blind alley containing several dilapidated three-roomed houses was known variously as 'Palmer's Folly', 'Chinaman Court', 'New Court' and, on at least one occasion, 'Victoria Court'.[6] Sometimes the name was not specified, but the consistent descriptions of the low, arched, tunnel-like entrance and what lay beyond leave little doubt that almost every reporter for nearly two decades beat the same path. One observer insisted that the den he visited was 'the only establishment of the sort'.[7] At the other extreme, the highest number cited with any specificity came from an anonymous missionary writing for the anti-opium *Friend of China* in 1877: he claimed personal knowledge of three such establishments in Bluegate Fields and two more in Limehouse.[8] But given that the *raison d'être* of the *Friend of China* 'was to decry the evils of the Indo-Chinese opium trade', the accounts printed there often beg for a grain of salt. In fact, the numbers given by a small coterie of missionaries always exceeded those of any of the other accounts published before the turn of the century. The East End missionary Joseph Salter seemed to suspect opium dens in every house that lodged Asian seamen, but he rarely confirmed his suspicions.[9] Another missionary, George Piercy, warned in 1883 that 'in our metropolis for years past there have been six or eight schools for opium smoking', but he refers explicitly to only two and describes the second in the vaguest of terms.[10] Citing Piercy as his guide, another writer refers in a similarly offhand manner to 'six or seven' dens, but again gives details of only one and refers vaguely to a second establishment that may or may not have been devoted to opium smoking.[11] It is clear that many Asian seamen smoked opium at least occasionally, but it is less clear that they did so in commercial establishments devoted to the purpose. Although it is possible that there were many such places, most reporters found no more than two, despite diligent searching.[12]

The details of the known establishments in 'The Fields' suggest two or possibly three separate but closely neighbouring dens.[13] The first two accounts – one in a *Daily News* article of 1864 and another in Dickens's miscellany *All the Year Round* in 1866 – seem to describe the same place: a cramped ground-floor room in New Court, dominated by a shabby bed made up into a kind of divan with pillows and bolster bunched along one side. Presiding is a very old Chinese man known as Yahee, 'whose pre-paration of the drug is so exceptionally skilful that Chinamen come from all parts of London to patron-ize him'.[14] Far from probing the hell-hole of a Fu Manchu thriller, these reporters present an oasis of dreamy calm amidst the threatening chaos of Tiger Bay, and Yahee's reputation appears to rest more upon 'the same stories of his cleanliness and quiet-ness' than his skill as an opium master.[15]

The next few published accounts differ more in their details. In 1868 two English periodicals reprinted a piece by the French journalist Albert Wolff, and both editors place the den in question in Whitechapel rather than Shadwell.[16] But given that Wolff was not a native Londoner, that the editors were paraphrasing his details and that the two areas are contiguous, it is more than plausible that the location was the same, especially since the very small Chinese community in London at the time was concentrated in Shadwell and Limehouse rather than Whitechapel.[17] The den is again in a small ground-floor room and presided over by a Chinese host known only by the generic nickname 'Jack'. Although this room again features the unusual bed cum divan, there is also a second 'room' up a ladder through a crude hole in the ceiling.[18] It is possible either that the first den was slightly altered in the two years since the previous account or that this was in fact a second den. But several other accounts, most of them published between 1868 and 1875, concur much more closely in their details, and these reporters were not the only slummers drawn to the place they describe: several accounts assert that the Prince of Wales himself once smoked there.[19] Like the first establishment, this one is in New Court, but instead of occupying the ground floor it is up a set of stairs. The room is still dominated by a sheetless bed made up sideways with as many as half a dozen smokers reclining upon it, and the host is again a Chinese man, but clearly younger than Yahee and with an English wife who assists him in preparing the opium. His name sometimes varies from one account to another (his wife's is never given): he is known as Chi Ki, Osee or, most frequently, Johnson (obviously an English nick-name). Although the different Chinese names may indicate different individuals, it is at least as likely, given the concurrence of so many other details, that two reporters mistook different Chinese words for their host's name or that the language barrier thwarted accurate transcription. As one reporter admitted: 'I think I could do better with the monkey language, or Volapuk.'[20]

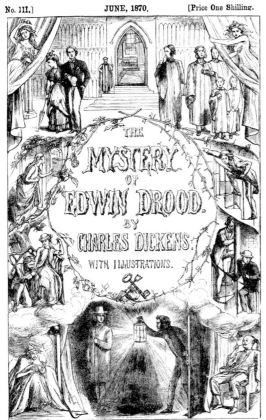

THE MYSTERY OF EDWIN DROOD. BY CHARLES DICKENS. WITH ILLUSTRATIONS.

LONDON: CHAPMAN & HALL, 193, PICCADILLY.
Advertisements to be sent to the Publishers, and ADAMS & FRANCIS, 59, Fleet Street, E.C.
[*The right of Translation is reserved.*]

Cover wrapper by Luke Fildes for monthly instalments of Dickens's *The Mystery of Edwin Drood*. The smoke from the opium pipes of the oriental characters in the lower corners frames and suffuses the other images.

Another common element among the accounts is the reporters' ambivalent fascination with the den's mixture of Asian men and English women, which leads – along with the mysteriously transformative influence of opium smoke – to a blending of racial identities. Several female regulars have acquired oriental nicknames such as 'Mother Addallah', 'Mrs Mohammed', 'China Emma', 'Calcutta Louisa' and 'Lascar Sally'. The opium master's wife, who 'is being gradually smoke-dried, and by and by will present the appearance of an Egyptian mummy', has 'a marvellous grafting of Chinese about her . . . Her skin was dusky yellow . . . and evidently she had, since her marriage, taken such a thoroughly Chinese

view of life that her organs of vision were fast losing their European shape.'[21] Most engrossing of all these hybridized women, however, is the English proprietress of a den across the court from Johnson's. Usually referred to as Lascar Sal,[22] she became a celebrity in her own right after Dickens used her den as a model for a setting in his last novel, *The Mystery of Edwin Drood*. She first appeared in an article published shortly after the novelist's death in 1870 and soon became a fixture.[23] Although she is often represented alone, she apparently had a Lascar husband and spoke Hindi and Hindustani. It is this familiarity with Asian culture that she blames for her seduction into opium smoking, claiming she 'used to be with those that spoke them, and one would say to her "Have a whiff", and another would say to her "Have a whiff", and she knew no better, and so she got into the habit, and now she cannot leave it off.'[24] Some reporters found her a more sympathetic and 'much more intelligent' figure than Johnson across the court, while others recoiled from her 'canting whine' or face in which 'it was difficult to see any humanity'.[25]

Dickens's version of Lascar Sal and her establishment brought the opium den into mainstream popular fiction, perpetuating several of the journalistic conventions and introducing some new ones for the next generation.[26] In the opening scene of *The Mystery of Edwin Drood*, an English choirmaster

'In the Court' by Luke Fildes for Dickens's *The Mystery of Edwin Drood* (1870). The Englishman on the right, having just awakened from a night of opium smoking in this East End den, mirrors the posture of the Lascar on the bed.

THE OPIUM SMOKER.

'The Opium Smoker' from Richard Rowe's *Saturday Night at the East End* (1870), the earliest graphic depiction of an English smoker caught in the act. Note his Asiatic features.

awakens in an opium den to the 'querulous rattling whisper' of his cockney hostess, who 'has opium-smoked herself into a strange likeness of the China-man' lying across the bed beside him. As he looks upon her and her Chinese and Lascar customers, 'some contagion in them seizes upon him ... until he has got the better of this unclean spirit of imitation'.[27] How successfully he has conquered the contagion is open to question, because the novel was left unfinished when Dickens died. But it is at least certain that the choirmaster takes his opium habit from the East End den back to his cathedral town, where he is a menacing figure who appears to have murdered his nephew. These sinister qualities are implicitly linked with opium's influence and the Arabian Nights-like violence of his opening visions, filled with 'ten thousand scimitars' and 'a rusty spike ... for the impaling of a horde of Turkish robbers'.[28]

Once *Edwin Drood* introduced the opium den as the portal between the halves of a middle-class Victorian's double existence, it became a stock motif of the burgeoning secret life genre. It appeared again most notably in two popular fictions of a generation later, Oscar Wilde's *The Picture of Dorian Gray* and Arthur Conan Doyle's Sherlock Holmes tale 'The Man with the Twisted Lip', both published in 1891.[29] Dorian Gray goes on secret binges of dissipation in 'dreadful places near Blue Gate Fields', most explic-

itly 'opium-dens, where one could buy oblivion, dens of horror where the memory of old sins could be destroyed by the madness of sins that were new'.[30] After travelling labyrinthine streets beneath the shadows of ships' masts, Dorian gives 'a peculiar knock' and is admitted into a veritable shopping mall of vice, where animalistic Malays gamble next to a garish bar lined with prostitutes.

> At the end of the room there was a little staircase, leading to a darkened chamber. As Dorian hurried up the steps, the heavy odour of opium met him. His nostrils quivered with pleasure ... Dorian winced, and looked round at the grotesque things that lay in such fantastic postures on the ragged mattresses. The twisted limbs, the gaping mouths, the staring lustreless eyes, fascinated him. He knew in what strange heavens they were suffering, and what dull hells were teaching them the secret of some new joy.[31]

Wilde's vivid and influential portrait of the den is all the more impressive given the improbability that he ever visited such a place (indeed Dickens may well have been the first and last fiction writer to draw his scene from direct observation). Nonetheless, the scandal caused by the novel – and the even greater scandal of Wilde's conviction a few years later for leading a secret, illegal life – helped to cement the opium den's image as the destroyer of seemingly respectable West Enders.

Doyle's den, in 'a vile alley lurking behind the high wharves which line the north side of the river to the east of London Bridge', seems to owe much to Wilde's, with its 'bodies lying in strange fantastic poses ... with here and there a dark, lack-lustre eye'.[32] Again it is the conduit between middle-class respectability and a secret East End existence for several characters including Sherlock Holmes him-self, who first appears in the story as a disguised patron of the den. Its effect, however, is more pernicious on two other characters. One is Watson's otherwise respectable acquaintance Isa Whitney, whom the good doctor rescues from an extended

Slummers and other gawkers look on as a serene Lascar prepares to smoke in an East End opium den, from Gustave Doré's *London: A Pilgrimage* (1872).

debauch. The other is Neville St Clair, a seemingly upright man of finance who actually funds his comfortable suburban family life by begging daily in the city after changing into his cadger's costume in the opium den. Doyle thus cleverly inverts a recurrent trope of the earlier magazine accounts, the repeated emphasis on the writers' careful donning of slumming costume *before* visiting the den. He also suggests that the opium den's insidious influence extends beyond the darkest East End to the very heart of English domestic life, a pattern reinforced by the striking resemblance between opium smoking and the strange ritual that Holmes enacts in St Clair's Kentish home. Having 'perched himself cross-legged' upon 'a sort of Eastern divan' made of sofa pillows, Holmes sits with 'an old brier pipe between his lips, his eyes fixed vacantly upon the corner of the ceiling, the blue smoke curling up from him' until 'the room [is] full of a dense tobacco haze'.[33] Doyle's den is also the first to be associated with a Moriarty-like criminal underground and to feature 'a trap-door at the back . . . which could tell some strange tales of what has passed through it upon the moonless nights',[34] points that resurface notably in the Fu Manchu novels.

Between the appearance of Wilde's novel and Doyle's short story came a piece in the *Strand Magazine* in which the reporter, John Coulson Kernahan, emphasized the predatory nature of the den's occupants, including 'a partly naked Malay of decidedly evil aspect, who . . . coiled himself up in the recesses of a dark corner, whence he lay furtively watching me'; the Chinese host with 'so evil a look upon his parchment-coloured features, and . . . small and cunning eyes'; and an attractive Englishwoman, who 'examined me so critically and searchingly from head to foot that I fancied once or twice I could see the row of figures she was inwardly casting up'.[35] In the last decade of the nineteenth century, the trend was clearly toward a more trepidant view of opium dens. There were fewer representations published at the turn of the twentieth century and these differed in their assessments of both the number of dens and their moral implications. One reporter asserts that

'A Malay', from *The Strand Magazine* (1891). The threatening Malay has a well-established lineage in the nineteenth-century opium-and-Orient tradition, hearkening back to Thomas De Quincey's reference in his *Confessions of an English Opium-Eater* (1821) to a Malay who visited his cottage and was afterward 'a fearful enemy for months' in his dreams.

'they used to be far more numerous than they are to-day . . . The days when the opium dens flourished and waxed rich were some fifty years ago', while another claims direct knowledge of six dens and fervently hopes 'that the local authorities will endeavour to stamp out this abominable opium-traffic in the East End of London without delay'.[36] But when Sax Rohmer took up the motif, the opium den emerged again firmly along the lines that Sherlock Holmes had sketched: as the sinister tool of an oriental underground.

Such quasi-hysteria has roots in several familiar fears that often accompany rises in immigration. Although England's population of Chinese and Indian immigrants was still relatively low before the First World War, it was clearly on the rise. Looking at the precedent of mass Chinese immigration to San Francisco, many Britons feared that they were 'in danger of being invaded by the "Heathen Chinese", not in his hundreds but in his tens of thousands' and that the common worker would 'be ruined by the competition of cheap Chinese labour' as well as lose his sweetheart to one of these supposedly

'In the Den', an illustration in *The Strand Magazine* (1891).

miscegenate competitors.[37] Thus full-fledged conspiracy scenarios such as Rohmer's touched a nerve, whatever their relationship to verifiable truth. Such anxieties were super-charged by the connection with opium, which had long been surrounded by fears that the Chinese would eventually seek revenge for Britain's having twice forced its own opium upon China from the helm of a gunboat. Although reports of existing opium dens declined with the Second World War, the idea of a vast network of such establishments in London's East End remains one of the most enduring myths about Victorian and Edwardian England.

Smoking and Sociability

MATTHEW HILTON

Ask any smoker why they smoke and the vast majority will answer that they started 'just to be sociable'. Sharing, offering and accepting a cigarette are some of the most visible formative rituals in the social development of about half the population of the Western world. Who really learns to smoke on their own? For the most part, we start to smoke because our friends and peers do. Smoking allows the young to 'join in', to demonstrate their arrival in the outside public world. Before the onset of addiction, habituation or even the knowledge of the joys of appreciating a cigarette by oneself, smoking is an act performed in a group. It is a compelling ritual. How many former smokers are there who will admit to having smoked only when young – in cafés and bars, pubs and restaurants – just to fit in?

Yet for all the social pressures to smoke, our image of the smoker is dominated by the great individualist icons of the twentieth century. When we think of 'the smoker' we think of Humphrey Bogart, Marlene Dietrich, Lauren Bacall and all the other cinema stars of Hollywood's golden age. Their smoking added to their allure, the exhaled wisps curling and framing their dimly lit portraits. We remember them as loners and individualists, tough guys and bad guys straight from the pages of a detective novel by Raymond Chandler. The curtain of smoke they created between themselves and the camera signified their aloofness from the world, their separateness from the rules and conventions of society and culture. Smoking established these characters as complete selves – they neither desired

nor required the company of others to confirm their identities. The tradition is encapsulated in an advertisement of 1959 that drew on the Bogart image and the *film-noir* aesthetic: 'You're never alone with a strand'. But this individualism is apparent also in a more aggressive iconography, in the images of the rugged cowboy of Marlboro country. And so too do we see it in a philosophical and intellectual context – what better way to visualize existentialism than with an image of Jean-Paul Sartre or Albert Camus smoking in a Parisian street or café?

The images and pleasures of smoking alone are not confined to the twentieth century. Charles Kingsley wrote that tobacco was 'a lone man's companion, a bachelor's friend, a hungry man's food, a sad man's cordial, a wakeful man's sleep, and a chilly man's fire'.[1] And, for Lord Byron, 'sublime tobacco' was a vital part of romantic self-expression.[2] In the second half of the nineteenth century smoking was celebrated as the embodiment of the individuality of the bourgeois gentlemanly amateur. In poetry, in the periodical press and in literary works such as J. M. Barrie's *My Lady Nicotine* (1890), odes and hymns were written and sung to tobacco, with each smoker simultaneously developing a distinctive mannerism in smoking culture.[3] As props to their smoking idiosyncrasies, devotees collected 'the paraphernalia of smokiania', including clay pipes, briar pipes, meerschaums, churchwardens, pipe cleaners, matches, cigar holders, cigar cases, ashtrays, pipe-lights, spills, spittoons, tobacco pouches, storage jars, snuff boxes and pipe racks, as well as

Marlene Dietrich in
a 1932 Paramount
Pictures photograph.

Humphrey Bogart
in a still from John
Houston's 1941 film
The Maltese Falcon.

their favourite smoking armchairs, tables, slippers, jackets and even hats. Most famously, Sherlock Holmes emerged as one of the greatest – and most individual – of all smokers. This most singular detective smoked the 'strongest shag' in an 'old and oily clay pipe', kept his tobacco in the toe-end of a Persian slipper, and was known to smoke 'all the plugs and dottles left from his smokes of the day before' for his before-breakfast pipe.[4] Even when the mass market substituted this diverse range of pipes and cigars with the standardized cigarette, smokers still constructed their self-identities and self-images through what was in practice an increasingly homogenous habit. So predominant has this individualist position become that confirmed smokers often imagine their own smoking histories as long processes of individual self-development. Eulogies to the weed continue to this day, with smokers ultimately seeing their enjoyment of this leisure pursuit as an individual rather than collective pleasure.

Yet the beauty of smoking is its adaptability to a variety of uses. It can act as a sedative, a stimulant, a soother of nerves, a relaxant, a retreat from the world and yet also a signifier of social cohesion. One can smoke purely for the enjoyment of the tobacco but, more often, one smokes to complement the multitude of other experiences encountered in work and popular culture. As the advertising for one cigarette proclaimed: 'Whatever the pleasure, Player's completes it.' The cigarettes and pipes smoked alone might be the ones remembered, provoking the thoughts and reflections that later seem central to the smoker's identity, but most tobacco is consumed in a social setting. Smoking together, then, is just as much fun as smoking alone.

The Victorians were great public and fraternal smokers. Despite the spatial escape that a pipe might afford through the retreat of a gentleman into his study – or even the temporal escape enjoyed by a lover of the weed while allowing his imagination to meander in unison with the patterns of smoke drifting from his pipe – tobacco permitted men to meet, converse and bond. 'Smoking concerts' were

The great detective.

a typical and regular event in the calendars of nineteenth-century voluntary associations. After sporting events, at annual conventions of trade associations and philanthropic organizations, or following meetings of civic dignitaries or members of chambers of commerce, men would dine, drink and smoke in private function rooms and public halls. It was to these men that an expanding periodical press was targeted, and for whom the short 'whiffs' or articles recounting the history of tobacco would be written. Readers were told of the great smoking companions of the past, from the sharing of pipes in Native American culture to tobacco's royal patrons in the seventeenth century. The literary circles of Alexander Pope, Jonathan Swift, Bolingbroke, Joseph Addison and William Congreve would be invoked to recreate the spirit of the eighteenth-century coffee house, and in the early nineteenth century the popularity of the cigar would be explained through the conviviality of the officer's mess. This was a culture not confined to

Cope's Tobaccos: *The Peerless Pilgrimage to Saint Nicotine of the Holy Herb.*

connoisseurs. Commercial companies sought to encourage a wider 'brotherhood of tobacco'. Most famously, Cope Brothers of Liverpool issued a series of cards, posters and calendars that featured illustrations of famous literary, cultural and political figures of the day. One such poster, released in 1878, was entitled *The Peerless Pilgrimage to Saint Nicotine of the Holy Herb*, and featured 65 Victorian celebrities travelling, like Chaucer's pilgrims, to worship at the shrine of tobacco'.[5] Another was entitled *The Pursuit of Diva Nicotina* and featured 30 characters in a style copied from Sir Noel Paton's painting, *The Pursuit of Pleasure*. An accompanying key plate was published along with the poster so that smokers could verify that the worshippers included William Morris, Canon Farrar, Lord Lytton, Lillie Langtry, Sir Stafford Northcote, Bismarck and the Emperor of Austria, collectively described as 'ardent votaries in ecstatic pursuit of our most gracious and glorious DIVA NICOTINA.'[6]

For the leisured bourgeois gentleman, however, the most glorified place of smoking companionship was the gentleman's club. The club was mytholo-

gized as an idealized smoking utopia of rest, meditation, loungeful conversation and, most of all, sheer dedicated concentration on the joys of one's cigar. Men came here to be solely in the presence of other men and their pipes or cigars. As the novelist Marie Louise de la Ramée put it in 1867:

> . . . that chamber of liberty, that sanctuary of the persecuted, that temple of refuge, thrice blessed in all its forms throughout the land, that consecrated Mecca of every true believer in the divinity of the meerschaum, and the paradise of the narghilé – the smoking-room.[7]

For less affluent smokers, a comparable smoking arcadia was found in the public house. Here, working men smoked a great variety of loose tobaccos in clay pipes, the names of which ranged from the 'alderman' and the longer 'churchwarden' of rural England, to the 'cutty' of Scotland and the 'dudeen' of Ireland.[8] The more intricately moulded pipes cost around one penny each, but most people were able to obtain their short clays free of charge from the public house. In 1896 *Tobacco Trade Review* estimated

The smoking room at the club.

that each publican gave away 'eighty to one hundred gross of pipes per annum (11,520–14,400)'.[9] This association of drink with tobacco is keenly reflected in the literature of the period, but it suggests also that smoking played a strong communal role in the life of ordinary working men. The fact that pipes were given away free further suggests the importance of hospitality in the smoking ritual, the publican now more formally taking the place of the private citizen of an older custom in which pipes would be given out ready to enjoy a shared smoking experience. It is a phenomenon noted in Wilkie Collins's *The Moonstone* (1868): on both occasions that Gabriel Betteridge takes visitors to Cobb Hole, a small country cottage, 'good Mrs Yolland performed a social ceremony strictly reserved for strangers of distinction. She put a bottle of Dutch gin and a couple of clean pipes on the table, and opened the conversation by saying, "What news from London, Sir?"'.[10]

What men put in their pipes differed by region and by type of work, depending on the local collective customs. 'Shag' (finely cut loose tobacco) was popular in the Eastern counties, South Wales and Monmouthshire, while Birdseye (so called because of the appearance of the finely cut stems) was enjoyed in Yorkshire. Rolls and thick twists such as 'nailrod' were smoked extensively in Ireland and the North of England. Roll was convenient and cheap for the working man; it did not require much manipulation before it was ready for the pipe in comparison to cake (pressed) tobacco; and it had a

certain versatility in that it could be simply bitten off and chewed if that method of tobacco consumption was preferred. Flake (slices of 'cake cavendish') was slightly more expensive since it was made of high-quality fine gold Virginia leaf and was popular among the better-paid clerks and tradesmen. Elsewhere, differences in taste seemed to be a product of one's work. Scottish miners were renowned for the high levels of consumption when on strike; Welsh miners were noted for their preferences for strong shags and rolls, dock labourers for their taste for thick twists and London cabmen for Irish roll. In jobs where smoking was not allowed, especially in the cotton and textile mills of Lancashire and Yorkshire, snuff continued to be commonly used – by women as well as men – as were varieties of chewing tobaccos that were also commonly used by miners when at the coal surface.[11]

The arrival of the mass-manufactured cigarette from the mid-1880s led to a revolution in smoking patterns, but the communal and social elements of the tobacco habit persisted. For juveniles, cheap Woodbines, selling at five for one penny, became symbols of adulthood, with boys often sharing what was an illicit pleasure for the under-16s from 1908. Gangs of youths would proclaim their entry into the world of work through the public smoking of cigarettes in the street, a phenomenon widely commented on and condemned by the many urban social investigators at the beginning of the twentieth century. The street became an arena for boys to assert precociously codes of masculinity that made them appear as a 'a species of man-child', 'overwhelmed by the feverish anxiety to become a man'.[12] The cigarette became a ritualistic communicator of the boy labourer's new social and economic position: 'The choice [of work] once made, . . . the boy very soon falls into the routine of work and in the first fortnight ages rapidly. Hitherto the smoking of cigarettes was a furtive prank, only delightful because forbidden; now it becomes a public exhibition, denoting manhood, independence, and wealth.'[13] The following passage, written by Alexander Paterson in 1911, provides some indication of the rituals that smoking boys would use to define themselves within the social world of the street gang:

> The great joy of the cigarette lies in the lighting of it, and in the first two whiffs. So much is the case that each one commonly lights his 'fag', draws in the smoke twice, inhaling deeply, breathes it out, spits, and says something, and then, holding his cigarette in his right hand, extinguishes it with the thumb and first finger of his left, and replaces it in the bottom right-hand pocket of his waistcoat. Ten minutes later the process will be repeated, and by this means, though the boy will seem always to be smoking, he will only consume a penny packet in a day.[14]

Such deliberately public methods of smoking – in which display was more important than taste or appreciation – continued into adulthood. In the late 1930s and '40s a team of social anthropologists called Mass-Observation investigated the smoking habits of the British working classes. It found that in pub-based culture the cigarette became an important tool in the public display of masculinity, either through bodily gesture or verbal communication. The proffering of cigarettes to friends and colleagues in the public house helped to define the group; it enclosed a community to the exclusion of non-smokers, and continued that public, communal mode of consumption associated with pre-industrial cultures, but which survived through and beyond the nineteenth century. Mass-Observation noted in particular an aggressively masculine culture among working-class smokers, where the very vocabulary built up around the ritual of smoking suggested a particular gender-based smoking identity:

> Smokers tend to talk of *pitching* and *throwing* the stub, rather than, more tamely, of *dropping* it; and quite often it is sent flying to some distance. Their actions, moreover, even more than their language, are frequently clothed in aggressiveness. Some speak of 'grinding', 'crushing', even 'killing' a stub, and a favourite trick is to burn it

to death in the fire or to drown it in the nearest available liquid. One man said: 'I cannot let a stub smoulder. I *must* crush it out.'[15]

Mass-Observation also interviewed dozens of smokers to discover why people start to smoke. Of smokers' own explanations for the initial introduction to the habit, social factors predominated – individual and psychological factors were more prominent when accounting for the maintenance of the subsequent habit. Smokers might mention tobacco's sedative or pharmacological effects, the tactility of the smoking ritual or even the visual aesthetics of the pipe, cigar or cigarette, but the importance of the social environment remained crucial. One smoker admitted to persisting with the habit for eight years in order to maintain an air of sociability, even though he had never actually enjoyed the taste of a cigarette. He also kept cigarettes to give out liberally to colleagues and new acquaintances in order to put everybody 'at their ease'. Another proffered cigarettes at 'that awkward moment when you have met a friend and enquiries to his welfare seem to have exhausted the conversational repertoire'.[16]

By the mid-twentieth century, cigarette smokers made up the majority of the population and advertisers sought to celebrate this great communal mass of tobacco lovers. Many would depict the world as a huge collective of smokers and feature crowd scenes at sporting events, the implication being that all were potential buyers of the particular cigarette. In the two World Wars, General Pershing of the US military recognized that tobacco supplies were more vital than those of food – cigarettes aided solidarity, morale and discipline.[17] The whole nation made a collective effort to support the great British smokers on the front line. Newspapers and traders ran campaigns to ensure that soldiers received cigarettes and tobacco in addition to the two-ounce weekly ration they received from the War Office. For instance, in the First World War *The People* called on its readers to send Woodbines – 'Tommy's favourite fag' – in bulk at prices as low as ten for

In the two world wars, the American General Pershing recognized that tobacco supplies were more vital than those of food – cigarettes aided solidarity, morale and discipline.

one penny, or else to contribute to their massively subscribed 'Tobacco Fund'.[18] Cigarettes helped to win the war for the nation and the two World Wars made Britain a nation of smokers. By the end of the 1940s, around four-fifths of adult men and two-fifths of adult women regularly smoked tobacco.[19]

It was this enormous collective smoking consciousness that commentators attempted to mobilize against the health scares linking cigarettes with lung cancer and heart disease in the 1950s and '60s. Cancer made smokers more aware of their identity as smokers. Writing in the *Daily Express*, Chapman Pincher attacked the medical establishment for seeking to destroy what he thought a harmless pleasure. He thought the Government and the Royal College of Physicians guilty of overbearing paternalism, their statements representing a major 'blow to freedom'. He called on smokers to unite in defiance against the 'interfering medics'[20] and was supported by many other commentators who appeared pleased to observe continued high smoking rates: 'the British don't scare easily', one proud journalist announced.[21] J. B. Priestley, too, worried about the implications of the health scare on the smoking community, fearing that it might even affect pipe smokers and lead to the sad cultural demise of the briar pipe, which had become the 'tribal badge' of the stoical, solid, common-sensical Englishman.[22]

But perhaps the most surprising consequences of the smoking and health scare were the new forms of sociability encouraged among smokers. The New Year immediately following the publication of the Royal College's report in 1962 gave birth to a new culture of 'giving up'. Smokers helped, cajoled and supported friends' and colleagues' efforts to quit, while they were ready to forgive and forget the failed attempts. In 1971 several *Daily Mirror* journalists tried to stop smoking at the same time, each experimenting with different stop-smoking devices. The newspaper reported on their progress every few days, inviting its readers to empathize with this new club of non-smokers.[23] Stopping smoking was an activity to be shared and was presented in the *Mirror* as almost a lifestyle choice in itself, as divorced from the health aspects of tobacco as much as Andy Capp's persistent 'drooper' cigarette. When some of the journalists admitted defeat and began smoking again their failure was reported with humour and high spirits as an understandable cycle that all smokers go through.

Today, a number of commentators have imagined a new smoker, that of the lone individual, the new rebel arising from the dark backstreets behind the gloss and shine of the chrome-plated shopping malls of the West's health-obsessed consumer culture. Here, they draw on that individualist tradition epitomized by Bogart and Bacall. But the flip side of the analysis is that the new smoking environment – of restrictions in public, of the exaggerated dangers of passive smoking, of warped assessments of the

Andy Capp, a famous British working-class cartoon character.

costs of smoking to national health services – draws as much on the persistent cultures of sociability and smoking. There is a new Marlboro land, not of lonesome cowboys, but of social-spirited urbanites, united against the perceived strictures of public health.

For a leisure-good whose use is so adaptable and diverse, a core identity among its users is difficult to establish. Fortunately, anti-smokers have always helped smokers to feel a part of a sociable and recognizable group. In the nineteenth century, a small group of radical temperance reformers created an Anti-Tobacco Society that frequently issued tracts against smokers and smoking. For the Cope's tobacco company, this was further propaganda material for its own cause. In *The Pursuit of Diva Nicotina*, tobacco's admirers are so eager to reach the holy herb that the anti-tobacco figures of the Revd John Kirk, Dr Charles Drysdale and Professor F. W. Newman are trampled underfoot. Above, in the clouds, is the 'denouncer of doom' with his 'umbrella of cant'. Other posters depicted an anti-smoker pointlessly lecturing to a group of pipe-smoking storks, herons, penguins and flamingos, and falling over roller-skating whilst others were clearly enjoying themselves. In *Cope's Tobacco Plant*, a long-running campaign mocked the dire financial situation of the movement, the manufacturers cheekily offering the society's leader, Thomas Reynolds, a testimonial of £1,000 if he would stop publishing the *Anti-Tobacco Journal*.[24] Later, so confident were they of the strength of their own position over the supposedly hysterical rantings of the anti-tobacconists that they offered to devote a page of each issue of *Cope's Tobacco Plant* to the anti-smoking cause. They suggested that Reynolds was his own worst enemy; they parodied his *Anti-Tobacco Journal* articles; and even proposed the setting up of an 'Anti-Teapot Society' to suggest the pointlessness of his task. Reynolds never rose to the bait, but had he done so he would at least have found himself communicating with a larger number of people than he had ever done before.

Today, the anti-smoking movement has much stronger support and a body of scientific evidence

Cope's anti-smoker lectures on and on.

behind it that gives its statement far greater authority. But this has not meant that the movement has been entirely successful, and up to a third of the adult population still continues to smoke in full knowledge of the widely publicized dangers of smoking. The new sociability of smokers is a product of both positive and negative factors. The negative are the reactions to the increased anti-smoking activity among public health officials and legislators. But the positive emerge from associations long-since acknowledged by the medical establishment. In 1958, just as the *Lancet* came to accept a causal link between smoking and lung cancer, one feature explained that smokers were 'restless, energetic, impulsive, independent, interesting men, ardent in the pursuit of enterprises which appealed to them, and seeking service during the war with combat units'. In contrast, non-smokers were 'bland, steady, dependable, hard-working, rather uncommunicative family men who tended during the war to gravitate to specialised non-combat units'.[25] Today, smokers might now be cold and wet, having been forced to smoke outside their offices, but at least they know what the *Lancet* knew nearly 50 years ago: smokers are better people. No wonder that smokers continue to smoke together.

Havana Cigars and the West's Imagination

JEAN STUBBS

> Smoking a Havana is universally recognised
> as a supreme form of pleasurable indulgence . . .[1]

In 1997, at the height of the 1990s cigar hype, the US magazine *Newsweek* ran two cigar features entitled 'Blowing Smoke' and 'Cool Fools'.[2] The latter addressed the Gen X market for hip imagery designer clothes, drinks, coffee and cigars. The former read:

> Cigars are smelly, expensive, and bad for you. They're also the hottest things going, as celebs, models and just plain folks-with-smokes fire up the trend. How could this happen? . . . You'd never guess it, but there are actually a few Americans left who've never smoked a cigar. Maybe you're even one of them.[3]

Well, I'm not an American, but I was one who had never smoked a cigar, until, that is, January 2001 in Cuba, down on the farm, in Vuelta Abajo, a mecca for any cigar connoisseur. Harvest in full swing, octogenarian grower Alejandro Robaina – who now has his own Vegas Robaina cigars and was voted Havana Cigar Man of the Year[4] – offered me a cigar rolled with his leaf. As we talked and rocked on his veranda, he autographed another in silver for me – the cigar historian – to keep. Later I purchased a metal canister (my own special humidor) from the *Casa del Habano* (Havana cigar shop) adjacent to the cigar factory in the neighbouring town of Pinar del Río, and now display it proudly on the bookshelf in my study at home. I haven't smoked since, but my addiction to researching and writing about Cuban tobacco continues unabated.

The supreme cigar experience is a visit to Cuba in January or February, to the green rolling fields of sun-grown tobacco or the sea of white cheese-cloth over shade-grown tobacco in Vuelta Abajo. Havana, however, is the city of the cigar, bringing in special cigar-lover trips and coveted revenue from tourists avid to buy at a fraction of the cost abroad. The 1990s cigar hype brought the paradox of quantity versus quality, since cigar tobacco was grown in less well-suited areas; young workers were crash-trained; and quality export brands – Cohiba Siglo III, Hoyo de Monterrey Double Corona, Montecristo A, Partagás, Ramón Allones Gigantes or the new Trinidad and Cuaba – were made in non-export factories outside Havana. This has now abated, and connoisseurs and neophtyes alike whiff the past at the old Partagás factory by the Capitol building in Havana or the recently refurbished cigar hotel, Conde de Villanueva Hostal del Habano, which are caught up in what one recently retired Cuban cigar expert has described as belonging to:

> the world of MAGICAL REALISM, as defined by the great Cuban and universal writer Alejo Carpentier to speak of Latin American cultures in which the Havana cigar is inscribed. The REALISM is that of the agricultural and industrial workers who fashion the leaf of Vuelta Abajo, Partido and other parts of Cuba in combination with the climate, winds and sun characteristic of these, the islands tobacco regions . . . The MAGICAL is

in its hedonism, its sublime gift to the smoker's palate . . .[5]

HAVANA MAGIC

The Cubans know cigars. When they spin a long yarn, they are said to be *contando la historia del tabaco en dos tomos*, telling the two-volume story of tobacco. Tobacco is clearly that important to the island and its people, and, of all its tobacco products, the cigar has reached mythical proportions: long considered the best in the world, and long imitated elsewhere. The early cigar belonged to the Amerindians, but, from the conquest of Columbus in 1492, the story became one of swashbuckling piracy, contraband and uprisings against Spanish colonial monopoly. Highly lucrative, the cigar was prey to German, British, French and North American capital, part of a nineteenth- and twentieth-century world cigar-tobacco economy whose tobacco blends were produced as far afield as Cameroon, Turkey, Java and Sumatra, and whose main markets were London, Amsterdam, Bremen and New York. The cigar was also at the heart of major political upheavals, exile communities and rival economies, from 1868 with the outbreak of Cuba's first War of Independence with Spain, through the Cuban Revolution of 1959 and the 1990s cigar hype.

The world mystique of the Havana cigar started more than five centuries ago, when Spanish envoys chronicled men with firebrands in their hands. Columbus, his eyes set on gold, attached no import-ance to this, although the indigenous people clearly did, calling it *tabacco*. The Cuban ethnographer Fernando Ortiz[6] would later delight in tobacco as the Indian's inseparable companion, part of mythology, religion, magic, medicine, ceremonies, collective stimulation, public and private customs, as well as politics and wars. For slaves from Africa transported to Cuba as human cargo, it was both profane and sacred – and it is still important today in Afro-Cuban religions. Tobacco travelled from the New to the Old World and back as one of modern history's commodities. In the case of Cuba, the

Gold-embossed 19th-century Havana cigar label depicting the palatial Calixto Lopez factory.

form observed by Columbus became *the* luxury smoke of the nineteenth and twentieth centuries: what in Cuba came to be popularly known in Spanish as a *tabaco* or *puro* (which literally translate as tobacco and pure), but more so *El Habano* (taking its name from Havana, home of the palatial factories producing cigars for the world's nobility) – the Havana cigar or simply Havana.

An iconography of cigar culture emerged and became fertile terrain for invented traditions, imagined communities and cultural contestations. Late nineteenth-century visual imagination was fired by tobacco art, from the cigar-smoking woman healer immortalized in Victor Patricio Landaluze's engravings to the splendid gold-embossed cigar labels on which chromolithography permitted the brilliant use of colours on an unprecedented scale.[7]

Writing on Florida's late nineteenth-century domestic 'clear Havana' industry, the historian L. Glenn Westfall commented: 'Cigars became synonymous with status, a barometer of a male's success and affluence . . . sales were augmented with more sophisticated printing techniques . . . manufacturers promoted brands and pictorial themes of a Spanish nature.'[8] The Spanish theme lost popularity in the 1920s in the United States with the rise of mass-produced, machine-made cigars, but made a comeback in the late twentieth century.

The cigar boom of the 1990s has been attributed in no small measure to the market-driven engineering of the New York-founded glossy *Cigar Aficionado*, first published in 1992 and edited by Marvin Shanken. The magazine has symbolized above all cigar smokers' anti-anti-smoking crusade. As one New Yorker expressed it in the very first issue:

> Each evening after dinner, accompanied by my two dogs, I stroll into Park Avenue to walk my cigar. Too many of my friends . . . have been swayed in recent years by the insidious campaign against cigar smoking, and this . . . has made me defensive at times, argumentative, even an activist against America's anti-smoking lobby . . .[9]

He went on to reminisce about Winston Churchill's waving to the crowds in the 1940s, with his 'Havana cigar (he even has a type of cigar named after him), 1950s public tolerance and respect for the fashion of cigar smoking among male members of the power elite, and the early 1960s Kennedy puffing a favourite Havana'. He ended: 'When America is not fighting a war, the puritanical desire to punish people has to be let out at home.'[10]

A year later, a Shanken editorial entitled 'Rise Up' clamoured: 'Cigar smokers are being recognized for something more than a scorned, isolated minority . . . Let the world understand how potent a force we can be.'[11] It was accompanied by a cartoon strip on the stigma attached to cigar-smoking pariahs, the greatest pariah of all being a Castro-like figure (see below). Castro might have given up smoking a decade earlier, but he was still the ultimate prohibition icon. He had, after all, been the target of failed CIA assassination attempts during the early 1960s that included a poisoned cigar, after which he had smoked only top-security Cohiba cigars rolled personally for him. Subsequent cover features, however, made it clear that the right to smoke included island Havanas, doubly attractive because they are illegal in the United States under Washington's 40-year trade embargo on Cuba. Despite issues over the years promoting cigar smoking among women, *Cigar Aficionado* is subtitled 'the good life magazine for men' and carries sensual, if not to say overtly sexual, ads – including a modern-day Miami-vice Carmen suggestive of cigars still being rolled on young women's thighs. *Cigar Aficionado* circulation has soared, and the web-based revolution ushered in www.cigaraficionado.com, complete with its 'Hall of Fame' and 'Cigar Stars', which honoured those leading the industry through its 1990s boom.

CIGAR COOL

A *Newsweek* feature in 1997[12] contained an inset: 'Will Cigars Stay Hot? How To Track the Trend'. The subheading ran: 'All trends – cigars, Rollerblades, tattoos – move through predictable stages of cool,

The ultimate cigar pariah: Fidel Castro, in a cartoon by 'Shoe' from a 1993–4 issue of *Cigar Aficionado*.

Miami-vice advertising: a modern-day Carmen rolling cigars on her thighs – a photo from *Cigar Aficionado*.

according to Lawrence Samuel of marketing consultants Iconoculture, Inc. Once mainstream, trends either die, mutate into microtrends or cement into national pastimes.'[13] Four stages are identified, from Fringe (pre-cool), through Trendy (cool) and Mainstream (post-cool), to Mutation (neo-cool). The pre-cool bankers, investors and lawyers of pre-1995 flout political correctness at smoke-out cigar nights; the cool yuppies, gender-benders and college students of 1995 puff up circulation of *Cigar Aficionado* (for boomers) and smoke (Gen X) in cigar bars and smoke-friendly eateries; post-cool Corporate America of 1996 cashes in, and Joe and Jane in Dockers lure 'nice-vice' cigars into suburbia; and in 1997 neo-cool down-town kids and smugglers of illegal Cubans produce backlash variations. US cigar sales would recede the following year, but elsewhere cigars, especially those from Cuba, held their own. In 1998 the UK journal *Economist* ran an article entitled: 'Cuban Cigars: Let the Good Times Roll':

> After Fidel Castro gave up smoking cigars in 1985, so did the rest of the world . . . It looked as though the Cuban industry would be stubbed out . . . But it has made a comeback. Cigars are an eloquent accessory for the rich, and there is a backlash against political correctness that has made smoking in public virtually impossible

in America and increasingly so in Europe. Libertarians (and libertines) are uniting in bars the world over.[14]

Havana cigar events became *de rigeur*. As reported in the *Cuban Review* of April 1997, a 700-strong gathering, from more than 40 countries, including 137 Americans defying US restrictions, thronged the famous Tropicana Cabaret for a gala dinner attended by Fidel Castro.[15]

CIGAR CITIES

The processes that originated in Cuba are emulated in cigars crafted outside of the country. 'A premium cigar', declared Mark Stucklin, 'is one that is made entirely by hand using whole and intact leaves for filler – only in Cuba [is] that bunching of the filler done by hand as opposed to a bunching device . . . To Cuba, more than anywhere we owe the development . . . of the long-filler handmade cigar . . .'.[16] Beyond Cuba, standard practice required cheaper cigars – known as stogies in the US – to be stuffed with a short filler of shredded tobacco and wrapped in a paper binder made from tobacco scraps pressed into a homogenous roll. Nonetheless, the quest for Cuban-quality cigars and leaf had led emigrés from the war-torn Cuba of the late nineteenth century and the revolutionary country of the late twentieth century to the surrounding Caribbean and Central America, but most of all Florida – from Key West, Tampa and Ybor City through what was once Marti City, where Ocala now stands, to Jacksonville, Tallahassee and Panhandle Gadsden County towns aptly named Amsterdam, Sumatra and Havana.

If Havana Cuba was cigar city, so in its time Key West was 'Cigar City USA' and Tampa (more specifically West Tampa and Ybor City) the 'Smoke Capital of the World'.[17] So linked were they that in 1892 the exiled independence leader José Martí sought in Tampa support for his Cuban Revolutionary Party. The most famous cigar ever rolled in Ybor City was smuggled into Cuba containing his order of 1895 for insurrection. Ybor City and Tampa may be ghosts of what they once were, but workers record a past of idealism, radicalism and nationalism – and also, it is all too often forgotten, a culture of smoking. An issue of the *Floridian* in 1972 described a good cigar of Ybor City as a 'burning brown torpedo full of history and romance and poetry', and wrote of one of the few remaining cigar makers, the 76-year-old Servando López:

> His eyes twinkle as he lights a cigar he's made. The sunlight filtering through the streaked windows bounces off his hair as he examines the even burn that is one of the signs of a fine cigar. He looks for the long ash, as would any connoisseur. López gets pleasure too from the old men who hobble in wearing shabby clothes, too poor to dress better but glad to hand over their centavos to buy the dignity of a fine cigar.[18]

Back in the mid-1980s – when cigar sales were at an all-time low and cigar mystique had become part of Hollywood nostalgia – local Tampa historians narrowly saved Ybor City from being razed to the ground by developers. Louis A. Pérez Jr interviewed José de la Cruz, who had left Cuba after a Havana cigar workers strike to arrive in Tampa in 1912 and later become an organizer of the great strike of 1931. To quote from an article that Pérez wrote, in which De la Cruz recounts the passions of the 1920s and '30s:

> a long silence came between us as Don José sent a billow of shapeless gray-white smoke rising to the ceiling. Moments passed as he proceeded to chase the lingering smoke away with the halfhearted pendulum swings of an arm heavy with age . . . 'We won, you know. I know what history is going to say . . . but I want *you* to know that it is not so.'[19]

The post-1959 successes of emigré growers, manufacturers and, to a lesser extent, workers came to pose a serious 'offshore Havana' challenge to the island Havana of post-1989 crisis-ridden Cuba. As its backer, the Soviet Union, disintegrated, so its enemy, the United States, tightened the noose – just when the cigar revival was beginning. In 1995 the Cuban-American writer Gustavo Pérez-Firmat wrote:

> Exiles live by substitution. If you can't have it in Havana, make it in Miami . . . Life in exile; memory enhanced by imagination. Like Don Quijote, every exile is an apostle of the imagination, someone who invents a world more amenable to his ambitions and dreams. It is no accident that for every twenty years the most popular eatery in Little Havana . . . is all cigar smoke and mirrors.[20]

The media war heated up. In the Miami *El Nuevo Herald*, the aggrieved writer Martin Mendiola in his regular 'Puro Humo' column declared: 'When asked which are the best cigars in the world, most,

Che Guevara, 1960s icon of the Cuban revolution, often depicted smoking a cigar.

Cuba's other 1990s icon: Buena Vista Social Club's Compay Segundo.

including *Cigar Aficionado*, tell us they're the Cuban cigars . . . but we find that many of the Dominican, Honduran, Nicaraguan, Jamaican and Canary Island cigars are much better quality . . . possibly created by or learned from Cuban forebears.'[21] Young Miami Cuban Americans who launched the magazine *Generation ñ*, their version of Gen x, and who had grown up in anti-smoking Florida redis-covered the Cuban cigar. The cover of August 1997 shouted: 'Cigars . . . finally! Blood's thicker than water.'[22] They were to be seen frequenting the Biltmore Hotel, built in 1926 and resurrected in the 1990s, in Coral Gables, with its Cigar Salon, Friday night 'Cigars under the Stars' courtyard and black-tie cigar dinners. Cigar festivals sprang up anew in Key West; cigar-smoke shops linked arms with baseball; bric-a-brac memorabilia included Havana Roller Pens, Havana Choco Grande Cigars and Habaneros candles, accompanying the usual ash-trays, mugs and baseball caps.[23]

And so, out of the parallel production and marketing of identical or similar brands – that of the island which is served by and serves primarily European markets, and that which is offshore and is integrally structured into the us cigar industry – have grown economic, political and cultural contestations that are fertile terrain for invented traditions and imagined communities. Yet, to quote a Fort Lauderdale cigar bar entrepreneur: 'American culture is coming of age. We smoke fine cigars. We drink fine wine. American culture is growing and maturing.'[24] If this is the case, the chances are that there might be an end to the 40-year us embargo that has made smoking real Havanas an illicit pleasure.

A Century of *Kretek*

MARK HANUSZ

Imagine the scene: after suffering from chest pains for a few days you finally decide to get something done about it. So you walk to your neighbourhood drugstore and consult the pharmacist as to what he would recommend to relieve you of your ailment. He nods his head understandingly and walks back to where he keeps his medicine. After searching for a short time, he comes back and hands you a pack of cigarettes and tells you to smoke them three times a day for a week.

Now a prescription for cigarettes may seem highly unlikely in today's world where cigarettes are advertised as harmful to one's health, but about 100 years ago in a small town called Kudus in Central Java cigarettes were the most popular prescriptive to alleviate the common cough. These cigarettes were no ordinary cigarettes, however; they were the clove-spiced *kretek* that today are a ubiquitous feature in the lives of more than 200 million Indonesians.

Around 1880 a Kudus resident named Haji Jamahri (the honorific term *haji* is given to a Muslim who has made the obligatory pilgrimage to Mecca) was suffering from a mild case of asthma. To relieve his suffering, he rubbed clove oil (eugenol) on his chest. Eugenol has been used for centuries as an astringent – most commonly in modern-day dentistry. While this eased his pain somewhat, he wondered if it would be more efficacious to bring the healing powers of the cloves in closer contact with his troubled lungs. What would happen if he mixed the cloves with tobacco and smoked it?

According to the legend, he did precisely that and his coughing ceased at once. He began to distribute his product through the local *apotik* (pharmacies) and soon his *rokok cengkeh*, or clove cigarettes, were considered a cough remedy as much as today's cough syrup.

Around the turn of the twentieth century this new smoking sensation began to capture a wider audience – one that did not use the clove cigarettes as a remedy, but rather for the taste of the tobacco and clove mixture. It was about this time as well that the new product was renamed *kretek* (kreh-TEK), because of the pop and crackle that the cloves make when burned (keretek-keretek). While Haji Jamahri failed to grasp the commercial potential of his invention, another Kudus resident did. This man, Nitisemito, was the originator of the *kretek* industry.

Nitisemito was holding various odd jobs around Kudus when he noticed that more and more people were taking up the habit of smoking tobacco mixed with cloves. At that time, all *kretek* were hand-rolled and the ingredients were bought separately. Nitisemito, in a flash of inspiration, decided to mix the ingredients, package the result and sell it as a branded product. He experimented with several names but finally settled on Bal Tiga (three balls), and in 1906 he founded his company as Bal Tiga Nitisemito.

Nitisemito marketed and distributed his product in ways that were unique in the Netherlands Indies (as Indonesia was then called). He set up stands at every fair on Java to distribute his *kretek* as well as

Hand-rolling *kretek*.

prizes such as teapots, cigarette cases and even bicycles – all branded with the Nitisemito logo.

While conventional 'white' cigarettes (made by companies such as BAT and Faroka) were the smoke of choice for most consumers, the success of Bal Tiga led other entrepreneurs to set up companies around Kudus and other points on Java. Most *kretek* were wrapped in cornhusk, but two companies, Mari Kangen in Solo and HM Sampoerna in Surabaya, wrapped their *kretek* in paper. Even today, Dji Sam Soe by HM Sampoerna is one of the most popular branded products in Indonesia. Interestingly, on the back of each pack of Dji Sam Soe is a claim that its special mixture is anti-*batuk* (cough) – no doubt a throwback to the days when *kretek* were sold in pharmacies.

During the 1920s and '30s there was a rapid rise of *kretek* production, but they were unable to unseat

Porcelain bowl featuring a *kretek* pack at bottom.

Cigarettes on display in an Indonesian shop.

white cigarettes as the number one cigarette. *Kretek* were still regarded as the cigarette for the middle classes, while white cigarettes conferred style and prestige. The Second World War and the Japanese occupation halted most *kretek* production due to the scarcity of tobacco and cloves. Shortly after the end of the war and subsequent independence, Indonesia revived production.

It was not until the late 1960s and early 1970s that the status of *kretek* changed from just a spicy cigarette to that of a national icon. Three factors contributed to the rapid rise of *kretek* production and consumption – not just on the island of Java but throughout the archipelago. The first was the oil boom in the early 1970s, which resulted in a cash windfall in the Government's coffers and an upsurge in domestic industries (*kretek* leading the way). The second was the policy of transmigration – the forced relocation of residents from the over-populated areas of Java, Bali and Madura to the outer islands. As the transmigrants settled in their new homes, they brought their favourite brands of *kretek* with them and the *kretek* companies began supplying this new market. The last and perhaps most important factor was a Government decision to permit selected companies to purchase machines to automate the *kretek* manufacturing process. Up to that time, all *kretek* were rolled by hand and looked rustic when placed alongside the machine-made white cigarettes. All of this was about to

change when Bentoel in Malang bought the first machine to mass-produce *kretek* in 1968. A British manufacturer, Molins Machines, agreed to supply Bentoel with one machine to produce *kretek*, and the first machine-made *kretek*, Bentoel Biru International, appeared on the market in 1974.

To put the numbers in perspective, in 1974 cigarette production was as follows: hand-rolled *kretek*, 27 billion sticks; white cigarettes, 24 billion sticks; and machine-made *kretek* just 51 million sticks. Three years later, hand-rolled *kretek* production was 38 billion, white cigarettes 23 billion and machine-made *kretek* ballooned more than 4,000 per cent to 4 billion sticks. As other companies began to buy machines and develop their own brands, machine-made *kretek* production surpassed even its hand-rolled rival in 1985.[1]

By the end of the twentieth century, *kretek* commanded roughly 85–90 per cent of the entire cigarette market in Indonesia.[2] There are now more than 500 independent *kretek* manufacturers in Indonesia directly employing more than 180,000 people, and more than 10 million indirectly.[3] The industry is one of the largest sources of the Indonesian Government's excise revenue, and it is one of the only domestic industries to survive the recent financial crisis almost unscathed. It is one of Indonesia's most well known cultural signifiers with its distinctive scent greeting each visitor – and it all started 100 years ago.

Ganja in Jamaica

J. EDWARD CHAMBERLIN AND BARRY CHEVANNES

As a Jesuit in training in 1967, I received permission along with a fully trained priest to go and live among the poor. We found accommodation in a tenement yard, not exactly in Trench Town, but in the adjacent Rose Town. There I was befriended by a number of Rastafari men, one of whom invited me to a reasoning they were having early in the evening; many hadn't yet reached home from work. I was very cordially received by the group of a dozen or more men, sitting, 'kotching' on logs, boulders and other makeshift benches. At the appropriate time a quantity of ganja was prepared and the chalice lit, and as I was their honoured guest it was passed to me first. I received it and, emulating what I saw the brethren who lit it did, I held the cup in my left hand, placed the tube in the circle of my right thumb and index, and sucked. Nothing happened. I sucked again. Nothing. No glow, no popping of seeds. The host took the chalice back. He sucked and sucked. He gave the impression by his effort and body language – close inspection, holding up to the light – that he did not know what could possibly be wrong with the herbs, and no one suggested anything. He sent for more of the substance and started all over again. But as he prepared it I became aware of a consensus that I should be spared the chalice, and so someone else built a splif which he lit and gave to me, while the rest of the group passed the chalice around. By the second puff I was so overcome with nausea that I had to be rescued by one of my friends.

What had happened, as I later – much later – found out was that I had wet up the herbs. I did not know about the tiny hole above the watermark, which served as a valve that one had to lock with the thumb as one

sucked. So instead of the smoke passing through the water, the reverse happened – the water passed up into the herbs. Perfect hosts that they were, the Rastas refrained from explaining what I had failed to do, and therefore spared me any feeling of guilt.
Barry Chevannes

Nothing can soak
Brother Joe's tough sermon,
His head swollen
with certainties.

When he lights up a s'liff
you can't stop him,
and the door to God, usually shut,
gives in a rainbow gust.

Then it's time for the pipe,
which is filled with its water base
and handed to him for his blessing.
He bends over the stem
goes into the long grace,
and the drums start

the drums start
Hail Selassie I
Jah Rastafari,
and the room fills with the power
and beauty of blackness,
a furnace of optimism . . . [1]

In Jamaica, smoking means marijuana. Asked 'how much do you smoke?', Bob Marley answered 'plenty'. He wasn't talking about Marlboros or Craven As or Dunhills or Coronas. He was talking about marijuana.[2]

In keeping with the opening excerpts, this essay will weave together poetry, music and the personal narratives of both authors and Rastafari to illuminate aspects of the material history and the spiritual significance of ganja smoking in Jamaica, an influence felt throughout the world as Rastafarianism has spread through its powerful musical expression: reggae. Many writers from the West Indies, especially its poets, have located ganja smoking at the centre of both redemption and resistance. In turn, ganja smoking has become a symbol not only of enhanced states of consciousness but also of anti-social behaviour, and associated with the defiance of both the young and the Rastafarian to the conventions of civil society. In a long tradition in literature, ganja smoking becomes the insignia of both the saint and the sinner, of the detachment of both the monastic cell and the prison cell. This essay strives to bring this contradiction into focus.

The poem 'Wings of the Dove,' by the Barbadian poet Kamau Brathwaite encapsulates both the significance of ganja for the poor, the desperate and the outcast as well as drawing out the significance of ganja for prophetic meditation. It describes a

Rastaman within a biblical discourse and a language of lament, transformed into New World rhythms of hope rising (like smoke) out of the depths of longing and despair, drawing on both contemporary fiction (specifically one of the first novels of modern Jamaica, Roger Mais's *Brother Man*), popular song and a tradition of religious poetry that includes both seventeenth-century mystics like George Herbert and Henry Vaughan and the modernist invocations of Gerard Manley Hopkins and T. S. Eliot.

> Brother Man the Rasta
> man, beard full of lichens
> brain full of lice
> watched the mice
> come up through the floor-
> boards of his down-
> town, shanty-town kitchen,
> and smiled. Blessed are the poor

in health, he mumbled,
that they should inherit this
wealth. Blessed are the meek
hearted, he grumbled,
for theirs is this stealth.
Brother Man the Rasta
man, hair full of lichens
head hot as ice
watched the mice
walk into his poor
hole, reached for his peace
and the pipe of his ganja
and smiled how the mice
eyes, hot pumice
pieces, glowed into his room
like ruby, like rhinestone
and suddenly startled like
diamond.[3]

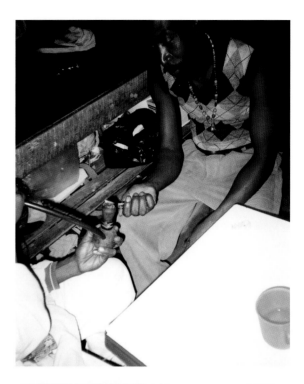

Hopkins's great double sonnet, 'That Nature is
a Heraclitean Fire and of the Comfort of the
Resurrection', figures here as Brother Man goes into
his meditation, resulting in a mystical experience.
In Hopkins's poem, the moment of transformation
is described like this:

> In a flash, at a trumpet crash,
> I am all at once what Christ is, since he was
>   what I am, and
> This Jack, joke, poor potsherd, patch, match
>   wood, immortal diamond,
> Is immortal diamond.[4]

The moment of revelation is religious; religion *is*
at the centre of Rastafari, after all. But for Brother
Man, there is still secular downpression – a typically
serious Rastafarian pun, in this case bringing the
meaning and the sound of oppression into align-
ment.

> And I
> Rastafar-I
> in Babylon's boom
> town, crazed by the moon

and the peace of this chalice, I
prophet and singer, scourge
of the gutter, guardian
Trench Town, Dungle and Young's
Town, rise and walk
through the now silent
streets of affliction,
hawk's eyes
hard with fear, with
affection, and hear my people
cry, my people
shout:

So beat dem drums
dem, spread
dem wings dem,
watch dem fly
dem, soar dem
high dem,
clear in the glory of the Lord.[5]

Ganja, the ways and cultural significance of smoking it, have a history no more than 150 years long in Jamaica. It is generally assumed that ganja was brought to Jamaica by indentured Indian servants, who began an in-migration lasting from the late 1840s to the early decades of the twentieth century. Prior to that, there is nothing to suggest that it was known, let alone used, in either historical record or oral tradition.[6]

Among Indians, smoking was a 'gendered' activity. Only men smoked ganja and they did so using a *kochi* and *saapi*. The *kochi* is a funnel-shaped receptacle in which the substance is stuffed, held in by a piece of charcoal. A damp rag called a *saapi* is placed over the small end of the funnel and the ganja sucked through. Women could smoke tobacco, but they used a *huka*, a more elaborate contraption, comprising a receptacle filled half-way with water, on which sits a *kochi*, and out of which comes the tube through which the smoke is inhaled by sucking.[7]

One difference between these two ways of smoking lies in the smoke itself. In the case of the *huka*, smoke passes through the water bringing with it vapour, whereas smoke from the *kochi* alone is dry. It could be, then, that the *huka* was thought of as a less harsh and more genteel way. Moreover, a labourer setting out to work in the sugar plantation could more easily carry his *kochi* and *saapi* than the additional water receptacle and tubing.

In the cultural diffusion to the African population, the pattern of using ganja was probably also transmitted. Indians and Africans lived and worked alongside each other on the estates, and those Indians who, following their indenture, received or bought tracts of land established households adjacent to or within the free villages and suburban settlements of the African population. The number of incoming Indians was at no time so large as to facilitate the kind of settlement pattern one finds in Guyana, where entire villages are almost entirely Indian. Rather, despite high concentrations in the sugar-producing parishes and townships, and in suburban settlements like Cockburn Gardens in Kingston, Indians lived in daily interaction with the Africans.

Nonetheless, up until the turn of the twentieth century ganja smoking was still very much associated with the Indian populace. The appropriation of ganja smoking by the African population is a twentieth-century phenomenon, spreading from plantation to rural community and, through internal migration, eventually to the city. Africans may well have also appropriated from the Indians the mythology surrounding ganja as a sacred herb from God, as well as the folklore on its effects as a medicine and a stimulant.[8] The pattern of use and implements of smoking seem also to have been adapted. Only one group of Africans, the group of Rastafari founded by Brother Lover, known as the Coptics, used the *kochi* and *saapi* method. Most Rastafari use the *huka*.

The *kochi* and *huka* are not the only methods of smoking ganja. Indeed, most ganja is smoked in the cigars and cigarettes known today as splifs. It is reasonable to assume that this method developed in Jamaica by simple transference, since the tobacco industry had been long established to service the acquired European habit. As the simplest method of smoking ganja, it was preferred by the rural small farmer, who grew it on his small plot. In the culture surrounding small farming, the small farmer rises early and sets off to 'the bush', his plot, having had only 'tea' (a herbal brew) and maybe a piece of bread. He works until very late morning, when his wife brings him 'brekfos', a heavy brunch of cooked staples and salted fish or salted meat. He returns to work until late afternoon before returning home. Sometimes the farmer does not work alone but with partners in a form of cooperative labour known variously as lend-a-day, or morning-sport, or digging, a retention of West African practices. The 'sport' aspect of it will come about when there is a large group, involving women who do the cooking on site, and children who contribute by, say, dropping the grains of corn and peas in the holes dug by the men. In this kind of atmosphere, the men will break out in 'digging songs', a call and response singing in which work becomes recreation, and tell stories and jokes during the brekfos.

The brekfos break is when the farmers would roll a splif and 'take a draw' before returning to work, their claim being that the ganja makes them work harder. This association between ganja and hard work is a culturally conditioned effect. Rubin and Comitas did find a greater energy output among those small farmers who smoked before returning to the work, though not necessarily a greater achievement. Today the ganja splif is commonly smoked *ad libitum* by workers on construction sites, on the waterfront, in their workshops, as they carry out their various crafts. There is, then, a work ethos guiding the Jamaican worker in the smoking of ganja. The claim is also made that it enhances greater concentration and focus. One will often come across a man silently getting on with his work, a splif hanging from his lips.

Until the association of ganja with the Rastafari, and Rastafari with reggae, only Indian men smoked for recreational purposes, in after-work sessions, during which they also consumed alcohol and sang folk and religious songs accompanied by their

musical instruments such as the tabalchi (fiddle), the dolak (drum) and manjira (bell). Such sessions served to reaffirm their cultural heritage and to bond the men together as a social group. As will become clear presently, in adopting the social use of ganja the Africans gave it a different, and exclusively religious, meaning. Their recreational use of ganja is now largely confined to the open-air stage shows, political rallies and 'sessions' (dances) where the substance may be openly bought and rolled into splifs.

Beginning in the early 1950s the second generation began to take issue with its elders for not extending the vision of Rastafari far enough, for being too compromising and apologetic. They first developed an attitude of defiance against white colonial authority, which they linked to the oppressive condition of the children of Africa, displaying it in a presentation of self that violated the norms of decency – the dreadlocks. Within the movement they became known as 'warriors', paralleling the Maasai of Kenya, or 'dreadful', 'dreads', 'dreadlocks'; while from outside the movement they accepted with satisfaction the designation of outcast. Attitude soon became part of the persona, and an entire philosophy of self, a new speech, dread talk, soon emerged. 'I', the subjective, replaced 'you', the objective, as all of Jah's children became 'I an' I'. And ganja they adopted as their sacrament. All this took place in their circles of reasoning, where the diffused Indian practices became transformed into Jamaican.

In September 2000 a National Commission was set up in Jamaica to consider whether or not ganja ought to be decriminalized for personal, private use. Among the many depositions received by the Commission was one from a spokesman on behalf of the Rastafari. His report aptly outlined the ritual function of ganja in Rastafari ritual. From the report, we can see that Rastafarian rituals have adopted and transformed the largely recreational use of ganja into a ritual of sacramental grace and power.[9] Rastafari insist on a relationship to ganja

that is equivalent to the relationship the Christian has to bread and wine, and defend their use by pointing to the fact that wine is an alcoholic drink. The Christian by consuming the bread and wine communes with God. The Rastafari by consuming the herbs in smoke achieves his union with Jah. However, this union is the divine knowledge or insight transmitted through the individual meditation thus induced by the herbs or the high-plane reasoning that it causes when the brethren sit together. The sacramental power of the herbs is meaningless without reflection and inward searching; therefore there is no magic, no leap of faith such as attends the transubstantiation of bread and wine. Each ritual act of smoking must leave the adherent more knowledgeable, and hence more powerful and closer to Jah. Bob Marley pointed to the use of ganja to heighten awareness and focus thought when he said: 'Maybe you could meditate without herb if you're somewhere that's quiet, but even if you go into the woods there's still the birds. But if you smoke herb the birds might sound sweeter and help you to meditate.'[10]

Thus reasoning opens limitless possibilities in an endless evolution. The Rastafari bring into the circle the unfolding external events and processes through which Jah makes his will and designs known. Through reasoning, a mosaic of daily responses is built, each fragment joined to others to create a picture of attitudes, interpretations, stances and tenets.

And there is another element, having to do with a larger sense of solidarity against a corrupt society. As Bob Marley said (in an interview in June 1976),

> Herb like fruit. Keep you healthy, mind clear . . . Devil make smoking illegal because Devil don't want people thinking one way. My friends feels the same as I when we smoke. We reach one another, y'know? Dat's what Babylon afraid of, that people think all the same.[11]

Thus there is a sense in which the very illegality of ganja is part of its power. It represents defiance of authority as well as delivery from the narrow utilitarian and moralistic values of contemporary society. Marley added:

> The authorities tell you that you mustn't smoke herb because it's bad for you. Yet if they catch you at it they'll carry you off to prison. I think it's better to be smoking herb out here free than being in prison.[12]

But it doesn't always turn out well. In Anthony McNeill's poem about Brother Joe, Babylon intervenes. The room may be filled with 'the power and beauty of blackness, a furnace of optimism', but

> The law thinks different.
> This evening the Babylon catch
> Brother Joe in his act of praise
> and carry him off to the workhouse.
>
> Who'll save Brother Joe? Hail
> Selassie is far away
> and couldn't care less,
> and the promised ship
>
> is a million light years
> from Freeport.
> But the drums in the tenement house
> are sadder than usual tonight
>
> and the brothers suck hard
> at the s'liffs and pipes:
> before the night's over
> Brother Joe has become a martyr;
>
> But still in jail;
> And only his woman
> who appreciates his humanness more
> will deny herself of the weed tonight
> to hire a lawyer
> and put up a true fight.
>
> Meantime, the musty cell,
> Joe invokes, almost from habit,

the magic words:
> *Hail Selassie I*
> *Jah Rastafari,*
> But the door is real and remains shut.[13]

The poets and fiction writers of Jamaica are caught up in two stories about ganja, one reassuring and redemptive and the other faithful to the realities of the everyday, in which bad things happen and martyrs end up dead, or in prison. This picks up the contradiction we began with, of the monastic cell and the prison cell, of spiritual retreat and criminal confinement. In an interesting way, ganja negotiates between the two in Jamaican life. It has compelling associations not only with anti-social behaviour but also with artistic inspiration, and not only with anti-rational intuition but also with religious revelation. In so doing, it raises the perennial question of whether these may possibly all be one and the same thing. In a poem about the 'intuitive' painter Brother Everald Brown, elder of the Ethiopian Church in Jamaica, Lorna Goodison describes the place he lives as one with the ganja – known locally as colly – that is grown there, and the reality of the landscape as one with the imaginings of the artist.

> An elder, an artist, a Rastafarian
> who dwells upon Murray Mountain
> St Ann, where springs the lambs' bread
> colly. He paints the dreamscapes alive
> behind his locks, Ethiopian Coptic scenery,
> multiple mountains and fallow clouds
> inclined to rain down angels.[14]

But the youth of the land are also in this, and for them it can be a very mixed blessing. On the one hand there is the call to join the outcasts, those living outside the laws of Babylon, those avoiding the responsibilities of the world. The old call. For others, ganja provides a more private escape, which Goodison catches in a scene at Bull's Bay, in the parish of Hanover, bringing smoking and dreamings together with the everyday goings-on of the place.

Here there is a mother
bathing a young baby.
She is sopping, stretching its limbs
reshaping the pliant body
in the salt water.

A child is building sand structures
testing the texture of the sand
between her fingers.

Sometimes she stops and stares
out to sea
with the liquid eyes of a dreamer.

There is a youth who has just emerged
from a one-room
barely high enough to stand in

he is now sitting on the low branch
of a coco plum tree.
he is smoking something . . .

so that the roof of the room can touch the skies
in imitation of the mercurial rise
of his dreams.[15]

In a poem entitled 'No sufferer', another
Jamaican, Dennis Scott, describes both the conditions and the consolations of the 'sufferers', a word
that in Jamaican speech refers to those who are
black and poor and mainly live in the wretched
slums of Kingston. As with many West Indian
poems, in its rhythm and phrasing it has affiliations
with the conventional English lyric. But it is unmis-
takably Jamaican in its diction and much of its
syntax. 'Mabrak', a word for black lightning and the
title of a famous earlier poem by the Rastafarian
'dub' poet Bongo Jerry, is mentioned here; while the
'dread time' is what it means to a non-Jamaican, a
time of fear; but it also has its Jamaican meanings of
Babylonian apocalypse and Rastafarian revelation,
'the blood's drum', playing on the tension between
fear and fascination that is part of ganja's appeal.
'Version' refers to the poet's rendering of the story,

his own words, but it has as well a specifically
Jamaican reference to the instrumental rendering
of a reggae song on the flipside of a 45-rpm record,
which is often 'dubbed' by disc jockeys with words
of their own. The phrase 'acknowledge I' is rich with
local associations: to the individual dignity of all
who join with Rastafarians in acknowledging the
authority of Jah, or God; to His acknowledgement
of them in their suffering; and to their collective
presence ('I and I' in Rasta talk) and acknowledgement of each other.

No sufferer,

but in
the sweating gutter of my bone
Zion seems far
also. I have my version–
the blood's drum is
insistent, comforting.
Keeps me alive. Like you.
And there are kinds of poverty we share,
when the self eats up love
and the heart smokes
like the fires behind your fences, when my wit
ratchets, roaming the hungry streets
of this small flesh, my city

: in the dread time of my living
while whatever may be human chains me
away from the surfeit of light, Mabrak

and the safe land of my longing,
acknowledge I.[16]

Scott's poem draws both on the literary authority of the lyric form, with all its engaging artifice, and on the credibility we give to speech that seems plain as life, which in this case involves using words of 'dread talk', originally a form of Jamaican speech reflecting the religious, political and philosophical beliefs of Rastafarianism and restricted to true believers – a secret language of sorts (exemplifying the exclusive codes of a closed community upon which poetry, too, often relies). The currency of dread talk is now much wider, and represents an affirmation of black consciousness and the advocacy of black power, especially by Jamaican youth. During the 1960s and '70s, the use of dread talk in the lyrics of reggae gave it prominence and popularity. In a nice turnabout, dread talk now has the same place in the orthodoxy of education as local dialect had a generation earlier. 'The middle class parent who yesteryear sweated and prayed lest another son might be "turning Rasta" when his language suggested it', notes the Jamaican linguist Velma Pollard, 'protests now on aesthetic and pseudo-educational grounds.'[17] In a poem called 'Rasta, Me Son', Ann Marie Dewar from Montserrat catches the pathos of this anxiety, once again in a way that involves the speaker in her subject. The poem's language represents Rastafarian speech, and provides an image of its independence. But it also conveys the feelings of a mother watching her son move out of reach, and calling to him in a language that binds them to each other, even – or perhaps especially – at the distance that now separates them.

So you tun Rasta now, me son!
An yu expec dat after eighteen years
O'callin you Emmanuel
Ah mus now forget de pride ah did feel
When you great granpa put ee han pan you head
An gi you ee's great granpa name!
Now you say you name Ras Ikido!
Jesus Christ did name Emmanuel!

It have any God name Ikido?

An when ah beg you fo comb you head
An go look fo wuk
You call you mudda 'daughter'
An tell me fo scant?
So you locks-up you head, me son!
An you callin pan Selassie
An pan Jah, who gi you
More overstandin dan de res o a-we!

You a dream bout Ithiopia!
While you a dream
Who a go look fo you youths?
Me know mudda milk a ital food!
You a go locks-up dem head!
School children wicked, you know!
Oh! you a go educate dem yourself
An gi dem some o de overstandin
Whey Jah gi you!
You say Jah leadin you to de hills
Fo meditate pan de holy weed
An de Holy Word!
When Ee call you, me son,
Me a go tan up somewhey,
Somewhey you cyan see me,
An me a go say 'Son, trod on, wid love'
An den me a go bawl![18]

In 'Zoo Story – Ja. '76' the St Lucian poet Kendel Hippolyte uses the language and the imagery of Rastafarianism, including the Lion of Judah, the red, green and gold colours of Rasta, and local words like 'Jamdung' (Jamaica) and 'dungle' (a version of dunghill, and the name of a now-demolished shantytown in Kingston to which Brathwaite's Rastaman referred in 'Wings of a Dove') to create a representation of Rastafarian experience in the dread time of the 1970s, a time of dark troubles and no black lightning.

dis dungle dread say:
'Lion!'
flash de colours

carry thunder on him head;
any heart-dead weak-eye
who try shake him faith
or break him righteous roots
him quake dem;
dis dungle dread roar:
'Rastafari!'

red-green-gold rainbow
lif' up from Jamdung
scatter de white thin clouds of heaven –
rest in I-tyopia . . .
but right now, right ya
earth weird
creation scared, it turnin' colour . . .
red-green-gold rainbow
dis man a-look a swif' way into Zion.

spliff use to take him dere
before –
but wha'?
spliff turn a white bone in him hand
rainbow faith bleach down,
city dry him roots to straw.
him still sight, but no lightning.[19]

The Rastafari movement did not, when it began, start out committed to the enlightenment that ganja could provide. That commitment came when the Rastafari began to take issue with the Jamaican state and society, denouncing their vilification of Africa and people of African descent, exorcizing the demon of racism and colour prejudice, and confronting them at the most basic level of questioning – ontology. They advanced Marcus Garvey's vision of pan-Africanism by cutting to the chase and bringing to the foreground the central issue of struggle, namely the self, the black being, the I, the I an' I. And there it set about re-appropriation and reintegration of a self alienated from itself and from its God. It is this more than any other attribute that has powered the Rastafari into artistic and philosophical consciousness. Who is to say that these penetrating in- (and out-) sights were not made possible by those chalices of lambsbread going (growing) up in smoke, transporting worshippers to the vantage points of the all-seeing Eye, the *I*, 'igh?

Smoking and All That Jazz

STEPHEN COTTRELL

In a dimly lit basement club a small jazz combo plays for a semi-attentive audience. A low conversational murmur, punctuated by the occasional clinking of glasses, provides the musicians with a permanent drone over which they weave their improvised counterpoint. A thick pall of smoke hangs over the entire proceedings, undiminished by the fruitless aspirations of the air conditioning system. The pianist, small beads of perspiration forming on his brow, plies his trade with a cigarette permanently drooping from the corner of his mouth, as does the drummer. Since neither of them require their mouths for their work, the ashtrays carefully positioned on their instruments become increasingly full as the evening wears on, the level of discarded butts signifying in inverse proportion the time remaining for this particular engagement. The saxophonist and trumpeter are also smoking, but each must wait for the other's solo before their next inhalation, their cigarettes kept close at hand by being wedged in their instruments, ready for a swift drag in the break afforded by a few bars rest.

This image, albeit stereotypical to the point of cliché, will appear familiar to many as a result of the myriad films, photographs and other media that present jazz musicians in settings similar to the one evoked above. Yet, like all stereotypes, while such images may embellish or exaggerate the facts, they contain kernels of truth. The evolution of jazz, that quintessentially twentieth-century musical genre, is indeed intertwined with the increasingly widespread use of tobacco products over the course of that century. Cigarettes, cigars and even pipe smoking have all played their part in creating and sustaining the

images we have of jazz musicians, stereotypical or otherwise, and the role of marijuana – particularly in the 1920s and '30s – is especially significant.

Moreover, the tobacco industry influenced the early development of jazz not only through the consumption of its products, but also because the paraphernalia associated with smoking appears to have furnished some musicians with rudimentary instruments. Jazz literature supplies us with several anecdotes of jazz and bluesmen of limited means using cigar boxes, particularly, to this end. Sidney Bechet, at the tender age of 13, is reputed to have fashioned such a box into a crude instrument, and played it in a club.[1] Big Bill Broonzy recounted a similar tale to Alan Lomax:

> I hung around Old Man See-See Rider till I figured out how his guitar and fiddle were made. Then I went to the commissary and they give me a cigar box and a big wooden box, and me and my buddy name Louis made a guitar out of the big box and I made a fiddle out of the cigar box. Then I went to the woods and cut a hickory limb and I stole thread from my mama to make a bow. Way we got strings, me an Louis would go to the picnics and barrelhouses and wait for See-See Rider to break a string. We would tie them broken strings together and put them on our home-made instruments.[2]

Among the impoverished underclasses of the southern United States, cigar boxes were clearly a valuable

Earl 'Fathar' Hines in New York, c. March 1947.

resource, and could be put to use in ways that were far beyond their manufacturers' expectations.

The origins of jazz remain controversial. While few dispute that it evolved in New Orleans in the first decades of the twentieth century, the common assertion that it arose in the brothels of that town's red-light district, where prototypical jazz musicians would be employed to entertain clients who were not otherwise engaged, is rather more contentious.

Certainly Bechet, whose significance in those early days rivalled that of Louis Armstrong, disputes this view. He writes in his (not always accurate) autobiography:

People have got an idea that the music started in whorehouses, [But] the musicians [*sic*] would go to those houses just whenever they didn't have a regular engagement or some gig they was playing, when there was no party or picnic or ball to play at . . . All that what's been

written about you got to play your instrument in a whorehouse, it's all wrong . . . How can you say jazz started in whorehouses when the musicianers didn't have no real need for them?[3]

Notwithstanding Bechet's observations, however, the musicians who constituted this early jazz fraternity were invariably tainted by their association with pastimes that were deemed either illegal or immoral, or both. Gambling, promiscuity and the consumption of alcohol – the last often to excess even in Prohibition times (1920–33) – were activities frequently associated with the musicians of the day, and not without good cause. Alcoholism was a particular problem and disrupted a number of careers, notably that of the great cornettist Bix Beiderbecke. Yet it was difficult for early jazz musicians to avoid the temptations of these disparate vices, since much of the illegal traffic in them occurred in the settings where the musicians themselves worked. This was true not only of the brothels and other nefarious institutions of New Orleans, but also later in the clubs of Kansas, Chicago and New York, where many of the musicians migrated during the 1920s and '30s.

Of course, smoking itself was never prohibited, and neither, in its earliest days, was marijuana. Thus, as the jazz tradition moved from the South to the North, so this mildly narcotic drug appears to have become increasingly popular among jazz players. Although initially more prevalent among white musicians than black,[4] it quickly became established on both sides of the colour divide. It was comparatively cheap, since it could be cultivated under backyard conditions, and appears to have been introduced into the Chicago area by migrant Mexicans and southern blacks.[5] It was referred to by a variety of monikers such as 'the mezzes', 'muggles', 'tea' or 'weed', and was smoked in the form of cigarettes called 'reefers', which were available both on the streets and in the clubs and dance halls where the musicians were usually employed. Users were referred to as 'vipers', and many of these slang terms found their way into the titles and lyrics of pieces composed at the time. Fats Waller's 'viper's Drag', Louis Armstrong's 'Muggles' and other numbers such as 'Golden Leaf Strut', 'Chant of The Weed' or 'Smoking Reefers', to give just a few examples, all testify to the widespread use and popularity of marijuana at this time, as well as the musicians' readiness to pay homage to it in their music.

There is some debate as to how much was actually smoked during performances, and much of its use apparently occurred in the socializing of musicians away from specific events. Those musicians who do admit to having used it seldom suggest that they actually played while under its influence. Hoagy Carmichael, for example, claims to have smoked marijuana only during social gatherings.[6] Many musicians suggest that it stifled creativity, or at least reduced their musical abilities in some way.[7] Given the many references to joints being rolled backstage or in intervals between sets, however, it is inconceivable that certain musicians were not under the influence of the drug during at least some of their performances. One significant individual – Mezz Mezzrow – certainly suggested that this was the case, and in fact went so far as to claim that marijuana was extremely beneficial to his musical performances.

Mezzrow is a central figure in the relationship between jazz culture and marijuana, since he was one of the main suppliers to musicians and others in the 1920s and '30s. Indeed, he was so closely identified with marijuana that it was from his name that the euphemistic description of the drug as 'the mezzes' evolved. Mezzrow's talents as a musician are much disputed; the bass player Pops Foster later wrote that Mezzrow 'just stands up there and goes toot-toot-toot. I like him, but man he can't play no jazz.'[8] Thus Mezzrow is perhaps remembered less for his playing (although he made numerous recordings) than for his highly stylized autobiography *Really the Blues*, a work written in a sometimes comical Runyon-esque language that nevertheless conveys a colourful if often fanciful memoir of his life and times. Mezzrow was a white musician of

Django Reinhardt at the Aquarium, New York, c. November 1946.

Jewish stock, although he attempted throughout his life to deracinate his origins by affecting the mannerisms and particularly the jive talk that were common among coloured musicians of the time. Indeed, so obsessive was his pursuit of 'negrification' that he later came to believe that he had actually, physically, begun to turn black.

Mezzrow was frequently to be found in bars and brothels, and demonstrated an unabashed fondness for the low life. But his openness surrounding his relationship with both marijuana and other musicians is illuminating. He expounds at length his belief that the drug, which he describes here as 'tea', could only enhance a musician's performance:

Tea puts a musician in a real masterly sphere, and that's why so many jazzmen have used it. You look down on the other members of the band like an old mother hen surveying her brood of chicks. The most terrific thing is this, that all the while you're playing, really getting off, your own accompaniment keeps flashing through your head, just like you were a one-man band. You hear the basic tones of the theme and keep up your pattern of improvisation without ever getting tangled up . . . You hear everything at once and you hear it right. When you get that feeling of power and sureness, you're in a solid groove.[9]

Mezzrow's idealistic claims for the drug are taken a stage further when he compares his own circles with those musicians who were overly fond of alcohol, going beyond simply comparing lifestyles and arguing for the greater musical achievements of the 'vipers' over the 'bottle babies':

> We were on another plane in another sphere compared to the musicians who were bottle babies, always hitting the jug and then coming up brawling after they got loaded. We liked things to be easy and relaxed, mellow and mild, not loud or loutish . . . Besides, the lushies didn't even play good music – their tones became hard and evil, not natural, soft and soulful – and anything that messed up the music instead of sending it on its way was out with us. We members of the viper school were for making music that was real foxy, all lit up with inspiration and her mammy. The juice guzzlers went sour fast on their instruments, then turned grimy because it preyed on their minds.[10]

Unfortunately, Mezzrow's idealism with regard to the beneficial effects of marijuana sits uncomfortably with his biographical details, and his book graphically describes his later descent into opium ('hip') addiction and his struggles to wean himself off it. But while many of his claims are far-fetched, and his association with the musical luminaries of his day probably rather more one-sided than he suggests, there is no doubting his pivotal role in the distribution of marijuana among jazz musicians of his time.

Mezzrow's name is also significant because he was a close associate of – and doubtless regular supplier to – perhaps the most high-profile user of marijuana, Louis Armstrong. Armstrong's own predilection for the drug was well known in the 1920s and '30s, and although he claimed to have later given it up – others dispute this – he retained fond memories of its effect. The following reminiscence, made just before his death in 1971, makes this clear. In his inimitable style Armstrong here reveals his own favourite slang word for the drug – 'gage' (gauge) – although he also refers to it as 'Mary

Warner'. He suggests that it was the legal penalties for being caught in possession that finally persuaded him to give up:

> As we always used to say, gage is more of a medicine than a dope. But with all the riggermaroo going on, no one can do anything about it. After all, the vipers during my haydays [sic] are way up there in age – too old to suffer those drastic penalties. So we had to put it down. But if we all get as old as Methusela our memories will always be of lots of beauty and warmth from gage. Well that was my life and I don't feel ashamed at all. Mary Warner, honey, you sure was good and I enjoyed you 'heep much'. But the price got a little too high to pay (law wise). At first you was a 'misdomeanor'. But as the years rolled on you lost your misdo and got meanor and meanor. (Jailhousely speaking.) Sooo 'Bye Bye,' I'll have to put you down, Dearest.[11]

Armstrong, who became increasingly famous during the 1930s, may also have been concerned about his image and reputation, particularly once he attained his later international stardom. And he never forgot that it was his use of marijuana that had landed him in a Californian jail for ten days or so in March 1931, while awaiting trial for possession. Even at this time he was sufficiently a celebrity for the case to have made the front pages of the Chicago newspapers, with some writers speculating that he was facing a six-month jail sentence. Eventually he was given a suspended sentence, perhaps even to the relief of the detectives who arrested him, since Armstrong later recounted that his arrest and detention were a surprisingly convivial experience, and only instigated after a tip-off from a rival band leader whose business was being affected by the popularity of Armstrong's shows; even the police agreed that the band leader in question was probably a marijuana user himself.[12]

Marijuana consumption became sufficiently widespread that it established itself as an integral part of jazz culture, even an essential prop in the oral/aural tradition by which musical and technical knowledge was disseminated. The trumpeter Buck Clayton recalls the occasion when he asked Armstrong how he performed a gliss (slide) on the trumpet; this resulted in an impromptu lesson given in a backstage toilet, accompanied by a shared joint:

And he gave me a cigarette. It was a brown cigarette, not the kind that I had been used to seeing. I looked at the cigarette and I guess he knew that I didn't know just what it was, so he said, 'Here, let me have it.' So he sat on the stool and lit it. He puffed on it and then he said, 'Now I'll tell you'. Then he puffed again and handed it to me, kinda grinnin' like. I took it and I puffed on it too. . . I puffed on it again and give it back to Pops, he puffed on it again and gave it back to me. This went on until the whole cigarette was gone.[13]

Not only was smoking 'tea' part of the socialization of musicians, but those who did not indulge were often under great pressure to conform to the behaviour patterns of those who did. Paul Berliner writes of the bass player Buster Williams that before he embarked on his first professional tour, his father 'took him aside and taught him how to smoke marijuana "without inhaling" – so as neither to offend other musicians nor pick up their bad habits'.[14] Another (unnamed) musician gives a similar insight into the peer pressures inherent within jazz culture:

I didn't go out with the others and hang out and get high. I remember the drummer once saying to me, 'Man. Why don't you ever hang out? You hold yourself apart.' I said, 'I have to play with you. That's my job. It doesn't mean I have to marry you and do what you do'. It's nice when everybody likes everybody in a group, but I'll be damned if I'm going to smoke dope and drink just so other people will think I'm nice.[15]

Nor was this pressure to conform only a characteristic of the marijuana-smoking 1920s and '30s; it

was also notable in the 1940s and '50s, when heroin had replaced 'tea' as the drug of choice. Charlie Parker's many acolytes, for example, felt that in order to play like him they had to share his addiction to hard drugs – a misguided idolatry that in many cases had tragic consequences. Although marijuana is non-addictive and appears to many as a relatively harmless recreational drug, those subscribing to the 'one-thing-leads-to-another' theory of narcotic dependency will find much ammunition for their cause in the historically close relationship between jazz musicians and stimulants of various descriptions.

Indeed, it is possible to read the evolution of jazz in terms of the substances that its musicians used and abused at any given time. The brashness and conviviality of the New Orleans tradition is suggested by the central role that alcohol played in sustaining it; whereas the smoother, even dreamier improvisations of swing players such as Lester Young appear well represented by the more mellow, reverie-inducing effects of marijuana. The fragmented and frenetic lines of bebop are a musical analogue of the psychotic heroin trips that destroyed the lives of so many jazz players in the post-war decades; and even the more modal lines of Miles Davis or the abstraction of John Coltrane's later work can be seen as a return to a cleaner, less drug-dependent lifestyle, with both of those artists having rejected their previous extensive use of hard drugs and alcohol (although Coltrane continued to smoke until the end of his life).

Drug usage among jazz players is decreasing as musicians, in common with others in the West, become more health conscious.[16] But it is still possible occasionally to smell the sweet edge of the 'wacky baccy' being consumed backstage at a jazz club, as the smoke drifts upwards to linger in the auditorium among the combined exhalations of a small jazz combo.

Coltrane on soprano saxophone, with a cigarette in his right hand.

Smoking in Modern China

ZHOU XUN

By the turn of the nineteenth century, the world was gradually moving towards a consumer society and China had become the world's biggest consumer market for opium, which challenged the very structure of imperial rule.[1] As the empire was about to crumble, the excessive consumption of opium became an epitome for that collapse. It became a 'silver drain' and opium smoking a source of internal corruption, a cause of military weakness and a distraction: too much leisure and not enough work.[2] Opium smoking had become China's 'biggest disease', an issue inextricably entwined with the country's economic, social and political destiny. It was not, however, a disease 'transmitted' by Western colonists, as conventional view tends to suggest,[3] but a symptom of an ill-functioning society. By associating it with 'dangerous' social groups, opium smoking had been transformed from 'pure pleasure' to 'evil habit'. Its consumers also expanded from the privileged and the wealthy classes to include coolies, the poor, prostitutes, criminals and anyone at the bottom of society. A new category of social group, the 'dope fiend', had emerged in China. As the opium users changed, its uses and meanings changed as well.

Despite two opium wars in 1840 and 1860, the downward spread of opium smoking in China quickened during the second half of the nineteenth century. According to an official estimate, by the 1880s the number of smokers in China had reached 30 million.[4] This, however, cannot be seen as merely an economic consequence or a result of power or privilege, and it cannot be simply addressed by the theory of social copying. Change is a complex issue and so are its causes and consequences. In view of changing patterns in modern consumption, many things must be taken into consideration. While it may be seen as a result of the fundamental transformations within Chinese society, it must also be linked to changes that took place in the outside world. The creation of the railway was a symbol as well as an engine of powerful change, which allowed the domestic market for opium, tobacco and other commodities to expand. Colonial expansion created new interdependencies and transformed the world. The combined effects of political and industrial revolutions in Europe endowed consumption with a 'modern life'.

As with all commodities, consumer taste was one important factor in determining the quality and variety of goods. The meaning of 'taste', however, transcends the mere sensation in the mouth. In the rise of the bourgeoisie in new urban centres after the end of nineteenth century, 'good taste' became associated with attributes such as 'refined', 'cultivated', 'high quality' or 'expensive', whereas 'bad taste' simply meant 'cheap'. While in the past the mere possession of opium had been seen as a sign of wealth and power, now one's 'taste' for opium became a measure of social standing: such class differences would be reflected in price levels as well as in the choice of opium houses. During the late Qing dynasty (1644–1911), there was a clear hierarchy of opium consumers, reflecting the hierarchy of

12 POST CARDS

A Manchu lady with a water pipe at the end of the 19th century.

contemporary Chinese society: Manchurian nobility, high state officials and the wealthiest merchants formed the upper-class consumers; a middle class of smokers comprised middle and lower rank officials, and the new urban elites such as lawyers, bankers and other professionals. Low-class opium consumers included coolies, performers, prostitutes, beggars and the criminal underworld. There was another category of opium smokers in rural areas, mainly consisting of peasants who produced opium. Most of these used opium for medicinal as well as recreational purposes. Upper- and upper-middle-class consumers smoked the foreign imports – which were the most expensive and therefore thought to be of the best quality – and the highest quality of domestically produced Yunnan opium. The lower middle classes normally smoked the less expensive opium from Sichuan, whereas the lower classes often smoked 'dross' made of the dregs left behind after boiling the opium.[5]

Social and economic differences among opium consumers were not only expressed in terms of quality and price, but also through quantity and forms of consumption. While the concept of

An opium warehouse in India in the mid-19th century.

pleasure continued to prevail amongst a few opium smokers, it was also considered a form of leisure. The modern conception of leisure was a development of industrialized society. It was a new way of defining the passage of time and of demarcating nascent urban societies. As in all modern industrializing societies, rapid economic development in certain cities of coastal China during the second half of the nineteenth century brought with it profound social changes. Like the old social elites, the rising bourgeois had extra income to dispose of, but they now earned their money through work. While sharing the old elites' desire for pleasure, they needed to separate their time between leisure and work. For this emerg-

ing new class, work was associated with the positive values of discipline, order, organization and control, whereas leisure represented spontaneity, disorder, relaxation and freedom. Leisure could be a measure of one's wealth and status while enhancing personal well-being, but could also be a cause of waste and over-indulgence, reducing productivity. It became an expression of recreational freedom, which implied that even members of the working classes could participate when their schedules allowed for it.

The separation of leisure and work also meant that leisure activities must be conducted outside the workplace. While the old elites and the wealthy continued to relax in their exclusive private gardens and mansions, guildhalls emerged in the middle of the nineteenth century to provide recreational spaces and meeting places for professional people. At the same time, temples, public parks – a new hallmark of urban society – as well as quickly proliferating theatres, teahouses and opium dens became the recreational grounds for a new 'public'.[6] As such, opium smoking had become a popular form of recreation and leisure by the second half of the nineteenth century.

When considering why a culture of smoking was particularly widespread in China, it is also important to bear in mind certain characteristics of traditional Chinese society. In order to maintain its control, the Government implemented policies supported by Confucian ideologies. Ordinary people were encouraged not to get involved in politics but to stay home peacefully, so that they would not stir up trouble.[7] While education, sports and the arts were seen as essential pursuits for a gentleman, the majority population had no access to such pastimes. For them, the only entertainment was gambling, drinking and smoking. Unlike gambling and alcohol, which can cause excitement and lead to dangerous acts such as fighting, opium is a sedative and tobacco is also known as 'peaceful grass'. They are both believed to produce a sense of well-being, have calming effects and to induce sleep.[8] Often people lay talking and smoking, passing the pipe around, until they fell asleep. Opium smoking indeed kept many peacefully staying at home or in opium houses and dens.

Opium houses and dens, like many other public recreational spaces, became social meeting places. Like the drug itself, there were different levels of opium houses and dens catering to different kinds of people. While the most upscale ones were reserved exclusively for the 'neo-opium connoisseurs', there were many cheap establishments for the poor and homeless.[9] Opium dens became their 'home', and opium smoking a diversion and a refuge from life's miseries and the pressures of urban life: 'For those who struggled to survive a life of hell, once they were able to get opium into their mouths, they immediately forgot all the pains and miseries.'[10] This phenomenon was not unique to China, since opium also provided an escape from the miseries and vicissitudes of working-class life in Victorian England: 'Men reverted to it to calm their fears of insecurity and poverty, to kill memories of long hours at the loom, the coal-face or the plough. Women took it to numb the grinding poverty in which they lived and worked, struggling to raise a family and feed a husband.'[11] For the toiling masses of late Qing China, smoking a few puffs of opium also served as a necessary 'refreshment'.

As well as designated opium dens, most hotels had dens, rather like contemporary hotel restaurants or cafés. In fact, there was rarely anything to distinguish the two, and there was not much difference between opium dens and restaurants. Often people's choice of an opium den, hotel or restaurant was based on whether they could also receive other services. In Chongqing most bathhouses had a smoking room for their customers, though the opium there was more expensive. One also expected to be served opium in brothels.

Every trade had its own guildhalls and auction centres where opium smoking was a ritual, since no business transaction could be carried out without it. On the passenger boats plying between Chongqing and Luzhou, boys would walk around offering tea as well as opium for smoking. Even on the famous Buddhist pilgrimage site of Mount Emei, monks sold opium to pilgrims, tourists and coolies. In the average home in Sichuan in southwest China, opium was an essential treat. It was considered to be improper and impolite for the opium lamp not to be lit when guests arrived. Many wealthy families often encouraged their sons to smoke opium, partly because an inability to smoke it, or not to smoke it in a proper way, was considered to show a lack of social grace.[12] Opium smoking was also praised as a good recipe for managing husbands, a family saviour, a more economical type of vice and a way to stop young people from wasting the family fortunes.[13]

Inside an opium den at Canton (*c*. 1900).

In the first half of the twentieth century, as China entered into the full swing of 'modernization', modern places of entertainment such as the cinema, pool halls and swimming pools emerged.[14] In cites such as Shanghai, urban Chinese who aspired to be 'modern' desired anything Western, which was also perceived as being 'exotic'. As a result, Western-style goods flooded the market. Soon investors discovered China as a major consumer market. Urban dwellers indulged in tinned food, powdered milk, chewing gum, foreign cigarettes and even Western-styled patent medicines. For them, smoking foreign cigarettes, taking Western medicine, going to the cinema and shopping were prestigious activities, whereas opium and pipe smoking and traditional styles of entertainment became increasingly seen as signs of China's 'backwardness'.[15] Consumers were partial

A man smoking tobacco in a yard while his hair is dressed (*c*. 1900).

to foreign cigarettes because they were elegant to smoke, convenient to carry, fashionable to have and tasted refreshing.[16] This was the image of modern life. Since travelling had become an increasingly popular modern occupation, several brands of cigarettes were marketed as 'the best companions of modern travellers'.[17] Some people also smoked cigars. The pressures of modern urban life were thought to drive many to seek more stimulating vices. Urban dwellers drank hard liqueur while listening to fast music, and smoked strong cigars in order to excite their nerves.[18] For those who could not afford expensive cigars, some manufacturers added morphine and heroin to improve the potency of relatively 'mild' cigarettes. Archival evidence shows that in 1936 fifty-three brands of cigarettes on the Shanghai market contained morphine or heroin.[19] The narcotics were added partly to reduce costs and to increase profits, for crude morphine and heroin were very cheap in China at this time. It was also a means of attracting customers. In the first half of the twentieth century, China was the world's biggest consumer market for narcotics. The

A 1930s *Double Crane Cigarettes* ad.

A 1930s *Three Cup* cigarette ad.

criminalization of narcotics led many to conceal the heroin or morphine in a pipe or in the top of a cigarette by mixing it with tobacco. They could thus 'drug' themselves openly without being noticed.[20] Cigarette manufactures exploited the opportunity, which ultimately resulted in an official drug ban.

Better still, consumers were regularly being offered deals such as 'try now and pay later', or 'buy one and get one free'. For instance, a pack of cigarettes often came with a lighter – also a trendy thing at this time – and it became fashionable to collect cigarette cards. Since smoking utensils were inconvenient for a modern lifestyle, they became increasingly viewed as antiques, and cigarette cards became the new and popular form of *objet d'art*. They often came in sets – one needed to buy hundreds of cigarette packs to collect a whole set – and children were also readily targeted. Zhu Xiang (1904–1933), one of China's celebrated but tragic literary figures, implied that his craving for smoking began with his childhood interest in cigarette cards.[21] Foreign cigarettes, lighters and cigarette cards had transformed the tradition of smoking into a modern pursuit.

As cigarette smoking became increasingly popular, choices of cigarettes became unlimited. To compete with foreign brands, Chinese products were promoted with patriotic slogans. In response, foreign companies such as British-American Tobacco localized their operations.[22] Domestic mass production and mass marketing were encouraged in the hope of achieving mass consumption. Clever promoters made fortunes in cigarettes through advertising. Like patent medicines, cigarettes were the pioneers of advertising in China.[23] Cigarettes and patent medicine ads paid for the rapid growth of the newspaper business in modern cities such as Shanghai. Newspaper columns were half-filled by their claims and beautiful pictures. From Shanghai to Chengdu, modern cities were covered with huge advertisements such as 'Please smoke a cigarette'. Odd ones such as 'Beauty is lovely; cigarette is also lovely. National product is even more lovely' also occurred.[24] It is, however, important to read these advertisements within the

context of the social and cultural changes that were taking place in China. While opium smoking had become associated with the nation's weakness and family misfortune, and was seen as a threat towards racial degeneration, cigarette advertisements sought to promote health, a modern lifestyle and nationalism. For instance, one advertisement appeared with a fashionably dressed housewife offering a tin of Golden Dragon cigarettes to her husband, dressed in traditional clothes though sitting on a modern sofa. The La Yebanan cigarettes, featured with a healthy, dark-coloured beauty, claimed to be able to smooth vital energies and reduce illness.[25]

The use of female images in many of the advertisements is particularly striking. Faces of classic Chinese beauties were often matched up to the bodies of modern female nudes. These images, however, should not be seen simply as fetish objects to attract male consumers, and they did not merely represent a new aesthetic trend in modern China. They were the embodiment of physical health – a new image of the modern Chinese and of tradition within modernity. They echoed the view that the modernization of China was reflected in the changing lifestyle of the new urban woman. Chinese women, according to some of China's modernizing male elites, were the most suppressed and exploited category in traditional China; they were virtuous, but deprived of personal freedom. In a modern China, it was believed, a 'new' woman must leave her home and become a citizen. She must no longer sacrifice herself for the sake of her family, but for the sake of her country and for the good of the community. In other words, for the progress of the country each individual Chinese citizen must attain the traditional female virtue or essence of self-sacrifice. Such virtue should be seen as the roots of modernity.[26] Educated modern women in China rarely smoked, however. The conventional belief was that women possessed virtue and vices were reserved for men. In traditional China, women smoked at home, which further symbolized their boredom and frustration. Smoking was a sign of their enslavement by the old society, and so the new and independent modern woman must be freed from the chains of smoking. She should leave the cage of her home and be fully equipped to serve society, to build a comfortable home, to bring up healthy children and to contribute to the progress of her country.

In addition to female images, popular traditional-style New Year pictures were also widely used in advertising to remind modern consumers of their national heritage and to appeal to a wider spectrum of population. Cigarette makers were also among the first businessmen to recognize the power of the catchphrase, the identifiable logo and trademark, the celebrity endorsement, the appeal to social status and the need to retain its everlasting attraction. The further development of the railway, steamship, telegraph and other manifestations of the communication revolution made a national and even international market increasingly viable. Waves of war and economic immigrants brought new consumers to the country. For instance, the population in Shanghai mushroomed from three million in 1937 to six and a half million in 1938. The newcomers did not have much money, but they would often venture a dollar for a 'smoke'. Mass production made cigarettes reasonably cheap and affordable. In comparison to opium, it was legal to smoke y were readily available: on sale at every street corner shop, teahouse, cinema, theatre and so on. If in the early twentieth century the cigarette was still a commodity for a few 'modernizing elites' in the cities, by the 1930s it had indeed become a mass consumer good, and its consumers were not only modern urbanites, but also traditional peasants. In 1934 a Chinese journalist wrote: 'many rural Chinese villages still don't know who in the world Sun Yat-sen is, but very few places do not know Ruby Queen cigarettes.'[27]

Although the Communist Government after 1949 eliminated many 'old' habits, it encouraged cigarette smoking and the tobacco industry. Today, one-third of the world's smokers live in China. The normalization of the culture of smoking in Communist China was achieved largely through Government sanction. Between 1949 and 1979 the Government issued no health warning on smoking, nor was it seen as bourgeois. On the contrary, it was and still is the mass commodity for the Communist masses. Most of the top Communist officials are heavy smokers. Deng Xiaoping even listed cigarettes as one of the ten merits that contributed to his longevity.[28] (After the death of Deng, Nury Nittachi, widely viewed as Hong Kong's bestselling English-language writer, joked: 'Deng is dead at the age of 92. Let us learn from this. Smoking kills.') Seen in this light, smoking cigarettes evokes power and prestige. It also plays an important and influential role in social relationships. It is sociable to smoke and China is a smoking-friendly environment. It is hospitable to offer a cigarette to guests and it is also polite to accept when one is offered. Cigarettes are often used in exchange for a favour, to win a promotion and to develop a good relationship with one's superior. They are one of the most popular choices of gifts. For instance, during the Mao era, cigarettes were often given as wedding gifts together with Mao's *Little Red Book*. Cigarettes are also a form of currency. In the early days they were used to purchase railway tickets, food and medicine; today they can buy drivers' licences and diplomas, among other things. Without a pack of cigarettes in China, 'one can barely move half an inch'. Smoking also plays an intrinsic part in the construction of sexual identities. Cigarette smoking is a display of masculinity and it is commonly believed that 'a man's life is not worthwhile if he does not smoke', while women who smoke are considered to be distasteful and improper.[29] Furthermore, smoking is a sign of one's intellect; as a popular saying goes: 'if what you write is rough, let smoke smooth it for you.'

In today's China, smoking is 'cool'. The mass media is covered with images of stars and celebrities smoking. Smoking is a display of wealth. A person's worth and fortune can be told through the brand of cigarettes he or she smokes. Smoking is a necessary part of being professional, since business can rarely be carried out without an exchange of cigarettes.

A *Pirate Cigarettes* calendar poster in the 1930s.

Cigarettes in a Beijing shop, 2004.

More and more professional women have picked up the habit of smoking. Smoking has also become connected to the small group of avant-garde in China. While it represents a spirit of rebellion, it can also provide comfort for their lost souls, as the words of the pop song *Strange Smoke* show:

> While mother was sleeping I crept out of the door
> And entered into that strange smoke
> I breathed in deep and flew up to heaven
> I have turned all my parents' money into strange smoke
> I was seduced by pleasure
> Strange smoke clouds my head
> I live in a dream
> I wake up and look around and all is as it was
> This evil fate beckons me with open arms
> For this I will cry my eyes dry
> Must my mother and father suffer for this?
> Must their hopes of a lifetime be shattered because of this?

> Oh my mother, take me back to your breast
> Save me from the strange smoke.[30]

Lyrics available on a commercial album, which make reference to yet other popular substance to be smoked, indicate that consumerism in China continues to expand. The words are heart-wrenching and the reality is that China is further submerged in clouds of smoke. The modern history of China is entwined with the culture of smoking. From pipe smoking to cigarettes, smoking has now become an enduring part of the contemporary Chinese cultural tradition.

A collection of Chinese cigarette packets. Photographed by Markuz Wernli.

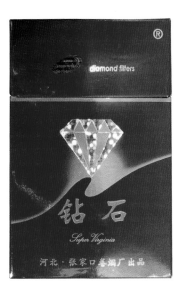

Smoking in Modern Japan

DANIEL GILMAN

A handsome Japanese man in his mid-thirties, wearing a dress shirt with rolled up sleeves, is sitting on a giant log in the midst of a silent, primeval forest. He is smoking. He takes a last leisurely drag on his cigarette and produces a small box from his shirt pocket. He opens it and puts the cigarette butt in. The screen fades to black and the words 'Smokin' Clean Style' appear.

All of the typical tools of advertising are there: a stylish person, a beautiful natural setting and the association of smoking with beauty, relaxation. It is not so different from a classic ad for Marlboro, one featuring a rugged cowboy similarly alone in the vast American desert. In the first advertisement, however, there is no mention of any brand name. This is the first indication that a slightly different dynamic from the Marlboro man is at work. To most native English speakers, the phrase 'Smokin' Clean Style' sounds like a reference to being cool, smooth and stylish. But ask a Japanese person what 'Smokin' Clean Style' means and you will hear a different answer: 'Mind your manners.'

The difference between the Marlboro Man and 'Smokin' Clean Style' seems even greater if you consider that the Japanese Government supports these commercials and has done so for at least a quarter of a century. Whereas American public service announcements about smoking feature such tempting slogans as 'Smoking Kills' and pictures of body bags, their Japanese counterparts have taken an entirely different direction.

In Japan, two commodities – tobacco and salt – were turned into Government monopolies. From 1985 the Government agency that regulated tobacco was transformed into Japan Tobacco (hereafter referred to as JT), a pseudo-autonomous company of which 66 per cent is owned by the Japanese Government. JT still holds a complete monopoly on locally produced tobacco but is traded on the stock market. Needless to say, JT is a major source of revenue for the Japanese Government, and cigarette taxes collected at the local level are a huge source of income for local and city governments. It is at this intersection of public responsibility and financial imperative that the Japanese tobacco industry and subsequent advertising have developed. While smoking in Japan has a long and deeply rooted history beginning in the sixteenth century, the associated health problems have forced the industry to create publicity and advertising that seeks to eliminate 'bad smoking' and create 'good smoking' – which is also 'Japanese smoking'. Thus, the Government has been able to maintain a positive image for smoking while actively addressing relevant social issues. To do this, JT has evoked two of the central concerns of Japanese culture: social responsibility and tradition.

Certain Japanese arts, like the tea ceremony, are given the name *do*, meaning 'path' or 'way'. For example, *sado* means 'the way of tea', and *judo* is 'the way of throwing'. These arts are not mere skills but potential paths to mental and spiritual enlightenment. 'Good' smoking in modern Japanese cigarette

草煙狗天

A poster for *Tengu* cigarettes.

advertising is limitless in its positive and ennobling powers. Issues such as addiction and disease are marginalized or relegated to 'bad smoking'. While JT does not go as far as creating a 'way of smoking', the implication is there.

An understanding of the history of tobacco smoking in Japan is necessary to proceed. Tobacco was almost certainly introduced to Japan from European traders sometime between 1570 and 1595. From as early as the beginning of the Edo period (1603–1868), smoking scenes began to appear in Japanese paintings. Imperial Prince Toshihito wrote in 1609 that 'among the common folk, lewd and learned alike, there are none who do not favor this herb'.[1] Traditionally in Japan, foreign imports undergo a rapid period of Japanization whereby they soon become distinct from the original and are gradually integrated into Japanese culture. For instance, deep frying was introduced by the Portuguese and soon developed into *Tempura* – fried vegetables and shrimp dipped in a delicate sauce. Smoking soon made the leap with the development of the *kiseru*, a long thin pipe that uses finely shredded tobacco.

The Meiji Era (1867–1910), which ended Japan's 350-year isolation, was marked by the mass import of Western technology and fashions, among them cigarettes, which became immensely popular. Cigarette sales were initially dominated by foreign imports, particularly American, but dozens of Japanese cigarette brands soon sprang up, beginning as early as 1874.

These companies were short-lived because the Government formed the tobacco monopoly in 1904. This is where the history of the modern industry begins. To give an idea of how little things have changed since the monopoly began, one brand that was started by the Government in 1906, Golden Bat, is still being sold today.

From the very beginning of the monopoly, Government influence was obvious. Cigarette packaging quickly became an extension of the publicity department, with commemorative brands such as 'Glory' marking the accession of Hirohito, and 'Peace', a still popular brand, marking the end of the First World War. During the Second World War all English words were banned, including the names of cigarette brands. Until the end of the war, 'Golden Bat' was called *kinshi*, which means 'Golden Kite'.

After the Second World War, the political connotations of cigarette advertising faded away and a more complicated cultural dynamic began to emerge. As a result of post-war rationing, a massive black market run mainly by Yakuza groups developed in cigarettes and tobacco. Although the Government tolerated the black markets, which were often the only source for food and other basic needs, cigarettes were particularly targeted. At this time the Tobacco Tax exceeded 20 per cent and was a critical source of income for the Government.[2] It needed to eliminate the black market while at the same time maintaining levels of smokers. To do this, advertising that appealed to social responsibility and cultural tradition was mixed with more traditional ads. A famous anti-

black-market poster from 1948 reads: 'Extinguish black market Tobacco, Light the fire of the culture.' Black market tobacco was marketed as bad, not just because it was illegal, but also because it undermined the culture: it was not Japanese tobacco. The underlying promotion was that, by buying solely from Government manufacturers, purchasers were not only supporting their country but were also reinvigorating a culture that had been devastated in the war.

An example of this can be found in the cigarette brand Peace: a beautiful, stylishly dressed woman against a background of lights, evocative of a city street at night. This associates cigarettes with beautiful women, wealth and exciting nightlife. This is an example of two ideas that are still being promoted. First, the Government is trying to sell cigarettes. Second, it is creating a moral and cultural distinction between good smoking and bad smoking – in this case between black-market tobacco and Government tobacco. Good smoking is always also Japanese smoking and is a loaded signifier for other powerful ideas: in this case cultural and economic renewal.

Carried along with the post-war economic boom, smoking rose to unprecedented popularity in Japan. In 1965, 82.3 per cent of Japanese men over the age of 20 smoked, and in 1967 they made 'Hi-Lites' the world's best-selling cigarette. The percentage for women, though much lower, only about 16 per cent, is still high enough for a woman smoker not to be seen as particularly unusual.[3] In contrast, only 51.9 per cent of men in America smoked, though 33.9 per cent of women did.[4] Thus not only was there a higher percentage of smokers in Japan but also most houses in Japan had a smoker, compared to the United States with little less than 50 per cent.

This was the golden age for the Japanese tobacco industry. The Government monopoly had no competition, extremely limited imports and half the population using the product on a regular basis. All this money went directly to the Government. Even today, in addition to the profits that go directly to the Government, almost 60 per cent of the price of cigarettes is tax and half of that goes to the local city hall. The golden age did not last long, however. After ten years of a slow decline in the percentage of smokers (though an increase in total sales), the industry saw a huge drop in the number of smokers between 1975 and 1985, nearly double the decline of the previous decade. The percentage of men smoking dropped from 76.2 per cent to 64.6 per cent and the decline would continue, losing around one percentage point a year through the 1980s and '90s. The start of this sharp decline also coincides with the last two major events of the history of modern Japanese smoking.[5]

The decrease in smoking followed an increase in the awareness of the health risks associated with cigarettes. In 1972 the Japanese Government first had health warnings put on cigarette boxes. This warning has still not changed substantially. While the US Government has a variety of specific and blunt warnings, such as 'Smoking may cause cancer', the Japanese labels merely say: 'There are fears that smoking too much may be bad for your health, so be careful of smoking too much.' Again there is a clear attempt to make a distinction between good and bad smoking in providing a public warning that will not greatly undermine the smoking industry itself.

This trend culminated with the introduction of the 'Smokin' Clean' campaign in 1974. One of the original ads features the caption 'Smoking clean, keep our town and nature beautiful' over a picture of a big green apple. While the adage 'an apple a day keeps the doctor away' is unknown in Japan, the imagery is similar. The association between eating an apple – the quintessence of a healthy act – and smoking may not be obvious, but the implication is similar. In this instance, minding your manners is not just to help others, it also transforms the act of smoking into something good and healthy. This campaign has continued up to the present day in various forms, including the commercial described at the beginning of this essay. In addition to advertising, JT has collaborated with Japan Railways to

スモーキン・クリーン 街を自然を美しく

Smokin' Clean cigarette advertisement.

create smoking areas on trains and station platforms. The 'Smokin' Clean' slogan appears in most of these areas, strengthening the association of the phrase while protecting non-smokers, and is also officially sanctioned. Thus the promotional aspects of the 'Smokin' Clean' ads are obscured by the strong association with the 'mind your manners' message and conversely strengthened by the association with a Government authority. Other public-service messages walk this fine line as well. For example, an advertisement in a convenience store has a picture of a dancing beer bottle and cigarette pack with the message: 'After you turn 20 buying alcohol and tobacco is OK!' Ironically, Japan has more than half a million cigarettes and alcohol vending machines.

In 2001 a new campaign was started: 'JT is changing!' This was the first step in the brand replacement for the 25-year-old 'Smokin' Clean Style' campaign. The new campaign is called 'Delight' and in the face of the continuing decline of smokers it has practically dispensed with subtlety. The posters and commercials all feature scenes where people are given a chance to 'mind their manners'. This is the text from one of the posters:

They say 'It is all right to smoke.' I say 'Thanks, I will smoke later.' I like smoking but I can also choose not to smoke. For example after a number of days I was coming back from a long trip.

On the train platform I was thinking, 'I would like a cigarette.' I had a sense of accomplishment and was a little tired. At times like these a cigarette is particularly delicious. When I was just sitting down on the bench and about to light up my cigarette, I noticed that a man sitting on the same bench was holding a hot dog. When he noticed that I had stopped lighting my cigarette he smiled and said, 'go ahead' and pointed to the ashtray (*meaning that it was a smoking area*). I thanked him but I put the cigarettes back in my pocket. Some sort of warm feeling slowly filled my heart. That time and any time: smoking is fun but not-smoking is also fun. That is the sort of adult I want to be.[6]

This ad emphasizes concern for others, self-control and politeness – all critical values in Japanese society. At the same time it stresses that the person has chosen to smoke, can control his smoking and, as an adult, has the right to smoke. This is a clear reaction against the growing awareness of the role of addiction in tobacco use. An addict is not in control but a 'good smoker' is, and moreover he exercises that control in the interest of others. Finally, while it takes the form of a public service gesture to protect people from second-hand smoke, it also says 'Smoking is fun. Cigarettes are delicious' in no uncertain terms.

The JT web page is an excellent source regarding smoking and its place in Japanese society. A section called 'Smoking: An Adult Taste' leads one into the world of JT, a world where the normal Japanese word for smoker (*Kitsuensya*) is replaced with *Aienshya*: a person who loves smoking. This area contains hundreds of pages of text, all extremely comprehensive. For example, the 'Other Names for Tobacco' section contains an entry that treats the reader to an extensive etymological discussion of the tobacco term, Memory Plant (*omoigusa*), which, however, is no longer in the vernacular. Clearly this web page is not an afterthought, but a central part of the company's merchandising policy.

'The Spiritual properties of Tobacco' section tells the interested that the word 'spiritual' is from the Japanese *kokoro*, which means heart, soul or mind. There are, according to JT, 29 of these uses. A few of them include 'Stylish Tobacco', 'Relaxing Tobacco', 'Idle Tobacco', 'Tobacco to cover one's confusion or nervousness', 'Love Tobacco', 'Friendship Tobacco', 'Daydream Tobacco', 'Gesture Tobacco', 'Tobacco for deepening sympathy with nature', 'Individual Tobacco' and 'Meeting Tobacco'. The format of the site, which adds to its accessibility, is written as a conversation between two characters using a somewhat archaic, rural style of Japanese. The style of language itself is evocative of an old, rural Japan, and the friendly bantering style of the writing brings to mind two grandfather-like figures reminiscing. Moreover, almost all of the discussions either centre around or begin with discussions of smoking in the Edo period. JT is not merely explaining to us the myriad wonderful ways in which smoking can enrich life; it is also demonstrating how smoking is an extension of a Japanese tradition.

While a list such as this may seem unusual from a Western perspective, it is a cultural norm in Japan. In the Japanese tea ceremony it is common to talk about the different uses in similar terms, such as 'Silent Tea' or 'Chatting Tea'. The tea ceremony originated in the Zen Buddhist tradition where the simplest act can have profound meaning. What one is doing is infinitely less important than the state of mind that accompanies it. Thus the simple act of making tea can become a ritual that can reflect all aspects of life – social and spiritual. JT markets smoking based on identical principles.

The twenty-ninth use, 'Stylish Tobacco', which is *iki* in Japanese, points out that it is a homonym of the words 'will', 'spirit' and 'life'. The discussion begins with a focus on women smokers, particularly in the context of theatre in the Edo period. For these women, they suggest, perhaps a better translation would be 'sexy'. Still, we are warned against thinking that this is merely fashion: 'Stylishness [*iki*] is a problem of the spirit. Even if you have the outward appearance of *iki* but your spirit

Race-course betting –
and smoking – in Kyoto.

is wrong you will end up being unrefined. *Iki* is connected to our modern problem with [smoking] manners.'[7] This is not, however, merely an issue of fashion! People with bad smoking manners are not only social outcasts but are also making a failure of the spirit. By extension, those people who maintain manners and smoke properly have their spirits properly in line.

As in the tea ceremony, the way one smokes becomes an expression of inner harmony as well as a marker of social status. This blurred line between the practical and the spiritual is characteristic of Zen thinking. Of course, smoking is not only an abstract expression of soul and style, it also has practical uses, as in this passage from 'Idle Tobacco' (the Japanese word *mui* does not have the negative connotations of the English):

There are those times when you have made a little free time, but don't know what to do and are looking aimless. When you notice that you have nothing to do, your manners become awkward. When you have that appearance and you start to

think that people are looking down on you your relaxation vanishes. For those times, lighting up a cigarette is just perfect. When you watch the slowly rising smoke you will cease to notice people's watching eyes, *for a moment, you are playing in your own world*.[8]

For a Japanese worker whose life has consisted of heavily rigorous schooling followed by an intensive work and social environment, the notion of being 'in your own world' is a powerful one. It is also practical advice. There is little or no break time in a typical Japanese office, and simply getting up and standing around for five minutes would be seen as irresponsible. Smoking, however, is a socially acceptable way to take a break without appearing indolent. But JT goes further, saying that the act of smoking itself removes one from the need even to consider such social pressures. This is a much more powerful endorsement of smoking than simply saying 'isn't it nice to take a smoking break?'

All the sections attempt to make smoking seem as Japanese as possible. Using smoking during the

Edo period as a historical base, the marketing then incorporates many other cultural references to smoking from plays, books and television shows. For example, Number 24 – 'Love Tobacco' – begins its detailed history in the Edo period and describes how prostitutes would initially approach men by asking for tobacco. A series of literary quotes follow, to illuminate how tobacco has been used in various classic love scenes in books and film. One book quoted is Kawabata Yasunari's *The Izu Dancer* (*Izuno Odoriko*, 1926), a well-known work of twentieth-century Japanese literature. In the scene the narrator is sitting in a teashop and preparing to smoke when the dancer pushes an ashtray nearer to him. JT regards this as a profound moment and further comments: 'Men and women can get closer by smoking together. Even if they don't actually smoke, for example when a man is about to light a cigarette and a woman lights it for him or pushes his ashtray closer. That is something that will make a man happy!'

In Japanese tobacco culture, tobacco represents the spirit of Japan. Positive or negative connotations are much less important than being recognizably Japanese. To illustrate this, the JT Tobacco and Salt Museum notes the writer Osamu Dazai as a famous smoker of Golden Bats, despite having a considerable reputation for drug and alcohol abuse, and multiple suicide attempts.

Smoking is thus intrinsically Japanese. It is a method of spiritual and social development, a tool for fitting into society and a way of rising above social restrictions. But even though most of the traditional Ways have some relation to Buddhism or Shinto, JT does not correlate tobacco with the religious. The only mention of this would be found under the section 'Prayer Tobacco', which discusses the ancient Mayan use of tobacco in religious ceremonies and humans' relationship to prayer. The section ends with the following comment: '[In these cases] unconsciously a feeling of prayer is at work. By offering up these prayers we can give our troubled feelings a moment of peace. Perhaps this is because when we watch the tobacco smoke drifting upwards we can think that the smoke is carrying our feelings with it up to heaven.'

The introduction of tobacco before Japan's global isolation period permitted nearly 300 years of national and cultural incorporation. The cultural significance of tobacco in Japan was so firmly ingrained that when Western-style cigarettes became available, the fundamental cultural and national perceptions dominated. If anything, the universality of smoking appealed to a Japan that was simultaneously trying to open to the West and protect its own culture. In addition to this cultural entrenchment, tobacco sales have been an important source of revenue on all levels of Government for nearly 100 years. Even the Tobacco Business law (which created JT) expresses the Government's interest in maintaining tobacco sales when it says: '. . . taking into consideration the role tobacco-related tax plays in financial income . . . this law thereby allows for the rightful growth of our nation's tobacco industry'.[9] Ignoring the health consequences of smoking is impossible to avoid, however; the World Health Organization lists smoking as one of the world's worst health problems. Between these two concerns the Government has chosen a middle path, one that attempts to protect the rights of both smokers and non-smokers. Since it cannot openly endorse smoking, the Government-dominated industry has created a Way of Smoking, which is distinct from normal, bad smoking. This 'good smoking' is socially responsible, controlled (and thus distinct from addiction), and a cultural and spiritual mode of expression that is modelled after traditional Japanese arts. The most obvious complaints of non-smokers are addressed without creating a negative image of smokers or marginalizing them. Smoking can be attacked and praised at the same time – anti-smoking posters in schools but 'Smokin' Clean Style' on the train; a cultural balancing act necessary to address health concerns while protecting a vital source of revenue, all projected to be for the greater social good. According to JT, 'Smoking like an adult might just be the first small step towards fixing the world.'[10]

Cigarettes in Soviet and Post-Soviet Central Asia

RUTH MANDEL

This essay presents an account of the symbols and practices of smoking and cigarette production and consumption in the Soviet and post-Soviet periods in Central Asia. It addresses some of the continuities and discontinuities in light of the enormous political and economic transformations that the region has experienced. Although the 'before' and the 'after' that frame this essay refer to the transition from 70 years of state-controlled command economy to a system struggling with the demands and pressures of a market, we will see that even during the period of state socialism the tobacco industry that was available to the Soviet people was implicated in global markets, events and geopolitics. As will be discussed below, however, the Soviet 'market' for cigarettes looked very different from the Western economics of smoking. Also addressed are the Soviet and post-Soviet visions of the relation between smoking and modernity, particularly evident in the way that smoking has been a gendered behaviour.

When discussing smoking, Kazakhstanis (citizens of Kazakhstan, as opposed to Kazakhs, members of the titular national group) sometimes mention a piece of Soviet propaganda that they were taught: 'A single drop of nicotine can kill a horse.' A powerful pictorial image of a dead horse was engraved in the memories of the schoolchildren who saw this picture in textbooks and on the walls of polyclinics. The potency of the image derives not only from a large and hardy beast being struck down by a miniscule drop, but also

from the fact that the horse was an essential part of traditional Kazakh culture, a nomadic society dependent on horses for transport and food. The fact that middle-aged Kazakhstanis can describe this image of a dying horse vividly 40 years after encountering it speaks to its profundity. In a mild form of dissent, however, a counter-phrase was sometimes bandied about: 'But a human is not a horse – you cannot kill him with only one drop.'

This description betrays a tension evident in the Soviet period, between the officially promulgated anti-smoking campaigns and a strong association with masculinity, manliness and, as shown below, patriotism and war. During the Soviet period other tensions existed as well, for the State that campaigned against smoking also produced and provided cigarettes. But before delving into the socio-economy of smoking, it might be useful to provide some background and context in which to situate Kazakhstan and its tobacco crop.

KAZAKHSTAN, COLLECTIVIZATION AND TOBACCO

Kazakhstan is the largest of the five former Soviet Central Asian states. It encompasses an immense land mass, extending from the Altai Mountains bordering Mongolia in the east to the Volga region in the west. Kazakhstan alone is the size of Western Europe. It shares a border with Russia (its most important political ally and trading partner) that stretches 6,846 kilometres; its border with its neighbour to the east, China, runs for

Packs of Russian
cigarettes: Apollo-Soyuz,
Alma-Ama, Belomorkanal,
Kazkstan and Medey.

1,533 kilometres. A landlocked country, it also borders on Kyrgyzstan, Turkmenistan and Uzbekistan. Rich in natural resources, Kazakhstan is currently one of the world's major players in oil geopolitics, and its rulers boast that its Caspian oil fields will make it the next Kuwait.

Primarily steppe, and not conducive to intensive agriculture, it was nevertheless the site of the famous 'Virgin Lands' project, carried out under Nikita Khrushchev, which aimed to transform the land into the Soviet bread basket. Although the wheat never materialized in the quantities anticipated, resulting in years of falsified statistics and accounting (common throughout the USSR), one result was a significant increase in the population size and diversity of the Soviet Socialist Republic of Kazakhstan, and its 'multi-national' character. This reinforced the minority status of the titular nationals, the Kazakhs.

The Soviets had imposed collectivization on a pastoral, semi-nomadic population in the early years of the USSR. In the process of collectivization, contiguous settlements were reorganized into institutions known as *Kholkhoz*, or *Sovkhoz*, collective farms or state farms. Near Almaty – formerly the capital Alma-Ata – were a number of tobacco-growing farms (in 1998 the capital was moved to Astana, a city in the northern steppe).

Each September, teenagers, organized into work groups, gathered tobacco leaves as 'harvest volunteers'. After the leaves had been collected, they were dried and fermented. Next, a solution of calcium hydrate – $Ca(OH)_2$ – derived from limestone was added to refine the burning qualities. The tobacco was then cut into *banderol* (a large roll of processed tobacco); finally it was sent to Alma-Ata where it was made into cigarettes at the Almatinski Tobachni Kombinat, or ATK, the Alma-Ata Tobacco Factory.

STRUCTURES OF SMOKING IN THE USSR:
PRODUCTION AND CONSUMPTION

Differences between the cigarette culture of the Soviet Union and that of Western countries included choice, brands, the nature of manufacturing and, of course, marketing and advertising. Cigarette manufacturing took place throughout the Soviet Union. One of the most famous factories was Yava, in Moscow, which still functions today. Every Soviet factory produced identical filter-less products – Prima, Pamir and Belomorkanal – all conforming to classificatory categories of weights, measures and quality control that were standardized throughout the USSR. Belomorkanal (named after the first Stalinist industrialization project, using a slave labour corps made up of political prisoners) is not, in fact, considered a cigarette, but *papirosa* (pl. *papirosi*), with a long hollow cardboard tip that the smoker squeezed and folded. During the Second World War, *papirosi* were the only type of cigarettes available, and they have been in production continually ever since.[1]

In the late 1960s, when filtered Orbita was introduced, all cigarettes were assigned one of four classes, 'Class 4', Orbita, being the highest quality. Cigarette prices were stable from 1961 until 1981: Pamir cost 12 kopecks and Belomorkanal 22 kopecks for a pack of 25, and Prima 14 kopecks for a pack of 20, making a pack of cigarettes several times dearer than a bus ticket of 5 kopecks. Pamir was so strong and foul-smelling that it was nicknamed 'thermonuclear', because, as one experienced informant explained, it was so awful that 'when someone smoked them near you, you wanted to commit suicide'. Polyot was introduced later, as an upgraded, more expensive version of Prima.

Orbita arrived in Kazakhstan, assembled at the Alma-Ata Tobacco Factory (ATK), in the late 1960s. Filtered, it became the most expensive on the market, selling at 30 kopecks. ATK was a popular place to work, since it was relatively easy for workers to steal tobacco and cigarettes and sell them, or to trade them for other goods and services on the black market.

A pipe-smoker in Central Asia.

The 1970s ushered in a new phase of Soviet cigarette production. Non-generic cigarettes – namely, anything other than Pamir, Belomorkanal, Prima or Orbita – were introduced. APOLLO SOYUZ, in production from 1975 to 1977, was issued in honour of the *détente*-inspired NASA–Soviet space mission. More costly at 60 kopecks, in Kazakhstan it was seen as quasi-foreign, thus prestigious, having been manufactured in Russia and Moldova. The pervasive sense was that all good things reached the Kazakhstani periphery from the Russian centre, Moscow, and thus like so much else, APOLLO SOYUZ assumed some of this reflected glory. Between 1977 and 1986 the same plants assembled Marlboro. At the time Philip Morris was the only Western tobacco company in the USSR. Marlboro, a blend of Turkish and Virginia types of tobacco, was sold for the princely sum of one rouble (100 kopecks), thus many times more

expensive than the generic brands. Other Philip Morris brands produced were Chesterfield and Bond Street.

Around this time 'global' (in a Soviet sense) cigarettes became localized, presumably in order to appeal to regional identities and interests in a safely controlled fashion. Thus, the generic filtered Orbita changed identity and began to be produced as Kazakhstan. Another brand designed to appeal to local residents was Medeo, named for the stunningly situated Olympic ice rink in the mountains just outside Alma-Ata. New national brands such as Kosmos and Kok Tyube (a popular viewpoint in the mountainous outskirts of the city) entered the market as well.

In the 1970s and '80s other foreign brands came and went: the Polish Sport and North Korean and Cuban non-filter cigarettes, all of which were considered inferior and never became popular. But

Bulgarian cigarettes were a class above, with TU 134, named after the popular Soviet jet, the Tupolev, and sponsored by Aeroflot; BT (Bulgar Tabak); Stewardess; and Shchipka. Western-produced cigarettes were available solely with nearly impossible-to-obtain foreign currency, at special foreign currency shops aimed at Western tourists, called *beriozka*.

Other non-generic cigarettes became available on a seasonal basis. Moscow's Yava factory produced, on an annual basis, S'novom godom, 'Happy New Year' cigarettes. To celebrate the Second World War 'Victory Day', 9 May, were Davai zakourim, meaning 'come, let's smoke', taken from the lyrics of a popular song. A parallel set of cigarettes was available only to military personnel. Comprising a vast segment of the population, the military enjoyed certain privileges and could purchase cigarettes for a mere 9 kopecks per pack. Without filters and of poor quality, two military brands, available only at special shops, were Ohotnichi, 'hunters', and Severnye, 'northern'.

It was more economical to roll raw tobacco in newspaper. Particularly prevalent in rural areas, this practice continues today, and one can see loose tobacco sold at markets throughout the former Soviet Union, often measured in drinking glasses. Rural families sometimes grew their own tobacco, called *samosad* (self-cultivated), popularized in song lyrics such as 'I have tasty samosad in my pocket.' Cheaper still was *makhorka*, a tobacco by-product made from crushed tobacco stems, as opposed to the leaves of the plant. A 250-gram package of *makhorka* cost a mere 6 kopecks. At one gram of tobacco per cigarette, a single package went far, indeed.

As mentioned above, prices remained steady until 1981, when Leonid Brezhnev, reacting to inflation, raised the costs. Belomorkanal went up to 25 kopecks, Prima to 20, and Kazakhstan rose by 30 per cent, from 30 to 40 kopecks. This was also the period when foreign imports first appeared, including the R. J. Reynolds brand Winston.

A Kazakh man who had been a student in Leningrad in the 1980s explained that the intelli-gentsia – his professors, researchers at the Academy of Science – all smoked Belomorkanal. 'All those who smoked Belomorkanal had lived through the war, and had smoked them then. But we students generally smoked Bulgarian cigarettes.' The preference of survivors for Belomorkanal suggests that the powerful memory of having lived through the Second World War was practised in a symbolic act of 'smoking-as-remembering'. Moreover, in wartime the civilians who were smoking perhaps knew that it was in the service of a munitions industry (see below), and could be read as a patriotic act.

The practices of smoking assumed different meanings throughout the USSR. When comparing the smoking practices in Leningrad and Kazakhstan, the former student said that while intellectuals preferred Belomorkanal in Russia, in Kazakhstan 'when young people smoke Belomorkanal they probably will be smoking hashish in it – if someone is smoking Belomorkanal in Almaty that is the first thing you think.'

Some claim that the Kazakhs traditionally did not smoke. One Kazakh man said that it was only with the urbanized, Russian influence that they began. Although not smoked, tobacco was used in southern Kazakhstan and in neighbouring Uzbekistan, where men sometimes chewed *nasfai*, tobacco fermented with lime. In addition to the introduction of smoking, a common Kazakh saying reflects the ambivalence towards the Russian influence: 'Russians taught us to drink, smoke, swear and piss in standing position' (squatting is a popular position of repose).

BULLETS AND TOBACCO

A former Soviet army officer mentioned that during his training he was taught that the diameters of cigarettes and bullets were intentionally identical. In theory, any cigarette plant could be converted into a munitions factory overnight. Belomorkanal, the 'cigarette' most available during the Second World War, matched the diameter of a 901 *vintofka* (rifle) used early in the war, until it was replaced by machine guns. Measuring 7.62 millimetres, the machine-gun bullets apparently matched the standard cigarette diameters. In the 1980s the popular Arktika emerged, its narrow diameter corresponding to a newly developed bullet, the 5.45, with a deliberately misplaced centre of gravity. This bullet, designed to enter a body but not to leave it in a straight line, was instead enabled to cause more damage by moving in different directions once it reached its target. This convergence suggests a powerful relationship between smoking and warfare, risk and patriotism, in the domain of State-controlled industrial production.

In the crisis years of 1990–91 that preceded the collapse of the USSR, the country experienced massive shortages. People received coupons, exchangeable for limited supplies of sugar, vodka, soap and tobacco (rationed at ten packs of cigarettes per month). A black market in coupons arose overnight, and in this non-monetary economy vodka coupons, for example, could be exchanged for cigarette coupons. The coupons ceased on 1 January 1992, coinciding with the official end of the USSR, the setting in place of Gaidar's shock therapy and the dismantling of the Ministry of Food Industry, which had overseen the production of cigarettes.

'SMOKING IS DANGEROUS FOR YOUR HEALTH'

In 1971 Yava cigarette packs were first printed with health warnings. In the final years of Brezhnev's rule an anti-smoking and anti-alcohol campaign was launched, and the legal age of smoking was raised from 14 to 16. (Later, Mikhail Gorbachev raised the drinking age from 18 to 21.) Smoking was not permitted in most public buildings, and, where it was allowed, there were often designated non-smoking areas. Gender governed the cinematic display of smoking: women were rarely shown smoking in films, although men might be.

Although it certainly takes more than the dramatic horse's drop, referred to above, to kill humans, the well-established deleterious effects of smoking are monitored internationally by the World Health Organization. While statistics gathered in the former Soviet Union are sometimes unreliable, it is nonetheless recognized that smoking contributes to the unprecedented decline in life expectancy. Bewildering to demographers, since this is the first time that a decline has been observed in an industrialized country, the stunningly low average male life expectancy is some 15 years lower than in Western Europe.[2] In the late 1990s the average male lifespan in Kazakhstan was 59.6; the female equivalent was 70.6, thus the average (combined) lifespan was 64. In the entire region that WHO identifies as 'EURO' (including every country from Iceland to Russia, Finland to Tajikistan), only Turkmenistan has a shorter life expectancy than Kazakhstan.

The vast majority of deaths are due to cardiovascular and respiratory illness, in other words they are smoking related. The WHO reported a decrease in smoking in the two years following the breakup of the USSR; it was short-lived, corresponding to the accompanying economic crash. In the mid-1990s it was estimated that one third of the total population (as opposed to adults only) smoked, supported by the high mortality figures.

Average annual (age-standardized) lung cancer mortality rates for the period 1991–1993 were 96/100,000 for men and 12/100,000 for women. Tobacco is estimated to have caused 25,000 deaths (20 per cent of all deaths) in 1995. Of these 20,000 were men, and 5,000 were women. About 30 per cent of all male deaths in 1995 are attributable to tobacco use (and almost half (46 per cent) of male deaths at ages 35–69).[3]

The government of Kazakhstan has taken contradictory stances about the promotion of anti-smoking practices. On the one hand, billboards scattered throughout the country advertise the president's 'Healthy Life Style' initiative and 'Kazakhstan 2030', the year by which the health and wealth of the nation will be assured. Competing billboards advertise the glamorous lifestyles of smokers. It is legal to sell cigarettes individually, unheard of in countries serious about minimizing smoking. (This practice is illegal in Russia.) Furthermore, the country's most popular television programme, a soap opera broadcast on the state network run by the daughter of the country's president (see below), advertised Lucky Strike and other British American Tobacco Products.

BRANDING – THEN AND NOW

The cigarette brands on the market today in Kazakhstan present a fascinating blend of continuity and change. During the Soviet period, a popular brand was called Kazakhstanskye, the Russian adjectival form for 'Kazakhstani'. One current brand has changed the packaging only slightly – the original Soviet pack is still readily recognizable in the new rigid carton – and the name has become Kazakhstan spelt in the Kazakh alphabet, not Cyrillic, printed on the front of the package, along with the Kazakh for '20 filtered cigarettes'. (The same information is in Russian on the back, in a smaller font.) When reading the fine print, however, one learns that the manufacturer is no longer the state monopoly, but Philip Morris. Similarly, the popular brands APOLLO SOYUZ and MEDEO have been bought by Philip Morris. Both are carry-overs from the Soviet period, and Philip Morris's decision has been to retain loyalty to Soviet packaging, except for the Kazakh language on the front and Russian on the reverse side. APOLLO SOYUZ, in fact, is still sold in soft packaging, unlike the others, and, like the original in 1975, is in English on one side, with APOLLO first, and Russian on the reverse side, with SOYUZ first.

New brands, ostensibly local, have emerged as well. One, bearing the name of 'Genghis Khan', is packed in a striking black box with a fierce-looking mythological creature in gold, a cross between a dragon, an eagle and a devil. Again, like the other brands, this is written in Kazakh on the front and Russian on the back. It is assembled in a Soviet-era candy factory in Shymkent, a city in the far south of Kazakhstan, and was originally brought out by R. J.

Reynolds. The fine print informs the reader that this brand is 'unique and made from the highest quality elite type tobacco, made for people who are free and proud, living in Kazakhstan, the former empire of Genghis Khan who ruled from the Pacific Ocean to the Black Sea'. Despite the historical inaccuracies on the carton, and its origins in a US firm, in this case the purveyor of Camel, such brands are meant to appeal to the neo-nationalism and increasing indigenization prevalent in the country.

WESTERN PENETRATION

Between 1996 and 2000 the only activity to be found at Kazakh Film, the largest film studio in Central Asia and now nearly deserted, was the production team making a soap opera.[4] But this was not just any soap opera, it was Kazakhstan's first. Begun as a private–public partnership initiated with British foreign aid, it was meant to be a didactic development aid project in which the sub-texts of the storylines taught the viewers important lessons about capitalism, privatization, the market, civil society and democracy. As a private–public joint venture in an environment alien to private sponsorship of any kind, the serial's producers struggled to find support. One of the primary sponsors that they found was British American Tobacco. Countless hours were spent by camera operators on the set to get the lighting just so, aimed at capturing a legible angle for the packet of Kent or Lucky Strike, since adequate product placement was the price of sponsorship.

Prohibited from television ads and product placement in the West, BAT, R. J. Reynolds and Philip Morris lost no time identifying emerging markets and lax regulatory environments in the former Soviet Union. BAT chose its market well – this soap opera, *Crossroads*, became the most popular programme in Kazakhstan, and its audiences noticed the brightly coloured cigarette packages and long drags inhaled by the glamorous young television stars. In interviews with viewers, many remarked that they took more notice of what the actors were wearing, their hairstyles, interior decor and cigarette brand than they did of the didactic messages meant to be conveyed in the sub-text of the soap opera.

Western tobacco giants have invested large sums on advertising elsewhere as well. Covering 7,270 square metres of public space, close to $300,000 are spent annually in Almaty on outdoor cigarette advertising; of this, Philip Morris spends 67.8 per cent. Next are JTI, Gallaher, Reemtsma and BAT.[5] Billboards punctuate the mountainous skyline of Almaty, showing rugged Marlboro men on horseback. Multi-storey murals decorate the sides of decrepit Soviet-era housing blocks, bearing the same message. The ubiquitous kiosks selling an improbably large selection of items, including vodka, juice, underwear, candy, cigarettes, sewing items and the like, often have vividly coloured cigarette advertisements painted or plastered on them.

But more striking still is the use of highly made-up young Kazakhstani women, dressed in flashy, provocatively skimpy outfits and stilettos, who roam the city's restaurants, youth festivals, concerts, parks and the like, passing out miniature packs of cigarettes to anyone who will take them. Even more proactive, the Western tobacco companies regularly sponsor huge music parties and other events oriented at youth, where free cigarette packages are liberally distributed.

The Western companies have devised clever means of advertising. For example, in neighbouring Kyrgyzstan the members of the public can obtain free West cigarette stickers and labels (a German tobacco company). If these are clearly displayed on cars, clothing, bags or in another visible place, and if they are spotted by the roaming West team, then attractive prizes can be won – for example, PCs, TVs and music equipment, with the First Prize being a trip to the Italian Grand Prix. Philip Morris, with an annual advertising budget of $2 million (in Kyrgyzstan), sponsors a live two-hour weekly show, aimed at youth, with cigarette ads intertwined with fun slots.

In 1993 Philip Morris bought 49 per cent of ATK; its share increased to 97 per cent in 1994. It now produces 20 billion cigarettes per year in Almaty.[6] The UK tobacco company Gallaher began exporting cigarettes to Kazakhstan in 1994. Their Sovereign brand has a 'significant market share', according to the company's literature. Gallaher has built a cigarette factory 32 kilometres from Almaty, with a capacity of three billion cigarettes per year. In 1998 it entered into a joint venture with Reemstma and, in addition to Sovereign, produces the brand State Line.

GENDERED SMOKING AND STATE COLLAPSE

With the use of young women to peddle their product, the Western companies have helped to instigate a shift in gendered smoking practices. During the Soviet period smoking in public was by and large a male practice; like drinking, it served as an escape valve as well as part of Soviet masculine identity formation. In pre-Soviet times drinking had been seen as a characteristic Russian trait, and, along with smoking, considered a permitted male vice. After the Revolution, these practices were incorporated into the Soviet ethos, as Russian notions of manhood evolved into Soviet ones. Women seen smoking in public were often looked down on, and it was a transgressive act. Although this changed somewhat with the introduction of filtered cigarettes and increasing exposure to Western popular images, the general ethos was that 'good girls' did not smoke.

Although a worldwide practice, smoking was indigenized to Soviet-ness, given a Soviet slant, for example by the deliberate renaming of existing cigarettes, and the new names selected. Recall, however, the tension referred to above, whereby the (admittedly mild) official discouragement in the USSR challenged, or was even undermined by, first the cavalier Soviet attitude toward public health and the environment, and second the association with martial values, which gave cigarettes a physical objective correlate.

A Russian soldier in Moscow, 1994.

In the post-Soviet years smoking has undergone yet a further transformation, from a permitted masculine vice to a deregulated consumer option. The former Soviet Union (FSU) has been the target of a virtual onslaught of a wide range of Western media images, primarily through advertising and satellite television. Closely tied to the introduction of new consumer goods and possibilities has been the potential of achieving what is imagined to be Western modernity, for many (particularly the under-30 generation) by definition far superior to anything Soviet. As Western governments and international development agencies pour in money to teach democracy and market economics, the road to the former Soviet Central Asia has been wide open to tobacco companies. These tobacco companies have thus become the successors to the Soviet regulators, since they base their campaign on the current climate of lax regulation, a result of a collapsed Soviet regulatory apparatus and weak Kazakhstani regulatory and enforcement mechanisms and environment. Furthermore, with the sea change in political and social values, foreign companies have taken full advantage of the post-Soviet desire for the symbols of Western modernity and have extended the cigarette market to young women. Ironically, these foreign firms have assumed the role of the new indigenizers, reviving Soviet brands and introducing new, neo-nationalist forms of smoking, such as Genghis Khan cigarettes. A shift in social meaning has taken place, since once specifically masculine-connoted commodities and practices have been attenuated, now crossing gender boundaries and feminizing the act of smoking. Mediating this change have been the new social engineers, represented by the international tobacco companies.

This essay has shown how smoking and cigarettes have been implicated throughout twentieth-century Russian, Soviet and post-Soviet history. At each historical juncture, whether the Revolution, the Second World War, *détente* or post-Soviet independence, the practices and symbols of smoking have reflected these transformations. Permeated with cultural meaning, smoking serves as a sort of litmus test of gendered economic, political and social relations. Furthermore, the analysis of cigarette production and consumption in the Soviet and post-Soviet periods reveals some of the uses of the local by the global, and vice-versa.

Smoking also performs memory and patriotic work, as seen in the context of world war, where symbolic ironies emerge, implying a democratization of war, putting civilians at as much, if not more, risk than fighting men. Ensuring the permanent state of readiness of munitions factories through smoking made the act one of collective patriotism.[7] Later, smoking Belomorkanal became a generational memory device, as patriotic, collective remembered identification with the most traumatic post-Revolutionary event the nation faced, the Great Patriotic War.

To return to the image of the dying horse, it is clear that such propaganda was not widely effective. According to the World Health Organization, it is becoming less and less effective almost on a daily basis, as predictions for increased smoking demonstrate. The post-Soviet period of independence has shown a vulnerability to Western symbols of modernity, in the form of popular cigarettes, along with State corruption at many related levels. Thus, by analysing smoking patterns, the symbolic dimensions of smoking and the practice as a feature of market competition, we can better understand contemporary Kazakhstan and its troubling social, political, and economic predicament.

The Cocaine Experience

ALBERTO CASTOLDI

At the turn of the twentieth century both in Europe and in the United States there spread an increasingly draconian opposition to the unregulated use of drugs. As early as 1914 the United States passed the Harrison Narcotic Act, which led to the severe repression of drug traffickers. Even before that, social concern had been made plain about the swift spread of drugs, as can be seen, for instance, in the fact that, from 1903, cocaine was removed from the recipe for Coca-Cola. But it was in the following decade that public opinion, stirred up by the press, was able to impose a strongly repressive line on the matter. In 1916 the French Parliament unanimously passed a law against the trade and use of narcotics, which was made more stringent in 1922; in 1970 French government health measures aimed at fighting drug dependency conferred on those who used drugs the double status of both patient and criminal: this marked the official birth of the drug addict. The prohibition of drugs stands out as a decisive turning point in the history of their use, since it brought about a range of entirely new social roles and behaviours. The creation of the cocaine addict, who was regarded as socially unproductive, ill and potentially dangerous because compelled to seek his drug illegally, was also accompanied by the spread of criminal organizations given over to the drugs trade and the quick setting up of an international traffic that nourished the most varied forms of illegal activity.

The medicalization of the cocaine addict made of him a victim of society and relegated him to the margins of collective life. It is not the cocaine addict's enjoyment in itself that is the cause of his being reprimanded, but the fact that the pleasure derives from something alien to human nature, something artificial: it is a pleasure that is perversely and unproductively bound to suffering. The defence of a 'natural' or 'original' body is expressed in the canonical terms of the foundations of Western culture: the I, conscience, reason, freedom, alienation, sexual difference, the unconscious, the relation with death, sublimation, reality and the law, and so on. As is well known, the prohibitions imposed by the law inspired Antonin Artaud to react violently in two 'official' documents – the 'Letter to the Honorable Legislator of the Law on Drugs' and the 'Liquidation of Opium'[1] – in which he regards the law as a threat to his physical existence and to his creativity. Thus there emerged into public discussion the question of the drug's therapeutic role, which has been too often ignored in diatribes about its social dangers.

Indeed, the history of cocaine, its discovery and use, refers to its beneficial side, even if a distinction should be made between the coca that was used by the inhabitants of South America and the cocaine that is a product of the white man. In a harsh landscape like that of the Andes, the hungry aboriginal could hardly avoid becoming a *coquero* in order to survive: 'Cocaine is not a drug, it is food.'[2]

The Inquisition condemned the use of coca and in 1552 the First Council of Lima determined that it was a 'work of the devil'.[3] Nevertheless, it was in constant use over the following two centuries, especially among soldiers. It was not until 1750 that the first samples were sent to Paris, by Joseph de Jussieu, and it was only in 1786 that Jean-Baptiste de Lamarck gave it a botanical classification, as *Erythroxylum coca*.[4] Nearly a century later, in 1859, Albert Niemann was the first to isolate the alkaloid in coca, which came to be known, from 1862, as cocaine.[5] Hugues d'Algernon Weddel,[6] Johann Jacob von Tschudi[7] and Paolo Mantegazza then confirmed the extraordinary nutritive and tonic qualities of the drug, virtues that had been proclaimed since the early seventeenth century by Garcilaso de la Vega in his *Royal Commentaries of the Incas*.[8] In particular, Mantegazza, who had used the drug himself while in South America, published his observation on the therapeutic effects of coca leaves in his essay of 1859, *Sulle virtù igieniche e medicinali della coca* (The Hygienic and Medicinal Properties of Coca).[9] Karl Koller, on the other hand, gave greater importance to the anaesthetic powers of cocaine:[10] when placed on a nerve ending, it eliminates sensations first of pain, then of hot and cold, and finally of touch. Cocaine is thus of the greatest use in surgery, and was frequently used as an analgesic even for children. In 1886, working in the Johns Hopkins hospital in Baltimore, William Halstead made use of it not only in surgery, but also on himself, injecting himself daily for years: he would later become a morphine addict.

From his reading of Theodor Aschenbrandt's *Clinical Observations*, Sigmund Freud learnt of Mantegazza's studies and decided to try cocaine himself.[11] He began to take the drug in 1884, while he was an assistant in the Laboratory of Experimental Medicine at the University of Vienna. He continued the practice regularly for three years and then occasionally until 1895. In his letters to his fiancée, Martha Bernays, he noted the progress of his research and his hopes for success: 'I hope that cocaine will be used alongside and in preference to morphine',[12] and the article he wrote on it appeared in July 1884.[13] Freud obtained his cocaine on order from the firm of Merck in Darmstadt and paid a high price for it, equivalent to $1.27 per gram.[14] The

experience turned out well and Freud could hardly contain his praises for cocaine, which was able to give 'an exhilarating sensation and a lasting euphoria'; one could carry out 'intense mental and physical work' without fatigue and without addiction. In view of these properties, as well as the anaesthetic effect, it is no surprise that Freud wanted his family and friends to join in the experience: he had Martha try the drug 'to strengthen her' and to improve her complexion.[15]

Riding on this wave of proselytism, Freud offered his colleague Ernst von Fleischl the chance to rid himself of his morphine addiction by replacing it with cocaine. The experiment turned out tragically, because von Fleischl soon became addicted to cocaine and died of an overdose of it, which made Freud feel deeply guilty. His critics, such as Friedrich Albrecht Adolf Erlenmayer, would accuse Freud of having promoted the spread of a new curse to go with alcohol and morphine by testifying to coca's harmlessness.

Among the advantages of morphine were the speed and ease with which it could be taken by means of a syringe (the Pravaz syringe). This enabled it to be used with appropriate casualness, even in public. By contrast, cocaine withdrew from this mixture of the clandestine and the ostentatious, and called for greater attention and a more elaborate ritual.

Cocaine can be taken in liquid form, diluted in water, which was the most common way at the end of the nineteenth century. In 1863 Angelo Mariani created the fashionable tonic drink 'Mariani's Peruvian Coca Tonic Wine',[16] which was so popular as to count among its supporters Colette, Thomas Edison, Henrik Ibsen, Victor Hugo, Jules Verne, Charles Gounod, Jules Massenet, Emile Zola and even Pope Leo XIII. Others drank cocainized champagne. In the United States, cocaine and whisky was preferred, but the greatest success was that of Coca-Cola, invented in 1885 by John Styth Pemberton. By far the strongest and most immediate effect is obtained by intravenous injection, which inserts the cocaine directly into the blood. Arthur Conan

Pope Leo XIII (1810–1903) endorsed Vin Mariani, a cocaine-laced wine very popular in Europe in the mid-19th century. When Colonel John Pemberton in Atlanta brewed up his first batch of Coca-Cola in 1886, he was trying to imitate Vin Mariani, but dropped the wine to avoid problems with Temperance groups. Pemberton did, however, leave in the cocaine, which remained in Coke for at least the next twenty years.

Doyle's fictional detective Sherlock Holmes makes use of a 'seven-per-cent solution' in *The Sign of Four* (1890), where there is a lengthy account of the ritual aspect of this practice. Under the worried gaze of his friend Dr Watson, Holmes takes

> his bottle from the corner of the mantlepiece, and his hypodermic syringe from its neat morocco case. With his long, white, nervous fingers he adjusted the delicate needle and rolled back his left shirtcuff. For some little time his eyes rested thoughtfully upon the sinewy fore-arm and wrist, all dotted and scarred with innumerable puncture-marks. Finally, he thrust the sharp point home, pressed down the tiny piston, and sank back into the velvet-lined armchair with a long sigh of satisfaction.[17]

Soon enough, however, the use of cocaine in liquid solution was replaced by the white powder, which is sniffed and carried to the brain by the blood vessels of the nasal scrolls. Still today, the most common way to take the drug is by sniffing it through a rolled piece of paper or banknote, or through a golden straw. Cocaine's colour adds to its fascination: while opium is blue, hashish green, ether transparent, mescaline yellow, LSD translucent and ecstasy a rainbow of colours, cocaine is white. Given also its extreme lightness, this has given it the name of snow.

Against Koller's emphasis on cocaine's anaes-thetic and analgesic properties, Freud made play of its euphoric effects in giving a feeling of being at the height of mental and physical vigour and being able to do without food and sleep. When Dr Watson remonstrates with him about his motivations for recourse to drugs, Holmes replies that he 'crave[s] for mental exaltation',[18] an exaltation that is supplied by abstruse problems or, in default of that, by drugs.

More than other drugs, cocaine seems to be able to call up the will to power and to exalt its vitality and strength, at the same time as accentuating the mechanisms of desire. Use of the drug is a perfect illustration of a theory of desire that reads the sub-ject as always in check. Desire is insatiable and to respond to it is to fall into a bottomless abyss. Instead of giving pleasure, the next dose brings only the relief of having avoided suffering: non-pain, which is a negative pleasure that is governed by a sort of chemically managed master–slave dialectic. In this respect, all drugs, including, paradoxically, the euphorics, are anaesthetics in their momentary quelling of a pain.[19]

It is not entirely implausible to think that Freud's experience with cocaine was associated with the formulation of his psychoanalytic theory, based as it is on the opposition between the pleasure and the reality principle. Growing up involves learning to defer pleasures and directing them to objects that are in line with the way the world is and with one's own self-preservation. In Freudian psychoanalysis, pleasure is the calming of an unsaturated tension, and cocaine fills a void even if it does not produce an increase in pleasure. Addiction thus appears as flight in the face of desire, as the negation of its insatiability. Even if we are not made for all the pleasures of which we are capable, nevertheless for Freud desires are not insatiable, except in neuroses, in dreams and in intoxication. On the other hand, Lacan postulates a desire that is always alive precisely because it is insatiable and the radical nature of desire has its unavoidable foundation in dissatisfaction.

In the very years that Freud and Doyle were coming face to face with cocaine, Robert Louis Stevenson was also being carried away by the marvellous effects of drugs. Although he most of all used opium to deal with his insomnia, he also had recourse to cocaine as a stimulant for writing. It is likely that the double figure of Dr Jekyll and Mr Hyde grew out of this experience. The mysterious potion that the character uses does not directly call cocaine to mind, but although its red colour would seem to indicate some tincture of laudanum, the effects are not sedative at all but euphoric, just like those of cocaine: 'I felt younger, lighter, happier in body.'[20]

The ambiguity that Stevenson brings to light became the very emblem of cocaine in approaches recorded from the early twentieth century. Although its use was at first restricted to an intellectual elite,

from the time of the First World War it spread quickly through the whole of the Western world and was freely sold on the streets of Paris, Vienna, Berlin, London and New York. Cocaine was the drug of preference for the armed forces, but all social classes used it, and there sprung up clubs where people gathered for 'drug parties' or 'five o'clock cocas'. As a direct result of this excessive use, and after various violent episodes, such as that involving the Hollywood actor Fatty Arbuckle, recourse to it began to diminish somewhat in all countries towards the end of the 1920s.

The reactions of intellectuals differed widely, ranging from a not uncynical irony to accounts of the most atrocious suffering. In France, the artistic avant-gardes were the most involved, not only in relation to their creative needs but also to help them deal with the difficulties of their social marginality. In 1919 the young poet Robert Desnos (1900–1945) wrote an 'Ode to Coco',[21] in which he plays on the many resonances of the word: the parrot, the cock's crow, the coconut, the word 'cocotte' and finally cocaine, although he declares his own preference for opium: 'I have fields of deceitful and pernicious poppies / That light up my eyes more than you do, Coco!'[22]

A few years later, also in France, Victor Cyril published an interview with a Montmartre cocaine dealer, *La Coca, poison moderne*.[23] Previously, it had been easy to get hold of cocaine in public places such as bars, perhaps by going to the lavatory or even at the till, where it was sold in small bottles (the till was called a pharmacy in slang). After it was prohibited, these ways came to an end and the drug circulated from hand to hand: 'You never find it left lying around anymore!'[24] Each individual would make up his or her own special cocktail, mixing cocaine with heroin, morphine or opium. The effects that are reported are identical to those that Freud had felt: everything becomes more beautiful and easier, and one feels superhuman or like God.

Likewise, in *Mort difficile*,[25] the young René Crevel (1900–1935) illustrates the way that drug lore had reached a popular audience with his amusing dialogue between the son and the mother of the family Dumont-Dufour. The mother rebukes the son for injecting himself with cocaine, and he replies that you don't take cocaine intravenously but by sniffing it; the mother replies indignantly that 'all these drugs are taken by jabs';[26] at which the son says ironically that if she knows more than him: 'Have you already given yourself a jab of cocaine?' Already in 1903 in their *Mortelle Impuissance*[27] Georges Normandy and Charles Poinsot had described in detail the dramatic effects of taking cocaine in liquid form. First of all the subject feels an excitement that seems to increase his creative powers; then the most painful hallucinations supervene and one has the sensation of being a corpse invaded by worms; to keep the devastating effect of the drug at bay one takes refuge in morphine. On the other hand, in his *Les Civilisés*,[28] Claude Farrère remarks on another way of taking, or, in this case, of giving coca: in Saigon, Dr Mévil prescribes cocaine pills for the ladies he wishes to seduce.

In 1930 the manuscript of M. Ageev's novel *Novella with Cocaine* arrived in Paris and soon became popular among the Russian emigré community, being published under the definitive title of *Novel with Cocaine*.[29] Nothing is known for sure about the author,[30] but the narrating voice in the novel belongs to the Dostoyevskian tradition, beginning with the subtitle, which describes the work as 'From the Notes of a Sick Man' (*Po zapiskam bol'nogo*). The narrator presents himself as a wicked, hateful and base being who is attracted by the voluptuousness of humiliation and pain. The highly detailed description of the use and effects of drugs is testimony to a close acquaintance with them, but does not add anything to what we already know. The narrator is initiated into the use of cocaine and stripped of his 'nasal virginity'[31] by Mik, one of his friends, who procures the doses for him. The first effect is anaesthetic: his teeth become completely insensitive so that 'touching one of them, you felt all the others coming easily along behind it'.[32] Gradually, this sensation spreads to the rest of the

body until it takes it over: 'My body has become cold, frozen, as if it had been cut off from the head.'[33] The next stage sets on foot a dramatic sequence involving spatial perception: to the narrator's terror, the room begins to spin and one side of it collapses: 'One corner slides down and slips under me, behind me, climbs up and appears above me and once again, but this time more quickly, to fall away.'[34] Once the drug's effect has worn off, the most anguishing state of mind takes over: 'the painful, lacerating and inevitable *reaction* (which the doctors call *depression*)'.

Soon enough, addiction to cocaine reduces the initial feeling of well-being so that one continues to take fresh doses pointlessly in the hope of recapturing the first experience, until dying of poisoning, as happens to the novel's main character. In *Morphine* (1927),[35] Mikhail Bulgakov also tries to get himself off the drug by taking refuge in cocaine, but with disastrous results. The main character does indeed feel a sensation of calm at his first injection, and this transforms itself into exaltation and well-being; but soon the effect vanishes and anguish takes its place. Bulgakov warns us against trying to replace morphine with cocaine: 'Cocaine is a terrifying and perfidious poison.'[36]

France is also the backdrop to the first Italian novel overtly given over to the drug: *Cocaina*, published by Dino Segre under the *nom de plume* of 'Pitigrilli'.[37] The leading figure of the novel is Tito Arnaudi, an Italian journalist in Paris who aims to break into the profession with an investigation into cocaine and cocaine addicts in the Montmartre quarter. The investigator's familiarity with circles in which cocaine is used lead him to observe, with an eye that is sometimes fascinated and sometimes disenchanted, an ensemble of rituals that he means to use to sum up an epoch. Pitigrilli is particularly struck by the aristocratic milieu in which not only cocaine is taken, but morphine and ether are also served together with champagne in goblets, as well as 'chloroform strawberries'. In these circles, the drug experience is part and parcel of social relations: men and women invite each other to 'cocaine parties' as if they were inviting each other to lunch. The craving for drugs rules their social behaviour, so much so that the pleasure of cocaine takes on the semblance of erotic pleasure: a cocaine addict sniffs the drug, and up pops a woman 'with moist and quivering lips' who throws herself on his mouth and 'licks his upper lip with relish and pokes her tongue into his nostril'.[38]

The drug's effects work on both the body and the mind. On the one hand, there is the euphoric effect, in accordance with which 'cramped ideas' open up and spread out like 'dried tea leaves in boiling water'.[39] On the other, there are many upsetting effects: 'cold feet and fireworks in the brain';[40] personality splits: 'the two individuals that are inside me disparage each other and condemn each other in such a way that my hatred for myself is shown up';[41] and perceptual alteration: 'cocaine performs the cruel trick of deforming Time'.[42] Tito Arnaudi dies at the age of 28 after falling in love with the dancer Maud-Cocaina, and his death is meant to be taken as the emblem of an epoch that is consciously killing itself in the cult of its own sterility.

Paris is once more the setting for the drug experiences of Aleister Crowley (1875–1947) recounted in his *Diary of a Drug Fiend* (1922).[43] Cocaine was only one of the range of drugs that he took, at a time when it was possible to have it sent by post from London and at a much higher grade of purity than that currently available. Crowley paints a glowing picture of cocaine, which is essentially an anaesthetic capable of suppressing physical suffering, but he is also aware of the drug's 'delicious perversity': one feels an extraordinary sensation of well-being and an unmotivated euphoria that frees one from all worry.

In the German-speaking world especially, the same climate of opinion affected other intellectuals, such as Georg Trakl and Gottfried Benn, both of whom were much taken with cocaine. After trying chloroform and veronal, Trakl moved to cocaine and died in 1914, probably from an overdose, after having praised 'the white sleep' and the 'black snow'.[44] Similarly, Benn would return to the night-time hallucinations undergone under the influence of the drug: 'Oh night! I have taken cocaine.'[45] By contrast, in his account of his very varied experiences of drugs (including ether, opium, hashish, hallucinogens, LSD and peyotl), Ernst Jünger is insistent in describing how taking the drug has a charm of its own: the little box full of white powder, white as snow, glistening like satin and tamped down like talcum, the metal spoon to carry a snort to the nose, and finally its frightful effect: the nose, the mouth, the forehead and the rest of the body become cold and insensitive.[46]

After the Second World War, it was the English-speaking world that made the most of drug experiences. Along with Timothy Leary, William Burroughs, whose life was dedicated to all sorts of drugs, was the prominent figure. At first he was interested only in opiates, particularly morphine and heroin, and it was not until later that he began to take cocaine, but, contrary to Bulgakov's indications, he would recommend taking it in combination with morphine injections. In *The Naked Lunch*[47] he maintains that cocaine is by far the most effective drug, but it lasts just a few minutes, which means that, even if it does not cause addiction, the pleasure can be extended in time only by continuing to take fresh doses. This gives rise to the need for morphine, which takes away the nervousness that cocaine induces and prevents overdose. Burroughs claims that cocaine addicts often stay up all night injecting themselves with alternate doses of heroin and cocaine, or with a mixture of heroin and cocaine in the same syringe so as to create a 'speed ball'.

In the 1960s and '70s, the great science fiction writer Philip K. Dick (1928–1982) experimented extensively with drugs but, unlike Burroughs, preferred cocaine and amphetamines to opiates. After a detox cure, he published *A Scanner Darkly*,[48] which offers a disquieting portrait of a gang of drug addicts who take pills of so-called Substance D, whose effects are very similar to those of cocaine. The drug returns in novels of the new generation of writers such as Bret Easton Ellis in *Less Than Zero*

Crack smoking in America in the late 1980s.

(1986)[49] and *American Psycho* (1991),[50] Jay McInerney with *Bright Lights, Big City* (1984)[51] and Carrie Fisher, whose *Postcards from the Edge* (1987)[52] recounts the author's own detoxication.

In the meantime, cocaine has been spreading at an increasing rate and its popularity has been enhanced by its use by musicians, from Keith Richards of the Rolling Stones to J. J. Cale, and by sporting heroes. But, although there is some rather doubtful evidence of its adoption in the 1920s, it was only in the last two decades of the twentieth century that smoking became a dominant mode for the consumption of coca derivatives. While snorting cocaine became fixed in the public imagination as the manner adopted by 'yuppies', as seen in films from Oliver Stone's *Wall Street* (1987) to *Boiler Room* (2000), the accelerating trade in cheaper by-products of the drug, such as crack, led to a split in perceptions of it. It has been conjectured that the very name of crack is onomatopoeic, from the sound that it makes when it is burnt to produce the smoke

that is inhaled, which allows the alkaloid to be assimilated into the blood system in larger quantities than an injection would permit. This ritual was increasingly associated with marginalized ethnic groups and with urban degradation. While the supply of drugs among white-collar workers was a seen as a personalized exchange between dealer and user, crack generated the image of the highly fortified and anonymous crack house, in which purchases would be made through a hole in the door. The association of smokable crack with squalor and desperation was by no means broken by the cases of prominent politicians and sportsmen being arrested for using it. If anything, it is significant that the bourgeois students who have recourse to free-basing in Soderbergh's *Traffic* (2000) are criticized by social workers for behaviour that is inappropriate to their class background: they are not ghetto kids. Just as smoking in general came to carry social stigma, so the consumption of cocaine as smoked crack became the object of special opprobrium.

Smoking & Sociability

Claude Lévi-Strauss assigns tobacco to a rather unique place in his dichotomy of all human relationships to the external world. In his From Honey to Ashes *tobacco is neither raw nor cooked – it is 'metaculinary'. It shares in all of the qualities of things found naturally in the world and things manufactured by mankind. Smoking defines the very nature of what it means to be human. We smoke together with others after meals, in clubs; we smoke in twos (ideally in bed, after sex); we smoke alone. In each case the very act of smoking reinforces our relationship to that network we call humanity. Even smoking alone underscores an alienation from all others. Yet smoking structures the best conversation. As William Cowper observed in 1782: 'The pipe with solemn interposing puff / Makes a half a sentence at a time enough.' Indeed, there is the tale told of a meeting in 1833 between Ralph Waldo Emerson and Thomas Carlyle in which they shared a pipe, sitting quiet until midnight, and when they parted congratulated one another on what a profitable and pleasant evening they had had. Smoking makes the best husband, wrote Robert Louis Stevenson in 1881: 'No woman should marry a teetotaler, or a man who does not smoke . . . Whatever keeps a man in the front garden, whatever checks wandering fancy and all inordinate ambition, whatever makes for lounging and contentment, makes just so surely for domestic happiness.' Smoking makes the best soldier. In the British medical periodical The Lancet for 3 October 1914, the editor noted that 'we may surely brush aside much prejudice against the use of tobacco when we consider what a source of comfort it is to the sailor and soldier engaged in a nerve-*racking campaign . . . tobacco must be a real solace and joy when he can find time for this well-earned indulgence.' Fifty years later the Argentine revolutionary Che Guevara, remembering himself in the Cuban hills, understands that 'a customary and extremely important comfort in the life of the guerrilla fighter is a smoke . . . a smoke in moments of rest is a great friend to the solitary soldier.' Smoking makes the best in society until the anxiety about its risk – an anxiety present from its very earliest use in the West – dominates and smoking itself is understood as the killer of individuals, and couples, and society. It is in the miasma (in the form of second-hand smoke) that infiltrates the unsuspecting body of the bystander and destroys not only the social network but also life itself. Here the very link of smoking as a bond between individuals is destroyed. But perhaps this is but another sign of the postmodern, as Robert D. Putnam notes in his Bowling Alone: The Collapse and Revival of American Community (2000). Putnam has warned us that our stock of social capital – the very fabric of our connections with one other – has plummeted, impoverishing our lives and communities. We have become less and less social. We belong to fewer organizations that meet, know our neighbours less, meet with friends less frequently, and even socialize with our families less often. Our number of dinner parties has plummeted by half. We are even bowling alone. More Americans are bowling than ever before, but they are not bowling together in leagues. And in all of these cases we are certainly no longer permitted to smoke, or we smoke alone.*

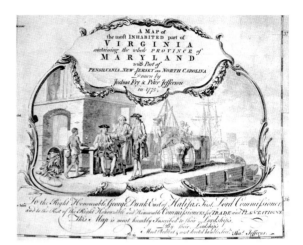

Detail from Joshua Fry and Peter Jefferson's 1775 MAP of the most INHABITED part of VIRGINIA . . . , depicting a wharf with ships, workers and a 'master' smoking a pipe.

Detail from Captain John Smith's 1612 *Map of Virginia with a Description of the Country. . .* , with Powhatan in a lodge smoking a pipe. 'POWHATAN Held this state and fashion when Capt. Smith was delivered to him prisoner, 1607.'

'Caught in the Act', an
illustration from *Frank Leslie's
Sunday Magazine* (1891).

'So many Bostonians flourished brown rolls
during the years just before the Civil War
that the city fathers set apart a special area
for cigar smokers on tree-shaded Boston
Common – the Smoking Circle.'

A man lighting a cigarette for another on a city street in the US, c. 1900–10.

H. R. Robinson, *The Smokers*.

'Time Off for a Smoke. *NCO*'s relaxing in a shell-hole. Poperinghe, 1917.'

Men smoking in Baghdad.

The New York smoking ban.

Paul Henried and Bette Davis in a still from Irving Rapper's 1942 film *Now, Voyager*.

Ho Chi Minh and Mao Zedong smoking, Vietnam, 1960.

Smoking in
Art and Literature

Symbol and Image: Smoking in Art since the Seventeenth Century

BENNO TEMPEL

These are hard times for artists. Police confiscate works of art and artists are prosecuted because their work is out of line with the consensus in society. Social deformations such as paedophilia and the social crusade against child pornography have stained the reputation of pieces showing nude children, for example. Depicting tobacco at a time when its use is so under fire has not yet led to the confiscation of works of art, but perhaps this is only a matter of time. The growing ban on tobacco advertising brings paintings such as Keith Haring's *Lucky Strike* series (1980) into the danger zone and could mean the loss of a popular theme in art. Smoking has not always been perceived as unhealthy, although the use of tobacco has provoked sharp reactions since the seventeenth century. Artists have made grateful use of this. The various portrayals of smoking in Western art since the seventeenth century reflect changes in social opinion, and just a few striking examples are cited below to stress the symbolic importance of pipe, cigar and cigarette.

THEMES OF SMOKING IN ART DURING THE DUTCH GOLDEN AGE

During the prosperous seventeenth century in the Netherlands, a period known as the Golden Age, a new and characteristically Dutch form of art appeared, in which tobacco and its attributes occupied a special place. Although it is hard to say who painted the first smoker, tobacco is very prevalent in Golden Age paintings, so much so that

it is impossible to discuss all its facets here. For southern European artists the pipe was too modern for their mythological and classical scenes. In Dutch art, however, apparent reality often served as a pretext for disguised symbolism, and these works are linked by a prominent moralism. In *The Way you Hear it is the Way you Sing it* by Jan Steen a father gives a bad example by allowing a boy to smoke a pipe; the child is introduced to a dissolute lifestyle at an early age.

Paintings commonly reflect the social reality that smoking was popular amongst the poor, who lost their cares in special smoking taverns. Any carefree life they may have enjoyed was disrupted by the plague epidemic in Amsterdam of 1601–2 and the earthquake of 1602. It was widely believed that tobacco fumes would keep away the plague, so the poor reached eagerly for their pipes.[1] Their social position made them vulnerable, but smoking gave them hope and reduced their hunger. Dutch painters such as Gerard ter Borch and the Flemish artist David Teniers the Younger specialized in painting the lowest social class: coarse types unhindered by the conventions of civilized society. The paintings served to entertain a well-to-do class that enjoyed poking fun at the rabble. Smoking became an indispensable element in such paintings, but they should certainly not be regarded as eulogies of smoking, because the use of tobacco came to be associated with social deviance.

It is often difficult to determine whether those who are portrayed drinking and smoking are in

Jan Steen, *The Way you Hear it is the Way you Sing it* (As *the Old Sing, So Twitter the Young*), c. 1665, oil on canvas.

taverns or brothels. According to popular belief, smoking desiccated people from the inside, making them thirsty, and this thirst was then quenched with beer. The result was a vicious circle. The moderation that was preached in the Calvinist Dutch Republic disapproved of such misbehaviour: smoking led to physical inertia, and thus to the waste of valuable time.[2]

There are relatively few portrayals of women smokers in the seventeenth century. When women do appear, they are often represented as bringing misfortune down on smokers and carousers. Women ran the smoking houses, and they were the ones who kept their wits about them and swindled the drunken pleasure-seeker when he was most vulnerable.[3] In fact, in these scenes it is the women who oversee what goes on. Artists did not intend to portray women in a negative light, and used them to convey a moral message. They are often positioned within the work to maintain engagement with the viewer, thereby making it clear to what fate such foolish behaviour leads. Another theme is that of an old woman filling a pipe. But these were not

for their personal use – such women were procuresses, and the gesture is obscene. The pipe is the symbol that makes this message clear.

The pipe was also often used in self-portraits. This offered the opportunity to give the portrait a symbolic meaning. When the artist is seen smoking with his back turned to an empty canvas, it stresses that he is wasting his time; when the artist is facing the canvas, the implication is that smoking brings inspiration.

With the commercial growth of the tobacco industry in the Dutch Republic, smoking became more respectable. To reduce the heat and noxious fumes, pipe stems became longer. This speeded up their social acceptance, and long pipes became status symbols.[4] The growing popularity of smoking among the prosperous classes went some way to driving the villainous peasants from the canvas. Smoking even became prestigious. From around 1660 figures at elegant parties – for example in the works of Dirck Hals – tastefully raise a pipe. Sumptuous still lifes depict objects associated with enjoyment. The prosperous growth of the Republic increased the predilection for ostentatious display. Smoking reflected the good life.

Smoking did not yet have an unhealthy stigma in the early seventeenth century, and tobacco was even thought of as a medicine. But such scenes as Adriaen van Ostade's *An Apothecary Smoking in an Interior*, which shows a man smoking as he sits among other medicines, are rare. Smoking in art enjoyed a higher reputation as a pleasure than as a remedy.

The passing of time was a recurrent theme in art. Pipes in *vanitas* still lifes – collections of objects chosen to remind the viewer of the transience and uncertainty of life – refer to the earthly pleasures that fail to bring salvation of the soul. Like the tobacco that goes up in smoke, life is short. In line with this theme, physical functions of the body were also represented. For example, people who are urinating are said to emphasize the transience of the body. A smoker combined with an allusion to a figure defecating can also stand for smell. Tobacco smoke is strikingly frequent in representations of

Adriaen van Ostade, *An Apothecary Smoking in an Interior*, 1646, oil on panel.

Jan Miense Molenaar, *Smell*, 1637, oil on panel.

Jean-Etienne Liotard, *A French Woman in Turkish Costume in a* Hamam *Instructing her Servant*, *c.* 1744, pastel.

the five senses. Besides standing for smell, it can also be a symbol of taste.

THE EXOTIC WORLD

The decline of the Dutch Golden Age was followed by a lean period of depictions of smoking in the arts. Relatively few representations of smoking are to be found in eighteenth-century art. The French painter Jean-Baptiste-Siméon Chardin, who was influenced by Dutch seventeenth-century art,

occasionally placed a pipe in his compositions, but he was an exception. Smoking lost much of its attractiveness not only in art, but also in daily life. In the Rococo age of elegance, smoking was replaced by the taking of snuff, which became a fashionable practice among the aristocracy and at court. Peasants and country folk smoked pipes, and thereby degraded the attribute as a symbol for the prosperous. The delicate sniffing of tobacco from the hand and gracious sneezing are rarely seen in art.

Looking at eighteenth-century art, the idea occurs that smoking was to a large extent non-existent in the Western world. There was, however, a place for the pipe in exoticism, of which works by Antonio Guardi, Joseph Vernet and especially Jean-Étienne Liotard provide splendid examples. Depictions of harem women smoking emphasize their erotic passivity and boredom. Sitars, long beards and pipes determined the exotic cliché. They satisfied the desire for the bizarre that the eighteenth-century public so loved. Such paintings also reflected the growth in trade between Europe and the East. The Enlightenment encouraged interest in other countries, as manifested, for instance, in science, art and literature. The association of smoking with unknown places was made for many years, and many examples of this exoticism can still be found today.

MIDDLE-CLASS PLEASURE AND ARTISTIC FREEDOM

In the late eighteenth and early nineteenth centuries, artists used smoking as a symbol of simple pleasure. The country dweller was idealized in the spirit of Jean-Jacques Rousseau. The 'noble savage' was at one with nature and enjoyed his pipe in tranquillity. The pipe even pops up in rustic arcadian landscapes depicting shepherds among Classical ruins. Smoking symbolized timeless contemplation. The days of farmers and shepherds were all similar, and smoking a pipe negated the passage of the hours: it killed time.

In the puritanical nineteenth century, smoking women were frowned upon.[5] A woman's place was in the home: she was its pure mistress, mother and angel. Smoking was confined to men's rooms – the smoking saloon, the billiard room and the library – and there it was a harmless part of the day's activities, a moment of middle-class pleasure. The pipe is a common attribute in the canvases of the German Biedermeier, evoking the calm of these bourgeois, contemporary genre scenes. Raising a pipe, however, was not dramatic enough for the heroic scenes of international Romanticism.

The Romantic period emphasized the individuality of the artist, who began to draw on personal interests and emotions for his themes, and wanted to distinguish himself from the bourgeoisie. As a result, over the course of the nineteenth century, smoking secured a place in European painting. Smoking proved to be a particularly useful way of characterizing the intellectual milieu depicted. Artists, writers and philosophers lost themselves in thought amid clouds of smoke curling into the air. The artist's contemplative gaze was recognizable by the fact that he smoked. The rising clouds of smoke wrote a 'poem' and brought inspiration, as in Edouard Manet's *Stéphane Mallarmé*. This painting aptly illustrates the supposed effect of nicotine: bringing bodily calm and spiritual stimulation. At the same time smoking was also a symbol of the independent spirit of the artist, as manifested in many self-portraits. Self-conscious and with a touch of arrogance, the artist presents himself as a bohemian who feels superior to bourgeois society. Here, smoking is emphatically modern, despite the fact that it had been around for centuries.

The Impressionists, known as the artists of the new era, painted few smokers.[6] In their 'snapshots' of everyday life, smoking attributes were interchangeable with such objects as a walking stick, hat or glove, and thus lost symbolic import. Post-Impressionism, on the other hand, with its stronger symbolic and psychological undertones, stimulated a renewed interest in smoking. New associations sprang up. Smoking and sport, for instance – a contradiction in terms today – formed an indissoluble duo in society and art around 1900 and continued for decades.[7] Noteworthy are the two smoking figures in Georges Seurat's famous painting *A Sunday Afternoon on La Grande Jatte* (1884–6; Art Institute of Chicago). To the left a pipe-smoking rower is reclining. Bodily exertion is succeeded by emotional relaxation. The fashionably dressed gentleman in the right foreground is smoking a cigar, thereby underlining the unequal relation between him and the woman he accompanies – a courtesan.

Edouard Manet, *Stéphane Mallarmé*, 1876, oil on canvas.

It is also significant that Seurat uses the cigar as a phallic symbol.

Women slowly started to put a cigarette between their lips, in both art and in society. The first were prostitutes. Henri Toulouse-Lautrec and Vincent van Gogh painted women sitting at a table in a bar. The viewer could immediately recognize their trade: their faces were whitened with *poudre de riz* to hide the marks of syphilis. Some artists captured the mystic atmosphere of an illuminated face seen through smoke rings in compelling yet sinister compositions. The women hoped to attract clients like moths to a flame. Smoking in public was out of the question for real ladies. But after 1900 it gradually became a charming and chic pastime in which women indulged, reaching great heights in

the 'roaring twenties'. Man Ray's photograph of Peggy Guggenheim (*c*. 1924) is a good example of this. A lady could no longer appear without a snow-white cigarette.

Another new theme that occurred in the late nineteenth century is that of the gloomy vision of life. Tobacco helped macabre scenes to gain in intensity, as in van Gogh's *Skull with a Burning Cigarette*, one of the earliest examples. Although some like to see this painting as an anti-smoking warning – much stronger than the ones that are printed on cigarette packets today – van Gogh was here playing a typical student stunt. The skeletons in studios were artistic props, but they often became implements in practical jokes.[8] Van Gogh, who smoked a pipe, did not want to moralize, but

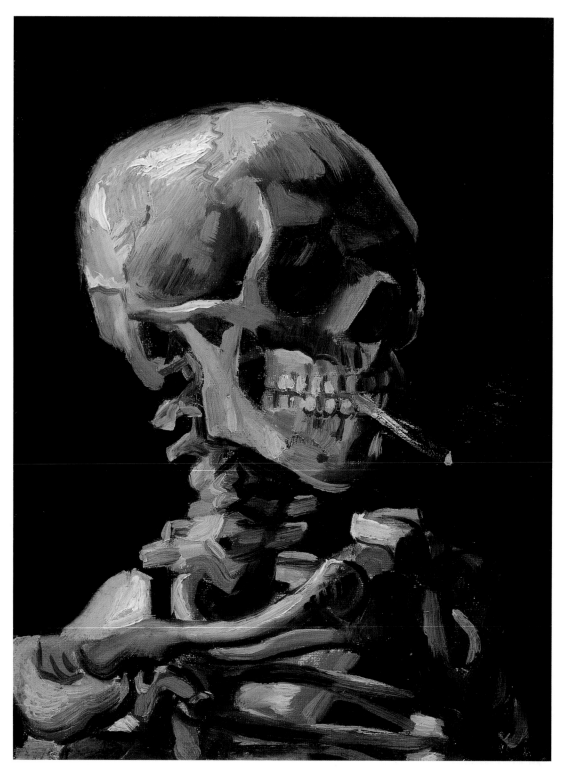

Vincent van Gogh, *Skull with a Burning Cigarette*, 1885, oil on canvas.

Pablo Picasso, *The Poet*, 1911, oil on canvas.

to play a sick joke. *Fin-de-siècle* fatalism was deliberately at work in the sinister works of Edvard Munch, where clouds of smoke reflect psychological troubles, as in the compelling *Self-Portrait* and *Evening in St Cloud* (both in the National Gallery, Oslo). It is as though they presage Sigmund Freud's vision of a sexually charged society in which human action is determined by instincts.

THE GAME OF THE CLASS SOCIETY

Although the cigarette and the cigar were introduced in the nineteenth century, it was only in twentieth-century art that the different sorts of smoking materials acquired particular significance. An artist could now create a particular image of a person by means of the way he smoked. It is striking that the pipe, cigarette and cigar have come to represent such strong archetypes in art that these images are now generally socially accepted. In general one can say that the pipe and the cigar both correspond to figures of authority, but unlike the cigar the pipe stands for thoughtfulness and calm. It is a telling fact that the pipe and literature seem to be inseparable. The fictional detectives Sherlock Holmes and Maigret depend on it, and artists characterized writers in a similar way. For instance, Pablo Picasso gave a pipe to *The Poet*, and Louis Marcoussis gave one to the poet Apollinaire (1912; Philadelphia Museum of Art). The cigar, on the other hand, connotes wealth: both tycoons and gangsters use it to reflect their powerful positions. It accentuates mean and heartless characters. Cigarettes stand for adventure, danger, strength and youth, as can be seen clearly from the cliché advertisements for the Camel survival and the Marlboro cowboy. But a cigarette can also typify the nervous worrier.

The pipe was particularly popular among the twentieth-century Cubists. It crops up repeatedly in their still lifes, with the guitar, the newspaper and spectacles. These are generally taken to be bar attributes that reflect the bohemian life of the artist, but in light of the play of opposites that the Cubists

deployed, another motive seems more plausible. Pre-eminently bourgeois objects became the subject of a new, avant-garde formal language. Thus the pipe and the other accessories represent the bourgeoisie. More than a bar attribute, the guitar was derived from the harp of Classical art, which often alluded to amorous relationships. The shape of the guitar stood for the female body. The pipe, on the other hand, personified the modern and the male. It is interesting to note that while the Cubists anatomized the traditional guitar, the modern pipe was often depicted realistically.

What was still an intellectual game for the Cubists became harsh satire in the cold and remote *Neue Sachlichkeit*. Cigars, pipes and cigarettes were used to show role divisions in bourgeois society. Because of the nightmares of the First World War, hope declined. Cynicism prevailed, caused by a lack of confidence in the modern age. In art, traditional society carried on smoking peacefully as though nothing had happened. Smoking representations in art accentuated lethargy. Such works reflect the unequal relations between man and woman, between employer and employee. Artists often made use of the symbolism of the different smoking attributes to show their disapproval of the hypocrisy of bourgeois morality: the working class with its fags opposed to the exploiter with his cigar. The cigar – as a social symbol – often characterized the potentate, as in *The Black Marketeer* by Heinrich Maria Davringhausen (1920–21; Museum Kunst-Palast, Düsseldorf). In addition, the macabre eroticization that had been introduced with the smoking prostitutes in the late nineteenth century continued. Artists such as Georg Grosz and Otto Dix painted brothel scenes in which the characters puff away. The fact that the prostitutes themselves are sometimes seen smoking a cigar is best explained by a citation from Bertold Brecht: 'Ein grosser Geist belibt in 'ner Hure stecken' (A mighty genius, stuck on prostitution):[9] the power of these women over men was so great and destructive that they plunged their weak clients into misfortune. With the rise of Nazism, the sometimes thoroughly cynical view

Christiaan Schad, *Portrait of Dr Hausbein*, 1928, oil on canvas.

of society raised menacing clouds of smoke that announced the approaching storm.

THE LAST PUFFS

After the Second World War, it was youthful rebel misfits such as James Dean and Marlon Brando who expressed their social impotence and the generation gap through the burning cigarette, which also gave them a sense of security. Pop Art, which turned ordinary, everyday objects into icons, often made use of the visual idiom of youth culture. In the 1960s, when smokers had not yet become pariahs and almost everybody seemed to smoke, the cigarette was omnipresent. Artists reinterpreted common cigarette advertisements.

The mass culture of capitalism provided strong images. The cigarette packs themselves were like miniature works of art and have become collectors' items.[10] The Dadaist Kurt Schwitters was already incorporating cigarette brands in his collages before the Second World War. Pop Art linked the humour of Schwitters's work to the stereotypes of smoking. Mel Ramos pokes fun at the world of advertising and the eroticization of products by depicting naked women crawling over cigars. Tom Wesselmann plays with the cliché of sex and cigarette by showing a naked breast bulging behind an ashtray with a cigarette. But the image of the consumer society is by no means always colourful, bright and breezy. In Daniel Spoerri's rancid assemblies of after-dinner tables, the butts have been stubbed in the food left on the plate. All the waste material makes smoking an ideal symbol for the wastefulness of consumer society: butts, matches, packs, paper for roll-ups and cigar bands simply contribute to the piles of refuse. Claes Oldenburg's sculpture *Giant Fagends* (1969; Whitney Museum of American Art, New York) reflects the disposable society. Oldenburg shows blow-ups of unappetizing fag-ends, which accentuate the addiction and destruction of the body. It is hardly surprising that he uses cigarette butts, because he once described his works as an illustration of 'towering banality'.

A chaotic and alarming image of human beings gradually emerges. Artists can use smoking to express the anxiety and boredom of people today. The ashtray is full of butts in Francis Bacon's *Two Studies of George Dyer* (1968; Sara Hildén Art Museum, Tampere, Finland), but this does not stop Dyer from lighting another cigarette. It is a portrait of a nervous, neurotic, compulsive chain-smoker. The loneliness and alienation of human existence are poignantly present in Cindy Sherman's photographs. They have become almost standard pictures, in which the cigarette sometimes plays an emphatic role.

As a result of the tightening up of legislation and negative publicity, smoking began to lose its

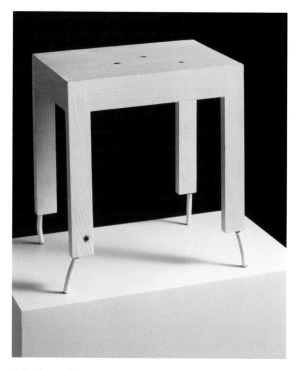

Miroslaw Balka, *Take Care*, 2000, mixed media.

attractiveness around the 1980s and its image has since changed drastically. What once was a model now became an outcast. The big glossy works by Richard Prince play with the stereotype of the emancipated smoker and the awareness that he has become an inconsolable lonesome cowboy. In anti-smoking campaigns in the USA it is not for nothing that the Marlboro man is an impotent cowboy. The World Health Organization has even commissioned artists (e.g. Miroslaw Balka) to create works that express the risks of smoking. Smoking has become asocial and associated with the consumer proletariat, as in Duane Hanson's *Supermarket Shopper*. The depressing, miserable smoker is a loser: unsuccessful, fat, greedy and lacking in will-power. Stripped of all its charm, all that is left is the addiction of the man or woman in the street whose life is dictated by what the supermarket and the television have to offer.

The growing call to prohibit smoking, however, also leads to a recalcitrant reaction. British artists associated with the Saatchi collection make no

Duane Hanson,
Supermarket Shopper,
1970, polyester, fibre
glass painted with oil
and mixed technique.

bones about being shocking. Sarah Lucas took her own photograph with a cigarette end in the corner of her mouth, and the title *Fighting Fire with Fire* leaves little doubt about the intention of her aggressive attitude. But is this attitude enough? After all the restrictive measures, it looks as though the end of four centuries of smoking in the West is in sight. Perhaps Lucas's attitude is

the right one after all: it is precisely at times when society tries to create taboos that art can break through them.

The *Houkah* in the Harem: On Smoking and Orientalist Art

IVAN DAVIDSON KALMAR

The pipe was an essential object in the fantastic scenes that nineteenth- and early twentieth-century artists passed off as pictures from the 'Orient'. This term, at the time, referred mainly to the Islamic world. In the multi-sensory delirium of their canvases, luxurious draperies – and, often, luxurious female bodies – appeal to the sense of touch, and musical instruments address the sense of hearing. To include taste and smell, there may be a brass pot of coffee with cups. The pipe, too, like coffee, evokes flavour and aroma. But what makes its role in creating the 'Oriental' atmosphere even more important is what smoking it could do to one's state of mind. It was reported, not without foundation, that Muslims sometimes filled their pipes with hashish and even opium. But even the standard pipe contents – aromatic tobacco – could intoxicate if smoked continuously.

Long, leisurely smoking is just what the orientalist artist imagined. Odalisques or soldiers around the pipe recline unhurriedly, oblivious to the world's demands. Each of the two types of pipe that appear in oriental art suggests taking one's time. The long-stemmed pipe, typically reaching 1.2 to 1.5 metres in length, is hardly something to smoke on the go. The octopus-like *houkah* – by far the most frequently depicted 'oriental' pipe – insists by its very shape that users sit around it patiently, passing its tubes from reveller to reveller. In short, the pipe was used in Western 'orientalist' art to associate the Orient with a sensuous high that was very, very slow. Oriental sensuality was seen as essentially lazy.

Such idleness was not without its appeal to the 'civilized' inhabitants of the West, who were familiar with complaints, voiced in every generation from Rousseau's to beyond Freud's, about the way that modern society prevents us from taking time to smell the roses. Being busy was recognized, even 200 years ago, as the distinguishing virtue of the bourgeois. The image of deep-reaching laziness offered by 'orientalist' art therefore provided some attraction to the anticapitalist instincts of a wide variety of people suspicious of work as understood by the bourgeois: aristocrats, the large numbers of semi-rich who lived on interest income and were known in France as *rentiers*, dandies, romantics, bohemians and artists themselves.

Orientalist art did not, of course, provide a radical critique of capitalism. Nor did it, in spite of the sincere admiration some felt for the Orient, provide a radical critique of Western domination. Ultimately, the lazy pleasures of the East were understood as but the reverse side of its inefficient sloth, and its sensuality was held to prove its underlying irrationality. In fact, the indolent pleasures suggested by the *houkah* could be seen as proof of the orientals' opposition to diligent work – or indeed their inability to perform it. Since there could be no progress without a work ethic, the inhabitants of the countries of Islam would need – in order to lift themselves out of what Westerners often described as sleepy stagnation – the intervention of the West.

In other words, what some individuals may have felt as an admiration of the slow, smoke-filled sensuality of the Orient was based on assumptions that also justified the West's colonial domination.

Consequently, the greatest flowering of orientalist art coincided with the expansion of European power in the Muslim East. It was prepared by Napoleon's expedition to the eastern Mediterranean in 1798, which unleashed a craze in Europe for anything 'Egyptian'. It took a new impetus from France's occupation of Algiers in 1830. And the heyday of orientalist art came during the period of high imperialism: the last decades of the nineteenth century until the outbreak of the First World War.

Of course, romantic orientalist fantasies (like the desire to control the Islamic world that they ultimately hide) survived long beyond that. The camel on the eponymous package of cigarettes, like the smoke inhaled by Humphrey Bogart and Ingrid Bergman in the film *Casablanca* (1942), comes from a period of early decline in the colonial empires. Perhaps some of its orientalism was experienced as nostalgia even when the film was new.

Regardless, Camel's advertising is among the best illustrations of the sexism that had characterized the artistic genre of the pipe-smoking Oriental from its beginning in the early nineteenth century. Orientalism almost always encodes not only the domination of East by West, but, perversely, also the domination of women by men.

The erotic image on Camel's bonus money means to associate the pleasures of smoking a Camel with the 'pleasures of the kasbah'. The curvaceous resident of the kasbah might be a belly dancer, such as one might see in one of the clubs where she would be available to a European's gaze – or more. But, more excitingly still, the Camel smoker is perhaps encouraged to imagine a 'kasbah pleasure' forbidden to him – gaining access to the forbidden possession of a Muslim male: a harem girl.

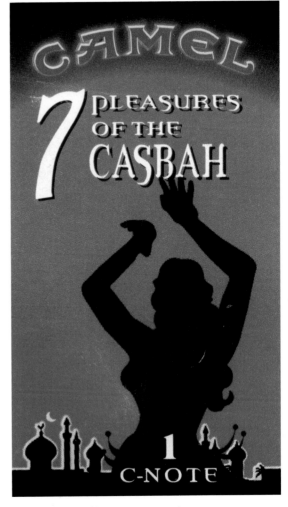

Camel's 'C-Note' bonus money card.

THE HAREM REVEALED

No doubt cigarettes evoking the harem sold well at a time when orientalist imagery was still quite popular. The harem had long been associated with smoking. More than in any sub-genre of classic, nineteenth-century orientalist art, in harem interiors a pipe is almost obligatory. The work of Jean-Auguste-Dominique Ingres clearly set the tone for much that was to come. In Ingres' 'odalisques' the invitation to touch extended by the exquisitely portrayed body is amplified by a profusion of sensuous textiles. A *hookah* or other type of pipe suggests the additional pleasure of a smoke.

J.-A.-D. Ingres, *Odalisque with a Slave*, 1839–40, oil on canvas mounted on panel.

It is possible that the odalisque (harem girl) herself has just used the pipe, causing her to exude as she does so a lazy sensuality, perhaps under the influence of a more powerful drug than tobacco. But, more probably, the pipe has been prepared for the odalisque's male visitor, who at one point after he enters this interior will pick up the pipe and sit down on the chair next to it. It is at him, the approaching male, that the woman is gazing already. We are asked to stand in his place and fantasize ourselves into his position: that of a man who can enter a harem unimpeded, to be welcomed by a beautiful odalisque.

Let us ask *whose* place it is that we thus occupy. The Muslim lord of the harem is never included in paintings of odalisques, and he is just as surely eliminated from the sexual fantasy being offered here. In television and film studies, much has been

made of the kind of social situation that is projected on to the viewer. The issue is also relevant to orientalist painting. The projected target for Ingres' work is a European male. He has penetrated the Muslim man's harem, encountering no opposition. (Presumably, his Muslim opponent has already been defeated.) The odalisque is waiting for *him*.

Like Ingres' odalisque, Eugène Delacroix's *Women of Algiers in their Apartment* of 1834, also in the Louvre, is a prototype of the 'harem interior' genre. The *houkah*, though in fact less common in Algiers at the time than in Beirut or Damascus, suits this type of work better than the single-stemmed pipe. In part this is because the *houkah*, which unlike the pipe can stand on its own, can more easily be placed in a prominent place in the composition. But another reason to use it is that in smoking it is passed around from person to person. This permits the presence of

Eugène Delacroix, *Women of Algiers in their Apartment*, 1834, oil on canvas.

multiple smokers. In Delacroix's image, the central position of the *houkah* indicates that the women have smoked it themselves, and smoked it together.

Replacing the single odalisque with a group stresses the harem's role as an important metaphor for a man's ability to possess a multitude of women. The orgiastic aspect of the fantasy is strengthened by the fact that the women smoke at the same time – their facial expression and posture indicate that all three have already been intoxicated. The master is still nowhere to be seen, but the group portrait continues, of course, to place the European male viewer in his position.

Very common in the background of harem scenes is the suggestion of a mysterious interior beyond, here indicated by the half-open doors. What we see here is probably only the beginning; there are further interiors beyond the interior revealed in the painting. The interiority, not coincidentally stressed in Delacroix's and other orientalist artists' titles, has obvious vaginal connotations, but it also stresses the male, European viewer's – and the artist's – feat in penetrating a forbidden, Muslim space. The further interior beyond the visible space amplifies this sense of penetration, and at the same time produces a fantasy of more inmates and more sexual experiences; in effect, an unending supply of compliant women in a harem without limits. If depicted, there is little doubt that each additional space would include another *houkah*.

In much orientalist imagery, the harem inmate who gazes at the white intruder turns out to be, surprisingly perhaps, white. Ingres' *Grande Odalisque* is physically French. If Delacroix's women are not quite so it is because they are presumably images of living models, probably Jewish ones. Their physiognomy departs somewhat from that of European women. This may be one reason why a black servant is included in Delacroix's picture. Her dark skin makes the odalisques appear more European by comparison.

No one painted more perfectly marble-white harem inmates than Jean-Léon Gérôme, one of the most important French orientalists. In spite of his many oriental voyages and reputation for veracity, Gérôme seemed to find exactly the same marble-skinned women regardless of whether they grace the banks of the Nile or the Seine. A particularly striking example is *The Harem Bath* (1899; whereabouts unknown), where three lily-white women abandon themselves to the pleasures of smoking, while another nude does her leisurely *toilette* in the foreground.

Yet although Gérôme's women are unambiguously white, he too sometimes includes a black servant in the composition, proving that the reason for the practice is not merely to create a visual contrast with the odalisque's white skin. In the *Moorish Bath* (1870; Museum of Fine Arts, Boston), Gérôme depicts one of his characteristic marble nudes accompanied by a very dark, masculine-looking female attendant. Her unfeminine features underline the fact that she is not to be imagined as the master's sexual partner. She is not the one bathed and perfumed for him; neither is the *houkah* for her.

There are innumerable examples of a black slave attending on a white harem inmate in orientalist art. It is European women that are here the willing prisoners in a harem that has been taken into the imagined possession of a male European spectator, in an ironic twist on the very old plot of European men rescuing white females, as in Mozart's *Die*

Entführung aus dem Serail (Abduction from the Harem) of 1782. To this extent, the orientalist harem painting is not a projection of the East into the West, but a perverse projection of the Western woman into the subject position of a powerless sex slave. It is a patriarchal response to the gender politics of nineteenth- and early twentieth-century Europe.

There is, however, more than that. As always in orientalist art, sexism and imperialism go hand in hand. There is a reason why white flesh alone does not suffice, and a black servant, though unattractive, is required to complete the scene. The black attendant universalizes the master–slave relation beyond what could be blamed on Europeans. Indeed, Western thinkers have long associated slavery with the figure of the 'oriental despot'.[1] If in the harem the white slave herself is given a black slave, it proves that Muslims too keep slaves, and African ones at that. In the Western world black slavery had recently been abolished, so the 'fact' that Muslims continued the practice helped to dispel any belief that occidentals were particularly prone to enslaving others. Indeed, it showed up the Muslims as worse than the Christians. Surely, it must have been felt, Muslims cannot object to the Western desire for power over them, when they themselves have, presumably for centuries, dominated others and still persist in buying and selling slaves – even white ones.

POSTCARDS FROM THE COLONIES

Marble-skinned women were rarely found in real as opposed to imaginary harems, however, and this posed a problem for the photographers who, towards the end of the nineteenth century, began to try to provide photographic documentation of the same images that painters had been selling – and were continuing to sell – to an eager public as Muslim women in 'their interior'.

Familiarity with the Orient grew through travel and, more importantly, through direct military and commercial expansion, and Westerners demanded 'realistic' information about the Muslim world. Gérôme's canvases were characterized by maximum precision and crispness; indeed, their apparent realism exceeded that of contemporary photography, which could not yet use colour. Nevertheless, the invention of photography introduced a medium that could claim verisimilitude for its products because of its ability to capture a 'real' moment in space and time. Photographers were no more successful than painters in gaining access to actual harems, so, like the artists, they continued the practice of arranging fictional harem scenes. Models, often prostitutes, were photographed in 'native costume' and in poses predetermined by Ingres, Delacroix and other orientalist painters of the previous generations. The orientalist habits of imagining the harem allowed the viewers of the resulting photographs to believe that they were looking at ethnographic truth, captured for them by the eye of the camera.

To heighten the sense of scientific reality, photographs often carried captions ostensibly presenting the models not as sex objects but as 'types' representing some racial or geographic variant of the 'oriental'. In Malek Alloula's fascinating study of French Algerian postcards, an identical woman is shown, in the same oriental costume, as a 'young Bedouin woman', a 'girl from the South' and a 'Kabyl girl'![2] These captions certified the model as genuinely exotic. In the place of an imaginary white slave now appears a truly 'oriental' woman whose fictional subjection in a harem masks – not always very deliberately as we shall see – her true subjection as a prostitute.

In the photographs the *houkah* is just as much present as in orientalist painting. In *Scenes and Types: Moorish Woman in her Interior* by 'L. L' (the studio photographs of Lehnert and Landrock), the smoking implement represents a rather rude intrusion into the composition, interrupting the graceful line of the model's long legs.[3]

As so often, there is a coffee set next to the *houkah*. Notice that there are three cups rather than one. The odalisque is never truly alone. She shares her 'interior', and her master's sexual attentions, with fellow harem women. If it is he who next

Lehnert & Landrock Studio, *Scenes and Types – Moorish Woman in her Interior*, postcard.

Scenes and Types – Type of Moorish Woman, postcard.

comes to drink the coffee and puff at the *houkah*, he will do so in the company of the odalisque in the picture – plus another.

Beyond earlier artistic models, postcards of harem women took as their model contemporary pornographic photographs whose models were prostitutes. Even more than orientalist painting, orientalist photography would suggest to European men a location with which many were quite familiar: the brothel. The harem was, to them, an exotic extension of the brothels they knew at home. (Indeed, brothels, like burlesque theatre, often included 'oriental' props – hence the term 'exotic dancer'.) The particular attractiveness of the harem inmate as an imagined version of the prostitute lay in the fact that she was available only to the one man who owned her. The fantasy appealed to the frustrated sense of power of the male who, at home, could typically afford to pay women to please him only if he shared them with others.

Alloula's postcard collection includes some 'works' where the emphasis on the canonical artistic tradition represented by Ingres and Delacroix is frankly replaced by the very thinly veiled desire to depict an 'oriental' whore. Such women were known carnally by many Europeans travelling or 'serving' in Muslim lands. Many photographers probably patronized them as well. In these 'ethnopornographic' works, the *houkah* is often replaced by the familiar sign of a prostitute: the cigarette.

In this medium, as in both orientalist painting and Western pornography, the depiction of more than one woman was popular. The photograph of the *Moorish Women of Algiers* borrows a modicum of respectability through its ethnographic title, which is reminiscent of Delacroix's famous painting. The presence of the cigarettes, however, as well as the facial expressions, especially of the woman on the right, suggests the sexual abandon associated with both prostitutes and 'oriental' women in general. In this context the title affirms the hidden thoughts that no doubt appeared in the minds of those who first beheld this image: 'all Algerian women are whores'.

Moorish Women of Algiers,
postcard.

Jean-Léon Gérôme, *Bashi-Bazouk Singing*, 1868, oil on canvas.

Jean-Léon Gérôme, *Bashi-Bazouk Chieftain*, c. 1881–2, oil on canvas.

All are – or should be? – available to the European.

Since even under colonial rule Muslim society managed to protect most of its women from predatory Europeans, such a statement remained a frustrated fantasy. But it represented a semi-conscious desire, the sexualized version of the wish to have unlimited rule over the people of the 'Orient'.

SOLDIERS AND NAKED BOYS

Since it was Muslim soldiers who were often the main obstacle to the European male's domination, both sexually and politically, it was encouraging for Europeans to see them depicted, in orientalist art, as languishing in the same lazy stupor as the harem girls.

Here again we find a mixture of superficial admiration mixed with underlying contempt. Gérôme's *Bashi-Bazouks Singing* (1868; Walters Art Gallery, Baltimore) is a scene of camaraderie that a Westerner might appreciate. The scene is almost Netherlandish in its folksy charm, recalling a canvas by Jan Steen. It would be a pleasure to join this group for a smoke.

In the diary of his Eastern voyage, Benjamin Disraeli, later Queen Victoria's favourite prime minister, fondly recalls his visit to an Ottoman dignitary in Albania: 'I am quite a Turk, wear a turban,

Jean-Léon Gérôme, *Odalisque*, undated, oil on canvas.

Jean-Léon Gérôme, *The* Hookah *Lighter*, c. 1898, oil on canvas.

smoke a pipe six feet long, and squat on a Divan. Mehemet Pacha told me that he did not think I was an Englishman because I walked *so slow*.'[4] To Disraeli, smoking a pipe with the Turks represented friendship and, beyond that, a willingness to participate, even if temporarily, in the habits of an alien culture: 'I am quite a Turk.' The act is reminiscent of smoking the peace pipe with the Native Americans, which was to become a cliché for friendly relations between 'whites' and 'natives' in North America.[5]

Yet, however admirable in some way, the 'slowness' of the Muslim soldier always carried with it a connotation of ineffectuality: such a soldier was ultimately easy to defeat. In *Arnaut Blowing Smoke*

at his Dog (1882; whereabouts unknown), Gérôme transforms the fierce cruelty that was the reputation of the Muslim soldier into an ineffectual, childish act of malice towards his pet. Alhough belittling Muslims was never Gérôme's conscious aim, it is clear that such a warrior could never be a serious threat to the power of the West.

The perception that Muslim males were not men enough to challenge a Western male partly explains the Western preoccupation with oriental homosexuality. In Gérôme's *The Serpent Charmer* (1870; Sterling and Francis Clark Art Institute, Williamstown), warriors wearing costumes from different parts of the Ottoman Empire watch

Charles Gleyre, *Arab Woman, Cairo, c.* 1835, watercolour on paper.

a naked boy make a cobra rise to the sounds of a gourd pipe. They repose indolently on each side of the green-turbaned elder, who holds a long-stemmed pipe. The pipe's long shape here echoes that of many of the weapons and the flute: the phallic, homoerotic and paedophile connotations are obvious. Work such as this no doubt helped some Western men (including the artist himself?) to externalize troubling features of their sexuality by projecting them on to the Muslim male.

Such ineffectual, emasculated Muslim warriors could hardly be imagined to keep the Western male at bay for long. Under the surface of the relatively innocuous ethnographic image there is in orientalist art a hint of the classic military victory that ends in the 'elimination' of men and the sexual subjection of women. In this delirious imperial fantasy the conqueror is free to enter the luscious odalisque's chamber with not a Muslim man in sight. She will offer herself to the triumphant Western male. When he is ready for a smoke, she will soothe him with a peacock-feather fan.

Smoking in Opera

LINDA HUTCHEON AND MICHAEL HUTCHEON

Both on and off stage, the act of smoking has always been given contradictory meanings in Western culture. As both a relaxant and a stimulant, tobacco has been associated with both the medicinal and the deadly; with both sensual pleasure and sexual danger; with both the companionship of society and the alienation of the rebel. Another example of this double nature is observed within gender issues. We know that both men and women smoked in sixteenth-century France and the seventeenth-century Dutch Republic, but smoking fell out of favour and fashion for respectable bourgeois women over the next century in Europe. As Richard Klein rather pointedly puts it, some women continued to smoke – specifically those who 'got paid for staging their sexuality: the actress, the gypsy, the whore'.[1] Some women who sought to challenge patriarchal society's privileges specifically smoked, just as they took to wearing men's dress: think of the trousered George Sand with her cigar.[2] But, as is made abundantly clear in Théophile Gautier's poem of 1852 to Marie Mattei called 'La Fumé', one of the strongest gendered associations was between smoking and sexual transgression – once again with those twinned connotations of both excitement and dissipation.

This same contradictory discourse about smoking was played out on the operatic stages of Europe in the nineteenth and early twentieth centuries. Opera, like other cultural forms, proves to be both a reflection of and influence upon social practices. For example, the companionship and male bonding so familiar in the West from cigarette advertising even today can be found in musical representations of smoking in works from John Gay's *The Beggar's Opera* (1728) to Jacques Offenbach's *Les Contes d'Hoffmann* (1881; The Tales of Hoffmann). However, smoking associated with the lone rebel figure that is so popular in movies is also found on the operatic stage. Jack Rance, the cigar-smoking sheriff of Giacomo Puccini's opera *La Fanciulla del West* (1910; The Girl of the Golden West) is the prototype of those film characters later played by Humphrey Bogart, James Dean and Clint Eastwood.

Given opera's long-standing fascination with love and death, passion and violence, it is perhaps not surprising that one particular set of associations with the staging of tobacco consumption came to prevail. The gendered connection of smoking with sensual pleasure and with specifically female sexuality was retained and even exploited, but it was joined by another, more disturbing linkage: male jealousy and violence. The idea that these two associations would make for engaging and intense stage drama might explain why they are found so frequently in opera. We find that even their most benign invocation ends up being fraught with the possibility of danger. For instance, in Ermanno Wolf-Ferrari's and Enrico Golisciani's opera of 1909, *Il segreto di Susanna* (Susanna's Secret), we witness a woman's defiant, yet innocent, hymn of praise to the sensual sweetness of smoking: *Sottile vapor mi carezza* ('Fine smoke caresses me'). What Susanna calls her *vizietto profumato* – her perfumed little vice

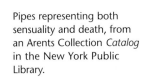

Pipes representing both
sensuality and death, from
an Arents Collection *Catalog*
in the New York Public
Library.

Lucrezia Bori as Susanna in Wolf-Ferrari's *Il Segreto di
Susanna*.

Right: Pasquale Amato as Jack Rance in the 1910 premiere
of Puccini's *La Fanciulla del West*.

– is, however, something she chooses to keep secret from her new husband of a month, knowing that it is not appropriate for a woman of her class to smoke. Prostitutes might advertise their profession and availability by lighting up a cigarette, but a new bourgeois bride would never be suspected of this particular habit. In this level of society, only men smoked. And so, when her husband smells tobacco smoke he can assume only that his wife has taken a lover. He finally does learn the truth, but not before he has vented his jealous fury in violent action on stage. While his extreme response is presented as comic, we are always aware that its violence is potentially as tragic as Othello's jealousy. Yet, at the end of the opera, the jealous husband decides that his wife need not give up her pleasure: he will smoke with her. She then lights his cigarette from hers, mouth to mouth, and they sing together about how true love smokes without rest (*fuma sensa tregua*). In an interesting symbolic gesture, they then re-light their cigarettes (which, not surprisingly, have gone out during the duet), but this time they do so ostentatiously with a more domestic object, a candle – before heading off to the conjugal bedroom, the socially approved site of bourgeois marital pleasure. This comedy acknowledges the various associations of smoking with sensuality and sexuality, but restrains any implied threat to middle-class order through humour and domestication.

To move out of the bourgeoisie and into the working class is to confront the idea of violence and jealousy more directly. It also means exploring the series of metaphors and clichés that exist in many European languages that link smoke, smoking and the lighting of matches to burning jealousy, flaming anger and smouldering suspicion. Giacomo Puccini's and Giuseppe Adami's one-act opera *Il tabarro* (1918; The Cloak) is based on Didier Gold's naturalistic melodrama about a *crime passionel* among stevedores working on the Seine in Paris. The work opens with Michele, a barge owner, sitting on board his boat at sunset, holding his unlit pipe in his hand. His much younger wife, Giorgetta, enters and at once calls attention to the fact that no smoke rises from his pipe. Michele does not miss the sexual implications of this remark and counters with an assertion that his pipe may be out but his passion is not: *Se la pipa è spenta / non è spento il mio ardor.*

This opening scene frames the story of Michele's jealousy over Giorgetta's attraction to Luigi, who is a younger worker on the barge and also a jealous man who threatens to kill anyone who comes near her. The associations with smoking continue, as the lovers' 'all-clear' signal for their nocturnal amorous trysts is the lighting of a match – a metaphor for the flaring up of their mutual passion. The opera climaxes with Michele, rather than Giorgetta, lighting a match (in order to try to light that extinguished pipe) and this sets the tragic scene for the lover's error and the husband's murderous revenge. Offering at once a source of effective imagery, a piece of crucial stage action and a means of characterization, the act of smoking is anything but accidental or incidental in the plot of this opera.

Perhaps the most well-known opera that is necessarily framed by smoke and smoking is Georges Bizet's *Carmen* (1875), which tells yet another tragic tale of male jealousy and female sexual independence. While the plot is set in Spain, its whole cultural world of associations is decidedly French. Its source text was a popular novella of 1845 by Prosper Mérimée that had been based on both literary lore and the Frenchman's personal experiences in Spain. But the opera's premiere at the Paris Opéra-Comique was a fiasco since it had simply broken too many local stage taboos. One of these involved a rather less than docile chorus of women who both smoked and physically fought each other. In the story, these are workers in the famous (and historically real) cigar factory in Seville, outside of which the librettists Henri Meilhac and Ludovic Halévy chose to set the opening scenes. In the nineteenth century, this large building, then on the outskirts of the city, had to be guarded by armed men. This was in part because it housed hundreds of women (whose small agile hands were needed to roll cigars), some of whom elected to deal with the intense summer heat by partially undressing. While

A chorus of tobacco workers in the 1952 production of Bizet's *Carmen*, at the Metropolitan Opera, New York.

men needed a permit to be allowed to enter the premises, many indeed went to the trouble of obtaining one. In fact, a trip to the Seville tobacco factory soon became a necessity for males travelling to Spain from other parts of Europe. Before long, a visit to this building and its inhabitants came to form an important part of the French erotic imaginary – thanks to writer-travellers such as Théophile Gautier, Pierre Louÿs and Maurice Barrès.[3] Their descriptions of this 'harem' of women – in various stages of undress – provoked a whole range of associations from the appalling to the appealing.

It was precisely these associations that the French librettists knowingly drew upon when they decided to have their Carmen work at the Seville cigar factory and the female chorus of her fellow tobacco workers sing of smoking and love. Unlike the secretive Susanna and her husband who, in true bourgeois fashion, linked true love to constant smoking, these more cynical working-class women instead connected the transience of smoke to the short-lived nature of love; but they also emphasized the importance of the sensual pleasures of smoking. This is one delight that appears to transcend class barriers. Into this smoking framework, the librettists insert their Carmen, a seductive woman singing of love but in terms that also describe herself: it is capricious, and has a rebellious gypsy nature. In many productions, Carmen enters with a cigarette in her mouth. We know of Carmen's intense sexual appeal because the soldiers and other men standing around outside the factory – also smoking – tell us of it in their words, and then underline it in their music. Her passionate and rebellious temperament is further demonstrated when she is arrested for fighting with another woman worker, and her independence and will are proven when she persuades the soldier who arrests her, Don José, to let her escape.

The story of the love of Carmen and Don José is well known, as is its tragic conclusion in which her jealous former lover murders the gypsy femme fatale, now enamoured of the toreador Escamillo. This ending managed to shatter yet another taboo, for Carmen was the first woman to die on the stage of the Opéra-Comique. From the recorded responses, this transgression was clearly just too much for the Parisian audience, coming as it did after so many other affronts. As the co-director of the theatre, Camille Du Locle, put it: 'Gypsies, cigarette girls – at the Opéra-Comique, the theater of families, of wedding parties?'[4] The reviews of the premiere condemn the murdered protagonist, sympathizing instead with the poor innocent man who was seduced by her.[5] To comprehend why the members of that late nineteenth-century Parisian audience might agree with Don José that the tragedy was all the fault of the 'devil' Carmen and not the result of his passion, jealousy or desire, we need to understand the French construction of both Spanish women and gypsies at this time.

Victor Hugo's Les Orientales of 1829 had placed Spain somewhere between Africa and the Orient in European cultural-geographical terms, thereby setting the scene for the French 'orientalizing' of this part of Europe.[6] Spanish women, in particular Andalusian women, came to be specifically associated with passion.[7] But it was with stage (and literary) representations of gypsy women that the full implications of this stereotyping were exhibited. Like the Jew, the gypsy was the foreigner whom French people of this time could see daily, and on their home turf. Consequently, both developed into familiar metaphors for European 'otherness'. Mérimée's gypsy Carmen is described in animal imagery, presumably to give a sense of her strange and savage beauty and her ferocious and alien moral nature; she is presented as alluring, but also as dishonest and vicious. The operatic Carmen's personality was tamed considerably for that Parisian family audience, but she remains a classic, if exoticized, image of the femme fatale: sensual, lascivious and charming – she is both attractive and dangerous. The fact that she is a gypsy as well would have brought with it at this time racial associations of nomadic freedom from society's constraints. Historically, the Roma people have been highly organized in terms of their language, history and morality, yet in many European countries they were (and are) persecuted and seen as satanic as well as superstitious, frightening as well as exotic. These negative associations were invoked throughout Mérimée's novella, but especially in a final chapter that he added for the edition of 1847 on gypsy women and their supposed lack of morals.

The social and sexual autonomy that is part of Carmen's gender and racial identity here makes her the opposite of the domestic and the bourgeois. The middle-class French audience would have found her smuggling activities morally reprehensible, but also her smoking. It is no accident that there is a brand of French cigarette named after gypsy women – Gitanes. In addition to this, Carmen is also presented as working class, and her music, as Susan McClary has argued, shows her familiarity with the cabaret versions of popular dance music from Spain and Latin America – the habañera and the seguidilla.[8]

In the twenty-first century – when the cultural meanings of everything from the act of smoking to representations of class, race and gender have changed – how can an opera director stage Carmen's cultural and moral misbehaviour in such a way as to capture both the allure and the threat? In our time, tobacco has been shown to be a health hazard and not a protection against cholera or the plague, as it was once thought to be. We know from the evidence of films that the earlier connotations of sexiness and exoticism with smoking women persist nonetheless. A director, therefore, could choose to deconstruct the stereotypes and reveal their social and cultural

A *Gitanes* cigarette packet.

roots in the past. The Romanian director Lucien Pintilie's production for the Welsh National Opera in the 1980s chose to address in a self-reflexive way the meaning of *Carmen* and Carmen for a modern audience who knew little about the original social context. The cigarette-workers' song to the joys of smoking offered Pintilie the opportunity to highlight the differences through self-conscious irony and parody. The sexy women came on stage accompanied by comically immense volumes of cigarette smoke, as if to underline the inescapability of the association. They proceeded to display themselves for our (and the men's) consumption on a rotating stage that looked like what is called in culinary terminology a 'lazy Susan'. These workers were all sexy; they all smoked ostentatiously. But at the end of the song, the audience learned that some of them were not women, but rather transvestites. The illustration of sexual transgression can be shown in different ways depending on different periods in history.

There can be little doubt that the more recent negative associations with tobacco use are going to be in the minds of audience members, so directors must be alert to them. In staging Harry Somers's and Rod Anderson's opera of 1992, *Mario and the Magician*, for the Canadian Opera Company, the director Robert Carsen and the designer Michael Levine used as their major backdrop for the opening frame – a lecture given in Munich – a sign with the prominent words *Nicht Rauchen* ('No Smoking'). This injunction was picked up in the set for a theatre in Italy, the scene of the performance of the magician of the title, Cipolla. This time the sign is in Italian: *Vietato di fumare*. Cipolla enters, openly and heedlessly smoking, clearly caring not a whit about either the public's safety or its health. An allegorical figure of the fascist demagogue, Cipolla impudently blows smoke at the characters on stage as well as at the members of the audience, both those within the opera's theatre scene and those in the auditorium. Counting on a modern understanding of the negative connotations of smoking – from second-hand smoke to fire risk – the production team supplemented the libretto's pejorative portrayal and ensured a negative reaction from the audience. The dual nature of the usual associations with smoking gives way here to a singular politicized idea.

Like all live dramatic forms, opera has to take into account its audience. In the nineteenth century, librettists could call upon the double-sidedness of smoking to complicate and deepen the tensions of their staged action. Today, any such attempt would be considerably more problematic, given the shifts in the cultural and medical meanings now attributed to tobacco use. In most contemporary productions of *Carmen*, however, the protagonist and her fellow factory workers still smoke. Perhaps this is because of the plot's use of the more negative connotations of tobacco with male violence and jealousy, in contrast with smoking as both sensuous pleasure and signifying female sexuality. Operatic representation, as in other art forms, is not universal but very culture-, place- and time-specific. Yet perhaps there are continuities that can be exploited to powerful dramatic ends.

In Praise of Lady Nicotine: A Bygone Era of Prose, Poetry . . . and Presentation

EUGENE UMBERGER

As W. A. Penn put it, 'With probably the single exception of religion, there is no subject on which so much printer's ink and paper has been expended as on tobacco and the practice of smoking.'[1] This statement is arguably still as true today as it was when he made it a century ago, in *The Soverane Herbe: A History of Tobacco*, since, in the early twenty-first century, the stream of tobacco literature continues unabated.

The last 50 years have witnessed a veritable explosion of publications on a whole range of tobacco-related topics: industry and company histories, tobacco advertising, 'how to' books (chiefly on pipe and cigar smoking), cultural and social histories of tobacco smoking, tobacco in art, referential material (dictionaries, encyclopedias and bibliographies), history and appreciation of antique and contemporary pipes, the smoking controversy, accoutrements of smoking (from lighters to tobacco stoppers), Havana cigars, clay tobacco pipes and so on. These books are often richly and colourfully illustrated, particularly foreign-language publications. But there is one category of books largely absent from this continuing profusion of tobacco literature.

Books in praise of tobacco in prose, verse and song may seem incongruous in this age of anti-smoking sentiment, but at one time they were quite popular, and offered in various kinds of 'get-up' (to use trade lingo) to broaden their appeal. Such tomes reached their apogee in the first decade of the twentieth century, when they were targeted at

'the man who smokes'. These books first began to appear in noticeable numbers in the 1880s, but by the 1930s, when the cigarette had clearly emerged as the dominant form in which tobacco was consumed, they had largely disappeared.

Not surprisingly, their appearance coincided with a significant increase in the per capita consumption of tobacco, which at this time was principally consumed in the form of cigars, pipe tobacco and the 'chaw' (chewing tobacco), and indulged in mostly by men. Not until the First World War was there a dramatic change in the fortunes of the cigarette, when it was supplied on a massive scale to the armed forces, thus popularizing it among a younger generation. Following the war, increasing numbers of women took up the habit. Despite the contemporary anti-smoking (specifically, anti-cigarette) movements, smoking became more and more socially acceptable, and the tobacco industry enjoyed a level of respect that is hard now to imagine. The social environment, on the whole, was conducive to the publication of pro-smoking tomes.

Although many books published during this period might not at first appear to be specifically in praise of tobacco, on closer inspection they are suffused with prose, poetry and anecdotes of the allure and lore of the herb. One classic in the field was Frederick W. Fairholt's *Tobacco: Its History and Associations . . .* , published in 1859 and charmingly illustrated; it proved so popular that a second edition appeared in 1876. Associations with liter-

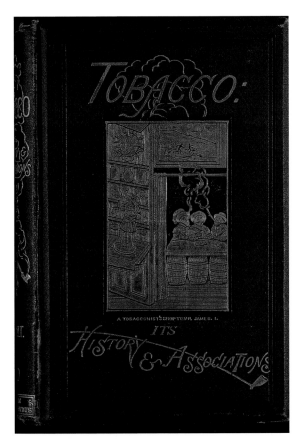

Frederick W. Fairholt, *Tobacco: Its History and Associations*, 2nd edition (London, 1876), cloth. The central image is a slight variation on the earliest known illustration of an English tobacco shop, found in Richard Brathwait's *The Smoaking Age* (London, 1617).

ature are evidenced throughout the entire book, as they are in E. R. Billings's generously illustrated *Tobacco: Its History, Varieties, Culture, Manufacture and Commerce . . .* (1875). Promoted as a book for the 'Tobacco Grower', 'Dealer' and 'User', as well as the 'Scholar and Library', it was also used as a marketing tool by the tobacco trade, which offered a complimentary copy for a specified minimum order of product. Penn's *The Soverane Herbe* of 1901 covered a similar range of material, but included a chapter specifically on the literature of tobacco.

In 1915 W. A. Brennan published *Tobacco Leaves: Being a Book of Facts for Smokers*, observing 'how few books there are written expressly for the smoker . . . [who] will find it difficult to get a book just giving him the facts concerning tobacco and smoking, which he ought to know, and omitting matters, which, although are interesting, are not necessary.'[2] And facts it contains, with none of the romance of smoke. Yet apparently there is quite a bit that a smoker 'ought to know', since he plunges right in to discuss not only the expected various modes of consuming tobacco, but the cultivation and chemical composition of the tobacco plant, the production of tobacco, the curing and marketing of tobacco leaf, and even the re-handling and fermentation of tobacco leaf!

Just why this may be so, and why coverage of such a range of topics ties together these books (and others yet to be mentioned), becomes clearer in Matthew Hilton's fascinating and revealing book *Smoking in British Popular Culture, 1800–2000: Perfect Pleasures*. The heart of his explanation for the mass phenomenon of smoking is that

> smoking has remained central to individual and group identity. However, this identity is firmly rooted in a specific liberal notion of the self, which was especially promoted by bourgeois gentlemanly smokers of the pipe and cigar in the mid to late nineteenth century. How they thought about their smoking habit provided the dominant meaning of tobacco which has subsequently come to be shared by other social groups in later periods.[3]

Indeed, he maintains that we are still living with and influenced by this legacy. And what these men thought about their habit was largely influenced by what they read in periodicals and books about smoking.

These sources of information routinely, even repetitiously, covered similar topics about tobacco, including history, botany, cultivation, production, manufacture, use and anthropology. All of this 'provided a body of knowledge about tobacco . . . which could form the basis of men's numerous eulogies to their favourite indulgence'. Further, 'rooting such devotion to an object within the masculine spheres of production, science, medicine and history would legitimate its use', that is, clearly separate it from the perceived world of feminine consumption.[4] While recognizing that his interpretation is based on British culture, which has its own distinctive history, Hilton feels that liberal assumptions about smoking, with an emphasis on individuality and independence, are at least partially applicable to other areas of the Western world (most obviously the United States, whose tobacco history is closely inter-twined with that of Britain).

A number of books that focus on the pleasures, the humour and even the 'seductiveness' of the divine herb form a natural grouping because they were all published between 1890 and 1909, during the apogee of such fumophile literature.[5] They are representative of many such books published at the time, and, indicative of their popularity, of the lengths to which the publishers would go to make the books physically appealing to the reader.

Joseph Knight's *Pipe and Pouch: The Smoker's Own Book of Poetry*, which was published in 1895 by his firm, the Joseph Knight Co., was made available in cloth (including a 'large-paper edition' limited to 250 signed copies) or leather. To give just a sampling, Kate Carrington's poem, 'The Scent of a Good Cigar', offers a poignant testament to the power of the sense of smell as it describes a woman rocking alone in a room:

Just as a loving, tender hand
Will sometimes steal in yours,
It softly comes through the open doors,
And memory wakes at its command, –
The scent of that good cigar.

And what does it say? Ah! that's for me
And my heart alone to know;
But that heart thrills with a sudden glow,
Tears fill my eyes till I cannot see, –
From the scent of that good cigar.[6]

Samuel Rowlands's poem of 1611, 'In Favor of Tobacco', speaks to the sufficiency of the plant:

Much victuals serves for gluttony
To fatten men like swine;
But he's a frugal man indeed
That with a leaf can dine,
And needs no napkin for his hands,
His finger's ends to wipe,
But keeps his kitchen in a box,
And roast meat in a pipe.[7]

Knight's book is one of the very few such compilations that was reprinted many years later (in 1970, by Books for Libraries Press).

In 1896 the Joseph Knight Co. published James Barrie's *My Lady Nicotine: A Study in Smoke*, again in cloth and leather editions. Barrie is better known for his play *Peter Pan* than for this book on smoking (it was first published in 1890), which is one of the very few fictional works in the genre that is generally considered to have true literary merit: 'With rare charm and humour are the subtle pleasures of smoking discussed, and its practice placed in its true position, not merely as a physical habit, but as a cult, with its mental and *spirituelle* aspects.'[8] Barrie's fiancée made it clear that, if they were to marry, he must give up smoking, not an easy task given his observation that,

I know, I feel, that with the introduction of tobacco England woke up from a long sleep. Suddenly a new zest had been given to life. The glory of existence became a thing to speak of. Men who had hitherto only concerned them-selves with the narrow things of home put a pipe into their mouths and became philosophers. Poets and dramatists smoked until all ignoble ideas were driven from them, and in their place rushed such high thoughts as the world had not known before . . . The whole country was stirred by the ambition to live up to tobacco. Every one, in short, had now a lofty ideal constantly before him.[9]

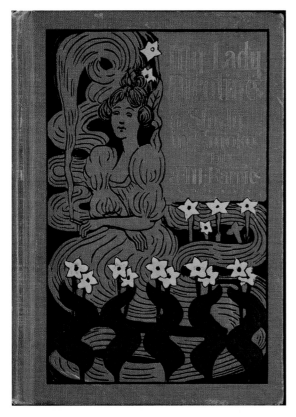

J. M. Barrie, *My Lady Nicotine: A Study in Smoke* (Boston, 1896), cloth.

Also in 1896, *Tobacco in Song & Story* (with a cigar ribbon bookmark) was published by Arthur Gray & Co. The author, John Bain Jr, was also the owner and publisher of *Tobacco Leaf*, the oldest tobacco trade paper in the USA. The book contains a pleasant mix of prose and poetry, with several entries on the practical value of smoking: '"Tobacco smoke", says Carlyle, "is the one element in which, by our European manners, men can sit silent together without embarrassment, and where no man is bound to speak one word more than he has actually and veritably got to say . . .".'[10] And as if in confirmation of his attitude, legend has it that 'on the one evening passed at Craigenputtock by Emerson, in 1833, Carlyle gave him a pipe, and, taking one himself, the two sat silent till midnight, and then parted, shaking hands, with congratulations on the profitable and pleasant evening they had enjoyed'.[11]

A recurrent theme is that of a man having to choose between tobacco and marriage. Edmund Day's bachelor, in 'A Bachelor's Soliloquy', seems to have chosen marriage, until we get to the last stanza:

And so farewell, a long farewell –
    Until the wedding's o'er,
And then I'll go on smoking thee,
    Just as I did before.[12]

The firm of H. M. Caldwell Co., which intended 'to excel all previous successes in attractiveness of *Get-up*', specialized in reprints of the classics, popular series, children's books and books for special occasions and holidays. In 1901 it published both cloth and leather editions of *My Lady Nicotine*, *Tobacco in Song & Story* and *Bath Robes and Bachelors and Other Good Things*. (The last was Arthur Gray's retitled *The Good Things of Earth: For Any Man Under the Sun* of 1897, which contained essays entitled 'My Pipe' and 'Cigars'.) The leather editions of the last two titles came housed in a cardboard imitation cigar box. In 1902 Caldwell also packaged these leather editions together in a cedar imitation cigar box as a 'Holiday or Presentation Edition'.

In 1905 the firm published its own edition of the continually popular *Pipe and Pouch*. The cloth edition could be purchased with or without a distinctive leather pouch, complete with drawstring. During this year, it also brought out 'The Smoker's Library' (described as 'A Unique Gift for Whist or Euchre Prize'), which extended the concept of the 'Holiday Edition' of two leather books housed in a cedar imitation cigar box to one that now included four: *Tobacco in Song & Story*, *My Lady Nicotine*, *Tobacco Leaves* and *Pipe and Pouch*.

Tobacco Leaves (1903) by John Bain Jr, intended to be a companion volume to his *Tobacco in Song & Story*, was the first of three new contributions by the Caldwell Co. to tobacco literature. One of the selections in *Tobacco Leaves*, David Curtis's essay entitled 'My Lady Nicotine and How She Seduced Me', corresponds to Hilton's comments that 'what was perhaps specific to the late nineteenth-century

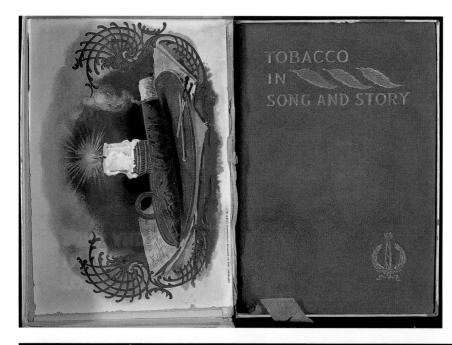

John Bain, Jr, *Tobacco in Song and Story* (New York and Boston, 1901), ooze leather (housed in a cardboard imitation cigar box).

Joseph Knight, compiler, *Pipe and Pouch: The Smokers Own Book of Poetry* (New York and Boston, 1905), cloth (housed in a leather pouch).

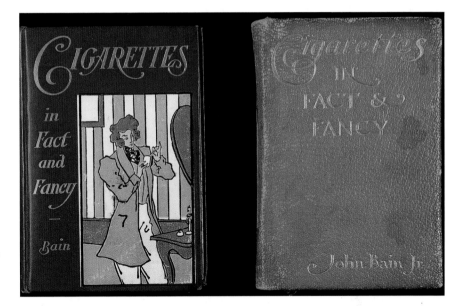

John Bain, Jr, *Cigarettes in Fact and Fancy* (Boston and New York, 1906), cloth (left) and pigskin (right) editions.

praise of smoking was the degree to which tobacco was anthropomorphised into a trusty companion, feminised into a wife or lover, and even deified into a God itself.'[13] Curtis states that there is no one 'who is not welcome to her close embrace, her sweet, perfumed kiss, and the languorous, delicious content that follows a brief hour's dalliance with her charms. And yet I love her!'[14]

Three years later the company followed this up with another of Bain's books, *Cigarettes in Fact & Fancy*. The leather edition of this book differed from the rest in that it was bound in pigskin. It also came in its own distinctive packaging – a cardboard imitation cigarette box. This is a book in praise of cigarettes, so we find in P. W. W. Hart's 'Rings Blown in Rhyme: Comparisons' a series of stanzas comparing the three forms of smoking:

> A pipe – for home, on couch, with book:
> Cigar – for joys where friendships twine:
> But the cigarette is the daintiest sip,
> Of all nicotian draughts divine.[15]

Caldwell's third original – and last – tobacco publication, *A Smoker's Reveries: A Companion Book to Pipe and Pouch* (1909), was by Joseph Knight, compiler of *Pipe and Pouch*.

In 1914 the Caldwell Co. was sold to the Dodge Publishing Co., which had already made a contribution to tobacco literature by publishing in 1907 Charles Welsh's *The Fragrant Weed: Some of the Good Things Which Have Been Said or Sung about Tobacco*. The book was initially sold in a grass cloth binding and in a special 'Smoker's Edition', boxed with a package of tobacco and a pipe; it later became available in ooze leather and cloth bindings. It includes a number of amusing poems, such as Tom Hall's 'A Bachelor's Views', in which the poet questions the merit of marrying – especially if one has 'a pipe, a book, a cosy nook' – and finally concludes:

> So let us drink
> To her, – but think
> Of him who has to keep her;
> And *sans* a wife
> Let's spend our life
> In bachelordom, – it's cheaper.[16]

The Dodge Publishing Co. continued to offer the Caldwell line of tobacco publications until 1917, when it came out with its own editions of all the titles in that group, except for Arthur Gray's *Bath Robes and Bachelors*.

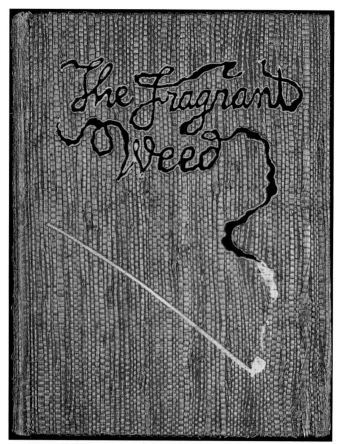

Charles Welsh, *The Fragrant Weed* (New York, 1907), grass cloth.

Below: Cope's Smoke-Room Booklets: *The Smoker's Garland* (Part One), no. 2 (Liverpool, 1889); *Pipes and Meerschaum*, no. 9 (Liverpool, 1893); *Cope's Mixture*, no. 8 (Liverpool, 1890); paper. The illustrator's initials, 'G.P.', stood for 'George Pipeshank' (in honour of George Cruikshank, the well-known illustrator of Dickens), pseudonym of John Wallace, who illustrated many of the Cope publications as well as their advertising material.

Walter Hamilton, ed., *An Odd Volume for Smokers: A Lyttel Parcell of Poems and Parodyes in Prayse of Tobacco* (London, 1889), cloth; J. W. Cundall, *Pipes & Tobacco: Being a Discourse on Smoking and Smokers* (London, 1901), cloth; Andrew Steinmetz, *The Smoker's Guide, Philosopher and Friend* (London, 1877), cloth.

A variety of other tobacco publications of this period are similarly appealing. Between 1889 and 1894 Cope Brothers and Co. Ltd of Liverpool published a series of Smoke Room Booklets. These drew heavily from the pages of *Cope's 'Tobacco Plant'*, a monthly periodical that the firm had published between 1870 and 1881. Reflecting the literary interests of both Thomas Cope and John Fraser (the editor and printer), the periodical was intended to serve not only as a trade magazine for the tobacco industry, but as a general interest publication for the smoker: 'tobacco was considered in its historical, geographical, ethnological, societal, physiological, literary, and every other conceivable relation; the periodical became, indeed, a monthly encyclopaedia of nicotian learning'.[17]

Fourteen booklets in all were published. They included, as one author so aptly put it, 'the highlights of the *Tobacco Plant* with the duller bits left out'.[18] Titles included 'The Smoker's Text Book', 'Charles Lamb in Pipefuls' and even 'Amber: All About It' (amber was once used in making

stems for pipes and cheroot holders). Between the periodical and the booklets, Cope's moved far beyond the promotion of the tobacco trade – or even of its own brands – and sought, apparently successfully, to promote a culture of smoking.

Appearing the same year as the first Cope's booklet was Walter Hamilton's *An Odd Volume for Smokers: A Lyttel Parcell of Poems and Parodyes in Prayse of Tobacco*, which conveniently provides separate sections for poems on the pipe, cigar, cigarette and snuff. The section on 'Parodies Relating to Smoking' contains imitations of Shakespeare, Wordsworth, Longfellow and the like, in which the compiler has borrowed frequently from *Cope's 'Tobacco Plant'*. One such parody, 'Hamlet(?) on Smoking', starts off

> To smoke or not to smoke, that is the question?
> Whether 'tis worthier, in respect of morals,
> To cherish the narcotic as a dainty friend,
> Or shun, as dangerous, what some may call
> An evil, slavish habit . . .[19]

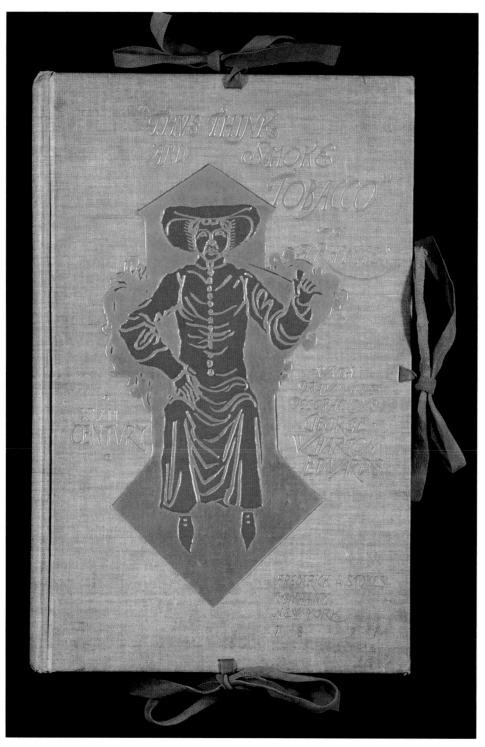

Frederick A. Stokes, *'Thus Think and Smoke Tobacco': A Rhyme (XVII Century)* (New York, 1891), cloth with leather thongs.

Written, of course, by 'Smokespeare'. Two years later, the Frederick A. Stokes Co. published '*Thus Think and Smoke Tobacco': A Rhyme (XVII Century)*, a book-length poem illustrated by George Wharton Edwards on heavy card stock. In addition to its striking cover, the book is provided with leather thongs on three of its sides so that it may be tied shut. *Whifflets*, predominantly a collection of poetry, was compiled in 1897 by J. M. Jenkinson as a promotional piece for the R. & W. Jenkinson Co., a Pittsburgh cigar manufacturer and retailer. The expanded second edition published three years later included not only a cigar ribbon bookmark, but a bound-in cigar label for its exclusive brand, 'Duquesne Bouquet'.

A number of books are more prose than poetry. *The Smoker's Guide, Philosopher and Friend* (1877), by A Veteran of Smokedom (Andrew Steinmetz), has as its sub-title *What to Smoke – What to Smoke With – and the Whole 'What's What' of Tobacco, Historical, Botanical, Manufactural, Anecdotal, Social, Medical, Etc.*, emphasizing, once again, the number of standard topics with which the smoker was expected to be conversant. And J. W. Cundall's *Pipes and Tobacco: Being a Discourse on Smoking and Smokers* (1901) includes chapters ranging from 'Soldiers and Tobacco' to 'The Pipe in Parliament', yet the author also felt compelled to include one on 'Cultivation and Manufacture'.

L. C. Page and Co., which also published its own editions of *Pipe and Pouch* and *My Lady Nicotine*, produced an interesting calendar in book form. Entitled *The Sov'rane Herb and The Smoker's Year*, Francis Miltoun wrote the text and his wife, Blanche McManus, illustrated each month with a representative smoker from around the world. A decorative imitation cigar ribbon was pasted around the front cover, spine and back cover. It too was offered in cloth and leather bindings for the two years, 1904 and 1905. Lastly, Wilfred George Partington's *Smoke Rings and Roundelays: Blendings from Prose and Verse since Raleigh's Time*, published in 1924, appeared towards the end of this era of nicotian celebration. Partington's book,

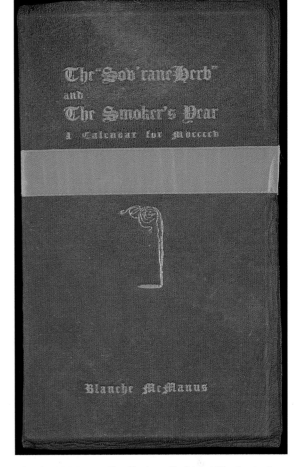

Blanche McManus, *The 'Sov'rane Herb' and The Smoker's Year: A Calendar of MDCCCCV* (Boston, 1905), leather.

available in a cloth or leather binding, not only includes the usual sections on pipe smoking, cigars, cigarettes and snuff, but also extends to a variety of other topics, such as 'Women and the Weed', 'The Philosophy of Smoke', 'Accessories to the Pleasure' and 'Recipes and Hints'.

Although the heyday of pro-smoking literature (and attractive bindings and packaging) was in the late nineteenth and early twentieth centuries, a few efforts were made to carry on this tradition. The cigar box, not surprisingly, proved to be an appropriate and useful adjunct to the packaging of tobacco books. The Caldwell Co. was not the only firm to take advantage of its ready appeal and intimate connection to the subject at hand. In 1949 Century

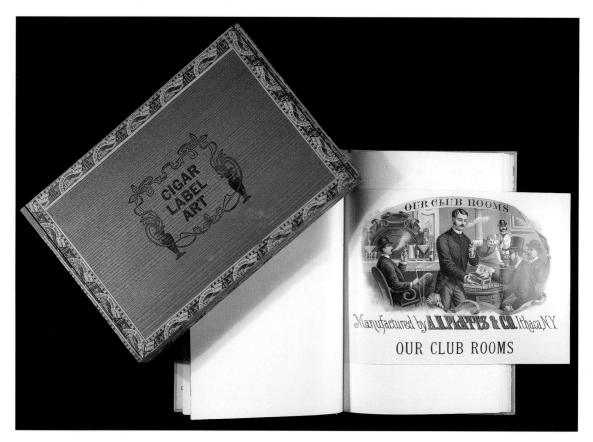

A. D. Faber, *Cigar Label Art* (Watkins Glen, 1949), cloth, housed in wood imitation cigar box.

House published A. D. Faber's *Cigar Label Art*, housed in a wood imitation cigar box. Tipped into one section of the book were numerous cigar labels and edgings (strips of paper trim applied to cigar boxes) in an effort to appeal to those interested in typography and lithography.

Exactly 50 years later, coincidentally, Ingrid Meraner KEG-Verlag of Austria published *Habanos Mi Amor*, by Ingrid and Peter Meraner. A tri-lingual (German, Spanish, English) production, subtitled 'An Hommage [*sic*] to the Cigar and in Particular to Those Who Produce It', it also came boxed in a wood imitation cigar box with a sliding lid. And in a natural evolution of sorts, a cardboard cigar box actually *became* a book: Robert Kemp's *The Consummate Cigar Book: A Three-Dimensional Reference Guide* (1997). As one opens the cover, three-dimensional illustrations automatically

pop-up to accompany the text, and continue to do so each time a page is turned.

Anthologies in the tradition of those just covered continue to appear, although on a much more irregular basis: Sylvestre C. Watkins' *The Pleasures of Smoking as Expressed by those Poets, Wits and Tellers of Tales Who Have Drawn their Inspiration from the Fragrant Weed* (1948), *In Praise of Tobacco: A Collection of Poems from Many Pens* (1960; published by the Reynolds Metals Co., the book appropriately came with a slipcase covered in aluminium-coloured paper) and James Walton's *The Faber Book of Smoking* (2000).

Historians have made their own particular contribution in this area. V. G. Kiernan's *Tobacco: A History* (1991) is anything but the dry content the title suggests. The author states clearly that he is not attempting a systematic history but has chosen to present, arranged by themes, periods and regions, a fascinating collection of 'anecdotes of all sorts about tobacco and its progress round the world, testimonies of how men and women and nations have thought of it'[20] that shows a close affinity to the types of anthologies just discussed. More recently, Hilton's *Smoking in British Popular Culture* provides a fascinating analysis of both books and periodical literature on the subject of tobacco and smoking, offering much of interest to the general reader of the kind of pro-smoking literature reviewed in this chapter.

A direct consequence of the premium cigar craze in the 1990s was not only the publication of a plethora of cigar books, but, somewhat ironically, a number of more general pro-smoking books (e.g., *The Smoking Life* by Ilene Barth and *Smoke: Cigars, Cigarettes, Pipes, and Other Combustibles* by K. M. Kuntz). Although this publishing frenzy was something of a fluke, and despite the increasing anti-smoking environment , there is still every reason to expect that a wide range of tobacco literature will continue to be published – if not overtly pro-smoking, then at least reflecting a detached fascination with the subject matter. As Walton states in his introduction to *The Faber Book of Smoking*, far from writing an epitaph on the smoking habit (one of the original purposes of his project), his research led him to the conclusion that 'smoking . . . may be here to stay'.[21]

Both 'pros' and 'antis' – as well as social commentators – would do well to recall Carl Avery Werner's comment of some 80 years ago:

> I like to regard tobacco, both making it and smoking it, not only as a sort of fellowship, but as a vast domain of democracy wherein we find gathered people of every class and race and creed, having, in pipe or plug or cigar or cigarette, a bond of sympathetic understanding and a contact of common interest and good fellowship. I like to contemplate the business of producing and the pleasure of consuming this exalted plant as really a realm, peopled by congenial spirits and ruled only by those kindlier

human emotions which the smoke of these fragrant leaves enkindles in the hearts of men.[22]

Despite the clear and serious health consequences of smoking, it is, as Walton concludes, a 'complicated, perverse and, above all, *mysterious* activity',[23] one that will continue to generate a vast literature that will decry, celebrate and document this most pervasive of social habits.

Cinematic Smoke: From Weimar to Hollywood

NOAH ISENBERG

Hovering anxiously around a trumped-up and increasingly fierce card game at one of the private clubs portrayed in Fritz Lang's early crime picture of 1922, *Dr Mabuse, der Spieler* (*Dr Mabuse, the Gambler*), a circle of transfixed players smoke incessantly, dragging on their cigarettes and cigars as if to suggest that deep inhalation might somehow heighten their gambling prowess. In this world, where all who enter are greeted with the inevitable question 'cocaine or cards?', smoking not only adds to the dim, shadowy, nihilistic atmosphere – the same atmosphere that eventually will set the tenor for much of Hollywood *film noir* in the 1940s and '50s – but also serves as a fundamental means of social and cultural exchange.[1] Indeed, Weimar cinema abounds with prominent smokers, at once nervous and composed, haunting and delightful, shrouded in thick clouds of billowy smoke. In Lang's *Mabuse* there is Countess Told (Gertrude Welcker) who languishes on her sumptuous divan, drawing idly from an elongated cigarette holder clasped daintily between her fingers, observing with her cold, blasé attitude the fate of the gamblers in her midst. Or in Karl Grune's *Die Strasse* (*The Street*) of 1923, there is the nameless philistine (Eugen Klöpfer), who leaves behind his wife and his dull, bourgeois – not to mention smoke-free – existence in favour of the big city, ultimately falling prey to a sly cigarette-toting vamp (Aud Egede Nissen), who reveals herself as co-conspirator in a murder and failed heist. Equally memorable is the extensive repertory of acclaimed *femmes fatales* emanating

from the German screen between the wars: the Kansas-born Louise Brooks, who would star as Lulu, the flirtatious nightclub dancer and call-girl, who dangles her cigarette with a potent mixture of self-assuredness and innocence, in G. W. Pabst's *Die Büchse der Pandora* (1929; *Pandora's Box*); and Berlin's own Marlene Dietrich, an overnight sensation in her role of Lola Lola, a singer in smoke-filled cabarets and an emasculating temptress, in Josef von Sternberg's *Der Blaue Engel* (1930; *The Blue Angel*). Smoking in Weimar cinema is as much a cultural code for bourgeois leisure – as, for example, in Robert Siodmak and Edgar G. Ulmer's urban escape *Menschen am Sonntag* (1930; *People on Sunday*) – as it is for big-city pathology and paranoia, as in Lang's *M* (1931). What is, however, most notable is its enduring legacy, the long shadows it has managed to cast over Hollywood and the well-trodden path that these images, like many of the filmmakers and actors themselves, have followed.

Let us consider one of the most distinguished cases of Weimar's silver-screen smokers, an example so widely recognizable that it has inspired a great many imitators, tributes – even a Web site devoted solely to the images of smoking – countless fans and a veritable cult following.[2] There is perhaps no one, in the entire history of cinema, who wields a cigarette quite like Marlene Dietrich. From her first triumph, in Sternberg's *Blue Angel*, to her last pictures directed in Hollywood and in Europe, Dietrich made her mark as a striking, sharp-tongued diva who knew how to brandish a burning

Marlene
Dietrich, in
a still from
Josef von
Sternberg's
1932 film
Blond Venus.

cigarette. Like other distinctive features frequently linked to Dietrich (e.g. her legs), smoking helps to define her persona and serves as a vehicle through which to articulate her appeal. One merely needs to recall a pivotal scene in *The Blue Angel*, in which the bumbling Professor Rath (Emil Jannings) returns to visit Lola Lola in her dressing room ('They all come back to see me!'), having made a fool of himself at her club the day before upon discovering a group of his smitten Gymnasium students there and, in the process of becoming equally smitten himself, having unwittingly taken a pair of Lola Lola's bloomers with him. Seated opposite Lola Lola at her vanity table, in a tightly framed medium close-up, the contrite, seemingly infantile Rath begs for forgiveness as Lola Lola places a cigarette coolly between her lips and hands him the pack. Visibly nervous at this point – perhaps owing to the heat already radiating from Lola Lola and her unlit cigarette – Rath mishandles the cigarettes and drops several on to the floor. As he proceeds to clean them up, von Sternberg has the camera follow Rath, on hand and knee beneath the table, thus granting the viewer the same low-angle perspective that Rath himself enjoys, focusing in on Lola Lola's sheer stockings and undergarments. Meanwhile, Lola Lola proceeds to light her own cigarette and to deliver one of her characteristic caustic remarks: 'Hey, Professor, when you've finished [down there], send me a postcard, will you?'[3]

For Marlene Dietrich, in her myriad screen roles, smoking tends to endow her with a kind of authority and sexual edge that elevates her above her admirers. Whether in von Sternberg's *Morocco* (1930), Dietrich's American debut filmed in the immediate wake of *The Blue Angel*, where in the role of Mademoiselle Amy Jolly she does her famous number in top hat and tails, drawing confidently on her cigarette as she glides about hypnotically above her seated onlookers; or in her memorable cameo as Tanya, the cigar-smoking Gypsy woman – who like Amy Jolly is shot frequently at close-up range with viscous smoke circulating throughout the frame – in Orson Welles's *Touch of Evil* (1958), Dietrich takes smoking to new levels. As Richard Klein has observed, in *Cigarettes are Sublime*, 'Smoking . . . is both a source of visible sensual pleasure and an emblem of women's erotic life. At least that is how it appears to men, for whom the sight of women smoking is both threatening and intensely, voyeuristically exciting.'[4] The target audience for Dietrich – that is, for the stock images of Dietrich puffing arousingly on her cigarette – was ostensibly male, though her appeal to women, both on and off screen, was equally strong; it was, in the words of critic Kenneth Tynan, 'sex without gender'.[5] Indeed, Dietrich became so associated with the powerful, sexy allure of smoking that at the age of 49 she was selected to serve as the poster girl for the Lucky Strike advertising campaign of 1950. Not a far cry from Countess Told in *Mabuse*, Dietrich reclines elegantly upon a plush love seat, her cigarette holder propped nonchalantly between her lips; the advertisement's endorsement reads: 'Marlene Dietrich says: "I smoke a smooth cigarette – Lucky Strike!"' Since her heyday on the screen, Dietrich and the grand images of her smoking have remained in circulation, reproduced endlessly in fashion photographs and other forms of homage (Madeleine Kahn's brilliant parody, playing the role of the Western chanson-singer Lili von Shtupp in Mel Brooks's film of 1974, *Blazing Saddles*, still stands out).

Yet it was not only the actors of Weimar (Fritz Kortner, Peter Lorre, Emil Jannings) who, like Dietrich, enjoyed a long-standing association with the art of smoking, but also the directors (Ernst Lubitsch, F. W. Murnau, Lang and others) who mastered the use of smoking in their films. Take, for instance, Lang's classic *M*, a film in which smoking literally engulfs the spirit of a city under siege. From the first moment that news of Hans Beckert (Peter Lorre), a compulsive child murderer on the loose, hits the city streets to the last scenes portraying the combined forces at work to stomp him out, the *mise-en-scène* is constantly infused with smoke. Early on in the film, five men sit around a local *Stammtisch*, the regulars' table at

Scientific tests prove Lucky Strike milder than any other principal brand!

These scientific tests, confirmed by independent consulting laboratory, prove Lucky Strike mildest of 6 major brands tested!

MARLENE DIETRICH *says:*

"I smoke a smooth cigarette—Lucky Strike!"

LUCKY STRIKE

CIGARETTES

L.S./M.F.T.

Let your own taste and throat be the judge! For the rich taste of fine tobacco — for smoothness and mildness . . . THERE'S NEVER A ROUGH PUFF IN A LUCKY!

UMP-Collection

L.S./M.F.T. — Lucky Strike Means Fine Tobacco

So round, so firm, so fully packed—so free and easy on the draw

Marlene's 1950 Lucky Strike campaign.

a neighbourhood bar, chomping on cigars and washing down their smoke with swigs of beer as they listen incredulously to the sensationalized report being read aloud from a special-edition tabloid devoted to the murderer. Then, several scenes later, with the two main eradicating forces – the gangsters from Berlin's criminal underground and the police inspectors and city officials – assembled in their own bunkers, Lang simultaneously juxtaposes and links the separate worlds, both vying for dominance, in a feat of precise cross-cutting, camerawork and editing of synchronized smoking scenes in the two spaces. With the announcement of each new scheme to catch the murderer, more smoke enters into the frame, adding further visual intensity. As Anton Kaes has noted:

> While the editing establishes the common goal – the capture of the child murderer – thick smoke

blurs differences of status and position. Smoking among men establishes a curious commonality which even includes Beckert, who betrays himself by leaving three cigarette butts at the crime scene as evidence . . . M's inordinate focus on smoking points to a society under unbearable stress.[6]

It is simply impossible to imagine Police Inspector Lohmann (Otto Wernicke) without a cigar in his mouth, just as it is impossible to forget that the serial murderer himself smokes while writing in to the tabloid newspapers in order to exploit the public fears concerning the unsolved crimes, and that, perhaps most significantly, it is his preferred brand of cigarette (Ariston) that finally helps to divulge his identity to the police.

It was not long after the release of Lang's urban thriller, his first German talkie, that the fusion between smoking and personal identity – or, more precisely, between smoking and the identity of those linked to the film industry – took on charged political meaning. In an incendiary Nazi tract of 1937, *Film-'Kunst', Film-Kohn, Film Korruption: Ein Streifzug durch vier Film-Jahrzehnte* (Film-'Art', Film-Kohn, Film Corruption: An Excursion through Four Decades of Film), one discovers amid the various inflammatory items a photo composite under the heading *Der Mann mit der Zigarre* ('The Man with the Cigar'), a document that amounts to a kind of cinematic smear campaign.[7] In the composite, there are six portraits of easily recognizable film luminaries, all smoking: from the directors Ernst Lubitsch and E. A. Dupont to the German actor Fritz Kortner (listed as 'Fritz Kortner-Kohn') and the world-famous Charlie Chaplin. All are identified (in the case of Chaplin, mistakenly) as Jewish and therefore as political, cultural and ethnic pariahs.[8] As early as 1931, however, when *M* took the German cinemas by storm, the lead actor Peter Lorre (*né* Laszlo Loewenstein), playing the role of the supreme social outcast, was widely known as a Jew. In his role of the child murderer, Lorre's pathological behaviour and claims to

Der Mann mit der Zigarre

Ernst Lubitsch

Fritz Kortner-Kohn

Otto Wallburg-Wasserzug

E. A. Dupont

Kurt Ehrlich

Charlie Chaplin

'The man with the Cigar', a montage from the Nazi-Herzschrift *Film-'Kunst', Film Kohn, Film Korruption. Ein Streifung durch der Film-Jahrezehnte* (Berlin, 1937).

mental disorder were not necessarily understood in light of the actor's Jewish background, but, nonetheless, that identity – and the smoking attached to it – should not be wholly disregarded when attempting to understand the greater cultural implications of Lang's film.[9] (For his part, after emigrating to the United States in 1933, Lorre would go on to play a series of devious chain-smoking types in such unforgettable roles as Joel Cairo in John Huston's *The Maltese Falcon* of 1941 and as Ugarte in Michael Curtiz's *Casablanca* of 1942.)

Like numerous other refugees from Weimar Germany's film industry, Fritz Lang came to Hollywood in 1934 (with a handsome contract from Metro-Goldwyn-Mayer in his hand). Once in America, he continued to draw on certain themes, motifs and cinematic effects that he had explored during his German career, among them the clever handling and astute placement of smoking in his films. Already in his first American picture, *Fury* (1936), starring Spencer Tracy and Silvia Sidney, Lang has the protagonist Joe Wilson (Tracy) – who later becomes a victim of mistaken identity and an ensuing outburst of mob violence – smoke a pipe as a kind of folksy, all-American embellishment that further symbolizes the John Doe figure's pursuit of a wholesome dream of marriage and standard bourgeois comforts.[10] Indeed, in a remark he once made referring to his next film, *You Only Live Once* (1937), Lang revealed a sustained preoccupation with smoking as a vital on-screen prop: 'I wanted to have a kind of ironic touch when [Henry] Fonda and [Silvia] Sidney flee from the law and she goes and buys him some cigarettes, which ultimately provide the means of betrayal. I wanted her to buy Lucky Strike cigarettes to stress the irony of the bad luck they bring him.'[11] Lang succeeded, in many of his subsequent films, in giving smoking that ironic touch, whether in the pipe-smoking shadow image looming over the film's protagonist (Ray Milland) in the dramatic opening of *Ministry of Fear* (1943) or in the early celebration scene in *Scarlet Street* (1945), championing the faithful service of that film's hero, Chris Cross (Edward G. Robinson), with a round of fine cigars, just before he heads down an immoral path toward his doom.

Throughout American crime film of the 1940s and '50s smoking came to be viewed in large measure as a harbinger of existential despair, a psychological and emotional crutch used to prop up a character's flagging spirits. Think of Walter Neff (Fred MacMurray), the hard-boiled insurance man in Billy Wilder's *Double Indemnity* (1944), taking deep drags on his cigarette, nursing his wounds with tar and nicotine while giving his retrospective voice-over account, his so-called 'confession', of the murder plot in which he became ensnared.[12] Neff plays alongside two other noteworthy screen

Spencer Tracy as Joe Wilson in a still from Fritz Lang's 1936 film *Fury*.

smokers: the platinum blonde, cigarette-toting femme fatale Phyllis Dietrichson (Barbara Stanwyck), a woman whose sexual mystique combines the *noir* staples of power and deception; and Neff's man's-man supervisor Barton Keyes (Edward G. Robinson), a fellow who seems unable to pass a moment of the day without a cigar, even if he does not always have a light. As is by now well known, many of the great Hollywood *film noir* pictures were directed by the same émigré filmmakers (Lang, Wilder, Otto Preminger, Robert Siodmak, Edgar G. Ulmer and others) who had once honed their vision – either as apprentices and aspiring artists or as full-fledged directors – through the repeated exposure to the flourishes of chiaroscuro lighting and the rich, smoky shadows pervading German film of the 1920s.

One of the rawest examples of *film noir*, indebted to its Weimar antecedents, is Ulmer's *Detour* (1945), an extremely low-budget picture contracted by a poverty-row studio, Producers Releasing Corporation (PRC), and shot in less than a week.[13] As Wilder had done in *Double Indemnity*, Ulmer arranges for the film's voice-over narration to come from his distraught, traumatized protagonist Al Roberts

(Tom Neal). And like Wilder's Walter Neff, Roberts is a man driven to murder – if unwittingly in his case – and, finally, to confronting his ghastly misfortune while the swirling smoke and ashes emanating from his cigarette evaporate into the night. Before his luck turns on him, Roberts is portrayed as a passionate artist, a classically trained pianist in a New York jazz club, who exhibits the talent for making it big someday; in a scene after hours at the club, he takes deep, confident drags on a cigarette dangling from his mouth while banging on the piano keys in frenzied improvisation. However, on his ill-fated journey to be reunited with his love Sue (Claudia Drake), a singer from the same club who has gone to Hollywood to pursue her dreams, he not only becomes an accessory in the death of a motorist who gives him a lift, but later finds himself caught in the web of a treacherous vamp named Vera (Ann Savage). (Vera had earlier been travelling with the same motorist, and she holds her precious information about his untimely end over Al in order to keep him under her control.) Like everything else that Vera does – such as spouting rapid-fire scurrilous prattle or tossing back glasses of booze – she smokes with reckless abandon. Pent

After hours: a still from Edgar Ulmer's 1945 film *Detour*.

up in a cheap hotel room, trying to figure a way out of their misery, Al and Vera live in a sordid world in which the very cigarette butts left in an overflowing ashtray, together with empty liquor bottles strewn about, form a social tableau. Cigarette smoking, at least in terms of its overall design and mood, is so essential to the film that the publicity materials depicted both figures (Al and Vera) leaning against a city lamp post with cigarettes in their hands.

To this day, the style of smoking cultivated in Weimar cinema and then later in Hollywood *noir* – and, needless to say, in a host of other eras and genres – can be discerned in contemporary pictures. Most obvious in this vein are the neo-*noirs*, a flurry of which have appeared in recent years, many of them with conspicuous smokers occupying centre frame. Joel and Ethan Coen's *The Man Who Wasn't There* (2001), a retro existential drama shot in luscious black and white, deals with the main character of Ed Crane (Billy Bob Thorton), a simple barber who, not unlike Walter Neff or Al Roberts, is ultimately left tormented, painfully introspective and given to deep cravings for tobacco. Thorton's co-star Frances McDormand is said to have remarked: 'all Thorton's character does on screen is smoke and breathe'.[14] And indeed these very simple actions set the tone for this sharp throwback to *film noir*. There is mounting evidence that the Coen brothers are not alone. A recent piece in the *New*

Billy Bob Thornton and James Gandolfini in a still from the Coen Brothers' 2001 film *The Man Who Wasn't There*.

York Times, focusing on the apparent revival of cinematic smoking after 1990 – up to which point smoking in movies had reportedly been on the wane – termed the new (and, of course, old) phenomenon: 'Lights! Camera! Cigarettes!'[15] Another reporter, writing in the *Seattle Times*, described Hollywood's recurrent obsession in plain terms: 'Smoking is still very, very cool, and very, very sexy.'[16] Although smoking on screen, especially in the United States, has come up against fierce opposition, and much of the media attention it has received has been the result of negative medical studies, it continues to fascinate and to allure spectators. Despite anti-smoking activism, it still seems unlikely that this vital prop and cultural icon

– a fundamental device for romance and rebellion, introspection and conviviality – will vanish from our midst in the near future. Historically, in times of war and of peace, cinema has served as a form of cultural escapism, a medium that transports its audience to a world in which beauty, intrigue, fantasy and imagination still triumph over concerns of mortality. As one critic has put it, 'Everything people deny about smoking is true in movies. It is sexy. It is glamorous. It is cool. Smoking onstage may be problematic. Smoking in restaurants is unwelcome. But on camera, there's simply no more compelling way of doing nothing.'[17]

Emblems of Emptiness: Smoking as a Way of Life in Jean Eustache's *La Maman et la Putain*

DAWN MARLAN

Tobacco owes its botanical name – *Nicotiana* – to the savvy of Jean Nicot, the French ambassador to Lisbon in 1559.[1] When he introduced tobacco to the French court, it became known as a panacea, a mysterious and potent cure for sundry ailments. The smoking of tobacco emerged in France under the same premiss, as an activity or regime that belonged not to pleasure but to medicine. This scientific/medical frame, and its emphasis on whether tobacco was perceived as good or bad for one's health (a question that cannot help but become morally inflected), is cited in much of the historical literature concerning the introduction of tobacco, and finally smoking, in Europe. Ned Rival, a prominent historian of tobacco, notes: 'it is remarkable, in effect, to observe that in the pre-history of tobacco, smoking is rarely evoked as a pleasure or a relaxation. At most, chroniclers insist on the fact that tobacco calms hunger, soothes fatigue, and procures intoxication.'[2] But what does a substance that calms, soothes and intoxicates produce if not pleasure? While the connection between tobacco and pleasure has been explicitly underemphasized, it is implicitly present in these chronicles. In spite of the medical frame that controlled the discourse about tobacco when it was introduced to Europe, the question of pleasure always played a part in its reception, even (if not especially) when it was suppressed and/or denied. For this reason, the French relationship with smoking is inextricable from the cultural history of pleasure of which it is a part.

This relative silence about the pleasure of smoking might be due to the complexity of the question, 'what kinds of experience can be properly called a pleasure?'. Richard Klein is one of the few scholars both to address this question and to emphasize the pleasure of smoking unabashedly. His *Cigarettes Are Sublime* (1993) is the only study that provides intricate and compelling readings of smoking in the major cultural texts that deal with the subject in France. But while Klein's research, both in its coverage and in its insights, is indeed my point of departure, I have drawn different conclusions about the French relationship to smoking. For Klein, the pleasure of smoking is an order of experience that belongs to the Kantian sublime. In my view, smoking in the French cultural tradition has been represented above all as a pleasure that involves an experience of emptiness.

If the explicit mention of pleasure is rare in the history of tobacco, it is not everywhere equally marginal. In Molière's *Don Juan* – played before Louis XIV in 1665 despite widespread smoking prohibitions both in prisons and among the bourgeoisie – tobacco is announced as a necessary pleasure. Because the declaration 'A life without tobacco is not worthy of being lived' is made by Don Juan's valet, we must understand it as a statement in the service of seduction.[3] Not only does this utterance indicate that tobacco is associated with pleasure – the kind of erotic pleasure that is the seducer's apparent aim – but the statement also exposes a specific relationship to pleasure structured around emptiness. Tobacco makes men virtuous,

Sganarelle argues, because it inspires unsolicited generosity; one offers tobacco to others before they wish for it ('au-devant du souhait des gens').[4] To satisfy desire before it has a chance to develop properly would seem to forestall emptiness. Yet in his attempt to prevent emptiness, the seducer guarantees it.

In her book *The Literary Speech Act* (1983), Shoshanah Felman interprets Don Juan in terms of the figure anaphora, the formal repetition of beginnings that works here to de-negate ends.[5] Don Juan's repetition of beginnings can lead only to a multiplication of women, who become part of an infinite series of the same according to the principle of equivalence, an interchangeability of identical women without identities. For Don Juan, erotic plots must not develop. They must remain as empty as his proliferating marriage promises. The objects of desire are emptied of their specificity. And Don Juan's method of seduction lies in teaching his victims that 'separation [i.e. emptiness] is an essential aspect of seduction'.[6] The opening praise of tobacco in Molière's play highlights his philosophy of pleasure as an erotics of emptiness.

The discourse of empty pleasure is prevalent in most of the central literary texts to address pleasure in modern France, although its value fluctuates from one to another. For example, alongside Molière in the seventeenth century, Madame La Fayette's *La Princess de Clèves* (1678) proposes pleasure as empty, accessible to women as a fantasy only by remaining unrealized. In the eighteenth century, Pierre Choderlos de Laclos's quintessential libertine text, *Les Liaisons dangereuses* (1782), describes pleasure as empty insofar as it is subordinated to power. And in the nineteenth century, both Gustave Flaubert's realist *Madame Bovary* (1857) and Joris Karl Huysmans' decadent *A Rebours* (1884) show pleasure to be empty because it fails to satisfy.

It was in the nineteenth century, when cigarettes became popular – both in response to Louis Napoleon's chain-smoking example and to the revolutionary upheavals of 1848, which encouraged tobacco consumption – that the value of smoking became openly adjudicated in relation to its aesthetic rather than its medical status. And yet Klein's description of cigarette smoking, in which 'every single cigarette numerically implies all the other cigarettes, exactly alike, that the smoker consumes in a series; each cigarette immediately calls forth its inevitable successor . . . ' is strikingly similar to Felman's description of the snuff-taking Don Juan's eroticism (involving quantification, the absence of meaning, and the principles of addition and equality).[7] In the shift from snuff to cigarettes (a shift that occurred over centuries), the same structure of pleasure is preserved.

Klein's book offers an array of illustrations of the pleasures of smoking in nineteenth-century literary and critical texts. Theodore Burette's *La Physiologie du fumeur* (1840) equates smoker and *grisette* (a naughty, intoxicating lady).[8] In Charles Baudelaire's *Les Salons de 1848*, lower-class prostitutes, called *lorettes*, appear holding cigarettes.[9] Jules Laforgue's ode of 1861, 'La cigarette', identifies cigarettes with beautiful, dangerous women, again *lorettes*.[10] And in Prosper Mérimée's novella *Carmen* (1845), the heroine accepts a cigarette for the first time in literature, identifying her, Klein contends, as outlaw, sorceress and whore.[11] According to Klein, smoking among women began

with those who got paid for staging their sexuality: the actress, the gypsy, the whore. Such a woman violates traditional roles by defiantly, actively giving herself pleasure instead of passively receiving it . . . she [a woman smoking] may in fact be more desirable because she appears to be more free.[12]

Klein exoticizes the image of the smoking woman because his underlying commitment to smoking's sublimity slants his reading. What is central to constructing the desirability that he notices in these images – more central perhaps than the offer of pleasure they seem to announce – is emptiness.[13] While the desirability generated by emptiness appears as an affront to subjectivity, emptiness offers contradictory promises. On the one hand, it offers the fantasy of presence, an erotic exchange unburdened by individual histories; on the other, an exchange that takes on texture and pathos precisely through the encounter with absence (that is, encountering an emptiness in the other that is conditioned by an individual history). But Klein's emphasis here, despite the prominent role of death in his schematization, is not on emptiness, but rather on a kind of delicious empowerment. When smoking is placed within the Kantian category of the sublime, whores give themselves pleasure; hovels are 'transcended by rising cigarette smoke'; and smokers 'can be thrilled by the subtle grandeur of the perspectives on mortality opened by the terrors in every puff'.[14]

It is the resolutely unphilosophical category of the banal that differentiates my reading of smoking as an aesthetic phenomenon from Klein's. When it is banal, far from providing a constant thrill, smoking may not even be noticed. When it is banal, the *lorette*'s smoking, hardly a sign of unburdened freedom and self-pleasure, can be placed firmly in the French tradition outlined above, in which smoking signifies an eroticism, not of transcendence or freedom, but of emptiness.

If we associate smoking in France with the kind of eroticized abandon that might well be readable as a sublime 'intimation of eternity',[15] it is because the lasting iconic images of French smoking – images that represent a departure from French tradition – are cinematic. It is the *nouvelle vague* (French New Wave) that provides so many of these images. Inaugurated by Godard's *A bout de souffle* (*Breathless*) of 1960, the last frame of which shows Jean-Paul Belmondo inhaling smoke with his last breath, smoking begins to signal 'a peculiarly Parisian attitude – sexual, cultural, above all spiritual – in which self-destruction is an absolute freedom: the right to die, with style'.[16] As a gesture of defiance and self-sufficiency, smoking becomes what Gus Parr has called 'a *nouvelle vague* tic'.[17]

The French relationship to smoking for which I have been arguing – in which smoking works to characterize pleasure as involving emptiness – is nowhere more evident than during the moment when pleasure becomes dislodged from its association with freedom. Jean Eustache's prizewinning film of 1973 at Cannes, *La Maman et la Putain* (*The Mother and the Whore*), links smoking, in all its banality, to post-1968 disillusionment. Its use of smoking comments both on the student uprising and on the *nouvelle vague*, movements engaged in the disruption of traditional pleasures and in the creation of new ones specifically associated with freedom.[18] For Eustache, smoking interrupts the discourse of pleasure-as-freedom that the *nouvelle vague* and the uprising represented, replacing it with a conception of pleasure more consonant with the traditional French respect for the category of emptiness. A reading of this film, then, will serve to illustrate in detail the relationship to the 'empty pleasure' of smoking that is so characteristically French.

For more than 220 minutes, the primary action of *La Maman et la Putain* is in the build-up of undirected conversations punctuated by sex. Almost every conversation – in cafés, apartments, a borrowed car and on the bank of the Seine – is accompanied by smoking. The biggest talker is Alexandre (Jean-Pierre Léaud), who has no apartment and no job. He lives with Marie (Bernadette Lafont), a slightly older woman, who begrudgingly consents to Alexandre's free-love charm. Enter Veronika (Françoise LeBrun), a nurse with nothing but a small room in the hospital, and a habit of sleeping with anyone who wants her. The tension of the film is in the choice and opposition between Marie and Veronika, and in their mutual mounting jealousy, which devolves into Marie's suicide attempt and in a final, ill-timed marriage proposal.

While smoking is prominent in the visual landscape of the film, it hardly emerges as a topic of conversation and might appear to have a merely decorative function. But the objects in the background of the film are not used for their realist invisibility. Rather, smoking is dominant in the *mise-en-scène* as a visual element deliberately placed before the camera as part of the filmic discourse.

Stills from Jean
Eustache's 1973 film
La Maman et la Putain.

Like the record player that Eustache considered 'as much a character as Jean-Pierre, Bernadette or Francoise', Alexandre's cigarettes have a central function, not as characters but as emblems.[19]

Eustache, who began his career as Godard's assistant, and finished it by expanding or culminating the *nouvelle vague*, is certainly interested in the kind of 'image-building' that characterizes Godard's work.[20] Peter Wollen explains this process as 'images liberated from their role as representation and given a semantic function within iconic codes, a baroque code of emblems'.[21] An emblem is an image that allegorizes abstract qualities, virtues and, perhaps most aptly, states of things. Smoking concretizes emptiness by defining the interior of the body (and interiority as such) as a space that smoke fills. It illustrates the act of consumption. By marking the emptiness of values, and by signifying a position beyond health and happiness, smoking provides an answer to the film's ideological and philosophical contradictions. And finally, smoking-as-emptiness appears as a negative form of freedom, inverting the understanding of pleasure prominent in the decade between the birth of the *nouvelle vague* and the end of the student uprising.

Surprisingly, it is this inversion of freedom – not into non-freedom but into emptiness – that prevents the film from being what critics have called a 'profoundly reactionary' one.[22] There are several reasons invoked to support the film's reactionary politics: its *mise-en-scène* of the 'fascist playground'; its nostalgia for past certainties; its misogyny; and its final turn towards Catholicism. And yet, many of the same critics who denounce its politics are moved in ways that are inconsistent with their critiques. Either Eustache makes reactionary politics seductive, or, as I will show, critics mistakenly fill the emptiness with an inappropriate political content.

Alexandre's point of view controls the film until the very end, and it is through him that its politics are initially formulated. Named after the conqueror, Alexander the Great, Alexandre inverts his namesake's colonial impulse by conquering nothing but a woman who has already been ravaged. His sexual conquest, Veronika, is a ruin. Theoretically imperialist, viscerally anti-socialist and yet verbosely anti-capitalist, Alexandre's politics inhere in his stance against consumer society, which is focused specifically against production, allowing him, ironically, to become a radical consumer. Alexandre's politics can be understood only in relation to this economy of consumption.

The scene in the restaurant, *Le Train bleu*, establishes the dominance of useless consumption. While eating is highlighted as an act of consumption that is supposed to be, but is not useful, smoking is conspicuously absent. As he eats, Alexandre invokes emptiness as his guiding economic principle. In answer to Veronika's question, 'How do you live?', Alexandre responds with a quotation that echoes French Decadence: 'I am rather in favour of boredom . . . nothingness.'[23] But far from being confined to an intellectual position, emptiness is also proposed as a condition of the body. The beginning of this scene, filmed from the exterior of the restaurant through the transparent, revolving door, provides an architectural metaphor for describing the bodily economy as a cyclical passage between exterior and interior, a passage through virtually empty space. Moreover, neither Alexandre nor Veronika are hungry when they go to the restaurant, and each eats – on borrowed money – without signs of pleasure. The meal is utterly gratuitous, designed to prove their emptiness, which substitutes for hunger.

Because smoking has been excluded as an emblem here, in order to establish eating as a useful act of consumption that has become gratuitous, the intellectual, physical, and economic forms of emptiness that structure this scene (the principle of the void, lack of hunger, debt) rely on other signifiers. What differentiates smoking as an emblem from, for example, the revolving door, is its portability and plasticity. The emblem's adaptability mirrors Alexandre's own.

In fact, Alexandre's adaptability to contradictory and mutually exclusive world-views makes the film's politics difficult to track. But despite the various positions from which he borrows, the film endorses neither fascist nor bourgeois solutions.[24] First, neither Alexandre's unnamed friend (incidentally, also a cigar smoker) nor his former lover, Gilberte (the fascist and the complacent bourgeoise, respectively),[25] control the point of view.[26] Second, Alexandre is visibly upset by the images of people being hanged in his friend's book on the ss. Finally, Alexandre and Veronika adopt various other politico-philosophical orientations, among them: decadence, existentialism and nihilism.

While these orientations are not all compatible, all share a privileged relationship both to the concept of emptiness and to the activity of smoking. In decadence, as with smoking, sensations are pursued to the point of numbness. As an utterly illogical activity, smoking is also compatible – with whatever complicated ambivalence – with existentialist absurdity. But of all of the discourses that Alexandre appropriates, however unrigorously, nihilism is the one that best describes the link between a philosophical world-view and smoking as a way of life. In a system that calls for the re-evaluation of all values, or that demonstrates the emptiness of traditional hierarchies of values (even while producing a futile longing for them), smoking is not an activity that compromises the value of health and happiness, as much as one that argues for overcoming health and happiness as values at all. ('No one believes anymore. That's the advantage of Paris . . . people are sad.' 'I wasn't hung up on you but on my suffering.')[27] Nihilism does not just allow Alexandre and his friends to smoke; it insists on a culture of smoking demonstrated in nearly every scene, a culture outside an economy of health and strength.

The best example of a nihilistic reversal of values is Alexandre's critique of work. He refuses to work even in the service of his own pleasure, whether to seduce a woman ('I can't be interested in someone unless she is already interested')[28] or to break up with one ('I let time do it . . . You don't think I should do someone else's work . . .').[29] It is in this context that the smoke and talk-filled café becomes the central site of the passive activity characteristic

of smoking.[30] Although he announces his intention to read in Flore every afternoon, 'like a job', Alexandre never gets to the task. Instead, he talks. But rather than advancing through dialogue, Alexandre produces a stream of smoke and of contradictory verbiage, as if he were insuring the non-productiveness of his discourse, elevating smoking as his least self-undermining activity.

It is the very impossibility of productive ideological discourse for Alexandre that accounts for his interest in people who speak like dictionaries. His example of such speech, however, resembles a dictionary only in its confidence in meaning:

I'm reminded of an Arab who said, drawing out each syllable, 'it appears that black women make love in an extraordinary manner. When the man introduces his sexual organ in the vagina of the woman, it appears that it creates there [*qu'il y fait*] the heat of a furnace [*fournaise*]. It was an administrator of the colonies who told me that'.[31]

In wishful identification with the colonizing power, an Arab man envies a position that he cannot occupy: having sex with a black woman from a position of power. This position allows the administrator to transform a site of violence into a site of personal consumption: violent burning becomes exoticized as a native specialty. Whether 'it' (*qu'il y fait*) refers to the male organ or to the vagina (*le vagin*), the cause of the heat is effaced in favour of emphasizing the sexuality of the black woman, transforming, in effect, the colonial cause of violence into an attribute of sexuality and subjectivity based on race and gender. The black woman is described both as empty (furnace as receptacle), and as dangerously consuming (like the smoking *femme fatale* in the cinema of the 1920s and '30s). Not surprisingly, the word for furnace (*fournaise*) is related to the word for the bowl of a pipe (*fournau*), overlaying an image of neutral (or empty) pleasure (smoking) on to the image of annihilation. The linguistic relationship between *fournaise* and *fourneau* highlights colonial violence by making reference to an industry that depended on slave labour.[32] In repeating the speech of the Arab man who repeats the speech of the administrator, Alexandre reproduces not the content of his speech, but his position of envying the other across an unbridgeable gulf, because he cannot, like the Arab man, be consistently and unabashedly ideological.

In this example, Alexandre's empty imitation of speech with a reactionary character proves not that he is reactionary, but precisely that he is not. Similarly, the apparently Catholic ending to the film, when procreative love replaces free love, actually critiques this very gesture as naively romantic. Reading the ending as reactionary depends on ignoring the factors that contextualize Veronika's emerging Catholic voice.

The emblem of smoking as a sign of empty love is one of these contextualizing factors. Marie, for example, reads a spilled ashtray, ostentatiously sullying her apartment, as both a sign of Alexandre's and Veronika's frenzied love-making and a sign of their own emptied love. And Alexandre, for his part, leaves Veronika with a pack of cigarettes to keep her company while she sits in the car, waiting for him to finish his fight with Marie, whom, he tells Veronika, he will always love. In addition to serving as a tool to relieve the boredom of waiting, cigarettes function as a substitute for love that is directed elsewhere.

If smoking emblematizes emptiness in love (relying on the classical conception of love as lack), it is not by chance that, in the sequence marking the central event of the film, love operates according to a structure that emerged in the reception of tobacco when physicians regarded it both as a 'panacea for every ill', and as a 'poison that is more dangerous than hemlock, deadlier than opium'.[33] While individuals decided between these positions, tobacco's circulation in culture can be understood according to what Jacques Derrida has called the logic of the pharmakon, in which poison and cure coincide.[34] In the scene that leads to Marie's suicide attempt, 'empty love' can be understood according to this same logic.

This scene takes place just after Alexandre leaves Veronika in the car with cigarettes, and after his jealousy results in Marie's aborted dinner party. Back in Marie's apartment, Alexandre addresses Veronika:

Alexandre: You who operate on cancer, who cures the most unbelievable pain . . . Have you never sought a remedy to stop this suffering? Still, it's not new . . . Since the first love. You know, before, at the beginning of time, people fucked, coupled, without problems. Everyone with everyone. That should have been good. And one day, someone decided to keep a woman for himself, exclusively for himself . . . he didn't know what he had done. Well, isn't there a remedy? Shots, an operation . . . to suffer like that . . .

Veronika: One has to take vitamin 'M' (*Aime*/Love).[35]

Alexandre's speech situates love as a sickness that causes suffering, while Veronika posits love as its cure. These positions indicate not just a difference of opinions between which it is possible to choose, but that, like the *Pharmakon*, love is both poison and cure. The structure of impasse saturates free (or empty) love ideology, an ideal they cannot attain.

The empty love that Veronika offers as a remedy (Vitamin M – *aime*) is as likely to spread suffering as to check it. We recall that she mentions how much she would like to pierce Alexandre in his 'beautiful veins', or cure him, during the scene in which Veronika characterizes her own interior emptiness (her offering) as a fact of anatomy. When he enters her before she can remove her tampon, she claims that it will come out of her nostrils. In a similar confusion of remedy and cause of suffering, Marie announces Veronika's expected arrival in the role of nurse just as Alexandre is going out the door to 'buy cigarettes'. When he returns, Veronika is sitting on the bed with Marie. Alexandre displays not his cigarettes, but roses, which he throws on the bed between the two women. 'Very beautiful', Marie says with a touch of irony, 'Are they for me?'[36] If Alexandre intended the flowers as a reconciling gesture, he immediately evacuates the gesture of its potential by offering the flowers to both and neither of the women. The roses he gives are indeed the cigarettes – the emptiness – that motivated his departure. Ultimately, the cure that Veronika offers for Alexandre's sickness is not vitamin M (*aime*/love) but vitamin C (*c'est*/this is), substituting hard realism for romanticism. When Alexandre flinches, Veronika tells him that it will be his own fault when his cure causes a bump, in a further illustration that cure and illness are indistinguishable.

But if the film argues against free love by framing it as a cure that is also an illness, the same logic – the logic of smoking – argues against the necessity of procreative love, contextualizing the film's Catholicism. Veronika's motherhood must be read in the context of her whoredom, her finale with her debut. Alexandre represents his first meeting with Veronika, when they each, exchanging gazes, inhale their cigarettes in alternate frames: 'I met a girl. She was smoking Gauloises.' As Klein has noted, Gauloises is the brand of the soldier.[37] Veronika is a sex soldier, extinguishing herself in the (misleading) name of freedom, perversely inverting a notion of duty. She smokes the way she talks about having sex, quickly, without enjoyment or attention. Like a whore, she is available for sex without pleasure. But she accumulates sexual contacts without any corresponding accumulation of wealth. Far from making her richer, or fuller, Veronika's consumption makes her emptier.

> I took a maximum of lovers . . . And I got fucked. And maybe I'm a chronically sick person . . . chronic fucking . . . And lots of men have desired me like that, you know, in the void [*dans le vide*]. And they often fucked me in the void . . . But you know, I believe that one day a man will come and will love me and will make me a baby, because he loves me. And love isn't valid except when

people want to make a baby together.[38]

Veronika's 'chronic fucking' appears here as an addiction to emptiness analogous to her smoking. The cure that she proposes (making a baby) requires the same activity – 'fucking into the void', the empty unknown – that comprises her illness. That is, in proposing a cure for her malady, Veronika maintains the impasse of the panacea/poison structure.

The probable pregnancy that ends the film is hardly an argument for conservative values. Having just announced that she might be pregnant by Alexandre, Veronika is surprised that he follows her to her room. Written into the screenplay, under Veronika's question to Alexandre ('What are you coming to do here?'),[39] is the direction 'She speaks like Madame Bovary.' *Madame Bovary* marks the end of the convention of the seduction plot in which seduction naturally leads to death. Madame Bovary's end is not death, but suicide. By comparing the end in pregnancy to the end in suicide, Eustache suggests the destructive and artificial character of pregnancy as a resolution. A Catholic solution would be more optimistic in tone. And if there were any doubt, Veronika begins to vomit, a sign of drunkenness indistinguishable from that of morning sickness. This recalls the moment when Alexandre makes Marie vomit to get rid of the poison she ingested in her suicide attempt, poison that was actually too much of Veronika's medicine. The marriage proposal that closes the film recalls Alexandre's response to Gilberte's engagement, which questioned the possibility of reliable signs. And finally, the ending returns us to Veronika's own mocking deconstruction of romantic love ('No one but you can fuck me like that').[40] As the closing act of the film, highlighted by a final shot of Alexandre cringing in the corner, engagement guarantees nothing.

Rather than presenting a politics, Eustache's film concerns the failure of politics (and, to a lesser extent, the failure of the *nouvelle vague*) to articulate the relationship between freedom, non-freedom and pleasure, a relationship that is better articulated through emptiness, given solid form in the visual

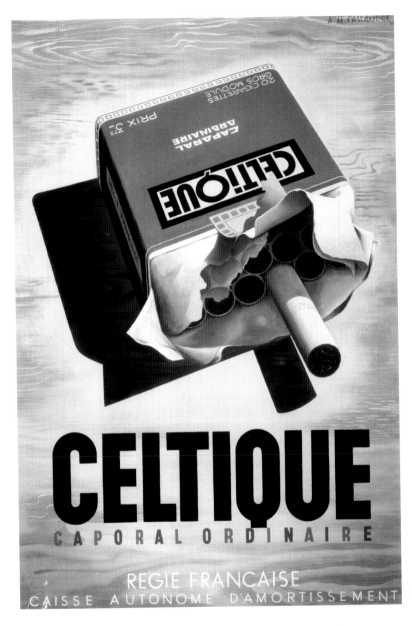

A 1934 advertising poster for CELTIQUE cigarettes.

emblem of smoking. Initially represented as the mother and whore respectively, both Marie and Veronika are smokers. Emptiness belongs equally to mothers, left alone on the bed listening to Edith Piaf, to whores, alone in their most intimate encounters, and to the insufficiency of the very categories mother and whore. Eustache has us value emptiness, just as we regret it. If it is universal, a bridge between mothers and whores, Marie's

reading of Alexandre's self-contradicting humanism is confirmed. Waving his cigarette before a static camera, shot in close-up, Alexandre celebrates the moment when 'the man on the street . . . flips out', suggesting that if emptiness, fragility and even madness are not rejected, 'there is the risk that something interesting will happen.'[41]

Smoking & Art

The Weimar cultural critic Walter Benjamin, writing in his essay 'One-Way Street' (1928), observed 'if the smoke from the tip of my cigarette and the ink from the nib of my pen flowed with equal ease, I should be in the Arcadia of my writing'. Smoking is a sign of creativity. It is of no surprise, therefore, that there is an obsession about representing smoking and smokers in art after the sixteenth century. The act of smoking – whether opium or tobacco or marijuana – is not merely connected with the creative act, it becomes a surrogate for it. Smoking is both hot and cool – it functions in multiple ways, representing not only creativity but also the society in which it functions. From a contemplative Dutch still-life by Willem Claesz. Heda, Still Life with Tobacco, Wine and Pocket Watch (1637) to the exotic luxury in Delacroix's Women of Algiers (1834), to Renoir's cozy portrait of a relaxed Claude Monet smoking a pipe (1872), Western art uses tobacco to mirror the very creativity that every artist desires. Thus in La tabagie, Chardin's still life of 1737 in the Louvre, the viewer is captured by an unassuming shelf in an ordinary room. A smoker has just carelessly set down his long clay pipe against the wooden box; a faint plume of smoke curls up from the still glowing bowl. 'In these objects', writes the art historian Charles Sterling, 'Chardin . . . finds and expresses one of those balanced systems that seem to be everywhere, buried in the chaos of the everyday spectacle, awaiting only their painter'. Thus the plume of smoke is itself the ephemeral yet aesthetic nature of art's own world.

That plume of smoke leads to the world of film. Both Gloria Swanson's elegant yet passé cigarette holder with its wisp of smoke in Billy Wilder's Sunset Boulevard (1950) and Humphrey Bogart's clenched cigarette with smoke rising into Rick's eyes in Michael Curtiz's Casablanca (1942) evoke memories of smoking. The use of smoking flashbacks places the act of smoking as the key for the viewer to comprehend the differences in the meaning of the ephemeral smoke. Even the 'citation' of smoking from one film to another comments on how all such images are linked. In his Touch of Evil (1958), Orson Welles has the jaded Mexican madam Tanya played by Marlene Dietrich talk with a cigar dangling from the side of her mouth to Sheriff Welles, evoking a very different scene in Josef von Sternberg's The Blue Angel (1931), in which smoke and sex are present. Marcel Proust was right – and not just about cookies – when he wrote in Remembrance of Things Past that 'let a noise or a scent, once heard or once smelt, be heard or smelt again in the present . . . It is a minute freed from the order of time . . . one can understand that the word 'death' should have no meaning for him; situated out of time, why should he fear the future?' Thus the representations of smoking are of the past and of the present, but as representations that are also of the future, a future in which pleasure and danger exist but are mediated by our dedication not to the realities but to the memories and their representations.

Jan Steen (1626–79), *Seated Man with a Pipe*, oil on canvas.

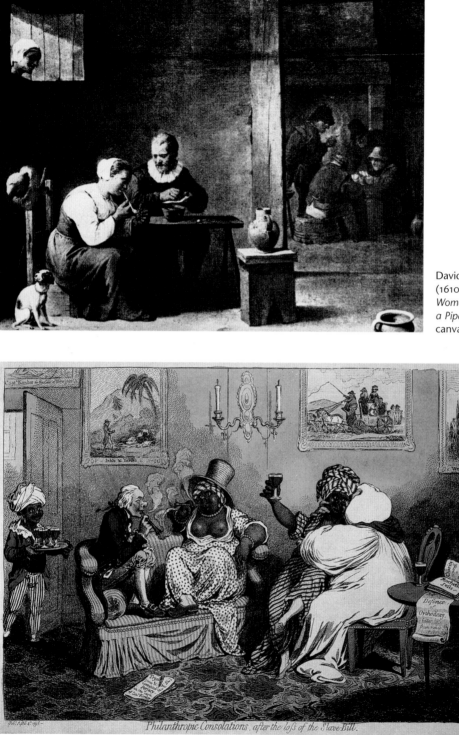

David Teniers
(1610–90),
*Woman Smoking
a Pipe*, oil on
canvas.

James Gillray, *Philanthropic Consolations, after the Loss of the Slave-Bill*, 1796, hand-coloured etching.

Edouard Manet, *The Smoker*, 1866, oil on canvas.

Paul Gauguin,
Night Café, 1888,
oil on canvas.

Paul Cézanne,
The Card-players,
1890–95, oil on canvas.

Georges Braque, *Still-life with Pipe*, 1914, oil on canvas.

George Grosz, *Dusk*, 1922, watercolour.

Ernst Ludwig Kirchner, *Self-portrait with Model*, 1910–26, oil on canvas.

Susie Freem and Dr Liz Lee, *A Packet a Week*, 2002, nylon monofilament yarn, cigarette ends; pocket knitting.

Maggi Hambling, *A Conversation With Oscar Wilde, 1854–1900*, 1998, bronze. Adelaide Street, London WC2.

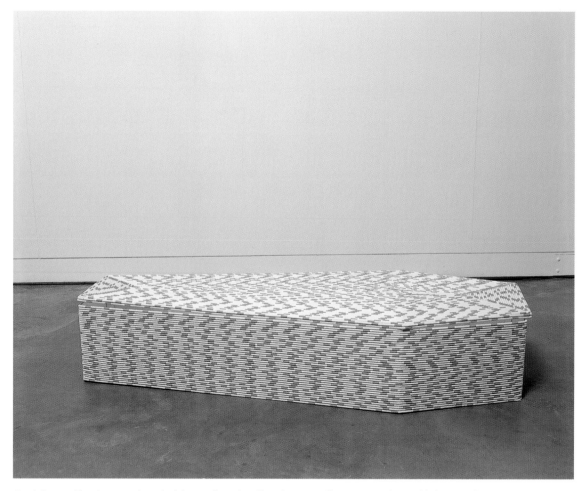

Sarah Lucas, *Thank you and good night*, cardboard coffin, cigarettes, fluorescent tube, red lighting gel, 2003.

Smoking, Gender and Ethnicity

Jews and Smoking

SANDER L. GILMAN

The myth supporting a connection between Jews and smoking seems to begin at the very beginning. On 2 November 1492 Christopher Columbus, having landed on what would be called Cuba, sent two of his crew to spy out the land. They returned to him on 6 November, announcing that they had found a village of people who 'drank smoke'. They 'light one end of the tabuco [sic] and by the other suck . . . by which they become benumbed and almost drunk.' One of the two men was Luis de Torres, Columbus's interpreter, who 'knew how to speak Hebrew and Chaldean [Aramaic] and even some Arabic'.[1] It was this Luis de Torres who, according to the legend, introduced tobacco and smoking into Europe.[2] Torres, modern scholars assume, was one of the hidden Jews who remained in Spain after the expulsion of the Jews and Moors that year. The fact that this account, written by Columbus's later companion, the priest Bartolomé de Las Casas, as a commentary on Columbus's widely circulated diaries, was not published until 1825 – and his magisterial *History of the Indies* not until 1875 – places this 'legend' very much within the nineteenth-century debates about Jews and tobacco. And that late nineteenth-century scholars quickly associated de Torres with the expulsion of the Jews at the moment of the East European pogroms and the strong, negative association of Jews with tobacco should also not be of much astonishment.[3]

Before the publication of the Las Casas account during the 1820s – which was also earlier than the Jewish acculturation to European society – the connection between Jews and smoking was seen as a positive one. It was also an association that was made largely about Sephardi Jews, primarily those Spanish Jews who had settled in European cities after their expulsion from Spain in 1492. These Jews were visible as outsiders within society, since they noticeably came from somewhere else. They were seen as exotic, and their association with tobacco simply made them seem more exotic. After Jewish acculturation in Europe, however, when Jews were no longer so visible, the non-Jewish pseudo-scientific world came to use this alleged connection between smoking and Jews to support their claims that Jews had a racial essence that was different from that of the Europeans. When they were making these claims, these so-called scientists were no longer referring to Sephardi Jews, but to the mind and body of the East European Jew, who lived in their midst. The connection between smoking and Jews functioned to posit a racial category and to place that category outside Europe in the exotic, primitive world of the Middle East, where the East European Jew was assumed to belong. The tragic, political ramifications of this manoeuvre are obvious only with hindsight.

The association between Jews and smoking was never purely a symbolic one. Jews, as individuals, did play a substantial role in the tobacco industry in early modern Europe.[4] As early as 1612 the City Council of Hamburg permitted Sephardi Jews from Portugal to reside in the city. The Jews of Hamburg, while not permitted to live in the inner city, were also not required to live in ghettos. They were trades people who specialized in the wholesale commerce of exotic wares such as tobacco, sugar, coffee, cocoa, calico and spices. The Sephardi Diaspora became associated with exotic wares such as tobacco. Sephardi Jews settled in the Dutch province of Groningen in 1683, again as tobacco merchants. The long association of Jews as merchants dealing in exotic products shaped the popular view that they were naturally associated with them. As exotics in northern Europe, they were associated with the positive aspect of tobacco as a luxury product.

As tobacco became a major European staple, Jews were also involved in its growing, treatment and processing. In areas outside the traditional settlements of Jews in cities such as Amsterdam and Hamburg, Jews were primarily engaged in rural occupations or lived and worked in small towns. In south-west Germany during the early nineteenth century, in states such as Baden, Jews, unlike those in Prussia and the Rhineland, grew as well as processed and traded tobacco. This area was the centre of German tobacco production, and Jews, beginning in the early nineteenth century, took an increasingly larger role as middlemen, buying, curing and manufacturing cigars and pipe tobacco. Indeed, by the beginning of the twentieth century, Jews owned about 40 per cent of all the tobacco-related companies in the city of Mannheim, which had a Jewish population of about 4 per cent.[5] In the more rural Russia Empire, Caucasian Mountain Jews (also known as Tats and Dagchufuts) were not permitted to own and till land until the nineteenth century. While their oldest occupation was growing rice, they also grew tobacco and thus became associated with the tobacco trade. In the Habsburg Empire, it was only after Jewish civil emancipation at the end of the eighteenth century that Jews were permitted to engage in the tobacco trade. Diego d'Aguilar, still of Sephardi origin, held the tobacco monopoly in Austria, using Christian nobles as middlemen, from 1743 to 1748, while Israel Hönig established the State Tobacco Monopoly in 1788.[6] From the

nineteenth century the Jews were seen as the face of the tobacco trade in Eastern Europe as well as the United States.

Companies such as Loeser and Wolf (in Berlin) became hallmarks of the tobacco trade. In partitioned Poland, Leopold Kronenberg produced 25 per cent of the cigars and cigarettes manufactured there in 1867.[7] In post-First World War Europe the association between Jews and the smoking industry changed. Polish Jews were actually forbidden employment in the state tobacco monopoly. In the early 1930s, before the Nazi seizure of power in Germany in 1933, SA officials accused one of the major producers of cigarettes of making 'Jewish cigarettes', because a member of the board of directors was a Jew.[8] As is evident, after the First World War Jewish participation in the tobacco industry was observed through the lens of anti-Semitic rhetoric, and was no longer associated with the comforts of a luxury product brought to Europe by an outsider group.

From the seventeenth century, European Jews also became the workforce of American tobacco. At that point Jewish merchants, such as the firm of Asher and Solomon, dominated the snuff trade. The Jewish firm of Keeney Brothers, whose cigarettes, 'Sweet Caporals', were the best-selling brand of the nineteenth century, employed 2,000 Jewish workers. The trade union movement began when Samuel Gompers organized the cigar makers in the 1870s and '80s. Jews became identified with the retailing of tobacco. Since the history of the connection between Jews and smoking follows a different path in America, we will only concentrate on the European example here.

The power of the association between Jews and smoking, however, was not simply grounded in the social reality that individual Jews were involved in the tobacco industry. In Iceland, where there were de facto no Jews before the twentieth century, one imported product was strongly associated with Jews. This was the Jewish tobacco that Danish Jews had been exporting to Iceland since the early eighteenth century.[9] This social fact was read as part of the mythology of Jewish difference that grew up in the course of the nineteenth century around Jews and tobacco in Europe as well. The fact that it was known as far away as Iceland shows the power of this connection. Anti-Semites used this association to their advantage. Those who saw tobacco as weakening the social fabric laid its very origin at the feet of the Jews. This view is documented in the Christian anti-Semitic literature of the nineteenth-century German Romantic poets. One example is a contribution of the poet Clemens Brentano to the 'German-Christian Table Society', created in 1811. For him, it was the Jews who 'in the year 1696 planted the first tobacco in the Mark Brandenburg':

Thus they hindered the development of our countrymen and generated the many sinful and confused thoughts that arose in the devilish steam bath of this plant that already stank while it was growing. Indeed one can survey all of the destruction that this horrid herb generated. One sees in the fall the tall, leafless stems that dominate the poverty-stricken land like gallows. At that moment, one can believe the old Jewish myth that Christ admonished all trees not to bear his body, so that every cross that was made collapsed. Then a Jew bound such plant stems out of the devil's garden together to a great height until he was crucified.[10]

The Jews themselves are so addicted to this narcotic, states Brentano, that they even subvert their own laws against smoking on the Sabbath. They blow smoke into a barrel on Friday that they empty on Saturday in order to inhale the fumes without creating fire, in this case lighting up. Brentano associates such views with the 'remarkable inherited diseases' of the Jews, diseases that he considers a punishment for their denial of Christ. Tobacco consumption came to be a means of describing yet another sign of the innate physical and psychological difference of the Jews.

The debate about smoking and Jews reappears in late nineteenth-century science in the context of those 'horrid and unmentionable' diseases that

writers such as Clemens Brentano attributed to the Jews. In 1858, at the very beginning of his career, the French neurologist Jean Martin Charcot created 'Claudication intermittente' as a medical diagnosis.[11] He described it as the chronic recurrence of pain and tension in the lower leg, a growing sense of stiffness and finally a total inability to move the leg, which causes a marked and noticeable inhibition of gait. This occurs between a few minutes and a half hour after beginning a period of activity, such as walking. It spontaneously vanishes, only to be repeated at regular intervals.

Charcot's diagnostic category became part of the description of the pathological difference of the Jew. Intermittent claudication became one of the specific diseases associated with East European Jews. In 1901 H. Higier in Warsaw published a long paper in which he summarized the state of knowledge about intermittent claudication as a sign of the racial make-up of the Jew.[12] Most of the twenty-three patients he examined were Jews, and he found that the etiology of the disease was 'the primary role of the neuropathic disposition [of the patients] and the inborn weakness of their peripheral circulatory system'. By the time that Higier published his paper, this was a given in the neurological literature. Such illnesses were to be found among male Jews from the East, from the provinces. Heinrich Singer regarded intermittent claudication as proof of the 'general nervous encumbrance born by the Jewish race . . .'.[13] This is both a sign of anti-Semitic discourse as well as a restatement of the Jewish Haskalah's view that the Eastern Jews were diseased because of their form of religious practice, as well as their '2,000' years in the ghetto. Jewish reformers saw the sole transformation of the diseased Jewish body in liberating the Eastern Jew from his social bondage. These reformers located disease in the East European body to distance their own Jewish bodies from them. It is ironic that Jews participated in positing racial discourse too.

One attempt to move this classification away from a sign of the general weakness of the modern Jew's body was taken by Samuel Goldflam in

Mei' Cigarrenfpitz.

Was? — Er wird fchon „fchwarz"!

At the close of the nineteenth century the Viennese anti-Semitic periodical *Kikeriki* represented the black face of the Jew as a cigar holder, with the contradictory images of the traditional religious sidelocks and the top hat of the modern city dweller. The Jew is in pain because of the cock's attention ('Kikeriki' is the sound that a German rooster makes).

Warsaw.[14] Goldflam was one of the most notable neurologists of the first half of the twentieth century.[15] What was noteworthy in Goldflam's analysis of his patients with intermittent claudication was not that they were all Eastern Jews, but that they were almost all very heavy smokers. Thus it is not the ill Jewish body that bore the stigma of nervous disease but rather tobacco intoxication.[16]

In a major review essay on the 'nervous diseases' of the Jews, Toby Cohn, a noted Jewish neurologist, included intermittent claudication as one of his categories of neurological deficits.[17] While com-

In this image from a 1953 Passover Haggadah, the good father doesn't smoke; the purse-thief is also a smoker.

menting on the anecdotal nature of the evidence, and calling on a review essay by the Jewish neurologist Kurt Mendel (who does not discuss the question of 'race' at all[18]), he accepted the specific nature of the Jewish risk for this syndrome while leaving the etiology open. Two radically different etiologies had been proposed: the first reflected on the neuropathic qualities of the Jewish body, especially in regard to diseases of the circulatory system. The other potential etiology noted by Goldflam and Cohn did not reflect on the inherent qualities of the Jewish foot, but on the misuse of tobacco and the resulting occlusion of the circulatory system of the extremities. It is tobacco that, according to Wilhelm Erb, played a major role in the etiology of intermittent claudication.[19] In a somewhat later study of 45 cases of the syndrome, Erb found, to his surprise, that at least 35 of his patients showed an excessive use of tobacco.[20] (This meant the consumption of 40–60 cigarettes or 10–15 cigars a day.) Indeed, the moral dimension that the latter provide in their discussion of the evils of tobacco misuse is an answer to the image of the neurological predisposition of the Jew's body to avoid military service.[21] The misuse of tobacco is a

הגדה של פסח.

יְמֵי חַיֶּיךָ הָעוֹלָם הַזֶּה. כֹּל יְמֵי חַיֶּיךָ לְהָבִיא
לִימוֹת הַמָּשִׁיחַ:

בָּרוּךְ הַמָּקוֹם בָּרוּךְ הוּא. בָּרוּךְ שֶׁנָּתַן תּוֹרָה

denotes this time only; but ALL the days of thy life, denotes
even at the time of the Messiah.

Blessed be the Omnipresent; blessed is he, blessed is he who
hath given the law to his people Israel, blessed be he: the

A Passover Haggadah first published in Hebrew and English by Rabbi H. Lieberman in Chicago in 1879. Evil is represented here in the image of the child who smokes. He represents the seduction of the modern, secular world. The turbaned father represents traditional ('oriental') values.

sign of the Eastern Jew, not the Western Jew. Goldflam's patients were all seen in Warsaw. The noted Berlin neurologist Hermann Oppenheim observed that of the cases of intermittent claudication in his practice (48 cases over five years) he found that the overwhelming majority, between 35 and 38, were Russian Jews.[22] The Eastern Jew's mind is that of a social misfit and his body reifies this role, but this is not a problem of Western Jewry except by extension. In other words, when Sephardi Jews, recently uprooted, were associated with the tobacco trade, they did not pose a threat to their surrounding community. However, because Western Jews had assimilated and were no longer a visible group in society, it was necessary for the pseudo-scientists to posit one, and they latched on to the image of the East European Jew. Since Western Jews wanted to preserve their transparency in society, they too targeted the East European male body.

That desire to locate the etiology of intermittent claudication in the heavy use of tobacco by Jews played directly into the racial theory of the day. By the close of the nineteenth century, Jews were already labelled as a 'race' with a particular susceptibility to tobacco poisoning. In the classic literature on the pathology of tobacco at the close of the nineteenth century, such as the work of L. von Frankl-Hochwart, all Jews were tagged as susceptible because of the appearance of intermittent claudication, as well as certain types of cerebral events, such as aphasia.[23] Intermittent claudication was seen as a disease of Western Jews, too, because he claimed that they were really misplaced Orientals. Since 'Orientals' smoked in the open in their native surroundings, they were less susceptible to tobacco-related diseases,[24] but when Jews came to Europe, he believed that they were unable to adapt their Oriental essence to new challenges. So, because in Europe they smoked in closed spaces, they became ill. These same 'Orientals', now displaced into a hostile, modern environment, became diseased. In this view Jews were 'Orientals' out of their appropriate place, the Middle East (and its practices). This view continued in complicated ways through the late 1930s. Fritz Lickint, whose work on tobacco went back before the First World War, repeated the claim that it was intermittent claudication that marked the major effect on the Jewish body of tobacco. His further claim, which is a social one, is that the overuse of tobacco is the result of the religious prohibition against the use of alcohol, ludicrous since Jews have no such prohibition.[25]

Who poisons whom with tobacco? The debate about Jews and the nervous illnesses caused by smoking was found beyond the case study of intermittent claudication. In seeking for a root cause for a degeneracy perceived as tied to life in the modern world, tobacco was also designated as one of the origins of hysteria and, by Theodor Billroth, the great Viennese surgeon, of the 'nervousness' of modern society.[26] This nervousness was a result of the competition for survival, and the result that 'tired nerves need the stimulation of tea and alcohol and strong cigars' to function.[27] Here again, Jews were the target of pseudo-scientists. And by Jews, it must be stressed that these were Jewish men, who were seen as the ultimate victims of the modern world, since they were congenitally unable

The stereotyped Nazi image of the Eastern Jew as the stock market speculator before 1933. (In pseudo-Yiddish he says: 'In any case, I am doing better here in Germany than in Galicia.') The cigar is a standard part of the image of the Jew as capitalist.

to deal with the pressures of modern life, or so said the early non-Jewish pseudo-scientists, as well as Jews themselves, such as the Zionist and physician Max Nordau. In the nineteenth century Jewish men were assumed to be a group highly predisposed to specific forms of mental illness such as hysteria. And, indeed, there was the view that one of the primary forms of undiagnosed mental illness of the *fin de siècle* was *Nicotinismus mentalis*.[28] If smoking caused hysteria, then male Jews from the East were, according to common medical wisdom, the classic hysterics. Yet if excessive smoking caused nervousness, Leopold Löwenfeld saw moderate smoking, three cigars a day, as a potential therapy to 'reduce nervousness'.[29] Jews were seen as those who suffered most from all forms of diseases of the modern world and smoking might actually cure them!

The disease of modern life included the cancers attributed to smoking, especially the smoking of cigars. Certainly the most famous Jewish case was that of Sigmund Freud, who was diagnosed with buccal cancer in 1923. For Freud, a cigar was much more than a cigar. He even attributed his ability to work to tobacco.[30] Being without a cigar, he complained, 'was an act of self-mutilation such as the fox performs in a snare when it bites off its own leg. I am not very happy, but rather feeling noticeably depersonalized', he wrote to Sandor Ferenczi in 1930 after another heart attack.[31] The cigar was a central attribute of his own sense of self; without it, he ceased to be a complete human being.

For Freud, his father was the model for the productive smoker: 'I believe I owe to the cigar a great intensification of my capacity to work and a facilitation of my self control. My model in this was my father, who was a heavy smoker and remained one for his entire life.'[32] In Vienna it was the Eastern Jew of Jacob Freud's generation who was understood as an abuser of tobacco,[33] but by Freud's own generation of Westernized Jews, cancers of the hard palate had come to be called 'rich man's cancer' because of the cost of purchasing the fifteen to twenty cigars a day deemed necessary to cause the disease.[34] Cancer of the buccal cavity became a sign of success, much as did cardiac infarctions during the 1980s in the United States. It was no longer understood as a sign of inferiority, but of acculturation. What had been a quality ascribed to foreign Jews became a quality associated with a specific economic class, as Jews became increasingly integrated into the economic life of Vienna. Indeed, from 1900 to 1930, about the time that Freud's cancer was discovered, Jewish scientists, such as Maurice Sorsby, recorded that the incidence of cancer among Jews, except for genital cancer, seemed to be approaching the level of the non-Jewish population.[35] By becoming ill they were becoming like everyone else.

A predisposition to those diseases, including irrationalism, that are attributed to smoking is an aspect of the image of the Jewish body from the eighteenth century through the early twentieth century. As science came to define the Jew as a race, qualities associated with smoking that were present in the religious and cultural models of Jewish identity were transformed into medical categories. This world of myth making is far from any real association of individual Jews with the actual world of tobacco farming, curing, sale and manufacture.

The Commodified African American in Nineteenth-Century Tobacco Art

DOLORES MITCHELL

The nineteenth-century media explosion, based on the power press, mass-produced paper, lithography, rail distribution and an expanding consumer economy, gave advertising art unprecedented power to stimulate desire and mould visual consciousness in the United States.[1] Images of African Americans alluded to dark colour or its elimination in advertisements for shoe polish, tobacco, bleach, soap and other products.[2] In advertising for cigars and cigarettes – with white consumers as the prime targets – such images reverberate with the history of the cultivation of tobacco by slaves,[3] and with psychological overtones based on its consumption for sensual pleasure.

Tobacco ensured the wealth of the Chesapeake Bay settlers and, along with indigo, cotton and sugar, encouraged the slave trade in the New World.[4] Tobacco demanded such high prices in Europe that the leaf itself was often exchanged for slaves.[5] An engraving in J. S. Buckingham's *The Slave States of America* (London, 1842) illustrates the bidding for both slaves and hogsheads of tobacco in the same room.

The colonial use of black slaves for the intensive cultivation required by tobacco was so well established by the seventeenth century that black boys on tobacconist shop signs in Bristol and London indicated the sale of Virginia leaf.[6] Some signs combined Indian and black attributes in a single figure, so that a black boy would wear 'a headdress and kilt of tobacco leaves, instead of feathers', and be carrying 'a rope of tobacco under one arm, and

holding a long-stem pipe with the opposite hand'.[7] In a trading card of 1902, based on earlier prototypes, the slave is linked to tobacco since he sits on tobacco bales and touches a plant. His blank expression and near nakedness suggest that both he and the tobacco were regarded as raw materials.

The last quarter of the nineteenth century was the 'golden age' of cigar-box labels, a period of 'wars' between hundreds of manufacturers in the highly competitive cigar industry. Large Northern cities in the USA, with New York and Philadelphia in the lead, were the primary sites of cigar manufacturing and advertising. Although cigars were expensive in comparison to pipe or chewing tobacco, or cigarettes, and were purchased by a comparatively small percentage of tobacco users, they claimed nearly 60 per cent of all tobacco revenues. Cigars became a signifier of white masculine affluence and power. The manufacture and packaging of loose smoking tobacco, chewing tobacco and snuff took place largely in the South, typically with white owners supervising a black workforce. The few companies that monopolized such production used distinctive labels and posters to establish the product identity.[8]

Advertising for most tobacco products was supplied by ten major lithographic firms, situated mainly in Northern cities. In the 1870s a number of German lithographers emigrated to Philadelphia and New York, supplying the skills needed for labels that required as many as ten colour separations, as well as gilding and embossing.[9] They

'Sweet Scented . . . ', a colour lithograph trading card for Drake, Hulick & Co., Easton, Pennsylvania, manufacturers, c. 1890.

enriched an existing repertory of American commercial imagery, with traditions drawn from European fine art, such as paintings by Pieter Bruegel the Elder and George Stubbs that show stooped, depersonalized workers immersed in crops, while a supervisor stands over them, perhaps elevated on a horse.

White artists, working largely for white lithographic firms that served white manufacturers and tobacconists, tended to 'commodify' African Americans, especially on cigar-box labels that were meant to attract affluent white consumers. Even art for cheaper tobacco products rarely used dignified images of blacks to appeal to black consumers. 'Commodification' devices include placing blacks within nostalgic scenes of pre-Civil War plantation life, comparing their colour with that of tobacco, equating them with farm animals and showing them giving pleasure to those they serve, while unable to act on their own desires. Although images of African Americans appear in only a small percentage of nineteenth-century tobacco art, they reveal

much about how white Americans wished to relate to the newly freed black population.

In the 1890s George S. Harris & Sons, a lithographic firm of Philadelphia, created numerous nostalgic images of plantation life that ignored the swelling migration of African Americans to the North to work in a variety of industries.[10] In 'Southern Planter', a large figure of a white master commands the foreground, while tiny, faceless blacks, placed below the horizon line, merge with the crop and the earth. The planter sits in an upright position, his features visible against the sky, a traditional placement device that emphasizes rationality and dominance over nature. His cigar smoke resembles smoke from the steamship that will transport the crop to market. Such labels encouraged a potential cigar buyer to fantasize about mastering a docile black workforce, which would give him the leisure for such pleasurable activities as smoking a good cigar.

Written and visual representations of happy blacks working on plantations originated before the Civil War, when 'In the face of increasing criticism against slavery, slave owners, clergy, newspaper editors, and college professors in slave states created arguments that slavery was somehow good.'[11] These representations ignored the numerous ways in which slaves displayed anger and unhappiness, through such means as sabotage and running away. Leading literary magazines of the period, such as *Harper's*, also romanticized plantation life, and ran caricatures of Negroes that suggested low intelligence and the need for white paternal control.

In the cigar-box label 'Havana Ruddy', the tropical setting and 'Havana' suggest a Cuban product, but this label was designed by the Harris lithographic firm of Philadelphia for an American manufacturer who used Cuban leaf as cigar wrappers and interior tobacco from Virginia.[12] 'Ruddy' describes the colour of a variety of tobacco when dried. The artist established the dominance of the white master by giving him a straight posture, frontality and a white, tailored outfit. He indicated the black labourer's submissiveness

HAVANA RUDDY

TITLE & DESIGN REGISTERED

Two colour lithograph cigar-box labels for George Harris & Sons, c. 1890.

No. 2505. $20.00 per 1000. $2.10

ALSO FURNISHED BLANK

through a profile view, slumped posture, dark, tattered clothing, and by depicting him leaning on a hoe while waiting for orders. Their roles are clearly defined: the black worker cultivates the tobacco and the white master uses it to his own benefit.

Representations of African Americans created in the decades after Emancipation and Reconstruction, when theories of Social Darwinism were current, both reflected racial attitudes and contributed to their formation. In 1885 *Harper's* published John Fiske's 'Manifest Destiny' lecture, which argued for the inevitable progress of Teutonic and 'Aryan' races and the decline of so-called lesser races.[13] In the European theories of J. C. Lavater and Julien Joseph Vireys, popularized by American eugenicists, Africans were placed low on the evolutionary scale, and, in many illustrations, compared with orang-utans.[14] Similarly, in a 'premium' offered by Duke Tobacco, a black man casts a shadow that resembles the profile of an ape.[15]

Ironically, the concept that blacks occupied a lower rung on the evolutionary ladder than whites made them well suited for certain types of advertisements, just as in the 1950s 'dumb blondes' were considered ideal to sell cars. Artists can simplify and exaggerate one or two physical characteristics to make selling points obvious. When African Americans are thought of as 'uncivilized' and close to nature, an artist can effectively compare their skin colour with the colour of tobacco (whose raw materials were traditionally cultivated by slaves). In the label 'A full hand', the same brown ink is used for the man's skin and the cigar. This grinning, elderly 'Uncle' with missing teeth was a non-threatening stereotype. Blacks appear in tobacco art commonly at either the end or beginning of the life cycle – both vulnerable states. In some labels, crawling babies bring to mind four-legged animals and the crouched position of field labour. Children at play allude to the supposedly childlike nature of Africans.[16] Artists can exploit such concepts through showing blacks taking uninhibited pleasure in consuming tobacco, without overtones of guilt or concern for dignity.

'A Full Hand!', a colour lithograph label for Knapp & Co, 1890.

As early as the seventeenth century, both African Americans and Native Americans appear on tobacco trading cards, and it is instructive to compare their representations in nineteenth-century tobacco art.[17] It was widely known that, unlike blacks, Indians, in advance of Europeans, had cultivated tobacco through their own volition. Most images of Native Americans on cigar-box labels derive from fine art 'noble savage' traditions, as in paintings by Benjamin West. In contrast, commercial artists ignored the dignified depictions of blacks by Théodore Géricault, Henry Ossawa Tanner, Winslow Homer and others, and drew upon caricatures, including anti-abolitionist depictions of happy-go-lucky slaves. Black-face minstrel shows, first appearing in 1842 and performing 'oddities, eccentricities, and comicalities of that

Sable Genus of Humanity', provided further source material.[18]

African Americans were generally depicted as comic figures of servitude, and Native Americans as free, nomadic peoples, even though, in these decades, the latter were being confined to reservations. Native Americans are shown in harmony with, or in control of animals, while African Americans, once regarded as livestock themselves, are depicted as incapable of mastering beasts. The many labels that combined blacks and animals served as reminders that slaves had been considered chattels.[19] Animals often dominate blacks through their size or aggressiveness. Even a mere fly is capable of throwing a black person off balance, as in the popular 'Shoo Fly' label. Compare the ease with which Native Americans ride galloping horses in an 'Indian Brand' label with the helplessness of a group of black men who explode into the air with the collision of their electric car and a mule. By the mid-eighteenth century, the use of wooden or metal sculptures of cigar-store Indians had become ubiquitous; most expressed the imposing dignity of Roman

'Indian Brand', a colour lithograph label for Chas. R. Messinger, Toledo, Ohio, manufacturer, The Calvert Lithographic Company, Detroit, c. 1890.

An American Tobacco Company colour lithograph label of 1902, advertising *Duke's Mixture* and *Old Virginia Cheroots*.

'Sparkling', a colour lithograph label for George Harris & Sons, c. 1890.

No. 2593. $20.00 per 1000. $2.10 per 1(

ALSO FURNISHED FLATS

orators. If a tobacconist wanted to be different, he might order a 'Black Boy', a contemporary Northern street urchin, dressed in picturesque, shabby clothing and holding out a bunch of cigars,[20] a figure likely to inspire responses ranging from amusement to pity, rather than respect.

It is important to consider how black people are *not* shown in tobacco art. There are no depictions of vigorous males, brave historic figures, attractive women, complete family groups or males bonding through the act of smoking.[21] A black man is seldom shown smoking an elite cigar, but, when he is, the artist makes it clear that he is incapable of doing so with dignity. Common associations of class and race with types of tobacco products appear in a blatantly racist novel by Charles B. Lewis, *Brother Gardner's Lime-Kiln Club*, which was published in the 1880s and reprinted in the 1890s. In it, only a flamboyant and corrupt black politician flaunts cigars. Most blacks in the novel use pipe or chewing tobacco, as these quotes in dialect – meant to demonstrate an inability to master white culture – indicate: 'Ize chawed terbacky for forty y'ars, an' Ize gwine to chaw her till I die'; 'De man who would take away my pipe would pick my pocket.'[22]

Although many blacks, especially in the North, practised a variety of professions, and some attained wealth, in tobacco art they are generally shown as field labourers, waiters or house servants who offer to the master or customer what they are not to sample themselves. The singularity and marginal placement of blacks – often boys or old men – on these labels encode a lowly status, and extend traditions that were well established in European art by the sixteenth century.[23]

In the cigar-box label 'Sparkling', a jet of champagne from a bottle that the waiter grips with his thighs suggests ejaculation. While the servant's expression is ecstatic, his marginal placement, with his back to the banquet table, implies that, much as if he were a slave, he cannot possess what stimulates his desires. More than 2,500 blacks were lynched in the United States between 1884 and 1900, often for the supposed rapes of white women. Such a label, therefore, reveals much about the myth of black sexuality, yet an elderly servant would be less threatening than a younger man.[24]

Thomas Jefferson, in his *Notes on Virginia* of 1784, voiced the belief that Negroes were more influenced by sensation than by thought.[25] The popular belief that Africans had unusually acute powers of smell and taste, and were governed by their appetites, made them well suited to express ecstatic responses to the pleasures of tobacco. The late eighteenth- and early nineteenth-century European theorist Julien Joseph Vireys stated that: 'In the negro species, the forehead is retreating, and the mouth projecting, as if he were made rather to eat than to think.'[26] Those who took social status seriously in the nineteenth century were cautioned by etiquette books to exhibit dignity and self-control, and, 'when eating or drinking [to] avoid any kind of audible testimony to that fact'.[27] Temperance campaigns, which expanded in the 1890s to rail against tobacco use, acted as further inhibitors to displays of sensual enjoyment while smoking.[28]

The function of the black waiter in 'Corker' is to demonstrate intense desire for the product, providing the white buyer with vicarious pleasure. The waiter serves as a surrogate 'id', whose closed eyes, flaring nostrils and tipped-back head imply that smells from the cigar box on his tray have filled him with a desire that he cannot satisfy, but that the buyer may. A white man shown expressing such feelings might have been judged as degraded and unmanly.

During the post-Civil War period, when the slave/master distinctions between the races were dissolving, no commercial motivation apparently

'The Best in the World', Seal of North Carolina, a colour lithograph trade card for Marburg Bros. manufacturer, c. 1890.

'Corker', a colour label by Schwencke & Pfitzmayer Lithographers, New York City, c. 1890.

existed for making black women appear desirable in tobacco art that was meant primarily for white male consumers. Black women are seldom shown stylishly dressed, do not appear to flirt with the buyer and are usually accompanied by a black man. In 'Best in the World', a man costumed as a dandy of the 'Zip Coon' minstrel type, blows smoke in the face of a woman dressed as a kitchen servant, or 'mammy' type.[29] She grins with pleasure. In 'Golden Slippers', viewers are encouraged to laugh at the plump, elderly black couple, who fly through the air in their night clothes.

In the 1890s, as voting rights and state rule issues were being hotly debated, and as increasing

'Golden Slipper', an engraved ad for Bitting & Whitaker, manufacturers, of Winston, North Carolina, *c.* 1890.

numbers of blacks moved north to compete for jobs, white anxieties were expressed through ever more aggressive mockery of blacks within minstrel shows, and in some Broadway musicals.[30] In tobacco art, such anxieties surfaced in the theme of the black servant who steals his absent master's cigars – symbols of power and masculinity. In a typical label, a servant has laid aside his duster, his symbol of service, to recline and smoke, his feet on the table. The situation threatens the power structure, but the comical drawing style calms fears. It is unlikely that such a lazy-looking servant would dare take liberties on his master's return.

The decades after Emancipation and Reconstruction were ones in which tobacco art flourished. Uncensored expressions of prejudice in such art provide insight into white attitudes towards a newly freed black population. Displayed in shop windows, and mounted in albums as part of a repertory of private entertainment in pre-radio, film and television times, such commercial art may have had as much social impact as fine art in museums.

Women and Nineteenth-Century Images of Smoking

DOLORES MITCHELL

The creators of advertising art, caricatures, fine art, poetry and novels included increasing numbers of women in smoking scenes as the market for smoking products grew in the nineteenth century. Advertisers, aiming to entice smokers and potential smokers, used attractive female images as a lure, but seldom depicted women in the act of smoking. Caricaturists did depict female smokers, but showed them as ugly and immoral. Painters and novelists, especially when seeking modern subjects, tended to depict women smokers in a negative light as well. Only a few women artists and writers created positive, self-assured images of women smokers.

The paucity of females shown smoking in nineteenth-century art corresponds to the social practices of the time. Smoking was an important element in male bonding rituals, both in club smoking rooms and at home. After dinner, when women left the table, men would talk of sex, money and the important affairs of the day. That it was unusual for middle-class women to smoke in public is indicated by a comment made in 1846 by Charles Dickens. He found himself trapped in a room of a grand hotel with ladies who began to light up: 'in five minutes the room was a cloud of smoke . . . I never was so surprised . . . for in all my experience of ladies of one kind and another, I never saw . . . not a basket woman or a gypsy smoke before.'[1]

In the nineteenth century, pipes and cigarettes became as much an attribute of assertive masculinity as the omnipresent – and equally phallic – top hat. The cigar accompanies the moneybag in caricatures of bankers; politicians puff away, the unfurling smoke suggesting their vitality. Creators of erotica, such as Félicien Rops, emphasize the phallic nature of smoking projectiles. Edvard Munch alludes to ejaculation in his etching of 1895, *Tête-à-tête*, in which a man and a woman sit drinking in a room, and the smoke from the man's pipe travels across her smiling face.[2]

While correspondences between an erect penis and a cigarette or cigar were emphasized in visual art, in literature the object that a man smoked was usually described as feminine, following a tradition dating from Elizabethan times, when tobacco was personified as female. Carl Werner's poem 'She' refers to his cigarette: 'I pressed her fondly to my lips.'[3] The anonymous author of 'Choosing a Wife by a Pipe of Tobacco' writes: 'Let her have a shape as fine/ Let her breath be sweet as thine/ Let her, when her lips I kiss/ Burn like thee, to give me bliss.'[4] Rudyard Kipling referred to his Havana cigars as 'a harem of dusky beauties fifty tied in a string.'[5]

By the third quarter of the nineteenth century, when cigarettes became cheaper and more easily available, a few more women of all classes began to smoke. Many suffragettes and 'new women' adopted smoking as a highly visible way to challenge stereotypes about 'natural' female behaviour. Male artists discovered a new, modern subject in the female smoker. She might look worn out and depressed, as in Manet's *The Plum* (c. 1877; National Gallery of Art, Washington, DC) and Vincent van Gogh's *A Woman in the Café Le Tambourin* (1888; Vincent van Gogh

A moneybags cartoon from the 1890s.

Foundation, Amsterdam). She could be a suffragette who neglected her family to smoke and drink in taverns, or a courtesan who appeared enslaved to her vice. Caricaturists ridiculed the 'new woman' who smoked brazenly in public – even on trams – as oblivious to male disapproval.

At the turn of the century, as suffragettes demanded the vote and 'new women' rode bicycles and smoked, the image of the middle-class woman as a secret smoker, or intruder in the smoking room, became a popular subject in the arts. In Max Pemberton's short story 'A New Intruder', published in *Punch* in January 1890, a young wife,

angered at her husband's neglect, disguises herself as a man and sneaks into the smoking room of his club. Later that night, her husband is dismayed that 'Babs' fails to meet him at the door, where she usually 'kisses the point of his chin and relieves him of his hat and papers'. He finds Babs in his study, smiling slyly as she leans back in an easy chair. Like a man in his club, she holds a glass of vermouth as she smokes, blowing a 'cloud of smoke from her cigarette and look[ing] deliciously aggravating'. She repeats conversations that she has overheard at the club. Her husband suspects that some club members 'had played such a scandalous

Edvard Munch's *Tête-à-tête*, an etching of 1895.

Vincent van Gogh, *A Woman in the Café Le Tambourin*, 1888, oil on canvas.

trick as to repeat the gossip of the smoking-room to his wife' and leaves home in a state of shock. Babs regrets having committed 'an offence so heinous that all London would ring with the story of it presently'. The story ends with reconciliation and restoration of the usual order between the sexes.

The assertive, educated 'new woman' was becoming a popular subject in both literature and the visual arts. Smoke from a woman's cigarette curls up the border of the poster advertising the London production of Sydney Grundy's play of 1894, *The New Woman*. Grundy dramatizes the battle between the sexes by having men use their cigars as weapons. A husband who dislikes a book that his wife has written about sexual equality drops 'cigar ash on the final chapter'.[6] A middle-class unmarried woman who smokes 'on principle',[7] and believes that women should have latch keys so that they can slip in and out of the house as men do, is passed over by an eligible bachelor; he selects instead an old-fashioned, non-smoking woman who once was a housemaid. An elderly colonel winds things up by denouncing everything that casts discredit on the institution of marriage and weakens a community's moral fibre.

In Ermanno Wolf-Ferrari's and Enrico Golisciani's opera *Il segreto di Susanna* (Susanna's Secret), first performed in 1909, Susanna's husband smells

R. Vignesot, 'Smoking en Déshabillé', *La Vie Parisienne* (1893).

smoke on her breath and assumes that she has a lover. Susanna's real secret is her smoking – a reversal of the older literary theme in which women perceive their husbands' cigars and cigarettes as rivals. Although husband and wife are reconciled in the last act, Susanna's willingness to deceive her husband by smuggling cigarettes into her bedroom hints that she might do the same in the future with a lover.

Nineteenth-century caricatures of women smoking alone in their bedrooms sometimes show them in a state of collapse that suggests masturbation – then considered a disorder leading to moral and physical ruin. Suggestions of women withdrawing from men to seek private pleasure awakened male fears. The turn-of-the-century writer Arthur Symons stated: 'the deeper woman was drawn into herself, the further she drew away from man's civilizing influence and the more dangerous she became.'[8]

Smoking as a sign of a bad wife and mother appears in seventeenth-century Dutch moralizing art. In Jan Steen's painting *A Man Blowing Smoke at a Drunken Woman* (c. 1660–65; National Gallery, London), an unconscious woman slumps in a tavern, her pipe resting over her crotch; she is clearly unable to defend herself from male advances and is a threat to family stability. Anti-smoking campaigns during the eighteenth and nineteenth

She 'Smoked like a man', from the British *National Police Gazette* (1896).

centuries – often connected with temperance movements – condemned women smokers because of their perceived custodianship of family morality. J. H. Cohausen MD exhorted: 'Freedom in smoking and drinking goes with freedom in morals . . . Smoke destroys virtue and beauty together. But smoke if you must, misguided girls. It will make you weep, and that is woman's lot.'[9]

The frequent depiction of prostitutes, *grisettes* and *lorettes* smoking with men at masked balls and in billiard rooms and boudoirs imbued the cigarette with dangerous associations. In his novel *Nana* (1880), Emile Zola linked the courtesan's sexual drives and smoking habits: 'Nana kept rolling cigarettes, rocking backwards and forwards on her chair as she smoked them.'[10] Nana's powerful odour of lovers' sperm and tobacco enhanced her sexual attraction. Many writers, such as Zola, as well as medical practitioners, warned that prostitution – common in Paris – would transmit the disease of the 'dangerous classes' into middle-class homes. Some prostitutes were said to emit the stench of the sewers and contagion – Nana literally putrefies in her last illness.[11] Men, Zola seems to be saying, wasted not only their seed but their fortunes on Nana. The cigarette in Nana's, or some other temptress's hand, was a castration symbol, representing the appropriation by women of men's powers. It is significant that Nana had both male and female lovers.

During the 1890s manufacturers and commercial artists began increasingly to use beautiful women to sell products, including cigarettes and smoking paraphernalia.[12] Women still provided an insignificant market for tobacco products, however, even with the small increase in their smoking; advertising campaigns used women enticingly in campaigns directed toward men. Then, as now, advertising images hinted at illicit eroticism. The women on posters were often actresses and dance-hall girls; Jules Chéret's cigarette girls on posters for JOB Cigarette Paper appear to offer their bodies as well as their cigarettes. Georges Meunier's *Papier à JOB* (1894), includes a black cat as his cigarette girl's

companion, bringing to mind Manet's notorious *Olympia* of 1863 (Musée d'Orsay, Paris).

The blonde Medusa-haired woman in Alphonse Mucha's poster of 1896 for JOB swoons in a cigarette-induced orgasm. Her posture – head tipped back, eyes closed and lips parted – was, according to Martha Kingsbury, 'reserved almost exclusively for women, touching men only on rare occasions when they too exhibited a kind of mastery or power simultaneously with submersion of themselves'.[13] The cigarette becomes the woman's substitute lover. By appropriating the male smoking habit, she wields the phallic cigarette for her own pleasure.

Turkish, African, American Indian and Spanish women, all from regions that cultivated tobacco or prepared tobacco products, were frequently depicted in advertising. Thus, the woman on a cigar-box label – whose frank sensuality was surpassed only by

Alphonse Mucha, *JOB*, 1896, colour lithograph.

pornographic images – became identified with a product that was consumed for pleasure, inserted in the mouth to be 'kissed' and sucked. A man might enjoy this pleasure alone in his den, or share the pleasure with other males in a bar or club as part of a bonding ritual.

Turkish women on cigar-box labels lounge about within harems, with water pipes nearby. The artist makes it clear that the sole function of such a confined female is to give pleasure to a master who has absolute control over her. There are parallels between Western paintings of beautiful slaves being auctioned off and the auctioning of tobacco. Prized cigars must be stored in special containers to keep them in perfect condition, much as harem women are depicted as being pampered. Sources for such tobacco labels as *White Slave* include the harem paintings of the French artist Ingres.

The deep brown of an African woman's skin was compared to the colour of cigars in advertisements that hinted at a 'primitive' smoking experience. Native American women were idealized as living in harmony with nature, rather like present-day Marlboro cowboys.

Although beautiful women are used in tobacco art to associate sexual with smoking pleasures, they are seldom shown smoking. An exception is the Spanish woman, a 'Carmen' type who takes bold pleasure in smoking and flirting. Such images encouraged male buyers of tobacco products to fantasize about the possession of both cigars and women.

Prosper Mérimée's novel of 1845, *Carmen*, popularized smoking as an attribute of the femme fatale, although threatening images of female personifications of tobacco as a witch had already surfaced in the sixteenth century.[14] Carmen, a gypsy, works in a cigarette factory that seems a cross between a harem and a brothel. When Mérimée's narrator first meets her Carmen tells him that she is 'very fond of the smell of tobacco'. He gives her a cigarette and comments: 'We mingled our smoke.'[15] Carmen's appetite for smoking prepares the reader for her appetite for sex, with smoke serving as a metaphor

for her fatal fickleness. She undermines her lover's loyalty to his mother and his childhood sweetheart. He can free himself from his addiction to Carmen only by stabbing her to death.

At a time when most male artists and writers portrayed women smokers as deviant, dangerous and deceitful, a small number of women artists and writers used smoking as a sign of independence and strength. The popular English novelist Marie Louise de la Ramée ('Ouida') created a plucky heroine called 'Cigarette' in her novel of 1867, *Under Two Flags*. Cigarette shares with Mérimée's Carmen free attitudes toward smoking and sex. Even though 'she had tossed about with the army', having 'as many *affaires* as the veriest Don Juan among them' and answers a man's insult by 'blowing a puff of smoke at him',[16] she is portrayed in a positive light. Smoking is her way of defying social conventions, 'making scorn of her doom of sex, drinking it down, laughing it down, burning it out in tobacco fumes'.[17] Rather than destroying the man she loves, she becomes his 'comrade-in-arms': she rides into an ambush meant for him and dies fighting. Ouida gives Cigarette traits that are usually associated with male heroes: physical and moral courage, free will and the ability to relish pleasure – preparing the way for a new iconography involving women who smoke. Ouida herself refused to leave the room when men lit their pipes and cigars, saying: 'Now gentlemen, suppose my mother and myself are out of the room. Smoke and drink as if you were at the club; talk as if you were in the smoking-room there.'[18]

In the last years of the nineteenth century, Frances Benjamin Johnston and Jane Atché were among the few women artists who appropriated the iconography that had empowered male smokers for depictions of female ones. Neither allegorical nor exotic, the costumes indicate that their subjects are contemporary middle-class women. When the English artist William Frith dared in 1870 to paint a middle-class woman smoking in a public garden, he was 'mercilessly attacked for painting such a subject at all'.[19] Johnston and Atché were part of

White Slave and *El Mulo*, two colour lithograph cigar-box labels, *c.* 1890.

a growing category of women who presented a genuine challenge to their societies. Their professional skills enabled them to earn their own livings. As artists they questioned visual stereotypes and created iconographies with a social impact.

One of the first American women to make a commercial success of photography, Frances Benjamin Johnston was born in 1864 in Washington, DC, where her father worked for the US Treasury Department. From 1883 to 1885 she studied drawing and painting at the Académie Julian in Paris, intending to become an illustrator.[20] On her return to Washington, realizing that photography would soon supplant drawn illustration in newspapers, she obtained a Kodak camera and underwent an apprenticeship in the Smithsonian Institute's photographic laboratory. She began her professional career in 1889, photographing notable personalities such as Susan B. Anthony and taking on challenging documentary assignments, such as shooting inside the Kohinoor Coal Mines in Shenandoah.

When Johnston created the striking self-portrait illustrated here, she was about 32, and had been a successful practitioner of her craft for some seven years. She posed in one of the six rooms of the studio that she had added to her parent's Washington home in 1894, showing herself as woman of substance surrounded by her collection of art objects and photographs, holding a cigarette in one hand and a beer stein in the other. She sits with one leg crossed jauntily over a knee, calves and petticoats showing, yet her clothing is not provocative in itself, or her expression seductive. Johnston never married; she smoked, drank and had bohemian as well as socially prominent friends. Her cigarette and beer stein are not arbitrary props but reflect real aspects of her life. Her faint smile and the flaunting manner in which she displays her 'attributes' indicate that she has quite consciously selected three aspects of behaviour that the conservative viewer would deem outrageous in a woman. In control of her image and her pleasures, she defies social conventions, yet retains her hearth and other rewards of middle-class life.

A *Punch* caricature of 1900 of a 'new woman' smoking by a fireplace with art objects on the mantel resembles Johnston's *Self-portrait*. The caricature, however, shows the 'new woman' seated on the floor on top of pillows with her thighs open to the heat of the fire – the traditional iconography of lust.[21] The caption gives the male visitor, Dr Prim, these words: 'Miss Lucy!! Smoking!' Miss Lucy (described as 'an advanced young lady with Classical knowledge') responds: 'It's classical and correct. "*Ex Lucy dare fumum.*"' The caricature indicates how closely the education and the smoking and sexual habits of the 'new woman' were linked in the popular imagination.

Frances Benjamin Johnston, *Self-portrait*, c. 1896.

By the late 1890s Jane Atché, born in Toulouse, was known for her colour lithographs of women, which were published as commercial posters and decorative panels. Little is known about her life.[22] Her poster of about 1896 for JOB contrasts greatly with Mucha's poster for the company. Mucha's woman appears to be inhaling so deeply that tobacco fumes fill her body, causing the hair on top of her head to rise and mimic the behaviour of smoke. Her contorted grasp of her cigarette conveys sexual tension. Atché's woman is not overwhelmed by the act of smoking, although her posture, expression and gesture convey sophisticated enjoyment of the experience. Atché's image brings to mind Mary Cassatt's *At the Opera* (1880; Museum of Fine Arts, Boston), in which an unaccompanied woman shown in profile takes pleasure in viewing an afternoon performance.

Gail Cunningham, in *The New Woman and the Victoria Novel*, states: 'the New Woman is regarded as a highly sexual being, all the more dangerous since she cannot be dismissed as a prostitute or a fallen woman'.[23] Indeed, Johnston and Atché provide no clues, no flirtatious glance or provocative dress that suggest their well-dressed smokers are anything but respectable middle-class women. They are the sort of woman that alarmed writers such as Marcel Prevost, who in *Les Demi-Vierges* (1894) warned of the dangers posed to society when women give out mixed signals. He bemoaned that it had become difficult to tell bad and good women apart, since fashionable women had taken to behaving like the fallen: 'shamelessly flout[ing] all the genteel conventions to which modest, well-brought up young girls were expected to adhere'.[24] Implicit as a subtext is the fear that such women will introduce disease and degeneration into middle-class households.

The images by Johnston and Atché share an iconography of restraint, one traditionally used to empower male figures. The profile poses distance the women smokers from the viewer; none of the smokers seeks an admiring eye. Unlike the orgiastic, wild-haired female smokers of Mucha and the cari-

Jane Atché, *Papier a Cigarettes JOB*, c. 1896, colour lithograph.

caturists, their hair is pinned securely to their heads. Their costumes are buttoned, their breasts covered. Although they wear no jewellery, they are fashionably, even expensively dressed. Their expressions are also restrained. Johnston's faint smile suggests that she enjoys projecting a socially defiant image. Atché's woman, with head held high, looks like a Parisian sophisticate and connoisseur of sensual pleasures.

These women recall figures from Classical reliefs: they are in profile, with arms confined within a narrow plane and positioned to clear their torsos – such devices classicize and dignify the figures. The pose may even allude to the educated status of the 'new woman' who could think for herself, since higher education in the nineteenth century commonly involved the study of Classical art and literature. Both women artists use formal devices traditionally associated with portrayals of men. For example, their women enlarge their bodies visually through elbow-out arm positions. None has the languishing or sinuous postures typical for women in Victorian art or art nouveau but sit straight, or, as in the Johnston, lean forward. Both works use strong value contrasts and incisive lines, rather than the light colours, diaphanous forms and wandering, broken lines often used to depict women by their contemporaries, as in Mucha. The black cloak in the Atché also serves as a powerful design element, as does the dark, plaid outfit worn by Johnston.

Nineteenth-century art theorists were fascinated by the expressive potentials of lines; the vertical line tended to carry associations of authority, and hence masculinity. For example, David Sutter, a theorist who affected Seurat's art, stated: 'The vertical line is the line of nobility, of grandeur, majesty, and authority.'[25] (Prostitutes were jokingly called grand horizontals.) The straight vertical line formed by the cloak edge in the Atché is one of the poster's most conspicuous formal elements. A vertical buttress appears behind Johnston in her *Self-portrait*. The figures are both centrally placed, a position of spatial command.

Why would Ouida, Johnston and Atché want to appropriate typical male images and apply them to portrayals of female smokers? An obvious answer is that smoking carried associations of a wider knowledge of life from which women were excluded. Suffragette movements gained momentum at the turn of the century and stimulated public debate about restrictions on women's lives – including smoking. By smoking, a woman might claim publicly – in the words of Ouida's heroine, Cigarette – 'her right to do just whatsoever pleasured her'.[26]

There is another possibility that relates specifically to these women as artists: nineteenth-century smoking lore held that smoking aided creativity by stimulating fantasies and associative memories (tobacco was often stronger and less heavily processed then, and other drugs were sometimes added). Many nineteenth-century artists and writers, including some women, were conspicuous smokers – George Sand is one example. Charles Baudelaire praised the pipe as the writer's consolation.[27] In Charles Lummis's poem 'My Cigarette', he says: 'me seem's a poet's dreams / are in the wreaths of smoke ascending.'[28] A verse by an anonymous writer states: 'when smoking all my ideas soar/ When not they sink upon the floor.'[29] The Sherlock Holmes novels popularized the notion that tobacco induced profound thoughts. In numerous *Punch* caricatures of artists or philosophers struck by or waiting for inspiration in the 1890s, more than 90 per cent are shown smoking. Women eager to broaden their horizons might have applied to themselves James Barrie's statements in *My Lady Nicotine* (1895). Speaking of the introduction of tobacco to England, he says: 'Men who had hitherto only concerned themselves with narrow things of home put a pipe into their mouths and became philosophers.'[30] Ouida, Frances Benjamin Johnston and Jane Atché chose to portray in a positive light women who nourish their thoughts with smoke, and because they invested these women with dignity, they seem to have thoughts worth nourishing.

Toward a Queer History of Smoking

ROBYN L. SCHIFFMAN

There was a touch of the swashbuckler in the
way Rosalba was carrying herself, something
of a rapier in that long cigarette-holder.
Compton MacKenzie, 1928[1]

In the middle of Book Two of Jean-Jacques Rousseau's
Confessions, Rousseau recalls a man described as a
Moor who attempted to seduce him. With his char-
acteristic honesty and naïveté, he writes:

> One night he tried to get into bed with me; I
> protested, pointing out that my bed was too
> small; he pressed me to get into his; I again
> refused; for the miserable fellow was so dirty
> and stank so badly of chewed tobacco, that he
> filled me with revulsion.[2]

This incident occurred sometime in the late 1720s,
after Rousseau had left Geneva at the age of 15. In
his recollection of the evening, he maintains that
he had no idea what the young man wanted or why
he was behaving the way he did. When Rousseau
told others what had happened, he was warned
about the *Chevaliers de la manchette*, or Knights of the
Cuff, as homosexuals were referred to in the early
eighteenth century. He was also strongly cautioned
to keep silent.

The incident had a remarkable and profound
effect on the young Rousseau. He vowed henceforth
to be kinder and gentler to women, since he imagined how terrified they might be when in a similar
situation. But what is also striking about this
passage, apart from Rousseau's genuine absence
of irony, is that he seems more upset that the man
smelled of tobacco than anything else and it is this,
along with his filth, that disgusts him. Indeed, in
Rousseau's mind, there is a very strong connection

between the tobacco smell and the seemingly
strange sexual behaviour.

In the early part of the twentieth century, which
was more than a century after the posthumous
publication in the 1780s of Rousseau's *Confessions*,
the link between smoking and homosexuality
would only get stronger. In a passage in Christopher
Isherwood's autobiography, in which he describes
his years as a young man in Berlin and elsewhere,
the writer recalls sitting at a café working on the
novel that would become *The Memorial* (1932).
Isherwood, who refers to himself alternately in the
third and first person, considers how the smell of
smoke functions as an aphrodisiac and enables him
to remember his first love, a Czech boy called Bubi:

> With his manuscript in front of him, a tall glass
> of beer on his right, a cigarette burning in an
> ashtray on his left, he [Christopher] sipped and
> wrote, puffed and wrote. The beer, of course, was
> German: Schultheiss-Patzenhofer. The cigarette
> was a Turkish-grown brand especially popular in
> Berlin: Salem Aleikum. Bubi had introduced him
> to both, so the taste of one and the smell of the
> other were magically charged.[3]

To remember Bubi is to remember smoking and
drinking; the oral activity of the smoking and
drinking recalls the orality of fellatio. The substitu-
tion of sex for smoking and drinking becomes
complete when we later read that Bubi had taught
Isherwood all he knew about sex. In contrast to

Rousseau, there is clearly no repulsion here, only increased desire, which makes the memory both pleasant and poignant.

In the years between Rousseau and Isherwood, smoking had been linked with creativity, especially with the writing of poetry, and also with heterosexuality. Ross Chambers coins the term *le poète fumeur* to describe the well known – and lesser well known – writers from France (Charles Baudelaire, Stéphane Mallarmé and Jules Laforgue) and England (Charles Lamb, William Cowper and Charles Calverley) who introduced their late eighteenth- and nineteenth-century readers to a new literary subject: cigarettes, cigars, pipes and smoking. But after the trials of Oscar Wilde in the 1890s and Radclyffe Hall's notorious lesbian novel, *The Well of Loneliness* (1928), which was banned and also brought to trial for obscenity in the year that it was published, queer culture and smoking yet again found themselves linked. The simple act of smoking and the presence of a cigar or cigarette invite a reading of behaviour that Radclyffe Hall called 'inversion' and Virginia Woolf, distinguishing between men and women, called 'buggery' and 'Sapphism'. It becomes possible, then, to read the cigarette in selected early twentieth-century texts as one of many signs and symbols that gay men and women used to recognize each other.

It is true that there a many queer characters who smoke, and queer texts with smoking characters, and they are not any more interesting or dull than anyone else. But what emerges from this study is that there is a place for a history of smoking within queer culture. The cigarette, in other words, can queer a text in certain visual and textual media. This shift gained currency precisely at the time when a modern subjectivity about homosexuals was born, when the medical communities of, for example, Sigmund Freud and Magnus Hirschfeld, as well as the new literary interlocutors such as Wilde and Hall, were bringing new attention to a growing homosexual population and identity. It is not surprising, then, that also at this time a 'fag' became both a synonym for a cigarette and a derogatory name for a male homosexual.

The cigarette became part of a complex network of fashion accessories that began to carve out a discernible homosexual style and culture, and that became recognizable to those in the know. In his monumental study of the beginnings of modern and urban gay culture, *Gay New York*, the historian George Chauncey documents what some of these discernible traits were. 'Some clothes', he writes, 'such as a green suit, were so bold that few dared wear them.'[4] The green suit mentioned by Chauncey became transformed into a green carnation on the lapel of a dinner jacket in Robert Hichens's thinly disguised *roman-à-clef* about Oscar Wilde and Lord Alfred Douglas of that title: *The Green Carnation* (1949). The carnation is worn by Lord Reginald Hastings and Esmé Amarinth, the models for Douglas and Wilde in Hichens's novel.

In addition to the carnation, which provokes commentary and wonderment from other characters in the novel, there is another important accoutrement: a gold-tipped cigarette. Hichens, in the preface to the novel, recalls his first meeting and impression of Douglas and Wilde. He writes: 'I had . . . seen Mr Wilde . . . with a gold tipped cigarette in his smiling mouth.'[5] Esmé Amarinth also smokes gold-tipped cigarettes. The cigarette and the carnation queer this text, in other words.

Chauncey continues to enumerate other ways of knowing: 'Other items of apparel . . . were worn more commonly. Perhaps the most famous of these in the early years of the century was the red necktie.'[6] Combining the red tie and the cigarette as a medium in an economy of sexual exchange, Chauncey mentions Paul Cadmus's *The Fleet's In!* of 1934. In this painting, a male civilian offers a cigarette to a sailor. The look on both men's faces suggests that the sailor knows exactly what is being offered to him, as he takes in the man's shaped eyebrows, bleached hair, the rouge on his face and the red tie. The cigarette occasions the connection, enables the contact between the two men, whereby one reads the signs on his body.

Perhaps one of the best examples to illustrate a queer narrative with characters who both smoke

Paul Cadmus, *The Fleet's In!*, 1934, oil on canvas. The painting is suggestive and very crowded, but the area under discussion is the civilian and sailor to the left of the canvas.

and wear red ties is Thomas Mann's famous story of 1912, *Death in Venice*, a story about a trip to Venice by an elderly German writer, Gustave von Aschenbach, and the Polish boy, Tadzio, he sees there, becomes obsessive about and loves. Critics, it should be said, have long recognized homosexual themes in this work: in June 1999 *Death in Venice* topped the Publishing Triangle's list of 100 great gay novels of all time.[7] What is notable about Mann's work is that there are two characters who fit the gay male patterns identified by Chauncey in the early 1900s, by dress and by behaviour, and that they also smoke: a passenger on board the boat and Aschenbach himself. An examination of how these various codes are played out in the pages of the narrative reveals how this story emerges as a model text in examining the conjoining of smoking and queer cultures in the early part of the twentieth century.

On his arrival in Venice, Aschenbach notices 'one . . . in a dandied buff suit . . . and a red cravat'.[8] Aschenbach, who is horrified and fascinated by this man, with his painted face and wig, is drawn to his hands: there is 'a cigarette between

his shaking fingers'.[9] His uncanny relationship to the man, who is never named, is based on the recognition of sameness of desire. Aschenbach, on the other hand, is mentioned as smoking only once; but his name, suggesting 'ash', carries from beginning to end this association, since the first words of the story announce his undisputed title and name him most certainly: 'Gustave Aschenbach – or von Aschenbach, as he had been known officially since his fiftieth birthday.'[10] He does not need to smoke because he is already ash. As his love for Tadzio grows, and he participates in this self-knowledge, Ashenbach decides to go to the barber for a make-over. He dies his hair, has his eyebrows shaped, has rouge put on his cheeks, is given eye make-up and lip gloss. In short, Aschenbach becomes the figure in Cadmus's painting and becomes like certain Bloomsbury homosexual men that Virginia Woolf, writing to Jacques Raverat in 1925, would identify by the fact that 'they paint and powder' their faces.[11] And when Aschenbach emerges from the barber, the narrator reports: 'Aschenbach went off . . . in his red neck-tie.'[12]

Although he does not smoke, there is a third red tie- wearing character in *Death in Venice*: Tadzio. It is his clothing that makes him instantly recognizable to Aschenbach: 'His eye found him out at once, the red breast-knot was unmistakable.'[13] By reading and recognizing the constellation of queer characteristics of these three men, the modern homosexual literary subject is born. And this modern homosexual subject seems to do a lot of smoking.

The entrance of women into the narrative of smoking queers really began in 1928 with publication of two novels: Radclyffe Hall's famous *The Well of Loneliness* and Compton MacKenzie's *Extraordinary Women*. By 1928, the year in which Woolf published *Orlando* and went on holiday with Vita Sackville-West, when, it has been claimed, they first had sex, the queer sign had become personal and more localized. Moving from a discernible fashion with regard to clothing, at least with women, it became written on the body, an extension of the body. Stephen Gordon, the invert of Hall's novel, goes to visit Valérie Seymour, a character modelled on Nathalie Clifford Barney. On meeting Stephen for the first time, Valérie says: '"I am so delighted to meet you at last, Miss Gordon, do come and sit down. And please smoke if you want to." [she adds] quickly, glancing at Stephen's tell-tale fingers.'[14] Here, it is Stephen's smoking fingers that enable Valérie to read her body, and to read it queerly. And in MacKenzie's text, Aurora (Rory) Freemantle, a cigar-smoking lesbian, uses the actual smoke of her cigar as the canvas in which she paints a fantasized picture of her life with the woman she loves, Rosalba Donsante: 'She [Rory] did make pictures in the smoke of her cigars of that life with Rosalba – of the house they would live in, of the garden they would plan, of the view Rosalba's window would frame, and of the uniform of their maids.'[15] The smoke enables, in fact creates, the fantasy whereby the two women can be together.

Reading smoking and certain fashion accessories in early twentieth-century writing in this way allows for a queer presence in any history of smoking. This connection between queer culture and smoking changed, not surprisingly, with the intervening births of feminist and queer theory and cultural practices. A culture that no longer needs to rely on a practice of decoding and symbolization, a culture such as the late twentieth-century one, forcefully finds these links in playful and self-conscious ways. By releasing her seventh album with the mischievous title of *Drag*, the Canadian lesbian, vegetarian, animal-rights activist and Country musician Kathryn Dawn Lang, more commonly known as k. d. lang, suggested that this link runs true and deep, and that she is the medium to announce it loud and clear.

Although neither a record-breaking nor a best-selling album, *Drag* (1997) was nonetheless a highly anticipated follow-up to her previously themed record, *All You Can Eat*. On the album's cover, Lang made play with the word 'drag', solidly connecting both registers by wearing a man's suit (with a red tie!) and being poised to smoke. Known for her performances, costumes and penchant for covering old tunes, Lang did not disappoint her fans, since *Drag* is a collection of some famous songs – such as Peggy Lee's hit of 1948, 'Don't Smoke in Bed' – that all focus on smoking and addiction. In other words, the album is a palimpsest of musical styles and genres that recall an earlier era in both music and gender. It should be said that Lang does not encourage smoking in any way: the ultimate (and rather banal) message on the album is that smoking is as dangerous and addictive as love. In addition to the obvious pun on the album's title, the metaphors of smoke relate to interests in textual layering, both with respect to Lang as a woman who wears men's clothes and a country-turned-pop musician who sings and records many songs she has not written.

But what is the rich, lexical field in which Lang finds herself playing and invoking? Words such as drag and fag, as any dictionary of American slang will show, have registers in both smoking and queer cultures. The word drag, which first appeared in the late fourteenth century, was not used as a term to describe feminine attire as worn by men until the early 1870s.[16] The entry for 'Transvestitism/

Theatrical' in the *Encyclopedia of Homosexuality* reveals that being 'in drag' was a term taken from '"thieves" cant that compared the train of a gown to the drag or brake on a coach, and entered into theatrical parlance from homosexual slant around 1870'.[17] Drag's association with costuming has continued in our age of, among other things, essentialist debates regarding homosexuality, as RuPaul, an (un)likely deconstructionist, famously declared that 'we are born naked. The rest is drag.'[18] At least from the seventeenth to the twentieth centuries, the word drag has been connected with smoke. In the early seventeenth century, dragoon or dragon, the word from which drag derives, was considered an old name for a musket and the soldiers who carried these firearms were called Dragons or Dragoons.[19] It was not until the 1910s that drag began to be used as a synonym for inhalation, to describe the action of pulling on or at a cigarette.[20] And though slang usage with respect to drug culture is an enormous lexical field unto itself, it was in 1961 that the phrase 'to chase the dragon' was coined for smoking heroine, since the movements of the smoke after inhalation are said to mimic the tail of a Chinese dragon.[21]

The usage of the word fag functions in a similar manner. Fag, a shortened form of faggot or fagot, is often used as an example of how gay men and lesbians have reclaimed and reappropriated originally pejorative words toward a new, and somewhat liberationist, cause – queer being the most obvious example. But a careful reading of the etymological literature on fag reveals a complicated set of possibilities for its origin. Used now as a slang term for homosexual men, fag's origins in the Middle Ages and Renaissance link it with female prostitutes: 'In the 1500s', according to the editors of *When Drag Is Not a Car Race: An Irreverent Dictionary of over 400 Gay and Lesbian Words and Phrases*, 'disagreeable/objectionable women were called faggots as a term of abuse.'[22] The evolution of fag built upon this association with woman, since more commonly – and more recently – cigarettes were called fags in Britain during the First World War.[23] The argument holds that the smoking of cigarettes was considered

unmanly, since they were understood to be weaker, inferior versions of cigars. Thus to smoke a smaller penis, if you will, was a sign of less masculine behaviour. But it was in American English at this time that fag as a slang term for a homosexual man was coined,[24] thus indicating that fag, at least on both sides of the Atlantic, had become a term used to mean both a thing and a person. Other widely held derivations of the word are highly contested. Warren Johansson maintains that there is actually no connection to the practice in nineteenth-century English boarding schools that employed a system of fagging, in which junior pupils performed certain duties (including sexual) for senior ones. And, he continues, in early modern times, it was hanging, not burning, that was the punishment for homosexual activity, thus erasing a connection between the faggots, or burning bundles of sticks, that were placed under homosexuals in order to execute them.[25] It is clear that the derivation of this word is still in need of explication and analysis, but contained within this history are links between gender, sexual behaviour and smoking.

This attempt at a construction of a queer history of smoking has cut across national languages, literatures and artistic media. And with the Internet, whole new chapters can be written; just a quick canvas of Microsoft's and Yahoo's Internet male smoking communities reveals that of the thirteen devoted exclusively to men who smoke, eight of them are for gay men. A recent contribution to *The New Yorker*'s 'Talk of the Town' quotes a member of CLASH (Citizens Lobbying Against Smoker Harassment) considering about how to get more people involved in the cause. Unapologetically, the member offers the following suggestion: 'we have to . . . get the gay people involved. They smoke a lot.'[26] This may or may not be true, but a comprehensive examination of the role of smoking in visual and literary culture must take into account the ways in which cigarettes, cigars and the act of smoking emerge as crucial intertexts in the construction of a queer history of smoking.

Gender & Ethnicity

'TOBACCO SYMBOLIZES THE SYMBOLIC', wrote Jacques Derrida in his 1991 Counterfeit Money. For him, smoking has multiple, simultaneous meanings functioning in multiple systems of significance. But if this is true, if everyone smokes, and if it means infinitely different things simultaneously, then we need to differentiate between those whose smoking we imagine is like ours, however we define ourselves, and those who only mimic smoking. Gustav Flaubert in 1857 puts his emphasis on the falseness of Emma Bovary's freedom of action by writing of her smoking while puffing on his cigar: 'By the mere effect of her love Madame Bovary's manners changes. Her looks grew bolder, her speech more free; she even committed the impropriety of walking out with Monsieur Rodolphe, a cigarette in her mouth, "as if to defy the people".' People unsure of their identity smoke in order to look like 'real' people. Thus the 'New Woman' in Europe and Asia mimicked men smoking, as does T. S. Eliot's 'Miss Nancy

Ellicott', who in 1915 '… smoked / And danced all the modern dances; / And her aunts were not quite sure how they felt about it, / But they knew it was modern.' In the multiple images of outsiders – women and ethnics and colonial subjects who smoke – there is a powerful sense of the world in which smoke takes on constant shifts in meanings. What in the early twentieth century is a shallowness ascribed to women's and ethnics' mimicry becomes a lifestyle by the late twentieth century. The motto of the 1980s Virginia Slims cigarette ads, 'You've come a long way, baby', gives way to more recent ads that show a woman holding a cigarette with the slogan "Tis a woman thing!' This certainly is true, as we know: we have a world in which lung cancer cases for women exceed those for men, and non-Western use of tobacco, especially in East Asia, has set the stage for a new meaning attached to the modern. There is no longer any thought that such smoking might be inauthentic – only dangerous. Yet risk sells.

In Brazil, André Thevet in 1555 noted that *petun* (tobacco) was believed to be 'wonderfully useful for several things'. One was medicinal: here a sick man is being 'fumigated' with smoke from a large cigar. Another shakes a tammaraka or rattle, now a musical rather than a medical instrument.

'GENUINE HAVANA', an 1868 lithograph advertisement.

Jean-Louis Forain, 'Finally Alone!', a prostitute from his weekly *Le Fifre* (1899).

Schaufensterplakat for the Dresden Cigar manufacturers Jedicke & Sohn.

A model with a cigarette in an artist's studio, *c.* 1900.

Smoking with a water pipe in Algeria, *c.* 1910.

Women smoking in Paris.

Melpa tribesman in New Guinea, 1985, smoking a cigarette.

Smoking at a festival in the Philippines.

Man smoking a pipe, India, 1995.

A woman smoking a cigar, Havanna, Cuba, 2002.

Smoking:
The 'Burning Issue'

Why Do We Smoke?: The Physiology of Smoking

LESLIE IVERSEN

Drugs are chemical substances that are taken deliberately to obtain some desired effect. They can be administered in many different ways – by mouth, injection (sometimes directly into the bloodstream), eye drops, nasal spray, topical application to the skin or inhalation into the lungs.[1] The last route offers many advantages, since the inhaled substance is exposed to the large internal surface of the lungs and is often absorbed very rapidly into the blood. The lungs consist of a system of highly branched tubes (bronchi) that end in minute delicate bulbs (alveoli), through which oxygen is absorbed and carbon dioxide excreted. The human lungs contain some 300 million alveoli, with a total surface area of approximately 70 square metres (equivalent to the floor area of two large rooms). Inhalation is used to administer a number of medically useful drugs. These include the gaseous anaesthetics and medicines used to treat lung diseases (e.g., asthma). In order for a drug to be delivered in this way it must usually be a gas (e.g., the anaesthetics halothane or nitrous oxide), a volatile liquid (e.g., chloroform or ether) or a substance that can be converted to gaseous form by heating (smoked drugs); alternatively, the drug can be dispersed in fine droplets in an aerosol device and the fine cloud of droplets inhaled (e.g., asthma medicines).

This chapter focuses on those psychoactive drugs that are inhaled by smoking. To be suitable for this form of intake, the substance must have certain particular physicochemical properties. Smoke is generated by heating or burning, using either plant materials that contain an active drug or the pure substance itself. The active drug is a substance that can be converted into a gas at high temperatures (usually in the range 200–300°C). Such a gas would be far too hot to be inhaled directly into the lungs, but in the smoking device (pipe or cigarette) the gaseous drug rapidly condenses back into liquid or solid form as the gas cools. This forms a smoke (i.e. a fine dispersion of minute particles) containing the active drug. The smoke is inhaled into the lungs and rapidly delivers the drug to the bloodstream. Smoking provides the rapid delivery of drugs that many users crave. In the case of heroin and cocaine, this gives a sudden wave of euphoria, the so-called rush. Taking the same drugs by mouth produces a much slower absorption into the blood and thence to the brain; in addition, drugs absorbed from the gut may be removed and degraded as they pass through the liver before entering the general circulation.

Not all drugs can be smoked. For example, a common form of cocaine is the sulphate derivative, but although this can be insufflated on to the nasal membranes as a powder, it cannot be smoked, since it cannot be converted to a gas by heating. It was the production of crack cocaine (the free base form of the substance) in the 1980s and '90s that first made cocaine smoking possible. Although opium smoking was common in China in the nineteenth century, opium and the synthetic derivative heroin were not commonly smoked in the Western world. Taking opium preparations by mouth – or by injec-

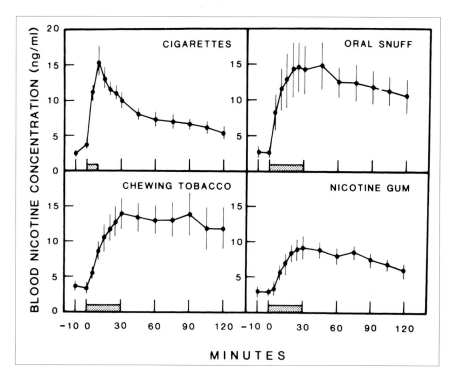

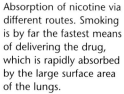

Absorption of nicotine via different routes. Smoking is by far the fastest means of delivering the drug, which is rapidly absorbed by the large surface area of the lungs.

tion in the case of heroin – were the usual methods. More recently, however, with the increased availability of purer forms of heroin, smoking or inhaling the vaporized drug has become more common. The latter method, known as 'chasing the dragon', appears to require considerable skill:

Chasing involves heating some powder on creased silver foil and inhaling the fumes through a tube of rolled foil or, for those with less steady hands, the outer case of a matchbox. Chasing is quite a skill. The amount of heat applied has to be just right so as to get the heroin to liquefy and run along creases to avoid charring. At the same time the tube has to be manipulated to follow and inhale the wisp of vapour that resembles a dragon's tail. Opening up the foil tube reveals smoke deposits which can be vaporised in their turn to minimise waste. The rush (sudden euphoria) achieved by this method is almost as good as that obtained by injection. On the other hand it is less economical since some of the

smoke is lost into the atmosphere, and demands better quality heroin.[2]

Although some active drug is lost by combustion and some in the exhaled smoke, smoking is, nevertheless, a very efficient way of rapidly delivering psychoactive drugs. The experienced tobacco or cannabis user learns to exert a fine control over the amount of drug absorbed and entering the brain. This is achieved by varying the frequency of inhaled puffs and the depth of inhalation and by holding smoke in the lungs to prolong absorption of the active substance. A number of research studies have shown that both tobacco and cannabis smokers will vary their smoking behaviour to obtain the required dose of active drug when given unmarked cigarettes or joints containing different amounts of active drug (nicotine or delta-9-tetrahydrocannabinol [THC]). When given weaker cigarettes or joints, smokers automatically inhale more deeply and more frequently. Table 1 lists some of the psychoactive drugs that are commonly smoked, and

Illustration 1 shows how efficient this route of drug administration is by comparison with other means of administration.

TABLE 1 – DRUGS THAT ARE SMOKED

COMMON NAME	ACTIVE DRUG SUBSTANCE	BOILING POINT, °C
Cannabis (marijuana)	THC	200
Crack Cocaine	Cocaine	187
Heroin	Diacetylmorphine	272
Opium	Morphine	252
Tobacco	Nicotine	247
Speed, Ice	Methamphetamine	circa 200

Unfortunately, inhaling the smoke generated from burning plant leaves is not good for the lungs. Tobacco smoke contains carbon monoxide, a product of incomplete combustion, and when this is absorbed it impairs the ability of the blood to carry oxygen. One of the consequences of this is to impair the growth of an unborn baby if the mother smokes – leading to low-birth-weight babies, who are more prone to various diseases. Other poisons in tobacco smoke have even more serious consequences for the long-term smoker – with an increased risk of early death from more than two dozen different causes, of which lung cancer is the most common.[3] Tobacco-related illnesses and deaths represent the single most important public health problem for most countries in which smoking is common. In the United States of America, tobacco smoking is responsible for more than 500,000 deaths annually. A recent survey in China suggested that as many as one third of young adult men will eventually die prematurely from smoking-related illnesses.[4]

The smoke generated by smoked cannabis (marijuana) contains many of the same ingredients as tobacco smoke, and is consequently also a serious potential health risk for long-term users – although there is as yet no reliable scientific data to show that this is the case.[5]

ACTIONS OF SMOKED DRUGS ON THE BRAIN

The reason that people smoke the drugs listed in Table 1 is because all of them have desirable actions on the brain. These range from the mild stimulant or relaxant actions of tobacco to the intoxicant effects of cannabis and the intense euphoriant 'highs' experienced by heroin, crack cocaine and 'speed' users. Experienced users report that it is the rapid delivery of the active drug to the brain, which is made possible by smoking or direct injection into the bloodstream, that generates the most intensely pleasurable 'high' – although exactly why this should be so remains unclear. The psychoactive drugs that are smoked are each recognized by particular groups of nerve cells in the brain – which possess specific receptor molecules on their surface to which the drug molecules attach.[6] When this happens, the drug triggers an alteration in nerve-cell function, making it more or less excitable and consequently altering patterns of brain activity, which are in turn interpreted as pleasurable experiences by the user. Psychoactive drugs act by 'hijacking' natural brain mechanisms.[7] Messages in the brain cross the gaps between nerves by means of chemical messengers (neurotransmitters) that are manufactured and stored in the end of the nerve and released in response to electrical impulses arriving at the nerve end. The released neurotransmitter passes into the gap, latches on to receptors on the other side, and triggers changes in the activity of the nerve carrying those receptors. Thus, nicotine is recognized by brain receptors that normally respond to the naturally occurring chemical messenger acetylcholine. This chemical is used in a system that has an important function in alerting attention mechanisms in the brain – processes that are vital to normal cognitive function. Heroin is recognized by receptors that are normally targeted by naturally occurring chemicals known as endorphins, which play a crucial role in regulating the sensitivity of the brain to painful and/or pleasurable events. Cocaine and methamphetamine both work by causing a greater availability of another naturally

occurring chemical messenger, dopamine, in the brain. An increased release of dopamine in a brain region located deep in the forebrain (the 'nucleus accumbens') seems to play an important part in drug craving – the desire to seek further exposure to the drug. An important research finding in recent years has been that not only cocaine and meth-amphetamine, which act directly on dopamine-containing nerve cells, but also other drugs of abuse (cannabis, heroin and nicotine) lead indirectly to increased dopamine release in this brain region.[8] Some scientists go so far as to suggest that dopamine release here may represent the final common pathway in a 'reward' or 'pleasure' circuit that is activated by various drugs of abuse. Laboratory rats will repeatedly press a lever to obtain electrical stimulation of the dopamine pathways in the brain, and they will incessantly press a lever to obtain injections of cocaine – which also causes dopamine release. On the other hand, many drugs of abuse can

also trigger an increased activity in the opioid (endorphin) systems in brain – and this may also be related to the pleasurable effects induced by these drugs.

WHY DO WE GO ON SMOKING? MECHANISMS OF ADDICTION AND WITHDRAWAL

Why do people go on smoking cigarettes when the very real medical dangers of doing so are very well known? The answer is that nicotine is a powerfully addictive drug.[9] The tobacco industry strenuously denied this fact for many years. But the intensive investigations undertaken by the former Commissioner of the US Food and Drug Administration, David Kessler, and others in the USA during the 1990s eventually forced even the industry to admit that this was the case. These investigations showed, furthermore, that the industry had for many years systematically manipulated the nicotine content of cigarettes by a variety of means – including even the breeding of genetically modified strains of tobacco with exceptionally high nicotine content.[10]

What do we mean by 'addiction'? The term tends to be replaced nowadays by a broader definition of 'substance dependence' – a chronic condition that has many manifestations but also several common components. Two key characteristics are a compulsion to go on taking the drug, and a withdrawal syndrome that results in psychological and sometimes physical discomfort when the drug is withheld. The compulsion to continue taking the drug may be extremely pressing in some cases – as with some heavy tobacco smokers who wake up in the middle of the night in order to smoke a cigarette – or less so in others. The compulsion is driven by 'craving' for the drug and may become so strong that it comes to dominate all other aspects of life and the drug user loses control and is unable to limit intake. On the negative side, 'withdrawal' may be accompanied by severe physical discomfort that can even become life threatening. Thus, heroin addicts can suffer severe gastrointestinal pain, headaches and convulsions during withdrawal. Milder physical signs accompany withdrawal from nicotine, but the psychological distress is very real – including depressed mood, unhappiness, irritability, anxiety, frustration and difficulty in concentrating. These unpleasant psychic symptoms of nicotine withdrawal persist for long periods, during which the ex-smoker experiences intense craving. It is possible that, in the case of nicotine and other drugs of dependence, the continued use of the drug is importantly driven by the wish to avoid the unpleasant consequences of withdrawal.[11] Indeed, some have even suggested that it is really only the first cigarette of the day that gives any real pleasure; the rest are taken to stave off withdrawal. A further complication is that the pleasurable effects of smoking become blunted by the development of 'tolerance' during the day – an increasing resistance of the reward mechanisms in the brain to further drug stimulation:

The daily smoking cycle can be conceived as follows. The first cigarette of the day produces substantial pharmacological effects, primarily arousal, but at the same time tolerance begins to develop. A second cigarette may be smoked later, at a time when the smoker has learned there is some regression of tolerance. With subsequent cigarettes, there is accumulation of nicotine in the body, resulting in a greater level of tolerance and withdrawal symptoms become more pronounced between successive cigarettes. Transiently high brain levels of nicotine after smoking may partially overcome tolerance. But the primary (euphoric) effects of individual cigarettes tend to lessen throughout the day. Overnight abstinence allows considerable resensitization to the actions of nicotine.[12]

In tobacco smokers, nicotine, at least in the first cigarette of the day, does produce positive reinforcing effects including mild euphoria, increased energy, heightened arousal, reduced stress and anxiety and appetite suppression. These positive effects are crucial in establishing a pattern of repeated administration – and we assume that this repeated administration eventually causes some long-term adaptation of the brain mechanisms leading to dependence.[13] Psychologists also believe that so-called secondary reinforcers can become important components that drive continued drug taking. These factors often relate to the context in which the drug is taken. In the case of smoked drugs, the paraphernalia associated with smoking – the pipe, bong and lighter – can themselves become rewarding emblems associated with the pleasurable experience of smoking. Nicotine dependence affects a high proportion of smokers – possibly more than 90 per cent. Only 10–20 per cent of those who try to quit smoking succeed in maintaining this for twelve months or more – and most relapse much earlier. Drugs vary in their liability to cause dependence (see Table 2). Surprisingly, the notorious narcotics heroin and cocaine do not cause dependence in as high a proportion of users as nicotine does, and cannabis leads to dependence in only about 10 per cent of users. Cannabis smokers often take the drug only at infrequent intervals – unlike the 15–30 a day cigarette smoker.

TABLE 2 – PERCENTAGE OF DRUG USERS WHO ARE DEPENDENT [14]

DRUG	% DEPENDENT
Nicotine	80
Heroin	35
Cocaine	21
Stimulants	11
Cannabis (Marijuana)	11
Alcohol	8

Despite much research on the subject, scientists still do not understand the nature of the changes that occur in the brain during the development of drug dependence. Biological systems are pro-grammed to restore themselves to their original state when perturbed. When the balance of brain chemistry is upset by the persistent presence of a drug, compensatory mechanisms will be activated. Drugs that cause over-activity in dopamine-containing nerve, for example, may lead to a down regulation of dopamine-related brain mechanisms. This in turn could cause an unnatural and troubling under-activity of dopamine nerves when the drug is suddenly withdrawn. It seems increasingly clear that the changes involved in the development of drug dependence involve alterations in the patterns of genes that are switched on or off in the brain – and modern techniques for studying the thousands of genes involved in brain function may soon lead to some important clues in this hunt.[15]

Neither do we have a very good understanding of the brain mechanisms that are responsible for the negative features of withdrawal. One important research finding that has emerged from studies of animal models is that withdrawal is often associated with an increased release of a particular hormone in the brain, known as corticoptropin release factor (CRF).[16] CRF is thought to act as a co-ordinator and final common pathway involved in the reaction of the body and the brain to stress. Drug withdrawal thus appears to activate one of the emergency signals in the body, which is normally triggered by stressful events. Other research suggests that among its many actions CRF can cause increased levels of anxiety. New medicines are being devel-oped that act to block the actions of CRF on its receptors in the brain – and these may prove valuable in combating some of the negative physical and psychological symptoms associated with drug withdrawal.

HOW CAN WE HELP THOSE WHO WANT TO
   QUIT SMOKING?

As already noted above, most tobacco smokers find it very hard to quit. Few successful treatments have been discovered to treat this or other forms of drug dependence, for those who want to break their habit. For some smokers, behavioural training or hypnosis may prove effective; others have found success with medicines that have been designed to help.[17] For tobacco smokers, one method that has proved reasonably successful is to use nicotine itself as a substitute for smoked tobacco. One problem is that nicotine is not well absorbed when given by mouth, so alternative means of delivery have been developed. One form of nicotine is taken in the form of chewing gum – taking advantage of the fact that the environment in the mouth is slightly alkaline (unlike the acid conditions in the stomach), and this favours nicotine absorption. In addition, by altering the rate and intensity of chewing, the subject can to some extent control the rate of nico-tine delivery. Another popular device involves the constant delivery of nicotine through an adhesive patch stuck on to the skin. These devices can simu-late the blood levels of nicotine normally achieved by smoking. What they cannot do, however, is to mimic the sudden rushes of nicotine that are obtained through smoking. A recently developed artificial cigarette may help to overcome this short-coming. This small plastic device resembles a

therapy is to administer the drug naltrexone, which binds to the morphine receptors in the brain and blocks their function. This effectively prevents any of the pleasurable effects normally triggered by heroin. This approach is dangerous for addicts, however, since the sudden blockade of the actions of heroin by naltrexone can precipitate a violent and dangerous withdrawal reaction. But for heroin addicts who have successfully withdrawn from the drug, continuing treatment with naltrexone may help to reduce the likelihood of relapse. So far most heroin addicts have shunned this approach; the only group to whom this has appeal are physicians who have managed to break a heroin habit, for whom the danger of relapse can mean the loss of their medical licence and livelihood.

There are other medical developments on the horizon. The possible use of CRF antagonist drugs to combat some of the negative psychic features of withdrawal has already been referred to. Another development has been the potential use of antidepressant drugs to assist in treating withdrawal symptoms, helping to relieve the depression of mood which is often a prominent symptom. The drug Bupropion (®Wellbutrin), developed initially as an antidepressant, has recently been approved as an aid to tobacco smokers who want to quit.[19] The drug proved effective in large-scale clinical trials, and has been granted official approval for this use. It is interesting to note that Bupropion acts in part by making more dopamine available in the brain. Since this is an effect that is also triggered by nicotine, it may be that Bupropion's effectiveness is due to its ability to mimic this action. Anecdotal evidence suggests that fluoxetine (®Prozac), another of the newer generation of antidepressant medicines, may also assist those wanting to quit. Looking further into the future, one may hope that an improved scientific understanding of the molecular mechanisms that underlie addiction will permit the development of ever more effective treatments. Genetic research may also help to identify people who are at the greatest risk of becoming dependent on recreational drugs.

cigarette, and is charged with a nicotine-containing cartridge. On smoking by inhaling through the device, a dose of nicotine equivalent to that in a cigarette is delivered to the lungs. Another way of delivering a rapid burst of nicotine is by means of a nasal spray containing the drug. Although nicotine replacement has proved successful for some people, the success rates are still not all that impressive. Whereas after twelve months some 90 per cent of smokers will have relapsed in the absence of any treatment, 75–80 per cent of those receiving nicotine treatment experience relapse.

A similar approach has been taken for heroin addicts, many of whom are treated with the synthetic morphine-like substance methadone.[18] Methadone is taken by mouth and is slowly absorbed; it does not produce the same high as heroin, but it occupies the same brain receptors and helps to reduce the level of craving. A more drastic

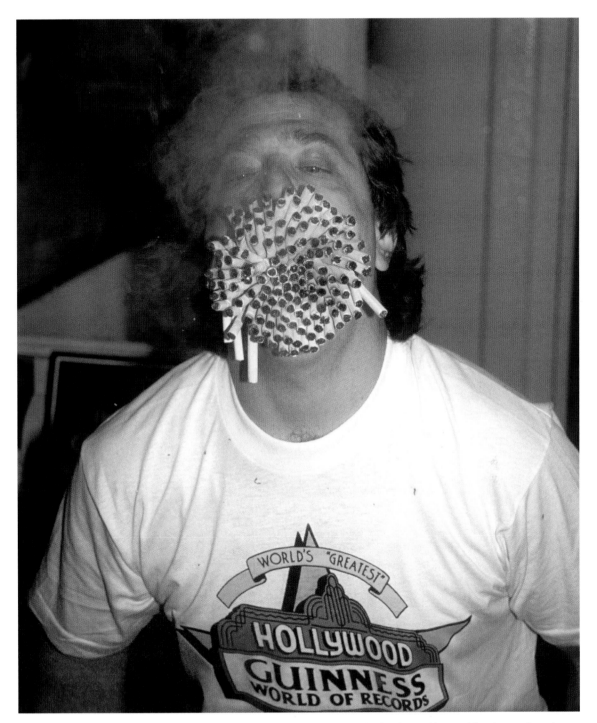

Jim Mouth smokes 154 cigarettes on American 'No Smoking Day', 1992. He broke the world record for the number of cigarettes being smoked at once.

Smoking, Science and Medicine

JOHN WELSHMAN

In August 2001 *The Times* carried a story that Richard Boeken, aged 57, a Californian dying of lung cancer, who had been awarded $3 billion in damages against the maker of Marlboro cigarettes, had agreed to take a substantially reduced award of $100 million.[1] It is easy to assume that, since the early twentieth century, the relationship between science and smoking has been the central issue in the cultural history of smoking. As we shall see, however, this association is comparatively recent, and seems only to apply to the period since 1950. This essay explores debates about smoking and health in three periods: 1850–1930, when concerns centred on juvenile smoking; the classic era of 1930–80, when the links between cigarette smoking and cancer were first established; and the period since then, which can be characterized as the era of the non-smoker. It also examines the way in which historians have explored the relationship between smoking and science, particularly in Britain and the United States. A range of arguments has been put forward, on the respective responsibilities of the individual, the tobacco companies and the state, and on the way that the science of epidemiology led to new concepts of risk. This essay tries to review and summarize this recent work, which has done much to further our understanding of the relationship between smoking, science and medicine.

THE AGE OF THE PIPE SMOKER: MODERATION AND ADULTERATION

It has been pointed out that the growth of the tobacco industry was dependent on developments in agriculture, the technology of production and the way that industry was organized, as well as the availability of safety matches.[2] In the nineteenth century it was through pipes – or cigars in the case of the middle classes – that tobacco was consumed. This had implications for the debate about tobacco and health. Analysis of the *Lancet* in the period 1830–1938 indicates that in the early years the main concerns were with the alleged links between tobacco and such general complaints as 'dyspeptic derangement', insanity, paralysis, hysteria, rickets, impotence and loss of memory.[3] The one specific issue linked to pipe smoking was cancer of the lip, but this was never pursued systematically. Instead, tobacco continued to be linked in a random way with 'muscular debility', jaundice, cancer of the tongue, 'weakness of the extremities', trembling hands and 'tottering knee'. In fact, one of the main sources of concern was over the adulteration of tobacco. Reports in *The Times* indicated numerous cases of the adulteration of tobacco, with sugar, alum, lime, flour, rhubarb leaves, starch, treacle, burdock leaves, endive leaves and red and black dye, among others.[4]

During this period tobacco was also seen to have health benefits, since it was noted that smokers rarely suffered from 'consumption', or tuberculosis, and its effects in alleviating stress, among such groups as labourers and soldiers, were well known. As early as 1872 it was reported that nicotine, cyanide, ammonia and sulphide were constituents of tobacco smoke, and insurance actuaries suggested that separate mortality records should be kept of smokers and non-smokers.[5] Pipes began to incorporate filters and perforations at the bottom of the bowl that allegedly kept the lower layer of tobacco dry and reduced the amount of oil in the smoke. Nevertheless, the principal emphasis of the *Lancet* was in favour of moderation. Lung cancer was still rare in the nineteenth century, and only a minority of doctors believed that moderate smoking was harmful to adults. As the *Lancet* declared in 1879: 'we have no sympathy with prejudices against wine or tobacco, used under proper restriction as to the time and amount of the consumption'.[6]

It is surprising how little this debate was affected by the advent of cigarette smoking in the 1880s. Some doctors began to experiment with filters, while others warned against the practice of inhaling smoke directly into the lungs. As with pipe smoking, however, the *Lancet* approved of smoking cigarettes in moderation, and what concerns there were tended to centre on the alleged adulteration of Egyptian cigarettes. As one historian has suggested, in many ways the stance of the *Lancet* was purity, not abolition, and it aimed at abuse, not use.[7] Manufacturers submitted cigarettes to the journal for medical approval. In 1902 the *Lancet* stated: 'when, however, the cigarette is rationally smoked, and not to excess, it is probably the mildest form of smoking, and this fact, coupled with its convenience and cheapness, is a sufficient reason for its immense popularity'.[8]

There were a large number of anti-smoking organizations, including the British Anti-Tobacco Society, the Anti-Tobacco Legion and the Scottish Anti-Tobacco Society. In France, the Société Contre L'Abus du Tabac was founded to encourage moderation, and to oppose smoking among children. The *Lancet* regarded these organizations as exaggerating the danger of smoking, noting in 1872 that 'it is very unwise to seize upon a cheap pleasure and label it with a bad name'.[9] Most were unsuccessful at mobilizing a mass of supporters. It was the anti-smoking organizations founded in the early 1900s to oppose smoking among children rather than adults that enjoyed some success.[10] These included the British Lads Anti-Smoking Union, the International Anti-Cigarette League and the Hygienic League and Union for the Suppression of Cigarette Smoking by Juveniles.

The campaign against juvenile smoking well conveys the cultural context for the relationship between smoking and science in the early 1900s. The Inter-Departmental Committee on Physical Deterioration of 1904 recommended that legislation should prohibit the sale of tobacco to children and its sale in sweet shops, suggestions that ultimately passed into law in the Children's Act of 1908. This legislation, however, had only indirect links with the earlier anti-tobacco movements, and had much closer connections with related debates about boy labour and 'national fitness'. The actual effects of smoking on the health of children were always ambiguous. From the point of view of the middle-class social reformer, the cigarette became a badge of identity for the working-class youth. Smoking was linked with swearing, gambling and hooliganism as the vices of adulthood – the solution was the games playing that was encouraged by boys' clubs and such specific organizations as the International Anti-Cigarette League. Most organizations that opposed smoking by children were established through churches and Sunday Schools, and had an essentially moral purpose in the context of wider debates about urbanization and physical degeneracy. Thus debates about juvenile smoking employed medical evidence in rather an opportunistic way, and were essentially concerned with morality and citizenship.[11]

THE PERIOD OF THE CIGARETTE SMOKER: CANCER

It has been shown that in the same way as the growth of the tobacco industry was dependent on

A British promotional poster issued by the Empire Marketing Board in 1929.

economic and technological trends, the cigarette marks the convergence of corporate capitalism, technology, mass marketing and advertising. If the nineteenth century was the era of the pipe and the cigar, the 1950s were the heyday of the cigarette. The cigarette is so commonplace today that it is easy to forget that it is a relatively recent invention. It was only with the invention of the Bonsack machine in 1883, and its adoption by the W. D. and H. O. Wills tobacco manufacturer, that the mass production of cigarettes became possible. Thereafter expenditure on advertising increased rapidly, as did consumption. Figures for Britain indicate that, by 1953, 64 per cent of men and 37 per cent of women smoked cigarettes. In the United States, per capita consumption rose from 49 in 1900 to 4,318 by 1965.[12]

The crucial steps in the realization of the health dangers of cigarette smoking are well known, and can be quickly restated here. In the 1930s statisticians employed by insurance companies had begun to link smoking to reduced life expectancy, and to cancer. What is not so well known is that smoking had also been the subject of scientific investigation in the 1930s in Nazi Germany, in the context of concerns about racial hygiene and bodily purity. Smoking was linked with cancer and heart disease, and there were concerns about its effects on reproduction. An ambitious anti-smoking campaign was launched, including health education, bans on advertising and restrictions on smoking in many

public places. Adolf Hitler himself was opposed to smoking. This was consistent with the so-called *Gesundheitspflicht*, or duty to be healthy. In fact, it was German scientists who in 1939 were among the first to link tobacco to lung cancer.[13]

The earlier era of moderation and adulteration has both continuities and contrasts with the post-war period, when the medical and scientific evidence against smoking was mobilized more effectively. By the end of the Second World War concern about lung cancer had intensified – in the United States, deaths had risen from 4,000 in 1935 to 11,000 in 1945. In Argentina, the experiments of Angel H. Roffo had demonstrated how tars derived from tobacco smoke could induce cancer in experimental animals. In Britain, these changes in mortality were investigated by Richard Doll and Austin Bradford Hill, although their initial hypothesis was that increases in car ownership and the tarring of roads might be more significant. Their famous article, which first established the link between cigarette smoking and lung cancer, was published in the *British Medical Journal* in 1950. Doll and Bradford Hill concluded from their research that 'smoking is a factor, and an important factor, in the production of carcinoma of the lung'.[14] E. L. Wynder and E. A. Graham reported very similar findings in the United States that same year.

It has been claimed that, henceforth, the scientific paradigm of epidemiology and statistical inference was now the most significant. Cigarette smoking remained an important social activity in the 1950s, however, and the health dangers of smoking were only slowly communicated to the general public. Criticisms of the original article by Doll and Bradford Hill (including by Sir Ronald Fisher) were only gradually allayed by their later cohort study. In Britain, the important, and influential, first report of the Royal College of Physicians, *Smoking and Health*, was published in 1962, and it clarified the arguments by stating that heavy smokers were 30 times more likely to contract lung cancer than non-smokers. Sir George Godber, then Deputy Chief Medical Officer, played a central role in the genesis of this report, but it also fitted in with the 'modernizing' agenda of the Royal College.[15] The American equivalent was the Report of the US Surgeon-General of 1964, which took a similar stance, and argued that smoking was more important than air pollution in causing lung cancer and bronchial disorders. It has been suggested that the report created new interest in the relationship between behaviour, risk and health.[16] Again, however, real action on the ground followed gradually. In Britain, cigarette advertising on television was banned only in 1967, and health warnings on cigarette packets appeared in 1971. In the United States, legislation passed in 1965 required that cigarette packets carry health warnings, with successively stronger messages.

Historians have attempted to understand the relationship between smoking, science and medicine in the second half of the twentieth century in a variety of ways. One strand has examined the relationship between science and policy.[17] Another has emphasized how the power of the tobacco industry has meant that attempts by the state to control smoking have been very limited. Governments have concentrated on attempting to change individual habits rather than directly controlling the industry, and resources allocated to health promotion have been very limited.[18] As the journalist Peter Taylor has written, 'the smoke ring is the ring of political and economic interests which has protected the tobacco industry for the past twenty years'.[19] In the United States, Congressional anti-smoking policies were limited, while tobacco subsidies remained in place.[20] Thus both governments and the tobacco industry wanted to keep people smoking because of the wealth that cigarettes created. The relationships between government and industry in this area are similar to the cases of food, alcohol and the pharmaceutical industry.

Other historians have focused on the limited nature of the response in the 1950s and '60s in Britain by the Ministry of Health and such bodies as the Central Council for Health Education. Despite the appearance of the article by Doll and Bradford

Hill in 1950, the Ministry of Health took little action until the publication of a report by the Medical Research Council in 1957. This declared that the link between smoking and lung cancer was one of direct cause and effect. Even so, the real meaning of causation remained problematic and a source of dispute. Responsibility for health promotion was delegated to the local authorities, the most demoralized branch of the National Health Service. The posters and use of vans by the Central Council in hindsight appears naïve and woefully inadequate, partly because of a failure to appreciate the scale of the behavioural problem involved. In the hands of these historians, the story is one of scientific caution, bureaucratic inertia, commercial pressure and caution about Government intervention. As Charles Webster has written, 'these efforts have constituted

A Norwegian poster of 1947 insisting on the health benefits smoking offers.

no more than a token response to the form of addiction having had the gravest effect on the people whose health the National Health Service is pledged to protect'.[21]

While some have stressed continuities in the record of the Labour and Conservative administrations, others have claimed that Labour emerges from the story with more credit than its political opponents. Despite lack of action at government level, it is claimed that Labour MPs were active in anti-smoking activity in the mid-1960s, and were influential in the decision to ban cigarette advertising on television. A more recent take on this has been the suggestion, by Paolo Palladino, that concerns about smoking, health and the making of a good society are rooted in aspirations to Christian community that were and remain fundamentally important in the development of British socialism. Palladino argues that this is as true of Tony Blair in the 1990s as of Horace Joules in the 1950s.[22] Matthew Hilton has looked at the wider cultural context for these medical debates by examining the ways in which the health dangers of smoking were conveyed to the British public through the medium of newspapers, radio and television in the period. He argues that the way that these health messages were received was shaped in important ways by the medium through which they were conveyed. Thus while the *Guardian* reported the issues in a thorough and serious manner, the *Daily Express* argued that smokers should be allowed to make up their own minds, and *The Times* opposed Government intervention. What was most striking was the diversity of the ways in which medical knowledge about smoking and lung cancer was produced and disseminated. Hilton concludes overall that 'popular printed, aural and visual forms of communication interpreted, accepted, rejected and constructed their own views of the smoking and health controversy in often fundamentally different ways from one medium to another'.[23]

THE ERA OF THE NON-SMOKER: PASSIVE SMOKING AND ADDICTION

By the 1970s the case against smoking had been proven and was accepted within the medical establishment, although rejected by other pressure groups, including the Freedom Organisation for the Right to Enjoy Smoking Tobacco (FOREST). A second report from the Royal College of Physicians was published in 1971, *Smoking and Health Now*, while the pressure group Action on Smoking and Health (ASH) was also established during this period. New developments were limited, but were significant in two areas. The first was in the recognition of the dangers of passive smoking, a development that has had a significant impact on attitudes towards risk. A crucial paper, on lung cancer rates among the non-smoking wives of heavy smokers, was published in the *British Medical Journal* in 1981. In the United States, where the dangers of 'side stream' smoke were stressed in a report of 1986 by the Surgeon-General, there was a rapid increase in the number of local communities that restricted smoking in public places. By the 1990s cigarettes had been banned from almost all domestic airlines. The second major change was in the recognition that tobacco was an addictive substance, since nicotine was the real cause of physical dependence. This increasingly called into question the idea that smoking was an essentially voluntary activity. As Allan Brandt has written, 'the innocuous habit had become the noxious addiction'.[24] Nevertheless, there continued to be tensions between rival cessation and 'harm minimization' models.

The effect on the tobacco companies was considerable, with evidence emerging that in the post-war period they had marketed cigarettes knowing full well the effect of tobacco on health. In the United States, numerous lawsuits have been filed claiming that tobacco companies continued to market products that were detrimental to health in full knowledge of the risks. We began this essay with the case of Richard Boeken, who successfully sued the Philip Morris Company. Similarly, and with more success, individual American states took to the courts in an effort to reclaim some of the costs of health care for smokers back from the tobacco industry. Rates of smoking cigarettes have fallen, among the middle classes, and in developed countries in particular. In Western Europe, there are signs that smoking is concentrated among working-class women, and tobacco companies have responded by concentrating their marketing efforts on developing countries. Progress in some areas has been matched by delay in others. In Britain, for example, the publication of the White Paper *Smoking Kills* in 1998 was accompanied by a failure to curb cigarette advertising through motor racing.

Historical writing has been less successful in showing why comparatively large numbers of people continue to smoke in face of the acknowledged scientific evidence of the dangers that cigarettes pose to health. Matthew Hilton argues that smoking has remained central to individual and group identity 'firmly rooted in a specific liberal notion of the self'. Children continue to smoke for the reasons they have always done – because cigarettes symbolize a rite of passage into an adult world. Adults, too, remain locked into a cult of individuality that opposes standardizing policy, and an ideology that has dominated the understanding of smoking since the nineteenth century. In fact, claims Hilton, there are signs of a backlash that ensures that the act of smoking continues to have 'a romantic status in popular culture'.[25] Nevertheless, Allan Brandt warns that this interpretation ignores the fact that cigarette smoking is increasingly stratified by education, social class and ethnicity. Since the 1970s an authoritative literature has explored the relationship between smoking and social deprivation, including notably in the case of working-class women. Figures for the United States indicate that smoking is more prevalent among blacks than whites, and that smoking has fallen more rapidly among college graduates than for those without a college degree.[26] Thus the emphasis on individual responsibility runs the risk of denying that some social groups may be more susceptible to behav-ioural risks, and ignores the fact that behaviour may not be merely a matter of choice.

CONCLUSION

Before the Second World War, the alleged health dangers of smoking were a relatively minor aspect of the history of tobacco. In the nineteenth century, when lung cancer was comparatively rare, and tobacco was consumed through pipes and cigars, the debate was about moderation and adulteration. Moreover, even after the advent of the cigarette in the 1880s, concern was limited to the specific case of juvenile smoking, and was probably concerned more with morality than health. Since 1950, however, when the acknowledged link between cigarette smoking and lung cancer was one of the first triumphs of the new science of epidemiology, the relationship between smoking, science and medicine has been a central theme in the history of the health of the public. How significant this theme has been to smokers themselves is open to question. Historians have explained the contrast between increasing scientific knowledge of the medical dangers of smoking on the one hand, and continuing public consumption of cigarettes on the other, in a variety of ways. Some stress the liberal, individualizing nature of smoking, while others place more emphasis on poverty and deprivation. But whichever interpretation is supported, the relationship between cigarettes, science and medicine seems likely to remain an important theme for the smokers of the future.

Engineering Consumer Confidence in the Twentieth Century

ALLAN M. BRANDT

The spittoon, ever present in the nineteenth century, became an antique, an artefact of 'pre-modern' tobacco use in the urban, industrial society of the twentieth-century United States. 'Plug tobacco . . . the chief form of nicotine dispensation in the mid-nineteenth century, is messy and socially disagreeable at the best, and in city life it is nearly intolerable', the economist Richard Tennant noted in 1950.[1] In contrast, the cigarette fitted well with the norms and values of the emerging 'modern' culture that developed in the first decades of the twentieth century. As early as 1889, the *New York Times* – an early critic of the cigarette – explained:

> Whatever its merits and demerits, one thing is certain – namely, that there is an ever increasing subjection to the influence of this narcotic, whose soothing powers are requisitioned to counteract the evil effects of the worry, overpressure and exhaustion which characterize the age in which we live.[2]

Certainly this quality had been noted during the First World War, when soldiers employed cigarettes to relieve their anxiety and boredom.[3] But, strikingly, cigarettes would also be cited as an antidote to a range of modern concerns about the frenetic pace of urban-industrial society. As the boundaries of where and when to smoke eroded during the 1920s and '30s, the cigarette was rapidly diffused into the public, urban landscape – the shop, stores, restaurants and transport – that comprised the new consumer world. Since smokers could light up quickly in factories and offices, on buses and trolleys, the introduction of breaks in the monotony of the modern work environment were now punctuated and calibrated by smoking a cigarette. The cigarette could be used anywhere – and at any time – an attribute widely noted by its advertisers. '*Now*', their ads proclaimed, was the time to light up. The advantages of a short smoke seemed particularly well suited to the pressures of a modern, driven culture.

Most historical assessments of the rise of cigarette smoking emphasize how deeply integrated smoking became in the modern cultural practice of the United States during the first decades of the twentieth century. The rise of a modern consumer society, urban mores and the triumph of new media are all powerfully associated with the cigarette. By most accounts, the cigarette embodied modernity, marking a critical watershed from earlier 'pre-modern' forms of tobacco consumption. But, rather than simply describing the emergence of the cigarette and its natural 'fit' with modern culture, this essay suggests that the tobacco industry worked assiduously to shape cultural change in the interests of its product. The product and the culture were brought into conformity by specific and often purposeful economic and industrial social forces. Fit required the adjustment of traditional boundaries and social expectations and the deployment of new techniques that structured both product and market. Perhaps the most sentient example of this

A 1930 R. J. Reynolds advertisement.

process was the concerted effort on the part of the tobacco industry to solicit women smokers. Through the effective and powerful use of innovative tools and strategies in advertising and marketing, public relations and packaging and design, the industry acted to reconstitute culture for the purpose of commerce. This essay therefore examines in particular the changing nature of American culture in the era of the rise of cigarette consumption, as well as the explicit attempts on the part of the industry to construct a cultural context in which to 'grow' tobacco. Adjusting the message to meet the moment tested the creativity and ingenuity of the cigarette's promoters.

Earlier models of markets had focused on the interrelationship between supply and demand. But a critical aspect of modern advertising in the consumer culture was the creation of both need and desire. Government policy makers also approved of the creation of demand for its positive effect on the country's economy. As President Calvin Coolidge explained in his speech of 1926 to the International Advertising Association, 'Mass production is only possible where there is mass demand. Mass demand has been created almost entirely through advertising.'[4] The increase in goods manufactured far outpaced increases in population, making the need for increased demand from individual consumers clear.[5]

The cigarette in particular suggested to many observers the important notion that demand itself could be fashioned, shaped and reshaped by the techniques of advertising, promotion and public relations. When advertisers for Chesterfields noted bluntly in the 1920s that 'They Satisfy', they explicitly subscribed to this psychology of needs met. Some executives in the tobacco industry offered impressively candid assessments of this process. For example, an analyst writing in *Advertising and Selling* in 1936 explained:

You know a large part of the public really doesn't know what it wants. Our big task in recent years had been to dig up new likes or dislikes which we think might strike the public's fancy, and sell them to the public. We have dealt with diet, weight, coughs, mildness, quality of tobacco, nerves, toasting tobacco, youthful inspirations and a host of other subjects. The public must be given ideas as to what it *should* like, and it is quite surprising sometimes how the public is sold on what might look, in sales conference, like the brainchild of a demented person. The old sales bywords 'know your customer's needs' have been remolded to 'know what your customer should need and then educate him on those needs'.[6]

Advertisers quickly picked up and utilized purported 'functions' of the cigarette: it 'soothed the nerves', 'aided digestion', encouraged a good diet, provided a 'lift' and was 'your best friend'. Cigarettes, ads suggested, offered special respite from the pace and demand of modern life. Advertisers promised relief from 'jangled nerves' and the frenetic rhythms of the urban society. 'Build yourself a CAMEL SMOKE SCREEN', counselled one ad, 'We claim with good evidence to back us that a cool cloud of CAMEL smoke is a practically perfect protective smoke-screen. Outside the charmed circle of its mellow fragrance, troubles and worries and sundry bothers hover baffled. Within, all is peace, pleasure, content.[7]

Another aspect of the cigarette advertisers' strategy was to emphasize the taste of their particular brand: blends of tobacco and flavourings constituted the top secrets of each company. Taste, of course, simultaneously possessed double meanings, both crucial to the success of the cigarette. When tobacco ads touted their brand's superior taste, they suggested much more than the experience of the individual smoker: they not so subtly implied that smokers of their brand had 'better taste', which had now been publicly demonstrated. And, in the structures of the consumer culture, consumption was a public act with great significance; although 'conspicuous consumption' used the examples of homes and cars, the cigarette – as advertised – offered important opportunities for a form of conspicuous consumption that crossed the lines of social class.[8]

Marketing both responded to and drove fashion and taste. Aggressive and successful promotion required understanding and exploitation of social change. But the cigarette had many meanings. For men, it could be a symbol of virility and strength, but also of sensitivity and mental acuity. Just as cigarettes came to denote masculinity, this same product – indeed, the very same brand – used by women could be deployed to invoke feminine beauty and attraction, as well as new social and political equality. Ironically, conforming to fashion and trends in behaviour and taste could be read within the consumer culture as acts of autonomy, independence and rebellion. If the cigarette signalled new norms and values concerning pleasure, it was not simply a mark of easing Victorian strictures. Pleasure had specific product-focused meaning in the context of

the modern consumer culture. Increasingly, pleasure would come to be associated with satisfying needs through the very process of consumption. Products promised the achievement of desires met.

The rise of aggressive national marketing and the powerful techniques of advertising and promotion that it utilised raised important questions about the character of the consumer culture. The ongoing debates about advertising, publicity and manipulation constituted a larger debate about the nature of rationality, agency and affect in the consumer culture.[9] And, indeed, advertising drew its share of critics on precisely these grounds. How powerful was advertising in its ability to bend consumer behaviour? And what if such power came to be used to support anti-social ends? The rise of national advertising with its claims of effectiveness generated new concerns about manipulation and behaviour in a mass society. And the cigarette as a popular icon of this consumer culture, built on the edifice of mass marketing, only intensified this question of agency.

But even as many worried about this manipulative power, advertisers developed and refined their field of work. Lord & Thomas, Albert Lasker's agency employed by American Tobacco, urged the 'professionalization' of advertising in a shrewdly self-promotional pamphlet of 1911, which discussed the role of the advertiser:

> To determine in advance that, through his will and skill, they [the buyer] shall make a concerted movement, toward a purpose of purchase they never previously contemplated, in direct response to his printed word –
>
> *That* is the mission, privilege and power of the modern advertising man who can live up to his opportunities.[10]

One aspect of this power was an expectation that the agency would be an 'altruistic' force spurring industry and consumer into relationships of social value. Lord & Thomas reckoned that *advertised* products protected consumers.

The opening up of cigarette advertising to target women provides a prime example of this creation of needs. If women were perceived to be the principal arbiters of the Moral in late nineteenth-century American culture, now they were understood to be the principal force in the ethos of consumption.[11] As one advertising psychologist explained: 'The advertiser, especially the one using large space consistently, has within his power not only to affect temporarily, but to mould permanently, the thought and attitude he wants his particular public to have with reference to the relative importance of style and beauty and such other factors as he may choose to play up by means of advertising.'[12] The tobacco industry – which grew by leaps and bounds during the first two decades of the twentieth century – clearly realized that women comprised half their potential market. While in no way given to gender exclusions in the creation of new patrons for their product, the tobacco industry was nonetheless aware that they entered into contested cultural terrain in their efforts to target women. This was an area in which the fit between product and cultural expectation was imperfect at best. Prohibitions against women smokers persisted well into the first decades of the twentieth century.[13] Advertisers and marketers recognized that if smoking was truly to become mass behaviour they would need to shape this territory. Early debates about the meaning of smoking for women offered opportunities, which they seized. Although smoking had appeal for women before the onset of targeted advertising, this does not reduce the significance of marketing mechanisms in the process of recruiting women smokers.[14]

Beginning with American Tobacco's 'Reach for a Lucky instead of a sweet' campaign in 1928, cigarette ads targeted at women made explicit appeals to both style and beauty. Not only was the cigarette an accoutrement of beauty, it became a powerful symbol of style as well, a symbol deeply embedded in the particular socio-politics of gender in the 1920s and '30s. Smoking for women – in this crucial phase of successful 'recruitment' – became part and parcel of the 'good life' configured in American consumer culture. The cigarette's symbolic meanings – of glamour, beauty, autonomy and equality – were inscribed through the powerful images of the advertisements. The effectiveness of these campaigns was heightened and reinforced by public relations campaigns geared to create a positive environment for these new images.

Advertising constituted but one technique in the shaping of the burgeoning consumer culture. George Washington Hill, President of American Tobacco, for example, understood that mass advertising was only one side of the marketing coin. Effective marketing required the deployment of a wide range of complementary techniques from public relations to corporate design. In pursuing his multifaceted promotional campaign, Hill enlisted the efforts of Edward Bernays. Born in Vienna in 1891, Bernays was a nephew of Sigmund Freud. His family came to the United States in 1892. After graduating from Cornell University, Bernays went to work for the Committee on Public Information during the First World War, where he first developed his communication skills and his theory of public opinion, public relations and the 'science' of propaganda.[15] After the war, Bernays embraced the new psychology and the new corporate order, eagerly making the techniques of propaganda and mass opinion a tool of corporate capitalism. Unlike his predecessors in the 'science' of public opinion, he did not see his role as an 'educator'. Rather, Bernays relied on exploiting the insights of psychology to shape mass behaviour and values.

Just as the cigarette emerged from the experiences of the First World War as a central element in culture, so too did public relations. Bernays quickly fashioned himself into the first 'counsel on public relations', offering his services to a wide range of industries in the United States and abroad. He soon became public relations' chief advocate and publicist. He came to define it as the science of the 'group mind' and 'herd reaction'. Central to his approach was an emphasis on the use of the media. In particular, Bernays emphasized what he called the 'created event'. 'The counsel on public relations not only knows what news value is, but knowing it, he is in a position to *make news happen*.'[16] The staging of public events, produced to draw news coverage, marked a central element of the 'counsel's' corporate responsibility. Bernays eagerly pointed out that generating news not only incurred no advertising costs but was also free of the expectations of self-interest and manipulation already being questioned within the advertising industry.[17] Although we often associate this idea of utilizing the media with the dramatic rise of electronic broadcasting later in the century, Bernays early on recognized the crucial connections between corporate interests, the media and the consumer culture.

The effective manipulation of public opinion, interest, values and beliefs would, in the 1920s, become a dominant aspect of the emergence of the consumer culture. Blurring the line between advertising and the news was a critically important technique in the new strategies of marketing, which would have far-reaching significance throughout the twentieth century. The emergence of national advertising and national 'news' operations were together crucial elements in the emergence of national culture. Bernays prized employing the power of the media precisely because it distanced – even hid – the interests of the industry. He understood that his behind-the-scenes machinations – typically conducted surreptitiously on behalf of clients – could easily disturb the delicate trust on which elements of the consumer culture rested. He objected to clients who were 'unsocial or otherwise harmful', and he argued that the counsel of public relations must have a central role in guiding corporate policy. Bernays devised a set of functions that were sharply distinguished from the publicist and the press agent; yet even his ingenuity and ego could not accomplish this distinction.[18]

Bernays's work on behalf of American Tobacco illustrates clearly this new approach to promotion. In 1929 he outlined the structure for a proposed public relations arm for American Tobacco. The 'Tobacco Information Service Bureau', he suggested,

A 1930 American Tobacco ad for Lucky Strike.

would provide news releases and information in an array of media and 'provide a certain scientific background for what the Bureau may from time to time say from a scientific standpoint'. Bernays argued that this Bureau would develop strong relations with the press, placing articles that would ultimately favour the interest of American Tobacco. Examples of stories, he suggested, might be 'INTERNAL REVENUE STATISTICS ON TOBACCO INTERPRETED', or 'DOCTORS SAY CIGARETTES REDUCE NUMBER OF BACTERIA IN YOUR MOUTH'. This 'educational work' would, he contended, help to overcome the current spate of criticism that Hill's campaigns had attracted, as well as ongoing concerns about the health effects of smoking.

Bernays also traded ideas with Hill to 'increase good-will and sales' for Lucky Strikes. He suggested, for example, planting photographs and news articles linking cigarettes, women, beauty and a range of smoking accessories:

> Feature story for fashion editors on importance of cigarette cases and holders to smartly dressed women as part of their ensemble. This with photographs. Propaganda to be injected into the story . . .

'If you approve of these . . . ideas', he concluded, 'We will be glad to do the necessary to carry them out.'[19]

A year earlier, Hill's first assignment for Bernays had been to assist in the campaign that he had begun for soliciting women smokers. Hill reportedly explained: 'It will be like opening a new gold mine right in our front yard.' According to Bernays,

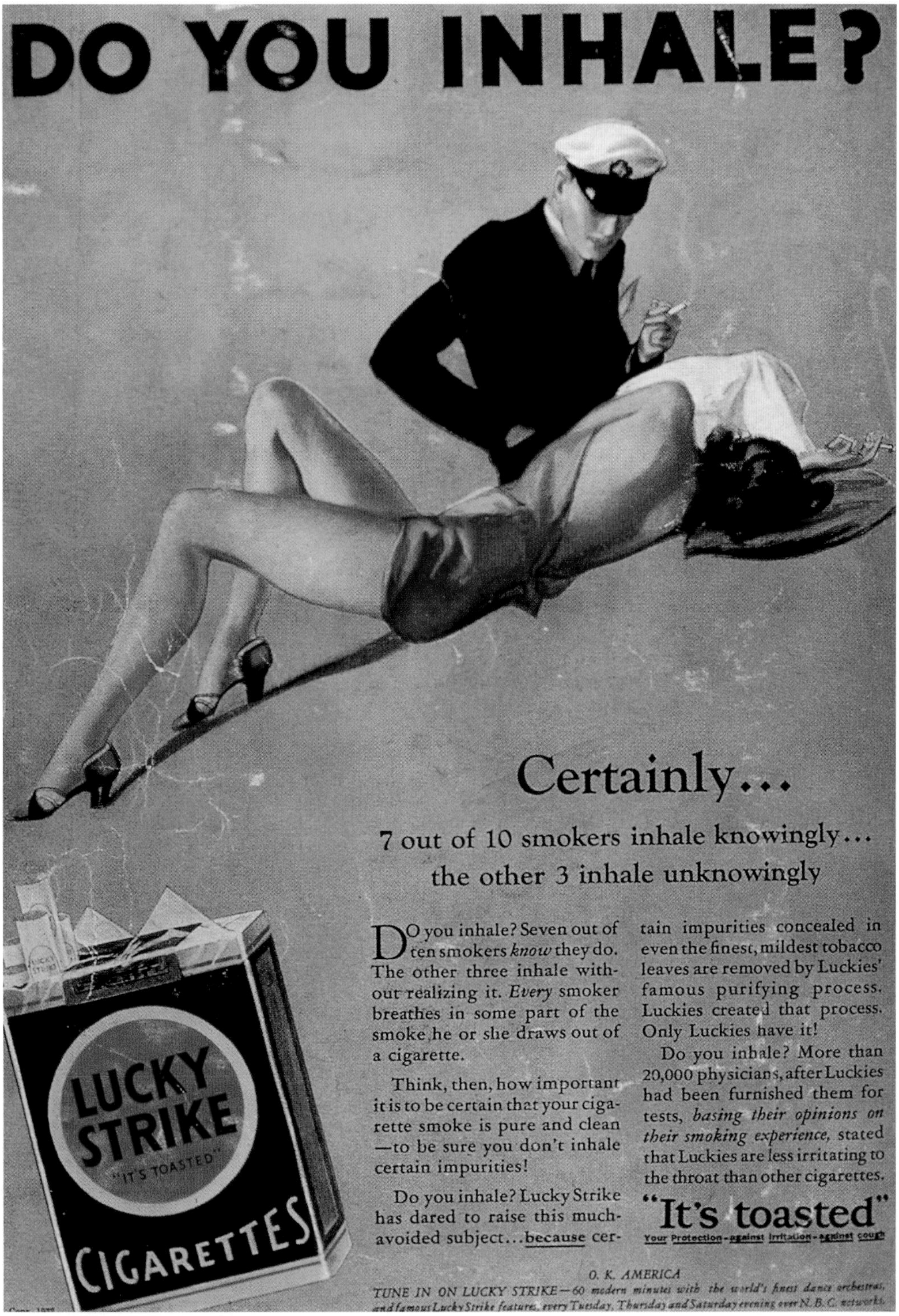

'Do You Inhale?' A 1932 American Tobacco ad for Lucky Strike.

An American Tobacco ad, from *Literary Digest* (5 April 1930).

'Hill became obsessed by the prospect of winning over the large potential female market for Luckies.' With Lasker's 'Reach for a Lucky instead of a sweet' campaign in production, Hill and Bernays set out to exploit the meaning and impact of this pitch. Recognizing that women's fashions were moving in the 1920s to a new emphasis on slimness, Lucky Strike ads now proclaimed that their product was a tool for beauty and physical attraction. Bernays sought to enlist the fashion industry, sending out hundreds of Parisian haute couture photographs of slender models. To strengthen his case, he solicited medical writings on the deleterious impact of sugar on the human body. With these results in hand, he made effective use of the media to broadcast the findings that he had gathered together.

He understood his role as creating a social context that would sustain the advertising campaigns and help to reach sympathetic consumers. To effect this goal, he argued vigorously that public relations must act behind the scenes to support the more overt marketing on which public attention and opinion would form.[20] On behalf of the 'Reach for a Lucky' campaign, Bernays – without ever noting his relationship with American Tobacco – sponsored a conference on the evolution of the modern ideal of beauty. At this meeting, artists insisted that the 'slim woman w[as] the ideal American type'. Another tool that Bernays employed was the survey – quick and dirty polls of social attitudes or practices. In Bernay's hands, the survey was not an instrument to measure public opinion, it was a technique for *shaping* it. Among Department Store managers, Bernays again found support for the emphasis on the modern figure that the Lucky Strike campaigns promoted. 'According to this survey', announced a Bernays press release, 'the slender, modish saleswoman is in demand and can earn more for herself and her employer than her heavier sisters.'[21]

Bernays also helped to shape public reaction to American Tobacco's attack on 'sweets'. When the campaign elicited protest and the threat of legal action from confectioners, he sought to portray such competition as in the consumers' interest. In his endeavour to define the battle between American Tobacco and the candy industry as characteristic of an important and timely shift in American economic life, Bernays built a new context around the dispute that – not surprisingly – favoured his client, typically seen as the aggressor. In particular, he was eager to sponsor 'news' articles, and then, if they served the company's interest, he would have them widely reprinted and distributed. He recommended, for example, articles by chemists, agricultural experts and physicians, written on themes that underscored the ongoing advertising campaigns. He recruited the physician Clarence Lieb to write in support of the 'moderation' campaign. Dr Lieb explained in language that echoed American Tobacco advertisement copy:

A 1930 American Tobacco ad, from *Literary Digest* (5 April 1930).

It may also be said that in every form of our complex civilization, whether in work or play, in social life, in eating and other forms of indulgence, particularly in eating between meals, excess seems to have become the rule instead of the exception and the thought of moderation is like a small voice crying in the wilderness.[22]

For Bernays, expertise was but a commodity that the public relations expert needed to purchase and exploit. Again, his efforts on behalf of recruiting

Humphrey Bogart, smoking.

in the mouth excites the oral zone. It is perfectly normal for women to want to smoke cigarettes.'[24] As Freud's nephew, Bernays was sympathetic to the notion that such insight could be used to modify patterns of consumption and cigarette use. As Brill suggested, 'Today the emancipation of women has suppressed many of their feminine desires. More women now do the same work as men do. Many women bear no children; those who do bear have fewer children. Feminine traits are masked. Cigarettes, which are equated with men, become torches of freedom.'[25] Bernays seized on this notion of 'torches of freedom' as a practical symbol for immolating the traditional taboos against women smoking in public.

In a publicity stunt of genuine historical significance, Bernays recruited debutantes to march in the New York City Easter parade of 1929 brandishing their 'torches of freedom'. The staging of such an event was, to say the least, precise, as Bernays's notes reveal:

OBJECT

women smokers proved a laboratory for his new technique and theory.

By 1929 Hill sought even more aggressive interventions to broaden the understanding of women's smoking and to attract this vast new market. As Bernays recounted, 'Hill called me in. "How can we get women to smoke on the street? They're smoking indoors. But damn it, if they spend half the time outdoors and we can get 'em to smoke outdoors, we'll damn near double our female market. Do something. Act!"'[23] In response, Bernays set out to identify and destroy the taboos associated with public smoking for women. He enlisted the advice of the noted Johns Hopkins psychiatrist A. A. Brill, who explained: 'Some women regard cigarettes as symbols of freedom. Smoking is a sublimation of oral eroticism; holding a cigarette

To increase the consumption of cigarettes by women and to gain publicity for Lucky Strikes. Specifically, pictures of women smoking to appear in papers on Easter Monday and in news-reels. In reading matter, stories that for the first time women have smoked openly on the street. These will take care of themselves, as legitimate news, if the staging is rightly done.

The women, Bernays counselled, must be carefully chosen: 'Discretion must be used in their selection.' He planned that the story should 'appear as news with no division of the publicity', suggesting that 'while they should be good looking, they should not look too model-y'. Bernays called for a meeting with the women on Good Friday when they would be 'given their final instructions . . . And furnished with Lucky Strikes.' Bernays even went so far as to provide his own photographer 'to guard against the possibility that the news photographers do not get good pictures for this purpose.'

In planning and organizing this event, Bernays remained behind the scenes, following a central tenet of his approach to public relations. For a man of his colossal ego, this, no doubt, must have been quite a struggle. Nonetheless, he eagerly arranged the event, fed news to the media and conducted surveys, all of which maintained his own and his clients' anonymity. Invitations to march in the New York City Easter Parade came from the feminist Ruth Hale:

Women!
Light another torch of freedom!
Fight another sex taboo!

The young women marched down Fifth Avenue puffing Lucky Strikes, effectively drawing together the symbol of the emancipated flapper and the symbol of the committed suffragist. Newspapers widely reported their exploit, touching off a national debate. Bernays eagerly expected protests, 'These should be watched for and answered in the same papers.' He had successfully reinvigorated the controversies of the previous decade, enlisting the cultural tensions over women's public smoking in his marketing campaign. While women's clubs decried the fall of the proscription on public smoking, feminists hailed the change in social convention. Reports of women smoking 'on the street' came from cities and towns across the nation. 'Age-old customs, I learned', wrote Bernays, 'could be broken down by a dramatic appeal, disseminated by the network of media.'[26] Bernays valued the fact that he had 'secretly' instigated news and controversy on behalf of his client and his marketing interests.

In 1934 Bernays once again intervened in American Tobacco's ongoing efforts to promote smoking among women. Hill was apparently concerned that women shunned Luckies because of the green packaging, which clashed with current fashions, and he urged Bernays to change the fashion. Bernays explained: 'That was the beginning of a fascinating six-month activity for me – to make green

the fashionable color.'[27] He developed an eclectic and far-reaching strategy, sponsoring fund-raising balls in which guests agreed to wear green gowns, and a 'Green Fashion Fall' luncheon to promote the colour green within the fashion industry, at which experts discussed the significance of the artistic and psychological meaning of 'green'. Bernays later explained: 'I had wondered at the alacrity with which scientists, academicians and professional men participated in events of this kind. I learned they welcomed the opportunity to discuss their favorite subject and enjoyed the resultant publicity. In an age of communication, their own effectiveness often depended on public visibility.'[28] The consumer age was predicated, Bernays had discovered, on providing a forum for voices that would do the industries' bidding.

Bernays understood early on the power of these new cultural mediums. Unlike advertising in which interest seemed so overtly exercised, he preferred the implicit qualities of other powerful forces in the culture of consumption. For example, while many focused on Madison Avenue, he looked West to Hollywood. Bernays quickly realized, for example, the importance of encouraging the use of cigarettes in film. Long before the term 'product placement' came to be enunciated as a core element of marketing and promotion, Bernays recognized the power of film to shape both cultural and consumer expectation. In an essay prepared for directors and producers, Bernays – anonymously (of course) – reviewed the range of dramatic meanings that the cigarette could be used to highlight effectively. 'Cigarettes have become chief actors in the silent drama or the talkie, for a great deal can be said with a cigarette which would ordinarily require a great many words to express', he noted.[29]

The goal in Bernays's film memo was to catalogue the range of applications for employing the cigarette in film. He suggested that this particular prop had come to represent a multitude of personal types and human affects.

There is many a psychological need for a cigarette

in the movies. The bashful hero lights a cigarette, the better to gain a hold of himself in this trying interview with his future father-in-law. The villain smokes hasty puffs to hide his nervousness or to ease his conscience. But perhaps the most dramatic scenes are those where the cigarette is not smoked. How much can be expressed by the habitual smoker, when he is too perturbed to smoke! The gambler in the Casino, who has staked his last thousand on one card, and has lost – his cigarette falls unlighted from his trembling hands, and tells us worlds of chagrin. The deceived husband, deserted by the heartless wife, reaches for a cigarette, but lets the package drop, to signify his utter loss, his absolute defeat. The enraged crook, who feels that his pal has double-crossed him, viciously crumbles his cigarette in his fingers, as if it were the body and soul of his once trusted comrade, on whom he is wreaking vengeance . . . Everything from the gayest comedy, to the most sinister tragedy can be expressed by a cigarette, in the hands or mouth of a skillful actor.

Just as Bernays had planned, by the 1930s the cigarette had become an important prop in movies, used to invest characters with a range of attractive meanings.[30] Even a cursory review of the great films of the 1930s and '40s would confirm just how central the cigarette had become in the telling social idioms of everyday life. Films both reflected and reified cultural and social norms at the same time that they created styles and fads.

In 1948 *Atlantic Monthly* catalogued the wide range of affect and emotion that could be served on screen or stage by the cigarette-as-prop (echoing Bernays's earlier memo). According to this assessment, cigarettes could easily demonstrate self-confidence or shyness, anxiety or surprise. In order to demonstrate anxiety, the authors suggested: 'Take quick and frequent puffs at cigarette, while moving briskly round stage or set. Discard a half-finished cigarette and straightaway light another.' To reveal 'acute distress' actors were advised to 'crush out a

half-smoked cigarette with awful finality'. Shyness could be portrayed by fumbling with a cigarette and matches. Finally, 'passion in the raw' could be exhibited as follows: 'Put two cigarettes in mouth at same time. Light both, then, with possessive air, hand one of them to adored.' It was precisely this act that Paul Heinreid had used in the blockbuster *Now Voyager* (1942) to 'consummate' his romance with Bette Davis.[31] And, of course, couples depicted in bed smoking had become a certain indicator of recent sexual activity.

Hill's and Bernays's multifarious – and nefarious – activities demonstrate how the tobacco industry came to employ a set of powerful cultural conventions and practices to expand the meaning of the cigarette and the mores of its use.[32] To suggest, however, that they were powerful conspirators in an insidious campaign to make women smokers would be to misrepresent the history of the era. No doubt, given the range of economic and social forces eroding prohibitions on female smoking, as well as the remarkable rise of cigarette consumption in the first decades of the twentieth century, women were marked as an important and inadequately tapped constituency for the product. Through their advertising and public relations efforts, based in part on the new professionalism of the public relations industry and of psychology as a scientific way to understand and manipulate human behaviour, Hill and Bernays – and their competition – shaped and promoted the cigarette's status as the symbol of the independent feminist and the bold, glamorous flapper. The cigarette revealed the importance of new techniques geared to make meaning and motivate consumption. It was this ability to recognize, shape – *and exploit* – cultural change that lay at the heart of successful consumer motivation – what Bernays would call 'the engineering of consent'. Bernays's approach represented central aspects of evolving techniques for promoting consumption in the new culture and a new economy.

If Bernays was the marketing manipulator par excellence – a master of mass motivation – he understood that it was crucially important for the individual to be sustained in his or her personal confidence in free choice and agency. It was perhaps for this reason that Bernays regarded advertising with some concern and scepticism. After all, in its overtly mass appeal it could erode the confidence of what he called 'consent', the belief in reflective and rational individual choice. In using the term 'engineering of consent', Bernays captured brilliantly the ethos of the consumer culture, which he came to service through the innovations of public relations. It was noteworthy that he employed the term engineering; in this word he captured the instrumental expertise associated with the modern profession. In 'consent' he implied that ultimately individual autonomy in democracy was maintained in spite of the power of corporate manipulation. The 'engineering of consent' in this respect was sharply ironic; it suggested that consumers achieved an effective autonomy through a closely manipulated *choice*. This illusion of consent marked a critical component of the consumer culture.

The tobacco industry had created a product that could be virtually all things to all people: a product with such an impressive 'elasticity of meanings' that it came to be defined by its promotion more than any innate characteristic. The success of the cigarette was nothing short of spectacular. Business writers, social critics and cultural observers could all agree as early as the 1930s that the cigarette had triumphed as a central icon of the new consumer culture. The use of tobacco – dating back to native cultures and colonial exploration – had reached its most impressive and widespread form of consumption in a new consumer culture driven by the emergence of powerful corporate entities.

If the cigarette emerged in the first half of the twentieth century as such an excellent 'fit' with the meanings and mores of modern culture, this was certainly not by happenstance. The very agents of the consumer culture discovered techniques to adjust the product to the culture and, perhaps more impressively, the culture to the product. In no other instance can this approach be so closely observed and analysed as in the case of the cigarette. The

innovations of the tobacco industry in advertising and public relations soon became national 'standards'; in the use of new advertising forms, new media and public relations, the tobacco industry had consistently opened up new territory in the colonization of the consumer culture. It was the tobacco industry that all others watched for a combination of striking attention-getting campaigns and ploys and an unprecedented combination of aggressiveness, psychological sophistication and effectiveness.

Even as the consumer culture triumphed, considerable criticism remained, often drawing upon deep, traditional American values that emphasized restraint and deferred gratification. Deeply embedded within the culture of consumption was a profound ambivalence about the nature of agency, individuality and risk. Later in the century, as the health risks of smoking became fully explicit, this ambivalence would resurface in powerful ways.

The rise of the modern cigarette forces us to re-examine the nature and character of cultural change. Without question the history of changes in values, beliefs and practices is complex and multivariate. What has often been overlooked in investigating such change, however, are the methods and processes of powerful economic interests that shape and reshape important cultural idioms to suit their industrial designs. Close examination of the promotional strategies of cigarette manufacturers in the early decades of the twentieth century demonstrates a sophisticated notion of culture and its operative mechanisms. Furthermore, these activities represent innovative notions of social and cultural 'engineering'. Looking back from the first years of the twenty-first century, perhaps the expectations of such manipulative approaches to creating demand seem *pro forma*. But, as this essay has suggested, these approaches to marketing were 'invented' around the commodity of the cigarette. In those instances where cultural norms and expectations marked an obstacle, the answer was: change the culture. Such approaches offer a darker meaning to the very idea of 'consumer confidence'.

Marlboro Man and the Stigma of Smoking

PATRICK W. CORRIGAN

Remember the Marlboro Man – a handsome cowboy smoking a cigarette on horseback? The icon has been prominent in American advertising for more than 50 years, inspiring potential and real tobacco users alike. His message was clear; people who smoke are cool! During the past decade or so, however, a new image has been challenging the Marlboro rider in the smoking consciousness of Westerners – the bad-breathed mope. This point was evident to me when driving to work this morning: on a roadside billboard along a major Chicago thoroughfare was a picture of a duck, dog and monkey each smoking a cigarette with the caption: 'It looks just as stupid when you do it.' Book covers, headbands, buttons, key tags, sports bottles, posters, T-shirts and refrigerator magnets all repeat the same message:

> 'Why don't they just call them what they are: cancerettes, phlegm balls, breath rotters . . .'

> 'If you're smoking around me, you better be on fire.'

> 'Don't make me choke on your secondhand smoke.'[1]

Perhaps most compelling of these images is a recent campaign highlighting what became of the Marlboro men. The wife of one model, David McLean, sued Philip Morris, alleging that he died from smoking. According to the lawsuit, in some instances McLean had to smoke more than five packs a day when posing for commercials.

Neither these anti-smoking campaigns – nor the genre of pro-smoking advertisements that preceded them – can be laughed off as meagre attempts to change behaviour. There is something inherently *personal* about both the Marlboro Man and the malodorous mope. In each case, the message extends beyond describing a simple behaviour – 'smoking tastes good and is fun' or 'smoking makes you smell and leads to cancer'– to a description of the person. On the one hand, smokers like the Marlboro Man are rugged individualists. On the other, people who are addicted to cigarettes are ignoramuses, playing with their lives. The aim of this essay is to consider the message propagated by the malodorous mope and to explore ideas of stigmatization.

The personal quality of statements about smokers is reminiscent of the stereotypes made about other stigmatized groups. Assertions about 'lazy coloured folks' implied far more than the speed with which a subset of people worked; it was an egregious slur against the very fabric of the social group. Might the same claim not be made against smokers? The anti-smoking campaign seems to be mean-spirited, going beyond the behaviour to denigrate smokers themselves. Yet, comparing the experiences of the smoker to, for example, the injustices experienced by descendants of slaves in the United States or by Koreans forcibly repatriated to Japan during the Second World War seems absurd. Hence, the primary question of this chapter: are smokers stigmatized? Answering this question requires a brief

Marlboro Man rides East: China in 1998.

Marlboro Man discovers a downside to smoking, as seen on Sunset Strip, Los Angeles in 1999.

review of definitions of stigma. This discussion leads to an equivocal answer and an equally curious realization: namely, that an experience that once was highly touted in Western culture (smoking) is now harshly condemned. What accounts for this evolution? Answers to these questions lead to a final round of queries. Is a stigma of smokers wrong? Most Western cultures hold stigma and its corresponding prejudice to be a gross social injustice. Does this concern apply equally to smokers? Might some of their experiences be recast as social indecency?

IS SMOKING STIGMATIZED?

Stigma has been a concern of social thinkers since the time of the Greeks. Under this rubric, people of different ethnic groups or religion, persons with physical or psychiatric abnormalities, and/or individuals with blemishes of character (e.g. addicts, the unemployed and the imprisoned) are grouped together. In the process, a variety of definitions have emerged to describe stigma. These definitions are briefly reviewed here as a first step in determining whether smoking is stigmatized. The resulting criteria are then juxtaposed to empirical evidence to evaluate whether smokers as a group meet these definitions.

DEFINITIONS OF STIGMA

Erving Goffman, a sociologist at the University of California, is often credited with focusing twentieth-century academia on concerns related to stigma. In his book,[2] Goffman defined stigma as a deeply discrediting group attribute. Central to his ideas is the notion of discreditability: that because of membership in a stigmatized group, people are somehow less than human and, therefore, not deserving of all the rights and privileges therein. The consequences of robbing a group of its humanity are many and terrible. The majority views the minority as inferior, incompetent or dangerous and uses this kind of logic to legitimize feelings of anger and hatred toward the stigmatized group.[3] They act on these feelings through discrimination, stealing the rightful opportunities that all humans deserve. For example, landlords will not rent safe housing to stigmatized groups and employers will not hire them. Even worse, the majority responds with terror. Stigma has led to such heinous crimes as the lynching of American blacks during Reconstruction, the prostitution of Chinese women during the Second World War and the torture of heretics during the Inquisition.

Goffman places the source of stigma in the individual; he or she has attributes from which discreditability results. The black skin of African Americans causes prejudice. Stereotypes about the physically disabled are activated by their wheelchair. Stigma about smokers comes from their cigarettes. These external signs are the marks that yield stigma. Ironically, the notion of stigma as an intrinsic attribute seems to add to the blame: it is a quality of the person from which prejudice results. Hence, might one conclude that if African Americans were not black then they would escape prejudice? Edward Jones and Albert Hastorf, working with a team from the Center for Advanced Study in the Behavioral Sciences at Stanford,[4] addressed this concern and refined the definition of stigma in the process. They recognized that an essential part of the definition is the perception of *labels*; namely, the act of stigma does not naturally follow when the mark is apparent to the majority but rather when the majority puts a label on the mark. Hence, black skin does not generate a label; rather, it is the European's perception that black skin means 'inferior' that leads to prejudice. The injustice lies in the eye of the beholder. Bruce Link, an epidemiologist at Columbia University,[5] summarized these discussions into four key tests, what might be considered the salutary criteria for deciding whether an outgroup is stigmatized:

1. People LABEL human differences.
2. Dominant cultural beliefs LINK labelled characteristics to negative stereotypes.

3. The labelled group is discriminated from the majority as US versus THEM.
4. Labelled people experience status loss and DISCRIMINATION.

DO SMOKERS MEET THIS DEFINITION OF STIGMA?

Smoking seems to meet the first of Link's criteria. Clearly, smokers have a publicly obvious mark (smoking cigarettes), which has been labelled by much of the public. In fact, it is a mark that most government health services, along with private foundations, have targeted for change.[6] For example, the World Health Organization has recommended that all countries develop a multi-targeted approach to stamp out smoking.[7] Moreover, the official goals of national governments have filtered down to the populace, especially in Western countries. Most children in these countries are now educated on the dangers of smoking, and know that 'those' people with cigarettes are different.

The second criterion – the label is linked to negative stereotypes – is supported by substantial empirical work. A variety of studies have highlighted the consensual ways in which smokers are negatively viewed. One qualitative investigation by Health Canada[8] summarizes the research: smokers are highly unattractive; cigarette smoking stinks; others think less of smokers; smoking causes premature ageing; and smoking can make you listless. Note how participants in these studies confuse the act (smoking is unhealthy and smells) with the actor (making critical and angry comments about smokers), an important point to which I will return. It is important to realize that these findings are fairly constant across the Western world and are becoming more prevalent in developing countries.[9]

Whether smokers meet the third and fourth criteria for stigma is less transparent. The third standard for a stigma is that stereotypes result in an 'us' versus 'them' mentality. There is a group status that separates those who belong to the stigmatized group from everyone else. Such differences are evident in restaurants, theatres, airports and other public places where smoking areas are clearly marked off from the rest of the environment. Smoking areas are the place to which smokers ('them') go to perform their discreditable act. That place often has the mark of shame attached, evident if one thinks of people sheepishly milling out in front of a public building, puffing on their hourly cigarette.

We should not assume, however, that the very presence of smoking rooms is evidence of a we/they mentality. Alternatively, restricted smoking areas may be construed as places to protect people from second-hand smoke; hence, the behaviour, and not the class of people *per se*, is targeted. If the distinction between those smoking 'over there' and non-smokers represents a true 'we/they' dichotomy, then the final criterion must be met to consider smoking a stigma: namely, do labelled smokers experience status loss and discrimination? Discrimination is defined here as a loss of opportunity or a penalty/punishment that results from membership in a stigmatized group. Clearly, smokers are treated with scorn by much of the public and suffer the consequences. The premiums for most health insurance plans are higher for smokers. Smokers can be precluded from obtaining some rental properties and many types of jobs. They may be banished from public settings because of their activity. It is interesting to note the extremes that these banishments may take. For example, staff members who work at the state hospital in which my office is situated must cross a football-size field and a busy road to get off grounds and smoke. If it were not so dangerous, the Keystone Cop efforts that smokers make in attempting to cross the road might be considered high comedy.

Once again, it is unclear whether these actions represent stigma against smokers or self-protective strategies to address the risks posed by smoking; more than likely, they mean both. Smoking is banished from public areas because laws are trying to protect non-smokers from ambient smoke and because smokers are undesirable people. The key to deciding which factor is prominent – social stigma or health behaviour – is the *link* among label,

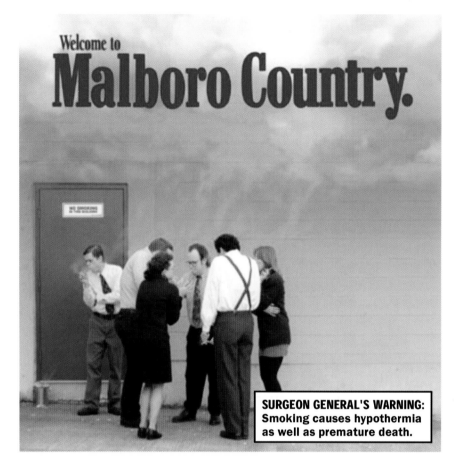

Another Adbusters
counter-promotion,
depicting 'Malboro
Country' as definitively
not the place to be.

negative stereotype and discriminatory behaviour. Members of the public who endorse this kind of discrimination because the group labelled smokers has weak character, is unattractive and smells, is committing a prejudicial act. Conversely, citizens who endorse smoking bans solely because of health concerns, thereby targeting smoking as a behaviour and not the smoker, are not stigmatizing the group.

FROM VALUED TO DEVALUED ACT

Perhaps one of the more interesting aspects of smoking is not that it is stigmatized, but rather that it seems to have changed its place in society significantly. What once was a behaviour touted as a sign of gentility and sophistication is now portrayed as foolish and unkempt. Consider such changes in the cinema. Positive representations of smoking in movies and television have diminished significantly since the 1950s. Common was the film where Humphrey Bogart or Bette Davis accentuated their dialogue with dramatic stabs of a cigarette. Early television was frequently punctuated by situation comedies and action dramas where stars puffed away in the midst of their lines. In part, this prevalence reflected cultural views that smokers were debonair and mysterious. In part, smoking was found in television and movies because of marketing efforts from the tobacco companies; they would buy time for actors to smoke their product.[10] Alternatively, cigarettes may have been nothing more than a prop, something that actors could do with their hands so that they did not seem awkward.[11] Regardless of the reason, smoking had been in the forefront and centre of the Western media.

Lauren Bacall in *Dark Passage* (1947).

Since that time, smoking on television and movies has been significantly reduced. Tobacco advertisements were banned from American broadcast media in 1971; many other countries have followed suit since then.[12] More subtly, there has been a noticeable effort to cut the amount of smoking as plot elements in films and on TV. Some notable actors, directors, writers and producers argued against smoking as an acting or marketing tool and participated in informal moratoria against on-air cigarettes. For a short time,

Smoking on screen seems to be limited to the 'bad boys' of Hollywood now: Johnny Depp in 1994.

the movie stars and television personalities who lit up as a device to accentuate their dialogue disappeared. Note, however, that there seems to be a recurring trend for more tobacco use in the media. Cigar smoking has increased significantly since the mid-1990s.[13] Films have reintroduced smoking as an acting device, especially by 'bad boy' actors such as Sean Penn and Johnny Depp.[14]

At the same time that smoking has decreased in the media, anti-smoking images have become omnipresent. Public service announcements in a variety of formats scream the message that smoking is dangerous and smokers are disgusting. Moreover, the recent tobacco settlement between the major American cigarette manufacturers and more than two dozen states has provided huge sums of money to further these campaigns. Other countries have latched on to this agenda and begun a broad-based effort to promote anti-smoking slogans. The World Health Organization has called for public education efforts to prevent young people smoking. Moreover, there is evidence that these campaigns are yielding positive effects. For example, national surveys completed at the University of Michigan show that, during the 1990s, teenagers endorsed negative attitudes about smoking more strongly and were less likely to take up the habit themselves.[15] Gallup polls show a steady increase in those who want to ban smoking totally in restaurants and workplaces from less than 20 per cent in 1987 to almost half the population in 2000.

With the recent explosion of anti-smoking concerns, we might think that the diatribes against smoking are a recent innovation and that stigma associated with smokers has evolved only over the past couple of decades. History, however, teaches us that a steady and petulant voice has harangued tobacco for centuries. More than a hundred years ago, for example, President William McKinley forbade a photographer from taking a picture of him smoking because of the subversive effects on the country's youth.[16] English writings of the nineteenth century overwhelmingly critiqued the role of smoking at that time. Hence, we should not conclude that the stigma of smoking is a new creation, but instead realize that it has become more prominent because of the mass media's endorsement.

Given this history, the question changes from why has smoking become devalued so quickly during the past decades to why is smoking – and not other health-related behaviours – socially reviled? Why are smokers labelled as weak and risk-takers? Why not equally lampoon couch potatoes for their lack of exercise or meat eaters because they risk arteriosclerosis? Once again, a myopic view of smoking may cause some readers to miss the other behaviours that are also touted as unhealthy: eating fatty food, drinking alcohol to excess and failing to exercise are all targets of public health agenda. Moreover, the disapproval of specific health behaviours frequently transfers to the people doing the behaviours. Overweight people are often the butt of prejudice (they are viewed as weak in character[17]) as are people who struggle with sobriety (they are sinners who are a danger to the community[18]).

There is, however, a unique aspect to smoking that exacerbates the prejudice experienced by smokers: *secondary smoke*. Unlike many of the other health-related stigmas, smoking is one of the few where the stigmatized act immediately impacts on others. Non-smokers report that the smoke of others is bothersome, causing their eyes to water and their throats to burn. Non-smokers also report that secondary smoke leaves a nasty odour in the environment and eventually causes draperies and walls to discolour. Perhaps most critical among these nuisances, research suggests, is that secondary smoke can lead to significant health problems in those exposed to it.[19]

The unique effects of second-hand smoke might be better understood in terms of the stigma-related notions of *contagion* and *contamination*, the idea that the curse that produces a stigma can be passed on to others.[20] Leprosy and leper colonies are centuries-old examples of this phenomenon. To protect the community, people with leprosy were doomed to live out the remainder of their life separated from family, friends and neighbours.

Sean Penn smoking on the set of the *The Interpreter*, New York, 2004.

We should not, however, think that leper colonies are things of the ancient past and foreign to the Western World. Hawaii's Kalaupapa colony was accepting banished lepers into its community up to 1969, when the State stopped this forcible expulsion.

Concerns about contagion are also prevalent in smoking. Surveys show that many people are concerned that they will get cancer and related diseases from second-hand smoke. But the public's concern about contagion goes beyond exposure to direct pathogens; it also reflects a moral contagion. Research suggests that the public is concerned about associating with people with mental illness in case they become infected with the disorder. For example, a survey of college students in 1981 showed that more than one third agreed with such statements as: 'I would not go swimming in a pool used by a group of mental patients' and 'I would wash my hands after touching a mental patient.'[21] Contamination worries go beyond the impact of pathogens and suggest something specifically dirty or blemished about the person. Jones and colleagues distinguished moral from physical contagion; namely, that associating with the diseased or addicted will transfer some of their sin to others.[22]

IS THE STIGMA OF SMOKING WRONG?

Most advocates for social justice quickly respond that stigma of any kind is a sin of the first degree. Anything that robs a group of their public respect and individual opportunity has egregious implications for the cultures in which these injustices occur. Hence, the reflexive response is that the stigma of smoking is indeed wrong!

An antagonist to this view, however, might remind the reader of the original purpose of stigma in ancient Greece. People were marked (with a brand on the cheek, mark on their clothes or wound on the shoulder) so that the public knew that there was danger in associating with them. 'Caution!', the mark would imply, this person is a criminal, or is a madman, or has an infectious disease. Although this idea seems ancient, Western cultures have con-

tinued to endorse the idea of a public mark. Most states in the USA require sex offenders to register on line so that people can find out if a paedophile lives in the neighbourhood. Criminal court judges have ordered drunk drivers to carry bumper stickers that warn people of their crime. In a similar fashion, it might be argued that efforts to mark smokers and smoking territories is a public service. People can protect themselves from moral and physical disease contagion by avoiding the smoker. Hence, questions such as whether a stigma like smoking is right or wrong seem to yield both positive and negative answers. Moral psychology is a paradigm that helps to explain why divergent answers are possible.

THE STIGMA OF SMOKING AND MORAL PSYCHOLOGY

Of its many goals, moral psychology attempts to frame human concerns about justice and sin in terms of the theories of psychology.[23] An important tenet of moral psychology, especially from the perspective of operant conditioning and humanistic theory, is the necessity of evaluating the *behaviour* separate from the *person*.[24] Determining whether a behaviour is good or bad and responding concordantly (reinforcing good behaviour and punishing the bad) has adaptive value for both the person and his or her community. In this way, children, for example, learn that hitting is bad and raising hands in class is good. Classmates benefit from the non-aggressive child who politely waits their turn. In like manner, health advocates punish smoking behaviour publicly by belittling the behaviour and reinforcing efforts to quit. As a result, smokers who abstain from cigarettes benefit from improved health, as does their community.

An epistemological error occurs when people mistake the behaviour for the person. This is the nature of stigma: equating the person with the blemish.[25] Many of the images of smoking go beyond statements about behaviour and suggest that the smoker is unworthy of our respect. This is the moral contagion discussed above. Research by social psychologists on attribution theory has identified variables that liken the wrongs of smoking with an immoral smoker.[26] The attribution theory is fundamentally a model of human motivation based on the assumption that individuals search for causal understanding of everyday events. 'Why did I get a pay raise?', 'How come Republicans were voted out of Congress?', 'Why can't that guy stop smoking?' The key to answering such questions lies in attributions of responsibility. People who are not considered responsible for their behaviour generally receive sympathy and help: 'that poor Harvey is a victim of cancer; can I drive him to the doctor's office?' Conversely, people who are viewed as responsible for a behaviour are disliked and punished: 'Harriet smokes because she is weak; I shouldn't have to pay taxes for her health bills.' There is mixed evidence whether the public views smoking and other addictions as a matter of personal responsibility (the smoker chooses to smoke) or as an uncontrollable disease process (the smoker is a victim of his or her genetic predispositions).[27] Clearly, however, individuals who view smoking as a matter of choice are likely to stigmatize the smoker as a result.

CONCLUSIONS

What was once considered to be a behaviour regarded as the epitome of sophistication has now become the act of the uncouth: 'Smoking stinks and kills!' In the process, negative attitudes associated with smoking behaviour have spilled over to the person guilty of the behaviour. Smokers are malodorous mopes who threaten their community with both physical and moral contagion. Following from this, smokers are considered to be a stigmatized group. The intriguing concern, however, is whether a stigma of smoking is wrong.

The reflexive appeal to social justice would suggest yes; smoking stigma, like any kind of discrimination, is iniquitous. On the other hand, the public mark of smokers may protect people from physical disease as well as moral contagion. Protecting people from illness caused by second-hand smoke is a reasonable public health goal. Hence, in this limited fashion, discrimination that arises from the stigma seems legitimate. The equation becomes murkier when the idea of moral contagion is introduced. Members of the public who avoid smokers because of ethical concerns ('they are weak-willed individuals who are playing roulette with their health!') are likely to commit the same error as the interdictions that have been touted against people of colour and all the other countless stigmatized groups. When viewed through this lens, stigma as a tool of discrimination is unacceptable.

Smoking & Advertising

Can you make someone want to smoke? Certainly one of the major industries that drove the rise of modern advertising in the late nineteenth century was tobacco. But is tobacco advertising inherently baneful? Does it drive the unsuspecting innocent into a life of addiction and dependency? In the first generation of European smokers, James VI, the king of Scotland who, in 1603, became James I, King of England, certainly believed so. In his screed against tobacco in 1604, he observed that those who 'smoke . . . are not able to forbeare the same, no more than an old drunkard can abide to be long sobre . . .'. What makes this claim difficult, even in the age of the mass appropriation of smoking, is that idea that we do have some claim to individual choice. Iago, not the most reliable of commentators in Othello, makes this clear in answering James's charge: 'Our bodies are our gardens, to the which our wills are gardeners: so that if we will plant nettles, or sow lettuce, set hyssop and weed up thyme, supply it with one gender of herbs, or distract it with many, either to have it sterile with idleness, or manured with industry, why, the power and corrigible authority of this lies in our wills' (I: v: 320–26). Of all human activities, smoking seems to define the predicament of modern autonomy: do we choose to do something that destroys our ability to choose again? Or is the seduction of smoking one that we enter into autonomously, engaging in those actions that give us pleasure even though/because they are inexorably intertwined with the very promise of risk.

By the 1940s and the triumph of tobacco advertising the American brand Philip Morris shouted in its ads that its version is healthful:

Dining a burlesque girl after the show – a lithograph for the Devere's High Rollers Burlesque Co., *c.* 1898.

'ALL SMOKERS INHALE – BUT YOUR THROAT NEEDN'T KNOW IT.' IT WAS FOUND AND REPORTED BY EMINENT DOCTORS WHO COMPARED THE LEADING CIGARETTES: 'SMOKE OF THE FOUR OTHER LEADING POPULAR BRANDS AVERAGED MORE THAN THREE TIMES AS IRRITATING – AND THEIR IRRITATION LASTED MORE THAN FIVE TIMES AS LONG – AS THE STRIKINGLY CONTRASTED PHILIP MORRIS!'

Their competition, Chesterfield, then claimed, 'TO GIVE YOU SCIENTIFIC FACTS IN SUPPORT OF SMOKING.' A responsible consulting organization then reports a study by a competent medical specialist and staff on the effects of smoking Chesterfields: 'It is my opinion that the ears, nose, throat and accessory organs of all participating subjects examined by me were not adversely affected in the six-months period by smoking the cigarettes provided.' It is neither addictive nor harmful – only pleasurable. By the 1950s the advertising claims of healthfulness were paralleled by the desire for pleasure:

NEW PHILIP MORRIS – *gentle for modern taste*
This smart new package is a symbol of something all Philip Morris smokers have enjoyed for months – a new cigarette – made gentle for modern taste. Born gentle, then refined to special gentleness in the making, this new Philip Morris meets the requirements of modern taste – of today's young.

Here in the mid-twentieth century the desire for pleasure and the acknowledgement as well as the recognition of danger was little changed from that of the seventeenth century. The voice of the advertising campaign demanded the recognition of choice in the light of the anxiety about risk:

Winston smokers believe that smoking should be fun. That means real flavor – full, rich, tobacco flavor – and Winston's really got it! This filter cigarette tastes good – like a cigarette should! Along with Winston's filter flavor, you get a filter that really does the job. The exclusive Winston filter works so effectively, yet lets you draw so easily and enjoy yourself so fully.

So enjoy – but also enjoy the risk! Today point-of-purchase advertisement for cigarettes – which of course are ads advocating smoking – are countered by equally seductive anti-smoking ads. These are not necessarily anti-tobacco acts. For they stress the risk over the pleasure of smoking.

'Giddap Uncle!', painted by Edward V. Brewer for the Cream of Wheat Co., c. 1921.

Advertisement for The Regent cigarettes.

A Lucky Strike ad of *c*. 1932, American Tobacco Company

Lucky Strike, *c*. 1936, American Tobacco Company.

An ad of *c*. 1934, Liggett & Myers Tobacco Co.

A Lucky Strike ad of *c*. 1934, American Tobacco Company.

Santa smoking Lucky Strike at Christmas.
c. 1936, American Tobacco Company.

An ad of *c*. 1936, Liggett & Myers
Tobacco Co.

'A light smoke' Lucky Strike,
c. 1936, American Tobacco
Company.

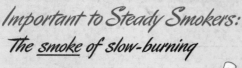

A Second World War Camels ad.

An ad from *Life International*, August 1962.

'Test it', an ad from the
Polish edition of *Playboy*,
May 1997.

An ad from *Paris Match*, June 1966.

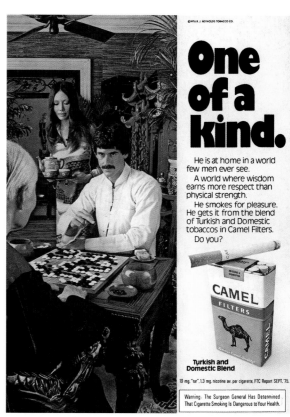

From *Playboy*, June 1976.

An advertisement for *bidi* cigarettes, India, *c.* 1992.

'The fat lady sings'.
Silk Cut mark the end
of tobacco advertising
in the UK, February 2002.

An anti-smoking poster in New York, 2001.

References

SANDER L. GILMAN AND ZHOU XUN: 'Introduction'

1 Las Casas's account first appeared with the publication of
Columbus's journal (Madrid, 1825). There are many accounts of
this as a given fact. See, for example, Jerome E. Brooks, *The
Mighty Leaf: Tobacco through the Centuries* (London, 1953), pp. 12–15.

2 Iain Gately, *Tobacco: The Story of How Tobacco Seduced the World*
(New York, 2001), pp. 1–20.

3 Sarah August Dickson, *Panacea or Precious Bane?: Tobacco in
Sixteenth-Century Literature* (New York, 1954), p. 119.

4 *Ibid.*, p. 95.

5 Cited in Gately, *Tobacco*, p. 27.

6 T. De Bry, *A Brief and True Report of the New Found Land of
Virginia* (Frankfurt am Main, 1590), p. 16, quoted in Alexander
von Gernet, 'Nicotian Dreams: The Prehistory and Early
History of Tobacco in Eastern North America', in *Consuming
Habits*, ed. Jordan Goodman, Paul E. Lovejoy and Andrew
Sherratt (New York and London, 1995), pp. 74–5.

7 J. W. Shirley, *Thomas Hariot: A Biography* (Oxford, 1983),
pp. 432–4.

8 Dickson, *Panacea or Precious Bane?*, p. 98.

9 Cited from James Walton, ed., *The Faber Book of Smoking*
(London, 2000), p. 22.

10 Numbers 16: 46–50.

11 Herodotus, *The Histories*, trans. Aubrey de Sélincourt
(London, 1927), p. 295.

12 Cited by Gately, *Tobacco*, p. 31.

13 Jasper Ridley, *The Tudor Age* (London, 1988), p. 333.

14 See Jordan Goodman, *Tobacco in History: The Culture of
Dependence* (London and New York, 1993), p. 66.

15 Thurstan Shaw, 'Early Smoking Pipes in Africa, Europe and
America', *Journal of the Royal Anthropological Institute of Great
Britain and Ireland*, XC (1960), pp. 272–305, as well as John
Edward Philips, 'African Smoking and Pipes', *Journal of African
History*, XXIV (1983), pp. 303–19.

16 See Barney T. Suzuki, *The First English Pipe Smoker in Japan / Le
Premier Fumeur de pipe anglais au Japon: William Adams, the Pilot and
the English Trade House in Hirato, 1600–1621* (Paris, 1997), pp. 5–11.

17 *Ibid.*, p. 15.

18 Timothy Clark *et al.*, eds, *The Dawn of the Floating World,
1650–1765: Early Ukiyo-e Treasures from the Museum of Fine Arts,
Boston* (London, 2002), pp. 109, 195.

19 Li Zhiyong, ed., *Zhang Jingyue yixue quanshu* [The medical
treatises of Zhang Jingyue] (Beijing, 1997), p. 1546; Fang Yizhi,
Wuli xiaoshi [Knowledge regarding nature] (Taiwan, 1974), p. 237.

20 Cited in Zheng Tianyi and Xu Bin, *Yanwenhua* [Smoking
culture] (Beijing, 1992), p. 62.

21 Cited by Wolfgang Schivelbusch, *Tastes of Paradise: A Social
History of Spices, Stimulants and Intoxicants*, trans. David
Jacobson (New York, 1993), p. 103.

22 Ye Mengzhu, *Yueshi bian* [A collection of observations],
(Shanghai, 1981), p. 167

23 L. Carrington Goodrich, 'Early Prohibitions of Tobacco in
China and Manchuria', *Journal of the American Oriental Society*,
LVIII (1938), p. 651.

24 Quoted in Walton, *The Faber Book of Smoking*, p. 33.

25 *Work for Chimney-Sweeper; or, A Warning for Tobacconists* (1601;
reprinted London, 1936), title page.

26 Quoted in Walton, *The Faber Book of Smoking*, p. 53.

27 Quoted in *ibid.*, p. 60.

28 Anon., 'A Resident Officer', *Madrid in 1835* (London, 1836),
vol. I, p. 242.

29 For a detailed description on opium pipes and the art of
opium smoking, see Peter Lee, *The Big Smoke: The Chinese Art
and Craft of Opium* (Thailand, 1999), pp. 34–65.

30 Roy Porter and Marie Mulvey Roberts, eds, *Pleasure in the
Eighteenth Century* (Houndsmills, 1996).

31 Edgar Pankow, ed., *Honoré de Balzac: Pathologie des Soziallebens*,
trans. Christiana Goldmann (Leipzig, 2002), pp. 176–84.

32 Arthur W. Grundy, 'My Cigar', in Joseph Knight, ed., *Pipe and
Pouch: The Smoker's Own Book of Poetry* (London, n.d. [1894?]),
pp. 2–4, here pp. 2–3.

33 J. H. Kellogg, *The Living Temple* (Battle Creek, MI, 1903), p. 453.

34 William McAllister, *Drug Diplomacy in the 20th Century: An
International History* (London, 2000); Jan-Willem Gerritsen,
*The Control of Fuddle and Flash: A Sociological History of the
Regulation of Alcohol and Opiates* (The Hague, 2000).

35 Paul Gootenberg, ed., *Cocaine: Global Histories* (London, 2000); Joseph F. Spillane, *Cocaine: From Medical Marvel to Modern Menace in the United States, 1884–1920* (Baltimore, 2000).

36 Howard Cox, *The Global Cigarette: Origins and Evolution of British American Tobacco, 1880–1945* (Oxford, 2000).

37 Press packet for the Artworks project on Smoking sponsored by the World Health Organization Regional Office for Europe (November 2000).

38 Steven Fanning, *Mystics of the Christian Tradition* (London and New York, 2001), p. 137.

FRANCIS ROBICSEK: 'Ritual Smoking in Central America'

1 Quoted in Bernal Díaz de Castillo, *The Conquest of New Spain*, trans. J. M. Cohen (Harmondsworth, 1963), p. 227.

2 Juan Díaz, *La primera noticia del descubrimiento de la Nueva España en Europa: el itinerario de la espedición del Capitán Juan de Grijalva (año 1518)* (Mérida, 1958).

3 G. Arents, *Tobacco* (New York, 1936), vol. I, p. 23.

4 A. M. Tozzer, *A Comparative Study of the Mayas and Lacadones* (New York, 1907).

5 M. J. Harner, *Hallucinogens and Shamanism* (New York, 1969).

6 C. Wisdom, *The Chorti Indians of Guatemala* (Chicago, 1940).

7 R. Asado, *Libro de Judeo* (US Peabody Museum, Harvard University, n.d.).

8 G. Benzoni, *Historia del Mundo Nuovo* (Venice, 1568).

9 P. Schellhas, *Representations of Deities in the Maya Manuscripts* (Cambridge, MA, 1904).

10 Francis Robicsek, *The Smoking Gods: Tobacco in Maya Art, History and Religion* (Norman, OK, 1978), p. 62.

TANYA POLLARD: 'The Pleasures and Perils of Smoking in Early Modern England'

I would like to thank the Wellcome Centre for the History of Medicine at University College, London, for support with research, and Roy Porter, Katherine Craik and Will Sternhouse for their thoughtful comments on this essay.

1 For a summary of the medical claims for tobacco, see especially Grace Stewart, 'A History of the Medicinal Use of Tobacco, 1492–1860', *Medical History*, XI/3 (1967), pp. 228–68; Sarah Augusta Dickson, *Panacea or Precious Bane?: Tobacco in Sixteenth Century Literature* (New York, 1954); and Jerome E. Brooks, 'Introduction', *Tobacco: Its History Illustrated by the Books, Manuscripts and Engravings in the Library of George Arents Jr* (New York, 1937), vol. I, esp. pp. 29–43.

2 Rudi Matthee points out that tobacco was the first of a number of 'psychotropic substances' spreading around the globe to become popularized; see 'Exotic Substances: The Introduction and Global Spread of Tobacco, Coffee, Cocoa, Tea and Distilled Liquor, Sixteenth to Eighteenth Centuries', in *Drugs and Narcotics in History*, ed. Roy Porter and Mikuláš Teich (Cambridge, 1995), pp. 24–51; p. 24. On the use of opium at this time, see, for instance, Angelus Sala Vincentinus Venetus, *Opiologia; or, a Treatise concerning the Nature, properties, true preparation and safe use and Administration of Opium*, trans. Thomas Bretnor (London, 1618). Medical writings of the time routinely referred to opium as a treatment for plague.

3 David Harley notes that the debate over tobacco 'was the first English campaign against an exotic psychoactive substance'; see 'The Beginnings of the Tobacco Controversy: Puritanism, James I and the Royal Physicians', *Bulletin of the History of Medicine*, LXVII/1 (1993), pp. 28–50; p. 50. On the identification of drugs with fears of foreigners, see Jonathan Gil Harris, *Foreign Bodies and the Body Politic: Discourses of Social Pathology in Early Modern England* (Cambridge, 1998).

4 The term tobacco encompassed two slightly different plants, *Nicotiana tabacum* and *Nicotiana rustica*. *N. tabacum*, from Trinidad, was generally seen as superior to *N. rustica*, the more common form found in North America and Mexico. On the distinction between the two, see Brooks, *Tobacco*, p. 13.

5 On the early history of tobacco in Europe, see especially Dickson, *Panacea or Precious Bane?*, and Brooks, *Tobacco*.

6 See, for instance, William Harrison's 1573 description of smoking in 'an instrument formed like a litle ladell, wherby it [smoke] passeth from the mouth into the hed & stomach', in 'Chronologie', in *Harrison's Description of England in Shakspere's Youth*, ed. Frederick J. Furnivall (London, 1877), vol. I, p. lv; Anthony Chute also refers to smoking in 'earthen or siluer pipes', in *Tabacco: The distinct and seuerall opinions of the late and best Phisitions that haue written of the diuers natures and qualities thereof* (London, 1595), p. 15.

7 On apothecary shops and their reputations in this period, see Patrick Wallis, 'Bad, Corrupt and Falsified: Medicines, Fear and the Material Culture of Apothecaries' Shops', paper presented at the Research Forum of the Oxford Wellcome Unit for Medical History, 14 February 2001.

8 Nicholas Monardes, *Joyfull Newes out of the newe founde worlde, wherein is declared the rare and singular vertues of diuerse and sundrie Hearbes, Trees, Oyles, Plantes, and Stones, with their aplications, as well for Phisicke as Chirurgerie . . .*, trans. John Frampton (London, 1577), fol. 35r.

9 Giles Everard, *De herba panacea, quam alii tabacum, alii petum, aut Nicotianum vocant, breuis commentariolus* (Antwerp, 1587). The first English translation was published in 1659.

10 Edmund Gardiner, *The Triall of Tobacco. Wherein, his worth is most worthily expressed: as, in the name, nature, and qualitie of the sayd hearb; his speciall vse in all Physicke, with the true and right vse of taking it, aswell for the Seasons, and times* (London, 1610), fol. 3v.

11 On inherited medical beliefs and practices, see especially Nancy Siraisi, *Medieval and Renaissance Medicine* (Chicago, 1990).

12 On associations of cold and wet humours with women, see, for example, Aristotle, *On the Generation of Animals*, trans. A. L. Peck, in *Women's Life in Greece and Rome*, ed. Maureen B. Fant and Mary R. Lefkowitz (London, 1982), p. 84. On the gendering of the transformation of agency attributed to tobacco, see especially Joan Pong Linton, 'Gender, Savagery, Tobacco: Marketplaces for Consumption', in *The Romance of the New World* (Cambridge, 1998), pp. 104–30.

13 William Barclay, *Nepenthes; or, The Vertves of Tabacco* (Edinburgh, 1614), sigs A8r–v.

14 John Deacon, *Tobacco Tortured; or, The Filthie Fume of Tobacco Refined: shewing all sorts of Subiects, that the inward taking of Tobacco fumes, is very pernicious vnto their bodies; too too profluuious for many of their purses; and most pestiferous to the publike State* (London, 1616), p. 51.

15 Barclay, *Nepenthes*, sigs A8b–B1r.

16 Deacon, *Tobacco Tortured*, p. 52.

17 See, for instance, Hippocrates, 'On Diseases of Women', 2.126, 123, and 'Nature of Woman', 8, 3, trans. Mary R. Lefkowitz, in *Women's Life in Greece and Rome*, pp. 93–4; also, Hippocrates, 'On Diseases of Women', trans. A. Hanson, *Signs*, I (1975), pp. 567–84. Heinrich von Staden discusses this form of treatment in 'Women and Dirt', *Helios*, XIX (1992), pp. 7–30.

18 Leonardo Fioravanti, *A Compendium of the rationall Secretes, of the Worthie Knight and moste excellent Doctour of Phisicke and Chirurgerie, Leonardo Phiorauante*, trans. I. Hester (London, 1582), pp. 130–31.

19 Discussing the introduction of 'much quantitie of Liquid Amber to Spaine', Monardes writes 'the smoke and smell doth seeme to be the same, and also they doe put it into other confections of sweete smelles to burne, and such like thinges . . . It serueth muche in medicine, and doth therein great effect . . .', Monardes, *Joyfull Newes*, fols 6v–7r.

20 *Tarltons Jests* (London, 1611; reprinted 1638), sig. C3v. I am grateful to Lucy Munro for calling this reference to my attention.

21 Monardes declared that 'his complexion is hot and drie in the seconde degree' (*Joyfull Newes*, fol. 34v). Later writers on tobacco echoed him; see, for instance, Gardiner, *The Triall of Tabacco*, fol. 9r.

22 Tobias Venner, *A Briefe and Accurate Treatise, Concerning The taking of the fume of Tobacco* (London, 1621), sigs B3r–v.

23 A number of critics have commented on literary portrayals of tobacco at this time; see especially Jeffrey Knapp, 'Divine Tobacco', in *An Empire Nowhere: England, America and Literature from Utopia to the Tempest* (Berkeley, CA, 1992), pp. 134–74; Craig Rustici, 'The Smoking Girl: Tobacco and the Representation of Mary Frith', *Studies in Philology*, XCVI/2 (1999), pp. 159–79; and Linton, 'Gender, Savagery, Tobacco'. On Jonson's pre-eminence as a literary chronicler of tobacco, see Dickson, *Panacea or Precious Bane?*, p. 190. I would like to thank Michael Clark for calling my attention to the enormous body of epigrams written about tobacco at this time.

24 Ben Jonson, *Every Man in his Humor* (London, 1601), sig. G1r.

25 Henry Buttes writes: 'It cureth any griefe, dolour, opilation, impostume, or obstruction, proceeding of cold or winde: especially in the head or breast: the leaues are good against the Migram, cold stomackes, sick kidnies, tooth-ache, fits of the mother, naughty breath, scaldings or burnings . . .'; see Henry Buttes, *Dyets Dry Dinner* (London, 1599), sig. P4v.

26 Gardiner, *The Triall of Tabacco*, sigs A2v–a3.

27 J. H. [Joseph Hall], *Work for Chimny-sweepers; or, A warning for Tobacconists* (London, 1601), sig. B.iii.v.

28 James I, 'A Counterblaste to Tobacco' (1604), in *The Workes of the most high and mighty Prince Iames, by the grace of God Kinge of Great Brittaine France & Ireland Defendor of the Faith &c.* (London, 1616), pp. 219–20. Much has been written on the roots of James's hostility to tobacco; see, for instance, Harley, 'The Beginnings of the Tobacco Controversy', and Susan Campbell Anderson, 'A Matter of Authority: James I and the Tobacco War', *Comitatus: A Journal of Medieval & Renaissance Studies*, XXIX (1998), pp. 136–63.

29 James I, 'A Counterblaste to Tobacco', p. 220.

30 Venner, *A Briefe and Accurate Treatise*, sig. D3r.

31 On medical uncertainty, see, for example, Andrew Wear, 'Epistemology and Learned Medicine in Early Modern England', in *Knowledge and the Scholarly Medical Traditions*, ed. Don Bates (Cambridge, 1995), pp. 151–73. On Paracelsus, see especially Walter Pagel, *Paracelsus: An Introduction to Philosophical Medicine in the Era of the Renaissance* (Basel, 1958), and Charles Webster, *From Paracelsus to Newton: Magic and the Making of Modern Science* (Cambridge, 1982). On the impact of Paracelsus in England, see Allen Debus, *The English Paracelsians* (London, 1965), and Paul Kocher, 'Paracelsan Medicine in England', *Journal of the History of Medicine*, II (1947), pp. 451–80.

32 Barnabe Rich, *The Irish Hubbub; or, The English Hue and Crie* (London, 1617), p. 46.

33 On early modern preoccupation with melancholy, see, for example, Robert Burton's *Anatomy of Melancholy* (Oxford, 1621); Lynn Enterline, *Tears of Narcissus: Melancholia and Masculinity in Early Modern England* (Stanford, CA, 1995); Juliana Schiesari, *The Gendering of Melancholia* (Ithaca, NY, 1992), and William Engel, *Mapping Mortality* (Amherst, MA, 1995).

34 Barclay, *Nepenthes*, sig. A4r.

35 Hall, *Work for Chimny-sweepers*, sig. F4v.

36 Venner, *A Briefe and Accurate Treatise*, sig. D2r.

37 Gardiner, *The Triall of Tabacco*, fol. 9v.

38 Buttes, *Dyets Dry Dinner*, sig. P5v.

39 Venner, *A Briefe and Accurate Treatise*, sig. B3r.

40 Barclay, *Nepenthes*, sig. A7r.

41 *Thomas Platter's Travels in England 1599*, ed. and trans. Clare Williams (London, 1937), pp. 170–71.

42 Barclay, *Nepenthes*, sig. A4r.

43 James I, 'A Counterblaste to Tobacco', p. 222.

44 *Ibid.*, p. 220.

45 Gardiner, *The Triall of Tabacco*, fol. 19r.

46 Venner, *A Briefe and Accurate Treatise*, sig. B2v.

47 James I, 'A Counterblaste to Tobacco', pp. 220–21.

48 John Beaumont, *The Metamorphosis of Tabacco* (London, 1602), sig. B1r.

49 Barclay, *Nepenthes*, sig. A4r.

50 John Cotta, *A Short Discoverie of the unobserved Dangers of seuerall sorts of ignorant and vnconsiderate Practicers of Physicke in England* (London, 1612), p. 5.

51 Monardes, *Joyfull Newes*, fol. 39r.

52 See, for instance, Gardiner, *The Triall of Tabacco*, fol. 20v; Venner, *A Briefe and Accurate Treatise*, sigs B2r–v.

53 See Knapp, 'Divine Tobacco', p. 134, on the application of the epithet 'divine' to tobacco.

54 Oenoz Thopolis [Richard Brathwait], *The Smoking Age; or, The Man in the Mist: with The Life and Death of Tobacco* (London, 1617), p. 152.

55 See Knapp, 'Divine Tobacco', p. 167, on the conflation of 'the two kinds of ceremonial reverence'.

56 Joshua Sylvester, *Tobacco Battered; & The Pipes Shattered About their Eares that idly idolize so base & barbarous a weed; or at least-wise ouer-loue so loathsome vanitie* (London, 1614), p. 82.

57 George Chapman, *Monsieur D'Olive* (London, 1606), sig. D3r. I would like to thank Lucy Munro for calling this episode to my attention.

58 Hall, *Work for Chimny-sweepers*, sigs B1r and B1v.

59 Monardes, *Joyfull Newes*, fols 40r–40v.

60 *Ibid.*, fol. 40r.

61 On the excitement and ambivalence generated by the Americas, see Stephen Greenblatt, *Marvellous Possessions: The Wonder of the New World* (Oxford, 1991), as well as Knapp, 'Divine Tobacco', and Linton, 'Gender, Savagery, Tobacco'.

62 Rich, *The Irish Hubbub*, p. 43.

63 James I, 'A Counterblaste to Tobacco', p. 218.

64 Hall, *Work for Chimny-sweepers*, sig. A.iii.r.

65 James I, 'A Counterblaste to Tobacco', p. 221.

66 Deacon, *Tobacco Tortured*, p. 55.

67 James I, 'A Covnterblaste to Tobacco', p. 214.

68 Deacon, *Tobacco Tortured*, p. 8. On fears towards foreigners in early modern England, see especially Harris, *Foreign Bodies and the Body Politic*.

69 *Thomas Platter's Travels in England 1599*, p. 170.

70 On the new tax, see, for instance, Brooks, *Tobacco*, pp. 58–9, 88–90.

ALLEN F. ROBERTS: 'Smoking in Sub-Saharan Africa'

1 Soapstone pipes dating to around 1000 BCE have been discovered in Tanzania (personal communication, Merrick Posnansky 2001). On medicinal smoking, see, for example, Christopher Davis, *Death in Abeyance: Illness and Therapy Among the Tabwa of Central Africa* (Edinburgh, 2000), p. 237 and passim.

Wolfgang Cremer of Cologne is preparing a book on the smoking of Sub-Saharan Africa, and has been kind enough to comment upon a draft of the present paper; but I was not able to consult his manuscript before publication of my piece.

2 Jacques Dopagne, *Magritte* (Paris, 1977), p. 9.

3 Nicholas Thomas, *Entangled Objects: Exchange, Material Culture and Colonialism in the Pacific* (Cambridge, MA, 1991), p. 143 and passim.

4 Dopagne, *Magritte*, p. 9.

5 Brian du Toit, 'Man and Cannabis in Africa: A Study of Diffusion', *African Economic History*, I (1976), pp. 17–35; John Edward Philips, 'African Smoking and Pipes', *Journal of African History*, XXIV (1983), pp. 303–19; Berthold Laufer, Wilfred Hambly and Ralph Linton, 'Tobacco and its Use in Africa', *Field Museum of Natural History Anthropology Leaflet*, XXIX (1930).

6 Daniel Beaumont, '*Alf Laylah wa Laylah; or, The 1001 Nights*', www.arabiannights.org/index2. The flip assertion that Sindbad may have been smoking cannabis is my own.

7 Philips, 'African Smoking and Pipes', pp. 308, 313 and 315. Other scholars suggest that water pipes were invented – or at least developed and enjoyed – in ancient Persia and brought from there to eastern Africa (W. Cremer, pers. comm., 2002).

8 Philips, 'African Smoking and Pipes', pp. 317–18. For competing theories, see Christopher Decorse, *An Archaeology of Elmina: Africans and Europeans on the Gold Coast, 1400–1900* (Washington, DC, 2001), p. 163; Thurstan Shaw, 'Early Smoking Pipes: In Africa, Europe and America', *Journal of the Royal Anthropological Institute of Great Britain and Ireland*, XC (1960), pp. 272–305; and Ivan Van Sertima, *They Came Before Columbus* (New York, 1976). Alternatively, the Portugese may have introduced tobacco to western Africa in the late sixteenth century (W. Cremer, pers. comm., 2002).

9 Philips, 'African Smoking and Pipes', p. 318; see also Decorse, *An Archaeology of Elmina*, pp. 163–7, 240; and Brian Vivian, 'Searching for the Smoking Gun', unpublished conference paper, 31st Annual CEMERS Conference (1997), Binghamton, NY. Taking snuff is more popular than smoking in some parts of Africa.

10 Ann Wanless, 'Public Pleasures: Smoking and Snuff-taking in Southern Africa', in *Art and Ambiguity: Perspectives on the Brenthurst Collection of Southern African Art*, exh. cat., Johannesburg Art Gallery (1991), pp. 126–43, p. 127.

11 George Metcalf, 'A Microcosm of Why Africans Sold Slaves: Akan Consumption Patterns in the 1770s', *Journal of African History*, XXI/1 (1987), pp. 377–94.

12 *Ibid.*, p. 382.

13 *Ibid.*, p. 388. See also Claude Savary, 'African Pipes', *Tribal Arts*, V/1 (1998), pp. 72–83, p. 76; and Brian Vivian, 'People, Pipes and the Production of Smoke', unpublished conference paper, Society of American Archaeology Annual Meetings (2001), New Orleans.

14 See David Calvocoressi, 'European Trade Pipes in Ghana',

West African Journal of Archaeology, V (1975), pp. 195–200; Iain
Walker, 'The Potential Use of European Clay Tobacco Pipes
in West African Archaeological Research', West African Journal
of Archaeology, V (1975), pp. 165–93; and Jean Lecluse, 'Pipes
d'Afrique noire', 2 vols, privately mimeographed (Liège,
Belgium), vol. II, p. 28.

15 Wanless, 'Public Pleasures', p. 128.

16 Ibid.

17 Ethnography concerning Tabwa people of the Democratic
Republic of the Congo is from my own research as a doctoral
candidate in Anthropology at the University of Chicago,
1974–7. On Tabwa notions of animals that eat cannabis, see
Allen Roberts, Animals in African Art: From the Fantastic to the
Marvelous (Munich, 1996), p. 54.

18 Charles Delhaise, 'Chez les Wabemba', Bulletin de la Société
Royale Belge de Géographie, XXXIII (1908), pp. 173–227, 261–83,
pp. 216–17.

19 See Staffs of Life: Rods, Staffs, Scepters and Wands from the Coudron
Collection of African Art, ed. Allen Roberts (Iowa City, IA, 1994);
and William Dewey, Sleeping Beauties: The Jerome L. Joss
Collection of African Headrests at UCLA (Los Angeles, 1993).

20 Lecluse, 'Pipes d'Afrique noire'; Savary, 'African Pipes'; see
also Enid Schildkraut and Curtis Keim, African Reflections: Art
from Northeastern Zaire (Seattle, 1990); and Arthur Bourgeois,
'Pipes Figuratives de la région du Kwango au Zaïre', Arts
d'Afrique Noire, XCIV (1995), pp. 17–26.

21 See Chokwe! Art and Initiation among Chokwe and Related Peoples,
ed. Manuel Jordán (Munich, 1998), pp. 52, 180.

22 See Julius Lips, The Savage Hits Back (New Haven, CT, 1936),
pp. 128, 150 and 195; and Schildkraut and Keim, African
Reflections, p. 16.

23 Vivian, People, Pipes and the Production of Smoke', 'with
reference to Paul Ozanne, 'Tobacco Pipes of Accra and Shai',
roneo-duplicated and in limited circulation, University of
Ghana Department of Archaeology (Legon, 1964).

24 Johannes Fabian, Out of our Minds: Reason and Madness in the
Exploration of Central Africa (Berkeley, CA, 2000), p. 9 and
passim. I have written a longer review of the book for a forthcoming issue of Africa Today, from which sentences in this
paragraph are adapted.

25 Ibid., pp. 162, 67 and 65.

26 Ibid., pp. 155 and 163.

27 Ibid., pp. 174–5, 163–4 and 172–9.

28 Paul Gebauer, 'Cameroon Tobacco Pipes', African Arts, V/2, 1971,
pp. 28–35, p. 28; Wanless, 'Public Pleasures', p. 128.

29 Gebauer, 'Cameroon Tobacco Pipes', pp. 28–30.

30 Wanless, 'Public Pleasures', pp. 128–30, citing Colin Murray,
E. Krige and V. Gitywa; personal communication, Dana Rush
2001.

31 Auguste Van Acker, 'Dictionnaire kitabwa-français, français-
kitabwa', Annales du Musée Royal du Congo Belge, serie V
(Tervuren, Belgium, 1907), p. 52; Delhaise, 'Chez les

Wabemba', p. 211.

32 Wanless, 'Public Pleasures', p. 131, citing V. Gitywa; and personal communications from Manuel Jordán, Robert Papini
and Merrick Posnansky, 2001.

33 Allen Roberts, 'Difficult Decisions, Perilous Acts', in Insight
and Artistry in African Divination, ed. John Pemberton
(Washington, DC, 2000), vol. III, pp. 83–98, pp. 86, 95; Philips,
'African Smoking and Pipes', p. 314, citing Jean-Paul Lebeuf;
James Fernandez, Bwiti: An Ethnography of the Religious
Imagination in Africa (Princeton, NJ, 1982), pp. 4 and 383.

34 Wanless, 'Public Pleasures', p. 130, citing Colin Murray. The
Sotho saying has an equally ribald French counterpart in
'faire une pipe'.

35 The Luba pipe is illustrated and discussed in an entry by
Allen Roberts in Masterpieces from Central Africa, ed. Gustaaf
Verswijver et al. (Tervuren, Belgium, 1995), illus. 175; the
Tabwa pipe is illustrated and discussed by Allen Roberts in
The Rising of a New Moon: A Century of Tabwa Art, ed. Allen
Roberts and Evan Maurer (Ann Arbor, MI, 1995), pp. 178–9,
with further stylistic comparison on p. 246. Lecluse, 'Pipes
d'Afrique noire', illustrates two other anthropomorphic Luba
water pipes, another is mentioned in Delhaise, 'Chez les
Wabemba', and a fourth in A. Swann, Fighting the Slave Hunters
in Central Africa (London, 1910).

36 Figurative stools and several other Luba art forms are
mnemonic, as discussed in Mary Nooter Roberts and Allen F.
Roberts, Memory: Luba Art and the Making of History (Munich,
1996).

37 Roberts, Rising of a New Moon.

38 See Anita Jacobson-Widding, 'Red–White–Black as a Mode of
Thought', Uppsala Studies in Cultural Anthropology, I; and Allen
Roberts, 'Insight; or, NOT Seeing is Believing', in SECRECY:
African Art that Conceals and Reveals, ed. Mary Nooter (New
York, 1993), pp. 64–9.

39 K. Slama, 'Why Tobacco Is an Urgent Problem for Africa
Today', www.ingcat.org/html/slama1.html.
Other relevant information can be obtained by calling up
'tobacco in Africa' on any Web browser.

RUDI MATTHEE: 'Tobacco in Iran'

1 Adam Olearius, Newe Beschreibung der Muscowitischen und
Persischen Reyse (Schleswig, 1656; facsimile reprint, Tübingen,
1971), p. 645; Egon Caesar Corti, A History of Smoking, trans.
Paul England (London, 1931), p. 144.

2 Garcia de Silva y Figueroa, Comentarios de D. Garcia de Silva y
Figueroa de la embajada que de parte del rey de España Don Felipe III
hizo al rey xa Abas de Persia, 2 vols (Madrid, 1903), vol. II, p. 403;
see also Thomas Herbert, Travels in Persia, 1627–29, ed. and
abridged by William Foster (London, 1928), p. 261.

3 ʿAqili Khurasani, Makhzan al-adviyah (Tehran, 2535 Sh./1976
CE), p. 275.

4 Hasan Simsar, 'Nazari bih paydayish-i qalyan va chupuq dar Iran', *Hunar va Mardum*, XVII (1342 Sh./1963 CE), pp. 14–25; 'L'Apparition du narghileh et de la chibouque', *Objets et Mondes*, XI (1971), p. 84.

5 It is said that tobacco was brought to India in 914 AH/1508–9 CE, although it did not become popular until the reign of Sultan Akbar (1556–1605 CE). See Sahba'i Dahlavi, *Shar-i Mina Bazar* (Kanpur, 1903), p. 105.

6 Shahnaz Razpush, 'Galiān', *Encyclopædia Iranica* (2000), vol. X, p. 263; Jakob Tanner, 'Rauchzeichen: Zur Geschichte von Tabak und Hanf', in *Tabakfragen: Rauchen aus kulturwissenschaftlicher Sicht*, ed. Thomas Hengartner and Christoph Maria Merki (Zurich, 1996), p. 23.

7 Thus in the early nineteenth century the French traveller Perrin noted that the Afghans were not nearly as addicted to the *qalyan* as the Iranians. See N. Perrin, *L'Afghanistan; ou, description géographique du pays théatre de la guerre* (Paris, 1842), p. 128.

8 Early images of water pipes all show this straight reed. See, for example, the drawings in Johann Neander, *Tabacologia medico-cheirurgico pharmaceutica* (Leiden, 1622), p. 247; Jean Chardin, *Voyages du chevalier Chardin en Perse, et autres lieux de l'Orient*, 10 vols and atlas (Paris, 1810–11), atlas, plate XIX; Bedros Bedik, *Chehil sutun, seu explicatio utriusque celeberrimi, ac pretiosissimi theatri quadraginta columnarum in Perside orientis* (Vienna, 1678), p. 288. This strengthens the assertion by a Persian source that the coiled tube was invented during the reign of Shah Sultan Husayn (r. 1694–1722 CE). See Muhammad Muhsin Mustawfi, *Zubdat al-tavarikh*, ed. Behruz Gudarzi (Tehran, 1375 Sh./1996 CE), p. 138.

9 Edward Ives, *A Voyage from England to India in the Year MDCCLIV* (London, 1773), p. 224. Another creative way that poor people used to construct a water pipe was by using the tibia of a sheep, observed by O'Donovan in Central Asia in 1881. See Edmond O'Donovan, *The Merv Oasis: Travels and Adventures East of the Caspian during the Years 1879–80–81*, 2 vols (London, 1882), vol. II, p. 440.

10 Ibrahim Pur-i Davud, *Hurmazdnamah* (Tehran, 1331 Sh./1952 CE), p. 208.

11 C. Elgood, *Safavid Medical Practice* (London, 1970), p. 41.

12 Neander, *Tabacologia*, pp. 247, 249.

13 Heinrich von Poser, *Tage Buch seiner Reise von Konstantinopel aus durch Bulgarey, Armenien, Persien und Indien* (Jena, 1675).

14 Olearius, *Newe Beschreibung*, p. 597; Chardin, *Voyages du chevalier Chardin*, vol. III, p. 302; Thomas Herbert, *Some Years Travel into Divers Parts of Asia and Afrique* (London, 1638), p. 198; H. Dunlop, ed., *Bronnen tot de geschiedenis der Oostindische Compagnie in Perzië, 1611–1638* (The Hague, 1930), pp. 35, 176.

15 Ange de St Joseph, *Souvenirs de la Perse et autres lieux de l'Orient (1664–1678)*, ed. Michel Bastiaensen (Brussels, 1985), pp. 103–5; John Fryer, *A New Account of East India and Persia, Being Nine Years' Travels, 1672–1681*, ed. W. Crooke, 3 vols (London, 1909–15), vol. II, p. 228.

16 Chardin, *Voyages du chevalier Chardin*, vol. III, p. 302; vol. IV, pp. 165–6.

17 Sr Poullet, *Nouvelles relations du Levant . . . Avec une exacte description . . . du royaume de Perse*, 2 vols (Paris, 1668), vol. II, pp. 328–9. One observer of early nineteenth-century Iran noted that all who smoked in the army were followed by cinder-bearers, 'who were of themselves sufficient to compose a small army'. See Moritz von Kotzebue, *Narrative of a Journey into Persia in the Suite of the Imperial Russian Embassy in the Year 1817* (London, 1819), pp. 142–3.

18 Jean-Baptiste Tavernier, *Les six voyages de Jean-Bapt. Tavernier en Turquie, en Perse et aux Indes*, 2 vols (Utrecht, 1712), pp. 598–9.

19 Fryer, *A New Account of East India and Persia*, vol. II, p. 248.

20 Cornelis De Bruyn, *Reizen over Moskovie, door Persie en Indie* (Amsterdam, 1714), p. 137.

21 Engelbert Kaempfer, *Die Reisetagebücher Engelbert Kaempfers*, ed. Karl Meier-Lemgo (Wiesbaden, 1968), pp. 65, 77–8.

22 Du Mans, 'Estats de 1660', in Francis Richard, *Raphaël du Mans missionnaire en Perse au XVIIe s.*, 2 vols (Paris, 1995), vol. II, p. 104. The term *dukkan-i tanbaku-furushi* appears in a *waqfnamah* issued by Shah Sultan Husayn in 1118 HQ./1706–7 CE, which turned a great many shops and ateliers, including tobacco shops, in Isfahan, into *waqf* (religiously endowed) property. See Sayyid Husayn Umidyani, 'Nigarishi ba yik vaqfnamah-i tarikhi az dawrah-i Safaviyah', *Ganjineh Asnad*, XXI–XXII (1375 Sh./1996 CE), p. 23.

23 David T. Courtwright, *Force of Habit: Drugs and the Making of the Modern World* (Cambridge, MA, 2001), p. 20.

24 Wolfgang Schivelbusch, 'Die trockene Trunkenheit des Tabaks', in G. Völger, *Rausch und Realität: Drogen im Kulturvergleich*, 2 vols (Cologne, 1981), vol. I, pp. 216–23.

25 In Sir William Ouseley, *Travels in Various Countries of the East* (London, 1819), p. 341.

26 Yet early references to hashish suggest that in medieval times it, too, was consumed in solid form rather than smoked. See Franz Rosenthal, *The Herb: Hashish versus Medieval Muslim Society* (Leiden, 1971), pp. 64–5.

27 Courtwright, *Force of Habit*, p. 105.

28 Berthold Laufer, *Tobacco and its Use in Asia* (Chicago, 1924), p. 27; Jordan Goodman, *Tobacco in History: The Culture of Dependence* (London and New York, 1993), p. 88.

29 For the hypothesis that the water pipe and hashish smoking were originally linked, see Carl Hartwich, *Die menschliche Genussmittel* (Leipzig, 1911), p. 231, quoted in Tanner, 'Rauchzeichen', p. 24.

30 Fryer, *A New Account of East India and Persia*, vol. III, pp. 99–100. According to Du Mans and Tavernier, the Uzbegs had (recently) taught the Iranians to mix tobacco with cannabis. See Richard, 'Estats et mémoire', vol. II, p. 104; and Tavernier, *Les six voyages*, vol. I, pp. 716–17.

31 Du Mans, 'Estats de 1660', vol. II, p. 106; Neander, *Tabacologia*, p. 247.

32 Olearius, *Newe Beschreibung*, p. 597; and Ambrosio Bembo, 'Viaggio e Giornale per parte dell'Asia di quattro anni incirca fatto da me Ambrosio Bembo Nob. Veneto', MS James Ford Bell Library, University of Minnesota, Minneapolis, fol. 244. Edward Ives makes a reference to *qalyans* made of a coconut shell and a bamboo reed being used on the island of Kharq in 1758. See Ives, *A Voyage from England to India*, p. 224.

33 Neander, *Tabacologia*, p. 247. Silva y Figueroa in 1619 mentioned *qalyans* made of gold at Shah ʿAbbas I's court, and various foreign envoys were treated to such water pipes during audiences at the court of Shah Sultan Husayn. See Silva y Figueroa, *Comentarios*, vol. II, p. 403; François Valentyn, *Oud en nieuw Oost Indien*, 8 vols in 5 tomes (Amsterdam, 1726), vol. V, p. 277; and P. P. Bushev, *Posol'stvo Artemiya Volynskogo v Iran v 1715–1718 gg.* (Moscow, 1978), p. 119.

34 Du Mans, 'Estats de 1660', vol. II, pp. 78, 267; De Bruyn, *Reizen over Moskovie*, pp. 102–3.

35 Fryer, *A New Account of East India and Persia*, vol. II, p. 259. This rule must have been instituted under Shah Sulayman, for, according to Tavernier, the Armenians were privileged over other non-Muslims in being allowed to ride richly caparisoned horses. See Tavernier, *Les six voyages*, vol. I, p. 468.

36 T. M. Chevalier Lycklama a Nijeholt, *Voyage en Russie, au Caucase et en Perse*, 4 vols (Paris and Amsterdam, 1873), vol. II, p. 244.

37 Pur-i Davud, *Hurmazdnamah*, p. 205.

38 Tavernier, *Les six voyages*, vol. I, p. 675.

39 Kaempfer, *Die Reisetagebücher Engelbert Kaempfers*, p. 79; Du Mans, 'Estats de 1660', vol. II, p. 104. Illustrations in *Treasures of Islam* (London, 1985), p. 119; and J. M. Rogers, ed. and trans., *The Topkapi Saray Museum: The Albums and Illustrated Manuscripts* (London, 1986), pp. 124, 182.

40 Bedik, *Chehil sutun*, p. 286.

41 Poullet, *Nouvelles relations du Levant*, vol. II, pp. 327–8.

42 Du Mans, 'Estats de 1660', vol. II, pp. 75, 81; Tavernier, *Les six voyages*, vol. I, p. 714; De Bruyn, *Reizen over Moskovie*, p. 172.

43 Fryer, *A New Account of East India and Persia*, vol. II, p. 210.

44 Michael Glünz, 'Das Vorspiel zur Revolution: Der iranische Tabakboykott von 1891/92 und der historische Kontext des Rauchens in Iran', in Hengartner and Merki, *Tabakfragen*, p. 148, quoting Samuel Greene Wheeler Benjamin, *Persia and the Persians* (Boston, MA, 1887), p. 103.

45 C. J. Wills, *In the Land of the Lion and the Sun or Modern Persia* (London, 1883), p. 29.

46 Harry de Windt, *A Ride to India across Persia and Baluchistan* (London, 1891), pp. 46, 86.

47 Muhandis Muhammad Sadiq Ansari, 'Sanʿat-i tutun dar Iran', *Kaweh*, IV (Munich, 1345 Sh./1966 CE), p. 178.

48 K. Seligmann, *Ueber drey höchst seltene Persische Handschriften* (Vienna, 1833), p. 41

49 Khurasani, *Makhzan al-adviyah*, p. 275.

50 Felix Klein-Franke, 'No Smoking in Paradise: The Habit of Tobacco Smoking Judged by Muslim Law', *Le Muséon*, CVI (1993), pp. 155–83.

51 Rasul Ja ʿfariyan, *ʿIlal-i bar uftadan-i Safaviyan* (Tehran, 1372 Sh./1993 CE), p. 352; a list of Shia anti-smoking tracts appears in Aqa Buzurg Tihrani, *al-Dhariʿah ila tasanif al-Shiʿah* (Najaf, 1378 Sh./1959 CE), vol. XI, pp. 173–5, and in Rasul Ja ʿfariyan, *Safaviyah dar ʿarsah-i din, farhang va siyasat*, 3 vols (Qum, 1379 Sh./2000 CE), vol. III, p. 1145.

52 For a repeal of the ban, see Muhammad Maʿsum b. Khajigi Isfahani, *Khulasat al-siyar, tarikh-i ruzgar-i Shah Safi Safavi* (Tehran, 1368 Sh./1989 CE), p. 39; Abu'l Hasan Qazvini, *Favaʾid al-Safaviyah*, ed., *Maryam Mirahmadi* (Tehran, 1367 Sh./1988 CE), p. 48.

53 Tavernier, *Les six voyages*, vol. I, p. 599.

54 ʿAbd al-Hayy Radawi Kashani, 'Hadiqat al-Shiʿah', in Rasul Jaʿfariyan, *Din va siyasat dar dawrah-i Safavi* (Qum, 1370 Sh./1991 CE), p. 350.

55 Ange de St Joseph, *Souvenirs de la Perse*, pp. 102–5.

56 Heinz Pampus, 'Die theologische Enzyklopädie Bihār al-Anwār des Muhammad Bāqir al-Maǧlisī (1037–1110 Sh./1627–99 CE): Ein Beitrag zur Literaturgeschichte der Šiʿda in der Safawidenzeit', inaugural dissertation, Friedrich Wilhelm Universität, Bonn, 1970, p. 45.

57 Tavernier, *Les Six Voyages*, vol. I, p. 599.

58 Du Mans, 'Estats de 1660', vol. II, p. 106; Fryer, *A New Account of East India and Persia*, vol. III, p. 7.

59 Public Record Office, London, FO60/482, Arthur Herbert, *Report on the Present State of Persia*, May 7, 1886, fol. 143.

60 Public Record Office, FO/60/480, enclosure in Nicholson, *Tehran to London*, Oct. 23, 1886, fols 199–202.

61 Nikki R. Keddie, *Religion and Rebellion in Iran: The Iranian Tobacco Protest of 1891–1892* (London, 1966), and Ann K. S. Lambton, 'The Tobacco Régie: Prelude to Revolution', *Studia Islamica*, XXII (1966), pp. 71–90; amd Shaykh Hasan Isfahani Karbal'i, *Tarikh-i dukhaniyah*, ed. Rasul Jaʿfariyan (Tehran, 1377 Sh./1998 CE).

P. RAM MANOHAR: 'Smoking and Āyurvedic Medicine in India'

1 Srisatyapala Bhisagacharya, ed. and trans., *Kasyapa Saṃhitā* (Varanasi, 2000), pp. 172–3.

2 K. P. Sreekumari, ed., *Vagbhata's Astāṅga Samgraha* (Trivandrum, 1982), p. 172.

3 Narayan Ram Acharya, ed., *Suśruta Saṃhitā* (Varanasi, 1996), 4.40.15; Harinarayana Sharma, ed., *Astāṅga Hrdayam* (Varanasi, 1996), 1.21.1, 22.

4 *Astāṅga Hrdayam*, 1.3.15, 47.

5 *Ibid.*, 6.3.47–8, 58; 6.6.18; *Kasyapa Saṃhitā*, pp. 172–3.

6 P. V. Sharma ed., *Caraka Saṃhitā* (Varanasi, 1983), 1.11.54.

7 *Astāṅga Samgraha*, p. 63.

8 Ramavalamba Shastri, ed. and trans., *Harita Saṃhitā* (Varanasi, 1985), 2.7.1–4.

9 *Kasyapa Saṃhitā*, pp. 170–75.

10 Kenneth Zysk, *Medicine in the Veda: Religious Healing in the Veda* (Delhi, 1996), p. 14.

11 *Caraka Saṃhitā*, 1.5.20–56; *Astāṅga Hṛdayam*, 1.2.6.

12 *Suśruta Saṃhitā*, 4.40.10; *Astāṅga Samgraha*, p. 407.

13 *Caraka Saṃhitā*, 1.5.37; *Suśruta Saṃhitā*, 4.40.3; Indradev Tripathi, ed., *Cakradatta* (Varanasi, 1991), p. 689; Parasurama Shastri, ed., *Sarngadhara Saṃhitā* (Varanasi, 1985), 3.9.1; K. R. Srikanthamurthy, ed. and trans., *Bhavaprakasa* (Varanasi, 1998), vol. I, p. 595.

14 *Suśruta Saṃhitā*, 4.40.14, 18.

15 *Caraka Saṃhitā*, 1.5.41–5; *Suśruta Saṃhitā*, 4.40.11; *Astāṅga Samgraha*, pp. 407–8; *Astāṅga Hṛdayam*, 1.21.2–4; *Sarngadhara Saṃhitā*, 3.9.3–6; *Bhavaprakasa*, p. 595.

16 *Caraka Saṃhitā*, 1.5.33–5; *Suśruta Saṃhitā*, 4.40.13; *Astāṅga Samgraha*, p. 408.

17 Girijadayalu Sukla, ed., *Bhela Saṃhitā* (Varanasi, 1999), 1.6.32–43.

18 The plants mentioned are: *Aquilaria agallocha, Commiphora mukul, Cyperus rotundus, Taxus baccata, Parmelia perlata, Nardostachys jatamansi, Vettiveria zizanoides, Cinnamomum zeylanicum, Madhuca longifolia, Aegle marmelos, Prunus cerasoides, Pinus roxburghii, Shorea robusta, Vateria indica, Cymbopogon citratus, Randia dumetorum, Boswellia serrata, Crocus sativus, Phaseolus mungo, Hordeum vulgare, Sesamum indicum, Nelumbo nucifera, Nymphaea alba, Ficus bengalensis, Ficus racemosa, Ficus religiosa, Ficus lacor, Symplocos racemosa, Glycyrrhiza glabra, Cassia fistula, Prunus cerasoides, Rubia cordifolia, Celastrus paniculatus, Curcuma longa, Terminalia chebula, Terminalia belerica, Emblica officinalis, Gmelina arborea, Oroxylum indicum, Stereospermum suaveolens, Premna integrifolia, Solanum indicum, Solanum xanthocarpum, Desmodium gangeticum, Pseudarthria viscida, Tribulus terrestris, Piper nigrum, Piper longum, Zingiber officinale, Ferula foetida, Balanites aegyptiaca, Tinospora cordifolia, Pistacia integerrima, Mesua ferrea, Plectranthus vettiveroides, Santalum album, Elettaria cardamomum, Liquidamber orientalis, Callicarpa macrophylla, Delphinium zalil, Angelica glauca, Cinnamomum tamala, Commiphora myrrha* and *Calophyllum inophyllum. Caraka Saṃhitā*, 1.5.20–23, 25–7; *Suśruta Saṃhitā*, 4.40.4; *Astāṅga Hṛdayam*, 1.21.13–18. Also see references 19–27 and 50–52.

19 *Caraka Saṃhitā*, 1.5.27; *Suśruta Saṃhitā*, 4.40.4; *Astāṅga Hṛdayam*, 1.21.17.

20 Tendons of animals such as cows, cat skin, shed snake skin, hoof, horns, crab shell, dried fish, worms, dried meat, clarified butter, yoghurt, fat, bone marrow, tallow, lac, beeswax, human hair and bile, urine, faeces and claws of fox, bull, ram, owl, mongoose and vulture. *Caraka Saṃhitā*, 6.10.51; *Suśruta Saṃhitā*, 4.40.4.

21 *Caraka Saṃhitā*, 1.5.26; *Suśruta Saṃhitā*, 4.40.4; *Astāṅga Hṛdayam*, 1.21.18.

22 *Boswellia serrata* (gum), lac, *Elettaria cardamomum* (seeds), *Nelumbo nucifera* (stamens), *Nymphaea alba* (tubers), *Ficus bengalensis, Ficus religiosa, Ficus lacor, Symplocos racemosa* (bark), sugar, liquorice roots, *Cassia fistula* (bark), *Prunus cerasoides* (heartwood), *Rubia cordifolia* (whole plant) and aromatic drugs such as *Aquilaria agallocha* (wood), *Cinnamomum zeylanicum* (bark) and *Commiphora mukul* (exudate). *Astāṅga Hṛdayam*, 1.21.16–17.

23 Tallow, clarified butter, beeswax, *Leptadenia reticulata* (tubers), *Roscoea procera, Microstylis wallichi, Microstylis musifera, Habenaria* species, *Teramnus labialis* and *Phaseolus trilobus* (roots). *Caraka Saṃhitā*, 1.5.25–6.

24 *Clitoria ternatea* (roots), *Celastrus paniculatus* (seeds), orpiment, realgar and aromatic drugs such as *Aquilaria agallocha* (wood), *Cinnamomum zeylanicum* (bark) and *Commiphora mukul* (exudate). *Ibid.*, 1.5.26–7.

25 *Solanum indicum* (roots), *Solanum xanthocarpum* (roots), *Piper longum* (dry fruits), *Zingiber officinale* (rhizome), *Piper nigrum* (dry fruits), *Cassia occidentalis* (whole plant), *Ferula foetida* (exudate), *Balanites aegyptiaca*, Realgar, *Tinospora cordifolia* (stem) and *Pistacia integerrima* (galls). *Suśruta Saṃhitā*, 4.40.4.

26 Ligaments, skin, hoof and horns of animals such as cow, dried fish and dry meat. *Ibid.*, 4.40.4.

27 Fibres of *Linum usitattisimum, Hordeum vulgare* (grains), clarified butter, *Prunus roxburghii* (exudate and wood), *Shorea robusta* (exudate) and *Cedrus deodara* (wood). *Ibid.*, 1.37.21.

28 *Caraka Saṃhitā*, 1.5.51; *Suśruta Saṃhitā*, 4.40.5; *Astāṅga Samgraha*, pp. 408–9; *Astāṅga Hṛdayam*, 1.21.7–8; *Bhavaprakasa*, p. 597.

29 *Caraka Saṃhitā*, 1.5.51–2.

30 *Caraka Saṃhitā*, 1.5.50; *Suśruta Saṃhitā*, 4.40.5; *Bhela Saṃhitā*, 1.6.29; *Astāṅga Samgraha*, p. 408; *Astāṅga Hṛdayam*, 1.21.8–9; *Sārṅgadhara Saṃhitā*, 3.9.11–14; *Bhavaprakasa*, p. 597.

31 *Astāṅga Samgraha*, p. 408.

32 *Caraka Saṃhitā*, 1.5.49–50; *Suśruta Saṃhitā*, 4.40.5; *Astāṅga Hṛdayam*, 1.21.8, 21.

33 *Caraka Saṃhitā*, 1.5.23–5; *Suśruta Saṃhitā*, 4.40.4; *Astāṅga Samgraha*, p. 409; *Sārṅgadhara Saṃhitā*, 3.9.15–18.

34 *Caraka Saṃhitā*, 1.5.46–8; *Suśruta Saṃhitā*, 4.40.8; *Astāṅga Samgraha*, p. 409; *Astāṅga Hṛdayam*, 1.21.9–11; *Sārṅgadhara Saṃhitā*, 3.9.17–18.

35 *Caraka Saṃhitā*, 1.5.36; *Suśruta Saṃhitā*, 4.40.18; *Astāṅga Samgraha*, p. 410.

36 *Caraka Saṃhitā*, 1.5.37; *Astāṅga Samgraha*, p. 410; *Astāṅga Hṛdayam*, 1.21.11–13; *Bhavaprakasa*, p. 598.

37 *Caraka Saṃhitā*, 1.5.37; *Suśruta Saṃhitā*, 4.40.18; *Astāṅga Samgraha*, p. 410; *Astāṅga Hṛdayam*, 1.21.11–12.

38 *Suśruta Saṃhitā*, 4.40.18; *Astāṅga Samgraha*, p. 410.

39 *Suśruta Saṃhitā*, 4.40.18; *Astāṅga Samgraha*, p. 411.

40 *Caraka Saṃhitā*, 1.5.52–3.

41 *Ibid.*, 1.5.53–4.

42 *Ibid.*, 1.5.54–6.

43 *Suśruta Saṃhitā*, 4.40.12; *Astāṅga Samgraha*, p. 407; *Astāṅga Hṛdayam*, 1.21.4–5; *Sārṅgadhara Saṃhitā*, 3.9.7; *Bhavaprakasa*, p. 596.

44 *Caraka Saṃhitā*, 1.5.39; *Astāñga Samgraha*, p. 407; *Astāñga Hṛdayam*, 1.21.5; *Sārñgadhara Saṃhitā*, 3.9.7–8.

45 *Caraka Saṃhitā*, 1.5.27–33; *Suśruta Saṃhitā*, 4.40.15–16; *Bheḷa Saṃhitā*, 1.6.31–40; *Astāñga Samgraha*, p. 407.

46 *Bhavaprakasa*, p. 595–9.

47 *Caraka Saṃhitā*, 6.3.314–15, 6.9.93, 6.10.53.

48 Ibid., 6.3.308–9, 6.9.93, 6.10.53, 6.14.48; *Suśruta Saṃhitā*, 4.40.19.

49 *Caraka Saṃhitā*, 6.3.308, 6.9.75, 6.17.77–9, 6.18.75, 130; *Astāñga Hṛdayam*, 6.7.33.

50 *Astāñga Hṛdayam*, 4.4.11–12.

51 Ibid., 3.4.2.

52 *Caraka Saṃhitā*, 6.14.48; *Astāñga Hṛdayam*, 4.8.18.

53 G. J. Meulenbeld, *Studien zur Indologie und Iranistik: The Search for Clues to the Chronology of Sanskrit Medical Texts, as Illustrated by the History of Bhanga-Cannabis Sativa* (Reinbek, 1989), pp. 59–70; Jharkande Ojha and Umapati Mishra, eds, *Dhanvantari Nighantu* (Varanasi, 1996), pp. 48–9; P. V. Sharma and Guruprasad Sharma, eds, *Kayyadeva Nighantu* (Varanasi, 1979) p. 648.

54 Sadashiva Shastri Joshi, ed., *Yogaratnakara* (Varanasi, 1939), pp. 26–7.

55 Indradev Tripathi, ed., *Raja Nighantu* (Varanasi, 1998), pp. 110–11.

BARNABAS TATSUYA SUZUKI: 'Tobacco Culture in Japan'

1 Diary of Richard Cocks, 1615–22, *Historical Documents in Foreign Languages Relating to Japan*, vol. III, part ii (Tokyo, 1980), p. 311.

2 C. R. Boxer, *The Christian Century in Japan, 1549–1650* (Los Angeles, 1974).

3 For further reading, see Razan Hayashi, *Razan Bunshu* [Razan anthology] (n.p., 1661); Hitsudai Hitomi, *Honcho Shokkan* [Food encyclopedia of Japan] (n.p., 1692); Shinken Mukai, *Enso-koh* [A study of tobacco] (n.p., 1708); Ekken Kaibara, *Yamato Honzo* [A herbal of Japan] (n.p., 1708); Ryo-an Terashima, *Wakan Sansai Zue* [Illustrated encyclopedia of Japan and China] (n.p., 1715); Yuzan Daidoji, *Ochibo-shu* [Gleanings] (Edo, 1728); B. T. Suzuki, *Kitsuen Denraishi no Kenkyu* [A historical study of smoking introduction into Japan] (Kyoto, 1999), pp. 13–25.

4 Suzuki, *Kitsuen Denraishi no Kenkyu*, pp. 33–82.

5 S. A. Dickson, 'Panacea or Precious Bane?', *Arents Tobacco Collection* (New York, 1954), vol. V, p. 78; M. Fleiuss, *Apostilas de historia do Brasil* (Port Alegra, 1940), pp. 69, 76.

6 Suzuki, *Kitsuen Denraishi no Kenkyu*, pp. 68–82, and B. T. Suzuki, 'Ryukyu Ohrai Koh' [A study of Ryukyu correspondences], *Tabako-shi Kenkyu* [A study of tobacco history], no. 74 (Tokyo, 2000), pp. 18–21.

7 Suzuki, *Kitsuen Denraishi no Kenkyu*, pp. 222–9.

8 Rom von Dorotheus Schilling OFM, 'Der erste Tabak in Japan', *Monumenta Nipponica*, V (1942), pp. 128–9.

9 J. Alden Mason, *The Use of Tobacco in Mexico and South America* (Chicago, 1924), pp. 8–9; Suzuki, *Kitsuen Denraishi no Kenkyu*, pp. 212–13; B. T. Suzuki, 'Tabako, Kitsuen Denrai Manila (Spain) Setsu no Shomondai' [Various questions on the views that tobacco and smoking was introduced from Manila or by the Spanish], *Tabako-shi Kenkyu* [A study of tobacco history], no. 73 (Tokyo, 2000), pp. 17–26.

10 Seiichi Iwao, *Shinpan Shuinsen Boeki no Kenkyu* [A study of Shuinsen trade, new edition] (Tokyo, 1985), pp. 293–4, 313; 'Copie Missive door Jeremias van Vliet naer Japan in dato 8 Juni Aº1634. Judia op 't Compt Siam' (Kol. Archief 1025).

11 *Journaal van de Negotie des Comptoirs Firando, Anno 1638, 1639, 1640, 1641*, General State Archives of the Netherlands, The Hague; *Hirado-shi Shi* [The history of Hirado City/Overseas Historical Record] (Hirado, 1998, 2000).

12 Suzuki, 'Tabako, Kitsuen Denrai Manila (Spain) Setsu no Shomondai', pp. 17–26.

13 Before tobacco cultivation started in Japan, the price of tobacco was extremely high; a leaf of tobacco was sold at 3 *momme* (approx. 11 grams) of silver in 1599 (Ishizaki). Early documents such as *Rokuon Nichiroku* [Diary of Rokuon Temple] (Kyoto, 1593) and *Ryukyu Ohrai* [Ryukyu correspondences] (Ryukyu, 1603) describe the tobacco or smoking pipes used by Buddhist priests and people of Kyoto high society. See: Taichu, *Ryukyu Ohrai* (1603); Shigeru Yokoyama, *Ryukyu Shintohki* [A history of Ryukyu Shinto = Taichu anthology] (Tokyo, 1970), p. 144; Zennosuke Tsuji, ed., *Rokuon Nichiroku* (Tokyo, 1961); Juroh Ishizaki, *Tabako no Hon* (Tokyo, 1967), p. 19; Suzuki, *Kitsuen Denraishi no Kenkyu*, pp. 118–19.

14 T. Hayashi, *Zuroku Sadoh-shi* [Illustrated history of the tea ceremony] (Kyoto, 1980), pp. 58, 60, 72, 92, 103–6, 214–15, 307.

15 See T. Nishimura, *Kirishitan to Sadoh* [Christians and the tea ceremony] (Tokyo, 1948); Peter Milward, *Ocha to Misa* [Tea and the mass] (Kyoto, 1995); Sohichi Masubuchi, *Sadoh to Jujika* [The tea ceremony and the cross] (Tokyo, 1996).

16 Yoshichika Kiyonakatei, *Mesamashi-so* [Awaking herb] (Edo, 1815).

17 Diary of Richard Cocks, vol. II, part ii (Tokyo, 1979), p. 238.

TIMOTHY BROOK: 'Smoking in Imperial China'

1 Quoted in Chen Cong, *Yancao pu* [Tobacco manual] (1805; repr. Shanghai, 1998), 5.12b.

2 Wu Han, ed., *Chaoxian Li chao shilu zhong de Zhongguo shiliao* [Historical materials concerning China in the veritable records of the Yi dynasty of Korea] (Beijing, 1980), p. 3755, cited in He Lingxiu, 'Qingchu jingshi xiyanfeng deng jige wenti' [Some questions regarding the fashion for smoking and other pleasures in the capital in the early Qing], *Qingshi luncong* [Essays on Qing history] (Beijing, 1999), p. 382.

3 Jonathan Spence, 'Opium Smoking in Ch'ing China', in *Conflict and Control in Late Imperial China*, ed. Frederic Wakeman and Carolyn Grant (Berkeley, CA, 1975), pp. 155–6;

· L. Carrington Goodrich, 'Early Prohibitions of Tobacco in China and Manchuria', *Journal of the American Oriental Society*, LVIII/4 (December 1938), pp. 648–57.

4 Quoted in Yuan Ting, *Zhongguo xiyan shihua* [A popular history of smoking in China] (Beijing, 1995), p. 35.

5 Yao Lü, *Lu shu* [The dew book] (repr. Shanghai, 1998), 10.46a.

6 Yang Shicong, *Yutang weiji* [Bundled writings from Jade Hall] (repr. Taipei, 1968), p. 80.

7 Goodrich, 'Early Prohibitions'.

8 Ye Mengzhu, *Yueshi bian* [A survey of the age] (repr. Shanghai, 1936), 7.13a–b.

9 Wang Pu, *Yin'an suoyu* [Desultory comments from Yin hermitage], quoted in Chen Cong, *Yancao pu*, 1.1b–2a.

10 Yao Lü, *Lu shu*, 10.46a.

11 Quoted in Yuan Ting, *Zhongguo xiyan shihua*, p. 35.

12 Shen Lilong, *Shiwu bencao huizuan* [Complete handbook of edible plants], quoted in Yuan Ting, *Zhongguo xiyan shihua*, p. 129.

13 *Qingpu xianzhi* [Gazetteer of Qingpu county] (1879), 19.43b–44a.

14 These and the following poems appear in Chen Cong, *Yancao pu*, 5.8a; 7.6a–7a.

15 Lu Yao, *Yanpu* [Smoking manual] (1833; repr. Shanghai, 1998), 3b–4b.

16 J. H. Gray, *China: A History of the Laws, Manners and Customs of the People* (London, 1878), vol. II, p. 149.

17 Chen Cong, *Yancao pu*, 3.3b.

18 In his history of Chinese Christianity in Fujian province, Ryan Dunch describes a village scholar rapping a foreign missionary on the head with his pipe for challenging the authority of Confucius; *Fuzhou Protestants and the Making of a Modern China, 1857–1927* (New Haven, 2000), p. 1.

19 The poem, entitled 'Making Fun of my Long Tobacco Pipe', is quoted in Yuan Ting, *Zhongguo xiyan shihua*, p. 71. The author is identified only as the wife of Master Lü of Jinghai.

20 Der Ling, *Old Buddha* (New York, 1928), opposite p. 226.

21 Carl Crossman, *The China Trade: Export Paintings, Furniture, Silver and Other Objects* (Princeton, NJ, 1972), pp. 112–13.

22 Bernhold Laufer, 'Tobacco and its Uses in Asia', Anthropology Leaflet no. 18, Field Museum of Natural History (Chicago, 1924), p. 17.

TIMON SCREECH: 'Tobacco in Edo Period Japan'

1 Herman Ooms, *Tokugawa Ideology: Early Constructs, 1570–1680* (Princeton, NJ, 1985), p. 145.

2 Kobayashi Tatsu, ed., *Horisasareta toshi, Edo, Nagasaki, Amasureudamu, rondon, nyūyōku* [Great cities: Edo, Nagasaki, Amsterdam, London, New York], (Tokyo, 1996), pp. 192–3.

3 Carl Peter (Charles) Thunberg, *Travels* (London, 1796), vol. III, p. 265.

4 Otsuki Gentaku, 'Enroku zufu' [Illustrated treatise on smoking],

in *Bansui zonkyō* [Bansui's echoes] (Tokyo, 1912), vol. I.

5 Kimura Yōjirō, *Edo-ki no nachurarisuto* [Edo naturalists] (Tokyo, 1988), p. 182.

6 Morishima Chūryō, *Bankoku shinwa* [True tales of the myriad nations] (Tokyo, 1948), p. 195.

7 Richard Cocks, *Diary* (London, 1926), vol. I, p. 213.

8 For an overview, see Donald H. Shiveley, 'Bakufu Verses *Kabuki*', *Harvard Journal of Asiatic Studies*, XVIII (1955), pp. 126–64

9 Cocks, vol. I, p. 99.

10 Hōseidō Kisanji, 'Nochi wa mukashi monogatari' [The rest is history], in *Nihon zuihitsu taisei* [Japanese commonplace books], series 3 (Tokyo, 1912), vol. XII, pp. 286.

11 Kimuro Bōun, 'Mita kyō monogatari', in *Nihon zuihitsu taisei*, series 3 (Tokyo, 1929), vol. IV, p. 569. Bōun was in Kyoto in 1780.

12 Shiba Kōkan, 'Shunparō hikki' [Shunparō's jottings], in *Nihon zuihitsu taisei*, series 1 (Tokyo, 1927), vol. I, p. 64.

13 'Mezamashi-gusa' [Wake-up grass], in *Nihon zuihitsu taisei*, series 2, trans. and ed. Seichū-tei Tokushin (Tokyo, 1973), vol. VIII, p. 239.

14 Koike Tōgorō, *Santō Kyōden* (Tokyo, 1961), p. 101. Kyōden was a widower. On marriage, Tama-no-i changed her name to Yuri.

15 Santō Kyōden (Kitao Shigemasa, ill.), *Sakusha tainai totsuki no zu* [Ten months of pregnancy in the author's womb]; for a convenient reproduction, see Timon Screech, *The Lens Within the Heart: The Western Scientific Gaze and Popular Imagery in Later Edo Japan* (Cambridge and New York, 2001), fig. 113.

16 Screech, *The Lens Within the Heart*, p. 117. See also Tani Minezō, *Edo no kopïraitā* [Edo copywriters] (Tokyo, 1986), pp. 55–9.

17 *Ibid.*, p. 56.

BEN RAPAPORT: 'How Do We Smoke?: Accessories and Utensils'

1 Philip Collins, *Smokerama: Classic Tobacco Accoutrements* (San Francisco, 1992), p. 3.

2 This sentence is literally translated into English from Robert Cudell, *Die Sammlung Haus Neuerburg: Ein Büchlein vom Rauchen und Rauchgerät* (Coeln, [i.e., Cologne] 1930), p. 53.

3 H. F. Reemtsma and P. F. Reemtsma, *Tabago: A Picture-Book of Tobacco and the Pleasures of Smoking* (1960), pp. 79, 81.

4 The British Museum established a working party in the 1980s '. . . to analyse the terms used to record object names in the museum, and to incorporate them into an on-line thesaurus . . .'. A wealth of tobacco accessory terms is found on the Internet at http://www.mdocassn.demon.co.uk/bmobj/ Objintro.htm

5 Salmon & Gluckstein Ltd, *Illustrated Guide for Smokers* (January 1899), p. 143.

6 George Zorn & Company, *Pipes & Smokers Articles*, catalogue, 5th edn, with preface by S. Paul Jung Jr [c. 1892], n. p.

7 http://64.21.33.164/cigarh.html and http://www.antiquere-sources.com/articles/stone.html

8 For evidence to this, subscribe to the *Cigar-Label Gazette*

(www.cigarlabelgazette.com), a bi-monthly journal for the cigar-box label and cigar-band collector; or obtain any of the following books: Joe Davidson, *Art of The Cigar Label* (Secaucus, NJ, 1989); Joe Davidson and Sue Davidson, *Smoker's Art* (1997); Jero L. Gardner, *The Art of the Smoke* (1998) and *Gals and Guys* (1999); Philippe Mesmer, *The Art of Cigar Bands* (2000); and Gerard S. Petrone, *Cigar Box Labels* (1998).

9 Deborah Sampson Shinn, *Matchsafes* (London, 2000), p. 9.

10 *Ibid.*, p. 10.

JOS TEN BERGE: 'The *Belle Epoque* of Opium'

1 J. M. Scott, *The White Poppy: A History of Opium* (London, 1969), p. 11.

2 Martin Booth, *Opium: A History* (London, 1996), p. 105.

3 Grevel Lindop, *The Opium-Eater: A Life of Thomas de Quincey* (London, 1981), p. 249.

4 Arnould de Liedekerke, *La Belle Epoque de l'opium* (Paris, 1984), pp. 97–8; Jos ten Berge, 'Het rijk van de grijze fee: Morfinomanie in decadent Parijs', *Kunstlicht*, XX/2 (1999), pp. 38–45.

5 Virginia Berridge and Griffith Edwards, *Opium and the People: Opiate Use in Nineteenth-Century England* (London and New York, 1987), pp. 195–205.

6 Paul Butel, *L'Opium: Histoire d'une fascination* (Paris, 1955), pp. 352–3.

7 De Liedekerke, *La Belle Epoque de l'opium*, p. 146.

8 *Ibid.*, p. 170.

9 *Ibid.*, p. 171.

10 Paul Bonnetain, *L'Opium* (Geneva, 1980), p. 281.

11 De Liedekerke, *La Belle Epoque de l'opium*, pp. 147 and 151–4.

12 Claude Farrère, 'Fou-Tchéou-Road', in *Fumée d'opium* (1904) (Paris, 1906), p. 146.

13 Roger Dupouy, *Les Opiomanes: Mangeurs, buveurs et fumeurs d'opium* (Paris, 1912), pp. 59–60.

14 *Ibid.*, p. 96.

15 *Ibid.*, pp. 101–3. This is in reference to Dr Michaut, 'Note sur l'intoxication, morphinique par la Fumée d'Opium, *Bulletin Génerale de Thérapie, Medicine et Chirurgre* (1893), p. 462.

16 *Ibid.*

17 De Liedekerke, *La Belle Epoque de l'opium*, p. 171.

18 *Ibid.*, p. 172.

19 Jean Cocteau, *Opium: Journal d'une désintoxication* (Paris, 1930), p. 86.

20 *Ibid.*, pp. 32 and 119.

21 *Ibid.*, p. 158.

22 Dupouy, *Les Opiomanes*, pp. 71–2.

23 Jean Dorsenne, *La noire idole* (Paris, 1930), p. 19.

24 Francis Carco, 'Préface', in *Les Veillées du 'Lapin Agile'* (Paris, 1919), pp. xvii–xviii.

25 André Salmon, *La Vie passionée de Modigliani* (Paris, 1957), pp. 84–8.

26 John Richardson, *A Life of Picasso*, 2 vols (London, 1991–6), vol. I, p. 320.

27 Salmon, *La Vie passionée de Modigliani*, pp. 81–2; Richardson, *A Life of Picasso*, vol. II, pp. 62–3.

28 Richardson, *A Life of Picasso*, vol. I, p. 320, and vol. II, p. 68; De Liedekerke, *La Belle Epoque de l'opium*, pp. 161–5; J.-P. Crespelle, *La Vie quotidienne à Montmartre au temps de Picasso, 1900–1910* (Paris, 1978), pp. 134–6.

29 Jean Mollet, *Les Mémoires du Baron Mollet* (Paris, 1963), pp. 93–4.

30 Francis Picabia, 'Guillaume Apollinaire' (1924), in *Écrits*, ed. O. Revault d'Allones and D. Bouissou (Paris, 1978), vol. II, p. 149.

31 Apollinaire, letters to S. Férat (4 January 1915) and F. Fleuret (21 December 1914), in *Oeuvres complètes* (Paris, 1965–6), vol. IV, pp. 780 and 746, and *Poèmes à Lou* (Paris, 1969), p. 91.

32 Fernande Olivier, *Picasso et ses amis* (1933) (Paris, 1954), p. 56 (compare pp. 165–6), and *Souvenirs intimes* (Paris, 1988), pp. 185–6

33 Richardson, *A Life of Picasso*, vol. I, pp. 120, 320–25, 386 and 464.

34 Alain Quella-Villéger, *Le Cas Farrère* (Paris, 1989), pp. 130–31.

BARRY MILLIGAN: 'The Opium Den in Victorian London'

1 Sax Rohmer, *The Insidious Dr Fu-Manchu: Being a Somewhat Detailed Account of the Amazing Adventures of Nayland Smith in his Trailing of the Sinister Chinaman* (New York, 1913), pp. 53, 65.

2 Terry Parssinen, *Secret Passions, Secret Remedies: Narcotic Drugs in British Society, 1820–1930* (Philadelphia, 1983); Matthew Sweet, *Inventing the Victorians* (London, 2001). Both directly quote several such headlines from the 1920s and '30s in a clipping collection in the Tower Hamlets Borough Library, London.

3 James Platt, 'Chinese London and its Opium Dens', *Gentleman's Magazine*, 279 vol. (1895), p. 274.

4 The names have changed over the years: Bluegate Fields and the Ratcliff Highway were Victoria Street and St George Street by the end of the nineteenth century, and they are Dellow Street and The Highway now.

5 J. Ewing Ritchie, 'Ratcliffe-Highway', *The Night-Side of London* (London, 1858), p. 77.

6 The name variations are readily explainable, with the possible exception of Victoria Court ('Chinaman Court' and 'Palmer's Folly' were merely popular names for New Court). But given that a map of 1888 shows another byway named after Victoria directly across Victoria Street (Bluegate Fields) from the entrance to New Court (*New Large-Scale Ordnance Atlas of London & Suburbs with Supplementary Maps, Copious Letterpress Descriptions and Alphabetical Indexes* [London, 1888], p. 17), perhaps the reporter (Richard Rowe, *Picked Up in the Streets* [London, 1880]) was confused regarding which name applied to the court itself. By 1895 New Court had been pulled down to make way for a school board playground (James Platt, 'Chinese London and its Opium Dens', p. 275).

7 James Greenwood, 'An Opium Smoke in Tiger Bay', *In Strange Company: Being the Experiences of a Roving Correspondent* (London, 1873), p. 229.

8 Anon., 'Opium-Smoking in London', *Friend of China*, III (1877), pp. 19–20.

9 Joseph Salter, *The Asiatic in England: Sketches of Sixteen Years' Work among Orientals* (London, 1873), especially p. 31.

10 George Piercy, 'Opium Smoking in London: To the Editor of the Methodist Recorder', *Friend of China*, VI (1883), p. 240.

11 Anon., 'London Opium Dens: Notes of a Visit to the Chinaman's East End Haunts, by a Social Explorer', *Good Words*, XXVI (1885), pp. 188–92.

12 Thus the whole genre of the opium den narrative seems to have been based almost exclusively on two or three neighbouring establishments. For a more detailed argument of this case, see the chapter 'Last Exit to Shadwell' in Sweet, *Inventing the Victorians*.

13 Salter (*The Asiatic in England*, p. 199) says there are two, but A. C. W. claims that there are three ('Opium Smoking in Bluegate Fields', *Chemist and Druggist*, XI [1870], p. 260).

14 Anon., 'Opium Smoking at the East End of London', reprinted from the *Daily News* of 1864 in *All About Opium*, ed. Hartmann Henry Sultzberger (London, 1884), p. 175. The name 'Yahee' is given only by Joseph Charles Parkinson in 'Lazarus, Lotus-Eating', *All the Year Round*, XV (1866), pp. 421–5. Salter gives an otherwise very similar description of a man he calls 'Old Latou' (*The Asiatic in England*, p. 285).

15 Parkinson, 'Lazarus, Lotus-Eating', p. 424

16 Anon., 'An Opium Den in Whitechapel', *Chemist and Druggist*, IX (1868), p. 275; Anon., 'In an Opium Den', *Ragged School Union Magazine*, XX (1868), pp. 198–200.

17 Chinese nationals had only very recently begun to settle in England (chiefly in Liverpool and London), after the opening of the Blue Funnel line's route to China in 1865 (J. P. May, 'The Chinese in Britain, 1860–1914', *Immigrants and Minorities in British Society*, ed. Colin Holmes [London, 1978], p. 111). Shadwell was often drawn under the Whitechapel rubric by slumming expeditionaries. A den whose location is specified as Bluegate Fields, for instance, appears in a chapter called 'Whitechapel and Thereabouts' in Gustave Doré and Blanchard Jerrold, *London: A Pilgrimage* (London, 1872).

18 The same detail is recalled in a retrospective account by the former magistrate of the area, Montagu Williams, in 'Ratcliff Highway', *Round London: Down East and Up West* (London, 1893), pp. 74–83.

19 Anon., 'East London Opium Smokers', *London Society*, XIV (1868), p. 72; Greenwood, 'An Opium Smoke in Tiger Bay', p. 229; James Platt, 'Chinese London and its Opium Dens', p. 275.

20 James Platt, 'Chinese London and its Opium Dens', p. 272. Matthew Sweet also notes that the census records for Shadwell are sometimes illegible, with numerous attempts at Chinese names ultimately scribbled through and replaced with 'NK' for 'not known'.

21 Anon., 'East London Opium Smokers', p. 72; Greenwood, 'An Opium Smoke in Tiger Bay', p. 233.

22 Although Richard Rowe calls her Eliza (possibly her proper name rather than nickname), she is Lascar Sal in Parkinson, 'Lazarus, Lotus-Eating', Ritchie, 'Ratcliffe-Highway', and Anon., 'Opium-Smoking in London', 'Lascar Sally' in Salter, *The Asiatic in England*, and 'Sally the Opium Smoker' in Frederick Wellesley, *Recollections of a Soldier-Diplomat* (London, 1947), p. 75.

23 The article in which she first appeared as Dickens's inspiration was A.C.W., 'Opium Smoking in Bluegate Fields'.

24 Rowe, *Picked Up in the Streets*, p. 39.

25 A.C.W., 'Opium Smoking in Bluegate Fields', p. 260; Rowe, *Picked Up in the Streets*, p. 39; Doré and Jerrold, *London*, p. 148.

26 There are good grounds for the equation of Lascar Sal and Dickens's 'Princess Puffer' asserted by many reporters after the novel's publication. Dickens's den is 'eastward and still eastward' from the General Post Office, presided over by a former alcoholic Englishwoman plagued by a dire cough (details mentioned by more than one interviewer of Lascar Sal), and in competition with 'Jack Chinaman t'other side the court' (Charles Dickens, *The Mystery of Edwin Drood*, ed. Margaret Cardwell [Oxford, 1972], p. 204). Perhaps most persuasively, James T. Fields recounts an expedition to Lascar Sal's den led by Dickens (*Yesterdays With Authors* [Boston, MA, 1890], p. 202). The point that clinched it for most reporters, though, was the unusual pipe with its penny ink-bottle bowl, used in both Lascar Sal's and Princess Puffer's dens.

27 Dickens, *The Mystery of Edwin Drood*, pp. 2–3.

28 *Ibid.*, p. 1.

29 An early version of *The Picture of Dorian Gray* was published in *Lippincott's Monthly Magazine* in 1890, but the opium den scene first appeared in the book edition of 1891.

30 Oscar Wilde, *The Picture of Dorian Gray*, ed. Robert Mighall (London, 2000), pp. 135, 176.

31 *Ibid.*, pp. 175, 179.

32 Arthur Conan Doyle, 'The Man With the Twisted Lip', *Strand Magazine*, 2 (1891), p. 624.

33 *Ibid.*, p. 633.

34 *Ibid.*, p. 626

35 John Coulson Kernahan, 'A Night in an Opium Den', *Strand Magazine*, I (1891), pp. 77–8.

36 Anon. 'In the Night Watches', *Argosy*, 65 vol. (1897), pp. 199, 209; Anon., 'Opium-Dens in London', *Chambers's Journal*, 81 vol. (1904), p. 195.

37 George Augustus Sala, *Living London, Being 'Echoes' Re-echoed* (London, 1883), p. 425.

MATTHEW HILTON: 'Smoking and Sociability'

1 This passage from *Westward Ho!* (1855) was written on the side

of every Westward Ho! Tobacco packet.

2 Lord Byron, 'The Island', canto II, verse xix (1823), in *The Poetical Works of Lord Byron* (London, 1857), p. 268.

3 J. M. Barrie, *My Lady Nicotine* (1890) (London, 1902).

4 This picture of Sherlock Holmes's smoking habits is taken from a sample of his adventures, though references are made in most stories. See especially 'The Hound of the Baskervilles', 'The Mazarin Stone', the 'Musgrave Ritual', 'The Naval Treaty', 'A Case of Identity', 'The Copper Beeches', 'The Engineer's Thumb', 'The Adventure of the Empty House', 'A Scandal in Bohemia' and 'The Adventures of the Cardboard Box', in A. Conan Doyle, *The Original Illustrated Sherlock Holmes* (Edison, NJ, 1997).

5 A. V. Seaton, 'Cope's and the Promotion of Tobacco in Victorian England', *Journal of Advertising History*, IX/2 (1986), p. 12.

6 *The Papers of John Fraser*, University of Liverpool Special Collections, file 680.

7 M. L. de la Ramée [Ouida], *Under Two Flags* (1867) (Oxford, 1995), p. 18.

8 Anon., 'All in the Clouds', *All the Year Round*, XV/369 (1866), p. 448; Anon., 'Old English Tobacco Pipes', *Chambers' Journal*, LXXIII (1986), pp. 495–6; 'Clay Pipes', *Tobacco Trade Review*, VI/70 (1873), p. 123; R. Quick, 'The Antiquity of the Tobacco Pipe', *Antiquary*, XLII (1896), p. 158.

9 'On Smoking', *Tobacco Trade Review*, II/22 (1896), p. 158.

10 W. Collins, *The Moonstone* (1868) (Ware, 1993), p. 282.

11 B.W.E. Alford, *W. D. & H. O. Wills and the Development of the UK Tobacco Industry* (London, 1973), p. 109; 'Increase of the Irish Roll Trade', *Tobacco Trade Review*, II/13 (1869), pp. 8–9; 'Decline of the Snuff Trade', *Tobacco Trade Review*, II/16 (1869), p. 56; 'On the Tobacco Trade', *Tobacco Trade Review*, X/115 (1877), p. 79; 'The Tobacco Trade of Scotland', *Tobacco Trade Review*, XIX/218 (1886), p. 42; 'The Tobacco Trade of Scotland', *Tobacco Trade Review*, XX/231 (1887), p. 78; 'Irish Roll', *Tobacco Trade Review*, XXIII/270 (1890), p. 158; 'Trade Topics', *Tobacco Trade Review*, XXIV/277 (1890), p. 24; 'Trade Topics', *Tobacco Trade Review*, XXIV/279 (1890), p. 68; 'Chewing Tobacco: Points for the Retailer', *Tobacco Trade Review*, XXVII/323 (1894), pp. 337–8.

12 E. J. Urwick, *Studies of Boy Life in our Cities* (1904) (New York, 1980), p. xii.

13 A. Patterson, *Across the Bridges; or, Life by the South London Riverside* (London, 1911), p. 125.

14 *Ibid.*, p. 142.

15 'Mass-Observation, Man and his Cigarette' (1949) in *File Report 3192* in *The Tom Harrisson Mass-Observation Archive* (Brighton, 1983), pp. 126–7.

16 Mass-Observation Archive, University of Sussex Library, Topic Collections, Smoking Habits 1937–1965, Box 3, File A, P. Moore (416).

17 Richard Klein, *Cigarettes Are Sublime* (Durham, NC, and London, 1993), p. 135.

18 *People*, 19 December 1915, p. 2.

19 J. W. Hobson and H. Henry, *The Pattern of Smoking Habits: A Study Based on Information Collected During the Course of the Hulton Readership Survey, 1948* (London, 1948), p. 4.

20 *Daily Express*, 9 February 1965, pp. 1, 8; *Daily Express*, 10 February 1965, pp. 5, 8.

21 *The Times*, 7 April 1958, p. 7.

22 *Guardian*, 23 December 1965, p. 5.

23 *Daily Mirror*, January–February 1971, various.

24 *Cope's Tobacco Plant*, II/7 (1970) p. 75.

25 *Lancet*, I (1958), pp. 680–81.

JEAN STUBBS: 'Havana Cigars and the West's Imagination'

1 Sergio Morera, Simon Chase and Bill Colbert, *Havanas: A Unique Blend of Sun, Soil and Skill* (London, 1993), n.p.

2 Kendall Hamilton, 'Blowing Smoke', *Newsweek*, 21 July 1997, pp. 54–61; and Mark Peyser et al., 'Cool Fools', *Newsweek*, 21 July 1997, p. 61.

3 Hamilton, 'Blowing Smoke', p. 54.

4 See *Cigar World*, Winter 1998–9, p. 2.

5 Adriano Martínez Rius, *Habano el Rey* (Barcelona, 1998), p. 11.

6 Fernando Ortiz, *Cuban Counterpoint: Tobacco and Sugar* (1940) (Durham, NC, 1995). Ortiz posed the classic Cuban counterpoint between tobacco and sugar, on which see Fernando Coronil's introduction to the 1995 edition of *Cuban Counterpoint*; Antonio Benítez-Rojo, *The Repeating Island: The Caribbean and the Postmodern Perspective* (Durham, NC, and London, 1990); and Gustavo Pérez-Firmat, *The Cuban Condition: Translation and Identity in Cuban Literature* (Cambridge, 1989). I posit a new counterpoint between the offshore and the island Havana cigar: 'Recentering Tobacco in the Contrapunteo: Reflections on Two 1990s Cuban Revivals – Fernando Ortiz and the Havana Cigar', in *Cuban Counterpoints: The Legacy of Fernando Ortiz*, ed. Mauricio Font and Alfonso Quiroz, (Lanham, MD, forthcoming).

7 For full-colour reproductions, see Antonio Nuñez Jiménez, *The Journey of the Havana Cigar* (Neptune, NJ, 1998); Joe Davidson, *The Art of the Cigar Label* (Secaucus, NJ, 1989); *Florida Cuban Heritage Trail* (Tallahassee, FL, n.d.); and Narciso Menocal, *Cuban Cigar Labels: The Tobacco Industry in Cuba and Florida: Its Golden Age in Lithography and Architecture* (Coral Gables, FL, 1995).

8 L. Glenn Westfall, 'The Cuban Cigar Industry and its Age', in *Ex Libris: The Special Collections in the University of South Florida Tampa Campus Library* (Tampa, n.d.), n.p.

9 Guy Talese, 'Walking my Cigar', *Cigar Aficionado*, Autumn 1992, p. 37.

10 *Ibid.*, p. 41.

11 *Cigar Aficionado*, Winter 1993, p. 9.

12 Feature article containing inset is Hamilton, 'Blowing Smoke', pp. 54–61.

13 'Will Cigars Stay Hot? How To Track the Trend', *Newsweek*, 21 July 1997, p. 59.

14 'Cuban Cigars: Let the Good Times Roll', *Economist*, 2 May 1998, pp. 59–60.

15 Francisco Isla, 'The Cohiba Has the World at its Feet', *Cuban Review*, II/23 (April 1997), p. 13.

16 Mark Stucklin, *The Cigar Handbook: A Buyer's Guide to the World's Finest Cigar Brands* (New York, 1997), p. 8.

17 See L. Glenn Westfall, *Don Vicente Martínez Ybor, the Man and his Empire: Development of the Clear Havana Industry in Cuba and Florida in the Nineteenth Century* (New York and London, 1987) and *Key West: Cigar City USA* (Key West, FL, 1984); Armando Méndez, *Ciudad de Cigars: West Tampa* (Tampa, FL, 1994); José Rivero Muñiz, *The Ybor City Story* (1958) (Tampa, FL, 1996); and Gerald E. Poyo, *With All and for the Good of All* (Durham, 1989).

18 Allen Cowan, 'A Good Cigar is More than a Smoke', *Floridian*, 26 November 1972, p. 24.

19 Louis A. Pérez Jr, 'Ybor City Remembered', *Tampa Bay History*, VII/2 (Fall/Winter 1985), pp. 170–71.

20 Gustavo Pérez-Firmat, *Next Year in Cuba: A Cubano's Coming-of-Age in America* (New York, 1994), p. 82.

21 Martin Mendiola, 'Puro Humo', *El Nuevo Herald*, 22 July 1997, p. 8.

22 See *Generation ñ*, II/13 (August 1997).

23 See *Generation ñ*, II /16 (December 1997).

24 Stephen Schatzman, 'There's an Entire New Generation of Cigar Smokers', *South Florida Gourmet* (July 1998), p. 14.

MARK HANUSZ: 'A Century of *Kretek*'

1 GAPPRI (Gabungan Perusahaan Pabrik Rokok Indonesia / Indonesian Association of Kretek Manufacturers) Annual Report, 1999.

2 *Ibid*.

3 Mark Hanusz, *Kretek: The Culture and Heritage of Indonesia's Clove Cigarettes* (Jakarta, 2000 and 2003).

J. EDWARD CHAMBERLIN AND BARRY CHEVANNES: 'Ganja in Jamaica'

All efforts have been made to contact copyright holders of poetry reprinted in this essay.

1 Antohny McNeil, 'Ode to Brother Joe', *Reel from 'The Life-Movie'* (Kingston, Jamaica, 1975), p. 29.

2 *Bob Marley: In His Own Words*, ed. Ian McCann (London, 1993), p. 82.

3 Kamau Braithwaite, 'Wings of a Dove', *Rights of Passage*, in *The Arrivants: A New World Trilogy* (Oxford, 1973), p. 42.

4 Gerard Manley Hopkins, 'That Nature is a Heraclitean Fire and of the Comfort of the Resurrection', *The Poems of Gerard Manley Hopkins*, ed. W. H. Gardner and N. H. MacKenzie, 4th edn (Oxford, 1970), pp. 105–6.

5 Brathwaite, 'Wings of a Dove', pp. 42–3.

6 Vera Rubin and Lambros Comitas, *Ganja in Jamaica* (Mouton, 1975), pp. 15–16.

7 Barry Chevannes, 'Background to Drug Use in Jamaica', *Working Paper No. 34*, Institute of Social and Economic Research (University of the West Indies, Mona), p. 10.

8 Ajai Mansingh and Laxmi Mansingh, *Hindu Influemces on Rastafarianism*, Caribbean Quaterly Monograph (University of the West indies, Mona, 1985).

9 Barry Chevannes, Webster Edwards, Anthony Freckleton, Norma Linton, DiMario McDowell, Aileen Standard-Goldson and Barbara Smith, *Report of the National Commission on Ganja* (Jamaica Information Service, September 2001), pp. 31–2.

10 *Bob Marley: In His Own Words*, p. 82.

11 *Ibid.*, pp. 81–2.

12 *Ibid.*, p. 82

13 'Ode to Brother Joe', pp. 29–30.

14 Lorna Goodison, 'Studio I: Brother Everald Brown', *Travelling Mercies* (Toronto, 2001), p. 63, reprinted with permission from the author.

15 Lorna Goodison, 'Bull's Bay, Lucea', *To Us, All Flowers Are Roses* (Chicago, 1995), pp. 66–7, reprinted with permission from the author.

16 Dennis Scott, 'No Sufferers', *Uncle Time* (Pittsburgh, 1973), p. 53.

17 Velma Pollard, 'Social History of Dread Talk', *Caribbean Quarterly*, XXVIII/4 (1982), p. 25.

18 Ann Marie Dewar, 'Rasta, Me Son', *Pacific Quarterly Moana*, VIII/3 (1983): *One People's Grief: New Writing from the Caribbean*, ed. Robert Benson, special edition, pp. 70–71.

19 Kendal Hippolyte, 'Zoo Story – Ja. '76', *Voiceprint*, ed. Stewart Brown, Mervyn Morris and Gordon Rohlehr, pp. 62–8.

STEPHEN COTTRELL: 'Smoking and All That Jazz'

1 David Perry, *Jazz Greats* (London, 1996), p. 77.

2 Alan Lomax, *The Land Where the Blues Began* (London, 1994), p. 428.

3 Sidney Bechet, *Treat it Gentle: An Autobiography* (New York, 1960). Cited in Robert Gottlieb, ed., *Reading Jazz: A Gathering of Autobiography, Reportage and Criticism from 1919 to Now* (London, 1997), p. 8.

4 Burton W. Peretti, *The Creation of Jazz: Music, Race and Culture in Urban America* (Urbana, IL, 1992), p. 139.

5 *Ibid.*

6 Hoagy Carmichael, *The Stardust Road* (New York, 1946), p. 53.

7 Peretti, *The Creation of Jazz*, pp. 140–41.

8 Pops Foster and Tom Stoddard, *Pops Foster: The Autobiography of a New Orleans Jazzman* (Berkeley, CA, 1971), p. 167.

9 Mezz Mezzrow and Bernard Wolfe, *Really the Blues* (London, 1993), p. 74.

10 *Ibid.*

11 Max Jones and John Chilton, *Louis: The Louis Armstrong Story* (St Albans, 1975), p. 138.

12 *Ibid.*, p. 133.

13 Cited in Gottlieb, *Reading Jazz*, pp. 70–71.

14 Paul Berliner, *Thinking in Jazz: The Infinite Art of Improvisation* (Chicago, 1994), pp. 40–41.

15 *Ibid.*, p. 438.

16 *Ibid.*, p. 453.

ZHOU XUN: 'Smoking in Modern China'

1 Qi Shihe, *Huang Juci Xu Laiji zouyi hekan* [A combined volume of Huang Juci's and Xu Laiji's Report] (Beijing, 1959), p. 69.

2 *Qing Renzhong shilu* [The official biography of the Jiaqing emperor], vol. CCLXX: 'Zhu xingbu niding fanmai xishizhe ketiaozhuiming shangyu' [Edicts on attempts to outlaw the selling and consumption of opium]. See also Yu Ende, *Zhongguo jinyan faling bianqianshi* [The changing history of opium prohibition in China] (Shanghai, 1934), pp. 72–3.

3 T. Chung, *China and the Brave New World* (Bombay, 1978), p. 144.

4 Li Gui, *Yapian shilue* [A short history of opium] (late nineteenth century), vol. II, pp. 3–6; republished in *Yapian Zhanzhen Shilao Huiban* [Historical documents on the Opium War], ed. Zhongguo Shixue Xuehui (Shanghai, 1954), vol. IX, pp. 203–50.

5 De Mei, 'Shanghai xiachen shehui jianying yiye' [A reflection on low life in Shanghai], *Judu yuekan* [Opium: a national issue], CI (May 1936), pp. 36–8.

6 For a general reading on public space, see Oscar Newman, *Defensible Space* (New York, 1965). For public space and urban culture in late imperial China, see Wang Di, 'Street Culture: Public Space and Urban Commoners in Late Qing Chengdu', in *Modern China*, XXIV/1 (January 1998), pp. 34–72; Shi Mingzheng, 'From Imperial Gardens to Public Parks: The Transformation of Urban Space in Early Twentieth-Century Beijing', *ibid.*, pp. 219–54; Li Deying, 'Public Space and Social Life in City: A Case Study of the Modern Urban Park in China', in *Urban History Research*, XIX–XX (January 2001), pp. 127–53.

7 Cf. Cai Bubai, 'Woduiyu jinyan de guangan' [My view on opium restriction], *Jinyan zhuankan* [A special publication on anti-opium movmement] (Shanghai, 1935), p. 9.

8 William Lockhart, *The Medical Missionary in China: A Narrative of Twenty Years' Experience* (London, 1861), p. 392; also Cai Bubai, 'Woduiyu jinyan de guangan', p. 9.

9 'Hangzhou tongxun: Qingmo Hangzhou' [Correspondence from Hangzhou: late Qing Hangzhou] *Judu yuekan* [Opium: a national issue], XCVIII (1935), p. 6.

10 *Ibid.*, p. 9.

11 Martin Booth, *Opium: A History* (London, 1997), pp. 60–61.

12 Xie Zhaoshen, 'Yi Sichuan yanhuo' [Memories of the opium problem in Sichuan], *Sichuan wenshi zhiliao jichui* [A collection of historical documents in Sichuan] (Chengdu, 1996), vol. VI,

pp. 499–500. See also Shang Kei, 'Jiu Chengdu de luguanye' [Hotel business in old Chengdu], *Longmenzhen* [Tales], VI (1983), pp. 17–24.

13 Cai Bubai, 'Woduiyu jinyan de guangan', p. 9.

14 Fen Zhicheng, ed., *Lao Chengdu* [Old Chengdu] (Chengdu, 1999), pp. 163–70, 199–202, 275–7, 280–82. See also Huang Jiren, *Lao Chongqing* [Old Chongqing] (Nanjing, 2000), pp. 101–6.

15 For foreign cigarettes in Chengdu, see Xu Borong, 'Xiangyan yu waishang' [Cigarettes and foreign merchants], *Longmenzhen* [Tales], IV (1996), pp. 96–7; Du Zhenghua, 'Ying Mei yanchao gongshi yu Chongqing juanyan shichang' [British and American cigarette companies and tobacco consumer market in Chongqing], *Sichuan wenshi zhiliao jichui* [A collection of historical documents], III (1996), pp. 279–91.

16 Xu Borong, 'Xiangyan yu waishang', pp. 96–7.

17 *Luyou zazhi*, III/3–4.

18 Taisheng, 'Mafei yu hongwan' [Morphine and the red pill], *Judu yuekan* [Opium: a national issue], LXXXIII (January 1935), pp. 6–7.

19 Number Two National Archive, Nanjing, 12/1188.

20 Shanghai Municipal Archive, U1/4/2690, 2691.

21 Zhu Xiang, 'Yanjuan' [Cigarette], in Lo Pin, ed., *Minjia bixia de yanjiuchadian* [Famous people talking about tobacco, alcohol, tea and dim sum] (Beijing, 1994), pp. 298–304.

22 For further reading on the foreign cigarette industry in modern China, see Sherman Cochran, *Big Business in China: Sino-Foreign Rivalry in the Cigarette Industry, 1890–1930* (Cambridge, MA, 1980).

23 For a reading on commercial advertising in modern Shanghai, see Sherman Cochran, 'Transnational Origins of Advertising in Early Twentieth-Century China', in *Inventing Nanjing Road: Commercial Culture in Shanghai, 1900–1945*, ed. Sherman Cochran, (Ithaca, NY, 2000).

24 *Liangyao huabao* [Good companion pictorial], XI (15 December 1926).

25 For the advertisement for Golden Dragon, see *ibid.* For those for La Yebanan, see *Luyou zazhi* [Travel magazine], III/3 (1929).

26 Wang Jingwei: 'Duiyu nujiede ganxiang' [Reflections on women's world], *Funu zazhi* [Women's magazine], X/1 (1924), pp. 106–8.

27 Quoted in Cochran, *Big Business in China*, p. 199.

28 Iris Cheng, Virginia L. Ernster and He Guanqing, 'Tobacco Smoking among 847 Residents of East Beijing, People's Republic of China', *Asia-Pacific Journal of Public Health*, IV/2–3 (1990), pp. 156–63.

29 *Ibid.*

30 *Strange Smoke (hailuk toman)* by Yasin Mukhpul, sung by Abdulla Abdurehim, 1996. *Sukuttike Sada* [Echoes of silence], Xinjiang Recording Co. I would like to express my gratitude to Rachel Harris of SOAS, University of London, for sharing this song with me.

DANIEL GILMAN: 'Smoking in Modern Japan'
1 Tobacco and Salt Museum Catalogue, English edition, Japan Tobacco Foundation (1988), p. 18.
2 Ibid., p 43.
3 National Cancer Center, Japan: http://www.ncc.go.jp/en/statistics/1997/index.html
4 American Lung Association: http://www.lungusa.org/data/smoke/smoke._1pdf
5 National Cancer Center, Japan: http://www.ncc.go.jp/en/statistics/1997/tables/index.html
6 JT Web page Delight Campaign: http://www.jtnet.ad.jp/www/JT/JTI/delight/welcome.html
7 JT Web page: http://www.jti.co.jp/jti/tobacco/touzai/essay29.html
8 JT Web page: http://www.jti.co.jp/JTI/tobacco/touzai/essay29.html
9 Anti-smoke site: http://anti-smoke-jp.com/keneneg.html
10 JT Web Page, http://www.jtnet.ad.jp.www/JT/JTI/shikouhin/essay/23.html.

RUTH MANDEL: 'Cigarettes in Soviet and post-Soviet Central Asia'
1 Papirosi (pl.; sing. papiros) pre-date the Soviet Union. James A. Shaw, as notes at http://www.wclynx.com/burntofferings/packsrussian.html
2 For more on this, see M. Fishbach, Ecocide in the USSR: Health and Nature under Siege (New York, 1992); M. McKee, 'Unraveling the Enigma of the Russian Mortality Crisis', Population Development Review, XXV (1999), pp. 361–6; M. McKee et al., 'Patterns of Smoking in Russia', Public Medicine, VII (1998), pp. 22–6.
3 'Tobacco or Health: A Global Status Report', World Health Organization (1999).
4 R. Mandel, '"A Marshall Plan of the Mind": The Political Economy of a Kazakh Soap Opera', in Media Worlds: Anthropology on New Terrain, ed. F. Ginsburg, L. Abu-Lughod and B. Larkin (Berkeley, CA, 2002), pp. 211–28.
5 Report on Competition in Tobacco Market, Kazakhstan. Gallup Media Asia (2001).
6 Respublika, 15 February 2001.
7 For the relationship between smoking and war, see N. J. Saunders, 'Bodies of Metal, Shells of Memory: "Trench Art and the Great War Re-cycled"', Journal of Material Culture, V (2000), pp. 43–67; and also N. J. Saunders, Trench Art: A Brief History and Guide, 1914–39 (Barnsley, 2001).

ALBERTO CASTOLDI: 'The Cocaine Experience'
1 A. Artaud, 'Lettre à Monsieur le législateur de la loi sur les stupéfiants' (originally in Ombilic des Limbes, Nouvelle Revue Française, Paris, 1925), reprinted in Œuvres complètes, 26 vols (Paris, 1956–94), vol. I, pp. 80–84; and 'Sûreté générale:

Liquidation de l'opium' (originally in Révolution Surréaliste, II, 1925), reprinted in Œuvres complètes, 26 vols (Paris, 1956–94), vol. I, pp. 319–24.
2 'La coca non es una droga, es comida': on the distinction between the uses of food and coca, see Stephen Hugh-Jones, 'Coca, Beer, Cigars and Yapé', in Consuming Habits: Drugs in History and Anthropology, ed. J. Goodman, P. E. Lovejoy and A. Stewart (London, 1995), pp. 47–66.
3 See D. Streatfeild, Cocaine: An Unauthorised Biography (London, 2001), p. 29.
4 J.-B. Lamarck, Illustrations de genres: Dictionnaire de botanique méthodique (Paris, 1785); see also P. Browne, The Civil and Natural History of Jamaica (London, 1756), p. 278.
5 A. Niemann, On a New Organic Base in the Coca Leaves, PhD dissertation, University of Göttingen, 1860.
6 H. A. Weddel, Voyage dans le nord de la Bolivie (Paris, 1853).
7 J. J. von Tschudi, Peru: Reisekizzen aus den Jahren 1839–1842 (St Gallen, 1846).
8 G. de la Vega, Comentarios reales de los Incas (1609–17) (Madrid, 2000); as Royal Commentaries of the Incas, reprinted New York, 1981.
9 P. Mantegazza, Sulle virtù igieniche e medicinali della coca (Milan, 1859).
10 K. Koller, Historischen Notiz Über die Anfänge der Lokalanästesi (1928), cited in Un peu d'encre sur la neige, ed. D. Antonin (Paris, 1997).
11 For a detailed account of Freud's cocaine episode, see E. Jones, Sigmund Freud: Life and Works, 3 vols (New York, 1953–7), vol. I, pp. 113–36, from which some of the following material is derived.
12 Ibid., Letter of 25 May 1884.
13 'Über Coca', in Archiv für der Gesämmte Therapie (1884), p. 289; see English abstract in Standard Edition of the Complete Psychological Works of Sigmund Freud, 24 vols, ed. J. Strachey (London, 1953–74), vol. III, p. 233.
14 Between February and October 1885 the price that Merck charged fell from 23 German marks per gram to 1; see D. Streatfeild, Cocaine: An Unauthorised Biography (London, 2001), p. 80.
15 E. Jones, Sigmund Freud: Life and Works, 3 vols (New York, 1953–7), Letter of 21 April 1884.
16 In French: 'Vin Mariani'; and in Italian: 'Vino Tonico Mariani alla Coca del Perù'.
17 A. Conan Doyle, The Sign of Four (London, 1890), chapter 1, ad init.
18 Ibid.
19 See, in this connection, G. Sissa, Le Plaisir et le mal: Philosophie de la drogue (Paris, 1997).
20 R. L. Stevenson, The Strange Case of Dr Jekyll and Mr Hyde (London, 1886); this phrase is in the concluding chapter, 'Henry Jekyll's Full Statement of the Case'.
21 Robert Desnos, 'Ode à Coco', text reproduced in my Il testo drogato: Letteratura e droga tra ottocento e novecento (Turin, 1994),

p. 157. For a more recent survey concentrating on French experiences in this regard, see M. Milner, *L'Imaginaire des drogues, de Thomas De Quincey à Henri Michaux* (Paris, 2000).

22 Desnos, 'Ode à Coco': 'J'ai des champs de pavots sournois et pernicieux/ Qui, plus que toi, Coco! Me bleuiront les yeux.'

23 Victor Cyril and Dr Berger, *La Coco: Poison moderne* (Paris, 1924).

24 'On ne la trouve plus déposée nulle part' in Antonin, *Un peu d'encre sur la neige*, p. 70

25 René Crevel, *Mort difficile* (Paris, 1926; new edition with preface by Salvador Dalì, 1974); there appears to be no English translation of this text; reference is to the pagination of the Italian edition translated by M. Raffaeli (Turin, 1995).

26 *Ibid.*, p. 41.

27 G. Normandy and C. Poinsot, *Mortelle impuissance* (Paris, 1903).

28 Claude Farrère, *Les Civilisés* (1921), cited in Antonin, *Un peu d'encre sur la neige*, pp. 111–13.

29 M. Ageev, 'Novel with Cocaine' (*Roman s kokainom*), first published in *Chisyel*, no. 10 (1934); reprinted Moscow, 1990; as *Roman avec cocaïne* (Paris, 1990); pagination references refer to the Italian translation, *Romanzo con cocaina* (Rome, 1984).

30 But see N. A. Struve's discussion of the 'Mystery Novel' (*Roman zagadka*) in the Russian reprint of 1990 (appendix, pp. 200–21), which conjectures a connection with Vladimir Nabokov.

31 Ageev, 'Novel with Cocaine' (Italian edn), p. 115.

32 *Ibid.*, p. 117.

33 *Ibid.*, 124–5.

34 *Ibid.*, p. 127.

35 M. A. Bulgakov, 'Morphine' (*Morfiy*), originally published in *Meditsinsky Rabotnik*, December 1927; reprinted in *Sobranie Sochinenie* [Collected works], 10 vols (Ann Arbor, 1982), vol. I, pp. 99–129; reference is to the Italian translation, *Morfina*, by M. Curletto (Genoa, 1988).

36 *Ibid.*, p. 100.

37 Pitigrilli, *Cocaina* (1921), reprinted Milan, 1982, to which reference is made; English translation as *Cocaine*, trans. by E. Mosbacher (Feltham, 1982).

38 *Ibid.*: 'con le labbre bagnate, vibranti . . . e gli leccò ghiottamente il labbro superiore, gli introdusse la lingua nelle nari', p. 24.

39 *Ibid.*: 'le idee accartocciate . . . le foglie secche del tè sotto l'acqua bollente', p. 86.

40 *Ibid.*: 'freddo ai piedi, fuochi artificiali nel cervello', p. 35.

41 *Ibid.*: 'i due individui che sono in me si criticano, si condannano in modo che ne risulta l'odio di me contro me stesso', p. 106.

42 *Ibid.*: 'la cocaina compie il crudele prodigio di deformare il Tempo', p. 104.

43 A. Crowley, *Diary of a Drug Fiend* (London, 1922; reprinted 1979).

44 'Schwärzliche Schnee': see untitled poem in Nachlass ('Gedichte 1912–14') in G. Trakl, *Dichtungen und Briefe*, 2 vols (Salzburg, 1969), vol. I, p. 323.

45 Cf. 'O Nacht! Ich nahm schon kokain': 'O Nacht', in G. Benn, *Gesammelte Werke*, 8 vols (Wiesbaden, 1960), vol. I, p. 53.

46 E. Jünger, *Annährungen: Drogen und Rausch* (1970), in *Sämmtliche Werke* (18 vols) (Stuttgart, 1978–81), vol. XI, esp. pp. 193–219.

47 W. Burroughs, *The Naked Lunch* (1959), reprinted with introduction by J. G. Ballard (London, 1991).

48 Philip K. Dick, *A Scanner Darkly* (1977; reissued, London, 1999).

49 B. E. Ellis, *Less than Zero* (New York, 1986).

50 B. E. Ellis, *American Psycho* (New York, 1991).

51 J. McInerney, *Bright Lights, Big City* (New York, 1984).

52 C. Fisher, *Postcards from the Edge* (London, 1987).

BENNO TEMPEL: 'Symbol and Image: Smoking in Art since the Seventeenth Century'

1 Johann van Beverwyck, *Schat der Gesontheydt*, 1636; Ivan Gaskell, 'Tobacco, Social Deviance and Dutch Art in Seventeenth Century', in *Holländische Genremalerei im 17. Jahrhundert*, ed. Henning Bock and Thomas W. Gaehtgens (Berlin, 1987), pp. 117–37. For a thorough overview from the seventeenth century onward, see Benno Tempel, *Rookgovdijnen Kunsten: van olievert tot celluloid* (Amsterdam, 2003). *Holländische Genremalerei im 17. Jahrhundert*, Symposium (Berlin, 1984), p. 120.

2 Simon Schama, *Overvloed en onbehagen: De Nederlandse cultuur in de Gouden Eeuw* (Amsterdam, 1989), pp. 206–13. (I used the Dutch translation from Schama, *The Embarrassment of Riches*. The book has an excellent index.)

3 *Tot lering en vermaak: Betekenissen van Hollandse genrevoorstellingen uit de zeventiende eeuw*, exh. cat., Rijksmuseum, Amsterdam (1976), p. 124.

4 Ivan Gaskell, 'Tobacco, Social Deviance and Dutch Art in Seventeenth Century', in Bock and Gaehtgens, *Holländische Genremalerei im 17. Jahrhundert*, pp. 133–4.

5 Georg A. Bongers, *Nicotiana Tabacum: The History of Tobacco and Tobacco Smoking in the Netherlands* (Groningen, 1964), p. 196.

6 See, for example, Henri Loyrette, 'Modern Life', in *Origins of Impressionism*, exh. cat., Grand Palais, Paris, and Metropolitan Museum of Art, New York (1994–5), pp. 265–93.

7 Until the 1970s it was not unusual for professional athletes to make ads for the tobacco industry.

8 Ronald de Leeuw, *Van Gogh Museum* (Zwolle 1997), p. 116.

9 Bertold Brecht and Kurt Weill, 'Ballade von der sexuellen Hörigkeit', *Die Dreigroschenoper*.

10 Many publications on this topic have been followed by a large amount of information on the Internet. There are clubs, such as the Cigarette Packet Collectors in Britain.

IVAN DAVIDSON KALMAR: 'The *Houkah* in the Harem: On Smoking and Orientalist Art'

1 The most influential work on orientalism and imperialism is

Edward W. Said's *Orientalism* (New York, 1978). On the importance of the 'oriental despot' to the Western imagination and political philosophy, see Alain Grosrichard, *The Sultan's Court: European Fantasies of the East* (London and New York, 1998).

2 Malek Alloula, *The Colonial Harem* (Minneapolis, 1986), pp. 44–5.

3 *Ibid.*, p. 78.

4 Benjamin Disraeli, letter to Benjamin Austen, 18 November 1830 from Nauplia, Greece. British Library Add. MS 45908, fols 33–4.

5 Tobacco was associated in the West both with the Native Americans and the Muslim East. For a more general exploration of the parallels between stereotypes of the North American native and the Mediterranean Muslim, see Nabil I. Matar, *Turks, Moors and Englishmen in the Age of Discovery* (New York, 1999).

LINDA HUTCHEON AND MICHAEL HUTCHEON: 'Smoking in Opera'

1 Richard Klein, *Cigarettes Are Sublime* (Durham, NC, and London, 1993), p. 117.

2 See Anon., *Les Fumeurs de Paris* (Paris, 1856), p. 86, on the issue of social equality and the threat to male status.

3 For the specific remarks on these working women, see Théophile Gautier, *Voyage en Espagne* (1845; Oxford, 1905), p. 159; Pierre Louÿs, *La Femme et le pantin: roman espagnol* (1898; Paris, 1916), pp. 77–8; Maurice Barrès, *Du sang, de la volupté et de la mort* (Paris, 1894), p. 135.

4 Quoted in Susan McClary, *Georges Bizet: Carmen* (Cambridge, 1992), p. 16.

5 For example the review by F. de L. in the *Revue des deux mondes*, II (1875), pp. 475–80.

6 See Edward W. Said, *Orientalism* (New York, 1978).

7 See Dominique Maingueneau, *Carmen: Les Racines d'un mythe* (Paris, 1984), pp. 22–4, 49–53, 58–60.

8 See Jeremy Tambling, *Opera, Ideology and Film* (Manchester, 1987), p. 37; Susan McClary, *Feminine Endings: Music, Gender and Sexuality* (Minneapolis, 1991), p. 57.

EUGENE UMBERGER: 'In Praise of Lady Nicotine: A Bygone Era of Prose, Poetry . . . and Presentation'

1 W. A. Penn, *The Soverane Herbe: A History of Tobacco* (London, 1901), p. 217.

2 W. A. Brennan, *Tobacco Leaves: Being a Book of Facts for Smokers* (Menasha, 1915), p. 7.

3 Matthew Hilton, *Smoking in British Popular Culture, 1800–2000: Perfect Pleasures* (Manchester, 2000), p. 2.

4 *Ibid.*, p. 21.

5 For a detailed publishing history of these books, as well as an extensive listing of variant editions, see the author's article '"The Smoker's Library": Collecting Possibilities in Turn-of-the-Century Tobacco Literature', in *Biblion: The Bulletin of The New York Public Library*, V/1 (Fall 1996), pp. 118–46.

6 Joseph Knight, ed., *Pipe and Pouch: The Smoker's Own Book of Poetry* (Boston, MA, 1894), p. 61.

7 *Ibid.*, p. 52.

8 Penn, *The Soverane Herbe*, p. 231.

9 J. M. Barrie, *My Lady Nicotine: A Study in Smoke* (Boston, MA, 1895), pp. 105–6.

10 John Bain, Jr, *Tobacco in Song and Story* (New York, 1896), p. 28.

11 *Ibid.*, p. 83.

12 *Ibid*, p. 70.

13 Hilton, *Smoking in British Popular Culture*, p. 32.

14 John Bain, Jr, *Tobacco Leaves* (Boston, MA, 1903), p. 148.

15 John Bain, Jr, *Cigarettes in Fact and Fancy* (Boston, MA, 1906), p. 147.

16 Charles Welsh, ed., *The Fragrant Weed: Some of the Good Things Which Have Been Said or Sung About Tobacco* (New York, 1907), p. 2.

17 Richard D. Altick, '"Cope's Tobacco Plant": An Episode in Victorian Journalism', *Papers of the Bibliographical Society of America*, XLV/4 (1951), p. 337.

18 A. V. Seaton, 'Cope's and the Promotion of Tobacco in Victorian England', *Journal of Advertising History*, IX/2 (1986), pp. 21–2.

19 Walter Hamilton, ed., *An Odd Volume for Smokers: A Lyttel Parcell of Poems and Parodyes in Prayse of Tobacco* (London, 1889), p. 113.

20 V. G. Kiernan, *Tobacco: A History* (London, 1991), p. 4.

21 James Walton, ed., *The Faber Book of Smoking* (London, 2000), p. xiii.

22 Carl Avery Werner, *Tobaccoland* (New York, 1922), p. 9.

23 Walton, *The Faber Book of Smoking*, p. xiii.

NOAH ISENBERG: 'Cinematic Smoke: From Weimar to Hollywood'

1 For a more thorough discussion of *Dr Mabuse*, see Tom Gunning's chapter 'Mabuse, Grand Enunciator: Control and Co-ordination' in his recent book *The Films of Fritz Lang: Allegories of Vision and Modernity* (London, 2000), pp. 87–116. See also Lotte Eisner's fine treatment in her *Fritz Lang* (London, 1976), pp. 57–67.

2 See, for example, the website: http://smokingsides.com/asfs/D/Dietrich.html

3 All citations from this particular film sequence are taken from the English translation of the German continuity script. See Josef von Sternberg, *The Blue Angel* (London, 1968), pp. 58–9.

4 Richard Klein, *Cigarettes Are Sublime* (Durham, NC, and London, 1993), p. 160.

5 Cited in Steven Bach, *Marlene Dietrich: Life and Legend* (New York, 1992), p. 74.

6 Anton Kaes, M (London, 1999), pp. 45–6.

7 See Carl Neumann, Curt Belling and Hans-Walther Betz, *Film-'Kunst', Film-Kohn, Film-Korruption: Ein Streifzug durch vier*

Film-Jahrzehnte (Berlin, 1937). The photo composite is reproduced in Helmut G. Asper's new study 'Etwas Besseres als den Tod . . .': Filmexil in Hollywood: Porträts, Filme, Dokumente (Marburg, 2002). See also Eric Rentschler's brief discussion of the book's significance in the context of Nazi cinema in his Ministry of Illusion: Nazi Cinema and its Afterlife (Cambridge, MA, 1996), pp. 155–6.

8 In her essay of 1944, 'The Jew as Pariah: A Hidden Tradition', Hannah Arendt places the non-Jewish actor Charlie Chaplin – who had, admittedly, given 'Jewish' screen performances as, for example, in The Great Dictator (1940) – within the same cultural and political lineage as Heine, Kafka and company. See her The Jew as Pariah: Jewish Identity and Politics in the Modern Age, ed. Ron H. Feldman (New York, 1978), pp. 67–90.

9 See Kaes's discussion of Lorre's / Beckert's perceived Jewishness, Kaes, M, pp. 71–2.

10 On Fury, see Gunning, 'Mabuse', pp. 212–34, and Eisner, Fritz Lang, pp. 160–76.

11 Cited in Timothy Corrigan, A Short Guide to Writing about Film, 2nd edn (New York, 1994), pp. 22–3.

12 For a full description of this scene, as written in the original screenplay, see Billy Wilder, Double Indemnity (Berkeley, CA, 2000), pp. 10–11.

13 For a trenchant analysis of Ulmer's film, see Andrew Britton, 'Detour', in The Book of Film Noir, ed. Ian Cameron (New York, 1993), pp. 174–83.

14 Cited in Brian Rooney, 'Stars Smoke, Critics Fume: A New Study Finds Movie Characters are Lighting Up More Often', ABCNEWS.com, 19 January 2001.

15 See Rick Lyman, 'In the 80's: Lights! Camera! Cigarettes!', New York Times, 12 March 2002.

16 Misha Berson, 'Hollywood Fans Flames of New Smoking Craze', Seattle Times, 15 September 1996.

17 Mick LaSalle, 'Hollywood Lights Up Again at the Movies', San Francisco Chronicle, 5 November 1996.

DAWN MARLAN: 'Emblems of Emptiness: Smoking as a Way of Life in Jean Eustache's La Maman et la Putain'

1 Count Corti, A History of Smoking, trans. Paul England (New York, 1932), p. 60.

2 Quoted in Richard Klein, Cigarettes Are Sublime (Durham, NC, and London, 1993), p. 11.

3 Ibid., p. 181.

4 Molière, 'Dom Juan ou le festin de pierre', in Théatre complet de Molière (Paris, 1882), p. 218.

5 Shoshanah Felman, The Literary Speech Act: Don Juan with J. L. Austin; or, Seduction in Two Languages (Ithaca, NY, 1983), p. 40.

6 Ibid., p. 43.

7 Klein, Cigarettes Are Sublime, p. 26.

8 Ibid., p. 56.

9 Ibid., p. 8.

10 Ibid., p. 18.

11 Ibid., p. 114.

12 Ibid., p. 117.

13 It is not surprising that desirability is constructed less through the claim to fill the lack that structures desire in the French tradition (for example, in Jacques Lacan), than through imitating it.

14 Klein, Cigarettes Are Sublime, pp. 116–17, 2.

15 Ibid., p. 2.

16 See Gus Parr, 'Smoking', Sight & Sound, VII/12 (December 1997), pp. 30–31. Parr also points out that smoking was a sign of freedom, particularly of female independence, as early as the 1920s. But one must bear in mind that even in A bout de souffle the freedom from law (the right to die, etc.) is inextricable from slavery to a cultural order (seen in Belmondo's imitation of Bogart) that compromises this self-sufficiency.

17 Ibid., p. 30.

18 The student uprising challenged bourgeois pleasures, replacing an ideology promoting procreative love with one that promoted free love, while the nouvelle vague challenged bourgeois pleasures in favour of freedom both in its content and in its form. Auteur theory was derived from Alexandre Astruc's concept of the caméra-stylo and its free or spontaneous use of the camera. Film-makers such as Godard and Resnais were also committed to freedom from linear narrative. Louis Malle made films about transgression, and François Truffaut's early films were built on what Gerald Mast has called 'the central artistic idea of freedom'. For a reading of May 1968 as the birth of modern France as 'more democratic, more liberal, more hedonistic', see Claude-Jean Bertrand, 'A New Birth in France', Media Studies Journal, XII/3 (Fall 1998), pp. 92–9. For a good overview of the nouvelle vague, see Gerald Mast, A Short History of the Movies, 4th edn (New York, 1986), pp. 349–68.

19 Stephanie Lévy-Klein, 'Entretien avec Jean Eustache (à propos de la maman et de la putain)', Positif, 157 (March 1974), p 54.

20 Lisa Katzman argues (p. 32) that Eustache's 'investigation of female subjectivity and male insecurity' expanded the New Wave, in contrast to Alan Williams, for whom Eustache's film is 'a throwback to the height of the nouvelle vague'. See Lisa Katzman, 'The End of the World', Film Comment, XXXV/2 (March–April 1999), pp. 30–37. See Alan Williams, Republic of Images: A History of French Filmmaking (Cambridge, MA, 1992), p. 393.

21 See Peter Wollen, 'Godard and Counter-Cinema: Vent d'Est', in Narrative, Apparatus, Ideology, ed. Philip Rosen (New York, 1986), pp. 123–4.

22 See Jonathan Rosenbaum, 'Jean Eustache's La Maman et la Putain', Sight & Sound, XLIV/1 (Winter 1974–5), p. 55. See also Pascal Bonitzer, 'L'expérience en intérieur', Cahiers du Cinéma, 247 (July–August 1973), pp. 33–6.

23 Eustache, Scénario, p. 43.

24 This reading very much agrees with that of Keith Reader, for whom Eustache's film can be considered 'a documentary montage of different May or post-May discourses . . .' (p. 30). See Keith Reader, 'The Mother, the Whore and the Dandy', *Sight & Sound*, VII/10 (October 1997), pp. 28–30.

25 Proust's Gilberte, after whom Eustache's Gilberte is named, is the daughter of Odette, a whore as well as a mother.

26 In fact, there are only two departures from Alexandre's field of vision (when Marie and Veronika are each shown alone in their rooms at the very end), which indicates both his loss of control over the women's discourse and the importance of their subjectivity in the film.

27 Eustache, *Scénario*, pp. 20–21, 16.

28 *Ibid.*, p. 19.

29 *Ibid.*, pp. 83–4.

30 See Klein, *Cigarettes Are Sublime*, p. 35.

31 Eustache, *Scénario*, p. 72.

32 For an explanation of the circular nature of the tobacco economy, in which tobacco was used as barter to acquire more Africans bound for plantations, see David T. Courtwright, *Forces of Habit: Drugs and the Making of the Modern World* (Cambridge, MA, 2001), p. 149. For a further treatment of the changes from the industry's shift from indentured servants to African slave labour, see Jordan Goodman, *Tobacco in History: The Culture of Dependence* (London and New York, 1993), p. 183.

33 Corti, *A History of Smoking*, pp. 102–3, 185.

34 See Jacques Derrida, 'Le pharmakon', in *La Dissémination* (Paris, 1972), pp. 108–33.

35 Eustache, *Scénario*, p. 103.

36 *La Maman et la Putain*, Séquence 30. Marie's comment appears in the film but not in the screenplay.

37 See Klein, *Cigarettes Are Sublime*, p. 6.

38 Eustache, *Scénario*, pp. 118–19.

39 *Ibid.*, p. 122.

40 *Ibid.*, p. 118.

41 *Ibid.*, p. 94. Eustache, My translation here is not from the screenplay, in which the quotation appears as 'maybe something interesting will happen' (*il va peut-être arriver des choses intéressantes*), but from the film, 'il risque de passer des choses intéressantes . . .'.

SANDER L. GILMAN: 'Jews and Smoking'

1 There are many accounts of this as a given fact. See, for example, Jerome E. Brooks, *The Mighty Leaf: Tobacco through the Centuries* (London, 1953), pp. 12–15. It is part of a Jewish history of tobacco in the article 'Tobacco', *The Jewish Encyclopedia*, 12 vols (New York, 1905–26), vol. XII, pp. 164–6.

2 Guillermo Cabrera Infante, *Holy Smoke* (Woodstock, NY, 1998), pp. 6, 13.

3 The best scholarly article on the early history of smoking stresses this association: Charles Singer, 'The Early History of Tobacco', *Quarterly Review*, CCCCXXXVI (July 1913), pp. 125–42.

4 Wolfgang Schivelbusch, trans. David Jacobsen, *Tastes of Paradise: A Social History of Spices, Stimulants and Intoxicants* (New York, 1993); Jerome E. Brooks, ed., *Tobacco: Its History Illustrated by Books, Manuscripts and Engravings in the Library of George Arents Jr*, 5 vols (New York, 1937–43), and Count [Egon Caesar] Corti, *A History of Smoking* (London, 1931).

5 Frank Swiaczny, *Die Juden in der Pfalz und in Nordbaden im 19. Jahrhundert und ihre wirtschaftliche Akitivtäten in der Tabakbranche: Zur historischen Sozialgeographie einer Minderheit* (Mannheim, 1996).

6 Joseph von Retzer, *Tabakpachtung in den österreichischen Ländern von 1670–1783* (Vienna, 1784) and Sabine Fellner, Wolfgang Bauer and Herbert Rupp, *Die lasterhafte Panazee: 500 Jahre Tabakkultur in Europa: Ausstellung im Österreichischen Tabakmuseum, 11. Juni bis 4. Oktober 1992* (Vienna, 1992).

7 'Tobacco Trade and Industries', *Encyclopedia Judaica*, 16 vols (Jerusalem, 1972), cols 1175–8. This entry ignores the 'legend' of the Jewish origin of tobacco in Europe and stresses only the sociological aspect of this question.

8 Robert N. Proctor, *The Nazi War on Tobacco* (Princeton, NJ, 1999), p. 235.

9 Svend Larsen, *Kortfattet beretning om tobakkens historie: fortegnelse over Tobakkens museumsgenstande* (Odense, Denmark, 1948).

10 Clemens Brentano, 'Über die Kennzeichen des Judenthums', reproduced as an appendix to Heinz Härtl, 'Arnim und Goethe. Zum Goethe-Verständnis der Romantik im ersten Jahrzehnt des 19. Jahrhunderts', dissertation, Halle (1971), pp. 471–90, on tobacco farming, p. 474; on tobacco consumption, p. 473; on the disease of the Jews, pp. 484–6.

11 His first paper on this topic is Jean Martin Charcot, 'Sur la claudication intermittente', *Comptes rendus des séances et mémoires de la société de biologie* (Paris, 1858), Mémoire 1859, 2nd series, V, pp. 25–38. While this is not the first description of the syndrome, it is the one that labels it as a separate disease entity. It is first described by Benjamin Collins Brodie, *Lectures Illustrative of Various Subjects in Pathology and Surgery* (London, 1846), p. 361. Neither Brodie nor Charcot attempt to provide an etiology for this syndrome. Compare M. S. Rosenbloom *et al.*, 'Risk Factors Affecting the Natural History of Intermittent Claudication', *Archive of Surgery*, CXXIII (1989), pp. 867–70.

12 H. Higier, 'Zur Klinik der angiosklerotischen paroxysmalen Myasthenie ('claudication intermittente' Charcot's) und der sog. spontanen Gangrän', *Deutsche Zeitschrift für Nervenheilkunde*, XIX (1901), pp. 438–67.

13 Heinrich Singer, *Allgemeine und spezielle Krankheitslehre der Juden* (Leipzig, 1904), pp. 124–5.

14 Samuel Goldflam, 'Weiteres über das intermittierende Hinken', *Neurologisches Centralblatt*, XX (1901), pp. 197–213. See also his 'Über intermittierende Hinken ('claudication intermittente' Charcot's) und Arteritis der Beine', *Deutsche medi-*

zinische Wochenschrift, XXI (1901), pp. 587–98.

15 See Enfemiuse Herman, 'Samuel Goldflam (1852–1932)', in Kurt Kolle, ed., *Grosse Nervenärtze*, 3 vols (Stuttgart, 1963), vol. III, pp. 143–9.

16 Samuel Goldflam, 'Zur Ätiologie und Symptomatologie des intermittierenden Hinkens', *Neurologisches Zentralblatt*, XXII (1903), pp. 994–6. On tobacco misuse as a primary cause of illness, see the literature overview by Johannes Bresler, *Tabakologia medizinalis: Literarische Studie über den Tabak in medizinischer Beziehung*, 2 vols (Halle, 1911–13).

17 Toby Cohn, 'Nervenkrankheiten bei Juden', *Zeitschrift für Demographie und Statistik der Juden*, new series, III (1926), pp. 76–85.

18 Kurt Mendel, 'Intermitterendes Hinken', *Zentralblatt für die gesamt Neurologie und Psychiatrie*, XXVII (1922), pp. 65–95.

19 Wilhelm Erb, 'Über das "intermittirende Hinken" und andere nervöse Störungen in Folge von Gefässerkrankungen', *Deutsche Zeitschrift für Nervenheilkunde*, XIII (1898), pp. 1–77.

20 Wilhelm Erb, 'Über Disbasia angiosklerotika (intermittierendes Hinken)', *Münchener medizinische Wochenschrift*, LI (1904), pp. 905–8.

21 Compare P. C. Waller, S. A. Solomon and L. E. Ramsay, 'The Acute Effects of Cigarette Smoking on Treadmill Exercise Distances in Patients with Stable Intermittent Claudication', *Angiology*, XL (1989), pp. 164–9.

22 Hermann Oppenheim, 'Zur Psychopathologie und Nosologie der russisch-jüdischen Bevölkerung', *Journal für Psychologie und Neurologie*, XIII (1908), p. 7.

23 L. von Frankl-Hochwart, *Die nervösen Erkrankungen der Tabakraucher* (Vienna and Leipzig, 1912), pp. 30–31, 48–53.

24 Cited by R. Hofstätter, *Die rauchende Frau: Eine klinische, psychologische und soziale Studie* (Vienna and Leipzig, 1924), p. 179.

25 Fritz Lickint, *Tabak und Organismus: Handbuch der Gesamten Tabakkunde* (Stuttgart, 1939), p. 284.

26 M. A. Gilbert, 'Hystérie tabagique', *La Lancette française*, LXII (1889), pp. 1173–4, and Corti, *A History of Smoking*, p. 260.

27 Leopold Löwenfeld, *Pathologie und Therapie der Neurasthenie und Hysterie* (Wiesbaden, 1894), p. 46 (in the Freud Library, London).

28 See the detailed account of the literature compiled by Paul Näcke, 'Der Tabak in der Ätiologie der Psychosen', *Wiener Klinische Rundschau*, XXIII (1909), pp. 805–7, 821–4, 840–42.

29 Leopold Löwenfeld, *Die moderne Behandlung der Nervenschwäche (Neurasthenie) der Hysterie und verwandten Leiden* (Wiesbaden, 1887), p. 28 (in the Freud Library, London).

30 Felix Deutsch, 'Reflections on Freud's One Hundredth Birthday', *Psychosomatic Medicine*, XVIII (1956), p. 279.

31 *The Diary of Sigmund Freud, 1929–1939: A Record of the Final Decade*, ed. and trans. Michael Molnar (New York, 1992), p. 69. Molnar comments that: 'the fact that flight from his native land and abstinence from smoking could arouse the same imagery is one small indication – if any more were needed – of the importance of Freud's tobacco addiction' (p. 276).

32 Max Schur, *Freud: Living and Dying* (New York, 1972), p. 86.

33 Cohn, 'Nervenkrankheiten bei Juden', p. 85.

34 Sharon Romm, *The Unwelcome Intruder: Freud's Struggle with Cancer* (New York, 1983), p. 38.

35 Maurice Sorsby, *Cancer and Race: A Study of the Incidence of Cancer among Jews* (London, 1931), p. 34 (Sorsby's initial publications on this topic are under the same of Sourasky).

DOLORES MITCHELL: 'The Commodified African American in Nineteenth-Century Tobacco Art'

1 A version of this paper was presented at the College Art Association Annual Meeting, San Antonio, Texas, 24 January 1995.

2 Debra Newman Ham, ed., *The African American Mosaic: A Library of Congress Resource Guide for the Study of Black History and Culture* (Washington, DC, 1993), p. 26.

3 Dan Lacy, *The White Use of Blacks in America* (New York, 1972), p. 15: 'To operate profitably the large tobacco and rice plantations that were coming into being by the end of the seventeenth century, ambitious men needed a permanent and involuntary labor force whom they did not need to induce to sign an indenture or to cajole to remain at their task, who did not need to be replaced every few years with new hands, and who could be whipped to their labors.'

4 *Tobacco and Smoking in Art*, exh. cat., North Carolina Museum of Art, Raleigh (1960), p. 14. Discussing a design by Benjamin Labtrobe for a capital for the small rotunda of the old Senate Wing, using a tobacco leaf and blossom design instead of acanthus: 'The choice of corn and tobacco to symbolize the material culture of the young nation was particularly apt, since they were two of the most important of the many plants which the Indians had introduced into European diet and culture, and because they also formed the base of our Colonial economy.'

5 Joseph C. Robert, *The Story of Tobacco in America* (New York, 1949), p. 15.

6 David Dabydeen, *Hogarth's Blacks: Images of Blacks in Eighteenth Century English Art* (Athens, GA, 1987), p. 18. 'As Ambrose Heal reminds us, the "Blackamoor's Head" . . . and "Black Boy" and "Tobacco Roll" was one of the commonest motifs on such signboards.'

7 Ellwood Perry, *The Image of the Indian and the Black Man in American Art* (New York, 1974), p. 55.

8 Robert, *The Story of Tobacco in America*, pp. 86–7.

9 For a background on the history of labels and tobacco art, see Tony Hyman, *The World of Smoking and Tobacco* (Claremont, CA, 1988); Tony Hyman, *Handbook of American Cigar Boxes* (Elmira, NY, 1979); Joe Davidson, *The Art of the Cigar Label* (Secaucus, NJ, 1989); Robert Opie, *The Art of the Label* (Secaucus, NJ, 1987); Chris Mullen, *Cigarette Pack Art* (New York, 1979).

10 Thomas L. Morgan and William Barlow, *From Cakewalks to*

Concert Halls: An Illustrated History of African American Popular Music from 1895 to 1930 (Washington, DC, 1992), p. 10: [After the Civil War] 'a variety of industrial occupations were now open to black laborers, and as they became stevedores, hemp spinners, turpentine workers, and furnace crew-members on steamboats, and then on the railroads . . .'.

11 Douglas Congdon-Martin, *Images in Black: 150 Years of Black Collectibles* (West Chester, PA, 1990), p. 5.

12 Robert, *The Story of Tobacco in America*, pp. 86–7: 'As early as 1810 the cigar-makers of Philadelphia, rolling about thirty million cigars per year, were using "Spanish" tobacco in one out of every ten cigars, probably putting a West Indian wrapper on a Kentucky filler.' Although the clothing style of the master might suggest an early twentieth-century date, the Harris lithographic firm went out of business at the end of the nineteenth century.

13 Rayford W. Logan, *The Negro in American Life and Thought: The Nadi, 1877–1901* (New York, 1954), pp. 252–3.

14 For example, a popularized illustrated version of Lavater's theories appeared in Julien Joseph Virey's illustrated *Histoire naturelle genre humaine*, first printed in Paris in 1801, and reprinted in 1824, 1826 and 1834. One illustration compares profiles of Africans with those of orang-utans.

15 In the premium booklet 'Shadows', issued by Duke Tobacco, on a page titled 'At This Critical Moment', in the Library of Congress files on tobacco art.

16 Such attitudes, and associated stereotypes, are discussed in Sander L. Gilman, *Difference and Pathology: Stereotypes of Sexuality, Race and Madness* (Ithaca, NY, 1985); John S. Haller, *Outcasts from Evolution: Scientific Attitudes of Racial Inferiority, 1959–1900* (Urbana, IL, 1971); Withrop Jordan, *White over Black: American Attitudes toward the Negro, 1550–1812* (New York, 1977); Kenneth W. Goings, *Mammy and Uncle Mose: Black Collectibles and American Stereotyping* (Bloomington, IN, 1994).

17 For an in-depth discussion of contrasting representations in fine art, see Ellwood Perry, *The Image of the Indian and the Black Man in American Art* (New York, 1974).

18 For an overview of both fine and popular art depictions of blacks, see Hugh Honour, ed., *The Image of the Black in Western Art: From the American Revolution to World War I* (Cambridge, 1989). See also Guy McElroy, *Facing History: The Black Image in American Art, 1710–1940* (San Francisco, 1990).

19 Lacy, *The White Use of Blacks*, pp. 15–16: 'As in Roman law, the slave codes enacted in the Southern colonies in the eighteenth century conceived the slave as a *res*, a thing, whose person as well as whose labor was owned by a master. Whatever the personal relationship in individual cases, the legal relationship of the master to his slaves was much more nearly that of an owner to his cattle than that of an employer to his employees.'

20 Patricia A. Turner, *Ceramic Uncles & Celluloid Mammies* (New York, 1994), p. 65.

21 My statement is based upon study of such images in tobacco art archives in the Library of Congress, Arents Collection in the New York Public Library, New York Historical Society and the Metropolitan Museum of Art. Patricia A. Turner details similar conclusions in her study of black images in material culture, *Ceramic Uncles & Celluloid Mammies* (New York, 1994).

22 Charles B. Lewis, *Brother Gardner's Lime-Kiln Club*, reprint of 1970 of a Chicago, Donohue, Henneberry & Co. publication of 1890 (Upper Saddle River, 1970), p. 202.

23 For a discussion of the European tradition, see the chapter on 'Servants' in Jan Nederveen Pieterse, *White on Black: Images of Africa and Blacks in Western Popular Culture* (New Haven, 1992).

24 *Ibid.*, p. 134.

25 Erskine Peters discusses how Jefferson influenced later American writings about black Americans, as well as images of them, in *Ethnic Notions: Black Images in the White Mind. An Exhibition of Afro-American Stereotypes and Caricatures from the Collection of Janette Faulkner*, exh. cat., Berkeley Art Center, CA (1982).

26 Vireys, *Histoire naturelle genre humaine*, p. 92.

27 *Collier's Cyclopedia of Commercial and Social Information* (New York, 1883), p. 602.

28 Joseph C. Robert, *The Story of Tobacco in America* (New York, 1949), p. 107: 'Perhaps the three leading agitators for the abolition of the nicotine menace in the period from 1830 to 1860 were the Rev. Orin Fowler, Dr Joel Shew, and the Rev. George Trask. [Rev. Fowler stated:] "Rum-drinking will not cease, till tobacco-chewing, and tobacco-smoking, and snuff-taking, shall cease".'

29 For a discussion of this type, see Jack Young, *Black Collectibles: Mammy and her Friends* (West Chester, PA, 1988).

30 Morgan and Barlow, *From Cakewalks to Concert Halls*, p. 16. See also Robert C. Toll, *Blacking Up: The Minstrel Show in Nineteenth Century America* (New York, 1974); Henry Sampson, *Blacks in Blackface* (Metuchen, NJ, 1980).

DOLORES MITCHELL: 'Women and Nineteenth-Century Images of Smoking'

1 G. L. Apperson, *The Social History of Smoking* (London, 1914), pp. 214–15.

2 For a discussion, see my 'The Iconology of Smoking', *Source*, Spring 1987, p. 29.

3 J. Bain, *Tobacco in Song and Story* (New York, 1896), p. 51.

4 'Choosing a Wife by a Pipe of Tobacco', *The Gentleman's Magazine*, June 1757, p. 45.

5 Compton Mackenzie, *Sublime Tobacco* (London, 1957), p. 245.

6 Sydney Grundy, *The New Woman* (London, 1894), pp. 51–2.

7 *Ibid.*, p. 102.

8 Bram Dijkstra, *Idols of Perversity* (New York, 1986), pp. 137–8.

9 J. H. Cohausen, *Dissertatio satyrica de pica nasi* (Amsterdam,

1716), as quoted in *Morbid Cravings: The Emergence of Addiction*, exh. cat., Wellcome Institute for the History of Medicine, London (1988), p. 15.

10 Emile Zola, *Nana*, trans. George Holden (London, 1972), p. 57.

11 Alain Corbin, 'Commercial Sexuality in Nineteenth Century France', *Representations*, Spring 1986, pp. 209–19.

12 Jan Thompson, 'The Role of Women in the Iconography of Art Nouveau', *College Art Journal*, Winter 1971–2, p. 159.

13 Martha Kingsbury, 'The Femme Fatale and her Sisters', in *Woman as Sex Object*, ed. Thomas B. Hess and Linda Nochlin (New York, 1972), p. 87.

14 See Jeffrey Knapp, 'Elizabethan Tobacco', *New World Encounters*, ed. Stephen Greenblatt (Berkeley, CA, 1993), pp. 273–312.

15 Prosper Mérimé, *Colomba and Carmen*, trans. Lady Mary Loyd (New York, 1901), p. 32.

16 Maria Louise de la Ramée [Ouida], *Under Two Flags* (1867; reprinted London, 1912), p. 56.

17 *Ibid.*, p. 63.

18 Elizabeth Lee, *Ouida: A Memoir* (London, 1914), p. 44.

19 William Powell Frith, *My Autobiography and Reminiscences* (New York, 1888), p. 27.

20 For information on Johnston, see Anne E. Peterson, 'Nineteenth-Century Profile: The Early Years of Frances Benjamin Johnston', *Nineteenth Century*, Spring 1980, pp. 58–61.

21 See, for example, François Boucher's *La Toilette* (1742; Museo Thyssen-Bornemisza, Madrid), in which a woman sits fastening her stockings by a fireplace, skirts raised, knees apart.

22 See Edouard-Joseph, *Dictionnaire biographique: Artistes contemporains, 1910–30* (Paris, 1931), p. 337.

23 Gail Cunningham, *The New Woman and the Victorian Novel* (London, 1978), p. 14.

24 Marcel Prevost, *Les Demi-Vierges* (Paris, 1894), p. 20.

25 David Sutter, 'Les Phenomenes de la vision', *L'Art*, XX (1880), p. 76.

26 Ouida, *Under Two Flags*, p. 469.

27 Charles Baudelaire, 'The Pipe', in *The Flowers of Evil*, ed. Marthiel and Jackson Mathews (New York, 1963), p. 81.

28 In J. Knight, ed., *Pipe and Pouch* (Boston, MA, 1895), p. 35.

29 *Ibid.*, p. 36.

30 James M. Barrie, *My Lady Nicotine* (Boston, MA, 1895), pp. 85–6.

ROBYN L. SCHIFFMAN: 'Toward a Queer History of Smoking'

1 Compton MacKenzie, *Extraordinary Women: Themes and Variations* (New York, 1928), p. 31.

2 Jean-Jacques Rousseau, *Confessions*, trans. Angela Scholar (Oxford, 2000), p. 65. The French is: 'Un soir il voulut venir coucher avec moi; je m'y opposai disnat que mon lit étoit trop petit: il me pressa d'aller dans le sien; je le refusai encore; car ce misérable étoit si malpropre et puoit si fort le tabac mâché, qu'il me faisoit mal au coeur', in Jean-Jacques Rousseau, *Œuvres complètes de Jean-Jacques Rousseau, I: Les Confessions, autres textes autobiographiqes.*, ed. Bernard Gagnebin and Marcel Raymond (Paris, 1959), p. 67.

3 Christopher Isherwood, *Christopher and his Kind, 1929–1939* (New York, 1976), p. 22.

4 George Chauncey, *Gay New York: Gender, Urban Culture and the Making of the Gay Male World, 1890–1940* (New York, 1994), p. 52.

5 Robert Hichens, *The Green Carnation* (London, 1949), p. vi.

6 Chauncey, *Gay New York*, p. 52.

7 See the article by Hillel Italie on Salon.com: http://www.salon.com/books/log/1999/06/08/100gay

8 Thomas Mann, *Death in Venice and Seven other Stories* (New York, 1989), p. 17. In subsequent citations of this work, the German will follow in notes. 'Einer, in hellgelbem, übermodisch geschnittenem Sommeranzug, roter Krawatte, "Der Tod in Venedig"', in Thomas Mann, *Der Tod in Venedig und andere Erzählungen* (Frankfurt am Main, 1954), p. 21.

9 *Ibid.*, p. 19; 'eine Zigarette zwischen den zitternden Fingern', p. 24.

10 *Ibid.*, p. 3; 'Gustav Aschenbach oder von Aschenbach, wie seit seinem fünfzigsten Geburstag amtlich sein Name lautete', p. 10.

11 Virginia Woolf, *A Change of Perspective: The Letters of Virginia Woolf, Volume III, 1923–1928*, ed. Nigel Nicolson (London, 1977), p. 155.

12 Mann, *Death in Venice*, p. 69; 'Seine Krawatte war rot', p. 77.

13 *Ibid.*, p. 37; 'Der erste Blick fand ihn, die rote Masche auf seiner Brust war nicht zu verfehlen', p. 32.

14 Radclyffe Hall, *The Well of Loneliness* (London, 1982), p. 246.

15 MacKenzie, *Extraordinary Women*, p. 51.

16 J. A. Simpson and E.S.C. Weiner, eds, *Oxford English Dictionary*, 2nd edn (Oxford, 1989), vols IV–V, p. 1010.

17 *Ibid.*, p. 1318.

18 RuPaul, *Lettin' it All Hang Out: An Autobiography* (New York, 1995), p. viii.

19 *Oxford English Dictionary*, vols IV–V, p. 1012.

20 *Ibid.*, p. 1009.

21 *Ibid.*, p. 1012.

22 Jeff Fessler and Karen Rauch, eds, *When Drag Is Not a Car Race: An Irreverent Dictionary of over 400 Gay and Lesbian Words and Phrases* (New York, 1997), p. 7.

23 *Oxford English Dictionary*, vols IV–V, p. 662.

24 *Ibid.*, pp. 633–4.

25 Warren Johansson, 'Faggot', in *Encyclopedia of Homosexuality*, ed. Wayne R. Dynes (New York, 1990), p. 383.

26 Herb Allen, 'Smoke-Filled Rooms: Brooklyn Tobacco Party', *The New Yorker*, 29 July 2002, p. 32.

LESLIE IVERSEN: 'Why Do We Smoke?: The Physiology of Smoking'

1 L. Iversen, *Drugs: A Very Short Introduction* (Oxford, 2001), pp. 20–23.

2 P. Robson, *Forbidden Drugs*, 2nd edn (Oxford, 1999), pp. 185–6.

3 R. Peto *et al.*, 'Smoking, Smoking Cessation and Lung Cancer in the UK since 1950: Combination of National Statistics with Two Case Control Studies', *British Medical Journal*, CCCXXI (2000), pp. 323–9.

4 B. Q. Liu *et al.*, 'Emerging Tobacco Hazards in China: Retrospective Proportional Mortality Study of One Million Deaths', *British Medical Journal*, CCCXVII (1998), pp. 1411–22.

5 L. Iversen, *The Science of Marijuana* (New York, 2000), pp. 190–203.

6 J. Cooper, F. E. Bloom and R. H. Roth, *The Biochemical Basis of Neuropharmacology*, 7th edn (Oxford, 1996), pp. 82–101.

7 *Ibid.*, pp. 341, 386.

8 G. F. Koob, P. P. Sanna and F. E. Bloom, 'Neuroscience of Addiction', *Neuron*, XXI (1998), pp. 467–76

9 G. Block and J. March, eds, *The Biology of Nicotine Dependence*, CIBA Foundation Symposium 152 (Chichester, 1990).

10 R. D. Hurt and C. R. Robinson, 'Prying Open the Door to the Tobacco Industry's Secrets about Nicotine: The Minnesota Tobacco Trial', *Journal of the American Medical Association*, CCLXXX (1998), pp. 1173–81; David A. Kessler, *A Question of Intent: A Great American Battle with a Deadly Industry* (New York, 2001), pp. 191–7.

11 S. S. Watkins, G. F. Koob and A. Markou, 'Neural Mechanisms Underlying Nicotine Addiction: Acute Positive Reinforcement and Withdrawal', *Nicotine and Tobacco Research*, II (2000), pp. 19–37.

12 Neal L. Benowitz in *The Biology of Nicotine Dependence*, p. 199.

13 Hurt and Robinson, 'Prying Open the Door'.

14 Annual report US National Institute of Drug Abuse, National Household Survey on Drug Abuse (2000).

15 Koob, Sanna and Bloom *op cit.*, pp. 470–75.

16 F. Rodriguez de Fonseca, M.R.A. Carrera, M. Navarro, G. F. Koob and F. Weiss, 'Activation of Corticotropin-Releasing Factor in the Limbic System during Cannabinoid Withdrawal', *Science*, CCLXXVI (1997), pp. 2050–54.

17 J. R. Hughes, M. G. Goldstein, R. D. Hurt and S. Shiffman, 'Recent Advances in the Pharmacotherapy of Smoking', *Journal of the American Medical Association*, CCLXXXI (1999), pp. 72–6.

18 P. Robson, *Forbidden Drugs*, 2nd edn (Oxford, 1999), pp. 226–38.

19 Hughes, Goldstein, Hurt and Shiffman, 'Recent Advances in the Pharmacotherapy of Smoking'.

JOHN WELSHMAN: 'Smoking, Science and Medicine'

1 'Smoker Agrees to $100m Damages', *The Times*, 23 August 2001, p. 20.

2 Allan Brandt, 'The Cigarette, Risk and American Culture', *Daedalus*, CXIX (1990), pp. 155–76.

3 R. B. Walker, 'Medical Aspects of Tobacco Smoking and the Anti-Tobacco Movement in Britain in the Nineteenth Century', *Medical History*, XXIV (1980), pp. 391–402.

4 *Lancet* (1855), vol. II, p. 157.

5 *Lancet* (1872), vol. II, p. 789.

6 *Lancet* (1879), vol. I, p. 131.

7 Walker, 'Medical Aspects of Tobacco Smoking and the Anti-Tobacco Movement in Britain in the Nineteenth Century', p. 394.

8 *Lancet* (1902), vol. I, p. 906.

9 *Lancet* (1872), vol. I, p. 770.

10 Matthew Hilton and Simon Nightingale, '"A Microbe of the Devil's Own Make": Religion and Science in the British Anti-Tobacco Movement, 1853–1908', in *Ashes to Ashes: The History of Smoking and Health*, ed. S. Lock, L. A. Reynolds and E. M. Tansey (Amsterdam, 1998), pp. 41–63.

11 Matthew Hilton, '"Tabs", "Fags", and the "Boy Labour Problem" in Late Victorian and Edwardian England', *Journal of Social History*, XXVIII/3 (1995), pp. 586–607; John Welshman, 'Images of Youth: The Issue of Juvenile Smoking, 1880–1914', *Addiction*, XCI/9 (1996), pp. 1379–86.

12 Brandt, 'The Cigarette, Risk and American Culture', p. 157.

13 Robert N. Proctor, *The Nazi War on Cancer* (Princeton, NJ, 1999), pp. 173–247.

14 Richard Doll, 'The First Reports on Smoking and Lung Cancer', in *Ashes to Ashes*, pp. 130–40.

15 Virginia Berridge, 'Science and Policy: The Case of Postwar British Smoking Policy', in *Ashes to Ashes*, pp. 143–62.

16 Brandt, 'The Cigarette, Risk and American Culture', p. 156.

17 Berridge, 'Science and Policy'.

18 Lesley Doyal with Imogen Pennell, *The Political Economy of Health* (London, 1979), p. 83.

19 Peter Taylor, *Smoke Ring: The Politics of Tobacco* (London, 1984), p. xix.

20 Brandt, 'The Cigarette, Risk and American Culture', p. 166.

21 Charles Webster, 'Tobacco Smoking Addiction: A Challenge to the National Health Service', *British Journal of Addiction*, LXXIX (1984), pp. 7–16.

22 Paolo Palladino, 'Discourses of Smoking, Health and the Just Society: Yesterday, Today and the Return of the Same?', *Social History of Medicine*, XIV/2 (2001), pp. 313–35.

23 Matthew Hilton, *Smoking in British Popular Culture, 1800–2000: Perfect Pleasures* (Manchester, 2000), pp. 202–20.

24 Brandt, 'The Cigarette, Risk and American Culture', p. 169.

25 Hilton, *Smoking in British Popular Culture*, p. 11.

26 Brandt, 'The Cigarette, Risk and American Culture', p. 172.

ALLAN M. BRANDT: 'Engineering Consumer Confidence in the Twentieth Century'

1 Richard B. Tennant, *The American Cigarette Industry: A Study in Economic Analysis and Public Policy*, Yale Studies in Economics, I (New Haven, 1950).

2 'A Whiff from the Pipe: The Uses and Abuses of the Tobacco Plant', *New York Times*, 10 March 1889, p. 14.

3 See, for example, Edwin L. James, 'War Department Will Issue Tobacco Rations', *New York Times*, 23 May 1918, p. 1.

4 Quoted in Frank Presbrey, *The History and Development of Advertising* (Garden City, NY, 1929), p. 598.

5 According to Presbrey, *ibid.*, p. 598: 'During the first quarter of the twentieth century the value of goods manufactured in the US increased 400 percent although population increased only 50 percent.'

6 Peter B. B. Andrews, 'The Cigarette Market, Past and Future', *Advertising and Selling*, 16 January 1936, p. 27.

7 T. J. Jackson Lears, *Fables of Abundance: A Cultural History of Advertising in America* (New York, 1994), p. 183.

8 See Neil Harris, 'The Drama of Consumer Desire', in *Yankee Enterprise: The Rise of the American System of Manufactures*, ed. O. Mayr and R. C. Post (Washington, DC, 1981), pp. 189–230. There have, in recent years, been important analyses of the rise of consumer processes. For a formative work on the subject, see Richard W. Fox and T. J. Jackson Lears, eds, *The Culture of Consumption: Critical Essays in American History, 1880–1980* (New York, 1983). For more recent historical analysis, see Lawrence B. Glickman, ed., *Consumer Society in American History: A Reader* (Ithaca, NY, 1999), especially: 'Coming Up for Air: Consumer Culture in Historical Perspective', pp. 373–97.

9 Otis A. Pease, *The Responsibilities of American Advertising: Private Control and Public Influence, 1920–1940* (New Haven, 1958).

10 See Lord & Thomas, *Concerning a Literature which Compels Action* (Chicago and New York, 1911); and Lord & Thomas, *Altruism In Advertising* (Chicago and New York, 1911).

11 See T. J. Jackson Lears and Roland Marchand, *Advertising the American Dream: Making Way for Modernity* (Berkeley, CA, 1985).

12 Carl A. Naether, *Advertising to Women* (New York, 1928).

13 See Cassandra Tate, *Cigarette Wars: The Triumph of 'The Little White Slaver'* (New York, 1999).

14 Michael Schudson, *Advertising, the Uneasy Persuasion: Its Dubious Impact on American Society* (New York, 1984).

15 Obituary, *New York Times*, 10 March 1995, p. B7. See also Larry Tye, *The Father of Spin: Edward L. Bernays and the Birth of Public Relations* (New York, 1998), and Stuart Ewen, *PR! The Social History of Spin* (New York, 1996).

16 Richard S. Tedlow, *Keeping the Corporate Image: Public Relations and Business, 1900–1950* (Greenwich, CT, 1979), p. 43.

17 *Ibid.*

18 Upon reviewing the Edward L. Bernays papers at the Library of Congress (EBMSS, LC), I was impressed not only by the details of his publicity campaigns, but also by the recognition of seeing what had to be secret, internal documentation of his many interventions on behalf of American Tobacco. Why would Bernays maintain such scrupulous records of his hidden efforts? The answer, it seems, is that only such documentation could effectively demonstrate his success.

This accounts for the many scrapbooks, memos and ghost-written letters that reveal the instrumental activities behind a coherent and powerful initiative to generate media.

19 Letter from Edward L. Bernays to George W. Hill, EBMSS, LC, Box 56, Folder 2 (7 February 1929).

20 Edward L. Bernays, *Biography of an Idea: Memoirs of Public Relations Counsel Edward L. Bernays* (New York, 1965), p. 383.

21 EBMSS, LC, Box 86, Folder 1.

22 EBMSS, LC, Box 89, Folder 5 (January 1930).

23 Bernays, *Biography of an Idea*, p. 386.

24 *Ibid.*, p. 383.

25 *Ibid.*, p. 386.

26 *Ibid.*, p. 387.

27 *Ibid.*, p. 390.

28 *Ibid.*, p. 391.

29 EBMSS, n.d., Box 86, Folder 4.

30 See Richard Klein, *Cigarettes Are Sublime* (Durham, NC, and London, 1993), pp. 53–5, 162–80, 200–01, n. 4; 114–15, 575, 776, 645.

31 Giles Playfair, 'Smoke Without Fire', *Atlantic Monthly*, April 1948, p. 96.

32 See Herbert L. Stephen, 'How Hill Advertises is at Last Revealed', *Printers' Ink*, 17 November 1938, pp. 11–14 89–103.

PATRICK W. CORRIGAN: 'Marlboro Man and the Stigma of Smoking'

1 A more complete collection of these slogans can be viewed at two websites: http://www.buttout.com and http://www.kick-butt.com

2 Erving Goffman, *Stigma: Notes on the Management of Spoiled Identity* (New York, 1963), p. 147.

3 Bernard Weiner, *Judgements of Responsibility: A Foundation for a Theory of Social Conduct* (New York, 1995), p. 301.

4 Edward E. Jones et al., *Social Stigma: The Psychology of Marked Relationships* (New York, 1984), p. 347.

5 Bruce G. Link and Jo C. Phelan, 'Conceptualizing Stigma', *Annual Reviews*, XXVII (2001), pp. 363–8.

6 W. James Popham et al., 'Effectiveness of the California 1990–1991 Tobacco Education Media Campaign', *American Journal of Preventive Medicine*, X/6 (1994), pp. 319–26.

7 World Health Organization, *Tobacco or Health?: A Global Status Report* (Geneva, 1997), p. 312.

8 Health Canada, *Cigarette Smoking and Young Women's Presentation of Self* (1996), p. 94.

9 World Health Organization, *Tobacco or Health?*, p. 383.

10 William L. Weis and Chauncey Burke, 'Media Content and Tobacco Advertising: An Unhealthy Addiction', *Journal of Communication* (August 1986), pp. 59–69.

11 Fred Andersen, 'Smoking and Business', *American Heritage*, July–August 1998, pp. 74–6.

12 World Health Organization, *Tobacco or Health?*, p. 383.

13 F. Baker *et al.*, 'Risk Perception and Cigar Smoking Behavior', *American Journal of Health Behavior*, XXV/2 (2001), pp. 106–14.

14 Andersen, 'Smoking and Business', p. 75.

15 L. D. Johnston *et al.*, 'Cigarette Use and Smokeless Tobacco Use Decline Substantially Among Teens', *University of Michigan News and Information Services* (2000), p. 76.

16 Michael E. Starr, 'The Marlboro Man: Cigarette Smoking and Masculinity in America', *Journal of Popular Culture*, XVII/4 (1984), pp. 45–57.

17 Diane M. Quinn and Jennifer Crocker, 'When Ideology Hurts: Effects of Belief in the Protestant Ethic and Feeling Overweight on the Psychological Well-being of Women', *Journal of Personality and Social Psychology*, LXXVII/2 (1999), pp. 402–14.

18 Bruce G. Link *et al.*, 'On Stigma and its Consequences: Evidence from a Longitudinal Study of Men with Dual Diagnosis of Mental Illness and Substance Abuse', *Journal of Health and Social Behavior*, XXXVIII/2 (1997), pp. 177–90.

19 S. Jones *et al.*, 'Second-hand Smoke at Work: The Exposure, Perceptions and Attitudes of Bar and Restaurant Workers to Environmental Tobacco Smoke', *Australian and New Zealand Journal of Public Health*, XXV (2001), pp. 90–93; R. Stone, 'Study Implicates Second-hand Smoke', *Science*, CCLXIV/5155 (1994), p. 30.

20 Jones *et al.*, 'Second-hand Smoke at Work', p. 347.

21 Amerigo Farina *et al.*, 'The Impact of an Unpleasant and Demeaning Social Interaction', *Journal of Social and Clinical Psychology*, X/4 (1991), pp. 351–71.

22 Jones *et al.*, 'Second-hand Smoke at Work', p. 347.

23 Daniel K. Lapsley, *Moral Psychology* (Boulder, CO, 1996), p. 289.

24 B. F. Skinner, *Science and Human Behavior* (New York, 1953), p. 461; T. W. Wann, ed., *Behaviorism and Phenomenology: Contrasting Bases for Modern Psychology* (Chicago, 1964), p. 190.

25 Susan T. Fiske, 'Stereotyping, Prejudice and Discrimination', in *The Handbook of Social Psychology*, ed. D. T. Gilbert *et al.*, 4th edn (Boston, 1998), vol. II, pp. 357–411.

26 Weiner, *Judgements of Responsibility*, p. 301.

27 Jeffrey A. Schaler, *Addiction is a Choice* (Chicago, 2000), p. 179.

Select Bibliography

Collamer M. Abbott, 'Tobacco, Melville and the Times', *Melville Society Extracts*, CXXI (July 2001), pp. 1, 3–6

Susan Campbell Anderson, 'A Matter of Authority: James I and the Tobacco War', *Comitatus: A Journal of Medieval & Renaissance Studies*, XXIX (1998), pp. 136–63

Anon., 'From "Coffin Nails" to "Save The Kids": A History of Thinking, and Emoting, about Smoking', in *Public Perspective*, IX/5 (August–September 1998)

Anon., *Legislative History of the Comprehensive Smoking Education Act* (Washington, DC, 12 October 1984)

Eric G. Ayto, *Clay Tobacco Pipes* (Princes Risborough, 1994)

Ilene Barth, *The Smoking Life* (Columbus, MO, 1997)

Kathryn Beck, *The United States Tobacco Industry: Past, Present, Future?*, dissertation, 1995

Steven R. Belenko, *Drugs and Drug Policy in America: A Documentary History* (Westport, CT, 2000)

Virginia Berridge, *Opium and the People: Opiate Use and Drug Control Policy in Nineteenth and Early Twentieth Century England* (London, 1999)

Alan W. Bock, *Waiting to Inhale: The Politics of Medical Marijuana* (Santa Ana, CA, 2000)

Janet Brigham, *Dying To Quit: Why We Smoke and How We Stop* (Washington, DC, 1998)

Timothy Brook and Bob Tadashi Wakabayashi, *Opium Regimes: China, Britain and Japan, 1839–1952* (Berkeley, CA, 2000)

John Broughton, *Puffing Up a Storm* (Dunedin, NZ, 1996)

Christopher Buckley, *Thank You for Smoking* (New York, 1994)

John C. Burnham, *Bad Habits: Drinking, Smoking, Taking Drugs, Gambling, Sexual Misbehavior and Swearing in American History* (New York, 1993)

Campaign for Tobacco-Free Kids, *Show Us The Money: A Mid-Year Update on the States' Allocation of the Tobacco Settlement Dollars* (2002)

Minja Kim Choe and Corazon Mejia-Raymundo, *Initiation of Smoking, Drinking and Drug-Use among Filipino Youth* (Cebu City, Philippines, 2001)

Philip Collins, *Sargent, Sam, Smokerama: Classic Tobacco Accoutrements* (San Francisco, 1992)

Harold V. Cordry, *Tobacco: A Reference Handbook* (Santa Barbara, CA, 2001)

Gian Luca Corradi, *Toscani: A Burning Passion* (Florence, 2001)

Egon Caesar Corti, *A History of Smoking*, trans. Paul England (London, 1931)

Robin Crole, *Pipe: The Art and Lore of a Great Tradition* (Rocklin, CA, 1999)

Peter Davey and Allan Peacey, *The Archaeology of the Clay Tobacco Pipe* (Oxford, 1996)

Mitchell Earleywine, *Understanding Marijuana: A New Look at the Scientific Evidence* (Oxford, 2002)

Rosemary Elliott, 'Destructive but Sweet': Cigarette Smoking among Women, 1890–1990 (Elizabeth.Publication: [S.l. : s.n.], 2001)

Barbara C. Fertig, 'The Tobacco Tradition in Southern Maryland', *New Jersey Folklife*, XI (1986), pp. 8–13

Sean Gabb, *Smoking and its Enemies: A Short History of 500 Years of the Use and Prohibition of Tobacco* (London, 1990)

Iain Gately, *Tobacco: The Story of How Tobacco Seduced the World* (New York, 2001)

Carlo Ginzburg, 'On the European (Re)discovery of Shamans', *Elementa-Journal of Slavic Studies & Comparative Cultural Semiotics*, I/1 (1993), pp. 23–39

Stanton A. Glantz, *The Cigarette Papers* (Berkeley, CA, 1996)

Ilana Belle Glass, *The International Handbook of Addiction Behaviour* (London, 1991)

Conor Goodman, *The Smoker's Handbook: Survival Guide for a Dying Breed* (Dublin, 2001)

Jordan Goodman, *Tobacco in History: The Cultures of Dependence* (London and New York, 1993)

Stephen Greenblatt, *New World Encounters* (Berkeley, CA, 1993)

Mark Hanusz, *Kretek: The Culture and Heritage of Indonesia's Clove Cigarettes* (Tortola, BVI, 2000)

Richard Harp, 'Tobacco and Raymond Chandler', *Clues: A Journal of Detection*, IX/2 (Fall–Winter 1988), pp. 95–104

Jack Herer and Chris Conrad, *Hemp & The Marijuana Conspiracy: The Emperor Wears No Clothes: The Authoritative Historical Record of the Cannabis Plant, Hemp Prohibition, and How Marijuana Can Still Save the World* (Van Nuys, CA, 1990)

Chrystie Renee Hill, *Flaming Youth: A Cultural History of Gender, Class and the American Cigarette*, dissertation, 1999

Matthew Hilton, *Smoking in British Popular Culture, 1800–2000: Perfect Pleasures* (Manchester, 2000)

Philip J. Hilts, *Smokescreen: The Truth behind the Tobacco Industry Cover-up* (Reading, MA, 1996)

Arlene B. Hirschfelder, *A Century of Smoking & Tobacco* (Amawalk, NY, 1998)

—, *Encyclopedia of Smoking and Tobacco* (Phoenix, AZ, 1999)

Julian Holland and Neil Millington, *The World of Cigars: A Connoisseur's Guide, from History and Manufacture to Choosing and Smoking the Best Brands* (London, 1999)

Inter-University Consortium for Political and Social Research, *National Health Interview Survey, 1985: Health Promotion and Disease Prevention (HPDP) Smoking History during Pregnancy Supplement* (Ann Arbor, MI, 1992)

Susan B. Iwanisziw, 'Behn's Novel Investment in Oroonoko: Kingship, Slavery and Tobacco in English Colonialism', *South Atlantic Review*, LXIII/2 (Spring 1998), pp. 75–98

David A. Kessler, *A Question of Intent: A Great American Battle with a Deadly Industry* (New York, 2001)

V. G. Kiernan, *Tobacco: A History* (London, 1991)

Richard Klein, *Cigarettes Are Sublime* (Durham, NC, and London, 1993)

Richard Kluger, *Ashes to Ashes: America's Hundred-Year Cigarette War, the Public Health and the Unabashed Triumph of Philip Morris* (New York, 1996)

Jeffrey Knapp, 'Elizabethan Tobacco', in *New World Encounters*, ed. Stephen Greenblatt (Berkeley, CA, 1993), pp. 273–312

Edward L. Koven, *Smoking: The Story behind the Haze* (New York, 1996)

John L. Lakatosh, 'The Pipemaker', *Pennsylvania Folklife*, XXXII/4 (Summer 1983), pp. 156–7

R. Alton Lee, 'The "Little White Slaver" in Kansas: A Century-Long Struggle against Cigarettes', in *Kansas History*, XXII/4 (Winter 1999–2000), pp. 156–7

Jay A. Levenson, *Circa 1492: Art in the Age of Exploration* (Washington, DC, 1991)

William Luis, 'Cuban Counterpoint, Coffee and Sugar: The Emergence of a National Culture in Fernando Ortiz's Cuban Counterpoint: Tobacco and Sugar and Cirilo Villaverde's Cecilia', *Valdes Palara: Publication of the Afro-Latin/American Research Association*, II (Fall 1998), pp. 5–16

Patrick Matthews, *Cannabis Culture: A Journey through Disputed Territory* (London, 1999)

Gary E. McCuen, *Tobacco: People, Profits & Public Health* (Hudson, WI, 1997)

Keith McMahon, *The Fall of the God of Money: Opium Smoking in Nineteenth-Century China* (Lanham, 2002)

Karen Miller, *Smoking Up a Storm: Public Relations and Advertising in the Construction of the Cigarette Problem, 1953–1954* (Columbia, SC, 1992)

Barry Milligan, '"The Plague Spreading and Attacking our Vitals": Opium Smoking and the Oriental Infection of the British Domestic Scene', *Victorian Literature & Culture*, XX (1992), pp. 161–77

—, 'Opium Smoking and the Oriental Infection of British Identity', in *Beyond the Pleasure Dome: Writing and Addiction from the Romantics*, ed. Sue Vice, Matthew Campbell and Tim Armstrong (Sheffield, 1994), pp. 93–100

—, *Pleasures and Pains: Opium and the Orient in Nineteenth-Century British Culture* (Charlottesville, 1995)

Ev Mitchell, 'Folklore of Marijuana Smoking', *Southern Folklore Quarterly*, XXXIV (1970), pp. 127–30

R. K. Newman, 'Opium Smoking in Late Imperial China: A Reconsideration', *Modern Asian Studies*, XXIX/4 (October 1995), pp. 765–94

Capper Nichols, 'Tobacco and the Rise of Writing in Colonial Maryland', *Mississippi Quarterly*, L/1 (Winter 1996–7), pp. 5–17

William Robert Nowell, *California's Anti-Smoking Media Campaign: The History and Effectiveness of an Advertising War on the Tobacco Industry* (Ann Arbor, MI, 1993)

Auriana Ojeda, *Smoking* (San Diego, CA, 2002)

Stephen Orgel, 'Tobacco and Boys: How Queer Was Marlowe?', *Glq: A Journal of Lesbian & Gay Studies*, VI/4 (2000), pp. 555–76

Filip Palda and Patrick Basham, *The History of Tobacco Regulation: Forward to the Past* (Vancouver, 2000)

Mark Parascandola,'Cigarettes and the US Public Health Service in the 1950s', in *American Journal of Public Health*, XCI/2 (February 2001)

Tara Parker-Pope, *Cigarettes: Anatomy of an Industry from Seed to Smoke* (New York, 2001)

Gus Parr, 'S for Smoking', *Sight & Sound*, VII/12 (December 1997), pp. 30–33

Christina M. Pego, Robert F. Hill, Glenn W. Solomon, Robert M. Chisholm and Suzanne E. Ivey, 'Tobacco, Culture and Health among American Indians: A Historical Review', *American Indian Culture & Research Journal*, XIX/2 (1995), pp. 143–64

David Pietrusza, *Smoking* (San Diego, CA, 1997)

David Pollock, *Denial & Delay: The Political History of Smoking and Health, 1951–1964* (London, 1999)

Robert L. Rabin and Stephen D. Sugarman, *Smoking Policy: Law, Politics and Culture* (New York, 1993)

Benjamin Rapaport, *A Tobacco Source Book* (Long Branch, NJ, 1972)

—, *The Global Guide to Tobacco Literature* (Reston, VA, 1989)

—, David R. Wright and Tom Beaudrot, *Museum of Tobacco Art & History Guidebook* (Nashville, TN, 1996)

Bruc Reeves, 'Pipes and Pipe-Smoking in Great Expectations', *Dickensian*, LXII (1966), pp. 174–8

Jane Resnick and George W. Wieser, *International Connoisseur's Guide to Cigars: The Art of Selecting and Smoking* (New York, 1996)

Wendy A. Ritch, 'Strange Bedfellows: The History of Collaboration between the Massachusetts Restaurant

Association and the Tobacco Industry', in *American Journal of Public Health*, XCI/4 (April 2001)

Francis Robicsek, *The Smoking Gods: Tobacco in Maya Art, History and Religion* (Norman, OK, 1978)

Tamara L. Roleff and Mary E. Williams, *Tobacco and Smoking: Opposing Viewpoints* (San Diego, CA, 1998)

Ruth Rosenberg-Naparsteck, *The Kimball Tobacco Company and the Anti-Tobacco Movement* (Rochester, NY, 1998)

David Salsburg, *The Lady Tasting Tea: How Statistics Revolutionized Science in the Twentieth Century* (New York, 2001)

Laura R. Sauerbeck, *Smoking Cessation after Stroke: Education and its Effect on Behavior*, dissertation, 2001

Jeffrey A. Schaler and Magda E. Schaler, *Smoking: Who Has the Right?* (Amherst, 1998)

Richard G. Schlaadt, *Tobacco & Health* (Danbury, CN, 1994, 1992)

A. Sharp, 'The Clay Tobacco Pipe Collection in the National Museum', *Review of Scottish Culture*, I (1984), pp. 34–42

Sue Shephard, *Pickled, Potted and Canned: How the Art and Science of Food Preserving Changed the World* (New York, 2001, 2000)

Paul Slovic, *Smoking: Risk, Perception & Policy* (Thousand Oaks, CA, 2001)

Jean Stubbs, *Tobacco on the Periphery: A Case Study in Cuban Labour History, 1860–1958* (Cambridge, 1985),

C. W. Sullivan III, 'Tobacco U. of Tennessee P', in *Rooted in America: Foodlore of Popular Fruits and Vegetables*, ed. David Scofield Wilson and Angus Kress Gillespie (Knoxville, TN, 1999), pp. 166–87

Barnabas T. Suzuki, *Early 17th Century Tobacco Smoking In Japan (as Seen in the Jesuit Documents)* (Tokyo, 1993–6)

—, *Introduction of Tobacco & Smoking into Japan* (Tokyo, 1991)

Tatsuya Suzuki, *A Historical Study of Smoking Introduction into Japan* (Japan, 1999)

Cassandra Tate, *Cigarette Wars: The Triumph of 'The Little White Slaver'* (New York, 1999)

Leo Tolstoy, 'Tobacco and Alcohol in Crime and Punishment', in *Readings on Fyodor Dostoyevsky*, ed. Tamara Johnson (San Diego, CA, 1998), pp. 63–6

Molly E. Tomlin, *Effect of Interview versus Questionnaire Data Collection on the Consistency of Responses to Cigarette Smoking History Questions*, dissertation, 1998

Eugene Umberger, 'George Arents and the Case of the Errant Volume', *Biblion: The Bulletin of the New York Public Library*, I/2 (Spring 1993), pp. 168–74

—, *Tobacco and its Use: A Bibliography of the Periodical Literature* (Rochester, NY 1984)

US Department of Health and Human Services, Public Health Service, National Institutes of Health, National Cancer Institute, *Cigars: Health Effects and Trends* (Bethesda, 1998)

US Surgeon General, *Preventing Tobacco Use among Young People: A Report of the Surgeon General* (Washington, dc, 1994)

Alexander Dietrich von Gernet, *The Transculturation of the Amerindian Pipe/Tobacco/Smoking Complex and its Impact on the Intellectual Boundaries between Savagery and Civilization, 1535–1935* (Ottawa, 1991)

James Walton, ed., *The Faber Book of Smoking* (London, 2000)

J. McIver Weatherford, *Native Roots: How the Indians Enriched America* (New York, 1991)

Carol Wekesser, *Smoking* (San Diego, CA, 1997)

Phillip Whidden, *Tobacco-Smoke Pollution: The Intolerable Poison Tolerated Too Long: An Outline of the Major Issues and Health Effects of Environmental Tobacco Smoke and a Basic Resource Tool, Based on the Scientific Literature and on History* (Edinburgh, 1993)

Mary E. Williams, *Smoking* (San Diego, CA, 2000)

Thomas D'Oyly, Charles Williamson and John Heaviside Clark *et al.*, *The European in India: From a Collection of Drawings* (New Delhi, 1995, 1813)

Joseph C. Winter, *Tobacco Use by Native North Americans: Sacred Smoke and Silent Killer* (Norman, 2000)

Elizabeth Wyckoff, *Dry Drunk: The Culture of Tobacco in 17th- and 18th-Century Europe* (New York, 1997)

Jerry Wylie and Richard E. Fike, 'Chinese Opium Smoking Techniques and Paraphernalia', in *Hidden Heritage: Historical Archaeology of the Overseas Chinese*, ed. Priscilla Wegars (Amityville, NY, 1993), pp. 255–303

Xue Fucheng 'Reply to a Friend on the Banning of Opium Smoking', trans. Chiyu Chu, *Renditions*, XLI–XLII (Spring–Fall 1994), pp. 138–43

Contributors

ALLAN M. BRANDT is Kass Professor of the History of Medicine at Harvard Medical School and holds a joint appointment in the Department of the History of Science at Harvard University. He is the author of *No Magic Bullet: A Social History of Venereal Disease in the United States since 1880* (1987) and the editor of *Morality and Health* (1997). He is currently completing a book on the social and cultural history of cigarette smoking in the USA.

TIMOTHY BROOK is Professor of Chinese History at the University of Toronto. He is the author or editor of twelve books on Asia and a contributor to the Cambridge History of China. His most recent work is *Opium Regimes: China, Britain and Japan, 1839–1952* (2000), co-edited with Bob Tadashi Wakabayashi.

ALBERTO CASTOLDI is Vice-Chancellor of the University of Bergamo. He has written books on the literature of travel (*Il fascino del colibrì*, 1972), on eighteenth- and nineteenth-century novels (*Il realismo borghese*, 1976), on the role of the intellectual in the 1930s (*Intellettuali e Fronte popolare in Francia*, 1978), on fetishism (*Clérambault: stoffe e manichini*, 1994), on drugs (*I testo drogato*, 1994), and on the notion of whiteness (*Bianco*, 1998).

J. EDWARD CHAMBERLIN is Professor of English and Comparative Literature at the University of Toronto. His books include *The Harrowing of Eden: White Attitudes towards Native Americans* (1975), *Ripe Was the Drowsy Hour: The Age of Oscar Wilde* (1977), *Come Back to Me my Language: Poetry and the West Indies* (1993) and *If This Is Your Land, Where Are your Stories?: Finding Common Ground* (2003). For the past five years, he has been directing an international project on oral and written traditions.

BARRY CHEVANNES is Professor of Social Anthropology and Dean of the Faculty of Social Sciences, University of the West Indies at Mona. He is the author of *Rastafari: Roots and Ideology* (1994). He recently chaired the Jamaican National Commission on Ganja (*Cannabis sativa*).

PATRICK W. CORRIGAN is Professor of Psychiatry at the University of Chicago and Director for the Chicago Consortium for Stigma Research. He has recently published 'Don't Call Me Nuts: Coping with the Stigma of Mental Illness'.

STEPHEN COTTRELL is a Lecturer in Music at Goldsmiths College, University of London. His academic research is particularly concerned with ethnomusicological approaches to western art music, and a monograph on *Professional Music-making in London* will be published in 2004. He has contributed to a range of other publications, including *The Cambridge Companion to the Orchestra*, *Musical Performance* and the *British Journal of Ethnomusicology*. He also works professionally as a saxophonist specializing in contemporary music, and has released numerous CDs, both as a soloist and previously as leader of the Delta Saxophone Quartet.

DANIEL GILMAN is pursuing a PhD in Political Science at Boston University, focusing on the relationship between economics, politics and culture. He has just completed a year studying at the School for Oriental and African Studies (SOAS) at the University of London. He holds a degree in Jazz Saxophone and East Asian Languages from Indiana University, Bloomington.

SANDER L. GILMAN is Distinguished Professor of the Liberal Arts and Medicine at the University of Illinois, Chicago, and Director of the Humanities Laboratory. His books include *Seeing the Insane* (1982), *Jewish Self-Hatred* (1986), *The Fortunes of the Humanities: Teaching the Humanities in the New Millennium* (2000) and *A New Germany in the New Europe* (with Todd Herzog, 2000). He is a recipient of the Mertes Prize of the German Historical Institute (1997) and the Alexander von Humboldt Research Prize (1998).

MARK HANUSZ, a former banker, is the author of *Kretek: The Culture and Heritage of Indonesia's Clove Cigarettes* (2000).

MATTHEW HILTON is Senior Lecturer in Social History at the University of Birmingham. He is the author of *Smoking in British Popular Culture, 1800–2000* (2000) and *Consumerism in Twentieth-Century Britain* (2003), as well as editor, with Martin Daunton, of *The Politics of Consumption* (2001). He is currently working on a study of the consumer in global civil society.

LINDA HUTCHEON is University Professor of English and Comparative Literature at the University of Toronto; michael hutcheon MD is Professor of Medicine and Deputy Physician-in-Chief of Medicine for Education at the University Health Network, University of Toronto. In addition to their many individual publications in their specialist fields, they are the joint authors of *Opera: Desire, Disease, Death* (1996), *Bodily Charm: Living Opera* (2000) and *Opera: The Art of Dying* (2004).

NOAH ISENBERG is Chair of Humanities at the New School in New York City. He is the author of *Between Redemption and Doom: The Strains of German-Jewish Modernism* (1999), editor and translator of Arnold Zweig's work from 1920, *The Face of Eastern Jewry* (2004), and contributor to *New German Critique, Cinema Journal, Salmagundi, Partisan Review, Dissent, The Nation, The New Republic* and *The New York Times Book Review*. He is currently completing a monograph, *Perennial Detour: The Cinema of Edgar G. Ulmer*, and editing *A Companion to Weimar Cinema*.

LESLIE IVERSEN is Director of the Wolfson Centre for Research on Age Related Diseases at King's College London; Visiting Professor at the Department of Pharmacology, University of Oxford; and founder of the pharmaceutical company Panos Therapeutics Ltd. He is a Fellow of the Royal Society of London and a Foreign Associate of the National Academy of Sciences, USA. His most recent book is *The Science of Marijuana* (2000).

IVAN DAVIDSON KALMAR teaches anthropology at the University of Toronto. He is the author of *The Trotskys, Freuds and Woody Allens: Portrait of a Culture* (1994) and co-editor of *Orientalism: The Jewish Dimension* (2004).

RUTH MANDEL teaches in the Department of Anthropology at University College London. She has published widely on topics including international migration, Islam in Europe, Turks in Germany, media and development.

P. RAM MANOHAR is an Āyurvedic physician from India. He is Director of the AVT Institute for Advanced Research (AVTAR), Coimbatore, and the author of several essays and monographs concerning Āyurvedic medicine and the history of the Indian medical system.

DAWN MARLAN is currently Associate Director of the Humanities Laboratory at the University of Illinois, Chicago. She works on the history of the European novel, and film. She has published articles and reviews in PMLA, *Modernism/Modernity*, the *Chicago Review* and the *Chicago Tribune*.

RUDI MATTHEE is Professor of History at the University of Delaware. He is the author of *The Politics of Trade in Safavid Iran: Silk for Silver, 1600–1730* (1999), *The Pursuit of Pleasure: Drugs and Stimulants in Iranian History, 1500–1900* (forthcoming) and co-editor of *Iran and Beyond: Essays in Honor of Nikki R. Keddie* (2000) and *Iran and the Surrounding World, 1501–2001: Interactions of Culture and Politics* (2002).

BARRY MILLIGAN is Professor of English at Wright State University. He is the author of *Pleasures and Pains: Opium and the Orient in Nineteenth-Century British Culture* (1995), the editor of the Penguin edition of Thomas De Quincey's *Confessions of an English Opium-Eater and Other Writings* (2003) and co-editor of *Romantic Generations* (2001). His current work focuses on the cross-influences between popular culture and the evolution of the medical professions in nineteenth-century Britain.

DOLORES MITCHELL teaches art history at California State University, Chico. Her field of interest is the social uses of art, and she has published articles on tobacco art.

TANYA POLLARD is an Assistant Professor of English at Montclair State University in Montclair, New Jersey. She is the editor of *Shakespeare's Theatre: A Sourcebook* (2003), and author of *Drugs and Theatre in Early Modern England* (forthcoming in 2004). Her essays on early modern drugs, poisons and drama have appeared in Shakespeare Studies, Renaissance Drama and various edited collections.

BEN RAPAPORT, an avid pipe smoker, antique pipe collector and bibliophile, is the author of *A Tobacco Source Book* (1972), *A Complete Guide to Collecting Antique Pipes* (1979), *The Global Guide to Tobacco Literature* (1989), *Museum of Tobacco Art and History Guide Book* (1996) and *Collecting Antique Meerschaums* (1999). He is now preparing a book on the art and craft of the Chinese opium pipe and its associated utensils.

ALLEN F. ROBERTS is Professor of World Arts and Cultures, Director of the James S. Coleman African Studies Center, and an editor of African Arts journal at the University of California, Los Angeles. With his spouse, Mary Nooter Roberts, he has written *Memory: Luba Art and the Making of History* (1996) and *A Saint in the City: Sufi Arts and the Making of History* (2003) to accompany major museum exhibitions of the same titles. The Robertses are currently studying arts and AIDS awareness in Sub-Saharan Africa and visual cultures of the Indian Ocean world.

FRANCIS ROBICSEK is Chairman of the Department of Thoracic and Cardiovascular Surgery at Carolinas Heart Institute, Carolinas Medical Center; Clinical Professor of Surgery at the University of North Carolina; and Adjunct Professor of Bioengineering and Adjunct Professor of Anthropology at the University of North Carolina at Charlotte. He has written many articles in his specialist field, as well as five books on Central American anthropology and Maya history and culture.

ROBYN L. SCHIFFMAN is writing a dissertation on the rise and decline of the epistolary novel in Britain and Germany at the Department of Comparative Literature at the University of Chicago. She has previously published articles on Charles Dickens and psychoanalysis.

TIMON SCREECH is Reader in the History of Japanese Art at the School of Oriental and African Studies (SOAS), University of London. His most recent books are *The Shogun's Painted Culture: Fear and Creativity in the Japanese States, 1760–1829* (2000) and *The Lens within the Heart: The Western Scientific Gaze and Popular Imagery in Later Edo Japan* (2nd edn, 2001).

JEAN STUBBS is Professor of Caribbean History and Director of the Caribbean Studies Centre at London Metropolitan University. The author of *Tobacco on the Periphery: A Case Study in Cuban Labour History, 1860–1958* (London, 1985) and other articles on Cuban tobacco, she is currently completing a book exploring the last 150 years of the 'offshore' and island Havana cigar.

BARNABAS TATSUYA SUZUKI is the author of many monographs on tobacco and pipe smoking history, including Kitsuen Denraishi no Kenkyu [A historical study of smoking introduction into Japan] (1999). He is a member of *Académie Internationale de la Pipe, Confrerie Maitre de Pipier de St Claude, Comité International des Pipe Clubs,* The Pipe Club of Japan (chairman) and the Tobacco History Society of Japan.

BENNO TEMPEL is curator at the Kunsthal, Rotterdam, and organized the exhibition *Taboo and Tobacco: Four Centuries of Smoking in the Arts, from Jan Steen to Pablo Picasso* (2003).

JOS TEN BERGE is Assistant Professor of Art History at the Vrije Universiteit in Amsterdam. He is the author of *Drugs in Art: From Opium to LSD, 1798–1986* (forthcoming). His publications include *Marginalia: Perspectives on Outsider Art* (2001) and two museum catalogues for the Kröller Müller Museum in Otterlo, dealing with Odilon Redon and Vincent van Gogh.

EUGENE UMBERGER is Interim Director of the Neville Public Museum of Brown County in Green Bay, Wisconsin. He has published articles on the history of tobacco and smoking and is the author of a bibliography on the subject, *Tobacco and its Use* (2nd edn, 1996).

JOHN WELSHMAN is Senior Lecturer in Public Health at the Institute for Health Research, Lancaster University. He is the author of *Municipal Medicine: Public Health in Twentieth-Century Britain* (2001) and numerous articles on the history of health care and social policy.

ZHOU XUN is an ESRC Research Fellow at the School of Oriental and African Studies (SOAS), University of London. Her recent publications include *Chinese Perceptions of the Jews and Judaism: A History of Youtai* (2000) and *Wisdom of Confucians* (2001).

Photographic Acknowledgements

The editors, essayists and publishers wish to express their thanks to the below sources of illustrative material and/or permission to reproduce it. (Locations of artworks are also given below.) Generally essayists have not been credited separately below for the supply of picture material featured in their own essays.

Collection of Malek Alloula: 223, 224, 225 top; Appleton Museum of Art, Florida State University, Ocala: p. 227; photo Artothek: 273; reproduced with permission from Neal L. Benowitz, 'The Biology of Nicotine Dependence', ed. G. Bock and J. Marsh, CIBA Foundation Symposium 152 (Chichester, 1990): p. 319; photos Michael Berkowitz: pp. 282, 283, 284; photo bfi Collections: p. 254; Bibliothèque Nationale de France, Paris: p. 93; photos courtesy of *Cigar Aficionado*: pp. 136, 137; photo Culver Pictures: p. 270 bottom left; Ken Fenske Collection: p. 104 foot; Fogg Art Museum, Cambridge, Mass. (bequest of Grenville L. Winthrop), photo © 2003 President and Fellows of Harvard College: p. 220; photos Foto Focus/Isaac: pp. 69 (except right foot), 71, 72, 73, 74; courtesy of Susie Freeman and Liz Lee: p. 274; collection of Dean and Beckie Gardiner: p. 105 middle and foot; photo William Bruce Hale: p. 107; photo courtesy of the artist (Maggi Hambling): p. 275; photo Michael Hoehne: p. 104 foot; Anne Jolly Collection: p. 104 top; collection of Ivan Davidson Kalmar: p. 219; photo Koninklijk Bibliotheek, The Hague: p. 62; Kunsthalle, Hamburg: p. 273; Kyōsei Atami Museum, Shizuoka: p. 95; photos Michael R. Leaman/ Reaktion Books: pp. 169, 181; Library of Congress Prints and Photographs Division, Washington, DC: pp. 19 foot (Frank and Frances Carpenter Collection), 155, 156 (Gottlieb Collection), 201 (top D4-34415, foot USZ62-19528), 287, 289 (USZC4-3424), 301, 311 top left (USZ62-78340), 356 (USZC2-1399/USZC4-1703); *London Magazine* (1821): p. 124; copyright the artist (Sarah Lucas), courtesy Sadie Coles HQ, London: p. 276; Mary Evans Picture Library, London: p. 297; Royal Cabinet of Paintings Mauritshuis, The Hague: pp. 207, 208 foot; Metropolitan Museum of Art, New York (Jefferson R. Burdick Collection, gift of Jefferson R. Burdick): p. 290 foot; photos Metropolitan Opera Archives: pp. 231 bottom right, 233; Minneapolis Institute of Arts (gift of Mr. and Mrs. Bruce B. Dayton): p. 269; collection of the Mint Museum of Art, Charlotte,

North Carolina: p. 32; Musée Cantonal des Beaux-Arts, Lausanne: p. 229; © Musée d'Art et d'Histoire, Geneva (Cabinet des Dessins), photo Bettina Jacot-Descombes: p. 209; Musée d'Orsay, Paris: pp. 211, 221, 270 foot; Musée de la Publicité, Paris: pp. 298, 302; Musée de la Sieta, Paris: pp. 295 top, 300; Musée de l'Art Moderne de la Ville de Paris: p. 271; Museo Thyssen-Bornemisza, Madrid: p. 215; photo courtesy of the National Museum of Ethnology, Leiden (inv. no. 3206): p. 66; The Navy Museum, Washington, DC: p. 306; New York Public Library (Arents Tobacco Collection): p. 231 top, 288, 290 top, 291, 292 foot; New York Historical Society (Bella C. Landauer Collection): pp. 292 top, 293; photos courtesy of the Newberry Library, Chicago: pp. 10, 11, 13, 14, 17, 19 top, 21, 22, 23, 24, 27, 199, 200, 202 top, 310; Peabody Museum, Salem, Mass.: p. 90 left; Sarunas Peckus Tobacciana Collection (photos Sarunas Peckus): pp. 102 foot, 103 foot, 105 top; photos Chris Pinney: pp. 69 (right foot), 75, 362 foot; State Pushkin Museum of Fine Arts, Moscow: p. 270 top; Benjamin Rapaport collection (photo Gary L. Kieffer/PPI): p. 102 top; photos Rex Features: pp. 5 (Ray Tang), 28 (Nils Jorgenson, 430142F), 138 (SIPA Press), 183 (Eastlight Photo News, 232028 htk – 1332), 188 (232028 htk – 1332), 196 (David Browne, 147965D), 202 foot (Denis Cameron, 117871 DCA PIC. 22), 203 top (Charles Sykes, 242413 RUS), 203 foot (Austral, 316438A), 204 (SIPA Press), 249 (SNAP, 390897CV), 255 (USA Films/Everett 433118I), 314 (Michael Friedel, 113392), 315 top (SIPA Press, 71667), 315 foot (Arild Molstad, 253854H), 316 (Alex Sudea, 436073B), 321 (Henryk T. Kaiser, 233068 htk – 22), 324 (Henryk T. Kaiser, 233068 htk), 325 (Dave Lewis, 208103A), 345 top (Sinopsis, 290401F), 345 foot (PB, 304534B), 349 (SNAP, 390934DQ), 350 (Sam Teare/BSKYB, 229100A), 352 (Greg Allen, 450535AB), 363 top (Nils Jorgensen, 404087P), 363 foot (Clive Dixon, 374314AA); photos RMN: pp. 211 (Hervé Landowski), 221 (Le Mage); reprinted with permission from Francis Robicsek, *The Smoking Gods: Tobacco in Maya Art, History and Religion* (Norman, OK, 1978): pp. 30, 31, 32, 33, 34, 36, 37; collection of Bob Rogers-dba-Wick'd Ways: p. 107; photos Roger Viollet/Rex Features: pp. 8 (image 4072-15; RV -746857), 264 (FA-95528), 270 foot (RVB-03673), 312 (RV -38323), 313 top (CAP 1567), 313 foot (RV-42678), 264 (FA-45528), 357 foot (RV -81-11); courtesy of the Royal Ontario Museum, Toronto: pp. 84 (gift of E. K. Brown), 85, 90 top right; photos Rovang

Index